THE ETHICS
OF KARL BARTH

THE ETHICS
OF KARL BARTH

BY

ROBERT E. WILLIS

LEIDEN

E. J. BRILL

1971

for Elaine

TABLE OF CONTENTS

PREFACE

The present study represents an attempt to develop the form and substance of Barth's ethics within the framework of his theology. Whether it is successful or not must be left to the judgment of others. I wish here only to record my deep appreciation to the many persons who have contributed, in various ways, to its completion.

I am especially indebted to Professors Arnold B. Come (now President) and Benjamin A. Reist, of the San Francisco Theological Seminary, San Anselmo, California. Their patient, generous, and (above all) critically incisive guidance saw this venture safely through its initial presentation as a Th. D. dissertation at that institution. Professor Donald G. Dawe, now of Union Theological Seminary, Richmond, Virginia, worked through some of the early drafts of chapters, and offered helpful suggestions pertaining to style and content. Professor Lloyd A. Gaston of the religion department at Macalester College, St. Paul, Minnesota, allowed me unlimited access to his impressive German library, and permitted me to abscond for an unconscionable length of time with his set of the German edition of the *Dogmatics*. My former colleague at Hamline, Professor Ernest L. Steen, now of Wagner College, Staten Island, New York, offered helpful suggestions at various points along the way, and acted as a formidable sounding-board against which to test some of the ideas developed in this study. Miss Sally Ehlers, now a graduate student in medicine at the University of Minnesota, proved an able typist during the early stages of preparation, and displayed a sense of humor that went far to allay fatigue. A special note of gratitude must be extended to Mr. T.A. Edridge, Classical Editor, and the directors of E.J. Brill, Leiden, for their decision to undertake the publication of this work.

Finally, an attempt to express the inexpressible—my unending indebtedness to my wife, Elaine, and my children, Kathy, Mark, Paul, and David. The ambiance of joy, encouragement, love, and play with which they surrounded me throughout the long months of work made this project, in a profound sense, their undertaking as well.

10 May 1970
New Barnet, Herts
England

TABLE OF ABBREVIATIONS

CGBG	*Christengemeinde und Bürgergemeinde.*
EG	*Evangelium und Gesetz.*
FQI	*Anselm: Fides Quaerens Intellectum.*
HG	*"Das Halten der Gebote".*
KD	*Die Kirchliche Dogmatik.*
KGSG	*The Knowledge of God and the Service of God.*
LHG	*Zum Lehre vom Heiligen Geist.*
RÖM	*Der Römerbrief.*
RR	*Rechtfertigung und Recht.*
SI	*"Schicksal und Idee in der Theologie".*
TC	*Theology and Church.*
WG	*The Word of God and the Word of Man.*

These abbreviations appear in the bibliographical references in the footnotes.

As regards the abbreviated titles above, with the exception of the lecture, "Church and Culture", in *Theology and Church*, the collected writings in *The Word of God and the Word of Man*, and Barth's Gifford lectures, *The Knowledge of God and the Service of God*, only original sources have been used. All translations from these are my own. Further, although *Die Kirchliche Dogmatik* is, within the body of the discussion, referred to as "the *Church Dogmatics*", or simply as "the *Dogmatics*", all quotations and footnote references, unless otherwise indicated, are from the German edition.

INTRODUCTION

> It is not too much to say that whoever wishes to
> become a truly moral human being (and let us not
> ask whether or not this is possible; I think we must
> *believe* that it is possible) must first divorce himself
> from all the prohibitions, crimes, and hypocrises of
> the Christian church. If the concept of God has any
> validity or use, it can only be to make us larger,
> freer, and more loving. If God cannot do this, then
> it is time we got rid of Him.
>
> (James Baldwin, *The Fire Next Time*).

It might be thought strange to begin a study in the ethics of Karl
Barth with a quotation from James Baldwin, who bears no obvious
theological credentials, and whose relation to the Christian community
is at best tangential. In fact, however, it would be strange or out of order
only to those readers of Barth who rest content with a repetition of
accumulated caricatures and shibboleths about the "abstractness" or
"remoteness' or "irrelevance" of his thinking, over against the dilemmas
facing contemporary man in his individual and communal life. For-
tunately, it is becoming more difficult to accept this reading of Barth
as adequate or final. Part of the concern of this study, accordingly,
will be to indicate the way in which Barth's approach to theology, and
the ethical thrust which is imparted to it, far from bypassing or trans-
cending man and the world, are designed to lend structure and substance
to both.

Now, it is one thing to make an assertion about Barth's ethics, as
I have done. It is another matter altogether to explicate that ethic
and examine its adequacy. For the moment, then, it is instructive to
consider carefully the indictment levelled by Baldwin against the Church.
One might seek comfort in the thought that similar judgments have
appeared regularly, both inside the Church and out, thereby placing
this as simply one among many criticisms. Or one might attempt to
blunt it by appealing to the trite sophism that *really* to understand the
hypocrisy and failure of the Church, it is necessary to be a part of it.

Neither of these will do. First of all, because the Church has an
uncanny penchant for rendering innocuous its own prophets, those
internal critics who in love exhort it to become what it already is, to *be*
the people of God in the world (and this in itself needs stringent re-

defining), and to act accordingly. But second, and perhaps even more to the point, because the Church has no grounds whatever for writing the world off through a refusal to listen when it is addressed, particularly when the address is so poignant and passionate an appeal on behalf of the humanity of man.

The really startling thing about Baldwin's statement, however, lies in the exceedingly fine piece of extra-ecclesiastical theology with which it closes. How often have notions like love and freedom been used to describe the dynamics of Christian faith, the authentically human, and the fruits of a nature relationship with God? And how often, sadly enough, have they failed of exemplification in the life of the Church, both internally and in its behavior in the world? If this inconsistency persists, if the Church continues to appear less than human to those outside, if it manifests neither love nor freedom in its actions, it can neither avoid nor justify itself against the charge of idolatry, of claiming more for God than He can deliver.

What emerges from this is a clear indication of the need for a viable ethic under which the Church can live and act. There are obvious difficulties in supplying this need, which render its undertaking and execution perilous indeed. Christian ethics unfold within the context of the coming of God's grace in Jesus Christ, which entails immediately the assumption that this makes a difference in the lives of those who recognize and affirm this grace in faith; that they will be, in their attitudes, decisions, and actions, determined and directed by it. The existence of the Christian, then, will in some respects necessarily be different from that of non-Christians.

Can this difference be identified and described in such a way that its ethical dimension assumes meaning and form? Is there a way of formulating Christian ethics which will both free the Church and the Christian for significant involvement in the world through decision and action, and yet preserve the world in its givenness and integrity? What constitutes right human conduct in the world within the context of grace, and how does one go about deciding on a course of action or perhaps inaction in face of the multiplicity and acuteness of problems in the world which cry out for solution? Can a Christian ethic *provide* answers, solutions, and programs, or is it designed for an altogether different end?

It is with these questions in mind that I turn to an examination of the ethics of Karl Barth. In doing so, I do not assume *prima facie* the adequacy of his ethics to supply correctives or answers to the problems which have been raised. The only point I would argue is that an investigation of this aspect of Barth's thought needs no serious justification. His undisputed significance for an understanding of the main currents and options in twentieth century theology, the sheer massiveness of his accumulated writings, and the political thrust and interest which informed his activity, make him a tantalizing subject of investigation. Further, since it is the ethical adequacy of Barth's theology and public utterances which is most often labeled deficient or irrelevant, the enterprise of getting clear what his ethics comes to is timely, appropriate, and well worth the effort.

Indeed, within the context of American theological and cultural modes, the challenge of providing some indication of the viability of Barth's ethics is particularly acute. To be sure, he has met with criticism from his own Continental brethren, but there is present in this country both a resolute and a tentative rejection of Barth which argue either that he is ethically irrelevant to the complex of issues confronting the Western world as a whole, or that the cultural peculiarities of the American scene render his high powered treatment of ethics within the context of dogmatics innocuous. The former reaction is seen in Reinhold Niebuhr's comment that Barth

> has become irrelevant to all Christians in the Western world who believe in accepting common and collective responsibilities without illusion and without despair. We cannot protect the truth of the gospel by separating it from all the disciplines of culture and all the common experiences of our ethical life [1].

And the latter is encountered in William Hamilton's indication of the importance, on the American scene, of

> a common feeling among a good many pursuers of theology that the time of European hegemony is at an end; that while we will always be working on and loving our German and Swiss betters, the thing of being a Christian in America today is so wildly *sui generis* that our most precious clues are no longer expected to come from a *Zeitschrift* or a *Dogmatik* [2].

Now, it is no mean task to make out the relevance or irrelevance of Barth's thought for Western man, and it may be that the situation of American Christians is *toto caelo* different from that of, say, the Austrian or the Dane. Each of these issues, however, must be momentarily tabled

---

[1] "The Quality of Our Lives", *Christian Century*, Vol. LXXVII, No. 19 (May 11, 1960), p. 571.

[2] "Thursday's Child: The Theologian Today and Tomorrow", *Theology Today*, Vol. XX, No. 4 (January, 1964), p. 487f.

pending the outcome of the investigation. What they serve to do, initially, is to underline once again its importance.

How best to proceed? The issue of methodology is crucial. If we are to do justice to our subject, it is imperative that Barth's own methodology be kept clearly in mind, at two points in particular: (i) his insistence on grounding the whole of dogmatics in Christology; (ii) his refusal to divide dogmatics and ethics into two separate disciplines. Forgetfulness at these points can lead only to misinterpretation, distortion, and inevitable bewilderment at Barth's failure to deliver significantly on issues of decision and behavior confronting Christians.

A valid approach cannot, accordingly, consist in cutting into his writings at those places which appear to be directly ethical. The fallacy in such a procedure lies in overlooking Barth's insistence that dogmatics in its entirety, properly understood, is "directly ethical". Indeed, the *Church Dogmatics* can itself be interpreted as one long, sustained *ethical* treatise, which focuses throughout on the one overarching action of God in Jesus Christ as the revelation and fulfillment of the ethical, but which also encloses and determines the solution to the problem of correct human action. For Barth, the revelation of God in Jesus Christ *is* the solution to correct human behavior. This means that it is both ontologically and paradigmatically *prior*, and that human action in its widest ramifications and subtlest nuances can only comprise a recognition and acknowledgement and following of the action of God.

With these remarks behind us, I can indicate briefly the direction to be taken in the discussion. I begin with a sketch of the concerns and emphases discernible in Barth's ethical thought from (roughly) 1911 to the publication of his study, in 1930, on Anselm. This will provide the requisite background for an extended treatment of the central *locus* of Barth's thought, the *Church Dogmatics*. The approach here will be systematic rather than serial or chronological, and will consist essentially in moving through my own admittedly contrived schema of the key notions and thrusts enunciated by Barth. This will achieve two ends: (i) a clear elucidation of the ethics of Barth as it unfolds within dogmatics; (ii) consideration of the various theological objections raised against Barth's ethics, and an appraisal of their persuasiveness. At the same time, I shall take into account the fact of chronological development and shift where these are evident within the *Dogmatics*. I shall also examine Barth's shorter writings contemporaneous with the *Dogmatics* which bear on the topic. These will prove instructive in forming a clear notion of his doctrine of the relation

between Church and State, since this has not been explored at length in
the *Dogmatics*. Finally, in two concluding sections I shall draw together those more serious issues surrounding Barth's ethics which have
emerged from the discussion, and indicate their amenability or resistance
to solution; and I shall seek to suggest some possible directions in which
Christian ethics might move beyond Barth.

CHAPTER ONE

THE BACKGROUND AND DEVELOPMENT
OF BARTH'S ETHICS
(1911-1931)

A. THE EARLY PERIOD (1911-1920)

It is important, in a study of the ethics of Karl Barth, to begin at the point where his own engagement with the ethical question began to take shape. For Barth, that coincided with his becoming, in 1911, the pastor of a congregation in the town of Safenwil, in Canton Aargau, in north-central Switzerland. There, according to Henri Bouillard, Barth was confronted for the first time with some of the real problems of life [1].

To that situation, Barth brought a background and perspective informed primarily by the prevailing liberal theology and neo-Kantianism of the day. Having studied under Adolph Harnack at Berlin, and Wilhelm Herrmann at Marburg, he moved within a theological framework which gave priority to the role and response of man to God, rather than to the action of God towards man, and which also assumed a given *relationality* between the human and the divine. This was argued not as a *dependent* relation resulting from the impact of grace, but rather as an indigenous aspect of creaturely reality, as seen in man's activity in esthetic, moral, and cultural modes [2].

As a kind of latent counterpoise to his avowed standing within liberal theology, Barth also brought into the pastoral context a certain sensitivity to Reformation theology, and its emphasis on the sovereignty and priority of God. The subsequent development of Barth's thinking displays a continuation of both liberal and Reformation elements, though to be sure under the transforming impact of his own creative formulations [3]. What this means concretely is that it will evidence concern for both the life of man, as seen in liberal theology, and the priority

---

[1] Henri Bouillard, *Karl Barth* (Paris : Aubier, 1957). Vol. I, p. 85.
[2] Arnold B. Come, *An Introduction to Barth's "Dogmatics" for Preachers* (Philadelphia : The Westminster Press, 1963), p. 25ff.
[3] *Ibid.*, p. 29.

and reality of God, as seen in Reformation theology. This is summed up nicely by Eduard Thurneysen, who asserts that Barth's whole theological development unfolds within the polarities of "the existence, the life of man, on the one side, and on the other the Word of God that meets this life" [1].

In a sense, this is an obvious truism applicable to most, if not all, figures in the history of Christian thought. It applies to Barth in a peculiarly stringent fashion, however, for it was his unremitting search for a theology which would enable him to do justice to both sides of this polarity that moved him through the successive stages of development from the first edition of the *Römerbrief* to the imposing Christological architectonic of the *Church Dogmatics*. Given the persistency of these two concerns, it is perhaps not surprising that Barth should have come under criticism, on the one hand, for providing an apparently ambiguous treatment of man as agent and self over against God [2]; on the other, for providing an oblique continuation of liberal theology *precisely within* the stringent Christological contours of the *Dogmatics* [3].

His immediate engagement with the demands of the pastorate launched Barth on a theological and ethical pilgrimage [4] which would end only with the publication, in 1932, of the first part of the Prolegomena to the *Church Dogmatics*. Initially, this was set in motion on two fronts: the fact and necessity of Christian preaching, and the emergence of Christian Socialism.

The act of preaching became for Barth *existentially* problematic in the deepest sense of the word [5]. It marked, however, more than a merely private dilemma, for it forced him to face directly the question of man's prerogative and ability to speak *as man* of God, and so called into question the whole thrust of nineteenth century liberal theology. Barth's engagement with this question thus served to elicit a reexamimination of the accepted theological genre of his day, which was given

---

[1] James D. Smart, *Revolutionary Theology in the Making* (Richmond: John Knox Press, 1964), p. 14.

[2] Arnold B. Come, *Human Spirit and Holy Spirit* (Philadelphia: The Westminster Press, 1959), p. 83f., 190.

[3] So Hans Frei in *Faith and Ethics*, Paul Ramsey, ed. (New York: Harper and Brothers, 1957), p. 51.

[4] Cf. Thomas F. Torrance, *Karl Barth: An Introduction to His Early Theology* (London: S.C.M. Press, 1962), p. 16.

[5] Arnold B. Come, *An Introduction to Barth's "Dogmatics" for Preachers*, p. 33.

expression in a series of articles and lectures which appeared from about 1915 to 1922 [1], and which was epitomized in the second edition of the *Römerbrief*.

At the same time that the problem of preaching was moving him to what would be eventually a break with the assumptions of liberal theology, Barth's involvement with the tension in his parish between workers and management provided a point of direct contact with the social, and with the Christian Socialist movement.

The development of Christian Socialism in Switzerland centered in the activity of two men, Hermann Kutter and Leonhard Ragaz. Essentially, it represented an attempt to relate Christian categories to an awakened social consciousness and drive for justice among industrial workers. In an early writing, *Sie Müssen*, Kutter pictured social democracy as the means by which God would establish his kingdom "on the margin of the sleeping Church" [2]. The movement took initial form at a conference led by Ragaz in 1906 on "The Gospel and the Real Social Struggle" [3].

Theologically, stress was placed on the radical character of the kingdom of God revealed in Christ [4]. The message of Jesus was that God is God; that he wishes to reign over the world, which includes both the Church and history as a whole [5]. The coming of Christ manifested not a new *religion*, but a new *world* [6]. Within this movement of God, Christian Socialism was given the task of securing justice in *society*, a task hitherto neglected by the Church in favor of its concern for individual salvation and the inner religious life [7].

There was thus discernable in the doctrines advanced by Kutter and Ragaz a strong eschatological motif [8]. The revelation of God in

---

[1] Cf. especially the articles in *The Word of God and the Word of Man* trans. by Douglas Horton (New York: Harper and Brothers, 1957).

[2] Bouillard, *Karl Barth*, Vol. I, p. 85. The quotation is Bouillard, not Kutter.

[3] *Ibid.*

[4] *Ibid.*

[5] *Ibid.*

[6] *Ibid.*

[7] *Ibid.* Bouillard indicates clearly the way in which the Socialist program entailed a criticism of contemporary bourgeois culture and capitalism: "L'attente du Règne, l'espérance chrétienne ne doit pas se réfugier dans la vie intérieure, mais animer la lutte contre la satisfaction bourgeoise et l'argent, contre l'injustice et l'oppression des pauvres".

[8] Though this does not, of course, imply simple identity in their teachings.

Jesus Christ was seen to be the creation of a new world, which, though not given in any final way at present, provides the basis for Christian hope and activity in society. This eschatological thrust represents the influence of Johann Christoph Blumhardt, through his son, Christoph [1]. Like his father, Christoph Blumhardt laid strong emphasis on the power of Jesus against the forces of evil, and on hope in the Kingdom of God. His views were, however, less consistently apocalyptic than those of the elder Blumhardt. Christian hope in God's kingdom was fused with the Socialist program of economic transformation, and emphasis was placed on the possibility of gradual progress towards a realization of the Kingdom of God [2].

In April, 1915, Barth joined the Social Democratic party, though with some reservation [3]. By September of that year, it had becomes apparent that it offered no real solution to the ethical dilemmas facing man in the context of modern society, and he withdrew from active participation. However, this did not constitute a withdrawal from life and the problems of the ethical. It is best assessed as one aspect of a growing uneasiness and disenchantment with liberal theology, insofar as the Socialist movement evidenced continuity with it.

In a recent article, Barth placed the end of nineteenth-century theology for him, personally, in a proclamation issued by a group of German intellectuals in August, 1914, in support of the war policies of Kaiser Wilhelm [4]. Among those signing, Barth discovered, were most of his former theological instructors. This direct and (apparently) unproblematic support of German nationalist aims alerted Barth to the *ethical* insufficiency of liberal theology. At the same time, it called into question its understanding of dogmatics, the Bible, and history [5].

Within this development away from his initial theological moorings, Barth's encounter with religious socialism played a dual role. On the one hand, it alerted him to the possibility of God's activity and reality as "wholly other than the God confined to the musty shell of the Christian-religious self-consciousness" [6]. It thus drew attention, rightfully, to the

---

Cf. Barth's summation of their leading respective points at the time of his own break with the movement, in *Antwort* (Zürich: Evangelischer Verlag, 1956), p. 842.

  [1] Bouillard, *Karl Barth*, Vol. I, p. 87.
  [2] *Ibid.*
  [3] Cf. *Antwort*, p. 840.
  [4] *Humanity of God* (Richmond: John Knox Press, 1960), p. 14.
  [5] *Ibid.*, p. 40.
  [6] *Ibid.*

importance of the social, and the ethical question which it posed for the Church [1].

At the same time, it ultimately proved inadequate, not because of its somewhat "radical" emphasis on social justice, but because it ended by *identifying* the Kingdom of God and the Socialist hope for the future [2]. In doing so, it remained of a piece with nineteenth-century theology. The insufficiency of the Socialist program, from Barth's perspective, was that it was not radical enough in its attempt to lay down new theological and ethical lines [3]. The impetus for this would be supplied, finally, only by a new awareness of the message of the Bible, and a sharp distinction between the reality of God in his self-disclosure and all norms and programs drawn from general culture, contemporary idealist philosophies, and human self-consciousness. Despite a formal break with the Socialist program, however, Barth continued to be influenced by both its concerns and its constructs. Indeed, according to one writer, it accounts in large part for his treatment of contemporary tensions between Communism and the Western world [4].

We must now return to our discussion of Barth's engagement with the problematics of preaching, for it was this which finally drove him to a thorough reconsideration of the source of all theology and preaching, the Bible.

Shortly after his withdrawal from the Socialist movement, Barth began a program of intensive biblical and theological study with Eduard Thurneysen, who was at the time pastor of a congregation in the neighboring town of Lentwil. It was out of this activity of sustained exegetical and theological reflection that the way was cleared for a dramatic new awareness of the "strange new world" of the Bible, and of the sovereignty of God over against all human contrivance. As T.F. Torrance rightly observes, Barth at this time became

> determined to hear the Word of God out of itself, as it came straight from above, unfettered by a masterful culture, uncontrolled by the needs and satisfactions of bourgeois society, and before it had been sifted and diluted by being passed through some general frame of thought already worked out by modern man [5].

---

[1] A concern earlier raised by Troeltsch.

[2] *KD*, II/1, p. 714.

[3] Cf. *Antwort*, p. 842.

[4] Charles C. West, *Communism and the Theologians* (Philadelphia: The Westminster Press, 1958), p. 185. We shall be considering West's criticisms of Barth at length in a later section of this study.

[5] Thomas F. Torrance, *Karl Barth*, p. 35.

Needless to say, this program was not realized straight off in all aspects. However, the articles and lectures which appeared under Barth's name from 1916 to 1922 provide clear indications of new accents and soundings, and evince a gradual submersion of liberal motifs through a consistent sharpening of the lines of demarcation between God and man, revelation and culture, and divine and human righteousness.

An early indication of this new direction is found in "The Righteousness of God", a lecture given in 1916 in the Town Church of Aarau [1]. Barth begins with the assertion that the "surest fact of life" is given us by "the voice of conscience": the righteousness of God [2]. This sounds immediately like an assertion of continuity between human religious awareness or sensitivity and the reality of God. It becomes apparent, however, that a new critical note has been imported into the discussion. Conscience now functions as a reminder of an original righteousness beyond and above, not human *righteousness*, but human error and folly. The awareness of God given by conscience is not, if we listen with seriousness to it, one of comfort and reassurance, guaranteeing validity and providing substance to human intentions and programs. It is only when we refuse to listen, and turn quickly away from conscience, acting "as if" our plans were significant, "as if something were happening, as if we were doing something in obedience to the conscience" [3], that the righteousness of God is distorted and misunderstood in this fashion.

The initial function of conscience is that of *disturbance*, of introducing an element of restlessness into our lives, and so of pointing us *away* from all attempts to "better" the human situation on our own. So, whether we throw ourselves into "religious" activities per se, into moral endeavor, or into the structures of state and law, the result remains constant: a domestication of God and a loss of seriousness [4].

Instead of activity, man needs to listen to conscience. When this is allowed to happen, God may again be recognized as God, rather than as a continuation of humanly structured programs and ideals; then we are enabled to recognize his will as "wholly other" than ours, yet also as the condition for every activity of will in which we engage. Only by such an initial recognition of God's prior righteousness as God can we regain a proper foundation for culture, morality, state and Church [5].

---

[1] *WG*, pp. 9-27.

[2] *Ibid.*, p. 9.

[3] *Ibid.*, p. 15.

[4] *Ibid.*, pp. 16-19.

[5] *Ibid.*, pp. 24-26. Essentially the same point is made in "The Strange

Finally, the act of listening, of recognition, entails a dual movement of humility and joy, which conflate in the notion of faith. And by this is meant simply the acceptance of Jesus as the Son of God [1]. To this, Barth adds a statement both ironic and challenging:

> One may object that this method of squaring the circle is childlike and inadequate. I grant it. But this childlike and inadequate solution is the beginning of the vast plan of God. It remains to be seen whether the quaking of the tower of Babel which we are now experiencing will be violent enough to bring us somewhat nearer to the way of faith [2].

This lecture is instructive, not only because it announces a new direction theologically, but also for what it suggests about theological ethics. This may be indicated as follows: (1) The righteousness of God entails a measuring of the distance between God and man, and so between divine action and human efforts to do or achieve the good. In the first instance, then, the righteousness of God brings unrest, disturbance; only on the far side of this initial encounter in the movement of faith can the positive side of that righteousness be explicated.

(2) Correct theological thinking begins with a recognition of the righteousness of God; so then correct thinking about right human conduct is also directed there initially. This argues immediately against deriving norms or imperatives from given cultural structures or patterns, or from human conscience, when these are taken as independent phenomena. Human righteousness, as this pertains to issues of decision and action, is now a secondary possibility following from, and so dependent on, the prior righteousness of God. The ethical is thus set within the context of theology, and has to do with the action of God manifested in Jesus, not with human decision and activity in themselves.

New World Within the Bible" (an address delivered in Thurneysen's church in Lentwil in autumn, 1916): "At certain crucial points the Bible amazes us by its remarkable indifference to our conception of good and evil ... Time and again the Bible gives us the impression that it contains no instructions, counsels, or examples whatsoever, either for individuals or for nations and governments; and the impression is correct. It offers us not at all what we first seek in it ... Once more we stand before this "other" new world which begins in the Bible. In it the chief consideration is not the doings of man but the doings of God—not the various ways which we may take if we are men of good will, but the power out of which good will must first be created ... It is certain that the Bible, if we read it carefully, makes straight for the point where one must decide to accept or to reject the sovereignty of God". *Ibid.*, pp. 38-41.

[1] *Ibid.*, p. 26.
[2] *Ibid.*, p. 26f.

Assuredly, these points are not filled out in any detail, and their explication even provisionally involves a certain amount of interpretation. We note certain motifs, however (i.e., the emphasis on God as *God*; the notion of the "wholly other"; revelation as disturbance, tension; denial of a simple correlation between divine and human), which will become increasingly dominant in Barth's thinking from this point on, and which, though subject to some inner development and modification, are never lost to view.

At the same time, it is evident that this is a transitional piece. The notion of "conscience" is used throughout without apology, though perhaps with overtones foreign to its straightforward liberal connotations; and faith apparently remains, at the end, still a human possibility. Also, the human will retains a capacity for positive activities in the midst of the social. The righteousness of God does not yet represent a total attack on all human ethical endeavor. This must await a further sharpening of these first indications of a break with liberal theology.

A second address from this early period of importance for a clear view of the development of Barth's thought is his Tambach lecture, "The Christian's Place in Society", delivered at the Conference on Religion and Social Relations in September, 1919 [1].

The importance of this lecture may be gleaned immediately from its title: "The Christian's Place in *Society*" [2]. Barth will be concerned here to relate the "place" or activity of certain men (Christians) to the larger given context and structures within which that activity occurs (the social). In sum, Barth is raising the question of the relation between the service of God and the service of man [3].

Initially, a distinction is drawn between "the Christian" (Christ) and "the Christians":

> *The Christian:* we must be agreed that we do *not* mean *the Christians* ... the Christian is *the Christ*. The Christian is that within us which is not ourself but Christ in us [4].

What Barth means is not a subjective condition or experience. "Christ in us" is to be understood rather as a "presupposition of life" [5],

---

[1] *WG*, pp. 272-327.
[2] Italics added.
[3] *WG*, p. 276.
[4] *Ibid.*, p. 273.
[5] *Ibid.*

exhibiting both pervasiveness and universality [1]. The notion of Christ as "the Christian" functions as a transcendent designation predicable of, but not reducible to, individual Christians [2].

It is with this designated relation between Christ and individual Christians that Barth moves to a discussion of the way in which Christ's presence in us is made manifest in society. This issue is logically equivalent to the question: How may we locate and identify the presence of God in the human? [3] The answer to this is made problematic at the outset because Barth refuses to argue any sort of automatic relation between the two which would be initiated from the side of the human. So, there can be no legitimacy to attempts either to "use the thought-forms of Jesus as the law for every economic, racial, national, and international order" [4], or to "clericalize" society [5]. What must be recognized from the outset is the *autonomy* of society over against the religious or God, and the autonomy of God over against society:

> If today, with all propriety, though to our grief, the Holy asserts its rights over against the profane, the profane asserts its rights over against the Holy. Society is now really ruled by its own logos; say rather by a whole pantheon of its own hypostases and powers [6].

The correct approach to the issue is therefore not to be pursued by attempting to detect and delineate the movement of God immanently, but rather by becoming aware of the transcendent, vertical movement of God in history which receives definitive exemplification in the resurrection of Christ [7]. The human and the divine are thus not finally disparate, but the line of connection lies strictly on the side of God; in revelation,

---

[1] " 'Over us', 'behind us', and 'beyond us' are included in the meaning of 'in us'. And 'Christ in us' understood in its whole Pauline breadth is a warning that we shall do well not to build again the fence which separated the chosen from the rest ... The community of Christ is a building open on every side, for Christ died for all—even for the folk outside". *Ibid.*

[2] Barth's affinity with neo-Kantian categories at this time is suggested here. What he appears to have in mind is the notion of the Transcendental Ego, though it remains here in somewhat embryonic form. It becomes central in the *Römerbrief*, both to his view of man and to his notion of the object of right human action, the neighbor. Cf. John Cullberg, *Das Problem der Ethik in der Dialektischen Theologie* (Uppsala: Appelbergs, 1938), p. 29f.

[3] *WG*, p. 278.

[4] *Ibid.*, p. 279.

[5] *Ibid.*, p. 280.

[6] *Ibid.*, p. 279f.

[7] *Ibid.*, p. 283.

not in man's understanding, experience or inherent "godliness" [1]. It is only in revelation, in the movement of God (Life) into history and our life, that the "deadly isolation of the human from the divine" [2] can be overcome.

Seen from the event of Christ's resurrection, the present situation is an "instant" in the movement of God [3]. It is an occurrence along the way from creation to redemption, and so participates in the total unfolding of the Kingdom of God. But this will mean that our lives unfold in the midst of transition from death to life, from human unrighteousness to the righteousness of God. Even more, it means that our lives, and so the life of society, occur under a total development which, from God's side, is already completed in victory [4]. The difficulties and inconsistencies of society, of our lives in history, are infused with eschatological significance in that they stand under and within the total movement of God in history:

> God in history is *a priori* victory in history. This is the banner under which we march. This is the presupposition of our being here. The real seriousness of our situation is not to be minimized; the tragic incompleteness in which we find ourselves is not to be glossed over. But it is certain that the last word upon the subject has been spoken. The last word is the *kingdom of God*—creation, redemption, the perfection of the world through God and in God [5].

The participation of our lives in the movement of God in history has direct bearing on human activity within the orders and structures of society. Initially, it indicates a certain validity to current attacks upon established forms and structures as ends in themselves. Human restlessness at these points is not to be neglected or refused out of hand, since it has a certain God-given necessity [6], and so an ability to give meaning to the times [7].

At the same time, such protests and unrest are not the *first* things to be undertaken, since this would suggest some kind of necessary relation

---

[1] *Ibid.*, p. 286f.
[2] *Ibid.*, p. 292.
[3] *Ibid.*, p. 295.
[4] *Ibid.*, p. 297.
[5] *Ibid.*
[6] *Ibid.*, p. 293f.
[7] "To *understand* the meaning of our times in God, to enter into God-given restlessness and into critical opposition to life, is to *give* meaning to our times in God". *Ibid.*, p. 294.

between the Kingdom of God and social protest in itself, and would end by granting independent status to the human. The truth of the matter is rather that God's kingdom "does not begin with our movements of protest": [1]

> It is the revolution which is before all revolutions, as it is before the whole prevailing order of things. The great negative precedes the small positive. The original is the synthesis. It is out of this that both thesis and anti-thesis arise [2].

This passage is worth exploring, because it enables Barth to posit a total continuity between creation and redemption, within which society is organically included and continued. The "synthesis" to which Barth refers is the unity of all things in God as Creator and Redeemer. The "thesis" is society; the "antithesis" is the denial or attack upon societal structures which results from the inevitability of the Kingdom of God, manifested in the resurrection of Christ. Beyond this attack, society is moved, with the whole of creation, towards renewal and closure in synthesis.

Now, since the positing of society and the human (thesis) is not within the capability of man, neither is the attack and criticism (antithesis) which issues from God subject to human manipulation. The first move, ethically, will thus be affirmative, an acceptance of the world as it is. Positive acceptance of the world, commitment to the divine element present in its orders, and acknowledgement of the continuity between creation and redemption [3] constitute the initial requirement placed upon the Christian in society [4].

The present, however, is transitional in character. Inevitably, then, "the same moving force that bids us take life as it comes presently prohibits us from doing so" [5]. Initial cooperation within the given structures of society is followed by "radical and absolute opposition" [6]. To exist

---

[1] *Ibid.*, p. 299.

[2] *Ibid.*

[3] It is in this sense of continuity that Barth accords a positive reading to Hegel's view of the rationality of being. *Ibid.*, p. 300.

[4] "When we find ourselves in God, we find ourselves committed to the task of affirming him in the world as it is and not in a false transcendent world of dreams. Only out of such an affirmation can come that genuine, radical denial of which is manifestly the meaning of our movements of protest". *Ibid.*, p. 299.

[5] *Ibid.*, p. 313.

[6] *Ibid.*, p. 320.

under the aegis of the Kingdom of God (and it is impossible *not* to do so) means to follow the movement of God from creation to redemption, and this "necessitates our advancing from the defense to the attack, from the Yes to the No, from a naive acceptance to a criticism of society" [1]. The function of the Church (and so of Christians) in society cannot, then, be that of maintaining a balance. The dynamics of the divine within history presses for "a new approach to the whole of life" [2].

The transition of the Christian from acceptance to criticism cannot, however, be infused with final significance. Both are penultimate undertakings. Both are, humanly considered, no more than *analogies* [3] to the original thesis and antithesis which issue from God. And this will mean that human activity, even when carried on in recognition of the activity of God, will not bring about a final synthesis; that capability lies in God alone [4]. The most the Christian can do is to order both acceptance and criticism transcendently with reference to the "wholly other", thereby bringing them into a proper relationship:

> When we look from creation and redemption toward perfection, when we look toward the "wholly other" *regnum gloriae*, both our naive and our critical attitude to society, both our Yes and our No fall into right practical relation to each other in God [5].

It turns out, then, that the Christian in society finally can do only one thing: He can "follow attentively what is done by God" [6]. To do this, however, does not mean an alignment with some particular ethical scheme or program. It does mean that the activity of the Christian in society, his "place", will be describable in terms neither of simple conservatism nor simple protest. The correct posture ethically for the Christian is just openness to God's prior activity in revelation, which moves the world (and so the orders and structures of society) from creation to redemption, from thesis through antithesis to final synthesis, from the "No" to the "Yes" manifested in the resurrection of Christ.

There are obvious points of continuity between these two lectures. Both place priority on the reality of God in revelation, and delineate

---

[1] *Ibid.*, p. 316.

[2] *Ibid.*, p. 318.

[3] *Ibid.*, p. 321.

[4] "It is only in *God* that the synthesis can be found; but in God it *can* be found—the synthesis which is *meant* in the thesis and sought in the antithesis". *Ibid.*, p. 322.

[5] *Ibid.*, p. 324f.

[6] *Ibid.*, p. 327.

this by a central emphasis on the resurrection of Christ. Both reject the assumption of automatic lines of connection between God and the human, and so (by implication) between divine and human action. This will mean, further, a denial of independent status or significance to human ethical systems, values, and norms. Ethics cannot be grounded immanently, in man and society; on the contrary, both the latter are enclosed within the reality and activity of God. Every attempt to provide adequate foundations for the ethical within the context of human life and activity serves only to indicate the problematic character of man's life. The only dependable basis for human action lies in referring the whole of the human to its transcendent origin in God, which entails a relativizing of proximate goals and ideals in the light of the ultimate, eschatological goal of the world [1].

There is also discernible in the second of these lectures a motif which will become increasingly dominant, and which will attain its most intensive statement in the second edition of the *Römerbrief*: the utilization of dialectic. This may be seen here, in somewhat germinal form, in the employment of Hegelian categories, in the tension between the temporal and the eternal, and in the alternation between acceptance and criticism of existing social forms, which in itself constitutes a mirroring of the activity of God. The central motif employed by Barth to express this dialectical relation between God and the world is found in the linguistic play between the "No" and the "Yes" of revelation. In this lecture and subsequent writings prior to the *Church Dogmatics*, the emphasis falls on the "No" [2]. It is important to note, however, that this is a matter of emphasis. Barth does not come down exclusively on either the "No" or the "Yes". The function of dialectic is that of enabling both sides of the movement of God in history to be referred consistently to their origin [3]. This indicates an historical, rather than a speculative, use of dialectic, as a means of remaining faithful to what Barth takes to be the witness of the Bible [4]. This enables him to shift emphasis in the *Dogmatics* to the "Yes" of revelation without falling into inconsistency.

---

[1] Cf. Torrance, *Karl Barth*, p. 63.

[2] "We must honestly confess, even when we seek to comprehend our situation from the viewpoint of God, that we know the element of tragedy in it better than that element of sovereignty which might reconcile us to it. *We live more deeply in the No than in the Yes* ... more deeply in longing for the future than in participation in the present". *WG*, p. 311f. Cf. also "Biblical Questions, Insights and Vistas", *Ibid.*, p. 80.

[3] "The truth lies not in the Yes and not in the No but in the knowledge of the beginning from which the Yes and the No arise". *Ibid.*, p. 73.

[4] *Ibid.*

Ethically, the emergence of dialectic in Barth's method will have two consequences: (1) It will enable him to approach the issue of the ethical without falling into or adopting a particular world-view or ideology [1]. As we shall see, this has important consequences during the years of Barth's struggle with National Socialism, and it is not without importance for an understanding of his later pronouncements on Communism, despite his methodological shift from dialectic to analogy [2].

(2) It poses the issue of the possibility of concrete human action, and the direction this is to take. Put differently, this is the question of what it will mean, concretely, to "follow attentively what is done by God". The dual aspect of the Christian's role in society, expressed in the notions of acceptance and criticism, provides, finally, only a formal indication of this. What are needed are criteria or conditions enabling one to decide in particular cases, i.e. when the response at the human level is properly acceptance of existing structures, patterns, and norms, and when criticism, modification, or overthrow of these is required. We shall need to look carefully to discern what Barth offers by way of providing these, and whether they adequately speak to the dilemma of right *Christian* human action in specific contexts.

I have sought, in this first section, to suggest the point at which Barth's engagement with the question of ethics occurred, and the direction it took. This has been gleaned somewhat indirectly, as it appears within the larger theological shift away from the guiding assumptions and method of liberal theology [3]. What has been indicated thus far, and what is surely the single most important point to emerge from this period, is a new direction and approach to the whole theological enterprise. The lines no longer run from culture or human consciousness to God; the movement is, rather, exclusively from God *to* man, from revelation *to* the social. There is thus a clear suggestion of *diastasis* between the reality and activity of God in revelation, and human response

---

[1] Cf. Torrance, *Karl Barth*, p. 80.

[2] I shall discuse this in a later section dealing with the issue of method in the *Church Dogmatics*.

[3] It is not inaccurate, perhaps, to suggest that even in these initial lectures the dependence of ethics on prior theological statement is clearly maintained. To be sure, it is not yet set forth as a formal principle of method, as it will be in the *Dogmatics*. And since both Aquinas and Schleiermacher sought, in their ways, to keep ethics within a consistent theological framework, we are advised against pushing the point too strongly here.

and behavior. This *diastasis*, or "Krisis" [1] serves to underline the *distance* between God and man, and so overcomes the notion prevalent in liberal theology of an indigenous relationality between the divine and the human. Also, it has the result of rendering human ethics at the outset *problematic*, in that the impact of revelation, in relativizing all human activity, places a question mark at every point over its validity.

Now, neither of these points has as yet been developed with final stringency by Barth. Indeed, as Bouillard points out, even the first edition of the *Römerbrief* still provides for an organic unity between God and man in the notion of the Kingdom of God, and ethics does not constitute a final crisis of the human [2]. It is the second edition of *Römerbrief* which exposes the radical character of the distance between God and man in its full ramifications, and which views human ethics functionally, as an indication of man's total "sickness unto death" [3].

B. THEOLOGY OF *Krisis* (1921-1926)

An appointment in 1921 to the theological faculty at the University of Göttingen removed Barth from immediate involvement with the demands of the pastorate. In September of that year, the second edition of the *Römerbrief* was published. This proved to be a stringent reworking of the first edition of 1919, whose favorable reception had aroused Barth's suspicions [4]. What needed to be excised, it was apparent, was every suggestion of an organic relation between God and man. So long as this remained, the line of demarcation between them was ambiguous, and incurred the risk of removal through an appeal to immanent religious categories. It was the second edition, accordingly, which alerted European theology to the presence of a decisive new voice and direction, earning for its author the dubious encomium of having founded a new "school" [5]. Any consideration of the development of Barth's thought during the

---

[1] The term most regularly employed by Barth in the second edition of the *Römerbrief* to designate the vertical inbreak of God into history.

[2] *Karl Barth*, Vol. I, p. 91.

[3] Cf. "The Problem of Ethics Today", *WG*, p. 150.

[4] *RÖM*, p. vii.

[5] *Ibid.* T.A. Gill has provided a nice summation of the operative facets of "Barthianism" as it evolved out of the *Römerbrief* and later writings. Cf. *Recent Protestant Political Theory* (Great Britain: Hunt, Barnard and Co., Ltd., 1953), p. 57.

period from its appearance to the publication, in 1927, of the *Prolegomena zur Christlichen Dogmatik*, must consist primarily in a delineation of the central thrusts of this pivotal work [1].

The stronger impact of the second edition of the *Römerbrief* may be seen as the result of a heightened employment of theological dialectic, and a virtual reduction of the meaning of revelation to the *Krisis* motif. That this did not entail complete discontinuity between the two editions may be seen in the following points of similarity drawn by Bouillard [2]. Both stress the radicality of the Kingdom of God in its transcendent origin as a sheer gift of God. This emphasis is continued in Barth's treatment of the Holy Spirit, which is delineated as a "transcendental disposition" possessing man, not an immanent determination of the human. Further, historical and psychological aspects of reality serve primarily as indications of man's continued efforts to retain autonomy from God. Consequently, every mode of human activity, even those ostensibly "higher" forms exhibited in morality, religion, the Church, pacifism, and the social-democratic movement, are nothing more, finally, than manifestations of sin. Man has, in himself, no capacity or ability to reestablish immediacy with God. He is saved only by faith, by the action of God, which occurs always as miracle. Finally, Barth's theological realism is discernible throughout in the emphasis placed on the "objectivity" of God in revelation.

Despite these points of similarity, the second edition of the *Römerbrief* manifests a consistently stringent and heightened sensitivity to the *distance* between God and man, which is bridged only from God's side, in grace, and which absolutely precludes every possibility of organic continuity between them. As might be expected, this will bear important consequences for his reading of theological ethics. Before examining this, however, we shall need to indicate the content of the *Krisis* under which man stands, and the methodological significance of dialectic as a vehicle for getting this expressed.

T.F. Torrance has suggested that Barth's use of dialectic provides an epistemic counterpart to the doctrine of justification by grace alone [3]. Another way of expressing this, perhaps, is that dialectic enables Barth

---

[1] Additional writings from this period will, of course, be introduced where relevant.

[2] Bouillard, *Karl Barth*, Vol. I, p. 94f. Bouillard suggests a coincidental similarity between Barth's critique of man's inner religious awareness and Hegel's critique of the "good soul" in the *Phenomenology of Mind*.

[3] Torrance, *Karl Barth*, p. 88.

to explore the dimensions of the *event* of revelation without incurring
the danger of converting the Subject of revelation into a simple and
direct datum or object of human experience and knowledge. Dialectic
would thus function to insure that, within the context of theological
exposition and exploration, God remains God. The counter to this,
of course, is that man recognizes and abides by the limitations proper
to him as the *object* of revelation. The subject-object polarity of divine
and human reality is thus not only not abrogated in the theological
venture; in dialectic it is given methodological exemplification. Torrance
puts the matter succinctly:

> Theological thinking is inescapably dialectical because it must be a
> thinking by *man* not from a centre in himself but from a centre in *God*,
> and yet never seeks to usurp God's own standpoint. It is dialogical
> thinking in which man remains man but in which he meets God, listens
> to him, answers him, and speaks of him in such a way that at every point
> he gives God the glory. Because it is dialogical, it can only be fragmented
> on his side, for it does not carry its co-ordinating principle in itself,
> but derives it from beyond itself in God's Word [1].

Within this context, the term *Krisis* [2] becomes operationally significant in two ways. First, it points to the total transcendence of God
over the world. Defined negatively, this means that God is unknown,
hidden, remote, "totally other". There is no possibility of "detecting"
God immanently. The reality of God is set over against the reality of
the world, and the latter has only a derivative, dependent status. The
positive side of God's transcendence indicates the total freedom with
which God encounters the world in his revelation. It is precisely in the
event of revelation in Jesus Christ that the freedom of God becomes
most evident. The reality of this event does not lessen the stringency
of separation between God and the world. It offers no available *via media*
between the otherness and presence of God, and consequently provides
no categories capable of "explaining" or "understanding" the reality
of God without remainder [3]. The paradoxical character of reve-

---

[1] *Ibid.*, p. 83.

[2] This term has its roots in the Greek word "κρίσις", which means, among
other things, a separating, dividing, or judgment. Here, the original force of
the Greek is taken up and expanded into a shorthand expression for a total
theological perspective.

[3] "God is the unknown God. As such, he gives to all life and breath
and all things. Thus, his power is neither a power of nature nor a power of
men's souls, nor yet some sort of high and remote force which we now know

lation insures God's freedom against and within the world [1].

The second task assigned the term *Krisis* is that of indicating the status of the world. Within the *Römerbrief*, the world is placed unequivocally under judgment. This means that the first effect of revelation is the negation of the world in its present form. Expressed anthropologically, what is involved is a total relativizing and submerging of human activities, values, and structures. These have no validity or stability in themselves. Placed under the impact of revelation, they can only serve as indications of the incompleteness and deficiency of the world apart from God, and of the impossibility of locating points of security within the world which will somehow, in themselves, maintain continuity with God. The immediate result of revelation is that everything is called into question and made insecure. Yet, paradoxically, this *Krisis* is also the necessary condition for the emergence of a positive human freedom [2].

What is true of the world generally is also specifically applicable to religion and the Church. On Barth's reading, the "religious" man can claim no special exemption from the *Krisis* of revelation, for he, and the institutionalized forms in which he participates, are denied autonomous significance [3].

---

or perhaps can come to know. God's power is neither the most exalted of known forces, nor is it their summation or source. Being entirely different, it is the crisis of all powers (*die Krisis aller Kräfte*), according to whose measure all power is seen to be something and—nothing, nothing and—something". *RÖM*, p. 11.

[1] "It hangs entirely in the air. It is the pure, absolute vertical miracle". *Ibid.*, p. 35.

[2] "This calling into question (*Infragestellung*) of the whole complex of our participation and activity, of all our known ways, direct and devious, of our seriousness and frivolity, righteousness and sinfulness, belief or atheism or scepticism, even this final perhaps—perhaps not, which has been laid like an axe at the root of a tree, is indeed the freedom beyond the Law which we have in God. It is a freedom which we cannot avoid, because it is the truth, because it is the freedom of God himself ... We do not mean a position, nor a highest standpoint on which, perhaps, certain men stand. Neither do we mean a blessed redemption present in some corner of our unredeemedness, nor a warm sunset glow in some phase of our life stages, which is about to break through after the thunder storm. We mean the orientation which is given to man by God himself and by God alone". *Ibid.*, p. 275f.

[3] "What can be said of men generally can be said also of the men of God. As men they do not differ from other men. There is no special divine history existing as a part or quantity in the midst of general history. The whole history

Human experience and knowledge, of whatever variety, display only the negative condition for revelation: man's utter lack of knowledge of God, and, correspondingly, his total incapacity to speak of God. No man escapes the *Krisis* under which God has placed the world, and the disturbance, tension, and insecurity which this brings. Put propositionally, the *Krisis* of the world can be stated directly: God is God [1]. The *Krisis* of the world and human existence can be seen only as the result of the direction and decision taken by God to justify, reconcile, and redeem the world. It is the result of God's act of election [2].

Now, the negative thrust of revelation unfolds against the background of the positive actuality of grace disclosed in Jesus Christ, specifically in the resurrection event [3]. Indeed, it is this alternation between the negative condition of man and the positive reality of grace that make up the dialectical interplay between the "No" and "Yes" of revelation [4]. The "No" of revelation, the *Krisis* into which the world is plunged, thus becomes the necessary precondition for an appropriate recognition and acknowledgement of God. Within the context of judgment, the reality of grace emerges. The negative condition of the human functions parabolically to indicate the hiddenness of grace in its manifestation. Negativity, therefore, is not to be seen as an end in itself. God's "No" unfolds only against an equally strong "Yes", and this insures that the world, in being placed under the *Krisis* of judgment, is also already caught up in the *total* action of God. In a word, it participates in reconciliation and redemption, in mercy and the forgiveness of sins.

The appearance of grace in Jesus Christ, the givenness of the "Yes" in the midst of God's "No" over the world, is not a self-evident fact. For this reason, its apprehension is always problematic and paradoxical.

---

of Church and religion occurs in the world. What is referred to as the 'history of salvation' is no more than the continuing crisis of all history. It is not an affair 'in' or 'alongside' ordinary history. There are no holy men in the midst of the unholy. Precisely insofar as they have wished to claim this, they have succeeded only in being unholy". *Ibid.*, p. 32.

[1] "... daß Gott Gott ist". *Ibid.*, p. 62. Bouillard cites this as the "leitmotif" of Barth's thought. *Karl Barth*, Vol. I, p. 22.

[2] *RÖM*, pp. 153, 328.

[3] *Ibid.*, pp. 6, 8, 133, 183. Of course, the actuality of the resurrection is eschatological throughout: "Sie ist als solche nicht ein 'historisches' Ereignis neben den andern Ereignissen dieser Geschichte, sondern das 'unhistorisch'e Ereignis". *Ibid.*, p. 183.

[4] Cf. Ramsey, *Faith and Ethics*, p. 48.

It is apprehended only in faith, which always entails risk. There is no way whereby it can be guaranteed from the side of the world [1].

Barth's employment of paradox and dialectic indicates the strong eschatological orientation of the *Römerbrief* [2]. The new world presented in revelation is in no sense directly visible. Outwardly, everything remains as it was, in the grip of sin and death. Redemption, participation in the new world of God, is hidden, and is presently accessible only as hope [3]. And hope assumes the form of waiting, of continuing in a world which is overcome only eschatologically:

> Indeed, that is the strange thing, that we are men who wait throughout the full extent of our journey through time, as if we saw what we do not see, as if we beheld the unseen. Hope is the solution to this riddle, the removal of the "as if". Indeed, we do see. We see existentially what we do not yet see. Therefore we wait [4].

Hope enjoys more than the function merely of providing an orientation to the world. It is also an adumbration of the possibility of positive human action :

> Indeed, we are then in the astonishing position of being called into question, and with this question—which manifestly is a question addressed to us by Another—we thrust on to an eternal Ground. Then we are indeed united with Christ, and, grasped and known by God, we have the possibility beyond all possibilities, the impossible possibility of walking after the Spirit [5].

Here we touch on the ethical thrust of the *Römerbrief*. Before proceeding to an analysis of this, a few summarizing remarks are in order. It is clear, in all this, that Barth is determined to eliminate every

---

[1] "The vision of the New Day is, and remains, indirect. Revelation in Jesus is a paradoxical fact, however objective and universally binding its content is. That the promises of the faithful God have been fulfilled in Jesus, that Jesus is indeed the Christ to whom all promises point, all that is not, and never will be, a self-evident truth, because in him the faithfulness of God appears in its final hiddenness and deepest mystery ... To believe in Jesus is the most hazardous of hazards". *RÖM*, p. 72f.

[2] "Christianity that is not wholly and exclusively eschatological has nothing whatever to do with Christ". *Ibid.*, p. 298.

[3] "Redemption is the invisible, the inaccessible, the impossible, and it encounters us as hope". *Ibid.*

[4] *Ibid.*

[5] *Ibid.*, p. 265. The German brings out the oddity of the possibility in a more obvious way than does Hoskyns's translation. Edwyn C. Hoskyns (trans.): *The Epistle to the Romans* (London: Oxford University Press), p. 282.

vestige of anthropocentrism which might have clung to the first edition. Where knowledge of God is concerned, the world is viewed only negatively. It provides no supports for revelation, but is instead wholly submerged and overcome in the judgment of God. Human forms of knowing provide no basis whatever for encountering the being of God. This occurs only on a transepistemological basis in the event of faith, which takes the form of hope. No *reasons* can be given for this. It remains a mystery which occurs in spite of (but also, paradoxically, *because* of) the "infinite qualitative distinction" between God and the world, eternity and time. Barth achieves his objective by refusing to separate epistemic and ontic considerations, or, as Hans Frei suggests, by rejecting the distinction between an *ordo cognoscendi* and an *ordo essendi* [1]. The being of God in revelation encloses the possibility of human knowledge of God, and this can be expressed only as paradox. The *possibility* of knowing God is grounded in the *actuality* of grace in the cross and resurrection of Christ. Every suggestion of organic continuity between God and the world is thus eliminated. The polarity between them is bridged only from God's side.

The first thing to be noticed, on turning to the ethical content of the *Römerbrief*, is the continuity maintained between theological and ethical issues. This has already been noted, in connection with our discussion of the earlier essays. Here the point becomes more explicit, though it is not yet stated as a formal principle of method. What it amounts to, finally, is a conflating of theory and practice. So, in beginning his discussion of the twelfth chapter of the epistle, Barth emphasizes that the "theory" that has been examined and explicated in the preceding sections is "the theory of the practice of religion" [2]. From the beginning, "the ethical problem has nowhere been left out of account" [3]. Given this continuity, it is scarely surprising that Barth's discussion of ethics will be informed by the motifs of *Krisis*, paradox, and dialectic, and will be placed within an embracing eschatological context.

Ethical possibilities and actions, since they fall within the context of the human, stand in the first instance under the impact of the *Krisis* of God's revelation in Jesus Christ, and so can only be problematic [4].

---

[1] Ramsey, *Faith and Ethics*, p. 49.

[2] "... daß eben die 'Theorie' von der wir herkommen die Theorie der Praxis ist". *RÖM*, p. 412f.

[3] *Ibid.*

[4] "What else can the problem of ethics, appearing here again with force, mean than the great disturbance (*die große Störung*)?" *Ibid.*, p. 410.

Their problematic character arises from the fact that they are viewed from the perspective of eternity, rather than from values and goals susceptible of immanent realization. The hiddenness of God in revelation, the eschatological thrust of faith as commitment in the face of paradox and mystery, and the total denial of immanent connectives between man and God, disclose the full ambiguity of human ethical activity [1]. Man's total enterprise as ethical agent, and the structures and forms evoked in support of this, are, as aspects of the world, placed under the judgment of God's "No". The ethical side of the human is thus (in itself) relativized and denuded of any positive significance. Taken independently, it indicates only the movement towards death in which the world as a whole is involved [2]. The life of the natural man, as exemplified in history and culture, contains no positive ethical possibilities or significance [3].

The results of this analysis for ethics are devasting. Clearly, there is no way to build up a "positive" ethic [4]. Not only do ethical actions share in a pervasive ambiguity reflecting the (erotic) form of the world; they fail further to establish continuity between human and divine reality and action. Accordingly, they can be granted only the negative significance of standing under the judgment of God. The end of all ethical activity, seen as a purely human possibility, is "shipwreck" [5]. It is impossible to derive an answer to the ethical problem from within the human. The only possibility open to man is that of realizing a total inability to provide an answer [6]. Or, again, the only "answer" possible is that man in himself is not good [7].

This negative reading of human ethical possibilities discloses the positive background and presupposition of a viable approach to the matter: God is God [8]. This does not mean that man is given the capacity

---

[1] "The decisive word about ethics must disclose their full ambiguity ('... der Aufweis des tatsächlichen Bestehens dieses Problematik'), an ambiguity covering every aspect of human behavior". *Ibid.*, p. 414.

[2] "The assault upon our genius constitutes the crisis that announces our passage from death to life". *Ibid.*, p. 421.

[3] "The Problem of ethics contains the secret that man as we know him in this life is an impossibility. *This* man, in God's sight, can only perish". "The Problem of Ethics Today", in *WG*, p. 140.

[4] *RÖM*, p. 417.

[5] *WG*, p. 163.

[6] *Ibid.*, p. 166.

[7] *Ibid.*, p. 167.

[8] "Daß Gott Gott ist, das ist die Voraussetzung der Ethik". *RÖM*, p. 424.

to recognize and grasp this *as presupposition*, after which he independently deduces the appropriate consequences, making application of it in varying situations evoking decision and action. The presupposition of ethics identifies at once the primary subject of every good action: God in Jesus Christ. Strictly speaking, there is only *one* action which is ethical, and that is an action moving the world in its totality from death to life, from judgment to forgiveness. The action of God in Jesus Christ both demonstrates the enigmatic character of every humanly conceived and executed "solution" to ethics, and itself provides the answer. The answer to the problem of the ethical lies not in what man is doing or might attempt to do. It lies wholly in what God has done and continues to do for and to man and the world in Jesus Christ. The *meaning* of God's action is enclosed in the word "grace". And this means, quite simply, that God does one very definite thing: He forgives men their sins:

> Grace means that God does something. Grace does not mean that God does everything, but that he does some quite definite thing. Not something in general, not a thing here and a thing there, but something in men. Grace means that God forgives man his sin [1].

The action of God in forgiving man's sin exemplifies his mercy. The mercy of God, as grace, is thus the positive answer to the ambiguity of the human, and to the problem of ethics. But because it encounters and overcomes sin, it can issue initially only in judgment and death. It is in this way that the action of God constitutes the *Krisis* of every human action. It indicates a transition from sin to grace, from death to life, from slavery to freedom. In short, it indicates man's (forensic) justification by God through the forgiveness of sins [2].

The reality of grace in the context of the human evokes an inexorable tension. It points to the irreversible decision of God on the world, and so provides a new orientation for human decision and action. It is clear, however, that this possibility can only be indirectly indicated as an aspect of man's historical existence. It is never a directly predicable quality at all, but is indicative of a contradiction in man, or, perhaps better, *over* man. The possession of grace is an "impossible possibility"

---

[1] "Gnade heißt, daß Gott etwas tut. Gnade heißt nicht, daß Gott 'alles', sondern daß er etwas ganz Bestimmtes tut, nicht im Allgemeinen, nicht da und dort, sondern am Menschen. Gnade heißt, daß Gott dem Menschen seine Sünde vergibt". *RÖM*, p. 196.

[2] *Ibid.*, p. 180. Here we encounter the key to Barth's anthropology: Man is always *simul justus et peccator*. Cf. Bouillard, *Karl Barth*, Vol. I, p. 23.

devolving from God [1]. It indicates, finally, an eschatological transformation of man:

> For indeed the significance of the divine contradiction is that the new individual created and redeemed by God is proclaimed as the invisible truth of our existence, before which our visible truth becomes untruth [2].

The impact of grace signals an absolute translation of the human. In the resurrection of Jesus Christ there occurs an adumbration of the new world, beyond sin and death, into which all men have been transposed. This transposition expresses the indicative facet of grace, the eschatologically posited and determined reality of the new man.

The indicative, however, does not exhaust the content of grace. The action of God, in addition to establishing the (transcendent) reality of man, also presents him with a demand. At the point of human action and decision, grace ineluctably takes the form of an imperative:

> Grace, as the existential relationship between God and man, can only break out of the indicative of the divine truth concerning men into the imperative by which the divine reality imposes its demand upon them; They must now will what God wills [3].

The imperative of grace exhibits both a primary and a secondary level. Primarily, it entails an existential awareness of sin, and the shattering failure of every attempt on man's part to do the good [4]. Moreover, this side of grace persists. Where human action is concerned, there is no facile transition from sin to grace. Empirically, the man of grace remains only a possibility to be realized. Every effort directed towards its realization is limited by the eschatological reality of the new man in Christ. There is simply no way to claim direct embodiment of the possibility of living in grace. Human existence occurs always only under the judgment and forgiveness of God. For this reason, human action can never be self-contained or adequate. It can only point beyond itself to the prior action of God [5]. The refuge of a "system" of ethics is denied even (or perhaps especially) man under grace [6].

---

[1] "Solches Gnadehaben geschieht als die unmögliche Möglichkeit Gottes jenseits aller unserer eigenen Möglichkeiten". *RÖM*, p. 197.

[2] *Ibid.*

[3] *Ibid.*, p. 204.

[4] *Ibid.*, p. 208.

[5] "Anlaß ist alles menschliche Handeln oder Nicht-Handeln um auf das allein wirklich dieses Namens werte göttliche Handeln hinzuweisen". *Ibid.*, p. 417.

[6] *Ibid.*, p. 210.

The recognition of sin, as a "first order" fulfillment of the imperative of grace, takes the form of repentance. As a recognition and acceptance of the "ambiguity of human existence" [1], repentance is the touchstone by which all additional "second order" actions are appraised and illumined. Repentance consists essentially in "rethinking" [2], that is, a continually renewed acknowledgement of the primacy of the action of God, and a willingness to allow every human judgment and action to fall under this. What repentance does, then, is to focus and underline the eschatological origin and goal, announced in the resurrection of Christ, of man's total existence [3]. Initially, correct human action consists simply in man's willingness to make way for the action of God [4]. This receives direct embodiment in the act of worship [5].

Granting this, it becomes obviously important to ascertain what form or direction "second-order" ethical actions will take, and what content they will embody. It is clear they cannot amount to some sort of independently consistent ethic. Human actions in themselves can never solve the ethical problem, not even where this applies to specific, limited problems, or to contexts within which issues are joined in decision. Every specific decision and action is relativized when viewed from the transcendent, eschatological perspective of the action of God in Jesus Christ. At best, human action is capable of embodying parabolic meaning [6]. It achieves this to the extent that it manifests a counter-tendency to the present course of the world, a negation of the "form of this world", and so demonstrates "a behavior which contradicts its erotic course, and which protests against its great error" [7]. Such parabolic action exhibits both positive and negative possibilities. There will be things

---

[1] "... der Problematik seines Daseins". *Ibid.*, p. 422.

[2] "Dieses primäre Handeln aber, an das alles sekundäre sich anschliessen muß, aus dem es seine Leuchtkraft gewinnt, ist 'die Erneuerung eures Dendens' ". *Ibid.*

[3] *Ibid.*, p. 423.

[4] "Man kann ihn bitten, dieser ihm nur zu wohlbekannten Krisis, aller seiner Gedanken nicht auszuweichen, sondern sie zu bedenken, dem Wort Gottes Gehör, dem Werke Gottes Raum zu geben". *Ibid.*, p. 423.

[5] *Ibid.*, p. 437.

[6] This reading of human action appeared earlier in "The Christian's Place in Society".

[7] "Positiv-ethisch ist das Wollen und Tun, das der (vergebenden!) 'Gestalt dieser Welt' ... gegenüber negativ ist, das sich nicht in ihr Schema, das Schema des Eros, fügt, das gegen den großen Irrtum Protest einlegt". *RÖM*, p. 436.

willed and done, and things not willed and not done, which point beyond themselves to the inexorable future of the world in God [1].

This latter point concerning the futurity of the world in God is crucial to an adequate understanding of Barth's view of the possibilities open for viable human ethical action. It has the effect simultaneously of relativizing temporal modes and structures as these define and describe human life within history, and of forcing us to address the *form* rather than the *matter* of human actions. Materially, all human actions, positive and negative, fall within the world. If they are to gain significance as Christian ethical actions, this will emerge only on the basis of their form [2].

We should not be misled into assuming that Barth is here positing some immanent formal significance or meaning in human actions which might be made evident through either simple inspection or detailed analysis. If this were a feasible interpretation, it would perhaps suggest the possibility of deriving an ethic of principle based on continuity of form. It is clear that Barth is not setting forth this sort of ethic at all. The possibility of human actions displaying parabolic significance, even formally, remains an eschatological one. Viewed immanently, the form as well as the matter of human actions is locked within the "form of this world". What Barth intends by the possible parabolic function of the form of human conduct is the relation it bears to the "Primal Origin" (*Ursprung*) of the world, to the "unity of the acting Subject" (*der Einheit des Handelnden*) [3]. That human action in fact bears this relation to God is, obviously, a matter strictly of grace. It lodges exclusively in the freedom of God. The parabolic significance of ethical action can in no way be programed, so that certain possibilities are directly identifiable as correct, and others are, just as directly, excluded.

Given this analysis, it is obvious that any descriptive account of those possibilities which fall under the category of a "positive ethic" [4] can serve only a limited end. "Submission" or "subjection" to existing orders and structures account, descriptively, for the "Great Negative Possibility"; and *agape* love, as the "concrete analogue of election", stands as the "Great Positive Possibility" nudging us beyond simple

---

[1] *Ibid.*, pp. 435-459.
[2] *Ibid.*, p. 436.
[3] *Ibid.*
[4] *Ibid.*, p. 436.

acceptance of or accommodation to those same orders and structures [1]. In neither case, however, is it possible to move directly from the possibility to its actualization in action. These do not indicate "principles of action" to be introduced into specific contexts. They rather indicate immediate possibilities which from time to time, in different situations, might gain embodiment in decision. Moreover, there is no way to build up even an empirically continuous account of Christian ethics by focusing on assumed psychological continuities informing decisions. Ethical continuity lodges in the Holy Spirit, not in the human spirit or conscience underlying our actions. The latter is of a piece with the world of Eros which has been placed under the shattering and total *Krisis* of God's action [2].

There is a persistent insecurity pervading the human. Every action is not only relative in relation to its context; it is further *relativized* by the overarching action of God. Hence, both the reactionary and the revolutionary are warned against attempting to evolve final programs of social and political reform [3]. And the Christian exerts influence, ethically, within the existing order precisely by "disturbing nothing at all" [4]. Second-order ethical action is not based on principles, rules, or programs of reform. It is oriented at all points towards the revolutionary disturbance of God within the world, which includes every humanly conceived and executed order, structure, program and action. The action of the Christian, even those specific actions which emerge in decision, is eschatologically oriented at all points. Positively, this carries a freedom over against all existing possibilities. Decisions are forged amidst the tension of judgment, the immediacies of the context, and the necessity to act. Negatively, it excludes the possibility of setting up some kind of final order within time and history [5].

The eschatological orientation of the *Römerbrief* is given additional emphasis at two important points: The reality of the Christian community as a context of fellowship and action, and the identity of the "other", the neighbor to whom the Christian is enjoined to demonstrate love. "Fellowship", as a predicate of the Christian community, is not an

---

[1] *Ibid.*, pp. 459-486.

[2] *Ibid.*, p. 441.

[3] "Today, we must guard ourselves from the temptation of accepting either a philosophy of revolution or a philosophy of reaction". *WG*, p. 143.

[4] "Er bringt die große göttliche Störung, indem er durchaus kein Störefried ist". *RÖM*, p. 491.

[5] *Ibid.*, p. 488f.

empirically derived quality or phenomenon. It does not describe the aggregate form of the individuals in the community, nor does it refer to the Church as organism [1]. "Fellowship" indicates instead an original, primal synthesis and unity of believers in Christ. The fellowship of the Christian community refers to its identity as "the Individual, the One, the New Man" [2]. Individuals in the community take their existential identity from their eschatological identity as the Body of Christ. And it is in relation to this primal identity that ethical actions are to be undertaken and carried out [3]. In the end, secondary ethical actions are inevitably turned back to the primary action of God, and so back to the *Krisis* under which the world is irrevocably placed [4].

Similarly, the "thou" whom we encounter in the neighbor is no simple, directly present, empirical thou. The real, ethically significant "Thou" again refers to Christ, in whom all men are grounded. The "object" of ethical action is lodged at this level. It follows, then, that concrete individuals have parabolic significance in relation to their eschatological identity in Christ [5]. And it appears, further, that the real existentiality of the individual just is that same identity which he has in Christ. This would hold true whether we are referring to the subject of ethical action (the individual Christian), or to the object of that action (the neighbor). Both have their identity, finally, only in relation to Christ, that is, only at a transcendent, eschatological level.

Now, Barth's treatment of positive ethical possibilities, and of the individuals involved in carrying these out, is probably not designed, ostensibly, to neutralize the human completely. The neighbor, even as parable, still constitutes something quite real towards whom action must be taken [6]. And Christians are required to act, to do something quite

---

[1] "Denn Gemeinschaft ist wieder Aggregat nach Organismus". *Ibid.*, p. 428. Cf. Bouillard, *Karl Barth*, Vol. I, p. 68f.

[2] *RÖM*, p. 429f.

[3] *Ibid.*

[4] "Denn es biegt kraft dieser Erinnerung die sekundäre ethische Handlung des sich Besinnens zürück zur primären zu ihrem Anfang und nimmt mit ihrem Anfang Teil an der Kraft und Würde ihres Ursprungs". *Ibid.*, p. 429f.

[5] "Denn eben am Problem des Andern entsteht das Problem der Ethik, die Frage: Was sollen wir tun? Aber nicht die empirischen 'anderen' Einzelnen als solche sind hier gemeint als Subjekt und Objekt der 'Ermahnung'. Gemeint sind hier die Andern, sofern auch sie gerade in ihrer undurchsichtigen unerforschlichen Andersheit Glaubende, von der Not und Hoffnung der Gottesfrage Bedrängte, als Einzelne in Christus begründet sind". *Ibid.*, p. 427.

[6] "Schon der Begriff der Zeit, an dem für unser Bewustsein dieses Du, das empirisch-wirkliche Individuum, der konkrete Einzelne als der Ein-Malige

specific, even if this takes the form, occasionally, of refraining from action. It does not necessarily follow, then, that an emphasis on eschatological realities diminishes the importance of concrete situations and possibilities within the world, as these relate to the emergence of ethical decisions. It depends on how one takes eschatology, and on how eschatological and non-eschatological categories are related. If the former signals a merely transhistorical plane lacking utterly in relation to the temporal world and affairs of man, then certainly the result would be ethically disturbing [1].

It can be argued that this negative interpretation was not intended by Barth. An alternative reading is suggested by two central considerations about the general posture of the *Römerbrief*. First, the utilization of dialectic, and the resulting interplay between the "No" and the "Yes" of revelation, or (put differently) between the negative condition of the human *under* grace, and the positive actuality of grace itself, could entail assigning positive significance to human actions. It could mean that the activity of man as ethical agent would make a difference relative to the immediacies of context within which he acts. Second, eschatological categories appear to describe the *present* transformation of the world under grace. And this, again, could mean that human actions might be enabled to discern and follow the activity of God in the world in such a way that they would be infused, as human actions, with at least a relative positive meaning. An eschatological dialectic, then, need not result immediately in an elimination of the significance of the human.

Unfortunately, it seems extremely difficult to make out this case with any degree of persuasiveness. There are, true enough, negative and positive possibilities which fall under something called a "positive ethic". What is not clear is that these serve to establish and enhance

---

entsteht, zeigt deutlich, daß dieser als solcher nur ein Gleichnis, der 'Anlaß' für dem Ewig-Einzelnen, Existentiell-Wirklichen sein kann. Was aber wiederum nicht heißen darf, daß er dieses Gleichnis, dieser Anlaß nicht wirklich ist, daß dieses transzendentale Ich, gerade weil es das ewige Ich ist, nicht in jedem zeitlichen Moment gegenwärtig ist". *Ibid.*

[1] This interpretation is taken by T.A. Gill: "What have eschatological realities to do with present politics? More exactly, why, when we orient our lives around ultimates, do we bother any longer with proximates—less than ultimates? If we believe in a resurrection from the dead, why act and fight for right in the temporal community? What is really important about the 'important?' ". *Recent Protestant Political Theory*, p. 76.

the human and temporal in any decisive fashion. It is one thing to focus on the action of God in Jesus Christ as *the* ethically meaningful action, and to insist that human choice and action are now to be oriented exclusively towards what God does and continues to do in the world. It is quite another matter to translate this into the context of the human in such a way that the existential reality of the acting self, under the freedom granted in grace, takes on discernible contour and depth. It is at just this point that the difficulty emerges.

The reasons for this are not hard to identify, though they do not include the problem of an assumed separation between eschatological and temporal categories and structures [1]. Barth makes it perfectly clear throughout that the action of God, though eschatological through and through, impinges directly and inclusively on the world. The issue has rather to do with a transformation of the world so radical that it appears to leave no room for establishing any sort of independent status for the world or human action. And if this is the case, then it would mean either that the impact of revelation results, quite simply, in the total elimination of the world, including human action, so that one can speak only of the reality of God, or that the world and the human are somehow absorbed into the being of God. Now, Barth clearly does not allow the latter possibility to happen. The former alternative, however, is at least suggested in the following ways.

In the *Römerbrief*, the dialectic between the negative and positive aspects of revelation is by no means balanced. The emphasis falls most heavily on the "No", on the original *Krisis* inaugurated by God upon the world [2]. To be sure, the "Yes" of revelation emerges within and under the "No", but the relationship is not reversible, nor is the transition effected through the agency of the human. It is, obviously, wholly and exclusively the prerogative of God. Man's position ethically is that of being placed under a question to which he cannot possibly provide the answer. Only God can do that. Every specific decision made by man serves only to recall the situation of the world, and so of ethics, under God. It can never, even tentatively or "parabolically", suggest or display, in itself, transition to the positive side of grace. That remains consistently

---

[1] Here we take issue with Professor Gill's analysis of the difficulty. Cf. *Ibid.*, pp. 76, 92, 115, *et passim*.

[2] "En toutes les constructions humaines, il voit une image de la mort. La vérité réside pour lui dans le *non* plus que dans le *oui*". Bouillard, *Karl Barth*, Vol. I, p. 69.

an eschatological possibility. Man's situation is thus, to put it gently, perilous. He must attempt responsible, ethically meaningful decisions, remembering all the while that these are already under judgment, so that there is no way of guaranteeing that the possibilities open in the sphere of human decision and action can emerge as significant actualities.

There is another reason beyond this why Barth's treatment of the human appears deficient. This has to do with his utilization of Kierkegaardian categories. It is a mistake to assume that this entails an employment of existential motifs in quite the way intended by Kierkegaard. Barth's indebtedness to Kierkegaard, in the *Römerbrief*, lies in the latter's development and exploration of the idea of the "infinite qualitative distinction" between man and God, time and eternity, and the resulting paradoxical character of revelation actualized in Jesus Christ [1]. It does not embrace Kierkegaard's exploration of human subjectivity in relation to God [2]. Caution must therefore be exercised in interpreting the significance of what are ostensibly existentialist categories. As we have already suggested, man's real existentiality lies, for Barth, not in his immediate givenness as acting subject, but rather in his transcendent identity which results from his relationship with Christ.

Given this orientation, it is understandable that the reality of the self as ethical agent appears problematic. Bouillard is surely correct, in this regard, in suggesting that Overbeck, rather than Kierkegaard, must be taken as the primary influence at work in the *Römerbrief*, and that the former's emphasis on "primal" history (*Urgeschichte*) and death plays a decisive role in Barth's thinking at this time [3].

The upshot of our discussion is that the almost exclusive emphasis which is placed on the priority and transcendence of God in his revelation, and the eschatological reality of the human as grounded in Christ, raise serious questions about the existential identity of man in his historicity,

---

[1] Cf. Come, *Introduction to Barth's Dogmatics*, p. 40f., and Bouillard, *Ibid.*, p. 67. Barth's own comment in the second preface to the *Römerbrief* is also illuminating: "Wenn ich ein 'System' habe, so besteht es darin, daß ich das, was Kierkegaard den 'unendlichen qualitativen Unterschied' von Zeit und Ewigkeit genannt hat, in seiner negativen und positiven Bedeutung möglichst beharrlich im Auge behalte". *RÖM*, p. xiii.

[2] Come, *Introduction to Barth's "Dogmatics"*, p. 40f.

[3] *Karl Barth*, Vol. I, p. 99. See also Barth's essay, "Unsettled Questions for Theology Today", in: *Theology and Church* (New York: Harper and Row, 1962).

and thus about the possibility for there being meaningful ethical actions which move beyond the primary action of repentance [1]. To be sure, Barth undertakes to speak to these points. The results, however, remain dubious. Whether his subsequent shift from dialectical categories to a use of analogy allows a more convincing treatment of the human remains to be seen [2].

The question raised at the end of the first section has deepened significantly in the *Römerbrief*. The issue is no longer one simply of appropriate conditions and criteria enabling us to ascertain what is to be done, in specific contexts, in response to God's prior action in Jesus Christ. The difficulty now turns on whether, in addition to the *Krisis* inaugurated upon the world by God, and the ensuing eschatological transformation which results, there remains room for speaking convincingly of the existential structure and function of the human. It is one thing to order theological categories in such a way that human structures and actions are stripped of ultimate significance, leaving only the possibility of an immediate ethical response to the givenness of one's context. When this implies further a reduction of man's immediate existential identity as ethical agent, then it is not clear how one could ever move beyond eschatological hope. Ethics remains only a *question* to which man is unable to provide even tentative, penultimate answers [3]. And if this is the case, then it is not at all clear what would remain of the notion of *responsible* human actions [4], except, perhaps, as these focus on the primary action of repentance.

---

[1] Cullberg argues that even the primary ethical action of repentance is not, finally, an existential act involving the whole of man's subjective being; "Es kann als Denkakt und demonstratives Symbol festgehalten werden, es hat aber an sich nichts mit dem Willens- und Gefühlsleben des konkreten Menschen zu tun. D.h.: Es handelt sich hier tatsächlich um eine Abstraktion und Konstruction, nicht um einen konkreten existentiellen Lebensakt, der den *ganzen* Menschen in Anspruch nimmt". *Das Problem der Ethik*, p. 35.

[2] Barth focuses on this issue in the *Church Dogmatics* (*KD*, II/1, pp. 714ff.), and in a later essay, "The Humanity of God", (Richmond: John Knox Press, 1960).

[3] See Bouillard, *Karl Barth*, Vol. I, pp. 65f., 70.

[4] Cullberg comments pointedly on this issue: "*Von einen verantwortlichen Handeln des Menschen im eigentlichen Sinn kann überhaupt nicht die Rede sein. Deshalb dürfte wirklich mit vollen Recht gesagt werden können, daß die 'Ethik' des Römerbrief Kommentars den 'absoluten Angriff auf alle Ethik' bedeutet*". *Das Problem Ethik*, p. 44.

There is, then, a problem about the humanity of man, and therefore about his immediate existential identity and activity. Somehow, Barth will need to find a way to give the human its due without diminishing the significance of the covering action of God.

C. TOWARD THE CHURCH DOGMATICS (1927-1931)

The period from the publication of the second *Römerbrief* to the appearance of the first volume of the *Church Dogmatics* displays Barth's continued search for an adequate theological method. In the *Römerbrief*, the categories of dialectic, paradox and eschatology supplied a temporary and needed answer to this problem. It also entailed, as we have seen, a negative employment of existential categories which, when wedded to the strong eschatological thrust of that work, raised serious questions about the identity and activity of man as ethical agent. Developments beyond the *Römerbrief*, accordingly, may be expected to display a lessening of emphasis on dialectic, and a corresponding shift in ethical accent.

The first move beyond a theology of *Krisis* was sounded with the publication, in 1927, of the first of a projected three-volume work, *Christian Dogmatics* [1]. The title of this is significant, for it marks the transition from "prophetic" or "marginal" to dogmatic theology, and so moves, as Cullberg suggests, from a merely negative and critical stance to a more positive position [2].

The difference between this and the *Römerbrief* may be seen at two points. First, in the designation of this period of Barth's thought as "theology of the Word" rather than "theology of Krisis" [3]. Second, in the conscious attempt to ground theology in existential thought, which in its way went considerably beyond Barth's earlier employment of existentialist categories, since it involved placing man in a new way at the center of theological interest [4]. That this did not involve exchanging

---

[1] *Die Lehre vom Worte Gottes*, Prolegomena zur Christlichen Dogmatik (München: Chr. Kaiser, 1927), Listed as entry 116 in the *Antwort* bibliography.

[2] *Das Problem der Ethik*, p. 25.

[3] Cf. *Ibid.*, pp. 46ff., and Torrance, *Karl Barth*, pp. 95ff.

[4] Cullberg quotes Barth on this point: "Wir können zur Näherbestimmung der Predigt als des Ausgangspunktes und Ziels der Dogmatik nicht länger daran vorübergehen, daß es der Mensch ist, der da redet, aber auch hört, und

Christian faith, subjectively understood, for the priority of the Word of God, is made clear in a pointed statement from the *Dogmatics*:

> The significance and the possibility, the object of dogmatics is not the Christian faith but the Word of God. For the Word of God is not based on and contained in Christian faith, but Christian faith is based on and contained in the Word of God. These are two different things, no matter how much the opposing side may speak of the objective content of faith [1].

Nevertheless, it remained true for Barth that "the Word of God is a notion, which in general is accessible only to existential thought" [2]. And this suggests that an understanding of the *nature* of the Word of God, though assuredly distinct from its subjective appropriation in faith, will yet be derivable from an analysis of the latter. This point is argued by Torrance, who sees this as the fundamental weakness, methodologically, of this phase of Barth's thought.

> In trying to derive the nature of the Word of God at all from the analysis of the concrete situation of the hearer, he was misled by a false tendency derived from phenomenological and existentialist thinking. To put forward, as he was doing, an anthropology, even a Church anthropology, as the ground of knowledge for decisive statements about the Word of God, was to show reverence to false gods [3].

What will be required is a deeper penetration into the objectivity of the Word of God, and a new way of ordering the relation between faith and the rational activity of theology. This will gain expression and form in Barth's study of Anselm [4], and in an earlier essay, "Schicksal und Idee in der Theologie", which appeared in 1929. It is against this development that Barth's engagement with the threat of National Socialism [5], his later violent break with Gogarten and Brunner on the

---

bei der Näherbestimmung der Dogmatik nicht länger daran, daß es eben die für sich selbst sprechende Beziehung Gottes zum *Menschen* ist". (*Die Christliche Dogmatik*, p. 48), *Das Problem der Ethik*, p. 25.

[1] Quoted in Ramsey, *Faith and Ethics*, p. 45.

[2] "Das Wort Gottes ist ein Begriff, der nur einen existentiellen Denken überhaupt zugänglich ist". (*Die Christliche Dogmatik*, p. 49), Cullberg, *Das Problem der Ethik*, p. 25.

[3] *Karl Barth*, p. 141.

[4] *Anselm: Fides Quaerens Intellectum* (München: Chr. Kaiser, 1931). English translation by Ian W. Robertson (London: SCM Press, 1960). Future references, cited as *FQI*, are from the English edition.

[5] This has been nicely traced, from its earliest beginnings to the dramatic statement of the Confession of Barmen, by Arthur Cochrane in *The Church's Confession under Hitler* (Philadelphia: Westminster Press, 1962).

issue of natural theology [1], and his pointed statements in the first volume of the *Church Dogmatics* concerning the necessity to free theology from any dependence on existential philosophy [2], must be understood and assessed.

For the moment, however, I wish only to note the transition involved in moving from the *Römerbrief* to the *Christian Dogmatics*. Ethically, it is a bit difficult to determine precisely what this shift entailed. It is partly discernible in an address delivered by Barth at the conference of student Christians held at Aarau in 1927 [3]. The title of this, "Following the Command", is suggestive at two points. First, the verb employed, "following", is active, and thus contains at least the possibility of a positive delineation of the options open to man as ethical agent. Second, Barth's use of the term "command" signals an orientation which will continue to dominate his approach to ethics, and which exclusively determines his development of this in the *Church Dogmatics* [4]. For these reasons, and especially the latter, this address is deserving of careful examination.

The central thesis which informs Barth's discussion is that the "so-called ethical problem" (*das sogenannte ethische Problem*), epitomized in the question 'What are we then to do?', can have only one answer: Follow the command [5]! This is, to be sure, a universal question designating a universal problem. However, its true universality is correctly understood only within the context of the Church as the community within which the individual (Christian) exists. Only within this context is the ethical question unproblematically posed and answered [6]. The truth which emerges in this situation is ethical truth. As such, it is

---

[1] The most complete (and pungent) statements of both sides of this controversy are found in Brunner's *Natur und Gnade* (Zurich: Zwingli Verlag, 1934), and in Barth's reply: *Nein! Antwort an Emil Brunner* (München: Chr. Kaiser, 1934).

[2] Cf. *KD*, I/1, p. viii.

[3] "Das Halten der Gebote", in: *Theologische Fragen und Antworten*, Gesammelte Vorträge, Band 3 (Zürich: Evangelische Verlag A.G. Zollikon, 1957), pp. 32-53. Future references to this cited as *HG*.

[4] Cf. especially *KD*, II/2 and III/4.

[5] "The thesis which shall be represented and explained in this lecture is as follows: Regarding the so-called ethical problem, which is always both an old and a new question: What are we then to do? ... No answer can be given, except this: *Follow* the *command*, understanding both ideas in their plainest and deepest meaning, as they are to be understood in the Bible". *HG*, p. 32.

[6] *Ibid.*, p. 33.

distinguished from both mathematical and metaphysical truth in that it is never directly given, but rather presses for realization and embodiment [1]. Ethical truth is determined, given form, in part at least, by the decisions we make in response to the demands of a specific context. Further, the ethical situation in itself is not problematic. It is rather a wholly unproblematic reality (*ganz unproblematische Wirklichkeit*). Within this context, the notion of ethical truth is given a special focus through the dual notion of following the command [2].

The fact that we are to *follow* the command of God as it encounters us in specific situations indicates that our decision has no bearing on its content. The content of the command is already given and determined. It does not indicate a general truth or direction, from which we then derive specific meaning. The command is always concrete, encountering us immediately as obligation and claim. Ethical decisions, therefore, can only be for or against the command. They can only be decisions of obedience or disobedience. The determination of the good is thus wholly and exclusively bound up with the concreteness of the command [3].

The command encounters the individual with a claim, and so imposes direct responsibility on him as the hearer of the command. As a responsible hearer of God's command, man recognizes the claim laid upon him to be the Law [4]. Barth makes it quite clear that the Law, as it relates to the form of the command, does not describe an autonomous structure interposed between man and God. The command which confronts man, and the Law embodied in its claim, is grounded in God's election of man to be his covenant partner. Indeed, it is precisely the reality of the command as it impinges on the human that lets man know that he is elected and loved by God [5]. In the command, we are placed under God's gracious decision over man, and are enabled to

---

[1] "Ethical truth thereby distinguishes itself from both mathematical truth, and the truth perhaps discovered in metaphysical speculation, in that it is never immediately evident, but only *becomes* evident in the specific situation of the individual, in which we all really find ourselves". *Ibid.*

[2] "Ethical truth, as it becomes evident in a given situation, is not general truth. It is rather the truth of the Church, and it is that as the very particular truth which emerges at the moment of our decision". *Ibid.*

[3] "Es ist dir *gesagt*, Mensch, was gut ist. Es gibt keinen Appell von dem dir Gesagten an das dir nicht gesagte Gute, sondern das dir Gesagte *ist* das Gute". *Ibid.*, p. 37.

[4] "Der Anspruch, von dem du getroffen bist, ist selbst das Gesetz". *Ibid.*

[5] *Ibid.*, p. 46.

see that we are loved. Unless we hear the command in these accents, we have not really heard it at all [1].

What this comes to, finally, is the *unity* of Gospel and Law in the command of God [2]. Barth does not put the matter in quite those terms, but it is clear that this interpretation is the only one that will do justice to the intent of his words. He asserts, for instance, that it is through the Gospel that the Law first receives truth and power [3]. Further, unless man perceives the Law through the Gospel, he has not really encountered in the Law the command that binds him irrevocably to obedience [4].

The command encounters man with a decisive either—or in face of which he can only be obedient or disobedient, i.e., he can only express in his decision fidelity or infidelity to God's love [5]. This would appear to leave man with two possibilities, one good, the other evil. In fact, however, Barth argues that only the latter is realized in man's decisions. The reason for this lies in the concreteness of the command. If the command were universal or general in form, and so abstract, we might then argue a positive case for human decisions where these serve to "fill out" the command in specific contexts [6]. What always happens, however, is that, faced with the givenness of the concrete command, we add or detract in our decision from its immediate contour, do something other than what is commanded, and so finally do not follow the command [7]. Human decisions continually reflect only disobedience. Man therefore does not do the good; his actions under the impact of the command do not reflect the love with which God has first loved him [8].

---

[1] "The basis of the command is love, grace, election. If we have not heard it on this basis, then we have not heard it at all. We have not heard it as the command of *God*, and so clearly we have not heard it as a real *command*". *Ibid.*, p. 42. The themes of election and grace receive central focus in the treatment of ethics in the *Church Dogmatics*. Cf. *KD*, II/2 for an initial development of these points.

[2] Cf. *KD*, II/2, pp. 564, 567f, 598, *et passim*, for parallels to this relation.

[3] *HG*, p. 43.

[4] *Ibid.*

[5] *Ibid.*, p. 45.

[6] "It might appear easy to understand our decision as a decision for the command, and thus to consider ourselves justified, if we were involved simply with a general idea of command whose concrete fulfillment were left up to us". *Ibid.*, p. 44.

[7] *Ibid.*

[8] *Ibid.*, p. 46.

Seen in this light, the command operates exclusively as man's judge. This follows from the fact that every decision manifests only a violation of the command [1]. However, this is not the final word to be said on the matter. Our disobedience and infidelity are grounded in and enclosed by the overarching fidelity of the electing grace of God. And this is inexorable. The decision of God manifested in the eternal election of man has already determined man for obedience as one who follows the command. The love of God, his fidelity towards man, precedes anything man does in his decisions and actions, and so neutralizes the negative thrust of the human [2].

Human decisions, then, though in themselves always wrong, are made right through faith in the predetermining grace of God. Indeed, the *meaning* of human decision which enables us to believe in the justification of our continually disobedient actions, is found exclusively in the act of faith. Faith thus constitutes a decision for the command, for the full impact of God's grace and judgment on man, and so becomes a following of the command [3]. In faith we are enabled to hear the Word of God addressed to us as both Law and Gospel, and so become doers of the Word [4].

This does not mean, however, that faith is viewed as a final *human* possibility beyond disobedience. It provides no independent guarantee which lies within our power to produce. Humanly speaking, we can only *believe* that our faith is the right faith [5]. Faith remains always a prerogative of God. It becomes real only through the agency of the Holy Spirit. And since the activity of God, his grace, is always free, faith can never describe a condition in man's *being*. It refers always to

---

[1] "We have necessarily only inadequately understood the command once more, if we have not become aware that, in the moment in which our decision takes place, it becomes our *judge*, and we stand before it as its violators". *Ibid.*, p. 44.

[2] "*Before* our decision against the command took place, it was already decided that it should be, not disobedience but obedience, not a violation but a following of the command. *Before* we chose that absurdity, we were already elected, *supra lapsum*, as the correct belief of Reformed theology teaches ... God's fidelity has not been removed through our infidelity". *Ibid.*, p. 47.

[3] "Faith can be—that is to say, when we believe—the *final* meaning of our decision, in which its final meaning and content are pleasing to God, a decision for and a following of the command". *Ibid.*, p. 48.

[4] *Ibid.*

[5] "We must also *believe* that our faith is the *right* faith". *Ibid.*

possibility, to *becoming*. It depends on God's constancy, on his not taking his hand from us [1].

We are thus directed, in the end, to the proper context of faith, the Christian community. There it becomes clear that the proper referent of faith is not human subjectivity. It rather focuses on God's faithfulness towards man manifested in Jesus Christ. The obedience of faith granted by the Holy Spirit consists in accepting the judgment levelled by the command, thereby recognizing the fidelity of God. It carries no automatic guarantee of an empirically changed life. Where God's Word is grasped as Law and Gospel, where God's claim is really encountered in the Gospel, there can be no question of a transition on our side from possibility to necessity. Man's obedience collapses immediately into disobedience when this is forgotten [2].

Within the Christian community, however, the faith engendered by the action of the Holy Spirit issues in discipline, humiliation, and gratitude [3]. Man receives discipline, in that the command does not cease speaking concretely to him in his situation. To receive this discipline is to indicate respect for the command, and so to demonstrate a certain relative nearness to sanctification and obedience [4]. Similarly, the command brings us to humiliation, in that it introduces restlessness and insecurity into our lives by reminding us of the Lord and his mercy. And such restlessness and insecurity are also a part of our sanctification and obedience [5]. Finally, we are led to gratitude by the command, in that it reminds us of God's love for us. Gratitude functions as a sign that we have understood that love, and so engenders the hope of sanctification and obedience [6].

This should not be taken to mean that Barth is setting up some sort of identification between justification and sanctification. Though these are not to be separated, they must be distinguished. Sanctification relates finally to our hope of salvation, and this lies wholly in the future in God [7].

---

[1] "The truth of the decision of faith, and of our justification is, like the truth of the command and its judgment, which it means for us, not an obvious truth of our *being*, but rather of our *becoming* ... For we cannot lay hand on God, but live only to the extent that he does not take his hand from us". *Ibid.*, p. 49.

[2] *Ibid.*, p. 50.

[3] *Ibid.*, pp. 51f.

[4] *Ibid.*, p. 51.

[5] *Ibid.*

[6] *Ibid.*, p. 52.

[7] "Grace is justification. Grace is also sanctification. It is a necessity of

In assessing this lecture, two points emerge as relatively new accents moving us beyond the *Römerbrief*. First, the emphasis placed on the notion of command as a descriptive category embracing both the form and content of the ethical. Second, the unity of Law and Gospel in the Word of God. These will continue to play a substantive role in Barth's thinking, particularly in the *Church Dogmatics*, where the Christological grounding and focus of ethics becomes complete [1].

There is, in addition, an ostensible lessening of the earlier dominance of eschatology. This is perhaps only a matter of form, however. When the ethical has been delineated and its possibilities accounted for, there seems little room for any positive pronouncement on the human. There is no more guarantee here than in the *Römerbrief* that man is capable of significant positive ethical action manifesting obedience. In himself, man always falls into disobedience and unbelief. It is only through the electing grace of God that man is justified in spite of and beyond his disobedience, since this carries the possibility that, under the impact of the Holy Spirit, man's final action will take the form of faith.

A second indication of Barth's thinking about ethics during this period is to be found in the outline of a lecture on ethics given at Münster during the summer semester of 1928 [2]. This is especially interesting, since it approximates, in general outline, the development of ethics in the *Church Dogmatics*. After an opening statement defining ethics as the command of God, the discussion breaks down into the command as seen under Creation, Reconciliation, and Redemption [3]. The formal relationship between dogmatics and ethics is expressed by describing ethics as a "supporting science" to dogmatics (*Hilfswissenschaft der Dogmatik*) [4]. Theological ethics is given the task of explaining, within the context wherein reflection on the doctrine of sanctification takes place, "to what extent the Word of God proclaimed and perceived in Christian preaching results in a definite claim being levelled against man" [5].

---

life to know that these two ideas may not be separated, but *must* be distinguished". *Ibid.*, p. 52f.

[1] Though not for the first time, of course. In the *Christliche Dogmatik* Barth states; "Dogmatic thinking is from end to end thinking κατὰ τον κριστον or it is not dogmatic thinking at all". Quoted by Torrance in *Karl Barth*, p. 107.

[2] Cullberg includes this at the end of his book. Cf. *Das Problem der Ethik*, pp. 157-168.

[3] *Ibid.*, p. 159.

[4] *Ibid.*

[5] "Ethik als theologische Disziplin ist diejenige Hilfswissenschaft der Dogmatik, in der in Erläuterung der Lehre von der Heiligung Besinnung

The opening section of the lecture makes essentially the same points about the divine command that were found in *Das Halten der Gebote*. The "good" is no general or theoretical truth. It is manifested in the specific event of our actions as decisions for or against the command [1]. This does not mean that our actions in themselves determine the good. They serve merely to recognize and follow the good as it is presented in the command [2]. Further, the command encounters us as God's judgment, in that it shows our particular decisions to be violations of the command. In judgment, however, we encounter grace, since it is out of God's judgment that the sanctification of man issues. God executes obedience even from the distorted actions of man [3]. With these points in mind, the content of the command as it unfolds within the context of creation, reconciliation, and redemption can be indicated.

Barth's discussion of the command of God the Creator falls into four sections: The command of Life; Vocation; Order; and Faith. The command of the Creator is that man should live [4]. To the extent that God addresses us as his creatures, we recognize life in general as a necessity, and it becomes for us an object of reverence [5].

This reverence is not executed generally, however, but in specific contexts where we encounter God's command. It is at this point that the category of vocation becomes important. God's command constitutes a claim over the totality of our concrete situations. It is only in this way that our actions become responsible [6]. Vocation, then, *means* to have an understanding of our own reality in its specific determination under the command of God. Barth indicates the range of this in a brief listing of the "Life circle of vocation" (*Das Lebenskreise des Berufs*): Human

---

darauf stattfindet, daß und inwiefern das in der christlichen Predigt verkündigte und vernommene Wort Gottes eine bestimmte Inanspruchname des Menschen vollzieht". *Ibid.*

[1] *Ibid.*, p. 160.

[2] "The good has been said to us in the command. The decision has already fallen there, which we have been awakened to perceive". *Ibid.*

[3] *Ibid.*, p. 160f.

[4] "God's command concerns me, to the extent that I exist as his creature. Because he speaks with me, he recognizes me as a living being. And because he wishes something from me, he commands me to live". *Ibid.*, p. 161.

[5] *Ibid.*, p. 162. The parallel between this and the discussion in the *KD* is exact. Cf. *KD*, III/4, pp. 366-453. Even in this outline Barth notes the necessity of an "Auseinandersetzung mit A. Schweitzer". *Ibid.*, p. 161.

[6] *Das Problem der Ethik*, p. 162.

existence; sexuality, friendship (the root of the idea of the neighbor); family, old-age; leadership and ability; mortality and transitoriness [1].

The significance of order for ethics lies in the steadiness which it introduces into our actions [2]. Within order, the command of God reminds us that life is both an individual affair and an existence with other life. To the extent that our wills are subordinated to the will of God executed in the command, they are determined by order. By "order" Barth means a place "where reality is not only given, but is given as *regular* reality in the definite steadiness of its given existence" [3]. This regularity and steadiness is provided by "orders of creation" (*Schöpfungs-ordnungen*), "divinely willed orders, which come into question immediate-ly with the reality of our lives, and which can be given a relative descrip-tion" [4]. Barth lists four such orders: work (culture); marriage; family; and community life in general under the principles of equality and leadership.

Faith plays a central role within the ethic of creation, for it is only on that basis that we can know that our actions are good, i.e., that they evidence obedience to the command of life, and that our vocation is appropriate and in order [5]. We know this only to the extent that it is said to us, and that we allow it to be said to us, that our actions are in agreement with the will of the creator of life. And this occurs in the reality of faith, which is the work of the spirit of God the Father [6]. Faith is a human-existential acceptance of God (*eine menschlich-existentielle Bejahung Gottes*). It therefore has to do with the temporal existence of man [7].

The command of God the Reconciler consists, again, of four

---

[1] *Ibid.*

[2] *Ibid.*

[3] "Ordnung: 'wo die Wirklichkeit nicht nur gegeben ist, sondern als regelmäßige Wirklichkeit in bestimmter Stetigkeit ihres Wirklichseins gegeben ist' ". *Ibid.*, p. 163.

[4] "Schöpfungsordnungen: gottgewollte Ordnungen, die unmittelbar mit der Tatsache unseres Lebens selbst in Frage kommen, und die in Relativität beschreiben werden können". *Ibid.* In the *KD*, Barth drops the term *Schöpfungs-ordnungen* altogether, and speaks instead of certain "spheres and relationships" (*Bereichen und Verhältnissen*) within which obedience occurs. Cf. III/4, p. 31.

[5] *Das Problem der Ethik*, p. 163.

[6] "Daß mir das gesagt ist, und daß ich mir das gesagt sein laße, das ist das Werk des Wortes und Geistes des Vaters, oder die Wirklichkeit des Glau-bens". *Ibid.*

[7] *Ibid.*

sections: the Command of Law; Authority; Humility; and Love. Here we encounter the command not simply as creatures of God, but as members of the elected people of God. Since God judges and shows grace to us as sinners, we are obligated to his law; that is, by the claim passed upon us in the name of Jesus Christ, we are bound to our fellow-man [1]. The law under which we are placed is neither "fidelity in itself", nor Fate, nor a general, timeless truth. The law of faith is the law of the revelation of God in Jesus Christ. As such, it carries a threefold meaning. First, the bearer of the good appears as another man, Christ, and through him, the neighbor. Second, the goodness of God has been exhibited and made into the norm of a kind of human goodness which is freely opened, turned towards, devoted to, the other. Third, through the law the neighbor is shown to be our brother, from whose existence we cannot abstract ourselves [2].

The discussion of authority flows out of the point just made concerning the neighbor. It is through the definitness of the neighbor, the fellow-man (*Mitmenschen*) commissioned by God, that the command of God touches us [3]. The authority of the neighbor over us is thus a divinely ordained authority. It rests on the *givenness*, the immediacy of the neighbor (we do not "elect" the neighbor), and so on his identity as bearer of the command. The authority of the neighbor performs the function of providing a corrective to our self-rule (*Selbstherrlichkeit*) [4].

To live in obedience to the command presented in the neighbor is to allow our act of repentance before God to fall over into acts of service to the neighbor. The actions of the reconciled sinner constitute an offering of his life [5]. The Christian life just is the sacrificial life of the servants of God. As such, it entails repentance, "the renewal of thought" [6], and openness for God's will and service to one's fellow-man.

---

[1] "Gottes Gebot geht mich an, sofern ich als Christ ein Glied seines auserwählten Volkes bin. Indem Gott mich als Sünder richtet und begnadigt, verpflichtet er mich auf sein Gesetz, d.h. bindet er mich durch den im Namen Jesu Christi an mich ergehenden Anspruch des Mitmenschen". *Ibid.*, p. 164.

[2] *Ibid.*

[3] *Ibid.*

[4] *Ibid.*, p. 165.

[5] "The *content* of the command of God the Reconciler: subordination through repentance; service to the neighbor in obedience to God's order". *Ibid.*

[6] A key point in the *Römerbrief.*

It rests on the revelation of reconciliation, and in itself constitutes a sign, a witness, a symbol, and a demonstration of that event [1].

The command of God the Reconciler is fulfilled to the extent that we recognize that we are bound to God, and through him to the neighbor. That we do in fact recognize this, that it is said to us, and that we allow it to be said to us, is, as the work of the Word of God, the reality of love [2]. The reality of love in our lives constitutes an existential acceptance of God. It also presupposes that God is objectively present to us in the neighbor (*daß er sich uns durch unserem Nächsten als Gegenstand gibt*). Love is thus both grace *and* responsibility, an answer to God's word [3].

The discussion of the command of God the Redeemer falls under these headings: The Command of Promise; Conscience; Gratitude; and Hope. Here the command encounters us, not as God's creatures, nor as reconciled sinners, but as children of God, heirs of eternal life [4]. When God speaks to us here, it is to promise us his presence as our redeemer beyond the present, in which we are his creatures, and beyond the contradiction in which we currently exist as Christians. So we are called to both wait and hasten towards God's own future [5]. That man is a child of God is an eschatological reality, that is, a reality which lies in our future. The child of God is *redeemed* man, obedient man. This cannot be said of either created or reconciled man. To that extent it is removed, future. It is, however, a future *in* the present (*eine Zukunft in der Gegenwart*) which takes the form of promise [6].

It is within this eschatological context that conscience is set. Essentially, it indicates a human knowledge about what God alone can know, the goodness or evil of our actions. This is a possibility open only to the

---

[1] *Das Problem der Ethik*, p. 165.

[2] "God's command receives fulfillment in me, that is, my action is good, it is obedience to the command of Law, to the extent that it has been said to me, and I have allowed it to be said to me, that I am bound solely to God, and through him to my neighbor. That this has been said to me, and that I have allowed it to be said to me is, as the work of the Word of God, the reality of love". *Ibid.*, p. 166.

[3] *Ibid.*

[4] *Ibid.*

[5] "Indem er mit mir redet, verheißt er mir seine Gegenwart als mein Erlöser aus der Vorläufigkeit, in der ich jetzt und hier sein Geschöpf, und aus dem Widerspruch, in dem ich jetzt und hier ein Christ bin, und heißt er mich also warten und eilen auf diese seine Zukunft". *Ibid.*

[6] *Ibid.*, p. 167.

children of God in concrete community with God the redeemer. To have conscience is to have the Holy Spirit [1]. Conscience, accordingly, is no available possession of man, for it signals continuity between ourselves and God which will be ours only as *children* of God. The content of conscience thus lies in the relation between our present actions and the coming kingdom of God [2]. The form of conscience would thus be understood, on the one hand, to have God as its subject, and, on the other, the human "I" in its future reality. Conscience, therefore, remains a hidden reality as part of our future with God [3].

The content of the command of redemption takes a dual form as gratitude and hope. Gratitude expresses the spontaneity and joy of our actions within the freedom which has been promised us [4]. Hope is the eschatological fulfillment of the command. It becomes real in our lives through the work of the Holy Spirit, which enables us to look towards a final unity between our actions and the will of God. The proper human action under hope is, therefore, prayer [5].

This lecture is significant, even in outline, for it provides a rather complete delineation of the way a theological ethic would be developed within the context of dogmatics. It is perhaps not too fanciful to suggest, in this respect, that this might eventually have found its way into the unfinished volumes of the *Christian Dogmatics*.

Another point which has already been mentioned is the parallel between this and the overall development of ethics in the *Church Dogmatics*. Of course, this is not an absolute parallel. The ethical sections proper of the *Church Dogmatics* are not now, and will not be, completed. Nevertheless, the general outline remains the same in each. One major difference appears to be that in this outline the category of freedom is introduced only under the command of redemption, whereas in the *Church Dogmatics* it plays a central role in the special ethic of creation [6].

In addition, there is discernible in this outline a lessening of eschatological motifs as compared with the *Römerbrief*. To this extent, at least, ethics is given a more positive cast within the Christian life. It constitutes more than a total *Krisis* within and over the human, an indication of our continuing "sickness unto death".

---

[1] *Ibid.*
[2] *Ibid.*
[3] *Ibid.*, p. 168.
[4] *Ibid.*
[5] *Ibid.*
[6] Cf. *KD*, III/4.

It may still be questioned, however, whether this results in a more sanguine reading of human possibilities. The problem here arises from Barth's treatment of man's identity as a child of God as an *eschatological* reality only. And since our freedom is intimately related to this, the possibility of a fulfillment of the command within creation and reconciliation is rendered immediately problematic, despite the fact that both faith and love are defined as existential realities in man's life. Not even the identification of our eschatological reality as children of God as a future in the present would seem able to move us beyond the essential actions of gratitude and hope. If this is the case, then once again man's identity and historicity as ethical agent would seem to be vitiated.

Something of this same ambiguity may be seen in "Church and Culture", an essay also written in 1928. Barth's statements in this suggest a somewhat more positive reading of the human. He states, for instance, that

> The remembrance that God is in heaven and we are on earth must never serve as excuse for burying in a napkin the one talent we have received. The knowledge that God alone is absolute must not keep us from making relative decisions and judgments. God makes his demands on us as earthly and erring men. 'He knoweth our frame' ... but he makes demands on us [1].

This is essentially the position taken in the *Römerbrief*, but carries the implicit suggestion that man might be faced with something other than a merely impossible demand. This suggestion is reinforced when it is later asserted that

> Sin has not so wholly destroyed God's image in man that God's friendship for man is now without an object. Man has not become 'a stick or stone'; he is still a human being (*homo*), although a human sinner (*homo peccator*). As such, God speaks to him in Jesus Christ, and humanity is therefore promise [2].

There is, in addition, a continuity posited between creation and reconciliation which receives focus in the human:

> That which, viewed from the standpoint of the creation, is the promise given to man, is, when viewed from the standpoint of reconciliation, the law under which he stands. What God demands from man is called humanity [3].

---

[1] *Theology and Church*, p. 341.
[2] *Ibid.*, p. 343.
[3] *Ibid.*, p. 346.

And the "law" under which man is placed is grounded both in nature and in the divine command. The difference between these is that the latter makes actual the promise contained within the law of nature that men are to become what they are, i.e., that they are to be human:

> That command is merely taken and lifted out of the sphere of wishing, of choice, and is made actual, the divine command. The command revives the promise which from the creation lies dormant in the law of nature; the law of nature is given, just because of the promise, necessity ... Sanctification, election for God, doing the will of God, is always in content being human. Men are to become men, not more than men; but also not less [1].

In the end, however, man's immediate identity is left unclear, as is his ability to move ethically from possibility to actuality. True humanity is found only in Christ, and possibilities are actualized only in God [2].

The question about man's temporal identity as ethical agent comes to rest, in the end, on the issue of obedience. Is man capable of genuine obedience in those specific contexts in which he finds himself confronted by the reality of the divine command, and can this take the form of decision and action extending beyond the actions of repentance, gratitude, and hope? Another way of putting this is to ask whether, alongside the action of God, there is also room to speak of a corresponding action of man that makes a difference? Or, put in more traditional form, is there any possibility of a transition from justification to sanctification, so that the latter becomes to some extent a predicate of the temporal existence of man, even man as *simul justus* et *peccator*?

In our discussion thus far we have noted difficulties precluding an affirmative answer to these questions. In the *Römerbrief* this was occasioned by Barth's employment of dialectic and paradox within a consuming eschatological framework. The result was twofold. On the one hand, a negative reading of man's given existentiality, so that it functioned only to indicate the *Krisis* directed upon the world in the action of God, and the corresponding description of all humanly derived answers to the ethical problem as a "sickness unto death". On the other, a transposition of man's real existentiality into an eschatological framework, which, if we have understood Barth correctly, was not at all predicable of man in his immediate temporal givenness.

In *Das Halten der Gebote* and the 1928 outline of ethics, we have

---

[1] *Ibid.*
[2] *Ibid.*, p. 346f.

discerned some accents which lead beyond the position of the *Römerbrief*. It remains still unclear, however, what the possibilities for human action are, once the attempt is made to move beyond the initial discussion of repentance and faith. I have, therefore, argued that Barth's treatment of the issue leaves something to be desired. It should be noted that this caveat does not fall into continuity with the criticisms of either Brunner or Niebuhr [1]. The issue has nothing to do with any assumed ability on man's part, vestigial or otherwise, to be open for revelation. It has rather to do with the possibilities available, *within* and *under* the primacy of the Word of God, for describing existence and action in faith in a positive fashion.

At this point we are led back to the question about how justification and sanctification relate. It is fitting, in this respect, that we turn now to an analysis of *Zur Lehre vom Heiligen Geist* [2]. This was written in 1930 by Barth in collaboration with his brother, Heinrich Barth, who contributed a discussion of "The Idea of the Spirit in German Idealism". Barth's discussion in this of "The Holy Spirit and the Christian Life" marks an important stage in the development of his thinking about ethics. Here he concerns himself specifically with the relation between justification and sanctification, and the problem of obedience which emerges within faith.

Initially, a distinction is drawn between man's creaturely existence under God and his life as a hearer of the Word of God. Both of these are classified as miracles occurring in the life of man through the activity of the Holy Spirit. The basic miracle is simply the reality and place of man alongside God [3]. Beyond this, there lies a second miracle: the occurrence of the Christian life, a life lived in openness and response to the Word of God:

---

[1] Cf. Brunner, *Natur und Gnade*, pp. 7-9: "Die Falschen Konsequenzen Barths"; and Niebuhr, *The Nature and Destiny of Man*, Vol. I, p. 269; Vol. II, p. 64. Hans Frei gives a summary of the criticisms levelled against Barth, and argues that they were all misplaced, since the critics failed to take seriously the central point involved in Barth's position: the search for a theological method leading beyond any assumption about a "point of contact" (*Anknüpfungspunkt*) between man and God. Cf. Ramsey, *Faith and Ethics*, p. 43ff.

[2] Karl Barth and Heinrich Barth, *Zur Lehre vom Heiligen Geist* (München: Chr. Kaiser Verlag, 1930). Hereafter cited as *LHG*.

[3] "Das unerhörte Wunder der Liebe Gottes ist wahr: Gott hat uns geschaffen. Wir haben Raum und Bestand neben der Wirklichkeit Gottes". *LHG*, p. 40.

It must happen to him as a pure miracle, as a second miracle beyond the miracle of his existence, when his life becomes really the life of the Christian, a life lived in the hearing of God's Word [1].

Both of these occur through the Holy Spirit. It is only thus that we are brought to an awareness of ourselves as creatures of God, and opened to faith, to a hearing of God's Word as his command encountering us in our creaturely existence [2].

In each of these, the activity of the Holy Spirit corresponds to an aspect of the being of God. In the first, the action of the Holy Spirit corresponds to the being of God as Creator. In the second, to God's being as Reconciler [3]. That will mean, for Barth, that the Holy Spirit, as Reconciler, acts as the spirit of Jesus Christ. The result of this encounter is that man is enabled to recognize himself as reconciled sinner [4]. The Christian always exists *simul justus et peccator*. Human existence under the impact of the activity of God in the Holy Spirit is therefore existence in tension. Nor does it lie within man's power to remove this. This is accomplished only through the Holy Spirit, acting here as the spirit of God the Redeemer [5]. It is clear, then, that Barth's discussion moves throughout within the framework of an incipient trinitarianism.

Existentially, the result of the activity of the Holy Spirit as Reconciler is faith. Barth allows this to emerge as a viable existential occurrence and stance. It is always, to be sure, a miracle which, as the work of God, remains hidden to view [6]. It is, however, really our faith, and not some sort of hypostasis suspended over man. To say "I believe" is to exist in faith [7]. The emergence of faith points to the reality of reconciliation in our lives as a work of God.

Faith, however, cannot be taken as an end in itself. The Word of reconciliation addressed to man is also a commanding Word. The reality of faith as existential condition inevitably raises the question of obedience, and this is a question about the presence of sanctification in the midst of

---

[1] *Ibid.*, p. 54f.

[2] *Ibid.*, p. 55.

[3] *Ibid.*, p. 39.

[4] *Ibid.*, p. 69.

[5] *Ibid.*, p. 77f.

[6] *Ibid.*, p. 80f.

[7] Der Glaube mit seiner Erfahrung des Gerichts und der Rechtfertigung ist Gottes Werk, ganz verborgen und reines Wunder. Er ist aber darum keine über oder vor oder hinter dem wirklichen Menschen schwebende Hypostase ... 'Ich glaube' heißt: Ich existiere im Glauben". *Ibid.*

justification [1]. In its classical form, this issue focuses on the relation between faith and works. Barth argues a necessary relation between these. Faith cannot be legitimately abstracted from works, since it is precisely in works, in different actions, that faith receives confirmation. That there *are* actions corresponding to the situation of faith indicates the reality of sanctification as a concrete extension of justification, which occurs only as a gift of the Holy Spirit [2].

Sanctification becomes real at the point where grace intersects our existence. The truth of grace "falls in vertically from above" (*senkrecht von oben hereinfallend*), and at this (mathematical) point of intersection, the problem of Christian obedience takes form [3]. Both sanctification and obedience gain expression within the context of the divine disturbance levelled against us by God. The two ideas are not identical, however. Sanctification indicates the reversal of our lives that results from the impact of grace, which enables us to exist as both hearers and doers of the Word [4]. Sanctification, like justification, is forensic in character. It hinges exclusively on God's judgment on the human, which also constitutes its unavoidable reversal.

The question of obedience, however, is another matter. Obedience has to do with the empirical manifestation of sanctification. Are we really obedient? Do we really let the divine disturbance fall upon us, so that our lives are opened for service in love to God and our neighbor? There is no way of answering these questions directly. Obedience, like faith, is not a self-evident fact of our lives. It hangs entirely on the reality of grace within our lives, and so within our actions and decisions, and that is concealed in the darkness of faith, which can be dispelled only by the Word of God [5].

---

[1] *Ibid.*

[2] "It is in fact the case, that the full truth of the community between God and man on its subjective side, which in reconciliation through Christ becomes event, as a gift of the Holy Spirit also becomes concrete in the reality of sanctification, in that there are also actions alongside faith ... Faith cannot stand alone. It is always confirmed or not confirmed as faith in particular actions". *Ibid.*, p. 81f.

[3] *Ibid.*, p. 82.

[4] "The idea of sanctification can be summarized as follows: To us, as those forgiven by God, there also falls from the same God a radical and powerful opposition, in which the contradiction of our lives against him is refuted and made untrue, by a disturbance of our existence which is in the highest sense both necessary and true, which results in our existing as believers, as hearers of God's Word, and therefore also as doers of that Word". *Ibid.*, p. 84f.

[5] *Ibid.*, p. 85.

Sanctification, then, is real. It is obedience that poses a continuing problem. The answer to this lies in the fact of forgiveness. As a forgiven sinner, man is surrounded in his every action by the grace of God, which insures that his actions are really obedient. This means, however, that the question of obedience can never be answered out of the context of the human. Man lacks the capacity to tell himself that he is obedient, that his actions are performed in response to the command of God. The only possibility open to man, ethically, is that of entering continually into the problem of obedience in all its obscurity (from his side). Man must act, but he must leave the results, the assessing of those actions, entirely in the hands of God [1].

Barth's intention here displays a close parallel with the stance of the *Römerbrief*. If the issue of obedience is not to be decided by direct reference to specific actions and possibilities, then we are forewarned against any attempt to set up orders and structures within history to which the adjective "Christian" could automatically be attached. This occurs whenever we attempt to speak unambiguously of a "Christian" world-view, morality, or art; or of "Christian" personality, family, party, or newspaper [2]. These serve merely to mark human efforts to establish continuity between the actions of man and the prerogative of God; or rather, they involve a continual ignoring of that prerogative. Barth's treatment of obedience is thus designed, in the first instance, to safeguard the freedom of God.

It would also seem to carry a corresponding freedom for man. If human actions are no longer bound to specific possibilities as these emerge within history, but are responsible wholly to the command of God within concrete situations, then the possibilities for human action would appear to be, in principle, unlimited. That is, there would be no way of deciding, in advance, what particular form or direction human obedience would take. There would be no ideological restrictions or demands to be met. Man under grace could move out with complete freedom to fulfill the command. And it might receive fulfillment, i.e.,

---

[1] "Darum ist unsere Heiligung Wirklichkeit, unser Gehorsam aber Problem, das wir nicht auflesen, in dessen Finsternis wir nur immer wieder hineingehen können, ganz und gar und allein auf Gott geworfen ... Wir können wohl opfern mit unserer Tat und dazu sind wir aufgerufen, aber daß wir dabei Abel und nicht Kain sind, das steht nicht in unserer Macht. Wir können wohl dienen mit unserer Tat und dazu sind wir aufgerufen, aber daß wir damit Gott und dem Nächsten wirklich dienen, das ist Gnade". *Ibid.*, p. 91.

[2] *Ibid.*, p. 92f.

obedience might be forthcoming, under the guise of idealism or realism; as conservatism, revolution, Pietism, or Communism [1]. So far, so good. This sort of point would follow logically enough from an ethic grounded in the command of God as a specific Word addressed to man in the givenness of his situation.

It is clear, however, that Barth does not wish to allow this sort of freedom as a predicate of man in his immediate temporality. Man has this freedom only as promise, only in relation to his future as a child of God. Like conscience, through which man is able to distinguish between good and evil, the freedom of the child of God is a final, eschatological freedom. Both conscience and freedom are present in man's existence only through the Holy Spirit, that is, only as grace and promise [2].

In the end, then, gratitude is cited as the only possibility for a fulfillment of obedience. In the period between reconciliation and redemption, between our identity as the subjugated enemies of God and as the children of God, gratitude constitutes both the condition for, and the sum and substance of, obedience [3]. Even this possibility, however, is transposed into the future:

> Who is grateful to God? Who is a free child of God? I have not said that there are such people, nor have I said that the Christian is now at some time thankful and that he has the freedom of the child of God ... Our unredeemed consciousness and subconsciousness we know well enough, but we do not know ourselves as children of God. The gratitude and freedom of the children of God is indeed our final, our future reality [4].

At this point one is led to wonder how far Barth has moved beyond the position of the *Römerbrief*. To be sure, the stringent dialectic given expression there has ceased to dominate, and the distinction between reconciliation and redemption provides a sort of stability to the human that was not present earlier. The question remains, however, whether

---

[1] *Ibid.*, p. 101.

[2] *Ibid.*, p. 102.

[3] "Und im heiligen Geist gibt es Dankbarkeit, als Summe und Inbegriff des Gott wohlgefälligen wirklichen Gehorsam. Im Reich der Schöpfung sind wir Knechte, im Reich der Versöhnung sind wir unterworfene Feinde, im Reich der Erlösung aber sind wir, noch einmal: Kinder Gottes". *Ibid.*

[4] *Ibid.*, p. 103. Barth's comments here bear a striking similarity to his development of certain themes in the *Church Dogmatics*. Cf. IV/3.2, Par. 71, Part 6, "The Liberation of the Christian", and Par. 73, Part 2, "Life in Hope".

the shifts that mark Barth's thinking from the *Christian Dogmatics* to this present writing (and it should be recalled that this brings us within two years of the *Church Dogmatics*) result in any substantive revision of his ethics. It is unclear, at this point, that they have. Reconciled man is, true enough, always *simul justus et peccator*. The difficulty thus far is that the emphasis falls always on the latter point. Again, this may not have been Barth's precise intention. Nevertheless, some way needs to be found whereby meaningful reference can be made to human possibilities and actions within the present immediacies of existence. Eschatological categories cannot legitimately absorb historical actualities. And if the category of obedience, with all that this entails, is understood only as an eschatological predicate of man, then this would seem to be what has happened.

It is necessary here to return to the beginning of this section. I indicated there the difficulties occasioned by Barth's methodological employment of existential categories in the *Christian Dogmatics*, and his subsequent movement beyond this approach. It will be helpful now to sketch in the background of this shift.

In an article written in 1939, Barth said, in surveying the preceding decade, that he was conscious "only of having walked farther on the way which I had begun, and by so doing of having brought the grounds, the import and the consequences of that common beginning into a clearer light" [1]. This involved a deepening of the general emphasis on the Word of God as a methodological norm in theology, which may be detected at two points. First, in the excision of any suggestion that Christian faith might be given a philosophical foundation and exposition. In this regard, Barth states that his study of Anselm was "the one written with the greatest satisfaction" [2]. Second, in the gradual emergence of the conviction that Christian doctrine has to be "exclusively and conclusively the doctrine of Jesus Christ" as the living Word of God spoken to man [3].

The issue involved in determining the relation within dogmatics between philosophical and theological categories was examined in a lecture delivered at Dortmund in 1929: "Schicksal und Idee in der

---

[1] "How My Mind Has Changed in this Decade", *The Christian Century*, Vol. LVI (September 13 and 20, 1939), p. 1098. Taken by itself, of course, this statement would eliminate the possibility of any substantive shift in Barth's ethics.

[2] *Ibid.*, p. 1132.

[3] *Ibid.*

Theologie" [1]. In this, Barth focuses on the place and function of realism and idealism within the theological enterprise. In this connection he is brought to an analysis of the categories of Fate and Idea, as these become emergent within, respectively, a realist or idealist framework.

At the outset, Barth provides a definition of theology:

> We understand by theology the science attached to the Church (and this means, indeed, the Christian Evangelical Church) which has to do with God as the Object of the proclamation of that Church. Theology relates itself to the Church, as the theological sphere of life, in the same way that medicine, philosophy (understood in the broadest sense), and jurisprudence relate to physiology, psychology, and sociology, respectively. To say that theology is a science means that it is an objectively ordered investigation of truth with reference to God as the Object of Church proclamation [2].

Theology does not undertake to investigate the nature of God "in himself", however. It is only within the context of the Church's task of proclamation that God becomes the appropriate object of theological investigation [3]. Within that context, however, theology has its appointed and appropriate function, which it performs as a service to God, as he has revealed himself and as he is proclaimed by the Church [4].

To say that theology has God as the object of its investigation cannot mean, of course, that God gives himself over completely to man. To set the matter straight, it has to be stated that theology has God for its object only insofar as it also has him as its subject:

> Theology does not only have God as its Object, but it has him as Object only to the extent that, as Thomas Aquinas has profoundly said, it also has him as its Subject, if only in the deepest hiddenness [5].

That theology is, in this sense, a science about God does not elevate it to a special status. As a particular kind of response to God as Subject

---

[1] In: *Theologische Fragen und Antworten* (Zurich: Evangelischen Verlag, 1957). Hereafter cited as *SI*.

[2] *SI*, p. 55.

[3] "Dadurch und so, daß Gott verkündigt wird und werden soll, wird er ja zum Inhalt des besonderen Lebensbereichs der Kirche, auf den sich die Theologie als Wissenschaft bezieht, in dem sie ihren irdisch möglichen Ort hat, auf dessen Boden Menschen Theologen sein können. Dadurch und so wird er zum Gegenstand auch der Theologie". *Ibid.*

[4] *Ibid.*, p. 56.

[5] *Ibid.* A good discussion of the relation between subject and object in Barth's theology is found in James Brown's study, *Subject and Object in Modern Theology* (New York: The Macmillan Company, 1955), Ch. 6.

of revelation who graciously gives himself over to be the object of theological investigation, theology remains a definitely human thinking and speaking with its particular laws, possibilities and limits. In this respect it does not differ from other kinds of human investigation [1]. At this point, however, theology finds itself inescapably involved with philosophy. It lives out its life in proximity to this other discipline, just as the Church exists in proximity to the State.

The clearest indication of this occurs in the language employed by the theologian. The theologian employs concepts and terms drawn from a common vocabulary and context of meaning. In saying what he must say, the theologian does not move into the esoteric. There are no special categories which delimit his knowledge of the Word of God from that of the philosophers. It is therefore possible that the philosopher may, without difficulty, say the same thing, but with a totally different meaning [2].

This underlines the continual ambiguity of the theological enter- prise. As a human undertaking, it can never guarantee the results of its efforts. It can never presume in itself really to speak of God. That it does so at all is a miracle. Theology is enabled to speak of God only by grace [3]. It can continue only on the basis of a continued hearing of God's Word. This being the case, theology is faced at all points with the danger of becoming simply another form of philosophy [4]. It is in view of this danger that Barth assesses the place of realism and idealism within theology.

The initial thrust of theological knowledge is towards objectivity, the given, or reality. In pursuing this, it faces the possibility of adopting a realist ontology and epistomology, in which knowledge about the being of God is derived from an encounter with the world. This approach is found in classical philosophy and in medieval thought, where it received expression in the theology of Thomas Aquinas. The outcome of this is a doctrine of analogy based on the reality or being of things. This rests on the assumption "that every existent thing as such has a share in God, in the deepest dissimilarity as only a creature of the Creator, yet also in the deepest similarity, in that it has being" [5].

---

[1] *SI*, p. 56f.
[2] *Ibid.*, p. 57.
[3] *Ibid.*, p. 58.
[4] *Ibid.*, p. 59f.
[5] *Ibid.*, p. 62.

Realism of this variety displays both an inner and outer, or subjective and objective, aspect. In a post-Cartesian context, it takes the forms, respectively, of Pietism and Rationalism. Both make a theological criterion out of a particular kind of experience. In Pietism, it is the subjective experience of God; in Rationalism, the objective experience of the external world. In Neo-Protestantism, this is expressed in the dialectic between faith and history. The upshot of this is that God is understood as man's fate, as a necessary consequence of our subjective and objective encounter with the world [1].

Theology cannot avoid the issue raised by realism. It cannot attempt to answer the question Where is God?, or Who is God?, without speaking of the reality of God. Indeed, even to name God as the *object* of theology involves a "typical realist proposition" [2]. And the use of I - Thou language in theology carries both poles of a theological realism: the outer and the inner, the objective and the subjective [3].

The resolution of the problem posed by realism lies in drawing a firm distinction between a naive theological realism which takes its rise from inner experience or history, and a realism grounded in God's self-revelation as it is proclaimed in the Church. The point here is that the Word of God says something *new* to man. It is not simply a clearer and stronger statement of what we are already capable of experiencing or knowing. There is thus no automatic continuity between nature, history, human consciousness and the Word of God. And God is therefore not to be understood as Fate [4].

Barth next takes up the problem of Idea in the context of theology. Whereas the thrust of realism lay in the direction of reality, the notion of the Idea relates to the problem of truth. The two are not entirely separate, however, for in idealism an attempt is made, through the use of reason, to overcome the situation evolving out of the objective and subjective aspects of Fate [5]. And in this, idealism inevitably runs onto the question about the Ultimate or God, expressed as Idea. The thrust of idealism is towards inclusiveness. It pursues this, however, within a recognition of the distinction between the given and the not-given, i.e., between immanence and transcendence [6].

---

[1] *Ibid.*, p. 63f.
[2] *Ibid.*, p. 64.
[3] *Ibid.*, p. 65.
[4] *Ibid.*, p. 68ff.
[5] *Ibid.*, p. 73.
[6] *Ibid.*, p. 72.

Idealism, like realism, inevitably plays a role in theological thinking. Indeed, to the extent that it incorporates transcendence into its expression, Barth sees idealism as a suitable and even necessary theological vehicle, in that it leads beyond the dependence of realism on the given. Theological idealism can provide a critical understanding of the givenness of revelation, in that it breaks into the context of things as they are, and so places these in question [1].

The danger of idealism in theology is that it can become the basis for some sort of ideology. This can be avoided only by emphasizing that truth is *given* to theology in the Word of God. It is always with reference to this that a legitimate theological idealism is possible; never on the basis of our particular idea *about* God [2].

The solution to the issues of realism and idealism lie, finally, in a correct hearing of the Word of God, in obedience. And that means, for Barth, in Christology:

> True theology always begins in the concreteness in which the Word of God has come and continues to come to us. In truth, because it is God's Word; in reality, because it has become flesh, true God and real man and so the one, divine, binding, justifying and sanctifying Word. Theology is indeed theology of the Word, of election, of faith, where it is exclusively Christology [3].

This lecture manifests a decisive movement towards the theological orientation of the *Church Dogmatics*. It rejects any immanent criterion, whether objective or subjective. It recognizes the unavoidability of certain philosophical motifs within theology, but places these at all points under the Word of God, that is, under Jesus Christ. Finally, theology is understood to be essentially Christology. Indeed it is not too much to say that the definition of theology given here receives precise embodiment in the volumes of the *Church Dogmatics*.

Barth's book on Anselm provides a deepening and a further confirmation of this orientation. In it attention focuses on the reality of God in his revelation in Christ as the object of theological reflection. This provides the proper point of departure, not some datum of self or world. Theology thus becomes simply the effort to understand what has been given to faith. It aims at a confirmation of faith. In that sense, it indicates

---

[1] *Ibid.*, p. 76. This role was actually given to idealism in the *Römerbrief*. Cf. also Ramsey, *Faith and Ethics*, p. 51.

[2] *SI*, p. 81f.

[3] *Ibid.*, p. 92.

a striving of the human will into, rather than towards, God, and so a creaturely participation in God's mode of being [1]. Theology is thus assured that its knowledge will bear a proper correspondence to its object, even though God is only indirectly an object in theological reflection. A proper correspondence, however, does not mean identity. Theological propositions about God will, in the end, prove inadequate to their object:

> Every theological statement is an inadequate expression of its object. The actual Word of Christ spoken to us is not an inadequate expression of its object, though of course every attempt on our part, even the highest and the best, to reproduce that Word in thought or in speech is inadequate. Strictly speaking, it is only God himself who has a conception of God [2].

Nevertheless, under the impact of revelation and grace, it is possible for theology to attain a relative significance, a kind of adequate inadequacy:

> Every one of the categories known to us by which we attempt to conceive him is, in the last analysis, not really one of his categories at all. God shatters every syllogism. But just as everything which is not God could not exist apart from God and is something only because of God, with increasing intensity an "aliqua imitatio illius essentiae", so it is possible for expressions which are really appropriate only to objects that are not identical with God, to be true expressions, "per aliquam similitudinem aut imaginem (ut cum vultum alicuius consideramus in speculo)", even when these expressions are applied to the God who can never be expressed [3].

Theology is thus given, within its limits as a creaturely undertaking, a proper and legitimate task. When this gets expressed in the *Church Dogmatics*, theology for Barth, as Hans Frei remarks, will have turned "from a critical, dialectical instrument to a positive descriptive means" [4].

In concluding this first chapter, I shall confine myself to making some general observations. It is clear, first of all, that there is no possibility, on Barth's reading of the matter, of separating dogmatics or theology from ethics. The theme of their unity has been present since his earliest writings, and it of course is pursued unremittingly in the *Church Dogmatics*. But since Barth's theology, particularly in the *Römerbrief*, though

---

[1] *FQI*, p. 16.

[2] *Ibid.*, p. 29.

[3] *Ibid.* It is possible to discern here the suggestion, at least, of a theological method which will utilize analogy rather than dialectic as its key vehicle.

[4] Ramsey, *Faith and Ethics*, p. 50.

not only there, was a conscious attempt to eliminate every possibility that would lead either to a grounding of theology in anthropology or to the erection of an ideology, it is only to be expected that his ethics would take a similar direction.

This would account, in part at least, for Barth's persistent refusal to allow any real significance to the variable possibilities open to human action, or to sketch out the direction that obedience, empirically, would take. An ethic grounded in the free electing grace of God, which encounters man as command in his particular givenness and determination, would be expected to exhibit a corresponding freedom from fixed categories of response and action. There is a problem in this, which has to do with those ordinary stabilities and orderings which surround man in his creaturely life. Barth has indicated an awareness of this in the 1928 outline of ethics, which included a section devoted to the place of order within an ethic of creation.

When the point about the freedom of grace in revelation and the implication that this carries for ethics has been recognized, a further question presses for answer. To what extent is man, as a creature enabled through the Holy Spirit to respond to God's gracious love, capable of realizing the possibilities open to him as ethical agent? Here I have suggested a certain lack of clarity. To be sure, there is discernible a somewhat more hopeful treatment of this issue in the writings after the *Römerbrief*. It still appears to be the case, however, that the eschatological reality of the human, as promise, even though a future *in* the present, is provided with no meaningful point of contact with man's givenness and his need to act now. It is possible that a subsequent deepening and extension of Christology in the *Church Dogmatics* will take us beyond what seems, at present, an impasse.

Finally, we should note that, at this point, all of the categories which become central in the *Church Dogmatics* are present: Election, Christology, at least an incipient Trinitarianism (in the sense that the doctrine of the Trinity has not yet achieved the status of a formal methodological principle), the command of God, the unity of Law and Gospel, obedience, freedom, man as *simul justus et peccator*, and a corresponding tension between justification and sanctification. It remains now to determine what these will come to in the ethics of the *Church Dogmatics*.

CHAPTER TWO

THE ETHICAL CONTEXT

A. Theological Method

The *Church Dogmatics* represents the culmination of the methodological revision which engaged Barth's attention after the publication of the first volume of the *Christian Dogmatics*. That revision entailed, we saw, a definition of theology as a science attached to the church, an accentuating of Christology, and a focusing of attention away from the self existing in faith and towards the positive content of faith given in revelation, i.e., the faith of the church. What this amounts to is a sustained effort to ground theology in an independent method, that is, in a way of carrying on its task of reflection, criticism, and construction without borrowing presuppositions or criteria from other disciplines. This will mean that theology begins, traverses, and culminates solely on the ground of, and exclusively in reference to, its origin in revelation. In this respect, theology will function as a reflection of the aseity of God. Naturally, this does not mean that it is given ultimate place as an independent science. To the contrary, it is justifiable only as a "relative factual necessity" (*relative faktische Notwendigkeit*) [1], and is thus to be understood as a "stopgap in an unordered cosmos" [2]. This relative justification of theology is further insured in that it is, in its attachment to the Church as its proper locus of activity, always an act of faith and obedience. This indicates the continued dependence of theology on the free action of God in Jesus Christ, and so precludes the possibility of its becoming absolutized as a completed body of truth [3].

The method employed by Barth in carrying through this under-

---

[1] *KD*, I/1, p. 4. Future quotations from and references to the *Kirchliche Dogmatik* will be cited simply by volume number and page, and will refer, unless otherwise indicated, to the German edition.

[2] "Sie kann sich selbst durchaus nicht als Glied in einem geordneten, sondern nur als Lückenbüßerin in einem ungeordneten Kosmos verstehen". *Ibid.*, p. 8.

[3] *Ibid.*, p. 14f. Cf. I/2, pp. 963ff.

standing of theology can be described along the following lines. The task of theology, as dogmatics, is the analysis of the language peculiar to the proclamation of the Church [1]. The legitimacy of the language employed in proclamation is a question exclusively of its agreement with the revelation to which Holy Scripture is the primary witness. Scripture as the written Word of God thus assumes a normative role as the objective standard against which church proclamation, the Word of God in the form of sacrament and preaching, is measured. Dogmatic theology falls precisely within the sustained examination of the relation which holds between these [2].

However, both scripture and church proclamation are themselves grounded in and dependent on the Word of God as originally revealed. There is thus a movement to be recognized and kept intact, an irreversible order of priority. The Word of God as revealed has to do with God's own proper action (*Deus dixit*). Scripture, as the primary witness to original revelation, and the proclamation of the church grounded in that witness, are, as human responses, placed in a dependent position. They are not, in themselves, simply identifiable with the Word of God, though they may, from time to time, *become* the Word of God. This occurs when and where and as the Word of God continues to reveal itself in Scripture and proclamation [3]. What this means for dogmatics is that it is directed first of all to an explication of the *concept* of revelation as a means of determining the extent to which both Scripture and church proclamation "are to be understood as the Word of God, the sort of correspondence that stands between them, and the way in which the second is to be measured by the first" [4].

---

[1] "Dogmatik ist als theologische Disziplin die wissenschaftliche Selbstprüfung der christlichen Kirche hinsichtlich des Inhalts der ihr eigentümlichen Rede von Gott". I/1, p. 1. Cf. *Ibid.*, p. 296. To the extent that Barth grounds dogmatics within the Christian community, he is in obvious continuity with the theology of the nineteenth century. Cf. F. Schleiermacher, *The Christian Faith* (Edinburgh: T & T Clark, 1956), p. 82f.; and A. Ritschl, *Justification and Reconciliation* (Edinburgh: T & T Clark, 1902), p. 3f. Attention is also drawn to this point by Richard R. Niebuhr in his book, *Resurrection and Historical Reason* (New York: Charles Scribner's Sons, 1957), p. 46.

[2] "Scientific dogmatics inquires—and with that we come to the decisive point—into the agreement of church proclamation with the revelation attested in Holy Scripture". I/1, p. 299. Cf. *Ibid.*, p. 300, and I/2, Par. 23, "Dogmatics as a Function of the Hearing Church".

[3] I/1, pp. 121, 308.

[4] *Ibid.*, p. 310.

This does not mean, of course, that dogmatics is provided with an abstract concept of revelation which it wields independently as a criterion in assessing Scripture and church proclamation. The concept of revelation, the revealed Word of God as originally given, is present only through, and so only in unity with, the word of Scripture and proclamation. The unity of the Word of God in its threefold form provides a precise analogy to the unity of God in his being as Father, Son, and Holy Spirit [1]. The doctrine of the Trinity thus becomes the means to a correct explication of the concept of revelation.

The doctrine of the Trinity corresponds to the outer possibility of dogmatics, the explication of the fact of revelation. The question of the inner possibility of this fact, however, is answered in the propositions of dogmatics which relate to Christology and the effectiveness of the Holy Spirit [2]. This means that for Barth the sum of revelation is given in Jesus Christ, and the reconciliation that takes place in him [3]. The doctrine of the Trinity, and the corresponding doctrines of creation, reconciliation, and redemption, will therefore be developed along exclusively christological lines [4].

Here we come to one of the most pervasive aspects of Barth's method, his insistence on making the actuality of revelation as given to faith in the history of Jesus Christ the basis or "presupposition" for every phase of the discussion. The importance of this principle for Barth's method may be seen at the following points. Jesus Christ is the presupposition and content of creation and reconciliation, and so the eternal presupposition of the convenant between God and man [5]. Again, Jesus Christ is the "presupposition and condition of the being of all men" (*Voraussetzung und Bedingung des Seins aller Menschen*) [6], and so the ground of all knowledge about man in his reality as the creature of God [7]. This will mean that our knowledge of man as sinner, the judgment of God, justification and sanctification, the freedom of man

---

[1] *Ibid.*, p. 124f.

[2] *Ibid.*, p. 309.

[3] "Revelation in fact does not differ from the Person of Jesus Christ, and again does not differ from the reconciliation that takes place in him. Whoever says 'revelation', says 'The Word became Flesh' ". *Ibid.*, p. 122. Cf. p. 309; IV/1, Par. 57, Part 1, "Gott mit uns".

[4] I/1, pp. 410, 475.

[5] II/1, p. 587; IV/1, pp. 56, 70.

[6] IV/2, p. 38.

[7] III/4, p. 46.

under God, his response of obedience and love, and the formation of the Christian community, will be explicated only on the presupposition of the being and action of Jesus Christ [1]. Finally, Jesus Christ is, through the Holy Spirit, the presupposition of our participation in and recognition of revelation. The Holy Spirit operates always on the presupposition of the power and lordship of Jesus [2].

It is Barth's insistence on developing the doctrine of the Trinity along exclusively christological lines that has brought forth the charge of "Christomonism" from H. Richard Niebuhr [3]. And it is his parallel insistence on seeing Jesus Christ as the presupposition for every other proposition in dogmatics that is described by Hans Urs von Balthasar as the "central problem" (Kernproblem) in Barth's theology [4]. Von Balthasar's comment occurs within his discussion of Barth's anthropology, but it underlines the focal point of Barth's endeavor to construct a method appropriate to dogmatics as the particular science which takes place within the church. In this respect, it is arguable that Barth's utilization of this principle takes at least logical precedence over the place of analogy in his method, since theological language, as indeed all creaturely language, is itself grounded in the presupposition of revelation actualized in Christ [5].

The importance of Barth's emphasis on Christology for the construction of an independent method is particularly transparent at two points: In answering the problem of an adequate ontology, and in providing the grounds for a viable theological epistemology. Dogmatics, as an independent science, cannot borrow its criteria of reality or knowledge from the general human sciences. From these, Barth asserts, it has nothing to learn [6]. Instead, it is required to remain faithful at all points to its own origin in revelation, and thus to draw its criterion of reality and its grounds for knowledge from that source alone. For Barth, this will mean that Jesus Christ is both the standard of reality, and the condition for authentic knowledge about God and the human. Continu-

---

[1] II/2, p. 828; IV/1, p. 618; IV/2, p. 294.

[2] IV/2, p. 405f.

[3] "Niebuhr would have to say of Barth's Trinitarianism that its complete identification with revelation in Christ makes it not a Trinitarianism but simply 'Christo-monism' ". So Hans Frei in Ramsey, Faith and Ethics, p. 101.

[4] Karl Barth: Darstellung und Deutung seiner Theologie (Köln: Jacob Hegner Verlag, 1951), p. 129.

[5] II/1, p. 259f.

[6] I/1, p. 6.

ity is thus established immediately between the order of knowing and the order of being. Or, as Barth expresses it, Jesus Christ is the basis, ontically and noetically, for all being and knowing [1].

Here it must be emphasized that Barth does not mean that Christ becomes, in theological method, some kind of "ontological principle" from which everything can be deduced. Were this the case, the charge of "rationalism" that has been levelled against him would indeed hold true [2]. There may be a problem of rationalism in Barth, but it does not arise in this way. The being of God in Jesus Christ is always understood by Barth as being *in act* [3]. It is therefore viewed dynamically, as history, in the birth, life, death, resurrection, and parousia of Jesus Christ. It is this history, the history of salvation (*Heilsgeschichte*) centering in Jesus Christ [4], that provides the criterion of reality. Nor is the character of God's being in act limited to his external dealings with the world and man. Internally, in the eternal givenness of his triune being, God is already historical [5]. The history of Jesus Christ is thus the external manifestation of the inner history of God in his eternal being, which in revelation has been opened to man for participation. It is this continuity between the external and internal sides of salvation history that enables Barth to move from the actuality of revelation to its possibility, from external historical manifestation to internal historical ground [6].

It is in exploring the meaning and results of this history that the significance of Jesus Christ as the criterion of the real emerges. For the

---

[1] II/1, pp. 166ff.; IV/1, p. 47f.; IV/2, pp. 39ff.

[2] Cf. the comments of Stanley Romaine Hopper in his essay, "The Modern Diogenes: A Kierkegaardian Crochet", in *Religion and Culture, Essays in Honor of Paul Tillich*, Walter Leibrecht, ed. (New York: Harper and Brothers, 1959), pp. 104, 106f.

[3] Cf. II/1, Par. 28, Part 1, "The Being of God in Act". Cf. also IV/3.1, p. 199f., where Barth insists, against Berkouwer's interpretation, that he does not move deductively from a "Christ principle", but always in reference to the "living Person of Jesus Christ" (*der lebendigen Person Jesu Christi*).

[4] II/1, p. 576.

[5] "Gott ist ja nach dem Zeugnis der Heiligen Schrift—schon entsprechend seinem dreieinigen Wesen und wie es gerade durch den biblischen Begriff der Ewigkeit angezeigt wird—schon in sich selbst geschichtlich ...". IV/1, p. 122. Cf. p. 222.

[6] Cf. I/2, Pars. 13 and 16; III/1, Par. 41; IV/1, Par. 57, Part 2. The notion of "salvation history" and its relation to ordinary history will be examined at the end of this discussion of the main points in Barth's method.

meaning of revelation is that it has brought about a radical and final alteration in man's being. It is here that the ontological thrust of revelation is discernible in a thoroughgoing realist form. This is seen clearly in Barth's Christology. In the Incarnation, there occurred a union of the Son of God with the Son of Man, Jesus of Nazareth. The humanity of Jesus, however, is interpreted not as simply the humanity of an individual man, but rather as "the *humanum*, the being and essence, the kind and nature, which is that of all men, which marks them all as men, and distinguishes them from other creatures" [1]. Unless the humanity of Jesus is this kind of "concrete universal", there is no way to denote a "basic alteration and determination" (*grundlegenden Veränderung und Bestimmung*) of the human [2]. In Jesus Christ, humanity as such and totally is reconciled and sanctified. It follows, then, that the future of man has been irrevocably cast; sin, evil, and godlessness are only apparently real. Ontologically, they have no referents, and can only be seen as aspects of man's distorted past. They have nothing to do with his future, already decided and determined in Jesus Christ, though Barth recognizes that he may still choose these "impossible possibilities" [3].

The realism that emerges from Barth's use of the Christological principle of presupposition provides the background for a positive ontological description of the identity of man as creature. This is accomplished through the employment of analogy, specifically the *analogia relationis* [4]. Of course, the possibility of meaningful analogous statements about the human can only be secured on the basis of the actuality of revelation, never the reverse. This holds true of both the ontological identity of man (*analogia relationis*), and his epistemological participation in revelation (*analogia fidei*). The use of analogy is thus securely anchored in grace, and the possibility of an analogy of being (*analogia entis*), viewed by Barth as "the invention of Antichrist" (*die Erfindung des Antichrist*), is excluded from the outset [5]. This will not mean that nothing can be predicated analogously about the being of man. The *participatio*

---

[1] IV/2, p. 51f. Barth's christological anthropology will be explored in detail in chapter five of this study.

[2] *Ibid.*, p. 52.

[3] III/2, p. 162; IV/1, p. 324; IV/3.1, pp. 282, 503f. Cf. especially IV/3.1, pp. 287-299, where Barth discusses the strategems employed by man to escape the divine decision and determination.

[4] A term first suggested to Barth by Bonhoeffer. Cf. *KD* III/1, pp. 218ff.

[5] I/1, p. viii.

fidei entails also a *participatio entis* [1]. The being of the creature, however, is to be explained only on the basis of the prior reality of God's being. The analogy is never from the human to God, but always from God to the creature. As Hans Frei points out, Barth's use of analogy makes God the analogue to which man is the analogate; it is the creature, not the Creator, who is to be clarified by analogy [2].

Given this orientation, it is clear that Barth's use of analogy will not fall precisely within the context of the scholastic distinctions. It will not be an analogy of attribution, inequality, or proportionality. All of these depend on and assume a likeness between creature and Creator which is detectable immanently, receiving logical expression in the act of predicating continuous qualities of both, though in a mode appropriate to each [3]. The logical difficulties of this program are in themselves virtually insurmountable insofar as it is assumed to be capable of providing an adequate ground for cognitive statements about God [4]. However, Barth's quarrel with traditional types of analogy does not rest on their logical deficiencies; it focuses rather on the ontological and epistemological arrogance and confusion which ensues from man's assumption that natural reason and ordinary language are themselves capable of attaining positive insight into the reality of God, or, for that matter, of man. Thus, though Barth's use of analogy displays formal similarity to the traditional scholastic types, materially it is intended to indicate a decisively different program.

The *analogia relationis* is validated by the relation that holds, in Jesus Christ, between God and man, which is itself a reflection of the eternal relation between the Father and the Son in the Trinity [5]. Christ,

---

[1] But *only* as the latter is grounded in grace. Cf. II/1, p. 89f., where Barth comments on an interpretation advanced by Gottlieb Söhngen which places the *analogia entis* in strict dependence on grace and revelation. Since Söhngen writes as a Catholic theologian, Barth remarks that if his interpretation could stand as the official doctrine of the Roman Church, he would have to withdraw his earlier characterization of the *analogia entis* as "the invention of the Antichrist".

[2] Ramsey, *Faith and Ethics*, p. 52.

[3] Cf. Frederick Copleston, *A History of Philosophy* (New York: Image Books, 1962), Vol. II, Part 2, pp. 73-76; 228f., for a discussion of these types of analogy.

[4] Frederick Ferré gives a good review and summary of these difficulties in his book, *Logic, Language, and God* (New York: Harper and Brothers, 1961), Ch. 6, "The Logic of Analogy".

[5] III/2, pp. 158, 176.

as the temporal manifestation of God's eternal election of man to be his convenant partner, and in his unique identity as eternal Son of God *and* Son of Man [1], displays the inner and outer being of God as a *being-in-encounter*, a being which in its innermost depths and in its historical embodiment in Jesus Christ, includes the human. God's eternal being is thus to be understood as free event and encounter. In the passion, crucifixion, and resurrection of Jesus Christ, the "humanity of God" is shown decisively to be co-humanity; Christ exists supremely and exclusively as the man with and for other men [2].

Within the human, there are various relationship that can be indicated as reflections and analogies of the relations existing within God, and between God and the human. There is, first of all, what Barth describes as the "basic form of humanity", the being-in-encounter of man as male and female [3]. This relationship is analogous to the relationship between God and man in Jesus Christ, and between the Father and the Son in the eternal being of God. As the being of Christ is a being in freedom for other men, and as this is the embodiment of God's eternal freedom which he has in relationship to himself, so too the co-existence of man as male and female exhibits man's freedom to be with and for his fellows [4]. Man's identity as male and female, which takes the form of an I - thou confrontation, is the *imago Dei*, the image and reflection of God in the creature [5]. And it is because of this form of being that God is able to address man as a definite "thou", and that man is capable of responding as a particular "I" [6]. The I - thou relationality of the human is

---

[1] II/1, p. 169; IV/1, p. 55.

[2] IV/1, pp. 251f., 703f.; IV/2, pp. 53f., 486f. Cf. also *The Humanity of God*, pp. 46ff.

[3] III/2, Par. 45, Part 2, "Die Grundform der Menschlichkeit".

[4] "As man generally is modelled on the man Jesus, on his being for his fellow-man, and as Jesus is himself modelled on God, so it can also be said of man generally in his existence with his fellow-man, that he is created in God's image. He is in his humanity, and therefore in his co-humanity". III/2 p. 390. Cf. III/1, p. 219; III/2, p. 291. The issues raised by the *analogia relationis* for Barth's anthropology will be explored in chapter five of this study.

[5] III/1, p. 219. Cf. Bouillard, *Karl Barth*, Vol. II, pp. 197ff.

[6] III/1, p. 219. The influence of the thought of Martin Buber may be seen in Barth's use of the I-thou relationship in describing the *imago Dei*, and in his characterization of the creation accounts in Genesis as pre-history or "pure saga" (*reine Sage*) (III/1, p. 89), a description which Barth also applies to the resurrection (IV/1, p. 370). Cf. Buber, *I and Thou* (New York: Charles Scribner's Sons, 1955); and *Moses: The Revelation and the Convenant* (New York: Harper and Brothers, 1958), pp. 13-19, "Saga and History".

given its most dramatic fulfillment in marriage, which is an analogy of the relationship between Christ and the church [1].

Beyond this basic instance of the *analogia relationis*, there are other aspects of the world and man which can be given ontological description. The most general example of this lies in the relationship posited by Barth between creaturely history and occurrence and salvation history. The former is seen at all points as a reflection of the latter. As the broad context within which human service and action take place, it provides the proper locus of God's own activity, and so becomes the reflection and mirror of that activity [2]. Again, it must be emphasized that the status accorded creaturely history and occurrence as a likeness of the history and occurrence of salvation cannot be established independently of God's eternal election of man as his covenant partner, and the resulting continuity which this establishes between creation, covenant, and reconciliation. The analogical validity of creaturely history and occurrence depends wholly on God's decision and will; that it always has the character of being a mirror and reflection of God's own history lies exclusively in the fact that the providental rule of God over his creation never ceases [3].

More specific examples of the *analogia relationis* are given in Barth's discussion of the life of the Christian community. As the body of Christ, the "earthly-historical form of his existence" (*seine irdischgeschichtliche Existenzform*), the community becomes a "provisional representation

---

[1] III/4, p. 159.

[2] "It may not be denied or overlooked that creaturely history in its whole development is similar to the history of salvation; though dissimilar, yet similar, as a reflection is similar to its original. It is not for nothing that creaturely history is the theater of the great acts of God, the Father's house. On the contrary, from its source and throughout its structure it is designed to reflect and illustrate these actions of God ... World-occurrence is, in things great and small, a mirror and likeness of the occurrence of salvation". III/3, p. 58f.; IV/3.2, p. 786f. Cf. Bouillard, *Karl Barth*, Vol. II, p. 216.

[3] III/3, p. 60f. It could be argued that the relation between creaturely and salvation history falls more properly within the *analogia fidei*, rather than the *analogia relationis*. Indeed, some of Barth's statements in this section lend themselves to that interpretation. However, to the extent that Barth here purports to be making statements about what creaturely history *is* in relation to salvation history, he involves himself in ontological description. Of course, such statements, as they embody the *analogia relationis*, would necessarily be grounded in the *analogia fidei* as the epistemic basis for their being made in the first place. What is lacking thus far, then, is an indication of the epistemological grounding of the *analogia relationis* holding between creaturely and salvation history.

of the humanity sanctified in Jesus Christ" [1]. It will follow, then, that the establishment of the community in service to the world represents a likeness and reflection of the prophetic office of Jesus Christ, in whom God has called the world as a whole to service, and that the sending of the community into the world will be comparable with God's initial sending of his Son into the world in Jesus Christ [2]. Christians, then, will be those who exist in analogy to what Jesus Christ is:

> According to the evident tenor of the New Testament assertion, it is clear that the particular being of Christians as "children of God" consists decisively and commandingly in the fact that, as those whom Jesus Christ in the work of his Spirit has called and calls to himself, they exist in a special nearness to him and, by virtue of this nearness, in analogy to what he is [3].

And it is clear, when Barth speaks of the Christian community and the individual Christian existing in analogy to Christ, that he intends the latter to be understood in a subjective, existential fashion. Whatever Barth's strictures against "philosophy of existence" in general and the theological program of Rudolph Bultmann in particular [4], it is evident that his emphasis on the objectivity and actuality of revelation, and the corresponding ontological realism that results, is not meant to overrule the possibility of man's existential involvement. Indeed, unless there is a response and participation from man, the grace active in revelation becomes simply "a one-sided decision of power" (*eine einseitige Machtentscheidung*) [5].

Here we come to the second thrust of Barth's Christology. As we have indicated, the ground of both being and knowing is given in Jesus Christ. Theological epistemology, for Barth, takes the form of the second type of analogy indicated above, the *analogia fidei* [6]. An under-

---

[1] IV/2, pp. 788, 791.

[2] IV/3.2, pp. 878f., 908f.

[3] IV/3.2, p. 612. The precise formula which Barth uses to express this analogy is that of "real similarity along with complete dissimilarity" (*realer Gleicheit bei aller Ungliechheit*). I shall explore the logical and epistemological implications of this for theological language at the conclusion of this discussion of the place of analogy in Barth's method.

[4] Cf. Barth's statements in the foreward to III/4, p. viiif., and in IV/1, p. 858.

[5] IV/1, p. 823.

[6] Barth also describes this as an "analogy of grace" and an "analogy of revelation". Cf. II/1, p. 275; III/3, p. 59.

standing of this is of obvious importance, since it will provide the clue as to how statements about the relational being of man, world history, and the Christian community, as analogies to the being of God and man in Jesus Christ and the Trinity, are to be validated as knowledge.

Revelation, it is obvious, cannot be in any sense the actualization of human cognitive possibilities [1]. It will therefore be the case that revelation carries its epistemological ground and principle within itself. The "order of knowing" will unfold in a pattern similar to that displayed in our discussion of the *analogia relationis*. As the being of man depends on the prior being of God, so too man's knowledge depends on the self-knowledge of God. The proper and original Subject and Object of knowledge is God himself in his inner Trinitarian life. In that sense, knowledge of God takes place first as "an event enclosed in the bosom of the divine Trinity" (*ein in Schoße der göttlichen Trinität verschlossenes Geschehen*) [2]. It is not this in abstraction from the human, however, since man is included in the event of this knowledge "in the height, in the hidden being and essence of God" [3]. This does not mean that man is, in himself, in some sense "ready" for the knowledge of God. Man's readiness for revelation, and so for knowledge of God, is exhibited only in Jesus Christ, who is also the specific embodiment of God's readiness to be known. Jesus Christ, then, as the grace of God, is at once the knowability of God on the side of both man and God [4].

Our participation in God's self-knowledge is the result of grace. It depends on God's giving himself over, as the proper Subject of revelation, to become also the proper Object of human knowledge and reflection, and, finally, language. This occurs through the action of the Holy Spirit, the temporal presence of Christ within the Christian community, which brings about the response of faith. The Holy Spirit is therefore the epistemic *ground* of our knowledge of God; faith the epistemic *organ* [5]. This means that knowledge of God always occurs as

---

[1] Cf. II/1, Par. 27, Part 1, "Die Verborgenheit Gottes".

[2] II/1, p. 230.

[3] *Ibid.*

[4] "We can very simply anticipate the positive answer to our question: The readiness of man enclosed in the readiness of God is Jesus Christ. And so Jesus Christ is the knowability of God on our side, as he is the grace of God itself, and so also the knowability of God on God's side". *Ibid.*, p. 167.

[5] *Ibid.*, pp. 176f., 231. Cf. von Balthasar, *Karl Barth*, p. 149; "Der Glaube ... ist das Organ der absoluten Wahrheit, der Veritas increata. Und umgekehrt gilt: das Organ der absoluten Wahrheit ist keine anderes als der Glaube".

event, as human response to the self-presentation and unveiling of God, which is also, from our side, a veiling. That our knowledge of God inevitably takes the form of faith indicates that it is both limited and dependent. We know God only *by* his grace; this constitutes the self-disclosure of God to the creature, indicating that it is at all points a dependent knowledge. But we know God only *in* faith; this indicates that our knowledge, though real, is limited. We do not know God as he is known to himself [1]. Faith will therefore not indicate a static quality of man's being, but will rather be viewed appropriately only as event, as God's continuous self-disclosure through the Holy Spirit. Human knowledge of God will depend on our continual openness and response to God's activity.

There is, nevertheless, a real correspondence between our act of knowing in faith, and God, the Object of our knowledge. This correspondence, grounded in grace, is the *analogia fidei*. On this basis, there is a similarity between the possibility of knowledge in faith, and the realization of that possibility in revelation, and so a similarity between our knowledge of God in faith and God's own self-knowledge [2]. That this similarity depends exclusively on grace means that the knowledge of God which occurs within the Christian community is always contingent. Knowledge of God, in continuity with revelation, occurs always as miracle; the possibility of faith, as the form of human knowledge about God, is actualized only in the continued faithfulness of God's revelation of himself in the Holy Spirit. As James Brown indicates, God is for Barth the proper and available Object of knowledge in faith, and so in theology, only as he remains at the same time and continuously "indissolubly Subject" [3].

The significance of this, and so of the *analogia fidei*, for theological method, is seen in Barth's contention that knowledge of God can have only one adequate response: obedience. The knowledge given in revela-

---

[1] II/1, p. 235.

[2] "Despite its total dissimilarity, the human possibility of grasping the promise in faith is not without similarity to the divine possibility of its realization. Not in itself, not as a human possibility, but indeed, according to our first determination, from the standpoint of its object, as a possibility of grasping the promise. The force of this similarity is the possibility of knowing the Word of God, the possibility of a certain and clear knowledge, similar, though not identical, to the certainty and clarity in which God knows himself in his Word". I/1, p. 256.

[3] *Subject and Object in Modern Theology*, Ch. 6, "God, 'Indissolubly Subject' ". Cf. I/1, p. 367.

tion concerns what God has done to and for man in Jesus Christ, and so it includes the determination and direction given man in that action [1]. What this means for dogmatics is that it will always occur as response. The thinking and speaking about God that is given a certain relative form in the discipline of theology can never proceed in terms of its own insights and formulations. They must reflect a continual response to grace in its immediate impingement on the human [2]. This will mean that the essence of the Church, as this is identical with Jesus Christ, and so of dogmatic knowledge, is *actus purus*: the free divine action in which God gives himself to be known. The path to dogmatic knowledge, accordingly, lies only in the "present instant in which Jesus Christ himself speaks and is heard, and the divine light is created in our hearts" [3].

Given this presupposition for dogmatic knowledge, it is in order to ask what sort of meaning attaches to its language. To what extent are our words capable of embodying and expressing the content of revelation? In themselves, as the ordinary creaturely linguistic media which we employ in talking about our world, they lack all capacity for this task. The relation between human language and revelation cannot be solved by direct transference from one context to the other. However, there will of necessity be some relationship between them, else the possibility of meaningful statements about God is excluded immediately. Unless our knowledge of God is expressible in the ordinary language at our disposal, there can be no such knowledge [4].

Barth's move at this point is in its own way ingenious, though hardly surprising. Obviously, the way out of the dilemma posed by either a univocal or equivocal approach to the problem lies in analogy. Equally obviously, for Barth this will be *analogia fidei* or "analogy of truth" (*Analogie der Wahrheit*) [5]. The argument then would run as follows: What occurs in revelation is that words and concepts, ordinarily applied

---

[1] "We have to learn to read from what God has done for us, what he wants with us and of us". II/2, p. 621.

[2] "That God in his grace will take up residence in the confines of our thinking and speaking certainly cannot mean that he has given himself over to us as a prisoner. He dwells there, where our thinking and speaking about him take place in obedience: in obedience to his grace, which is his grace, which as such, whether we repeat ourselves or not, at all events will always be presented anew to us, and always sought anew by us". II/1, p. 241.

[3] I/1, p. 41.

[4] II/1, p. 253.

[5] *Ibid.*, p. 260. By "analogy", Barth here means "similarity, partial correspondence, and agreement". *Ibid.*, p. 254.

to the creaturely sphere, are elevated (*erhoben*) to their original and proper role, and so are enabled to refer to God. Revelation thus entails a linguistic restoration of creation. Our words and concepts all derive from the creativity of God. They are therefore used in a proper, literal sense only when applied to him; otherwise they serve only an "improper and pictorial" (*uneigentlich und bildlich*) function [1]. The ingeniousness of this move lies in the fact that it removes theological language from the sphere of the special and in effect makes it the proper standard and measure of all creaturely language. Such common words as "father," "son", "patience", "love", "arm", and "mouth", are given proper use and meaning only when applied to God [2].

Of course, dogmatics itself cannot guarantee this sort of proper use and correspondence between word and object. This depends always on grace and receptivity. So there is absolutely no way, from our side, of granting validity to what we do in fact say about God. The most that is possible is the recognition which occurs in faith that in Jesus Christ God has made man participant in his knowing. Our knowledge of God, and so the validity of our language about him, is real only as promise, never as possession. Its actualization takes place in the moment in which Jesus Christ in the Holy Spirit speaks to the Church [3]. So we have at this point come full circle back to the original point of departure: Jesus Christ as the presupposition of all being and knowing.

A number of questions can be raised about Barth's method. To begin with, the extension of Christology into a general presuppositional basis for every statement in dogmatics leads disquietingly near to a kind of "faith rationalism" capable of developing a completed body of theological truth. Even after allowing for Barth's strictures against any such final program, and his consistently dynamic reading of God as

---

[1] "Our words are not our property, but his. And as he disposes his property, he places it at our disposal—at the disposal of our grateful obedience —in that he allows and commands us to make use of them also in relation to him. The use to which they are put is thus not an improper, wholly figurative one, but their proper use. We use our words improperly and figuratively—as we can say, looking back from God's revelation—when we employ them within the limits of what is proper to us as creatures. When we apply them to God they are not estranged from their original object and truth, but, on the contrary, are restored to it". *Ibid.*, p. 259.

[2] *Ibid.*, Barth actually advances the astonishing assertion that such words as "arm" and "mouth" are to us "as such, incomprehensible" (*als solche unfaßbar*).

[3] *Ibid.*, pp. 265f., 284-287.

being-in-act, it is still not clear that the *fides quaerens intellectum* should
necessarily entail the ability to move from the actuality of revelation to
its possibility, to trace the inner Trinitarian relations between Father,
Son, and Holy Spirit, to exhibit the continuity that holds between
creation, covenant, and reconciliation, and to construct a completed
anthropology on the basis of a Christologically centered realist ontology.
In weaving these into a unified theological fabric, Barth exposes himself
to comparison with the whole line of German Idealism, and Hegel in
particular, whose emphasis on the unity of things under a principle
(Reason or Spirit) that both presupposes and posits itself finds a certain
obvious echo in Barth.

This similarity has been explored, positively by Hans Urs von
Balthasar, who argues that Barth has simply transferred Hegelian
categories into the framework of dogmatics [1]; negatively by Henri
Bouillard, who, though sensitive to certain Hegelian overtones in the
Dogmatics, feels that Barth, by replacing Hegel's "philosophical ontology" with a "Christological dogmatic", places emphasis exclusively
on what God says *to* man, rather than on what man develops out of his
own consciousness, and so supplies a totally different content [2].

Of course, Barth is aware of the danger of falling into a purely
deductive rationalism in dogmatics. We have already noted the criticism
delivered against G.C. Berkouwer's interpretation of the "triumph of
grace", which implied that Barth was working with an abstract Christological principle. In addition, Barth cheerfully recognizes that his
exposition embodies circularity, in that it begins and ends with revelation.
The Word of God in Jesus Christ is both the *terminus a quo* and the
terminus ad quem of theological thinking [3]. Barth insists, however, that
circularity in itself is not really a problem. The only question is whether
we are involved in a "vicious" or a "true" circularity [4].

The difficulty with circularity, however, whatever its context, is
that it lacks genuine movement. In this respect, Barth's utilization of
the principle of presupposition threatens to vitiate the very dynamism

---

[1] *Karl Barth: Darstellung und Deutung seiner Theologie*, pp. 218f., 230,
236, *et passim*.
[2] *Karl Barth*, Vol. III, pp. 295-299. Cf. also Arnold B. Come's discussion
of Barth's rationalism and his affinity with Hegel in *An Introduction to Barth's
"Dogmatics" for Preachers*, pp. 140f., 248f.
[3] II/1, p. 276f.
[4] *Ibid.*

he wishes to preserve. The inexorability of the development of the discussion veers towards predictability, and an air of analyticity permeates throughout. The upshot of this is seen in the aura of finality injected by Barth into dogmatics, which appears both to conflict with the very limitations set over the whole enterprise at the outset, and to lack relevance to human life in its concrete historicity.

Bonhoeffer thought the resulting difficulty of a "positivism of revelation" could be overcome by applying linguistic therapy along the lines of a "non-religious interpretation of theological concepts" [1]. Barth's indirect reply to this in a lecture given at Aarau in 1956, "The Humanity of God", finds him simultaneously overruling the objection and supplying the clue as to where the difficulty really lies:

> The question of *language*, about which one must speak in reference to the so-called "outsiders", is not so burning today as is asserted in various quarters. This is true in the first place because, again thinking in terms of the humanity of God, we cannot at all reckon in a serious way with *real* "outsiders", with a "world come of age", but only with a world which *regards* itself as of age (and proves daily that it is precisely not that). Thus the so-called "outsiders" are really only "insiders" who have not yet understood and apprehended themselves as such. On the other hand, even the most persuaded Christian, in the final analysis, must and will recognize himself ever and again as an "outsider". So there must then be no particular language for insiders and outsiders. Both are contemporary men-of-the-world—all of us are. A little "non-religious" language from the street, the newspaper, literature, and, if one is ambitious, from the philosopher may thus, for the sake of communication, occasionally indeed be in order ... A little of the language of Canaan, a little "revelation positivism", can also be a good thing in addressing us all and, according to my experience, in which I am certainly not alone, will often, though not always, be still better understood even by the oddest strangers [2].

What this passage underlines, apart from its obvious indication of Barth's approach to the problem of theological language, is the pronounced realism that pervades his thinking, the pressing reality of God in revelation, together with the ontological transformation of the human that occurred in Jesus Christ. It is the relentlessness of Barth's pursuit of these points, what Richard R. Niebuhr describes as his "fearlessness

---

[1] *Prisoner for God, Letters and Papers from Prison*, Eberhard Bethge, ed., and Reginald H. Fuller, trans. (New York: The Macmillan Co., 1957), p. 148.

[2] *The Humanity of God*, p. 58f.

before the idea of revelation" [1], that leads ostensibly into an analytic-deductive posture.

Actually, it is possible, and preferable, to take the issue of rationalism in Barth in a less strict, more informal way. This would involve seeing in the *Dogmatics* an incorporation of the notions of rationality and order prevalent in Classical philosophy. The Christological principle may then be taken as a basis on which to explore the "reason" of things, theologically speaking. To the extent that this would involve, in addition, seeing Christ as the "necessary condition" and "efficient cause" (in the sense of theological origin and goal) of things, Barth falls philosophically closer to Plato's use of the form of Good than to Hegel's Absolute. Even in this modification, the crucial difference remains that for Plato the form of Good is not historically but speculatively determined and discovered, whereas for Barth Jesus Christ is never separated (nor separable) from his history.

A dynamic reading of Barth's realism, however, does not remove all the difficulties. Indeed, it makes them even more evident. For in taking Christ as the standard of reality and knowledge, Barth posits a consistent distinction between two types or levels of history, "ordinary" and "sacred"', and on this basis is led into an attempted removal of the epistemological questions generated by revelation by absorbing them into ontology. We must now explore these issues, and indcate the consequences they carry for the epistemic claims of the Christian community, as these are expressed in the logical structure of theological language.

The history of Jesus Christ, Barth makes clear, is not simply a part of ordinary history. It forms rather the special history of revelation, *Heilsgeschichte* [2]. It is the manifestation of the eternal will of God in

---

[1] *Resurrection and Historical Reason*, p. 45. Cf. *Supra*, pp. 00ff., for an early indication of the realist motif in Barth's thought, and his assessment of the legitimate function it might play within theology.

[2] Barth takes issue with the use of this term, insofar as it is used to signal a revelational history evolving out of the matrix of general history, and so capable of direct recognition and development into a kind of *Weltanschauung*. I/2, p. 64. Once it has been purged of this association, and brought into strict relation to God's freedom and discontinuity in revelation over against ordinary history, it can be legitimately employed. Cf. III/2, p. 192; IV/2, pp. 914, 929; *et passim*. It is in this way that Richard Niebuhr's argument that Barth's view of the relation between revelation and ordinary historical occurrences, and his distinction between the temporal contingency of the latter and the "real" time of revelation, indicates conformity "to the specifications of *Heilsgeschichte*

his act of electing all men in the humanity of Jesus, and so the "limitation and determination" of all other occurrences [1]. The historical order, accordingly, never moves from general or world-history to the history of Jesus Christ; world-history is rather to be seen at all points as a "predicate" of revelation [2]. It is this insistence on making the special history of revelation the ontological fulcrum on which general history (and our experience of it) rests, that lends ambiguity to Barth's statements about the life of Jesus. Richard Niebuhr, for instance, speaks of "the entire absence of contingency in the sequence of events comprising the sacred history" [3]. Actually, the issue is rather more subtle than this, for Barth asserts that the history of Jesus Christ both is and is not a "contingent fact of history" (*zufällige Geschichtstatsache*) [4].

What this means is that, on the one hand, salvation history gained concreteness in the life of a specific entity within the ordinary space-time order, Jesus of Nazareth; this is the "contingency" of salvation history. On the other hand, it indicates that, when one undertakes to interpret the significance of Jesus' life, he is directed beyond the context of contingency and onto a plane of non-contingent meanings. The notion of the "history of salvation", then, has to do essentially with a distinction between two kinds of meaning; that given through the channels of ordinary historical research and reconstruction, which reflect the employment of (roughly) consistent epistemic categories and conceptual patterns; and that which devolves directly from the fact of revelation, which depends exclusively on it, and which therefore eludes these categories and patterns.

---

even though he rejects the term", must be understood. Cf. *Resurrection and Historical Reason*, p. 86.

[1] "The true humanity of Jesus Christ, as a history which took place in time, is thus the execution and revelation of not only *an*, but *the* intention of God's will, which is not limited and determined by any other, and thus by no other occurrence in the creaturely sphere, but is rather the content of all divine purposes, and thus the limitation and determination of all other world-occurrences". IV/2, p. 33.

[2] "Offenbarung ist nicht ein Prädikat der Geschichte, sondern Geschichte ist ein Prädikat der Offenbarung". I/2, p. 64. Cf. Emil Brunner, *The Christian Doctrine of Creation and Redemption*, Olive Wyon, trans. (Philadelphia: The Westminster Press, 1952), p. 237: "Jesus Christ cannot be understood from the point of view of world history, but world history is to be understood in the light of Jesus Christ".

[3] *Resurrection and Historical Reason*, p. 86.

[4] Cf. IV/2, pp. 32, 788.

This, in effect, is Barth's answer to the dilemma that emerged within theology in the nineteenth century, the relation between revelation and history, which was expressed in its most succinct form in Lessing's question concerning the relation between contingent facts of history and eternal truths of reason. The issue is resolved by inverting the order of world-history and the history of salvation, positing the former as a predicate of the latter, and claiming that the question of interpretation and meaning (the particular epistemological concern of the working historian) is answered from within the event of revelation itself [1]. This imposes an immediate and obvious tension and opaqueness on the theologian's statements about this event, insofar as he also wishes, and necessarily so, to claim that it is an event within general history. This is seen, for instance, in Barth's insistence that the "peculiarity" (*Eigenart*) of the resurrection, as a part of the history of Christ, precludes its being investigated by the historian, since it offers no "historical ground"

---

[1] Barth sometimes employs the notion of the "non-historical" (*unhisto-risch*) as an apparent synonym for salvation history, by which he intends to designate its resistance to ordinary historical methods of investigation. And, in stressing the non-historical character of, say, creation and resurrection, Barth argues that the concept of salvation history is in continuity with a *true* appreciation of events within ordinary history, which can themselves be understood only when both their "historical" and "non-historical" dimensions have been explored: "How can it be overlooked, that all history is properly and finally important and noteworthy only to the extent that it also has this element, and so is not only historical but also unhistorical? How can it be overlooked, that all historical writing must become spiritless and intolerable to the extent that it wishes to be merely historical and not also unhistorical?" (III/1, p. 85). Barth's use of the term "historical" suggests a certain bias regarding the nature of historical method and inquiry. If by "unhistorical" is meant that kind of sensitivity to events which leads the historian beyond a merely positivistic recounting of occurrences, and into an apprehension of their total inner significance and meaning in relation to a given context (an apprehension which the Germans denote by the term *Geschichte*), then it is a mistake to assume, as Barth at times seems to, that this attitude and approach are lacking in contemporary historical scholarship. Barth's strictures against "historicism" would be better informed if they displayed an appreciation of the subtleties involved in the employment of historical reason by working historians. Along this line, R.G. Collingwood's essay, *The Idea of History* (New York: Oxford Univ. Press, Galaxy Books, 1956), is particularly illuminating. Perhaps an exploration of the ways in which historical scholarship is ordinarily both "historical" (*Historie*) and "unhistorical" (*Geschichte*) would reduce the need for a special category (*Heilsgeschichte*) in which to place the events of revelation.

(*historischem Boden*) available to ordinary cognitive operations [1]. The resurrection is apprehendable only as *Geschichte*, never as *Historie*. At the same time, the claim is advanced that it is an event "actual and objective in time and space" [2]; the Easter story is "a happening that once became an event in dateable time" [3].

The upshot of this approach is that the events comprising salvation history are extruded from the ongoing context of "secular" history, and so, finally, from the enveloping matrix of nature. Richard Niebuhr sees in this, and in the general tendency among contemporary theologians to place the events of revelation into a special history, a "naturalization" of ordinary history under the impact of an uncritical adoption of Enlightenment and nineteenth century views of nature:

---

[1] IV/1, p. 370. An old position even for Barth, since he himself acknowledges the New Testament texts as the given historical element that can be approached objectively and impartially. Cf. IV/2, p. 167. Barth's central claim is that an event like the resurrection leaves no room for the "historicist" concept of history, by which is apparently meant the objective continuity in time and space of events which forms the presupposition for the subjective engagement of the historian in the act of examination, reconstruction, and interpretation. If this is the case, then the term as used is open to question, since it normally specifies a particular *philosophy* of history embodying a belief in general predictability. Cf. Karl Popper, *The Poverty of Historicism* (New York: Harper and Brothers, Torchbooks Edition, 1964), p. vif. It could be argued, in this connection, that the concept of *Heilsgeschichte* itself involves a kind of transcendent "historicist" approach, since it is given at once as a totally completed (teleologically) movement of God, thereby attaining a retrospective descriptive "predictability". When world history is made the "predicate" of salvation history, its dynamic configurations and unpredictability are minimized by a tendency to view it from the teleological perspective of the latter.

[2] IV/1, p. 371. Cf. IV/2, p. 159f.

[3] I/2, p. 128. The way taken by Barth out of the problem raised by the obviously elusive character of the temporal actuality and objectivity of the resurrection is to describe it, along with creation, as "saga" or "pre-historical occurrence" (*prähistorischen Geschehen*). It may fairly be questioned, however, whether this ploy does not carry the consequence of completely absolving the theologian from concern over the concrete historicity of the event. Does the resurrection still remain something over which the Christian community could take "rational trouble"? Cf. I/1, p. 388. It is also open to question whether the resurrection accounts are as easily paralleled with the creation stories in Genesis as Barth assumes, particularly when the parallelism is located in the *historical* character of each. Barth surely would not want to claim that the creation is "a happening that once became an event in dateable time".

Under the influence of this tendency, they see the relationship between history and nature as strictly univocal. Nature is regarded as the static arena or causal network in the midst of which history takes place and by which historical possibilities are strictly defined. In a word, the idea of history has been naturalized ... What cannot be thought as occurring in nature also cannot be conceived as an historical event, in the ordinary sense. Consequently, it is necessary to find a wholly transcendental kind of history, unrelated to the space-time continuum, in which a home can be provided for the miracles that have been exiled from mundane history [1].

The significance of this elevation of *Heilsgeschichte* above the normal plane of nature and history, and the interplay to which they give rise, may be seen in the epistemological consequences to which it leads. We have already noted the firm connection maintained by Barth between ontology and epistemology. Strictly speaking, this means that it is *improper* to inquire into the epistemological status of revelation, for this sort of inquiry can be generated only out of the usual cognitive modes employed in the encounter between self, nature, and history, and these have been ruled out by Barth as inappropriate to what is

---

[1] *Resurrection and Historical Reason*, p. 105. Philosophically, this was given initial expression in Descartes' separation of the self as free substance (mind) from the causal matrix of nature (body), and later in Kant's distinction between the phenomenal and noumenal aspects of the world, to which experiential and practical reason (faith), respectively, applied. This development, and the accompanying solution, are discernible in Bultmann's comment on the resurrection: "The resurrection itself is not an event of past history. All that historical criticism can establish is the fact that the first disciples came to belive in the resurrection ... The historical problem is scarely relevant to Christian belief in the resurrection". Hans Werner Bartsch, ed., *Kerygma and Myth*, Reginald H. Fuller, trans. (London: S.P.C.K., 1953), p. 42. Cf. also Emil Brunner, *The Christian Doctrine of Creation and Redemption*, Ch. 7, "History and Saving History". Perhaps the strongest dichotomy between nature and history is to be found in Carl Michalson's *The Rationality of Faith* (New York: Charles Scribner's Sons, 1963). Michalson takes it that these refer to different "structures in reality" (p. 24), which in turn evoke radically divergent types of methodology. The questionable aspect of this program, as we see it, lies in its description of nature as a context of sheer facticity in which "the question of meaning is not raised" (p. 29). The concern for meaning, which Michalson parallels with the existentiality of the self, is thus transposed exclusively into the realm of history. The upshot of this is that nature is neutralized and divested of its legitimate significance for the development and emergence of the self. Richard Niebuhr provides a nice corrective to this sort of dichotomizing tendency. Cf. *Ibid.*, pp. 105f., 126f.

given in revelation [1]. Moreover, an inquiry of this sort would presuppose that we are somehow noetically active in the event in which knowledge of revelation (faith in the resurrection) occurs. Barth makes it quite clear, however, that this is not the case. Revelation supplies its own epistemology; there is thus no basis whatever in ourselves for knowing Jesus Christ [2]. The knowledge which emerges in faith will always occur as the miraculous event in which God as Holy Spirit addresses himself to the Church, and so to the individual believer.

Faith itself, then, in no sense designates a "natural" capacity or response in man. It is not descriptive of a "higher" epistemic possibility resident within the self. It is, rather, the gift of God. The "leap to faith" is not in any sense our own; it is something that is accomplished in us by grace [3]. What happens, then, to the normal subject-object relation that underlies, and operates as a condition for, our encounter with the world? Is this simply volatilized under the impact of grace, so that our subjectivity is annihilated by the immediate subjectivity of Christ in the Holy Spirit? Richard Niebuhr takes this line of interpretation, and finds in Barth, despite an ostensible disinclination to give attention to epistemological questions, a strong subjective idealism:

> This program, for all the author's disclaimers of philosophical preliminaries, depends on a consistent epistemological attitude, whose direction becomes clear in Barth's insistence that the knower is wholly passive, wholly conditioned and possessed by the known in revelation. In actuality Barth's realism must enlist a subjective idealism, in which the sole acting subject is Jesus Christ. At the moment of encounter with the risen Lord, the "knower", who has nothing of his own to contribute to the "recognition", fades into the overpowering subjectivity of the Son of God [4].

If this is the case, then it would have to mean that in the event of revelation God comes to knowledge of *himself* in faith [5]. A helpful alternative is advanced against this by James Brown, who suggests a

---

[1] IV/3.1, p. 249f.

[2] IV/2, p. 356f.

[3] "The leap which is made when a man repents (*daily* repents) is from the beginning (and daily) too great to be interpreted as a leap that we ourselves have made, or at least prepared for or facilitated or made possible ... No one makes this leap. As Christians, we are all borne as on eagles' wings". IV/2, p. 344. Cf. I/1, Par. 6, Part 4, "The Word of God and Faith".

[4] *Resurrection and Historical Reason*, p. 49.

[5] Cf. James Brown, *Subject and Object in Modern Theology*, p. 145.

distinction between the grammatical and epistemological meanings of "subject". On this basis, it is possible to argue that God is the "grammatical subject" of his "originating, initiating, continuing and ending activity in revelation, reconciliation and redemption", but not the "epistemological subject" in the event of man's knowledge of God [1]. Man would thus remain subject-in-act in the event of faith, in his encounter with God who, as Subject, allows himself to become the Object of man's response; the subject-object relation is thus preserved. This is, of course (as Brown is well aware) precisely what Barth himself says:

> The reality of our knowledge of God stands or falls on the fact that God in his revelation is mediately present to man in a double sense; In his Word he moves over against the human subject, as object, and through his Holy Spirit he makes himself accessibly as the object of human contemplation and understanding. Authentic knowledge of God includes God both in his relation to, and in his differentiation from, man. We thus separate ourselves from those conceptions of the knowledge of God, which understand it to be a unity between man and God, and so not objective, but a knowledge in which the distinction between knower and known is omitted [2].

It should be noted, however, that this designation of the subject-object relation stands outside the normal connotation of that relationship, for the following reasons. First of all, because *God* is the object in this relationship, and so never simply and directly object, but also always subject [3]. But secondly, because the "subjective" dimension of the human indicated here connotes a totally new event, faith, and so a totally new level of subjectivity. Further, our coming into possession of this does not in any sense exhibit continuity with our previous range of subjective encounters and operations. It is to be seen as an aspect of human subjectivity only as it is posited by the immediate impact of grace. This, it would seem, is the significance of Barth's insistence that revelation supplies its own epistemology. To the extent that revelation comprises a unique history, it requires a correspondingly unique mode of

---

[1] *Ibid.*

[2] II/1, p. 9. Cf. Brown, *Ibid.*

[3] This would also be true, of course, of our encounter as subjects with the "objectivity" of other persons, who also always remain at the same time subjects. As we have noted, this provides the central example of the *analogia relationis* between God and man. The parallel breaks down when we come to the second point, however, for we are from the outset subjectively "equipped" for our encounter with other persons, whereas our encounter with God requires a *new* subjectivity, which is given in faith.

apprehension. But since the presupposition for this is completely lacking in the given structure of man, it must be introduced by a miraculous event which creates in us this level of subjectivity [1]. *→ miracle of grace*

It is clear that the retention of the subject-object relationship, though it trades on the Kantian notion of a transcendental ego [2], avoids placing the community or the individual believer in a merely passive position vis-à-vis revelation. To be sure, there is a definite note of passivity present, in that the epistemological ground for the reception of revelation in faith is itself supplied by revelation. At the same time, the community, since it exists only in the act of God's being in revelation, is called to a corresponding action of its own, which is exhibited in the response of obedience given in worship and acts of service and witness to the world [3], and in the interplay which emerges within the community between recollection (memory) and expectation [4]. *The central Point!*

The latter point provides, ostensibly, for an "impartial and object-ive" (*neutral und objektiv*) assessment of the New Testament witness,

---

[1] It might be objected that our interpretation is deficient, in that it begs the question of the significance of the "created constant" of human nature embodied in the givenness of man as male and female, which, as the *imago Dei* in man, provides an epistemic "ground" for the knowledge that occurs in faith. On this basis, continuity could be posited between the ordinary range of subject-object relations existing within the natural order, and the particular subject-object relation that occurs between man and God in faith, since created human nature bears "an inner relation to God's turning towards man, and to the salvation intended for him by God" (III/2, p. 418). The difficulty here, however, is that Barth does not allow this "constant" to stand as an immanent "property" (*Zuständlichkeit*) of the human; it is rather a "transcendental determination" (*transzendente Bestimmung*) that depends on God's repeated action of grace (*Ibid.*). Whether or not this implies some sort of "transcendental continuity" of the subject-object relation, generally and in faith, the point would appear to hold, that there is no ground in man as such which forms a preparatory basis for the latter.

[2] Cf. Niebuhr, *Resurrection and Historical Reason*, p. 115f. Niebuhr argues (p. 125) that the appeal to a "doctrine of the transcendental self" is as unnecessary to the development of a viable theological employment of historical reason as the original distinction between salvation and world history, on which it rests.

[3] Cf. I/2, Par. 18, "The Life of the Children of God"; IV/3.1, Par. 71, "The Vocation of Man", and Par. 72, "The Holy Spirit and the Sending of the Christian Community".

[4] Cf. I/2, Par. 14, Part 3, "The Time of Recollection"; III/2, Par. 47, Part I, "Jesus, Lord of Time"; IV/1, Par. 62, Part 3, "The Time of the Community".

which forms the objective historical data on which the recollection of the community rests [1]. The way is thus opened for a thoroughgoing exegetical program utilizing all the ordinary equipment of historical reason to arrive at an impartial estimate of the events comprising salvation history. And this would tend to bring these events, methodologically at least, into closer proximity with ordinary history, thereby reducing the distance between them.

The difficulty here, as Hermann Diem points out, is that Barth insists on an exceedingly close relationship between dogmatics and exegesis. Where exegesis exhibits conclusions or possibilities at odds with the "facts" of dogmatics, i.e., its understanding of the events of salvation history, and scripture as the primary witness to those, the only response left is to question either the integrity or ability of the exegete [2]. In this way, the concerns of the historian are excluded, and the events of salvation history, as we have suggested, are removed from continuity with the range of ordinary experience and knowledge [3].

At this point, it is in order to ask what implications follow from Barth's realism, as exhibited in his interpretation of salvation history and the event of faith, for the epistemic claims of the Christian community embodied in its language. Epistemologically, the difficulty would seem to be that the knowledge afforded to faith bears no discernible relationship to our ordinary knowledge of the world given through nature and history. It has to do with a "transcendent", i.e. independent, level of being and history that lies utterly beyond our given cognitive powers. We are thus placed at two removes from the facts of salvation history:

---

[1] IV/2, p. 167.

[2] *Dogmatics*, Harold Knight, trans., (London: Oliver and Boyd, 1959), pp. 62f., 98f. Barth's view of a theologically sound hermeneutics is found in I/2, Par. 19, Part 1, "Scripture as a Witness to God's Revelation".

[3] "Barth ... can pose the question of historical truth only in the sense of discovering the true meaning and interconnexion of the Biblical texts, and sees no further possibility, nor indeed any occasion, to pose the question of historical fact ... Barth presupposes that the events attested in the Bible, the revealing action of God, are exceptional events forming the real foundation of the basis of which all history is to be interpreted. He presupposes further that the canon of Holy Scripture contains exceptional literary documents, which because of the exceptional history to which they bear witness demand a specific hermeneutic procedure, which supplies the basic principles for general hermeneutics applicable to other texts". Diem, *Dogmatics*, p. 96. Essentially the same criticism is raised by Helmut Thielicke in his *Theologische Ethik* (Tübingen: J.C.B. Mohr, 1951-1958). Band I, Pars. 573, 577, 585.

we are removed, initially, by virtue of its discontinuity with ordinary history and the context of nature, and, secondly, by its discontinuity with ordinary epistemic modes. Its knowledge requires a special mode of cognition to which we are brought, under the impact of grace, in faith.

This raises a peculiar problem for the language of theology, however, when we come to examine its cognitive significance. In keeping with Barth's strenuous efforts to rid theology of every suggestion of the *analogia entis*, the knowledge of God given in faith is not such that it can be adequately expressed through the media of our ordinary concepts and words. The reason for this, as we have indicated, is that God's unveiling of himself in revelation, since it occurs only in God's freedom, constitutes at the same time, from our side, a veiling. And this carries the consequence that though we do in fact employ ordinary linguistic forms in the context of theology to speak about God, they remain finally inadequate to the task. As Barth puts it,

> The lines which we can draw to describe, figuratively and conceptually, what we mean when we say "God", do not permit their being drawn out so that this meaning is actually described and denoted; but they always break apart, so that actually it is not described, and so not denoted. The means of definition at our disposal are not sufficient, in relation to God, to reassure us, when we have applied them to him, that we have thought what must be thought and said here. The being grasped by us in thought and words is always either not yet or no longer the being of God [1].

The answer to the question, how we came to "mean" what is meant, and to "intend" what is intended, in our use of these thoughts and words, is answered only on the presupposition of grace [2]. But this carries the consequence that *apart* from grace, our words as applied to God *can have no meaning*. This is true not only of the "outsider", the neutral thinker who undertakes to speak on grounds extraneous to revelation. It applies with equal force to the believer as well; the negation of the significance and power of human language holds true even within the relationship of grace. The only reasonable course left is to renounce completely any notion of an ability to conceive God:

> By the grace of God we are like him, powerful from him, one with him; this can be said of his children in the name of his only begotten Son.

---

[1] II/1, p. 210.
[2] *Ibid.*, p. 210f.

But we shall honor and acknowledge the revelation of the judgment of truth, according to which we are not these things of ourselves; thus we shall deny to ourselves the capacity to comprehend God, or rather, we shall have to recognize that this capacity has been denied us. Here, when we think the being of this God, the being of God in Jesus Christ, as we can and must, the possibilities of our understanding this actually break apart, whether we attempt to express it with this word or with some other word [1].

The hiddenness of God in revelation thus constitutes a very real and persistent linguistic "crisis" which extends over every attempt to speak meaningfully of him, whether this is found in the words of the Bible, the proclamation which takes place in the Church, or the propositions of dogmatic theology [2]. Here the significance of the *analogia fidei* becomes apparent. Earlier, we noted a development in Barth's description of this within the *Dogmatics*, moving from an early formulation of the analogy as one embodying "similarity, partial correspondence and agreement" [3], to a revised statement of this as "real similarity along with complete dissimilarity" [4]. The "real similarity" obviously describes the meaning which is given our words under the impact of grace; the "complete dissimilarity" denotes their inability, in themselves, to convey any meaning when applied to God. The "crisis" of our language about God is thus neatly embodied in the *analogia fidei*. The only possibility open to us, in face of the reality of God in revelation, is to acknowledge our inability to speak properly of him, and respond in obedience to the permission which is given us to undertake an expression, in the "improper" words and concepts available to us, of the knowledge that is given in grace [5].

Barth's approach to the question of the capacity of language to express the knowledge of God given in revelation constitutes, it seems, a third side of his persistent realism. The ontological side of this was seen in his positing of world history as a predicate of salvation history. The epistemological side consisted in enclosing the condition for knowing within the event of revelation, so that faith is understood, not as an indigenous "property" or possibility resident in human subjectivity as such, but as a new mode of cognition introduced into the human through

---

[1] *Ibid.*, p. 212.
[2] *Ibid.*, p. 218f.
[3] II/1, p. 254.
[4] IV/3.2, p. 612.
[5] II/1, p. 218.

grace. And now the logical side of Barth's realism comes into view. It consists, first of all, in the assertion that language receives meaning and clarity only as it is applied to God [1], and secondly, in making the event of grace the condition on which theological language is "justified". As the issues of history and faith were answered from a "transcendent" perspective, so too the logical question of linguistic meaning is presented with a similar solution.

The problem with identifying the meaning of theological language with the "ultimate" event of grace is that it seriously compromises the cognitive force of its propositions. Can the propositions of dogmatics really mean what they, in themselves, seem to mean? Barth's approach would entail that they cannot, except as they are "elevated" to that meaning by grace. The concepts utilized in such propositions are always inadequate to their objects [2]. The problem here is not that Barth has no standards by which to measure the appropriateness or inappropriateness of the *use* made of theological language. These are supplied by the Bible and the Christian community, which function for theology as the linguistic "poles" within which it moves. The problem is rather that by making the truth and meaning of theological propositions dependent on the miraculous event of grace, Barth has eliminated ordinary criteria which serve to delimit these. This accounts for the fact, as Frederick Ferré points out, that the language of the theologian, as Barth understands it, "will not be open to the kinds of analysis to which it is often put" [3],

---

[1] II/1, p. 259f.

[2] Cf. Barth's statement on theological propositions as applied to the Trinity: "When one has said what is meant by Father, Son and Spirit in God, one must continue and say that one has said nothing". I/1, p. 387. Barth's remark is strangely reminiscent of Wittgenstein's comment at the conclusion of the *Tractatus*: "My propositions are elucidatory in this way: he who understands me finally recognizes them as senseless, when he has climbed out through them, on them, over them. (He must so to speak throw away the ladder, after he has climbed up on it)". *Tractatus Logico-Philosophicus*, C.K. Ogden, trans. (London: Routledge and Kegan Paul, 1922), p. 189. Cf. I/1, pp. 454f.; 458f.

[3] *Language, Truth, and Logic*, p. 88. The same point is argued by Bowman L. Clarke in an article, "Linguistic Analysis and Religion" in: *The Monist*, Vol. 47, No. 3 (Spring, 1963), p. 375f.: "Now if religious language, or a part of it, obeys God's rules and not man's, then apologetics is in trouble, unless the unbeliever knows God's rules. Or even more puzzling, how do two believers know they are confessing the same thing unless they can agree on God's rules? Not only does communication between believer and non-believer become questionable, but communication between two believers becomes questionable.

i.e., by philosophers. At this level, the language of theology can only appear "mysterious", since there are no immanent criteria of meaning present.

But if theological language is bereft of meaning at this ordinary level, then it cannot possibly be either true or false, since meaning is a prerequisite for determining the truth or falsity of any proposition. Further, it makes no sense, at this juncture, to appeal to an assumed "higher" level of truth that is somehow "infused" into the theologian's statements; if those statements as such have *no* meaning, it cannot be that they somehow come to have a *true* sense or meaning [1]. So either there is some way to make out a case for meaning attaching to our customary *use* of theological language, apart from any miraculous "ingression" of grace, or the theologian is awash on the limitless expanse of non-objectifying or "poetic" language. Indeed, it is perhaps not altogether astonishing that Barth, who stands par excellence as the

---

Perhaps at this point we should heed St. Paul's advice concerning speaking in unknown tongues. To retreat into God's omniscience which is hidden from man or to resort to a miracle for the justification of the meaningfulness of religious language, not only makes a philosophical analysis of religious language impossible, it runs the risk of making religious language itself impossible".

[1] Cf. *Ibid.*, p. 91. Cf. the remarks of Alasdair MacIntyre in his provocative discussion, "The Logical Status of Religious Belief", in: *Metaphysical Beliefs* (London: SCM Press, 1957), p. 175f.: "There has been a consistent strain in Protestant theology which has held that meaning is conferred on religious assertations by a special illumination of the believing mind. Certain statements of Karl Barth, for example, seem to suggest that the assertions of the Bible are meaningless to anyone who has not received a special miracle of grace. But to suggest this is to use the word 'meaningless' meaninglessly. For what would it be to confer meaning on an otherwise meaningless expression? Suppose the form of words: 'Mountain neither fire red here'. The syntactical rules of English render this meaningless. To make it meaningful one would have to provide a set of rules whereby such an expression could be decoded, could be translated into a syntactically recognizable expression. Unless the expression could be decoded it would be meaningless for anyone, whatever their special inner graces; if the expression could be decoded it would be meaningful for anyone, provided only that there was access to the code, to the rules of translation. But for most theological and biblical expressions there is not even a problem of decoding. Because most religious language utilizes familiar words with familiar meanings their sense is equally apparent to believer and unbeliever. Talk about 'the language of the Bible' or 'religious language' must not conceal from us that such language is nothing more nor less than Hebrew or English or what you will, put to special use".

contemporary theologian concerned centrally with the *objective* reality of God's revelation in Jesus Christ, should be brought into proximity by Heinrich Ott to something called the "later Heidegger" [1], and so moved from an objectifying towards a non-objectifying mode of language. This is not to suggest that Barth in any way opens the door to the sort of immanentism exemplified in Heidegger. However, if the cognitive status of theological language is in effect thrown onto a transcendent level, then *formally* the view of the capacities of ordinary language adequately to express the objective side of a subject-object relation would come to the same point. In this respect, theology can ill afford to ignore the warnings currently being sounded against any movement into non-objectifying language [2].

The problem in Barth's conception of how meaning attaches to theological language does not lead directly into a non-objectifying mode of language, provided one is prepared to accept the notion that *apart from grace* there is no meaning that can be attached to theological statements. Meaning *is* allowed, at the level of grace. As I have suggested, however, this is precisely where the problem lies, for it is unsatis-

---

[1] Ott's main work to date is *Denken und Sein, Der Weg Martin Heideggers und der Weg der Theologie* (Zürich, 1959). A shorter statement of his position is given in an essay, "What is Systematic Theology?" printed with several replies to Ott in *The Later Heidegger and Theology* (New York: Harper and Row, 1963).

[2] Cf. the essay by Schubert M. Ogden ("The Understanding of Theology in Ott and Bultmann"), in: *The Later Heidegger and Theology*. There is also a spirited examination of this new fascination of theology with a non-objectifying language by Hans Jonas in his article, "Heidegger and Theology", in: *The Review of Metaphysics*, Vol. XVIII (December, 1964). Jonas sums up the relation between objective and non-objective language as follows: "That there is a problem, that the issue troubling the theologian is a genuine one, has been granted ... That the conceptualization and objective language of theory do not do justice, to some extent do violence, to the primary content committed to theology's care, on this there is agreement. Also on this: that there is non-objectifying thought and speech. We find it in the prophets and the psalmists, in the language of prayer and confession and preaching, also in lyrical poetry; and in the life of the dialogue: much of what Buber has said about the 'I-thou' relation and its language as distinct from the third person 'I-it' relation and its language, falls squarely into the area of our problem. But the theologian *when* he attends to theology (which he does not do all the time), is neither prophet nor psalmist nor preacher nor poet, nor in the I-thou situation, but under the yoke of theoretical discourse and therefore beholden to objective thought and language. This burden theology has to shoulder, and not even the later Heidegger offers legitimate release from it". *Ibid.*, p. 230f.

factory from both a philosophical and a theological point of view. It is philosophically unsatisfactory because it leads to a separation between the logical form of language and its meaning; that the latter is present depends simply on the assertion of the theologian about the activity of grace. And it is theologically unsatisfactory in terms of Barth's own emphasis on the incarnational character of the event of revelation. Frederick Ferré points tellingly to this insufficiency:

> What can possibly be further from a genuinely "incarnational" view than this position of "logical docetism"? The value of the human is minimized, denied, and deplored ostensibly to glorify the miraculous inspiration of the divine; but such a policy can never lead to a genuine theory of the incarnation, only to a violation of the debased human by the divine which, instead of "inspiring" the human, assaults and replaces it [1].

Here we are brought again to the question of Barth's treatment of the human. It is much too early to arrive at a judgment on this point, Ferré to the contrary notwithstanding. This much can perhaps be ventured, however. If our analysis of Barth's view of the meaning of theological language is sound, then it becomes quite unclear what the propositions of theological *ethics* would come to. If they are also, in themselves, utterly unsuited to *their* object, then the possibility of a cognitively meaningful ethics would seem to be jeopardized at the outset [2].

---

[1] *Logic, Language and God*, p. 89.

[2] Except, of course, as the propositions of theological ethics are provided with meaning under the impact of grace. That they could attain meaning *only* in this way would follow from the unity Barth posits between dogmatics and ethics (see below, pp. 96ff.). It should be noted here that I have no particular stake in the phrase "a cognitively meaningful ethics". There may be other kinds of meaning, or a meaning discernible in the *use* of theological language, that would lead beyond a concern for the cognitive status of the propositions of theological ethics. It is clear, for instance, that current reflection in both philosophical and theological circles about ethical, moral, and religious language tends toward a non-cognitive approach. Thus William Frakena points out, in a recent article, that in current philosophical discussion, "except in Thomistic circles, the main effort toward understanding morality is based on the conviction that it is not a body of knowledge, natural or non-natural, empirical or a priori". ("Recent Conceptions of Morality", in: *Morality and the Language of Conduct*, Detroit: Wayne State University Press, 1963, p. 2). In recent theological literature, Paul van Buren takes a cue from contemporary philosophical analyses of religious language, argues forcibly against granting cognitive status to theological language, and cites Barth in support of this conclusion (*The Secular Meaning of the Gospel*, New York: The Mac-

B. DOGMATICS, ETHICS, AND THE CHRISTIAN COMMUNITY

We have seen that Barth's understanding of the nature and function of dogmatic theology is such that it is placed at all points within the decisive matrix of the existence of the Christian community. Our task now is to expose the relation that holds between dogmatics and ethics, which will make apparent the fact that the development of a "Christian ethic" can in no sense be extruded from the context of the Church, but is throughout, in Paul Lehmann's apt phrase, a "koinonia ethic" [1].

The position espoused by Barth in positing a unity between dogmatics and ethics is not unique to the *Church Dogmatics*. We have noted that it was at least suggested in his earliest writings and lectures, becoming more pronounced in the second edition of the *Römerbrief*. And in examining the "outline" of ethics given in 1928, it was evident that something like a "principle" was expressed in the designation of ethics as a "Hilfswissenschaft" to dogmatics.

In the *Dogmatics*, ethics is understood from the outset to be an "integral part" of dogmatics [2]. This designation carries both a formal

---

millan Co., 1963, p. 98). Van Buren's case is weakened, however, at least where the specific theological and ethical language of the *Dogmatics* is concerned, since he tends to direct his criticism against theologies which "build ... on a natural sense of the divine, on natural religion and a natural revelation" (*Ibid.*). Since Barth eludes entirely this approach, building instead on the discontinuous verticality with which revelation impinges objectively on the world, this would appear to confer cognitive status on both dogmatic and ethical propositions, even though that status is reached only by grace. To be sure, their joint dependence on grace would preclude the development of a "body of knowledge", completed or not. At the same time, Barth clearly is asserting that when grace *is* active in the context of our language about God, the meaning conveyed relates to something encountered and *known*, which in principle is not reducible to the human. This obviously rules out the possibility, on Barth's grounds, of translating "God statements" into "man statements" without remainder (Cf. Van Buren, *The Secular Meaning of the Gospel*, p. 103). It also suggests, as we have indicated, that Barth would wish to grant cognitive status to ethical propositions. A conclusive judgment on this point must await a full discussion of the concept of command as it functions in Barth's ethics. This will be given in chapter IV of this study.

[1] *Ethics in a Christian Context* (London: SCM Press, 1963). Cf. Ch. II, Part 1, "Christian Ethics as 'Koinonia Ethics' ".

[2] I/1, p. xii.

and a material significance. Formally, it signifies that ethics is not an independent "science" alongside dogmatics. The reason for this is that the formal criteria of theological ethics cannot legitimately be drawn from a general (i.e., abstract) consideration of man and the good [1]. Where this is allowed to occur, dogmatics becomes nothing more than the ancillary to an independent description of the Christian life, the latter being viewed no longer as an integral part of the content of revelation, but rather as something which is "directly perceptible, and thus self-evident, describable, and normative" [2]. The formal corrective to this posture lies in the way in which Barth concludes each of the central "loci" of the *Dogmatics* with a statement of the ethical consequences to which it leads. Thus, the theological development of the "general" doctrine of God closes with an initial or "general" discussion of ethics [3]; the volume devoted to the doctrine of creation ends with a development of the "special" ethic of creation [4]; and a similar pattern was originally envisaged for the doctrines of reconciliation and redemption [5].

The material significance of the unity established between dogmatics and ethics, which underlies its formal manifestation in the external structure of the *Dogmatics*, lies in Barth's insistence that the development of theological ethics does not indicate a "turning" or transition to topics previously omitted. It consists rather in making explicit what has been present implicitly from the beginning in the doctrine of God as the Lord who from eternity has elected man to be his covenant partner. It is therefore impossible to explore the doctrine of God given in revelation without at the same time raising the question of a corresponding reaction and response on man's side [6]. The ethical "problem"

[1] I/2, p. 875f.

[2] *Ibid.*, p. 875.

[3] Cf. II/2, Ch. VIII, "The Command of God".

[4] Cf. III/2, Ch. XII, "The Command of God the Creator".

[5] Cf. I/2, pp. 986ff. The fact that neither the ethics of reconciliation nor of redemption were completed before Barth's retirement and subsequent death, is not an insurmountable obstacle to an adequate appraisal of his ethics, owing to the way in which the themes of creation, reconciliation, and redemption intersect in the *Dogmatics*, in keeping with the motif of *perichoresis* attendant upon the adoption of a Trinitarian structure.

[6] "How could God be understood as the Lord, if the problem of human obedience has not thereby been set? But what is implicit must now be made explicit; what is self-evident must now in itself be made especially clear. The

is thus lodged securely within the development of the content of revelation.

We must be more circumspect than this, however, if we are to do justice to the full thrust of Barth's position. It is not merely the case that revelation "raises the question" of correct human action, thereby precluding the possibility of a neutral stance on man's part. If it did only this, there would still remain the possibility of a polarization of the Word of God given in revelation with man's response as the hearer of that Word, and so a turning from "the book of the holy God" to "the book of the holy man" [1]. Actually, there is never this sort of turning from revelation proper to its "consequences", for the consequences are themselves enclosed in the fact of revelation [2]. The fact, as Barth sees it, "that dogmatics itself must be ethics, and that ethics can only be dogmatics" [3], signals the unity of question and answer, form and content, concerning the issue of correct human action.

The unity between dogmatics and ethics is to be understood, finally, only from the perspective of Christology. On this basis, ethics cannot possibly be given independent treatment, for there is no "independent man" to whom such a treatment might apply; there is only the man whose being is enclosed in the being of Jesus Christ [4]. As the revelation of God's grace. Jesus Christ is the answer to the question of human action posed by grace:

> The man Jesus, who fulfills the command of God, does not *give*, but through God's grace *is* the answer to the ethical question raised by grace. The sanctification of man, his being claimed by God, the fulfillment of his pre-determination in his self-determination to obedience, God's judgment on man and his command to him in its true execution—everything is here as event in Jesus Christ [5].

---

doctrine of God must be explicitly developed and explained and denoted as what it is throughout, ethics. Otherwise, human carelessness and forgetfulness can all too easily overlook the fact that it actually is this, that everything previously said about the doctrine of God also has this meaning   the meaning of basically ethical reflection and insight". II/2, p. 568. Cf. *RÖM*, p. 412f.

[1] I/2, p. 884.

[2] *Ibid.*, p. 884f.

[3] *Ibid.*, p. 890. Cf. II/2, p. 670: "The propositions of Christian ethics are propositions of Christian dogmatics. However, that means that their truth content, like that of all the other propositions of dogmatics, rests and is contained in the Word of God, that it can be known only in the Word of God, and that it must be sought and taken hold of again and again in the Word of God, and so in faith".

[4] II/1, p. 186; II/2, p. 599.

[5] II/2, p. 573.

But since the specific humanity of Jesus is that of the eternal Son of God, the resolution of the tension between the ethical question and its appropriate answer occurs, in the first and proper sense, as a movement within the being of God. Within this event, the response (i.e., obedience) of all men is proleptically included. It is, accordingly, necessary to speak of a "divine ethics" (*göttliche Ethik*) in contrast to human ethics, and to locate the "problem of the good" (which has now ceased to be a problem), only in relation to the former [1]. The "real being" of both God and man, ethically speaking, though in themselves hidden and mysterious, become in Jesus Christ an "open mystery" [2].

The "way" of theological ethics will thus consist of an exploration of "the command of the grace of God", which forms the presupposition of all ethical truth, whether this is drawn from reason or history, the secular or the religious, the church or the fact of human community in general [3]. It thus assumes the responsibility to speak inclusively, so that its statements are properly understandable only as universally binding assertions [4]. The command issuing from revelation is a demand for

---

[1] II/2, p. 574f. At this point, I wish to raise a minor question about the interpretation of Barth's use of the term "good", in connection with his initial statement of a theological ethic, by Paul Lehmann (Cf. *Ethics in a Christian Context*, p. 273, footnote 1). Professor Lehmann levels a mild criticism against Barth for what is ostensibly a transposition of the ethical question (in Christian theology) into a question of the Good. This occurs in Barth's question: "What is the good in and over every alleged good human action?" (*Ibid.*, p. 569). What is not clear is that this is intended as a Christian formulation of the ethical question, since it occurs within what Barth describes as "a relatively general idea" of "ethics" which is advanced "γυμναστικῶς", i.e., as an "exercise". This general idea of ethics, it is true, does raise the question of the good. That Barth does not make substantive use of this is suggested, however, by his subsequent identification of it with the "conception of sin" (*Ibid.*, p. 574), and his insistence that the question of the good cannot legitimately be raised as a *general* question in Christian ethics, the answer to which can be supplied by man, but only as the specific question of man's *recognition* of the fulfillment of the good in the action of God in Jesus Christ (*Ibid.*). The issue, then, is not precisely that of avoiding any use of the word "good" in Christian ethics (Cf. Lehmann, *Ibid.*, p. 274: "Christian ethics always already knows the Good"). It is rather a question of recognizing that this word is given content and meaning only within the context of grace.

[2] III/4, p. 25.

[3] II/2, p. 584.

[4] "Gerade sie würde sich von der Verpflichtung, allgemein gültig zureden, auf keinen Fall dispensieren". *Ibid.*, p. 585.

obedience placed against all human actions. The issue of correct human action leading to a realization of the good can be decided only in relation to grace, never on the basis of independent standards [1]. The only ethical problem in church dogmatics, then, lies in the question "whether, and to what extent, human action constitutes a praising of the grace of Jesus Christ" [2].

The inclusiveness of Barth's approach to theological ethics, which excludes totally the possibility of an independent sphere of the human alongside revelation, displays both a positive and a negative side. Negatively, it represents a continuation of Barth's rejection of the *analogia entis*, the assumption of some sort of "natural" continuity or congruence between God and man. When this is applied to Christian ethics, it means, on the one hand, that it cannot proceed on the basis of this sort of relationship. To do so, it would have to assume that man is somehow fitted to be the partner to or recipient of revelation, and so of the command which it imposes for obedience. The impropriety of this assumption was underlined in our analysis of Barth's approach to the epistemology of revelation. There is no previously existing "point of contact" for revelation in man, and so no immanent principle of coordination between God and the human providing for a recognition of the command and a response of obedience. The only point at which man is "coordinated" with God is in the humanity of Jesus Christ [3]. But since the action of God in Jesus Christ constitutes the solution to the problem of the Good, it also calls into question, on the other hand, all attempts to locate and describe the Good out of the context of reason. The "ethical question" is not in any sense a "free" question of good and evil; it is rather a question wholly centered on the problem of man's response to the good accomplished and completed in Jesus Christ [4]. There can be no legitimate independent examination of the ethical which leads to a discovery of the Good. This is something that is *given* to man in revelation.

---

[1] II/2, p. 598f.

[2] *Ibid.*, p. 600.

[3] II/2, p. 589f.

[4] "Approaching the issue from the knowledge of the divine election of man, we can know of no human action which does not stand under God's command, and so of no human existence that does not in some way or other answer to God's command, which does not have the character of obedience or disobedience to God's command, no neutral action in regard to it. But just for this reason, we also know of no free inquiry about good and evil". *Ibid.*, p. 594.

The positive side of Barth's inclusiveness has already been exposed partially, in his insistence that theological ethics is not "esoteric", but carries binding force for all men [1]. This follows logically from the unity posited between ethics and dogmatics. Since the latter is given the task of explicating the objectivity of revelation in its significance for all men, the ethics implied in this will necessarily carry a corresponding universality [2]. This rules out immediately any attempt to limit the thrust of Christian ethics to the context of the church. The result of such a limitation would be the creation of a "special" ethic applicable only to Christians, and would thus permit the recognition of other equally independent ethical systems. The corrective to this is provided by a theological ethic which applies *de facto* to Christians, and *de iure* to all other men. Christian ethics will thus maintain continuity with the sanctification accomplished in Jesus Christ, which applies *de iure* to all men, and *de facto* to the Christian community [3].

C. The "Place" of Philosophical Ethics

Barth's treatment of philosophical ethics unfolds within the context of both the positive and negative sides of the inclusiveness of theological ethics just described. The point that emerges from a consideration of these is that the relation between theological and philosophical ethics will be such that the extremes both of synthesis and diastasis are avoided [4]. The relation between theological and philosophical ethics, however, is for Barth simply a continuation of the broader one holding between theology and philosophy. It will therefore be helpful to have the latter before us.

---

[1] *Ibid.*, p. 584.

[2] *Ibid.*, p. 715. Obviously, it is in precisely this way that the problem of generalization, a central issue in philosophical ethics, ceases to be an issue in theological ethics. The question of philosophical ethics, how a "right rule of behavior" can be expanded as a general obligation devolving upon all men, is transposed into a delineation of the fact of the action of God, and the demand for obedience which this imposes on men without restriction. A good discussion of the "logic" of the argument from generalization in philosophical ethics is provided by Marcus G. Singer in his book, *Generalization in Ethics* (New York: Alfred A. Knopf, 1961). Cf. the comments of Paul Lehmann on the efforts of meta-ethical analysis to resolve this issue. *Ethics in a Christian Context*, p. 277, footnote 1.

[3] IV/2, p. 589.

[4] II/2, pp. 581-584.

It is clear from our analysis of Barth's method that he will allow no substantive role to philosophy within dogmatics, despite the fact that the theologian unavoidably incorporates some philosophical scheme or other into his work [1]. This tells us very little, however, about the status Barth is willing to grant philosophy as an independent discipline. The clearest indication of this is provided in an article, "Philosophie und Theologie", which Barth wrote for inclusion in a *Festschrift* dedicated to his brother [2]. Barth begins by suggesting that the "opposition" (*Gegenüberstellung*) in question is not between "philosophy" and "theology", which are, in themselves, "slightly mythological" abstractions. What is really at issue is the tension that emerges between *men* having different interests, commitments, and tasks [3]. However, there could be no tension between them if they did not show continuity (*Miteinander*) at some points. Barth locates this in their common involvement with the unity of truth [4].

In this respect, the problem of the philosopher and the theologian remains the same. Discontinuity (*Gegeneinander*) sets in when attention turns to the way in which each approaches this problem. The theologian begins with the truth of God's freedom for man, which includes an interest

---

[1] Cf. Barth's comments on the unavoidability of this, and the necessary restrictions which accompany it. I/2, pp. 815ff. This would appear to provide at least an indirect response to attempts to "reduce" Barth's theology to a given philosophical framework, i.e., Plato, Kant, or Hegel. On our view, the only safe and permissible generalization here is that Barth displays an affinity (perhaps unavoidable) for the rationalist-idealist side of Western philosophy running from Plato to Hegel, and scarcely any for the empiricist and/or pragmatist strain exemplified in British and American philosophy.

[2] *Philosophie und Christliche Existenz*, Gerhard Huber, ed. (Basel: Verlag Helbing und Lichtenhahn, 1960).

[3] "Die Gegenüberstellung von 'Philosophie' und 'Theologie' ist eine (leicht mythologisierende) Abstraktion. Das Wirkliche, das mit ihr gemeint ist, ist das Gegenüber gewisser verscheiden interessierter, verpflichteter und beschäftigter *Menschen*: das Gegeneinander und Miteinander des Philosophen und des Theologen". *Ibid.*, p. 93.

[4] "Ihre Trennung erfolgt angesichts der einen, ganzen Wahrheit und in der Voraussetzung, das nicht nur der Eine, sondern auch der Andere eben sie vor Augen haben, bedenken und anziegen möchte". *Ibid.*, p. 94. Barth's description of the common involvement of theology and philosophy with "the one, total Truth" indicates his reading of philosophy in terms of idealism, where a definite metaphysical concern of this sort (i.e., unity and inclusiveness) is expressed. It is interesting to speculate how Barth would view the decisive thrust in British and American philosophy away from this sort of concern toward an almost exclusive interest in empirical and linguistic analysis.

in the freedom of man for God. This order is, for the theologian, irreversible. His inquiry will always involve these two "moments" in just this sequence. The philosopher, similarly, displays a dual concern in his approach to the truth. This is seen in the distinctions which he draws between appearance and Idea, primary and secondary causes, the "Ding-an'sich" and theoretical or practical apperception, or reason and Logos [1]. Though this leads, in the first instance, to a kind of "analogy of endeavor" (*Analogie der Bemühungen*), this ultimately breaks down when the question of method is raised. For the theologian, there will be an absolute dichotomy between the order of his thought, which always moves from Creator to the creature, and that of the philosopher, which, expressed theologically, always proceeds from the creature to the Creator [2].

It is this methodological discontinuity which introduces a tension which leads finally to a break, for it indicates that the theologian and the philosopher serve different lords [3]. The decisive point to be made here is Christological: the one truth determining the direction of theological thinking and speaking is Jesus Christ, not in the sense of an "Idea" or a "vehicle" or "symbol", but as event, Jesus of Nazareth, who, as true God and true man, is the personification of the covenant set up by God between himself and men, and thus the truth which lights the world, thereby becoming normative for *both* the theologian and the philosopher [4].

The conclusions that Barth draws from this point place a decisive question mark over the whole enterprise of the philosopher. It is clear, to begin with, that the theologian cannot in any sense take up the problem or methods of the philosopher, whether this is done openly, or under the guise of becoming a "crypto-philosopher" [5]. The philosopher,

---

[1] *Ibid.*, p. 96.

[2] *Ibid.*, p. 101.

[3] "Wie sollte ein Denken und Reden, das — ich formuliere wieder theologisch — beim Geschöpf, beim Menschen als dem Vorgegebenen einsetzt, von da aus sich zum Schöpfer, zu Gott erhebt, um von da aus zu seinem Ausgangspunkt, zum Geschöpf, zum Menschen Zurückzukehren, mit einem anderen zu vereinigen sein, für das das Wort und Werk des Schöpfers das Vorgegebene und ... also der Ausgangspunkt ist, von dem es zum Geschöpf herabsteigt, um wieder in Wort und Werk des Schöpfers zu seinem Ziel zu kommen? Wird da nicht handgreiflich zwei verschiedenen Herren gedient?" *Ibid.*

[4] *Ibid.*, p. 101f.

[5] *Ibid.*, p. 99f.

by the same token, cannot undertake the tasks and concerns of the theologian. Each must remain responsible to the particular discipline in which he is involved, even though there may be occasional points at which the activity of one will carry significance for the other [1]. This does not mean, however, that Barth acknowledges any real justification for philosophy. Indeed, *post Christum natum* the theologian "can only wonder at the apparent faculty and possibility that the philosopher has, for thinking and speaking in the opposite direction" from himself [2]. The event of Jesus Christ has for Barth made a philosophical approach to the world superfluous and out-moded. As an independent approach to truth, philosophy apparently lacks even the relative and provisional significance granted theology as a "stopgap in an unordered cosmos" [3]. However, Barth's approach is not one simply of rejection. In spite of the fact that the theologian can allow no substantive weight to the philosophical program, there can still be a continuity of practical significance between them [4]. The philosopher, as *advocatus hominis et mundi*, can serve as a reminder of the importance of man and the world, and so keep the theologian from becoming inhuman through an overly exclusive concentration on the Word and work of God:

> That God has created, and so loved, the *world*, that he gave his own Son for it, that in him he has reconciled the *world* with himself—Jesus Christ the light of the *world*—that is indeed the theme of the theologian. But in his zeal for God's Word and work he can forget the concrete relation between his Word and work, the appointment of the creature as a partner in covenant with God, and so the world reconciled with God in Jesus Christ. He can forget the "true man" beyond the "true God",

---

[1] "Es wird ja das Lernen des Einen beim Anderen nie das bedeuten können, daß er nun seinerseits auf den Weg des Anderen hinüberträte, sondern nur das, daß er, ohne seiner eigenen Verantwortlichkeit untreu zu werden, auf irgend einer Stufe seines eigenen Weges durch dieses oder jenes Element im Denken und Reden des Anderen zu irgendeinem weiteren Schritt auf diesem seinem eigenen Weg angeleitet wird". *Ibid.*, p. 103.

[2] *Ibid.*, pp. 100, 102.

[3] *KD*, I/1, p. 8. Cf. *Philosophie und Christliche Existenz*, p. 102: "Eben hier ist der Theologe über den Philosophen so verwundert, weil er nicht verstehen kann, daß dieser—post Christum natum mit ihm in der gleichen Situation!—noch immer Wege vom Menschen zu Gott, vom Geschöpf zum Schöpfer zu suchen, zu finden und zu gehen, unter diesen oder jenen Vorzeichen und Titeln die Konstruktion eines von rechts nach links laufenden Uhrzeigers zu unternehmen scheint, die doch in Jesus Christus auch für ihn ein für allemal antiquiert ist".

[4] Huber, *Philosophie und Christliche Existenz*, p. 103.

and his own freedom and that of his fellow men beyond the freedom of God. Or, if he does not actually forget these, he can treat them so casually, and give them so little notice, that he appears inhuman ... The existence of the philosopher may serve to remind him that he must not proceed in such a way that he pursues his calling to the point where it is no longer possible for him to think and speak in a worldly, natural, human enough way, and where he cannot adequately praise the condescension of the Creator to his *creature*, and the elevation of the *creature* to his Creator [1].

It is clear from our analysis that Barth's approach to the activity of the philosopher is both polemical and, after a fashion, conciliatory. It is polemical in its rejection of any substantive continuity between theology and philosophy, and in its somewhat condescending attitude towards the fact that a philosophical approach to the world is still taken by some to be both a possibility and a necessity. And it is at least moderately conciliatory in assigning to the philosopher the function of a "sign" reminding the theologian that he must not neglect man and the world in his work. The bearing this has on Barth's approach to philosophical ethics, must now be indicated.

At the beginning of this section, I argued that Barth avoids the extremes of both synthesis and diastasis in describing the relation between theological and philosophical ethics. A synthetic alignment of these is impossible, because it would imply either that both were live, and to that extent neutral, options within the ethical spectrum, which might be brought together from a third, possibly higher, position; or that philosophical ethics comprised a viable context of inquiry and action needing only to be filled out and brought to completion under the apologetic thrust of theological ethics. In either case, the assumption is made that philosophical and theological ethics address themselves to the same problem, so that the credentials of theological ethics can be assessed within the preceding, general framework of philosophical ethics. This sort of continuity, Barth asserts, is simply nonexistent. The problem broached in philosophical ethics centers on the discovery and elucidation of the Good, as this is embodied in values and prescriptive rules of conduct. The question of human response and behavior is always secondary to this primary concern. In theological ethics, however, attention focuses entirely on the latter point, the question of human response and behavior, and the former problem of the Good ceases altogether to be a problem [2]. Theological ethics, then, since it departs

---

[1] *Ibid.*, p. 105.
[2] "What is a problem in ethics generally—the law of the good or value,

exclusively from the reconciling and redeeming action of God in Jesus Christ, and the command under which man is placed as a result, can only reject as impossible any attempted synthesis between itself and philosophical ethics along apologetic lines. It simply does not lend itself to that sort of program [1].

The attempt to resolve the tension between theological and philosophical ethics through a final diastasis or separation is equally unsftisfactory, because equally impossible. This approach is similar to the preceding one, in that it also posits two distinct ethical contexts. Instead of moving apologetically towards synthesis, however, it absolutizes the distinction, and so trades on the assumed validity of a continuing duality of spheres. The impossibility of this lies in the fact that, from the perspective of the command of God, there can be no independent, isolated ethics, whether theological or philosophical [2].

The only way open to theological ethics is to stand firm in its insistence on the inclusive significance of the command of grace, and to

---

by which it seeks a standard with which to measure human action and modes of action, and according to which they are to be done, the problem of truth and knowledge of the good— is no problem at all in the conception of God immanent to Christian ethics, in the doctrine of the Command of God". II/2, p. 576. Cf. Paul Lehmann, *Ethics in a Christian Context*, p. 273f.

[1] "We cannot interpret the distinctive principle of theology in such a way as to obtain recognition for it, so that it might be judged from the perspective of some other possible or necessary principle. We cannot translate the truth and reality of the divine command into a necessary moment in the life of the human spirit, or in the development of human reason, or in the realization of the good brought to completion through the human, or in a value position securely anchored in transcendence. We can only do that, when we have nothing more to do with the command of God, and so have failed from the beginning to undertake a theological ethic". II/2, p. 578f.

[2] "The temptation which comes through the opposition encountering theological ethics can, however, take a wholly different, or at least apparently different, form. The desired adaptation to general ethical thinking and speaking can be attempted by way of a tidy isolation of theological ethics from the former, and a convenient distribution of roles between them. The attempt can be made to show, whatever the relation between them might be, that there is a double formulation of the ethical question, so to say, a "theological" and a "philosophical" formulation, which mutually touch and limit, but do not destroy, one another. By a friendly indication of the difference between them it can both denote and secure the special task of theological ethics, and undertake to protect its formal compatibility with general ethics ... But the diastasis thereby attempted is no less suspect than the synthesis of both previously mentioned and criticized". *Ibid.*, p. 582f.

move towards philosophical ethics on the basis of what Barth describes
as "annexation" [1]. This involves, as Paul Lehmann suggests [2], both a
polemical and a conciliatory or irenical posture. The polemical side
is seen in the refusal of theological ethics to temper the stringency of
the command by taking seriously the claims advanced in philosophical
ethics, or by acceding to the criticisms raised against it from that quarter.
Where philosophical ethics questions the legitimacy of the inclusiveness
of the command of God as the final ground of all ethical truth, and
attempts to derive independent principles of action and views of life
and the world, it can be viewed only as "wrong and false and perverted" [3].
This results in a "conclusive" (*endgültige*) differentiation of theological
from philosophical ethics [4]. The polemics involved in this, however,
should not be understood in a purely negative way. The point involved
is *critical*, not negative, and has to do with the absolute inability of
theological ethics to surrender its principle, which, as the command of
God, is both the final principle of philosophical ethics, and the (implicit)
goal towards which it moves [5].

The other, irenical side of the movement of theological toward
philosophical ethics emerges in the fact that, from the side of theological
ethics at least, the lines of communication are never closed off. The
refusal to compromise its principle does not lead to a withdrawal from
the sphere of general ethics. Indeed, we have seen that this sort of move
can lead only to a denial of the very inclusiveness on which both dogmatics and ethics rest. Theological ethics will therefore establish "a continuous relation in its thinking and speaking to the general human ethical
problem" [6]. It will be absolutely open to all that it can learn from that
context, insofar as it provdes material necessary to the completion of
its own task [7]. And, where a philosophical ethics evidences awareness
of its origin in the command of God, there is the possibility of an ethic
that is "Christian" without being, in the strict sense, theological. From
this, the differentiation of theological ethics would be "provisional"
(*vorläufige*) rather than conclusive [8]. Theological ethics, then, cannot

---

[1] *Ibid.*, p. 581.
[2] *Ethics in a Christian Context*, p. 271.
[3] II/2, p. 585.
[4] *Ibid.*, p. 584f.
[5] *Ibid.*, p. 575f.
[6] *Ibid.*, p. 581.
[7] *Ibid.*, pp. 581, 585.
[8] *Ibid.*, pp. 601f., 584f.

and does not reject philosophical ethics. It rather engages it comprehensively and critically, refusing to take with ultimate seriousness the apparent opposition between them, since this has already been resolved in the death and resurrection of Jesus Christ [1]. It is only in relation to this that the "place" of philosophical ethics can be indicated and discussed.

There are some questions to be raised about Barth's approach to both philosophy and philosophical ethics. In the first place, the attempt to locate the specific characteristics of theology and philosophy as disciplines suffers from Barth's apparent inability to allow philosophy any degree of continuing importance. In a context that views the world only from the perspective of the transforming event of Jesus Christ, there seems little room left to the independent constructions of the philosopher, and the theologian is left only the response of amazement that the philosopher persists in his approach to things. The problem with this position is that it suggests that philosophy, Christologically speaking, is not only expendable, but actually unnecessary. This view is inadequate, even on Barth's view of the task and method of dogmatic theology. It is one thing to separate oneself decisively from dependence on "existence" as a determinative category, thereby focusing primarily on the *objectivity* of revelation [2]. It is another matter altogether to set up the relation between theological and philosophical reflection in such a way that the latter appears less than relevant, not only to the theologian, but to itself as well. Barth must be aware, however, that the relation that holds between philosophy and theology is too entrenched and subtle to be handled at this level. Regardless of what one chooses to make of the various philosophical attempts in the area of descriptive and constructive metaphysics, it can scarely be questioned that *without* such efforts, the theologian would lack the conceptual and critical tools necessary to the undertaking and completion of his task. Without the apparatus of philosophical terms and categories, the theologian would either be reduced to the option of repeating the statements of the Bible, or he would have to provide the needed apparatus by becoming a philosopher himself. The issue here does not center on whether or not the theologian

---

[1] *Ibid.*, p. 581. Cf. Bouillard, *Karl Barth*, Vol. III, p. 229.

[2] Though it is questionable whether this succeeds altogether in eliminating the issue of the existential grounding of *all* theological language. Cf. the article by Van A. Harvey, "A Word in Defense of Schleiermacher's Theological Method", *The Journal of Religion*, Vol. XLII, No. 3 (July, 1962), pp. 151ff.

makes "substantive" use of philosophical material. Where the *content* of theology is concerned, it is clear that Barth at least is at pains to avoid this. The point is rather that every systematic theologian makes at least a certain limited *formal* use of the constructs and categories of the philosopher. Not even Barth could say what he feels bound to say without the availability of idealist and realist thought forms. To be sure, Barth is aware of this, as we have seen. But then this suggests that the work of the philosopher is not quite so expendable as it seems to be on Barth's interpretation.

Furthermore, even if the remaining significance of philosophy, *post Christum natum*, is that of being, as it were, a kind of "Hilfswissenschaft" to theology, in that the philosopher is now seen as the "advocatus hominis et mundi", it is surely of some importance to the theologian how the philosopher undertakes to carry out *this* task. If, as Barth himself indicates [1], some philosophies merit the positive attention of the theologian more than others, this can only mean that qualitative distinctions are of importance to the theologian in assessing the fruits of philosophical activity. But this suggests that theology obviously has a more than casual interest in philosophy, and that the theologian might derive more from the philosopher than simply a reminder of his own need not to lose sight of man and the world.

The inadequacy that has been suggested in Barth's view of philosophy generally appears to be at least indirectly recognized in his statements on the relation between theological and philosophical ethics. In asserting that the command of God serves as the ultimate ground of all ethics, Barth establishes a basis for a positive-critical relationship between the two, launched from the side of theology. This gives currency to his statements about the necessity for theological ethics to establish and maintain continuity with the ethical question as a whole, and to be open to whatever insights might be provided from the side of philosophical ethics.

The problem that remains, however, is that the unity maintained by Barth between dogmatics and ethics necessarily precludes the possibility of anything emerging other than a dogmatic relationship between philosophical and theological ethics. Paul Lehmann is quite correct in asserting that, on Barth's interpretation,

---

[1] Cf. Barth's discussion of Leibniz in III/1, pp. 446ff., and of Nietzsche in III/2, pp. 276ff. The point here is that, whereas the discussion of Leibniz is critically *positive*, the treatment of Nietzsche is critically *negative*.

Christian ethics neither repudiates nor ignores philosophical ethics. Barth is neither an ethical iconoclast nor an ethical obscurantist ... I think it could be said that Barth is the first Christian moralist to set the record straight. The methodological fact is that Christian ethics need not, cannot, and does not reject philosophical ethics; it is philosophical ethics which must and does reject Christian ethics [1].

Despite the pointedness of Lehmann's defense of Barth, and beyond Barth's own statements about the need for theological ethics to be in continual contact with its philosophical counterpart, a question still remains: Can a theological ethics understood essentially as "divine ethics", united with dogmatics and grounded exclusively in the command of God, remain open to continual *dialogue* with philosophical ethics? It would seem that Barth's description of the relation between philosophical and theological ethics as being essentially "annexation" proceeding from the side of the former jeopardizes this possibility, despite the distinction which is drawn between a "conclusive" and a "provisional" differentiation between the two. The problem is not that theological ethics abstracts itself from continuity with the general ethical question. It is rather that on Barth's particular reading of the facticity of revelation, and the ethical consequences enclosed within it, theological ethics is placed in the position simply of asserting its *right* to "annexation", and is deprived of the ability, and possibility of the concern, to look seriously at the questions that might be raised against or about that claim from within philosophical ethics.

The reason for this lies in the fact that the peculiarity of the command of God enclosing the human is such that the possibility of raising questions about it is excluded. But this can only suggest that theological ethics is lacking in an ability or concern to provide *reasons* in support of its claim. Indeed, as Barth asserts:

The man who obediently hears the command of God is not in a position to consider why he must obey it, and so not in any position of wanting to show himself or others, from the perspective of another principle, how he arrived at this law of human willing and acting. He knows that the command of God is not grounded in any other command, and so cannot be derived from another, or assessed in reference to any other, or have its validity proven in relation to any other. He knows that man cannot in any sense say this command to himself, but can only let it be said to him. He has not discovered this principle of theological ethics, and he cannot set it aside or conceal it. He has not given it its vexatious character, and so he cannot try to remove it [2].

---

[1] *Ethics in a Christian Context*, p. 275. Italics omitted.
[2] II/2, p. 579.

It must be remembered that Barth is speaking, in this context, against the attempt to establish an "apologetic" connection between theological and philosophical ethics. The point here is that it is impossible to move in this direction because the basis of theological ethics is itself non-demonstrable, and so not subject to inclusion within a balanced dialectic between what is discoverable to reason and what is given in revelation. If this is taken at the same time to mean that both the ground of theological ethics, and its relation to the context of general ethics, elude rational explication and examination, then there appears little left to the theologian except a continued reassertion of his point, and a corresponding rejection of the philosopher's questions. If this happens, however, it becomes difficult to see any positive significance attaching to Barth's concern to establish continuity with philosophical ethics, and to be open, wherever possible, to whatever insights it might provide. The most obvious query from the side of philosophical ethics, why it should *accept* the annexation presented by theological ethics, would have to be either rejected as an indication of the continuing arrogance of natural reason, or "answered" by appealing again to the fact of revelation and the command which it imposes.

I would argue that this approach is inadequate, even on Barth's reading of the situation. If, as he asserts, the event of Jesus Christ encloses the human at all points, then it ought to be possible to explore the consequences of this in a positive fashion in relation to philosophical ethics. This would not involve any attempt to "demonstrate" the validity of the "principle" of theological ethics, but it would assume the ability of the theologian to provide reasons (i.e., explanations) in support of his contention that the "problem of the human" is given decisive illumination only from a Christological perspective. Within the context of Barth's ethics, with its emphasis on command, this would mean that it would not be inappropriate to consider why one ought to obey it, since again this would not involve any attempt at demonstration, but simply a *description* of the contours of the human which it expresses [1]. In this respect, it might conceivably be permissible to speak in a limited, qualified way, of a valid apologetics [2]. The resources for this sort of

---

[1] The specific problems raised by an ethic of command will be considered in a later section of this study. See Ch. IV, below.

[2] An example of this, we feel, is given in Paul Lehmann's book, *Ethics in a Christian Context*. Professor Lehmann is obviously not engaged in "apologetics" in any traditional sense (e.g., as in Schleiermacher), but he *is* involved in a serious attempt to provide a reasoned case for the validity of Christian

undertaking may be present in Barth; some of his comments, as I have indicated, lead suggestively in this direction. What remains unclear, at present, is that these result in a transition beyond a merely dogmatic stance.

---

ethics considered descriptively in terms of its implications for the human. Cf. also an unpublished paper by Arnold B. Come, "The Possibility of a Scientific Ethic", the Epilogue especially, for an example of the kind of dialogical engagement between theological and philosophical ethics that we have been advocating.

CHAPTER THREE

THE THEOLOGICAL BACKGROUND OF ETHICS:
THE SOVEREIGNTY OF ELECTING GRACE

In the preceding chapter, attention was drawn to the close relationship established by Barth between dogmatics and ethics, and to the way in which human ethical activity is grounded at all points in the prior being and action of God, i.e., in what Barth calls "divine ethics". In this chapter, we shall explore the specific dimensions of the latter, and indicate the ramifications it carries for an understanding of the human enclosed within the action of God.

A. THE TRINITARIAN GROUNDING OF ETHICS

One of the most pointed and far-reaching indications of Barth's discontinuity with nineteenth century theology is found in the status accorded the doctrine of the Trinity in the *Church Dogmatics*. Unlike Schleiermacher, who considered the Trinity only at the end of his treatment of dogmatics, viewing it as both a defensive and a synthetic doctrine‛ and thus as "postlegomena" separable from the immediately given data and propositions of the religious consciousness [1], Barth places it at the beginning of dogmatics, as part of the prolegomena, and argues its necessity as the formal and material criterion of the Christian understanding of the self-manifestation of God in revelation [2]. The doctrine

---

[1] Cf. Friedrich Schleiermacher, *The Christian Faith* (Edinburgh: T. and T. Clark, 1928), p. 738f. Claude Welch argues that Schleiermacher's writings, together with the emergence of biblical criticism, were an important factor in "the reduction of the Trinity to a doctrine of the second rank" which occurred in the nineteenth century. *In This Name* (New York: Charles Scribner's Sons, 1952), pp. 3ff.

[2] "The decisive question for the concept of revelation, the question about the self-revealing God, cannot be answered by disregarding the answer given in the doctrine of the Trinity, but the doctrine of the Trinity is exactly the answer to be given here. With that, we say that we designate the doctrine of the Trinity as the interpretation of revelation, or revelation as the ground of the doctrine of the Trinity: We find revelation itself so attested in Holy Scripture, that our understanding of revelation, which itself is related to this

of the Trinity thus becomes normative for the development of every part of dogmatics, and, by virtue of the unity established by Barth between dogmatics and ethics, for the development of a theological ethic as well [1]. I have hinted previously at the importance of the trinitarian formulation for each of these [2]; this must now be developed in more detail.

As we have seen, when Barth speaks of "ethics", this can mean either of two things. It can refer, in an original and primary way, to the divine action manifested in Jesus Christ, which provides the solution to the ethical problem, and exemplifies the correspondingly appropriate human responce of obedience. Or it can indicate, in a secondary, derivative way, the general ethical problem of obedience placed before all men by the command of God which results from the action of Jesus Christ. In each instance, the doctrine of the Trinity provides for Barth the only adequate basis for a systematically complete statement of what is involved.

The doctrine of the Trinity is understood as an "analysis" (*Analyse*) of the statement of revelation contained in the biblical witness [3]. It is thus indirectly identical with the primary statement of revelation: "God reveals himself as the Lord", which Barth designates the "root" of the doctrine of the Trinity [3]. Here a distinction must be drawn between

---

witness, i.e., of the self-revealing God, must be the doctrine of the Trinity". *KD*, I/1, p. 329. Barth's full defense of the place of the doctrine of the Trinity in dogmatics is given in *Ibid.*, Par. 8, Parts 1 and 2. Barth has come under strong criticism for his position, as shown in this statement from Paul Tillich, who in many ways is the best contemporary representative of the theological tradition emanating from Schleiermacher that Barth seeks to overcome: "It was a mistake of Barth to start his Prolegomena with what, so to speak, are the Postlegomena, the doctrine of the Trinity. It could be said that in his system this doctrine falls from heaven, the heaven of an unmediated biblical and ecclesiastical authority". *Systematic Theology*, Vol. III (Chicago: University of Chicago Press, 1963), p. 285. Cf. also the reaction of Wilhelm Pauck, as quoted in Welch, *In This Name*, p. 53.

[1] This position is, as Barth himself remarks (I/1, p. 316), "very isolated" in the history of doctrine. For a recent treatment of theological ethics grounded in the doctrine of the Trinity, see Paul Lehmann, *Ethics in a Christian Context*, Ch. IV, Part 1, "The Trinitarian Basis of Christian Ethics".

[2] I/1, p. 325.

[3] "The proposition: 'God reveals himself as the Lord', understood thus, i.e., what this proposition intends to designate, and so the revelation designated in scripture, we name 'the root of the doctrine of the Trinity'. "*Ibid.*, p. 326.

the *doctrine* of the Trinity, and the Trinity itself. Revelation, the event of God's turning toward man in Jesus Christ, is the ground of the doctrine of the Trinity, but not of the Trinity itself. If it were the latter, this would mean that we could speak only of an "economic" Trinity grounded in the historical manifestation of God, but not of an "immanent" Trinity descriptive of the antecedent nature of the God who gives himself in revelation. Barth counters this possibility by asserting that what is given in revelation and explored within the framework of the trinitarian doctrine is the *eternal* being of God as Father, Son, and Holy Spirit [1]. The continuity thus maintained between the economic and immanent determination of the Trinity preserves the unity of God in being and act in the event of revelation [2]. On this basis, it becomes possible to explore the event of revelation in its christological formulation in light of the eternal will and purpose of God for man and the world, so that, as Paul Lehmann comments, the doctrine of the Trinity becomes "the most comprehensive statement of the christological dogma" [3].

The divine economy moves dynamically from creation to reconciliation to redemption. These comprise the "moments" in the divine ethics. The relations that hold between these reflect the inner eternal relations within God, as the one Subject of revelation, between Father, Son and Spirit [4]. Barth's insistence on the *unity* of God as the active

---

In relating this to the propositions connected with the Trinity, Barth states: "The proposition or propositions concerning the Trinity of God are of course meant to be not directly, but indirectly identical with the proposition about revelation". *Ibid.*, p. 326.

[1] "We do not thereby say that the doctrine of the Trinity is only an interpretation of revelation, and not also an interpretation of the God who reveals himself in revelation ... But from the doctrine of the Trinity we in fact gather who the God is, who reveals himself, and so we allow it to gain expression as the interpretation of revelation. We do not thereby say that revelation is the ground of the Trinity, as if God were the Three-in-One only in his revelation and for the sake of his revelation. But we certainly say that revelation is the ground of the *doctrine* of the Trinity; the *doctrine* of the Trinity has no other ground than this". *Ibid.*, p. 328f. Italics added.

[2] *Ibid.*, pp. 351; 503.

[3] *Ethics in a Christian Context*, p. 105.

[4] IV/2, p. 381. Barth sets forth several alternative synonymous triads expressing what is involved in the concepts of Father, Son, and Spirit as applied to God, i.e., Revealer, Revelation, and Revealedness; Creator, Reconciler, and Redeemer; Holiness, Mercy, and Love. Cf. I/1, pp. 311, 383f. Functionally, the relations between Father, Son, and Spirit are expressible as the divine Who, What, and How of revelation. I/2, p. 37.

Subject of revelation carries important implications for both the development of the trinitarian doctrine, and the unfolding of the divine economy in its movement from creation to redemption. What it implies for the doctrine of the Trinity is that the distinctions between Father, Son, and Spirit are not substantive, since this would lead to the positing of three divine subjects or "persons", and so to a form of tritheism. The distinctions are modal, indicating the different ways in which the one God is present to us and to himself as God [1]. There is thus a certain relationality to be observed in describing the order of the divine modes of being as Father, Son, and Spirit, which involves an inequality of order or procession. This is seen, as Barth puts it, in the fact that there is a "Begetter and a Begotten" (*Erzeugen und Erzeugtsein*) [2], and a "bringing forth" (*Hervorbringung*) common to both of these [3]. This inequality of order insures that the three divine modes of existence as Father, Son, and Spirit, remain distinguishable, yet without impairing or threatening the unity of God as the Subject of revelation [4]. Barth's intention is thus to avoid the pitfalls of both modalism and subordinationism, while preserving the integrity of the biblical witness to the different dimensions of the Lordship of God [5].

The central point here lodges in the importance of the doctrine of the "interpenetration" (*perichoresis*) of the Trinity, which applies equally to its essence and its operation. The modal distinctions permissible in the doctrine of the Trinity do not indicate separations in God's being, for each mode participates fully in the other modes of existence [6]. This rules out immediately the possibility of an independent doctrine of the Father, or the Son, or the Spirit. The Father is always known only as

---

[1] "This one God is God three times in a different way, so different, that it is precisely only in this three-times otherness that he is God, so different, that this otherness, his existence in these three modes of being (*Seinsweisen*) is absolutely essential to him, inseparable from his deity, and thus so different, that this otherness is irremovable". I/1, p. 380.

[2] *Ibid.*, p. 383.

[3] *Ibid.*

[4] "Everything that can be said, whether it is a question of the inner content or of the outer form of the being of God, must finally be said in like manner of Father, Son, and Spirit. There is no attribute, no act of God, which is not in the same way an attribute and act of Father, Son, and Spirit". *Ibid.*, p. 381f. Cf. IV/1, p. 221f.

[5] I/1, pp. 396ff.

[6] *Ibid.*, p. 390.

the Father of the Son, just as the Son is revealed only as the fulfillment
of the will of the Father. And the Holy Spirit is known and received
only as the Spirit of the Father and the Son [1]. The centrality of the
Filioque, the mutual procession of the Spirit from the Father and the
Son, for the community and continuity that holds between the divine
modes of existence, is suggested in the following:

> Since God is himself the Father from eternity, he brings himself forth
> from eternity as the Son. Since he is the Son from eternity, he goes forth
> from himself as the Father from eternity. In this eternal bringing forth
> of himself and going forth from himself, he posits himself a third time,
> as the Holy Spirit, i.e., as the love which unites him in himself ... And
> therefore God is love, therefore love goes forth from himself as his love,
> as the Spirit, who he himself is, because he posits himself as the Father
> and so posits himself as the Son [2].

The *perichoresis* of the divine modes within the essence of God
carries over to the operations of God *ad extra* in creation, reconciliation,
and redemption. By "appropriation" (*Appropriation*), creation is associated primarily with the Father, reconciliation with the Son, and
redemption with the Spirit [3]. This cannot mean, however, that these are
broken down into isolable "moments" in the divine economy. The
distinctions between creation, reconciliation, and redemption, like those
between Father, Son, and Spirit, signify a difference in order, not in
essence. There is a mutual interpenetration and community of the divine
modes of existence in the external operations of the Trinity, so that the
unity of God as the one active Subject is maintained throughout:

> Thus the Subject designated in the first article of the confession of faith
> is not only the Father, almighty, creator of heaven and earth, but with
> him, in the order and sense appropriate to them, also the Subjects of the
> second and third articles. And again, the Subject of the first article is
> not only the Father, almighty, creator of heaven and earth, but, again
> in the order and sense which pertains to it, also the Subject of reconci-
> liation, like the Subject of the second, and of redemption, like the Subject
> of the third article. Thus: not only the Father is the creator God, but
> the Son and the Spirit are that with him. And the Father is not only the
> creator God, but he is also, with the Son and the Spirit, the reconciler
> and the redeemer God ... Because God is the eternal Father as the Father
> of the Son, and, together with him, the source of the Spirit, therefore
> the one who acts in reconciliation and redemption, who reveals himself

---

[1] *Ibid.*, pp. 426f., 496.
[2] *Ibid.*, p. 507.
[3] *Ibid.*, p. 416f.

as the reconciler and redeemer, can not be a second and a third God, or a second and a third part of God; therefore, God is and remains, in his operation as in his essence, *unus et individuus* [1].

The *homoousios* of Father, Son, and Spirit, is thus maintained at all points in Barth's development of the doctrine of the Trinity. Where this applies to the action of God [2], the key principle is given in the phrase, "opera trinitatis ad extra sunt indivisa" [3]. The significance of this for the development of the *Dogmatics* may be seen in the schematism Barth establishes between creation and reconciliation [4]. The whole sweep of God's activity from creation to redemption is grounded in his eternal resolve to enter into covenant with man, and to establish man as his covenant partner [5]. This receives its central expression in the Incarnation, which is the center and goal, and so the hidden beginning, of all God's works [6]. The history of Jesus Christ as the Son of God constitutes a repetition *ad extra* of the relationship proper to the inner being of God [7], and so forms the "center" (*Mitte*) of the Trinity, providing the basis for a proper assessment of the relationship and continuity holding between the precise "moments" of the divine economy [8]. Creation and redemption will be seen only from the perspective of reconciliation, as

---

[1] *Ibid.*, p. 415f.

[2] Barth argues that *all* our assertions about God apply only to his action, and to his essence only as this is given in the action. The freedom of God in revelation is thereby preserved, and the possibility of doctrinal speculation is cut from the outset. Cf. *Ibid.*, p. 391. Paul Lehmann suggests, however, that Barth "fails to indicate the bearing of the *Filioque* upon the work of the Spirit", thus weakening the connection "between the inner-trinitarian and extra-trinitarian dynamics of the divine activity", leaving open the possibility of a lapse into doctrinal speculation. Cf. *Ethics in a Christian Context*, p. 110f., n. 4.

[3] I/1, p. 415, *et passim*.

[4] Barth's treatment of the doctrines of redemption and the Holy Spirit are now, and will remain, uncompleted. I shall therefore not attempt to project what direction these might have taken in relation to creation and reconciliation, since the point I wish to draw attention to is sufficiently indicated in the latter.

[5] Cf. II/2, Pars. 32 and 33; III/1, Par. 41; IV/1, Par. 57.

[6] II/1, p. 746; IV/1, p. 222.

[7] III/2, p. 260; IV/1, p. 223.

[8] "Therefore, God is constant, he does not change, when in Jesus Christ he becomes and is one with the creature. For what is here a "different" happening is wholly God himself, his free life, in which he is inexhaustible, untiring, imperturbable. God does not contradict himself in this act, but confirms and

the fulfillment of the covenant, and as the point of departure for a legitimate understanding of the thrust and meaning of the divine activity in
which the problem of human action receives focus and direction [1].

This does not mean that the distinction between creation and
reconciliation is blurred or eliminated. Reconciliation is understood
as a new act of God beyond creation; it is not simply a continuation of
creation [2]. The "order" of the divine economy that moves from creation
to reconciliation is irreversible. Beside this, however, another fact must
be placed, that creation and reconciliation, and so redemption, coalesce
in their common origin in revelation, as the manifestation of the covenant [3]. This leads to a consistently dynamic interpretation of the divine
activity centering in the covenant. Creation is viewed as the "external
basis" (*äußerer Grund*) of the covenant, while the covenant is taken to
be the "internal basis" (*innerer Grund*) of creation [4], and the "presupposition" (*Voraussetzung*) of reconciliation [5].

This dynamic reading of the unfolding of the divine economy in the
realization of the covenant requires a correspondingly dynamic account
of man's situation under the command of God. The first task of theological ethics, accordingly, will be to develop the command as event [6].
It will therefore trace the unity and diversity of the command in precise
continuity with the unity and diversity, or unity within diversity, encountered in the unfolding of the doctrine of the Trinity, and the doctrines of

---

reveals himself as the one he is, as the Creator and Reconciler of his creature.
He does this as the One he is because the Incarnation as such is the confirmation
of the trinity of God; without abolishing the unity of God it nevertheless
reveals the distinction of the Father and the Son and also their community
in the Holy Spirit. He does it as the Creator, because the Incarnation as such
is the confirmation of the creature in its different reality from God; the fact
that in it God becomes one with the creature, reveals that God and the creature
are two distinct and different realities, and therefore that the creature also has
its own reality over against God. He does it finally as the Reconciler and
Redeemer, because the Incarnation confirms anew that God has accepted
and will always accept his fallen creature, and that he will conduct it on to a
completed redemption". II/1, p. 579.

    [1] The anthropological implications of Barth's position here will be
examined in a subsequent section of this chapter.
    [2] I/1, p. 430f.
    [3] *Ibid.*, p. 433f.; II/2, pp. 339, 610f.
    [4] III/1, Par. 41, Parts 2 and 3.
    [5] IV/1, Par. 57, Part 2.
    [6] II/2, p. 608.

creation, reconciliation, and redemption [1]. The Word of God as his command will be explored in its entirety in each of these contexts, which can be seen as modes of the kingdom of Jesus Christ, or as manifestations of the pre-temporal, co-temporal, and post-temporal eternity of God [2]. These will correspond to man's determination for God, his relationship to him, and his ultimate perfection in God, all of which devolve initially from the humanity of Jesus Christ [3].

B. The Temporality of God

The fulfillment of the covenant in the reconciliation realized in Jesus Christ provides the basis for a descriptive account of the temporal dimensions of God's being. The temporality of God centers in his eternal decision to elect man as his covenant partner. It will therefore be necessary to provide a careful elucidation of Barth's treatment of the doctrine of election as the basis for understanding the temporal significance of the history of Jesus Christ and the determination of the human resulting from this. Initially, we must note that "temporality", as such, is not limited to God's external manifestation in revelation. It applies equally to God's eternal being as Father, Son, and Spirit [4]. The eternity of God is not a pure timelessness, but is rather filled out with the dimensions of pre-, supra-, and post-temporality, which, in their correspondence to creation, reconciliation, and redemption, relate centrally to the conditions of human existence [5]. This signifies that eternity is "the element that encloses time on all sides" [6], in its origin, development, and completion. Here again, in continuity with the trinitarian formula, there is an order to be observed which in its way is irreversible. This cannot become the basis, however, for either an absolutization or elimination of one or the other of these. The temporal modes of God's eternity also partake of the *perichoresis* found in the Trinity [7]. This precludes the

---

[1] *Ibid.*, p. 611f.

[2] *Ibid.*, p. 609f.

[3] *Ibid.*

[4] II/1, p. 691f.

[5] *Ibid.*, p. 698f.

[6] *Ibid.*, p. 702.

[7] "God is equally and truly really pre-temporal, supra-temporal, and post-temporal. But he is all of these, because he is God, in divine perfection. Thus, his 'before' does not imply 'not yet'; his 'after' does not imply 'no

possibility of an exclusive concentration on the supra-temporal side of God's eternity, which, as Barth indicates, entails the possibility of an independent significance attaching to the present and the life of faith [1]; or of an exclusion of the post-temporal, eschatological thrust of eternity toward the future [2]. This point carries particular importance for theological ethics. In its legitimate concern to develop completely the command of the supra-temporal God [3], it has to remember that God is also pre- and post-temporal, and so, as the Lord of all time, bound finally to none. It is precisely this threefold temporality of God that makes ethics problematic, and precludes the emergence of static formulae, requiring instead an attitude of continual openness and receptivity [4].

The pre- and post-temporal dimensions of God's eternity are, like the doctrine of the Trinity, discernible only within the manifestation of God's supra- or co-temporality given in the revelation of Jesus Christ [5]. The occurrence of revelation constitutes what Barth describes as "fulfilled time", which is to be distinguished from both originally created time and the fallen, lost time within which human existence occurs [6]. The time of revelation, which is just the time God has for us, is the only criterion for a proper expression and understanding of time. Revelation is not some sort of timeless truth hanging over man's temporal existence, determining and bounding it from above [7]; it is rather the manifestation of the genuine time that God has for man, which is given in Jesus Christ, the Lord of time [8]. The establishment of God's genuine time in Jesus

---

more'; and all the more his present does not imply transitoriness. In each of his distinctions of perfection there is a part of the others. In God's beginning is enclosed not only his goal and end, but also the whole way to it. In God's present there occurs both the beginning and the end. In God's end his beginning operates in full power, and his present, as before, is still present. One can and must speak here, as in the doctrine of the Trinity itself, of a *perichoresis*, of a mutual penetration and operation of the three forms of eternity". *Ibid.*, p. 721.

[1] *Ibid.*, p. 712.

[2] *Ibid.*, pp. 713ff.

[3] The terms "co-temporal" or "in-temporal" can be substituted for this. *Ibid.*, p. 702.

[4] *Ibid.*, p. 719.

[5] *Ibid.*, pp. 700ff.

[6] I/2, p. 52; III/2, p. 555.

[7] A view which Barth allowed to gain prominence in the *Römerbrief*. Cf. the warning issued against this in I/2, p. 55f.

[8] I/2, p. 57. Cf. III/2, Par. 47, Part 1, "Jesus, Lord of Time".

Christ means that our "improper" time is taken from us. It no longer
has the character of endless duration, but is bounded by the simultaneity of past, present, and future in Jesus Christ, who is the Creator
and Lord of all time in his mode of existence as the Son of God [1]. The
life, death, and resurrection of Jesus Christ are, therefore, decisive for
the present existence of all men, for they constitute an unveiling of the
full thrust of the eternal temporality of God as Creator, Reconciler,
and Redeemer. The time of Jesus Christ, as the Son of God, moves
through the past of the eternal triune being of God to the "primal"
time and history of creation and the subsequent unfolding of the prophetic time and history of Israel, and into his present and future coming
to the Christian community in the Holy Spirit [2]. It is thus the inclusive
basis for an understanding of God's co-temporality with man.

The co-temporality of God, which includes always his pre- and
post-temporality, can be described along two lines, both of which
evidence God's grace towards man. The first, and prior, of these, is the
specific event of reconciliation, which foreshadows the eschaton or goal
of created being in salvation. As the fulfillment of the covenant between
God and man, God's presence with man in reconciliation is the center
of both creation and redemption [3]. It is therefore possible, from that
center, to draw a distinction between the "general" grace of God operative in the creation, preservation, and ruling of the world, and the
"special" grace of the covenant fulfilled in Jesus Christ [4]. The former
will accordingly lead to an explication of Barth's development of the
providence of God in preserving his creation; the latter, to an examination of Barth's decisive restatement of the doctrine of election.

The doctrine of providence describes the fidelity with which God
remains with his creature from its beginning, as the Lord of its history [5].
It is grounded in both the eternal election of man through the Son of God,
and in the act of creation, and is, therefore, an operation of grace which
is recognized only in the event and act of faith [6]. The Christian doctrine

---

[1] I/2, p. 73f.; III/2, p. 546f.
[2] III/2, pp. 570f., 582ff.
[3] IV/1, p. 1f.
[4] *Ibid.*, p. 7f.
[5] "The simple meaning of the doctrine of providence may be summarized
in the statement that in the act of creation God the creator as such has associated himself with the creature as such, as the Lord of its history, and remains
faithful to it as such". III/3, p. 12.
[6] *Ibid.*, pp. 3; 14f., 32f.

of providence exemplifies the way in which the God who is "for us" in
Jesus Christ is also "over us" in the exercise of his fatherly lordship over
the world [1]. So, within the context of faith, there will be a certain parallelism between the overall development and direction of creaturely life and
history, and the specific unfolding and realization of the history of the
covenant. The former can be given appropriate meaning only as it is set
within the context of the latter [2].

The providential activity of God toward the creature consists in
his preserving, accompanying, and ruling it throughout its history. God's
act of preserving the creature, as a function of his love [3], indicates that
God keeps faith continually with the creature [4]. The *mode* of preservation just is God's faithfulness in maintaining the context in which the
creature has its being and existence, in fulfillment of its destiny as the
elect participant in the divine covenant [5]. It is only on this basis that the
creature is enabled legitimately to exist and actualize its limited potentiality *as creature*, within the freedom appropriate to it [6].

The faithfulness of God toward the creature is indicated further
in the divine accompanying and ruling of its being and activity. The
divine accompanying signifies the way in which the activity of the creature
is surrounded and determined by the prior activity of God in executing
the history of the covenant of grace [7]. The activity of God precedes
(*praecurrit*), accompanies (*concurrit*), and follows (*succurrit*) the activity
of the creature [8]. This means that the conditions, operations, and meaning (i.e., the history and goal), of creaturely activity, are at all points
grounded in the one, indivisible, providential action of God [9]. The

----

[1] *Ibid.*, p. 32f.

[2] *Ibid.*, pp. 41ff. This is, of course, merely a restatement of the points
already made about the relationship between world-history and salvation-
history, and creation and the covenant.

[3] III/3, p. 68.

[4] *Ibid.*, p. 70f.

[5] *Ibid.*, pp. 73, 91.

[6] *Ibid.*, p. 96f.

[7] "The activity of the creature takes place in its coexistence with God,
in the presence, that is, in the *praesentia actuosa* of God, and so it is accompanied and surrounded by this activity. Let us lift the subject immediately
above all merely formal considerations. Creaturely action throughout its
whole development occurs alongside the fatherly wisdom and omnipotence
of God. The history of the covenant of grace is with the act of the creature
in its occurrence from beginning to end". *Ibid.*, p. 104.

[8] *Ibid.*, pp. 134, 149, 171.

[9] *Ibid.*, p. 149f.

activity of God and the creature form "a single action" (*eine einzige Aktion*) [1].

This continuity between the activity of the creature and the providential ordering of the whole range of creaturely occurrence by God does not lead, however, to an abstract conception of God as "first cause", nor to a mechanistic-deterministic view of human possibilities. The divine concurrence is understood only from its center in Jesus Christ, so that it involves the reality of God's Word and Spirit in their operation throughout the created order [2]. The activity of God within the creaturely sphere is always a manifestation of his grace, which aims not at the elimination or absorption of the creature, but at its affirmation, deliverance, and glorification [3]. The divine concurrence is understood correctly only when placed within the overall divine governance of the world and its history, which moves the creaturely sphere inexorably toward its appointed *telos* of salvation and unity with God [4].

The general co-temporality of God's concurrence with the creature in the divine preservation and governance of the world displays the full dimension of God's specific co-temporality with the creature in the history of the covenant, which centers in the eternal election of all men in Jesus Christ. Because of Barth's unique restatement of the doctrine of election or predestination, and the implications this carries for the development of ethics as the command of God, we shall need to develop the former in some detail.

The special co-temporality of God manifested in Jesus Christ centers in the covenant. It is only in relation to it that the purpose of

---

[1] *Ibid.*, p. 150.

[2] "For the God who is active in Jesus Christ through his Word and Spirit reveals himself as the One beside whom there is never and nowhere no other being and activity. On the contrary, he is generally and always active, as he is revealed to us there; even there, where he does not encounter us directly in the history of the covenant in Jesus Christ, but is hidden. As we know and believe in him here, we know and believe in him at all points as the One who is always active in, with, and over all his creatures through his Word and Spirit". *Ibid.*, p. 161f.

[3] *Ibid.*, p. 168f. A discussion of the implications and adequacy of the view of creaturely freedom involved in this must await the full development of Barth's anthropology in Chapter 5 of the study. Here I are concerned only with the temporal actuality of God in its general and specific manifestations within the created order.

[4] *Ibid.*, pp. 175, 179f.

creation, the general co-temporality of God in providence, and the event of reconciliation can be properly seen and assessed. The fact of the covenant itself, however, is grounded in the grace of God's free, eternal decision to elect man as his covenant partner [1]. The doctrine of election thus becomes, for Barth, the sum of the gospel, since it comprises all that is to be said concerning God's turning to man in love. It is exclusively in terms of this doctrine that we begin and end our understanding and knowledge of the way in which God has related and continues to relate himself to man [2]. This is not to say, however, that the doctrine of election exhausts the content of the covenant. It is rather the first element in the covenant, indicating God's eternal resolve toward man. Beyond this, there remains, as a second aspect of the covenant, the development of man's appropriate response to God's decision and action under the divine command [3].

In emphasizing the centrality of election, Barth is quick to dissociate himself from another theological tradition, developing out of Calvin and continuing to the present, in which the doctrine of election is construed in relation to an abstract *decretum absolutum* of God resulting in the separation of men into two groups, the elect and the rejected, so that, as Barth puts it, the " 'Book of Life' began to be spoken of as if it contained a death-column" [4]. The way beyond this possibility is provided in Barth's refusal to allow any separation or distinction between being and act in God. The only basis we have for asserting anything about the being and purpose of God lies in the specific action he has taken in inaugurating and sustaining the covenant in the unfolding of salvation history. But since this becomes clear only at that point where the will and purpose of God from all eternity have been revealed, it follows that the only adequate foundation for the doctrine of election lies exclusively in Jesus Christ [5]. It is only in the free decision of grace and election shown in him that God is God. Without this, and the relationship between God and the creature which it signifies, God would no longer be himself:

---

[1] II/1, p. 571f.; IV/1, pp. 38ff.

[2] II/2, pp. 1, 13, 95f.

[3] *Ibid.*, p. 565. However, both aspects of the covenant are securely centered and anchored in Jesus Christ. The development of the divine command, and its fulfillment, will not permit a transition to the sphere of general anthropology.

[4] *Ibid.*, p. 15.

[5] *Ibid.*, p. 5f. Cf. III/2, p. 362f.

Jesus Christ is indeed God in his turning towards man, or, more exactly, in his turning towards the people represented in the one man Jesus of Nazareth, in his covenant with this people, in his being and activity amongst and towards this people. Jesus Christ is the decision of God for this attitude. He is himself this divine attitude. It is undoubtedly a relation *ad extra* of God, for this man and the people represented in him are creatures and not God. But it is an irrevocable relation, of such a kind that once God has willed to enter into it, and has in fact entered into it, he would no longer be God without it [1].

The inclusiveness of the divine predestination (*Gnadewahl*) and election accomplished by God in Jesus Christ means that there can be no question of a twofold meaning which applies ontologically to man; of election for some and rejection for others, of eternal life and eternal damnation, of light and darkness. Dialectically, Barth expresses the reality of election in terms of a "Yes" and a "No", but the "No" enjoys no independent status. It is only because of the "Yes" that the "No" can be spoken [2]. The basic thrust of election, since it is directed toward all men, is always positive, not negative:

It is evangel: good news; a delightful, uplifting, comforting, helpful message. Once and for all, then, it does not have to do with an announced truth which is neutral in face of the opposition between fear and terror, or need and danger; nor with a theorem whose content would form only instruction and explanation of certain facts which themselves remained indifferent to the distinction between good and evil or right and wrong ... It is not a mixed message of joy and terror, salvation and damnation. Originally and finally it is not dialectical but non-dialectical. It does not proclaim in the same breath both good and evil, help and destruction, life and death [3].

The key to Barth's approach to the doctrine of election is found in his Christology: Christ is at once both electing God and elected man [4]. This entails a difference of determination (*Bestimmung*) between the divine and the human in Jesus Christ: "Primarily, then, electing (*Erwählen*) is the divine, and being elected (*Erwähltsein*) the human, determination of the existence of Jesus Christ" [5]. The faithfulness of God in

---

[1] IV/2, p. 132f.

[2] II/2, p. 12. This was also true of Barth's employment of this dialectic in the *Römerbrief*.

[3] II/2, p. 11f. Cf. IV/2, p. 427.

[4] IV/1, p. 185; II/2, Par. 33, Part 1, "Jesus Christ, the Electing and the Elected".

[5] II/2, p. 111.

his freedom and love toward the creature is thus exemplified in his relationship to the man Jesus, in his election of him. This eliminates the possibility of an abstract will of God which lies behind Jesus Christ, about which inquiry is to be made. Here the importance of Barth's trinitarian grounding comes again into view. The fulness of Godhead is revealed in Christ, since "the Father is the Father of Jesus Christ and the Holy Spirit is the Spirit of this Father and the Spirit of Jesus Christ" [1]. It is thus impossible that there should be something of God's being that is not given in his action. There can be no *decretum absolutum* outside or behind the grace shown in Jesus Christ. There is no "higher" mystery to be penetrated, and so no will of God apart from the decision taken in Christ [2]. Further, the election of Jesus Christ is not something occurring only in human time and history. It is grounded in the eternal act of election exemplified in the inter-trinitarian relationship between the Father and the Son, which includes the specific humanity of the man Jesus:

> In this free act of election, the Son of the Father is no longer only the eternal Logos, but as such, as true God from eternity, he is also the true God and true man he will become in time. In the divine act of predestination, therefore, Jesus Christ pre-exists, who, as the Son of the eternal Father and the son of the Virgin Mary, will become and be the Mediator of the covenant between God and man, the executor of the event of reconciliation [3].

The question of the election of the individual will, accordingly, be answerable only on the basis of God's eternal election of man in Jesus Christ. Strictly speaking, only Jesus Christ is elect before God; all other men are elect only "in him" [4]. And even the election of Jesus demonstrates the freedom and sovereignty of grace, since it does not signify some sort of merit or independent choice on his part, but rather indicates the true destiny of human nature under the impact of God's eternal resolve and action. The reality of election as it comes to man in Jesus Christ can be formulated thus: In Jesus Christ, the electing God, by virtue of the steadfastness of his grace, elects the man Jesus, who as such demonstrates the destiny of human nature, i.e., that it is elected human nature [5].

---

[1] *Ibid.*, p. 123f. Cf. IV/1, p. 141.
[2] II/2, pp. 169f., 124.
[3] IV/1, pp. 54, 70.
[4] II/2, p. 124.
[5] "The man Jesus, from whom we begin, is the man elected by God. Election means a special decision with special intent in view of a special object.

The positive thrust of election is shown clearly in Barth's exploration of the christological point within the context of the doctrine of reconciliation. The event of reconciliation signals the fulfillment of the covenant. This means that the doctrine of reconciliation becomes the central word in Christian confession and dogma. But, since the covenant fulfilled in reconciliation is grounded in God's eternal election of man, it follows that the doctrine of election is the first and decisive word about the mystery of reconciliation [1].

The unity between election and reconciliation indicates that we are dealing with an action that is exclusively God's from beginning to end. This is seen clearly in the development of Barth's Christology, which follows Calvin's use of the "threefold office" of Christ, but in an inverted order, i.e., Priest, King, and Prophet [2]. Taken together, these serve to indicate the interrelatedness and unity of God and man in Jesus Christ in the event of reconciliation. Put succinctly, the schematism of the threefold office is designed to show that in Jesus Christ we have to do, first, with very God; second, with very man; and third, with very God and very man in their unity [3]. These are, then, simply different ways of talking about the same event. The first and third of these pertain centrally to our exploration of the co-temporality of God; the second to the "determination" of man as the reconciled, and therefore justified and sanctified, covenant partner of God [4].

The fact and meaning of the existence of the man Jesus, to the extent that he is also a creature, do not depend on his own choice. To be sure, it is always also his own choice that he gives himself to remain in community with God, and so to do the saving work of God, giving God the glory, providing room for his lordship, and engaging in his service. But even in this choice, he has not elected himself. He is elected by God to this choice. In all this an eternal decision breaks through in time, in the world of the creature the will of the Creator, in the self-determination of this man his divine pre-determination. Predestination, God's election, is the basis of this, that Creator and creature, God and man, are one here, that the kingdom of God has come in him. Why is all this true of the man Jesus? Because he is the creature, in whom God's election is already fulfilled". III/2, p. 170f. Cf. II/2, pp. 126f., 134.

[1] IV/1, p. 94; II/2, p. 95f.

[2] Cf. John Calvin, *Institutes of the Christian Religion*, Allen translation (Philadelphia: Presbyterian Board of Christian Education), Book II, Ch. XV.

[3] Cf. IV/1, Par. 58, Part 4, "The Three Forms of the Doctrine of Reconciliation".

[4] My disposition of the separate aspects of this schematism is admittedly not parallel with Barth's, whose development relates the first two as the "material", and the third as the "formal", sides of the doctrine of reconcili-

Barth's treatment of the doctrine of election in the *Dogmatics* embodies the same terminological alternation between the "Yes" and "No" of revelation that was seen in the *Römerbrief*. The difference is that in the *Dogmatics* this alternation is developed along exclusively christological lines, so that, as Otto Weber suggests, the notion of a "double predestination" is radically altered, in that God's "Yes" is now reserved wholly for man, while the "No" falls entirely on God himself [1]. It is the action of God in taking the judgment reserved for man upon himself that illuminates the priestly office of Jesus Christ, and that makes clear the way in which Christ is very God. Since both the negative and positive sides of election are exemplified in Jesus Christ, it follows that these are epitomized in his death and resurrection, which together indicate "the divine rejection of elected man, and the divine election of rejected man" [2]. This does not permit any easy oscillation between the death and resurrection of Christ as the negative and positive poles of God's action. Rather, Christ's death and resurrection exhibit a unity as the judgment and sentence of God, so that both display, negatively, the way in which God remains faithful to himself; and, positively, the way in which he remains faithful to man. Or again, they represent together God's negative response to the unfaithfulness of man, and his positive purpose beyond that response in man's redemption [3].

The action of God in Jesus Christ means, quite simply, that God became a creature, and so assumed the contradiction and judgment of man. In Jesus Christ, God took the form of a servant (*forma servi*), entering so fully into fellowship with man that he took his place and suffered what he had to suffer [4]. It follows, then, that the two decisive

---

ation (Cf. IV/3.1, p. 7). While not wishing to obscure the unity of Barth's presentation, I should like, nevertheless, to argue the particular importance of the first and third dimensions of the doctrine of reconciliation for an understanding of the temporality of God, and the second for an initial (Christological) indication of the determination of man or the human which follows.

[1] "Wenn es also auch nach Barth eine gemina predestinatio gibt, so besteht sie darin, daß Gott zwar gewiß das Ja für die Gemeinde derer, die das Evangelium hören, bestimmt hat, das Nein aber im eigentlichen Sinne für sich selbst, so daß also der Verwordene eine schlechthin unmögliche Position einnimmt, die zum Verschwinden verurteilt ist". *Grundlegen der Dogmatik*, (Moers: Neukirchener Verlag, 1962), Zweiter Band, p. 486.

[2] IV/1, p. 574.

[3] *Ibid.*, p. 573f. Barth also asserts that the crucifixion and resurrection of Christ together constitute God's "Yes", as this is expressed in the obedience of Jesus Christ, and in his resurrection. *Ibid.*, p. 341. See below, p. 132.

[4] I/2, p. 171; II/1, p. 746f.; IV/1, p. 202.

motifs operative in this action will be those of humiliation and obedience. These will form the center, descriptively, of God's action, and, as we shall see, will also be crucial for Barth's development of theological ethics [1].

The humiliation (or condescension) and obedience shown in Jesus Christ can be taken as the outer and inner sides of God's action [2]. In keeping with Barth's insistence on the continuity between the economic and immanent determinations of God, humiliation and obedience are taken to be eternal, and therefore proper, counterparts of his being [3]. But since the notion of obedience can be properly filled out only if there is something or someone to which obedience is rendered, it follows that there is, within the being of God, "a First and a Second, One who rules and commands in majesty, and One who obeys in humility" [4]. So then, there is a subordination within God which becomes manifest in Jesus Christ. It is precisely in his obedience in humility that Jesus shows himself to be the Son of God, for in it he does something that only God can do:

> What the whole world lacks, what it cannot bring forth out of itself —not as creature, and certainly not as sinful creature—is just this complement, this obedience which corresponds to the lordship of God, and portrays it. Jesus Christ performs it. He performs it self-evidently, naturally, in his own freedom and therefore perfectly. He knows and goes only this way. He enters it and treads it without error, without making mistakes; he pursues it to the end. His entire being lies therein, that he is this obedient One ... The One who in such obedience is the perfect image of the ruling God is himself—in distinction to every human, creaturely kind—God by nature, God in his relation to himself, i.e., God in his mode of being as the Son in relation to God in his mode of being as the Father, with this One, with this same essence [5].

The first aspect of the history of Jesus Christ, accordingly, will focus on the condescension active in it. It is in this action that God shows himself to be, and remains, God, i.e., the One who in love and freedom places himself beside man in obedience, and so makes man's rejection his own:

> If we wish to know what God elected for himself because he elected

---

[1] Cf. II/2, pp. 566, 594, 677, *et passim.*
[2] IV/1, p. 210f.
[3] *Ibid.*, pp. 211, 219.
[4] *Ibid.*, p. 221.
[5] *Ibid.*, p. 228.

fellowship with man, then we can only answer that he elected our rejection. He made it his own. He bore and suffered it totally, in its bitterest consequence ... He elected our suffering (what we as sinners towards him and before him must suffer from him) to be his own suffering [1].

The full force of this aspect of Barth's Christology gains clarity at just this point, for in asserting that Jesus Christ is true God in his humiliation, in his identification with man in his disobedient existence before God, he also asserts that God becomes the "Judge judged in our place" [2]. As man's judge, Jesus executes the necessary sentence against the disobedience of Israel, the original elect people of God. The history of Jesus thus represents the completion of Israel's history, in that it is the concrete embodiment of God's negation of the people elected to covenant with him. At this point, the grace of God remains "hidden under his verdict and judgment, his Yes under his No" [3]. But since the negative thrust of God's sentence and judgment is entirely assumed by God himself in his co-temporality with man in Christ, this will mean that the notion of rejection is descriptively applicable only to God, and not at all to man:

> Since the negative side of the divine predestination, the reckoning with the weakness, sin, and necessary punishment of man, is that part of the matter that God takes to himself, that says at the same time that that part is not, in any case, a No that falls upon man ... Faith in God's predestination in itself and *per se* means faith in the non-rejection of man, non-faith in his rejection. Man, indeed, is not rejected. In God's eternal decree it is God himself who is rejected in his Son [4].

The positive side of election, man's reconciliation with God, is secured in Jesus of Nazareth, the Son of God, who makes man's situation his own, doing for man, and so for the world, what it cannot do for itself [5]. In Christ, God became man's brother, existing within world-history "under the full burden, in the total peril of all world-history" [6]. This action, which underlines the way in which the God who is "over us" in his providential care and guidance of the whole range of creaturely history is also "for us", reaches its culmination in the crucifixion and death of Christ. This constitutes a fulfillment of God's judgment on

---

[1] II/2, p. 179.
[2] IV/1, pp. 231ff.
[3] *Ibid.*, pp. 189, 283.
[4] II/2, p. 181f.
[5] IV/1, pp. 234ff., 244f.
[6] *Ibid.*, p. 236.

man's disobedience [1], and, as the obedient (and therefore free) act of God himself, is also the condition for, and realization of, man's reconciliation [2]. God's condescension in undergoing man's rejection and judgment provides a confirmation of the covenant, for it testifies to his fidelity in the face of Israel's infidelity [3].

The history of Jesus Christ, however, is viewed appropriately only from the perspective of its *telos* in the resurrection. This event, as a new act of God beyond the death of Christ, is for Barth the "verdict" (*Urteil*) of the Father on the action of the Son [4]. Taken together, the crucifixion and resurrection of Christ form the "Yes" of God toward the creature, which is expressed both in the obedience of Christ, and in the verdict of the Father on that obedience, in which Christ becomes the first recipient of God's grace [5]. The resurrection is additionally significant, in that it is the event in which the specific history of Jesus falls over into eternal history, becoming thereby the manifestation of the first stage in the *parousia* of Christ [6]. The function of the resurrection is to make the humiliation and obedience of the Son of God manifested in the passion of Jesus Christ real as revelation [7]. It is, accordingly, the sole basis for human response and participation in the event of reconciliation.

At this point, we are led to an exploration of a further dimension of God's special co-temporality with man: his being present to us through the self-witness of Jesus Christ in the Holy Spirit. This is set forth in a lengthy discussion by Barth as the "prophetic" office of Jesus Christ [8]. What is involved here is the expression, disclosure, and mediation of the event of reconciliation. Or, as Barth puts it, it is a question of the "How" enclosed within (though not reducible to) the "What" of the event of reconciliation [9].

There is an important distinction to be made here, in keeping with

---

[1] *Ibid.*, p. 278.

[2] *Ibid.*, p. 283; I/2, p. 148f.

[3] II/1, p. 438.

[4] IV/1, pp. 311ff.

[5] *Ibid.*, p. 309.

[6] *Ibid.*, p. 351f. The second and third stages in the *parousia* are filled out respectively, by the impartation of the Holy Spirit to the Christian community and, eschatologically, by the final return of Jesus Christ. Throughout these different forms the *parousia* remains a unitive event, in keeping with the consistency of salvation history issuing from it. Cf. IV/3.1, p. 338.

[7] I/2, p. 122.

[8] IV/3.1, Par. 69, "The Glory of the Mediator".

[9] *Ibid.*, p. 7.

Barth's general concern for the objective status of the events comprising salvation history. The specific point in question has to do with the revelatory character of the event of reconciliation, i.e., its self-communication, impartation, and manifestation. It is in elucidating this that Barth distinguishes between what can be described as a primary "revelatory character" (*Offenbarungscharakter*) attaching to the event of reconciliation, which is an objective property of the event itself, and a secondary revelatory character productive of specific phenomena in the world, i.e., the Christian community and individual believers [1]. The former point is developed by Barth as the third part of his Christology; the latter gains expression in the development of the doctrine of the Holy Spirit in relation to the third aspect of the event of reconciliation [2].

This, of course, represents nothing new in Barth's treatment of the doctrine of reconciliation, or his approach to theology generally. It serves rather to underline once again his refusal to temper the objective actuality of revelation by making it dependent at some point on man's response. The action of God in Jesus Christ is at all points a *completed* action. It follows, then, that this will be as true of the communicational and declaratory dimensions of that action, as it is of the crucifixion and resurrection. The activity of the Holy Spirit is not that of creating hitherto non-existing facts which would somehow fill out or complete the event of reconciliation. It is rather that point in the temporality of God at which the revelatory character of reconciliation receives confirmation in the response evoked in man. The possibility of authentic human response to the event of reconciliation depends on the prior actuality of reconciliation as disclosure, declaration, and impartation [3].

---

[1] *Ibid.*, p. 9.

[2] The whole of chapter XVI of the *Dogmatics*, "Jesus Christ, the True Witness" (IV/3.1 and 2), enunciates Barth's overall concern. Within this, Par. 69, Parts 2 and 3, and Par. 70, Part 1, would apply specifically to the objective revelatory character of reconciliation; Pars. 72 and 73 to the subjective appropriation of this event under the impact of the Holy Spirit in the formation of the Christian community and individual believers. Because of this distinction, it seems appropriate to focus our discussion primarily on the Christological point involved in the self-manifestation of reconciliation, and to develop Barth's doctrine of the Holy Spirit somewhat later, in relation to a development of his anthropology, and the emergence of the Christian community. We shall indicate in this chapter, however, the importance of the Holy Spirit for a completed statement of the temporality of God.

[3] "There is human knowledge, and a theology of reconciliation, because reconciliation itself and as such is not only real, but true, proving itself in the illuminating work of the Holy Spirit, but both real and true first of all in itself, as disclosure, declaration, and impartation". *Ibid.*, p. 11.

In drawing this distinction, Barth does not mean to suggest that the question of human response to revelation is either superfluous or expendable. This is made clear in the continuity which he establishes between the Christological and anthropological points in the *Dogmatics*. So, as the crucifixion, resurrection, and self-manifestation of Jesus Christ correspond to the priestly, kingly, and prophetic dimensions of his action, they are provided with the anthropological counterparts of justification, sanctification, and vocation [1]. Further, Barth indicates that the objective fact of reconciliation, even with its indigenous revelatory property, does not in itself constitute salvation history. Salvation history consists in both the objective fact of reconciliation, and the subjective response to it engendered in the prophetic activity of Christ through the Holy Spirit. The history of Jesus Christ in its prophetic aspect creates salvation history in the form of human response to, and knowledge of, the event of reconciliation [2]. Properly understood, salvation history consists in the unity existing between Jesus Christ and his people, the Christian community [3]. The history of Jesus Christ, which constitutes salvation history, gains exemplification and continuation in the emergence and action of the community of men who hear and respond to his prophetic Word.

What seems to emerge from this is the necessity of distinguishing between reconciliation as completed event and the ongoing thrust of salvation history. Barth does this by drawing a distinction between the material and formal aspects of reconciliation. The former lies in the accomplished obedience of the Son of God and exaltation of the Son of Man in the crucifixion and resurrection of Jesus Christ. To this, Barth asserts, nothing (materially) can be added [4]. What occurs in the development of salvation history beyond this in the prophetic action of Jesus Christ in the Holy Spirit constitutes for Barth the formal side of reconciliation, the communication of its truth to, and the evoking of a response in, men. This does not mean, however, that the truth of reconciliation is in any way dependent on human response. The self-manifesting and declaratory truth of the event of reconciliation encloses all men (*de iure*)

---

[1] Though, as we shall see, even the anthropological counterparts are predicable initially only of Jesus Christ. They *become* predicates of other men, ostensibly, in a derivative fashion through the action of the Holy Spirit.

[2] IV/3.1, p. 241f.

[3] *Ibid.*, p. 247.

[4] *Ibid.*, p. 6.

from the outset, whether they are aware of it or not [1]. Given Barth's ordering of the factors, the response of men to the Holy Spirit can only constitute a confirmation of the reconciliation already achieved in Jesus Christ, not some kind of completion of it. This would seem to hold true even though Barth is also willing to assert that the event of reconciliation is "actually victorious" (*faktisch siegt*) in the work of the Holy Spirit [2]. What this suggests is that the activity of the Holy Spirit, as the manifestation of the prophetic action of Jesus Christ to his people, is to be seen as a continuation of God's graciousness in entering into covenant with man, a graciousness which in no way depends on the human for its justification or execution. To suggest that the effective communication of reconciliation adds to that event would be to indicate that God stands in some sort of dependence on human response, a suggestion which Barth is at pains to reject throughout the *Dogmatics*. With these remarks in mind, we can proceed to an elucidation of God's co-temporality with man in the prophetic witness of Jesus Christ.

That reconciliation as event is also revelation depends solely on the fact that Jesus Christ lives. The basic christological assertion, at once the simplest and most difficult, is that "he, Jesus Christ, lives" [3]. As he lives, Christ is his own primary and authentic witness. Barth adopts a Johannine metaphor to describe the self-manifestation involved here, characterizing Christ as "the light of life":

> We have to speak at this point of the "light of life", of the light which life itself and as such radiates and diffuses, because it is itself light. Because Jesus Christ lives, he also shines out, not with an alien light which falls on him and illuminates him from without, but in his own proper light proceeding from himself. He lives as the source of light, through whose brilliance the outside is made bright ... As he lives, he is the light that causes sight to occur in all the eyes which as such are created and determined to see him, and everything that he makes clear [4].

This activity of self-declaration, which constitutes the condition for all human acquaintance with God's action in Jesus Christ, is also an integral part of his being and act [5]. In it, Jesus provides his own witness to his history as salvation history. At this point, salvation

---

[1] IV/2, p. 589; IV/3.1, p. 321.
[2] IV/3.1, p. 9.
[3] *Ibid.*, p. 41.
[4] *Ibid.*, p. 49.
[5] *Ibid.*, pp. 49, 53.

history is made coincident with the history of revelation (*Offenbarungs-geschichte*) [1].

The total unfolding of the prophetic history of Christ is signalled in a phrase Barth takes over from J.C. Blumhardt, "Jesus is Victor" [2]. The indicative mood of this statement must not be allowed to obscure the dynamism it is intended to convey. As employed by Barth, it stands as a descriptive summation of the concrete historical process embodied in the self-declaration of Jesus Christ, which aims at, and achieves, the end of moving men from a *de iure*, implicit involvement with the event of reconciliation to a *de facto* recognition and acknowledgement of that event in their lives. It has to do with the overcoming of human apathy, indifference, and hostility [3], so that

> as the event of reconciliation is also an event of revelation or prophecy, as the life as such is also light, it emerges from the apparent distance in which it takes place for us men, and moves us directly, "in the belly", so to speak, so that we are not only implicated, but find ourselves directly involved in its occurrence [4].

The history of the witness of Jesus Christ is grounded in the "Yes" of God's grace with which he encounters all men. Its beginning, and the activity enclosed therein, is always understood as aiming at, and achieving, good [5]. This is not accomplished directly or easily, however, and it is at precisely this point that the significance of Barth's disinclination to work in merely ontological or conceptual categories is made explicit. The prophetic history of Jesus Christ emerges as a history of conflict in which the Word addressed to man evokes a human response or "word" of rejection. The resurrected Jesus Christ is himself the aggressor in this conflict. Against his witness, the world is powerless; its future has been irrevocably cast [6]. In one sense, then, the response engendered by Christ's prophetic Word, the resistance and rejection which it meets, poses no serious problem concerning the truth of that message. The world *is* reconciled, and human responses of unbelief and rejection can

---

[1] *Ibid.*, p. 50.

[2] *Ibid.*, p. 192f. The forcefulness of Barth's use of this phrase, which stands as the heading for Par. 69, Part 2, is brought out clearly in the German: "Jesus ist Sieger!".

[3] *Ibid.*, p. 208f.

[4] *Ibid.*, p. 207.

[5] *Ibid.*, p. 262.

[6] IV/3.1, p. 274f.

do nothing to alter this fact [1]. It is in view of the unalterable facticity of reconciliation that Barth describes evil as "nothingness", "impossible possibility", and an "ontological impossibility" [2]. These somewhat dramatic terms, which Barth himself insists be taken "cum grano salis" [3], can be given proper meaning only if taken historically *and* eschatologically, i.e., in light of the thrust of the prophetic history inaugurated in the resurrection of Jesus Christ.

It is at this point that the full sweep of God's co-temporality with man moves toward closure. The statement "Jesus is Victor" indicates both the present reconciliation of the world and its future redemption. It is for this reason that the history of Jesus Christ moves dynamically through conflict towards (final) victory, a victory which is not in any way open to question. Jesus is victor both at the beginning and at the end of his conflict. His prophetic witness is thus properly seen as "reconciliation in its transition to completion in redemption" [4]. This transition cannot be read off empirically from developments within the world, whether these focus on an assumed "progress of the human", the program and activity of the Christian community, or the inner confidence of believers [5]. Final victory, the eschatological goal towards which the world is moved, is discernible only in Jesus Christ, who as the Word of God's act touches the "real man" beyond the element of evil in man's resistance, the man to whom God's action has been directed from the beginning. It turns out, then, that the time alloted man between reconciliation and redemption functions as a sign of God's grace to man. Rather than act as a *Deus ex machina* toward his creature, God allows it both time and space in which to share in the event of reconciliation [6]. The prophetic manifestation of Jesus Christ thus attests the unity and continuity holding in God's action from creation to reconciliation to redemption, a unity and continuity grounded in the identity of Jesus Christ as the Elect of God from all eternity, "in whom and with whom the creature is also elect" [7].

---

[1] *Ibid.*, p. 275.
[2] *Ibid.*, p. 203f.
[3] *Ibid.*, p. 203.
[4] *Ibid.*, p. 303.
[5] *Ibid.*, p. 304f.
[6] *Ibid.*, p. 383.
[7] *Ibid.*

C. THE DETERMINATION OF MAN

The event of reconciliation is marked by a dual movement: from above to below, and from below to above. The former received expression in the motif of humiliation marking the obedience unto death of the Son of God, signalling thereby that in Jesus Christ we have to do with true God. The latter is given in the motif of the exaltation of Jesus Christ as the Son of Man, who thus becomes the paradigm for a humanity reconciled and restored to fellowship with God:

> The problem of the reconciled man is, like that of the reconciling God, grounded in Christology, and can be legitimately posed, developed, and answered only on that basis. It has its roots in the identity of the Son of God with the Son of Man, Jesus of Nazareth, in what this man as such was and did, in what happened to him as such. In and with his humiliation as the Son of God there took place also his exaltation as the Son of Man. His exaltation is the exemplary type and dynamic basis for what will take place and is to be known as the exaltation of man in his reconciliation with God. In his fellowship with God and in our actual fellowship with him, this One, there arises our fellowship with God, that movement of man from below to above, from himself to God [1].

The exaltation of the Son of Man signals man's return to peace with God as his elected covenant partner. In the being and action of Jesus Christ, there occurred an acceptance and affirmation of God's grace addressed to all men. So Christ, as the Son of Man, is the One who in faithfulness and obedience *keeps the covenant*, demonstrating thereby the original and final continuity holding between the divine activity and the place and status of the human [2].

Barth's discussion of Jesus' exaltation as the Son of Man focuses on three points: election, incarnation, and resurrection [3]. The first and third of these have to do, respectively, with the eternal basis of Jesus' identity

---

[1] IV/2, p. 19.

[2] *Ibid.*, pp. 31f., 34f. Cf. *The Humanity of God*, p. 46f.: "Jesus Christ is in His one Person, as true *God*, *man's* loyal partner, and as true *man*, *God's*. He is the Lord humbled for communion with man and likewise the Servant exalted to communion with God ... We do not need to engage in a free-ranging investigation to seek out and construct who and what God truly is, and who and what man truly is, but only to read the truth about both where it resides, namely, in the fulness of their togetherness, their covenant which proclaims itself in Jesus Christ".

[3] IV/2, p. 32.

as Son of Man, and the revelational ground on which its communication to men rests. I have indicated the importance of election and resurrection for an understanding of the condescension and humiliation of God in the event of reconciliation. And, since what is now being explored is simply another way of looking at that event, it follows that election and resurrection carry the same force here. What remains, accordingly, is to provide an indication of the temporal fulfillment of God's exaltation of the human in the incarnation.

The incarnation, for Barth, is "the great Christian mystery and sacrament, beside which, strictly speaking, there is no other" [1]. The most succinct description of this event is that "God assumed a being as man into his being as God" [2]. The unity thus achieved between the divine and the human does not consist for Barth in a blending of two equally independent factors. That man has a place in the event of reconciliation depends strictly on grace. There will thus be no way to provide a separate treatment of the reality of the human in the incarnation, which might utilize an abstract or general notion of man, and so allow an easy transition from Christology to anthropology [3].

Barth eludes this possibility by making the incarnation exclusively the work of God in his mode of existence as the Son. It is therefore an event that is grounded in the eternal being of God as Father, Son, and Spirit [4]. This entails, however, that the incarnation is to be understood exclusively as the work of God. A more precise and expanded statement

---

[1] IV/2, p. 42.

[2] *Ibid.*, p. 44.

[3] An approach which would also depend on an assumed understanding and definition of "divine nature". Commenting on the utilization of a "two natures" approach to the incarnation, epitomized in the Christologies of the 4th and 5th centuries, Barth states: "The concept of the two 'natures' of Jesus Christ, which came into prominence in the older doctrine and theology of the Church after the struggles and decisions of the 4th and 5th centuries, was exposed to serious misunderstanding, proving thereby to be at least in serious need of interpretation. One need not abandon it on that account. But it is well to consider that it is entirely too easy to read out of the word 'nature' a reference to a generally known or at least conceivable disposition of a being, so that by the concept of a 'divine nature' we are led to think of a generally known or knowable essence of deity, and by that of 'human nature' to a generally known or at least knowable essence of man, and so—what at present is our concern—what is to be understood by the humanity of Jesus Christ is determined by some sort of universal anthropology, a doctrine of man in general and as such". *Ibid.*, p. 26f.

[4] *Ibid.*, pp. 46f., 70. Cf. I/2, p. 146.

of that event, then, would be that in it "God the Son assumed a concrete possibility of human being and essence prepared and elected by him for this purpose, thereby conferring actuality on it by making himself its actuality" [1]. It is the Son of God, as the active subject of the event of incarnation and reconciliation, who establishes a union of divine and human essence in Jesus of Nazareth. The unification achieved in him, and so his identity as very God and very man, rest wholly on the action of the Son of God [2]. It is only in this action that "by and in him the divine receives a determination to the human, and the human receives a determination from the divine" [3].

It is clear from this that the incarnation, and the determination of the human resulting from it, cannot be viewed in any sense as an immanent possibility of the created order. It is a unique act of God, grounded entirely in his freedom [4], in which the Son of God, the eternal Logos, "became flesh" [5]. The only descriptively adequate statement concerning the incarnation, therefore, is that it constitutes "a new creation" (eine neue Schöpfung) [6]. This makes it imperative that we be clear about Barth's understanding of the humanity of Jesus Christ, and the way in which it manifests continuity with created human nature.

Barth begins with a deceptively straightforward assertion:

> That the Word was made flesh means first of all and generally that he became man, that is, true and real man, sharing the same human essence and being, the same human nature and form, the same historicity, that is ours [7].

Here, when Barth speaks of "true and real man", this is descriptive of God's assumption of fallen, Adamic human nature. This provides the

---

[1] IV/2, p. 53.

[2] Ibid., pp. 55, 67.

[3] Ibid., p. 75.

[4] I/2, p. 148.

[5] Barth takes a phrase from John 1:14, "the Word became flesh", as the decisively succinct statement of the incarnation. Cf. Ibid., p. 145f.

[6] Ibid., p. 147; IV/2, p. 48. Apropos this point, Hendrik van Oyen comments: "Barth radikaliesiert den Menschen von der sich offenbarenden Tat Gottes her und sieht so den Menschen in eine völlig neue Situation hineingestellt, nicht mehr bloß als eine Reintegration auf die Schöpfung zurück, sondern als eine Neuschöpfung auf die Vollendung der Werke Gottes hin". Theologische Erkenntnislehre (Zwingli: Verlag Zürich, 1955), p. 60.

[7] I/2, p. 161. Cf. IV/2, p. 75: "Jesus of Nazareth was and is a man as we are—our Brother"; and p. 101.

basis for statements about the "likeness" holding between the humanity of Jesus Christ and that of other men [1]. These, however, cannot stand alone. A full appreciation of the humanity of Christ emerges only when the assertion of its "likeness" is juxtaposed to the contrary assertion of its "unlikeness" to created human nature:

> But the fact that he is not only *a* true man, but *the* true man, is not exhausted by his likeness with all other men. He is not only wholly like us, but also wholly unlike us—and it is only as one accepts this that the *vere homo* applied to him receives its full meaning [2].

Barth explores the difference between Christ's humanity and ours along two lines. The first of these, which focuses on his identity as the incarnate Son of God, may aptly be described as the ontological factor marking the distinction. The second, focusing on the obedient action of Jesus as the Son of God who is also (and simultaneously) Son of Man, brings out the historical and ethical aspects of his humanity which set it off from ours. It is important to indicate the meaning and significance of each of these, and then to suggest how created human nature as such, despite its dissimilarity from the humanity of Christ, is made participant in it, and so given a positive determination.

The humanity of Jesus Christ has no independent status. It *is* only insofar as the Son of God assumes temporal and spatial form in the figure of Jesus of Nazareth. In making this point, Barth adopts the older distinction between *anhypostasis* and *enhypostasis* as applied to the humanity of Christ [3]. This distinction involves both a positive and a negative point. Negatively, it excludes the possibility of viewing Jesus as an independent man who is somehow brought into union with God. The action of God does not presuppose the human in this way. It is for this reason that Barth issues a warning against placing central emphasis on Jesus as "a man" [4]. This is not designed to minimize the specific existence and identity of Jesus [5]. It serves rather to bring out the positive thrust of *enhypostasia*, i.e., that Jesus Christ exists as a man only because the Son of God actualizes his potential to become and be this specific man, to assume human nature in this way. Jesus exists as

---

[1] IV/2, pp. 28, 79f.; I/2, p. 165f.
[2] IV/2, p. 28.
[3] I/2, p. 178ff.; IV/2, p. 52f.
[4] I/2, p. 163; IV/2, p. 50f.
[5] IV/1, p. 174.

man only as he exists as God. His humanity can be properly described only as "the humanity of God" (*die Humanität Gottes*) [1]. The identity of Jesus as the Son of God in human form thus indicates an ontological distinction between him and other men which persists even though the human essence assumed in the incarnation is common to all men. As Son of God, Jesus is something that no other man can be [2].

The full significance of this difference emerges when consideration is given to the specific history and action of Jesus Christ as the Son of Man, i.e., as the Son of God in human form in whom human essence is exalted to its original and ultimate place in unity and fellowship with God. Here the exaltation of the Son of Man follows inexorably from the prior humiliation and obedience of the Son of God, and the specific dissimilarity between Christ and all other men becomes strikingly transparent:

> What else shall the Son of God who humbled himself to man become and be but the Son of Man who is not divinized but exalted to the side of God? What else can the Lord who became a servant become and be but the servant who became a Lord? That is the mystery of the humanity of Jesus Christ, which has no parallel at all in us. That is the basis and power of the reconciliation that took place in him on this side—seen here from below, from man. Everything that has occupied us in this chapter has its root in the exaltation of this servant to be the Lord, of the man Jesus of Nazareth to the side of God the Father; and this exaltation itself is grounded in the fact that he is the humiliated Son of God, the Lord who became a servant [3].

The origin of Jesus as Son of God lies in the eternal election of man as God's covenant partner. It is this origin, grounded wholly in grace, that brings about the exaltation of his human essence to unity with God. What this means is that Jesus in his humanity realizes authentic freedom in obedience, so that he exists in complete harmony with God [4]. It is the *freedom* exhibited in the action of Jesus that stands finally as

---

[1] IV/2, p. 78.

[2] *Ibid.*, p. 28; I/2, p. 177f.

[3] IV/2, p. 29f. In the English edition, the translators have erroneously rendered *Versöhnung* as "atonement" instead of the more appropriate "reconciliation". Cf. IV/2 (Eng. trans.), p. 28: "... That is the basis and power of the atonement made in Him on this side—as it is seen from below, from man ...".

[4] IV/2, pp. 100ff.

the crucial factor determining his history and marking him off from other men. Existing within and under the full scope and weight of the human, Jesus of Nazareth, as the humiliated Son of God and exalted Son of Man, lives a life of free obedience, and so achieves a restoration of authentic human essence [1]. The difference between Jesus and other men, put succinctly, is that "in our human being what we do is omitted, and what we omit is done" [2]. Human essence, in Jesus Christ, is exalted to service [3].

So Jesus, the exalted Son of Man, lives and acts as "the second Adam", the "royal man" [4], who undergoes rejection, suffering, and death, reflecting thereby the humiliation of the Son of God [5]. In the being and act of Jesus, God places himself unreservedly at man's side, demonstrating that he is wholly *for* man. As the kingly man, Jesus "mirrors and portrays the divine Yes to man and his cosmos" [6]. In him, God identifies directly with everything that threatens man's authentic humanity, removes this, and establishes a totally different direction and determination for man's future. But this will have to mean, as I have already suggested, that there will be continuity between Jesus and other men in spite of, or beyond, or, perhaps, *within*, the discontinuity and difference marking his identity as Son of God and Son of Man. That continuity can now be indicated.

The first point to be made is that the being and act of God in Jesus Christ, and so the specific humanity of Jesus as Son of God and Son of Man, establishes an unavoidable *ontological* determination for the human, in which all men are immediately implicated:

> Because God was in Christ, he reconciled the world to himself, and therefore us, each one of us. In this one the human, our essence as such, was elevated and exalted. In complete likeness with us, as our true brother, yet he was and is completely unlike us in his unique nature as the true and royal man. To that in which a man is like all other men, and therefore a man, there now also belongs brotherhood with this one man, who is so unlike him and all other men. To human essence in its nature and corruption there now belongs the fact that in the one man Jesus Christ,

---

[1] *Ibid.*, p. 103.
[2] I/2, p. 170.
[3] IV/2, p. 109.
[4] *Ibid.*, p. 173.
[5] *Ibid.*, p. 186.
[6] *Ibid.*, p. 200.

who as the true Son of God was and is also the true Son of Man, it has become and remains participant in that elevation and exaltation. There is no human existence that is not also initially and finally determined and characterized by the fact that it can take place only in this brother-hood [1].

The determination of man is thus grounded objectively and ontolog-ically in the determination of Jesus Christ. It is in his identity and action that the lines of creation, covenant, election, and reconciliation coalesce dramatically to form a unified history and action grounded in the eternal triune being of God. The ontological significance of the event of Jesus Christ lies in the fact that all men have been chosen (i.e., elected) and determined from eternity to be "in Christ" [2].

Given this determination, it would seem that the dissimilarity between the human essence of Jesus and created human essence is drastic-ally minimized, if not finally dissolved, in the course of a full working out of the history of Jesus Christ, exemplified in the transition from reconcil-iation to redemption. For consider: The Son of God, in the event of incarnation, assumed our common human essence, and, through his obedience in freedom, brought about a fulfillment of the covenant, and thus a restoration of the original and final status accorded man as the originally elected covenant partner of God. The exaltation of human essence that occurred in Jesus Christ does not, therefore, constitute an alien manifestation. It is rather the occasion in which man's true being (and future) is displayed, a being which he shares even now (proleptic-ally) in Christ, and which, presumably, he will come to participate in directly (i.e., in his own actions and decisions) under the impact of the Holy Spirit.

There is thus no irreductible discontinuity between Adam (created human nature) and Christ. The "humanity of God" manifested in the man Jesus constitutes the eschatological form and goal determining all men. Created human essence, then, though it may in some sense have and retain its own integrity and distinctness, cannot be set over against

---

[1] *Ibid.*, p. 299. Cf. *The Humanity of God*, p. 52f.
[2] III/4, p. 663.

the humanity of Christ as its ontological contrary [1]. So an adequate reading of the human, Barth asserts, always moves from Christ to Adam, never the reverse:

> Human existence, as constituted by our relationship with Adam in our unhappy past as weak, sinners, godless, enemies, has no independent reality, status or importance of its own. It is only an indirect witness to the reality of Jesus Christ and to the original and essential human existence that He inaugurates and reveals. The righteous decision of God has fallen upon men not in Adam but in Christ. But in Christ it has also fallen upon Adam, upon our relationship to him and so upon our unhappy past. When we know Christ, we also know Adam as the one who belongs to Him [2].

Between Christ and Adam, there is "the formal identity of the one human nature which is not annulled or transformed even by sin" [3]. Beside this, however, must be placed the recognition that within this formal continuity there is a material discontinuity establishing a difference, but not a final separation, between them. What this means, again, is that created human essence receives an ineradicable grounding and determination in Christ which pertains to all men whether they are aware of it or not. Man's essential and original nature, the real meaning of his creaturely form and being, is given only in Christ:

> We are real men in our relationship to Adam, only because Adam is not our head and we are not his members, because above Adam and before Adam is Christ. Our relationship to Christ has an essential priority and superiority over our relationship to Adam. He is the Victor and we in Him are those who are awaiting the victory. Our human nature is preserved by sharing Adam's nature, because Adam's humanity is a *provisional copy* of the real humanity that is in Christ [4].

---

[1] As I shall examine this possibility in detail in Chapter V of this study, it will suffice here merely to indicate that Barth does discuss the common humanity of man in its integrity *apart* from its ontological determination in Jesus. Cf. III/2, Par. 45, Part 2, "The Basic Form of Humanity". Whether this is sufficient to establish man in his subjective identity as self and agent is a question that will need to be examined carefully.

[2] *Christ and Adam: Man and Humanity in Romans 5*, T.A. Smail, trans., Scottish Journal of Theology Occasional Papers No. 5 (Edinburgh: Oliver and Boyd, 1956), p. 7. Cf. IV/1, p. 53f.

[3] Barth, *Christ and Adam*, p. 9.

[4] *Ibid.*, p. 10. Cf. Paul Lehmann, *Ethics in a Christian Context*, pp. 118ff.

A working out of the ethical significance and thrust of the determination and identity given man in Christ will be taken up in the next three chapters of this study. Before moving to these, however, I must indicate a difficulty that emerges from a consideration of the total action of God viewed from its center in reconciliation, and the determination of the human resulting from this.

The difficulty can be put in this way. The event of reconciliation provides the basis and exemplification of authentic human essence as this occurs in Jesus Christ. This does not constitute a mere possibility, however. It is for Barth an indication of man's unavoidable ontological status as the one elected from eternity to be God's covenant partner. This assigns an ineluctable direction and goal for the human, however, which appears to vitiate man's status as the creature distinct from God. The reason for this lies in the fact that for Barth the identity of Jesus as a man is expressible only in terms of his identity as the Son of God. But then if the line between man and God attains ontological convergence in Christ, this at least suggests, if it does not directly entail, an "absorption" of humanity [1], in that man, ontologically and eschatologically considered, becomes simply an extension of a mode of God's own being.

The possibilities for man as ethical agent that emerge from this, will need to be examined carefully to see whether Barth is able to establish a real difference between men generally and the humanity of God in Christ. It is clear that a direction and goal have been set, ontologically, in which all men are participant. If this leads, in turn, to a loss of man's individual identity and subjectivity, then not only the notion of "Christian ethics", but also the relationship and (ostensible) distinction between the events of reconciliation and creation, both of which are grounded in God's eternal decision to enter into covenant with man, become inexplicable.

---

[1] Cf. Arnold B. Come, *An Introduction to Barth's 'Dogmatics'*, p. 154.

CHAPTER FOUR

THE ETHICAL THRUST OF ELECTING GRACE:
THE DIVINE COMMAND

A. The Actuality and Possibility of Christian Ethics

The possibility of ethically significant human action rests exclusively on what Barth has described as "divine ethics". Borrowing a suggestive phrase from Paul Lehmann, we can rephrase Barth slightly and say that man's ethical activity and participation is preceded and encompassed at all points by "the politics of God" [1].

The action of God in Jesus Christ forms for Barth the first and decisive element in the unfolding of the covenant existing between God and man. It is the concrete fulfillment of God's eternal decision to turn to man and be present to him as his gracious God; and it is the explicit manifestation of the destiny and goal of created human nature resulting from its election to covenant with God. Both dimensions of this action are seen clearly as event in Jesus Christ, who is both electing God and elected man, the humiliated Son of God and the exalted Son of Man. It is from this christological center that the total sweep of the divine purpose and activity is to be viewed. The event of reconciliation provides the exposed nerve of God's inclusive temporality in its movement from creation to redemption, and the attendant status and determination devolving onto the human through its inclusion in that event in Jesus Christ. A full treatment of the impingement of the divine activity on the

---

[1] *Ethics in a Christian Context*, pp. 86ff. In adopting this phrase, Professor Lehmann underlines the seriousness of intent and concern it embodies: "When we say, then, that God is a 'politician', and that what God is doing in the world is 'making or doing politics', it is the Aristotelian *definition* and the biblical *description* of what is going on that we have in mind. According to the *definition*, we may say that politics is activity, and reflection upon activity, which aims at and analyzes what it takes to make and to keep human life *human* in the world. According to the *description*, what it takes to make and to keep human life human in the world is 'the unsearchable riches of Christ ... the plan of the mystery hidden for ages in God who created all things; that through the church the manifold wisdom of God might now be made known to the principalities and powers in the heavenly places ... until we all attain ... to mature manhood, to the measure of the stature of the fullness of Christ' ". *Ibid.*, p. 85.

human thus necessitated (1) an indication of its ultimate foundation in the trinitarian being of God; (2) an exposure of its concrete manifestation in the threefold dimensionality of Jesus Christ; together with (3) a statement of the ontological locus and direction of behavior issuing from the latter [1].

What this leads to is the insight, expressed in our earlier sketch of Barth's approach to ethics, that the question and problem of locating the good and identifying right behavior, because already answered in Jesus Christ, cease to be legitimate concerns for Christian ethics. The "ethical problem", accordingly, "is exclusively bound up in the question whether and to what extent human action constitutes a praising of the grace of Jesus Christ?" [2]. With this, a universal directional indicative is brought to bear on the behavioral question. It is precisely in this way and at this point that every concrete possibility within the range of human ethical response and action is inextricably rooted in the actuality of grace manifested in the event of reconciliation [3]. It remains now to indicate the way in which the "divine ethics" actualized in Jesus Christ falls over into the context of human decision and action, providing it with directional structure and focus.

The most significant behavioral clue, in this respect, is provided in the *obedience* of Jesus Christ as the humiliated and suffering Son of God. Since the obedient action of Christ is the ontological pattern and

---

[1] This same order is taken over by Professor Lehmann as a means of providing Christian ethics with an adequate grounding. *Ibid.*, Ch. IV, "Christian Ethics and a Theology of Messianism".

[2] II/2, p. 600. Cf. *Christliche Ethik* (München: Chr. Kaiser Verlag, 1946,) p. 8f.

[3] The universalizing thrust of grace may be brought out in two ways. First, in the fact that *every* concrete action and mode of action is referred to the antecedent of behaviour in Jesus Christ. And secondly, in the fact that this locus exhibits an inclusive ontological and behavioral determination of the human (Cf. II/2, p. 601). An emphasis on the universalizing impact of grace should not obscure the point brought out by Professor Lehmann, that Christian ethics, empirically considered, *cannot* be universalized, i.e., through the agency of general rules or principles. Even so, the point is still to be made that Christian ethical behavior, whatever it comes to in specific cases, will always be a doing of "the will of God". Cf. *Ethics in a Christian Context*, p. 77. What emerges from this the is fact that although men are placed under a general determination by the grace of God, the empirical consequences of this, which constitute a glorification of the grace of Christ and thus a doing of God's will, are themselves incapable of generalization.

determination of all correct human ethical action, it follows that the latter will necessarily have this property, regardless of the specific empirical variations of the context in which it occurs. An exploration of the resources provided by Barth that make possible a transition from the *possibility* of obedience to its empirical actualization in specific decisions and actions [1] would lead into an analysis of the ontological and existential structure of the human apart from Christ. What would be crucial here, of course, is the degree to which independent status and function remain attributable to "the humanity of man" apart from, or beyond, "the humanity of God".

To begin at this point, however, would be to miss a prior question which comes logically into view, and which must be answered before the issue of man's identity as ethical agent can be examined. The prior question has to do with that which evokes human obedience, and which gives shape and direction to it. It is insufficient, in this respect, merely to refer to the grace of God evidenced in the action of Christ. The problem is not that this is an inappropriate response. Indeed, in a final sense it is the persistent point of reference to which all human action is referred and by which it is directed. If grace is not to become a merely formal referent, however, it must be precised and fleshed out in such a way that its dynamic impingement on human action will provide a sufficiently stringent and consistent basis on which to ground human obedience. This necessity is realized nicely in Barth's use of the notion of "the command of God" (*das Gebot Gottes*), which functions both as the locus of all ethical truth manifested generally within the human [2], and as the second element in the covenant between God and man [3].

B. Indicative and Imperative: The Order of Gospel and Law

There is no more stringent indication in the *Dogmatics* of the underlying unity of God's action than the relationship Barth establishes between Gospel and Law, which finds its continuation within theological ethics in the resulting interplay between indicative and imperative.

---

[1] A transition which was seen to be ambiguous, at bast, in Barth's reading of ethics prior to the *Church Dogmatics*.

[2] II/2, p. 584.

[3] *Ibid.*, p. 564f.

The unity of Gospel and Law stands as a dramatic exposure of the way in which the action of God in assuming responsibility for man necessitates a corresponding embodiment of responsibility in human action:

> As God makes himself responsible for man, he also makes man responsible. Ruling grace is commanding grace. The Gospel itself and as such has the form and shape of the Law. The one Word of God is both Gospel and Law. It is not Law by itself and independent of the Gospel, but it is also not Gospel without Law. It is Gospel according to its content, and Law according to its form and shape. It is first Gospel and then Law. It is the Gospel which includes and encloses within itself the Law, as the Ark of the Covenant the tables of Sinai. But it is both: Gospel and Law. The one Word of God as the revelation and work of his grace is also Law, and so also a prior decision concerning man's self-determination. It is the claiming of human freedom, and so also a regulation and judgment of the use made of that freedom [1].

Not surprisingly, Barth's unification of Gospel and Law as the content and form, respectively, of the one Word of God, which represents a studied attempt to move beyond the traditional Lutheran deployment of those categories, has drawn the fire of his critics [2]. A consideration of critical reaction to Barth on this point can proceed meaningfully, however, only on the basis of a prior examination of his position. The most complete statement of Barth's approach to the problem is found in a monograph which he wrote in 1956, *Evangelium und Gesetz* [3]. This monograph, together with statements scattered throughout the *Church Dogmatics*, will enable us to discern with some precision his reading of the matter.

---

[1] *Ibid.*, p. 567. Cf. IV/2, p. 605f.

[2] The sharpest criticism of Barth on this point seems to be that of Helmut Thielicke. Cf. *Theologische Ethik* (Tübingen: J.C.B. Mohr, 1951-1958), especially Band I, Pars. 569, 571, 573, 588, *et passim*. Less stringent, but equally pointed, are the questions raised by H. Richard Niebuhr in: *The Responsible Self* (New York: Harper and Row, 1963), pp. 66, 131, 158.

[3] *Evangelium und Gesetz* (München: Chr. Kaiser Verlag, 1956), hereafter cited as *EG*, published as number 50 in the series: *Theologische Existenz Heute*. This monograph made its appearance exactly a decade after the publication (in German) of Volume II/2 of the *Dogmatics*, where the unity between Gospel and Law is sounded at the outset of Barth's initial development of ethics as the command of God. It may therefore be assumed that it constitutes his considered position on the matter.

Barth begins with an acknowledgement that Law and Gospel indeed denote a duality in scripture, but argues that this duality is overcome in the *one* Word of God understood always as a Word of grace [1]. What this will mean is that the Law cannot be given independent status; it can be recognized and appropriated only within the context of the Gospel:

> The Gospel is not the Law, just as the Law is not the Gospel. But because the Law is given in the Gospel, and proceeds with it from beginning to end, it follows that we must first of all know about the Gospel, in order to know the Law, and not the reverse [2].

The Law, then, is meaningful within the context of theological ethics only when it is grounded in Gospel, i.e., when it is rooted in a revelation, benefit, and election already accomplished. The imperative presented in the notion of Law is thus removed from the abstract and made concrete [3]. In its concrete form within the Gospel, and relative to it, the Law is still legitimately to be seen as "no less God's Word" [4].

What follows from this is that both Gospel and Law will be interpreted as *grace*. The *content* of grace is given as Gospel; the *form* of grace is given as Law. The ordering center of grace serves to underline and exemplify once again Barth's persistence in grounding every theological (and so ethical) point squarely within Christology. To speak of grace, of the unity of the one Word of God, is to speak of Jesus Christ [5]. And, since Christ stands eternally at the beginning and ending of God's activity and its intent for man, it follows that the unity of Gospel and Law is grounded ontologically in God's eternal decision to enter into covenant with man, thereby electing him to fellowship with himself [6].

---

[1] "The Word of God is the one 'Word of Truth', the Word of the 'Father of Lights, in whom there is no alteration or change between light and darkness' ... The opposition of Gospel and Law indeed denotes, as regards the scripture, a duality. It can even denote a discontinuity. More important than their duality or discontinuity, however, is the harmony between them in the one Word of this Father". *EG*, p. 6.

[2] *Ibid.*, p. 5. Cf. I/2, p. 343.

[3] I/2, p. 423.

[4] *EG*, p. 7.

[5] *Ibid.*, p. 10f.; I/1, p. 342; II/1, p. 432; II/2, p. 624f; IV/1, p. 56.

[6] "Jesus Christ—not an empty *Logos*, but Jesus Christ, the Word who became flesh, the child born in Bethlehem, the man put to death at Golgotha and resurrected in the garden of Joseph of Arimathea, the man of this history,

Neither in the Old Testament nor the New, then, can Law be separated from Gospel and given independent status as an autonomous set of demands to which man is accountable. The Law is always located squarely within the "teleological order" (*teleologischen Ordnung*) of revelation in its dynamic movement from creation to reconciliation to redemption [1]. Within this order, the Law is given its appropriate place and function as the "taskmaster" (*Zuchtmeister*) of the Gospel [2]. In their respective roles as the content and form of revelation, then, Gospel and Law indicate the inner and outer dimensions of grace.

The christological ordering of Law may be seen in more detail when a delineation of the dimensions it exhibits as "taskmaster" to the Gospel is undertaken. The most inclusive aspect of Law in this respect is seen in the way in which it draws attention to the lordship of God over man [3]. The lordship of God exhibited in the Law can be further analyzed into the components of judgment and demand. The judgment contained in the Law reveals the opposition involved in God's encroachment on man. The outer side of grace, in the first instance, consists in a direct frontal assault on every humanly conceived attempt to secure self-justification. Such attempts occur when the Law is interpreted as a system of ordinances marking off negative and positive possibilities for self-fulfillment. A distortion of grace inevitably accompanies this, for now Christ is taken as the personification of man's highest ideals, and so as "the spirit and leaven of our century" (*dem Geist und Geschmack unseres Jahrhunderts*) [4]. In the end, man is left at the mercy of a series of abstract, fragmented laws which can lead only to a loss of that unity and order of self for which he has been ordained by God [5]. The antidote to this fragmentation lies in the judgment imposed in the Law, which simulta-

---

is the unity of both, is both wholly and together. He is the promise and the command, the Gospel and the Law, the consolation of God to man and the claim of God upon man. That he is both of these as God's Word spoken in his Word, as God's Word which has become Word, is his own possession as the eternal Son of God prior to us. He is, accordingly, the preexistent *Deus pro nobis*". IV/1, p. 56. Cf. I/2, p. 424.

[1] II/1, p. 267.

[2] *Ibid.*

[3] For Barth, the sum of revelation is given in the statement, "God reveals himself as the Lord" (*Gott offenbart sich als der Herr*). I/1, p. 323. Cf. III/1, p. 70f.; I/2, p. 552f.

[4] *EG*, p. 23.

[5] *Ibid.*, pp. 21, 24.

neously exposes the distance between God and man, the inability of
man to bridge this independently of God's self-manifestation, and the
resulting guilt when man forgets this and attempts to make himself
secure [1].

Concurrent with the judgment presented by the Law is the demand
it imposes. This is not a demand which focuses on the fulfillment of
regulations. Rather, it calls forth our unconditional trust in, and acceptance of, God's action in Jesus Christ. Taken together, trust and acceptance delineate (for us) the total answer to the question what it would
mean to fear and love God [2]. This is the positive meaning of the Law
as it is given to the covenant community (Israel and the Church) *together*.
Rightly understood, then, Barth is arguing that the status and role of
Law in the Old Testament is not different from that in the New. So,
when Barth asserts that Christians are those who "in virtue of the power
of the death and resurrection of Jesus Christ have really left the situation
of Israel behind, who are really free from the Law which finally can only
accuse and condemn, because it confirms that they are sinners" [3], this
must be understood to refer to the Law in its distorted form as an
independent set of regulations operating outside the framework of
grace. Within the embracing framework of God's election of man,
and the covenant initiated and sustained in fulfillment of this, Gospel
and Law display an inner dialectic and interplay representative of the
"Yes" and the "No", or of the freeing (pardoning) and binding, or of
the promise given man (in Jesus Christ) and the requirement this imposes
on him. The significance of Law for Israel (and all men) is that it establishes an inexorable direction for human existence [4]. To be sure, the
direction thus established presupposes certain conditions to be fulfilled.
The point is, these are not independent conditions to be incorporated
into man's behavior through his own power. Any fulfillment of the
conditions imposed on human existence by the Law will depend strictly
on grace, i.e., on the prevenient, embracing thrust of the Gospel. The

---

[1] *Ibid.*, p. 18f.; II/1, p. 393. The judgment imposed by the Law is not,
however, a momentary reality marking man's initial encounter with grace.
Within theological ethics understood as the command of God, it plays a
persistent role. Indeed, relative to the other dimensions of the command
(claim, decision), it is given a kind of priority by Barth.

[2] *EG*, pp. 15f., 30.

[3] III/2, p. 367.

[4] IV/2, p. 668f.; I/2, p. 312.

direction set for all men, then, is participation in God's own action. And the condition which this imposes, the "binding and indispensable content of the law of the covenant imposed on man", is the response of gratitude and thanksgiving [1].

Obedience to the Law *means* acceptance and recognition of grace as this encounters man in the Gospel [2]. The obedience given in man's grateful response to God's action is at the same time an acknowledgement of the judgment imposed by the Gospel against every humanly conceived scheme of self-justification, and so a recognition of the lordship of God over the human. At this point, we are in a position to indicate once again, but in a different way, the importance of the christological grounding of Law. The *fulfillment* of the Law, like the enactment of the Gospel, is enclosed within the embracing context of grace. It will therefore be the case that the judgment and demand imposed by the Law, and so the recognition of the lordship of God required by the Law, occur first as aspects of the history of Jesus Christ. In Christ, God himself is "the doer of the Law" [3]. The validity of the Law lies precisely in the fact that "God commands first and only on the basis that he himself has given and realized and fulfilled what he commands" [4]. By this action, man has been liberated from autonomous law, the law which leads only toward sin and death in alienation and estrangement from God. And by this same action, man has been set free for service [5], for a recognition of the lordship of God, and the judgment and demand which this includes [6].

---

[1] IV/2, p. 44.
[2] I/2, p. 338f.
[3] II/2, p. 627.
[4] *Ibid.*
[5] *Ibid.*, p. 656.
[6] It is clear, on Barth's analysis, that Law in itself cannot function as a propaedeutic vehicle bringing man to a point of despair in which the need for grace is recognized. Law does level a judgment against man, but only as it is enclosed within the Gospel. Barth would therefore reject Brunner's notion that after man's breaking of his original relation with God (a relation signalled by the absence of Law), he is confronted by Law as an impersonal and abstract substitute for God: "There is now a neutral or abstract authority between God and man. God no longer confronts man personally, but he is represented by an impersonal authority, by the Law". *The Christian Doctrine of Creation and Redemption*, p. 120. Barth would reject both the notion that man's original relation to God was grounded exclusively in the Gospel, to the exclusion of

The various nuances of the Law will be explored at length in the next section of this chapter, where the consequences of the command of grace for marking off and structuring the ethical context within which man's behavior will take place will be examined. For the moment, I wish only to indicate some of the implications suggested in our analysis thus far. It is clear, first of all, that the actualization of grace in Jesus Christ is at the same the establishment of the Law. This entails that the real meaning and significance of the Law become evident only on a christological basis [1]. Second, the Law thus established can in no sense be given independent status and function—anymore than the Gospel can be treated as a promise given man *beyond* the Law. Gospel and Law are inextricably tied together as the inner and outer sides of grace. From this it follows, third, that the covenant community, Israel and the Church in their unity, are obligated to make evident the significance of Law (freedom in responsibility) in its relation to Gospel (election and pardon) [2]. Fourth, because the Law as the form of the Gospel has to do with man's real being in Jesus Christ, i.e., with "real man" [3], it will not remain external, but will claim him from within [4]. Human action in accordance with Law (command) will therefore signal man's recognition, and perhaps his realization, of authentic being. Finally, attention should be drawn to the way in which Barth's analysis of the notion of Law appears to move beyond the limitations of prescriptive formation and expression. That prescriptive expression can be given at least a *relative* function is suggested in his discussion of the behavioral significance of the Old Testament decalogue and the Sermon on the Mount. It is also clear, however, that such prescriptive formulations enjoy no independent status. Rather, they are understandable only in relation to the total ontological and behavioral matrix provided by grace, which includes both Law *and* Gospel. When this is recognized, however, it underlines once again the character of grace as event, and so leads away from a static or formalized conception

---

the Law (Cf. III/1, p. 312), and that his subsequent relation was to an abstract, impersonal Law *outside* the Gospel. As we have seen, Gospel and Law hang together from the beginning in the *one* Word of God. So there can be no Gospel without Law, just as there can be no Law without Gospel (Cf. II/2, p. 567).

[1] II/2, p. 624f.

[2] *Ibid.*, p. 625f.

[3] Cf. III/2, Par. 44, Part 3.

[4] I/2, p. 423f.

of Law and onto an understanding of it that displays an incipient (although unexpected) congeniality with H. Richard Niebuhr's use of the concept of "responsibility", which attempts to move beyond the limitations occasioned by an exclusive dependence on teleological and deontological approaches to the moral life and existence before God [1]. This apparent congeniality can be better explored, however, in relation to Niebuhr's reservations about Barth's ordering of Gospel and Law.

It should be noted, at the outset, that Niebuhr's criticism of Barth on this point amounts to a *reservation* rather than an outright rejection. Barth's position (along with Bultmann's) is located by Niebuhr within the contours of a deontological approach to ethics [2], the primary ingredients of which are law (rules, commands) and obedience. The interpretive symbol that emerges from this is that of man-as-citizen involved in the continual and necessary process of recognizing existing, or legislating new, laws, and following this with consent (acceptance) and obedience.

---

[1] Cf. *The Responsible Self*, pp. 55ff., 98ff., 136ff., *et passim*. Niebuhr approaches the issue of responsible selfhood as an exercise in "Christian moral philosophy" (*Ibid.*, p. 42). This immediately sets a different tone than is found in Barth, and allows for a more obvious attention to extra-Christian and dogmatic sources, i.e., philosophy, sociology and psychology. It is at least worth wondering, however, whether, in spite of these differences, and the obvious divergence in linguistic form and expression to which they lead, Niebuhr and Barth do not fall into a closer proximity in their notions of responsibility than could be allowed on a casual inspection of their positions. To be sure, any attempt to make out a case for this proximity would depend on a careful interpretation and evaluation of both men. Charles C. West has already performed this sort of analysis and comparison of Barth and *Reinhold* Niebuhr (Cf. *Communism and the Theologians*, pp. 240ff., 314ff.). Considering the influence Barth has had on H. Richard Niebuhr's theological development (Cf. the opening essays by Hans Frei in: *Faith and Ethics*), a similar undertaking here might prove equally fruitful.

[2] *The Responsible Self* (New York: Harper & Row, 1963), pp. 60, 101, 126. Actually, in terms of the criticism Niebuhr directs against Barth, it would be more precise to identify Barth's position as a species of rule-deontology. Niebuhr specifies only deontology and deontological theories generally, without distinguishing between rule- and act-deontological theories. That distinction is important, however, for I believe that Barth's position is properly identified as one embodying an act-deontology. The distinction between act- and rule-deontological theories is drawn by William K. Frankena in his book, *Ethics*, in the Foundations of Philosophy Series, Elizabeth and Monroe Beardsley, eds. (Englewood Cliffs: Prentice Hall, 1963), pp. 15f., 21-25.

The "law" in question may be either individual, familial, societal, universal (nature) or cosmic (will of God). The function to which law is put emerges consistently as the creation of those conditions which make possible the emergence of a viable "republic", i.e., the establishment of *unity* between disparate and conflicting claims, tendencies, and drives, whether at a personal, social, or universal level:

> We come into being under the rules of family, neighborhood, and nation, subject to the regulation of our action by others. Against these rules we can and do rebel, yet find it necessary—morally necessary, that is—to consent to some laws and to give ourselves rules, or to administer our lives in accordance with some discipline ... Those who employ the citizen symbol for the understanding and regulation of self-conduct, have various domains in view. For some the republic that is to be governed is mostly that of the multifarious self, a being which is a multiplicity seeking unity or a unity diversifying itself into many roles ... Or the republic in view is a human community of selves in which the manifoldness is that of many persons with many desires and subject to many regulations issuing from each other ... Or again, the community we have in mind may be universal society, and the quest may be after those laws of nature or that will of the universal God which the person is asked to accept not only with consent but actively, as legislating citizen in a universal domain [1].

While recognizing the positive contribution of the symbol of man-as-citizen, with its accompanying emphasis on law, to "our quest for the truth about ourselves and ... our quest for true existence" [2], Niebuhr undertakes to explore the additional illumination that may be given to these concerns through adopting the "new symbolism of responsibility" [3].

---

[1] *Ibid.*, p. 53f.

[2] *Ibid.*, p. 56.

[3] *Ibid.* Niebuhr makes it clear that "the idea of the moral life as the responsible life" offers only "a key—not *the* key—to the understanding of that Biblical ethos which represents the historic norm of the Christian life" (*Ibid.*, p. 65). Niebuhr also seeks to move beyond an approach to man's existence and the moral life that makes use of the symbol of man the doer or maker within the framework of a teleological reading of human action. I have not considered this approach because it seems to me that Barth's view of *human* ethical activity is not teleological, despite his willingness to describe the embracing activity of God in its movement from creation to redemption along teleological lines. Within the context of human action, teleology is replaced by the ingression of man's real (eschatological) future (already posited and determined in and by Jesus Christ) into his present, and the accompanying necessity this entails for immediate response and activity.

It is in relation to this shift away from an approach to the moral life along the lines of a rule-deontology that Niebuhr raises criticism against Barth's ordering of the relation between Gospel and Law. At the outset, it should be noted that the notion of responsibility is not simply omitted in teleological and deontological theories. Rather, what happens in these approaches is that "it is usually translated with the aid of the older images as meaning direction toward goals or as ability to be moved by respect for law" [1]. A consideration of Niebuhr's criticism suggests both that Barth's notion of responsibility is not adequately expressed as "respect for law", and that the reason for this lies in the dynamic configuration and content that Barth gives to Law as the outer side of the total movement of grace understood exclusively as *event*. Or, to put the matter positively, Barth's notion of responsibility can be interpreted as "respect for law" only to the extent that the dynamic configuration and content of the latter within the context of grace is kept clearly and consistently in view.

Niebuhr's criticism of Barth proceeds along two lines. First, there is the accusation that Barth has introduced "non-Christian though not non-Biblical symbols, such as commandment, law, obedience, and permission" [2] into the context of Christian thinking about ethics. Actually, this caveat emerges against the background of what Niebuhr sees as Barth's excessive use of the Christ symbol, so that it brings us to the center of Niebuhr's disenchantment with Barth, the latter's attempt to ground the whole of theology exclusively in Christology [3]. The second point Niebuhr raises is that Barth's employment of (Kantian) legal terminology with its attendant notion of obedience, within theolog-

---

[1] *Ibid.*, p. 57.

[2] *The Responsible Self*, p. 158.

[3] "In our time the effort to achieve a completely Christocentric and solely Christo-morphic form of thinking and acting has been confined to theology, most notably to Karl Barth's theology. But actually in such theology, as in the case of the exclusive Christian communities of the past, other symbols have had to be employed if the symbol of Christ was to be used. Barth, to take this representative of the most consistent Christian symbolism as our example, attempts to dismiss all analogies, all metaphors, all symbols from Christian speech and conduct except Jesus Christ. But, of course, he cannot interpret the meaning of Jesus Christ without the aid of other metaphors and symbols such as Word of God, Son of God, Servant, Lord, covenant, humiliation, exaltation, reconciliation, salvation". *Ibid.*, p. 158. Cf. the comments of James Gustafson on this point, *Ibid.*, pp. 13, 15 footnote 7.

ical ethics, proceeds by means of a transformation in meaning resulting
in terminological ambiguity:

> At all times, moreover, but particularly among the German interpreters
> in whom the Kantian symbolism holds sway, the deontological inter-
> pretation of man the obedient legislator has been used not only as the
> key to Biblical interpretation but for the definition of the true Christian
> life. For Barth and Bultmann alike in our times, not to speak of most
> interpreters of the Old Testament, the ethics of the Bible, and Christian
> ethics too, is the ethics of obedience. How to interpret Christian freedom
> and what to make of eschatology within this framework has taxed the
> ingenuity of the interpreters severely ... Barth has had to transform the
> law into a form of the gospel and the commandment into permission
> in order to reconcile the peculiarity of gospel ethos with deontological
> thinking [1].

The apparent ambiguities in Barth's position, however, may as
easily result from a failure to note that the terminology in question is
put to a radically different use (and so given a totally different meaning)
from that found in Kant, as from any obvious inconsistency or slip-
periness on Barth's part. It is in relation to this difference in Barth's
use of legal terminology to express the outer side of grace that the
possibility emerges of a reasonably close juxtaposition of the concept
of responsibility operative in both Niebuhr and Barth. The preliminary
step in this direction will consist in indicating what Niebuhr wants to
mean by the term "responsibility".

The basic point involved in his approach can be stated directly:

> What is implicit in the idea of responsibility is the image of man-the-
> answerer, man engaged in dialogue, man acting in response to action
> upon him [2].

As with the symbols of man-the-maker and man-the-citizen, so also
with that of man-the-answerer, we are dealing with what Niebuhr calls
a "synecdochic analogy" [3]. This kind of analogy arises [4] when, in attempt-

---

[1] *Ibid.*, p. 66; Cf. p. 130f.

[2] *Ibid.*, p. 56.

[3] *Ibid.*

[4] Niebuhr implies that all analogies, models, etc., in terms of which we
attempt to understand our personal, social, and universal relatedness and unity
are synecdochic in character. It should be pointed out that there appears to
be no parallel between Niebuhr's notion of a "synecdochic analogy" and the
function of analogy in Barth's method, beyond the superficial point that both
use the same word.

ing "to understand ourselves in our wholeness we use the image of a part of our activity; *only now we think of all our actions as having the pattern of what we do when we answer another who addresses us*" [1]. The specific components that fill out the concept of responsibility underlying the symbol of man-the-answerer are response, interpretation, accountability, and social solidarity [2]. When these are brought together, we have a definition that is both operationally and contextually satisfying:

> The idea of pattern or responsibility ... may summarily and abstractly be defined as the idea of an agent's action as response to an action upon him in accordance with his interpretation of the latter action and with his expectation of response to his response; and all of this in a continuing community of agents [3].

I am not concerned here with the specific working out of this definition in Niebuhr's thought. What is of interest, I feel, is the dynamic character of Niebuhr's reading of the human situation generally, and man's moral life in particular, under the rubric of responsibility. Further, it should be kept in mind that what I am suggesting in drawing a comparison between Niebuhr and Barth is that their respective notions of responsibility are *similar*, not identical. It is not necessary, then, to locate precise parallels in Barth to the components of response, interpretation, accountability, and social solidarity found in Niebuhr's definition. This could perhaps be done, but not, I feel, without a certain amount of strain, which might end by blurring the fundamental similarity I wish to indicate. This similarity is grounded, I have tried to suggest, in the *dynamism* which both Barth and Niebuhr infuse into their reading of responsibility. When it is recalled that Barth's employment of the category of responsibility is inextricably related to to his notion of Law, the possibility emerges for an interpretation and understanding of the latter which moves beyond the somewhat formalized approach indicated by a rule-deontology, and into the more dynamic immediacy of an act-deontology. We are now at a point where the specific considerations in Barth's handling of responsibility and Law that seem to lead in this direction can be indicated.

The first thing to notice about Barth's notion of human responsibility is that it does not function independently. Rather, it is seen as a total response to the responsibility God assumes for man in Jesus Christ.

---

[1] *Ibid.*, Italics added.
[2] *Ibid.*, pp. 61-65.
[3] *Ibid.*, p. 65.

But since God's action in making himself responsible for man, his being totally with and for man in Jesus Christ, constitutes the dynamism of the Gospel and the "inner" dimension of grace, it will follow that the Law, as the "outer" dimension of that same grace, will serve to indicate the way in which the Gospel presses for recognition and affirmation in human decision and action. And, since the grace that is made evident in Christ is simply the external, historical manifestation of God's eternal decision to have man for his responsible partner, it becomes impossible to mark off a separation between Gospel and Law at any point within the total movement from creation to redemption in which God's decision is made actual. The Law in its relation to Gospel will always indicate the dynamic binding of man in responsible reaction to what God is doing in the world. There is, then, absolutely no way, from Barth's perspective, in which Law can be legitimately separated from Gospel. Every move in this direction, whether it proceeds in terms of an abstracting or a historicizing of Law, is categorically excluded from the outset [1].

The continuity between divine and human responsibility exemplified in Barth's notion of Law is additionally important in that it sets a direction for the latter. The direction of man's responsibility is established in relation to the judgment and demand contained within the Law. The judgment, as we have seen, falls at the point of our attempts to secure self-justification and adequacy. The point here is not that man is to forego his own independent systems of law and morality in exchange for the more viable "system of law" embodied within the Gospel. This would simply lead from one form of external bondage into another. The positive point that emerges beyond this misunderstanding (which inevitably allows for the subtle establishment of an autonomous Law) is seen in the interplay that Barth sets up between the judgment and the demand of Law as an integral dimension of grace. The *judgment* of Law is designed to set us free from dependence on alien laws which result in a diminishing of man's real humanity by distorting both the possibility and the actuality of his freedom. The actuality of human freedom has been demonstrated and determined by Jesus Christ. The possibility of human freedom focuses on the *demand* presented by Law. The demand in question has nothing to do with the fulfillment of prescriptive

---

[1] Cf. Barth's criticism of the latter, historicizing tendency, which occurred as an aspect of the older federal theology (IV/1, pp. 57ff.).

legal formulae. Instead, it centers on the necessity placed upon man to respond in openness and trust to God's grace presented in the Gospel by recognizing and accepting it as the condition on which his authentic being, i.e., being-in-freedom, is grounded. In this respect, it can be argued that for Barth "obedience to the Law" *means* the recognition and acceptance of grace [1].

The fact that authentic human freedom is intimately tied to the Law exposes a third consideration about Barth's employment of legal terminology. To get this clearly before us, it is necessary to recall that the Gospel presented in Jesus Christ includes the full reality of both God and man. In Christ, the proper destiny and goal of all men is given. It follows, then, that the Law (as the outer dimension of grace) and the responsibility it entails, cannot possibly constitute, from Barth's perspective, some kind of abstract, alien requirement placed *over* the human. Rather, the notion of Law (command) and responsibility are tied inextricably to man's own proper being in Jesus Christ. Thus, they will evidence existential continuity with man's given identity as moral agent, i.e., as one who acts in *response* to what God has done and continues to do in the world by way of nudging man toward a gradual acknowledgment and realization of that authentic humanity which is already his (ontologically) in Jesus Christ. The response in question focuses exclusively on immediate acts of obedience or disobedience, i.e., on ethical behavior which will necessarily exhibit continuity or discontinuity with the identity and direction set for man in Jesus Christ. Man's response, then, is not to a (formalized) universal law or laws that evoke "respect". A full delineation of the immediacy of Law as God's command would disclose that the notion of response is oriented totally toward the direct activity of God in giving substance, structure, and direction to the context within which man is called upon

---

[1] It is clear from this that for Barth the notion of obedience is as much an *indicative* as an imperative term. The significance of Law for man's authentic humanity is by no means new in the *Dogmatics*. In his 1926 essay, "Church and Culture", Barth stated: "That command is merely taken and lifted out of the sphere of wishing, of choice, and is made the actual, the divine command. The command revives the promise which from the creation lies dormant in the law of nature; the law of nature is given, just because of the promise, necessity ... Sanctification, election for God, doing the will of God, is always in content being human. Men are to become men, not more than men; but also not less". *Theology and Church*, p. 346.

to act [1]. So, for Barth, *all* human action will exhibit "the pattern of what we do when we answer another who addresses us" [2], where, in the first instance at least, this "other" is always God.

Finally, it should be noted that Barth's analysis of Law as command invoking responsibility involves a concern for, and leads to the establishment of, unity, which was seen earlier to be an important ingredient in Niebuhr's analysis [3].

What emerges from this discussion, hopefully, is both an indication of the similarity holding between Niebuhr and Barth in their respective notions of responsibility, and a softening of Niebuhr's criticisms of Barth. The upshot of this may be indicated in fairly summary fashion: Barth's identification of the Law as the form of the Gospel indicates neither inconsistency nor ambiguity, for the simple reason that Barth invests the whole notion of Law with a meaning drawn exclusively from the context of grace. The additional fact devolving from this, that the Law, in presenting itself as command, is given the operational aspect of *permission*, seems merely to underline again the importance of keeping to a dynamic rather than a static view of Law. In the end, this focuses persitently on the necessity (and inevitability) of man's *response*.

The logical move beyond this point in the discussion would be a careful delineation of the precise meaning of the Law as the "command" of God. Only after this has been completed can we attempt an assessment of the difficulties that attend Barth's deployment of the notions of Law and command in theological ethics. Before moving to this, however, it will be instructive to consider the objections raised by Helmut Thielicke against Barth's unification of Gospel and Law, as an indication of the response from the side of Lutheran theology to Barth's ordering of these.

Thielicke's objections differ from Niebuhr's in that they proceed along dogmatic rather than ethical lines. The underlying concern in Thielicke's reaction to Barth is that theology retain the tension between God's holiness and love. Another way of putting this is to say that

---

[1] See section C below of this chapter. It is in this way that Barth's reading of ethics, and of law in particular, proceeds along the lines of an act- rather than a rule-deontology.

[2] Niebuhr, *The Responsible Self*, p. 56.

[3] The importance of unity in Barth's analysis emerges clearly in his general statement of theological ethics as the command of God. Cf. II/2, Par. 38, Part 3, "The Goodness of the Divine Decision". This is explored in the following section of this chapter.

theology must exhibit a real distinction between judgment and grace, so that these are not collapsed or merged into unity [1]. In Barth, however, Thielicke sees a blurring of this distinction, and so a loss of tension, between judgment and grace. This emerges, Thielicke feels, from Barth's pronounced interest in the soteriological question, and from his concern that the *unity* of God (and his action) not be endangered or lost by allowing the disparity or tension between holiness and love in God to gain predominance [2].

It is this concern for the unity of God's action that leads Barth, Thielicke argues, to an abstract monism in theology, and to a "world-view" (*Weltanschauung*) of grace centering in the love of God [3]. The problem attendant upon this orientation is that it results in an inevitable loss of the possibility of attaching any sense of movement or progress to salvation history (*heilsgeschichtlichen progressus*) [4]. It is in connection with this difficulty that Thielicke considers Barth's ordering of the Law as the form of the Gospel.

Initially, there are two difficulties in Thielicke's criticism of Barth that should be noted. First, Thielicke seems content to rest his case primarily on a reading of the "early" Barth, citing in support an address delivered in 1920, "Biblical Questions, Insights, and Vistas", and, of course, the *Römerbrief* [5]. Insofar as any development or modification of the position espoused in these is concerned, Thielicke simply asserts a continuing tendency toward "timelessness" (*Zeitlosigkeit*) [6]. The possibility is thus at least suggested that important questions have been begged in this assumption of continuity, particularly where the use of

---

[1] Thielicke, *Theologische Ethik*, Band I, Par. 561, p. 190f.

[2] "What is perceived (perhaps from Barth's position) as a consequence of this tension to be an endangering of the unity of God does not rest upon speculation, but rather upon a pronounced soteriological interest, i.e., an interest in the contemplation, praise, and conceptual expression appropriate to the miracle, the absolutely ungrounded contingency, of the divine love". *Ibid.*, Band I, Par. 563, p. 191.

[3] "Wenn es stimmt, was wir bereits andeuteten: daß nämlich die monistische Entschärfung des Gegensatzes von Gesetz und Evangelium zur zeitlosen Ruhelage der *Idee* dränge (der Idee der Liebe, der Gnade), dann müßten sich an der Bartschen Theologie diese konsequenzen verfolgen laßen, da in ihr ja alle jene monistischen Voraussetzungen gegeben sind". *Ibid.*, Band I, Par. 570, p. 193.

[4] *Ibid.*, Band I, Par. 571, p. 193f.

[5] *Ibid.*, Band I, Par. 594, p. 202.

[6] *Ibid.*, Band I, Par. 596, p. 202f.

what is obviously for Thielicke a pejorative term, "timelessness", is concerned. This is not meant to imply that there are no problems in Barth where the question of the historical is concerned. I have drawn attention to some of these in earlier discussions of theological method in the *Dogmatics*, and of the "determination" of man in connection with the temporality of God [1]. It is obvious, however, that such problems as may center in Barth's handling of the historical will not emerge with any clarity simply on the basis of an assumed continuity between the dialectical and post-dialectical periods in his thought, if for no other reason than that in the latter the category of reconciliation is inserted between creation and redemption. In view of the *historical* importance Barth attaches to this category in the *Dogmatics*, it behooves any interpreter who seeks to do justice to his thought to examine carefully its significance relative to the total sweep of the divine action [2]. Further, it can be noted that even where obvious problems do appear in Barth's notion of the historical, it might be that they are only incidentally related to his treatment of the relation between Gospel and Law. I shall return to this point momentarily.

The second aspect of Thielicke's criticism worth noting is that it depends on an interpretation of the theology of Luther and Calvin which Barth would no doubt find questionable. What Thielicke takes to be the crucial point in Lutheran theology (and so, by implication at least, in Luther himself) is the "passionately emphasized tension between Law and Gospel, which is the unique guarantor of the maintenance of the *historicity of revelation* in theological reflection" [3]. In distinction to this, Barth is placed in continuity with the theological line laid down by Calvin:

> Calvin orders his thinking about Law and Gospel consistently in terms of the unity of his conception of God, and perceives the two, accordingly, not in a relation of tension, but rather in one of harmonious supplementation [4].

Now, it is certainly true that conservative Lutheran theology has

[1] Cf. above, Ch. II, Section A; Ch. III, Section C.

[2] Cf. above, Ch. III, Section B, for an indication of the temporal significance of reconciliation for man's existential participation in God's action in Christ. Actually, Barth moved beyond the simple polarity of creation and redemption at least as early as his 1926 essay, "Church and Culture".

[3] *Theologische Ethik*, Band I, Par. 588, p. 199f.

[4] *Ibid.*, Band I, Par. 614, p. 209.

consistently drawn a relatively sharp distinction between Law and Gospel, which has entailed rather immediate (and sometimes unfortunate) ethical consequences. As Charles West points out, it was precisely this ordering, and the consequences to which it led during the Nazi period in Germany, that provoked Barth to a strong rejection of it, and to an emphatic reordering of the whole relation between Gospel and Law [1]. It is clear, however, that Barth does not regard his position on this matter as one which follows Calvin to the exclusion of Luther. The reason for this, as Barth sees it, is that both Calvin and Luther take essentially the same position as regards the role of the Old and New Testaments as the witness to the *one* revelation of God in Jesus Christ. What this means is that the unity of scripture is strictly underlined in the action of God, and the possibility of a material distinction between the Old and the New Testaments along the lines of a separation between Law and Gospel is excluded. Any difference between them, Barth asserts, is purely formal in nature [2].

Barth's tendency toward a de-historicized theology emerges initially, Thielicke feels, out of his doctrine of election, which rests on an originating movement or "decision" within the being of God involving the Father and the Son. What this means is that there is no separation, on Barth's view, between the original decision or "decree" of God to elect man to fellowship as his covenant partner, and Jesus Christ, in whom and through whom all men are elected [3]. This tendency toward a de-historicized theology is continued, then, in the relation Barth sets up between Gospel and Law. With regard to the loss of genuine movement in salvation history resulting from interpreting the Law as the form of the Gospel, Thielicke's criticism appears to center on the (ostensible) hermeneutical confusion attendant upon taking Christ as the unifying center of both the Old and the New Testament. This leads, Thielicke argues, to a non-historical hermeneutics exhibiting a strong tendency to reconcile investigation with proclamation, which ends by allegorizing the Old Testament [4]. The upshot of this development will unavoidably be

---

[1] *Communism and the Theologians*, p. 291.

[2] I/2, pp. 82ff. Cf. also Barth's latest remarks on this point, and his pointed questions to his Lutheran critics. IV/3.1, p. 427f.

[3] *Theologische Ethik*, Band II/2, p. 716, note 2. Cf. above, Ch. III, Section B, "The Temporality of God".

[4] *Ibid.*, Band I, Pars. 573, p. 194; 577, p. 195. Attention was drawn earlier to the way in which Barth tends to ground hermeneutics in certain prior

"historical docetism" (*Geschichtsdoketismus*) [1], since Christ now functions as a general symbol used indiscriminately in both the Old and the New Testaments. Rather than exhibiting any historical movement or development, they are viewed as concentric circles whose center is Christ [2]. As regards the relation between Law and Gospel, Barth's understanding of the unity of scripture does not result in a removal of the character or nature of Law as a "curse" or judgment (*Fluchcharakter*) [3]. What does result from Barth's concern for unity, however, is, first, that the Gospel "makes itself manifest as the content of the Law", and, second, that "the temporal succession" (*das zeitliche Nacheinander*) between them is removed [4]. These developments would appear to constitute Thielicke's major reservations about Barth's theological method, and the hermeneutics to which it leads.

The possibility of countering these criticisms rests on an unambiguous apprehension of the claims embodied within them. Thielicke clearly is arguing for (1) an apparently fixed difference in *content* between Law and Gospel, which gains external expression in (2) a necessity for Law to *precede* Gospel, which would entail that man is confronted by Law apart from, or on the way to, Gospel. Each of these claims, however, leads inexorably to a common conclusion: On Thielicke's view, it is not only possible, but unavoidable, that God's dealings with man, and man's response to God, proceed (in part at least) independently of Jesus Christ.

From Barth's perspective, the difficulties in Thielicke's criticisms, and the counter-claims to which they lead, are twofold. First, they suggest some sort of independent divine action which proceeds apart from Christ. Where this is allowed, it opens the way for a separation between the *Deus revelatus* and the *Deus absconditus*, between God as he presents himself to man in Jesus Christ and "God as He is, and remains, outside of Jesus Christ" [5]. And this leads inevitably to a further

---

theological assumptions about the meaning and unity of scriptural texts. Cf. above, p. 89f.

[1] *Ibid.*, Band I, Par. 585, p. 198f.

[2] *Ibid.*, Band I, Par. 571, p. 193f.

[3] *Ibid.*, Band I, Par. 583, p. 197f.

[4] *Ibid.*

[5] Emil Brunner, *The Christian Doctrine of God* (Philadelphia: The Westminster Press, 1950), p. 173.

distinction between the *opus proprium* and the *opus alienum* of God. Where this distinction is extended to the relation between Law and Gospel, the former is inevitably given the essentially negative function of exposing the wrath of God, and so of bringing man to a point of recognition and acceptance of the love of God enclosed in the Gospel. The Law, in short, is both temporally and functionally prior to the Gospel.

The second sort of difficulty occasioned by Thielicke's position is that it suggests the possibility of knowledge or insight concerning God and man that falls outside the event of revelation, and which is grounded independently in the created order and natural man. Or, where the possibility of such knowledge does not emerge directly, then it is at least implied that there are dimensions of God's being and activity extending beyond Jesus Christ about which man might *eventually* know, or, to the contrary, about which he should remain both perpetually concerned and inevitably ignorant.

Barth's emphasis on the unity of God's action is designed to overcome both sorts of difficulties. In relation to the being and action of God, and man's knowledge of God, everything begins and ends with Jesus Christ. Ontologically and epistemologically, nothing in the relationship between God and man can or does fall outside the unifying center of Christology. This will mean, however, that the possibility of a distinction in content between Law and Gospel is excluded. Both will now be seen only in relation to the overarching context and movement of grace, and the continuing unity between indicative and imperative, between God's action in Christ and man's appropriate response, that this necessitates. The Law, then, cannot possibly be given the merely negative function of exposing God's wrath as a kind of preamble to man's encounter with grace and the Gospel. This would suggest that judgment is a preliminary affair on the way to an engagement with the "real thing". For Barth, however, the "real thing" just *is* the unity between indicative and imperative, forgiveness and judgment, the "Yes" and the "No" of God's action; and the interplay between these describes man's persistent place under grace. The Law, then, even as judgment, is essentially positive, not negative, in its impact. It removes man from the context of alien "laws" and ideologies, and sets him free to respond in love to God.

The danger of a tendency toward a de-historicized theology in Barth does not lie in the unity he establishes between Gospel and Law. These function consistently as the inner and outer sides of the total historical and teleological movement of grace, in which man is made participant. Further, it seems evident that Barth's discussion of the continuing witness of Jesus Christ, and the tension and conflict this engenders [1], is intended to give significance and substance to both the *movement* of grace and the given historicity of man. It is not clear, then, that Barth's particular ordering of Gospel and Law necessitates a loss of the historical. Where the givenness and reality of the historical *do* become problematic is in the pronounced realism pervading Barth's method, which in some ways appears to threaten both the distinctness of man as subject and agent apart from God, and to submerge the lines of demarcation between creation and reconciliation. It is possible that a careful analysis of Barth's reading of Law as the command of God will shed additional light on these issues.

C. THE CONTOURS AND DIMENSIONS OF THE COMMAND

The notion of command, as employed by Barth, lends itself to neither an abstract nor a preceptual interpretation. In its impingement on the concrete situation in which ethical reflection and action occur, it serves rather to underline the dynamic character of Christian ethics as *event* [2]. This needs to be emphasized at the outset, lest the use of the phrase, "the command of God", be interpreted as securing a place for the legitimate employment of ethical laws, norms, or ideals, so that the final testing point in Christian ethics emerges as consistency rather than obedience. Barth's opposition to an ethics involving rules or principles whose introduction and application in specific contexts is made a function of human sensitivity and discernment is just as strong and unremitting in the *Dogmatics* as it was in the *Römerbrief* and the writings after it previously examined. In exploring Barth's use of the concept of command, then, it is imperative not to lose sight of the fact that it is understood unequivocally as the command of *grace*. What this means is that it does not constitute the introduction of a new element beyond the primary action of God in Jesus Christ, which for Barth exhaustively delineates the good, and which provides the only perspective from which

---

[1] Cf. IV/3.1, Par. 69, Part 3.

[2] "The first thing that theological ethics has to exhibit and develop as a basic and comprehensive thesis is the givenness and range of the command of God as event". II/2, p. 608.

the full sweep of the divine economy from creation to redemption can be appropriately viewed and assessed. Rather, the command proceeds analytically out of that event itself, and is, in effect, no more than the appropriate means for describing and placing the ethical imperative issuing from man's ontological determination in Jesus Christ. As we shall see, this carries a dual consequence. It means, first of all, that Barth's reading of ethics will exhibit formal continuity with act-deontological moral theories. Second, it will underline and make explicit what has already been implicit in my analysis of the ontological reach of the event of reconciliation, namely, that human action carries no substantive significance. The substance of correct action, and so of the good, has been totally exhibited in Jesus Christ. Human ethical decisions will consist only in a recognition, celebration, and following of that action and the good it establishes. It follows, then, that the question of obedience or disobedience is the only serious issue that can be raised about human action [1].

The most complete indication of the dimensionality of the divine command is given in Barth's initial, general statement on theological ethics, which occurs at the end of his discussion of the doctrine of God. There, the thrust of the divine command into the context of human action is described simultaneously as claim, decision, and judgment [2]. Before proceeding to an examination of these dimensions of the command, it will be helpful to indicate the importance of Barth's discussion for the development of a completed theological ethic. The use here of the term "completed" gains significance relative to Barth's employment of the trinitarian structure of creation, reconciliation, and redemption. Within the framework of theological ethics, the notion of completeness signifies the diversity within unity and the unity within

---

[1] II/2, p. 594. Cf. *Ibid.*, p. 607: "The goodness of human action lies in the goodness with which God acts toward man. But God acts toward man through his Word. His Word is the embodiment and the plenitude of all good, because God himself is good. Therefore, man does good to the extent that he hears God's Word and acts as a hearer of that Word. In this action as a hearer he is obedient. Why is obedience good? Because it issues from a hearing, because it is the action of the hearer, namely, of a hearer of the Word of God. It is good because the divine address is good, because God himself is good".

[2] *Ibid.*, Pars. 37, 38, and 39. The trinitarian ordering of the discussion is immediately evident, i.e., it is God the Father who claims man in the decision passed on him in God the Son, and it is God the Holy Spirit who makes both claim and decision real (existentially) in the judgment brought against us.

diversity of the command of God, who relates himself to man as Creator, Reconciler, and Redeemer [1]. What is therefore decisively *not* signified by the notion of a "completed" theological ethic is the possibility of either an inclusive conceptualization and description of the "ideal" Christian life, or the unfolding of a series of empirically and behaviorally tight conditions which would carry prevenient force for all possible situations [2]. With this demarcation, the logical and behavioral priority of the divine action is again brought out. In its immediate thrust into the context of human decision and action, the line between the *command* of God and God himself as *commander* is tightened and made secure against every possibility of separation or distinction [3]. The emergence of a *formally* complete ethic is ruled out, and is replaced by a *descriptively* inclusive account of the ramifications for human behavior which result from God's direct presence in his command. The beginning of such an account may be seen in Barth's initial explication of the command as claim, decision, and judgment. As we shall see, this involves a piece of theological map-work whose function is to indicate the way in which man's ethical actions take place within a context whose primary ingredient is the sustaining and formative power of the continuing activity of God.

The first thing to be said about the command of God is that it makes a claim upon man, and so places him under obligation. This follows from the ontological determination given him in Jesus Christ, in whom both the good and the obedience which it requires were realized [4]. So, whether man acknowledges it or not, his future is inevitably bound up with that action. This indicates that the claim, as well as the decision

---

[1] *Ibid.*, p. 609f.; Cf. III/4, pp. 26f.; 34ff.

[2] II/2, p. 597f. Barth quotes with approval Bonhoeffer's objection to schematizing efforts of this sort: "An ethic cannot be a book in which is written out how everything in the world actually ought to be, but unfortunately is not, and the ethicist cannot be a man who always knows better than others what is to be done and how it is to be done. An ethic cannot be a compendium which guarantees irreproachable moral actions, and the ethicist cannot pose as the competent critic and judge of every human action. An ethic cannot be a retort leading to the production of ethical or Christian men, and the ethicist cannot be the embodiment and paradigm of an essentially moral life". III/4, p. 9. The quotation is from Bonhoeffer's *Ethik* (München: Chr. Kaiser Verlag, 1958), p. 208.

[3] II/2, p. 607f.

[4] *Ibid.*, p. 627.

and judgment embodied in the command, is given a christological basis and presupposition. To indicate this, however, is to underline once again the centrality and teleological power of *grace* in its encroachment on the human. And to speak of grace is to speak of Jesus Christ as the event and the person in whom both grace and its form, both Gospel and Law, are brought into focus and unity [1]. The "form" of grace in its teleological power (*der teleologischen Kraft der Gnade*) [2] is not limited to Christ, however; it also encloses the being and activity of the people of God. This is not to suggest that behavioral conformity to the will of God occurs only within that context, which on Barth's analysis includes both Israel and the Christian community [3]. Rather, since the grace of Christ asserts itself with sovereignty over all men, it follows that the will of God has been fulfilled continuously (and oftentimes better) *outside*, as well as within, the covenant community [4]. It is still true, however, that the existence of the people of God creates a specific empirical context within which the command of God and its claim are accepted and received openly; human action within that context will thus serve as a parabolic indication of the response demanded of all men [5].

---

[1] *Ibid.*, p. 631.

[2] *Ibid.*, p. 634. It is clear that Barth intends an exclusively theological reading of the notion of teleology. It is derived only from a description of the total, eschatological thrust of grace from creation to redemption, and so is radically differentiated from an immanently derived teleology, which always carries the possibility of solidification in the form of an ideology. Cf. Charles C. West, *Communism and the Theologians*, p. 275.

[3] *Ibid.* Barth prefers to speak of the community or "people of God" (*Volkes Gottes*) rather than the Church, in order to draw attention to the continuity holding between Old and New Testament, Israel and the Christian community. The basis for this unity is located in God's election of *all* men in Jesus Christ. Israel and the Church thus serve the parabolic function of indicating the unifying impact of grace. Cf. *Ibid.*, Par. 34, Pt. 1. As we have seen, this provides the basis for arguing a single, continuous *ethical* framework, evading thereby what Paul Lehmann characterizes as the "crucial difficulty" of a double standard in ethical thinking. Cf. *Ethics in a Christian Context* pp. 145ff.

[4] II/2, p. 632. It is important to note that the line of ethical continuity between believers and unbelievers is christologically, not anthropologically derived. It is thus the embracing action of God in Jesus Christ that makes for common ethical context and behavior, not "a natural goodness of man" (*einer natürlichen Güte des Menschen*).

[5] *Ibid.*, pp. 634; 638.

The precise content of the claim levelled against man by the divine command is that his actions reflect the rightness of God's action in Jesus Christ. This means that man is to do what corresponds to grace, in whatever situation he might find himself. Christian ethical action will thus consist of man's continual recognition of the basis of his existence in grace, and his continual remembrance of the graciousness with which God in Jesus Christ has met and dealt with him [1].

It is clear that the claim which is placed on man to live in conformity with divine grace will not lead to a blurring of the "infinite qualitative distinction" between himself and God. Rather, the claim focuses clearly the pressing question of his responsibility in the light of God's action. And that responsibility is to display the image of God in his actions; it can never be that of "the creation of a second God in human form, nor of a mixing or transformation of the human into the one divine form" [2]. Human actions will always retain their status as *human* actions. Conformity to the action of God does not mean identity. There can be no question of a succession of Christs, nor of an equality of status and relation between Jesus and the community of faith. The relationship is and remains that of Lord and servant; man's actions in witnessing to God's prior action can never mean that he becomes himself a god. The summation of the content of the divine claim and the responsibility which it places on man is, quite simply, that he should believe in Jesus Christ. Not, as Barth emphasizes, that he should believe *like* Jesus Christ—"that issue is better left alone, since he is certainly God and we are only men" [3].

In view of the content of the divine claim as the responsibility placed on man to conform in his actions to the action of God, Barth next takes up the question of its form. By this, he seeks to detect what it is that distinguishes the divine claim from other claims which press for attention. This is the question of the manner in which the divine claim meets man. The most succinct and encompassing statement here is that it meets us in the form of permission, that is, *freedom* [4]. This is the

---

[1] *Ibid.*, p. 645f. Cf. IV/1, p. 14.

[2] II/2, p. 641.

[3] *Ibid.*, p. 647. Cf. II/1, p. 433f.

[4] "The form in which the command of God is distinguished from all other commands, the special form which is its secret even when it takes shape in some other command, consists in the fact that it is permission—the granting of a quite definite freedom ". II/2, p. 650. The existential-structural and pheno-menological aspects of Barth's treatment of human freedom under God will

situation into which man is called by the command—the freedom really to be what God in his act of election has determined man to be. In this permission, man is freed of any dependence on former commands and authorities, and so from every form of self-dependence which might determine the course of his life [1]. In God's gracious decision, man recognizes that God is for him, and he is thus set free from every anxiety and fear which arise when he attempts to be for himself. The initial obligation, therefore, under which man is placed by God's command is to be and remain free in the grace which has overcome him and set him on his feet [2]. Obligation, in the first instance, *means* permission (*Sollen ... heißt Dürfen*) [3].

With this aspect of the form of the divine claim goes a second. The freedom of the command carries with it an additional obligation. This does not mean, however, that we are faced here with an abstract understanding of the relation between freedom and authority [4]. Permission and obligation, freedom and command, can be (and are) united only in the decision of faith in the Word of God given in Jesus Christ. To attempt on our own to stand in this paradoxical situation leads only to legalism or lawlessness. It is only because of the truth of God's grace that the polarity of permission and obligation can be grasped and comprehended in its unity [5].

The unity of permission and obligation in the divine command issues and comes to focus in obedience, which has as its basic content man's decision for Jesus Christ. All other demands for obedience which

---

be explored in the next chapter. The importance of the concept of freedom in Barth's ethics may be seen in his elucidation of the "special" ethic of creation (III/4).

[1] II/2, p. 661.

[2] *Ibid.*, pp. 663ff.

[3] *Ibid.*, p. 669.

[4] *Ibid.*

[5] "Nobody expects to find in himself, apart from faith, and so apart from God's Word—in conscience, thought, volition, or emotion, or perhaps in some kind of special experiences—a point or points where he is himself in such agreement with the command of God that what he ought to do according to this command is at the same time a permission, and that the great permission of this command, without more ado, has become an obligation ... The concrete truth of the unity of the two, through which we are preserved from the abyss on both sides, is the truth of the grace of God itself, which as such is always known and grasped in its promise, and which, as the promise given to us, is our sanctification". *Ibid.*, p. 671.

confront man in his existence are to be rendered only "in the Lord",
i.e., there are no demands for obedience which can stand on equal
footing with this one concrete demand for obedience [1]. But again, we
hear the demand for obedience to Jesus Christ correctly only if it is heard
joyously, as the answer to the question and problem of human existence,
and, concretely, of *my* existence [2]. But, because of the ultimate eschatological significance of this demand, it will have to be put to us again and
again, in every moment of our lives. Decision can never be a once-for-all
affair, because there is no time in man's life when he does not imagine
that he lives to himself. So, it is necessary that the grace of God continually recall us to obedience to, and remembrance of, our true situation
before him [3]. It is this character of repetitiveness embodied in God's
command as claim that underlines the penultimate significance and place
of Christian life and ethics. Human ethical action, rather than serving
as an end in itself, provides an indication of the eternal, eschatological
grounding and goal of correct behavior [4].

The command of God is not exhausted by the claim which it brings
to man. At the same time, it places him under a definite conclusion.
It not only indicates a requirement, but simultaneously reminds him of
the original divine decision which has been spoken concerning him.
The claim of the command meets man as permission and obligation;
as freedom, and responsibility under that freedom. But this freedom
becomes actual for man only as it works itself out in the multiplicity of
concrete decisions which face him. The command of God which meets
us as claim is thus concerned with the nature and quality of these decisions, for it is in them that we witness to our existence in God.

But if this is true, it is also true that every concrete decision which
man renders stands already under the sovereignty of the original decision
made in Jesus Christ. The sovereignty of God's decision over man must
therefore be taken afresh into each situation. Unless we see ourselves
under the command in this manner, we have not really understood or
taken seriously the act of God's grace in Jesus Christ, which forms the
beginning and end of the divine decision concerning us [5].

The divine decision, then, is understood always (and simultaneously)
as a judgment, because it is the act of God's grace which everywhere

---

[1] *Ibid.*, p. 676f.
[2] *Ibid.*, p. 679.
[3] *Ibid.*, p. 681.
[4] *Ibid.*
[5] *Ibid.*, p. 705.

precedes human actions, in the light of which human decisions can only undertake effectively to reflect the original decision of God. This leads inevitably to a heightening of emphasis on the responsibility continually facing man. Man's responsibility as such can only be an answer to the Word of God which we hear as his command [1]. The enactment of this responsibility would be described operationally as "doing the will of God" [2].

On Barth's understanding, the concept of responsibility can be conceived correctly only within the context of Christian ethics [3]. Only there can the uninterrupted quality of responsibility in man's life be sufficiently understood. This does not mean that non-Christians are therefore irresponsible. Rather, they are responsible only before the command of God—never autonomously, so that responsibility is allowed to serve as a generic description of man's situation. A generic description of man's situation is possible only within the givenness of man's determination in Christ, which receives formative embodiment and significance in the divine command. The Christian, therefore, can only confront the non-believer as one who is already bounded and determined by the responsibility which brackets humanity as a whole, and which has already been fulfilled in Jesus Christ. The responsibility which the Christian knows to be the basis of his existence becomes the means of witness to other men [4].

The sovereignty of the divine decision forces man to a consideration of the fulfillment of the responsibility which it imposes. Ethically, this means that in every situation he is confronted anew with the question of action—the nature, direction, and quality of his own decision. Barth takes up the consideration of this issue through an examination of the question, "What ought we to do?" [5], and develops the answer out of the preceding analysis of the way in which human ethical action is grounded consistently in the prior action of God. Here we must recall an earlier point, that the good is not discovered through human analysis

---

[1] "It is in the concept of responsibility that we have to recognize the most precise description of the human situation in face of the sovereign divine decision. We live in responsibility, that is, our being and willing, what we do and what we do not do, whether we know it and wish it or not, is a continuous answer to the command of the Word of God spoken to us". *Ibid.*, p. 713.

[2] *Ibid.*, p. 710.

[3] *Ibid.*, p. 714.

[4] *Ibid.*, p. 715f.

[5] "Was sollen wir tun?". *Ibid.*, p. 717f., *et passim*.

and insight in a given situation, nor is it deducible from general presuppositions or norms. The good is something that is *given* to man in
God's action. For Barth, this carries the consequence that the asking
of the question, "What are we to do?", can never result in our seeing
clearly what is required of us and doing it, even (or perhaps especially)
where we are seriously inquiring about the will of God. If this sort of
unity between God's will and human action were achievable, it would
mean that human actions would be self-justifying, since they would
exhibit total conformity to the will of God, and so become identical
with it [1].

For Barth, the upshot of this would be that serious moral reflection,
which always involves humility and penitence [2], is made both impossible
and unnecessary. Nor would moral reflection be the only thing made
superfluous were this sort of correspondence between God's will and
human action possible:

> So, too, would the command of God itself and as such—in distinction
> to what we say to ourselves. So, too, would Jesus Christ as the Mediator
> of the covenant between God and ourselves. We would of ourselves
> keep the covenant as faithfully as it has been kept by God [3].

This reading of human action would lead, finally, to the elimination
of grace as the constant factor in every concrete decision, which in turn
would mean that sanctification would not be exclusively the work of

---

[1] "What ought we to do? If our action occurs within an awareness of
what we are asked with this question, then the responsibility before God which
we are to execute in our action would signify simultaneously our own justification before him. It would then be the action of those who are holy in the
same way that God is holy. The will of God would thus occur in our lives
in such a way as to become our own, so that, willing what God wills, we
would ourselves carry it out. Our decisions would run parallel to God's, and
would to that extent actually be identical with it". II/2, p. 717.

[2] We are reminded here of the importance Barth placed upon the "first-
order" action of repentance and "rethinking" in the ethics of the *Rǫmerbrief*.
As we shall see, this aspect has by no means dropped out in the *Dogmatics*. Whether or not it is, in the latter case, augmented by additional
possibilities for human ethical action is, from one perspective, the most
pressing question surrounding Barth's ethics. It is clear, however, that the
answer to this is tied closely to his analysis of the independent structure and
significance of the human apart from the humanity of God in Christ. I
shall examine these issues in the next two chapters of this study.

[3] II/2, p. 717.

God, but the result of a parallelism between God and man which placed each on an equal footing. The *actual* situation in which man finds himself, however, is that of having to seek anew, in each context, the meaning of God's command "without having the answer already prepared, and really without being able to provide it outselves" [1]. To the extent that our action is controlled by this question, it is obedient action; but its obedience lies in a recognition of the sovereignty of the command, not in an assumed *knowledge* of it. The command of God, as it confronts man at every point, is "the norm, which is not *in* us, but *over* us" [2]. It is only in this way that Barth will speak of a "norm" within the context of theological ethics. It is in no sense a possession of human insight or knowledge, but is grounded exclusively in the sovereignty of God's command, which stands over every specific human condition and situation, and which always meets man anew as grace. It can only be approached as something which is not possessed or known, but which is humbly and penitently *sought*.

Viewed in this light, the question of human action relative to any given context will always entail a radical questioning of past behavior, decisions, hypotheses and convictions. These are not arbitrarily set aside, but they cannot serve automatically as bases providing insight into what the command will mean now, for this situation. The reason for this is that "the goodness of God—even and precisely the goodness of his work for our sanctification—is new every morning" [3]. This is seen clearly in the kind of awareness with which the question of the "ought" for particular situations is raised. It is never presented as a requirement that we give to ourselves. Instead, it is seen always as an imperative which transcends whatever insights we bring with us out of previous experience, or discover immediately through careful analysis of a situation [4]. What this means is that the command of God cannot be identified

---

[1] *Ibid.*, p. 718.

[2] *Ibid.*, Italics added.

[3] *Ibid.*, p. 718; Cf. III/4, p. 16.

[4] "If there is an imperative to which I really owe obedience, then it must in the most radical sense come to me from without, in order for me to accept the claim it imposes within. If there is a command that transcends our action, then it may not be reduced, finally, merely to the command that I have given myself on the basis of my perception and experience, or of my sensitivity to and consciousness of truth, goodness, and beauty. On the contrary, it must come to me as an alien command, as the command of Another, which as such demands of me that I make its content my own proper command". II/2, p. 725.

with some aspect of a given situation, whether this emerges as a specific line of possible action, or as a more embracing "law of the hour" (*Gebot der Stunde*) [1]. Authentic ethical reflection is to be distinguished from a bare analysis of the situation. Every context within which decisions are made and actions undertaken will require a consistent ordering of priorities. Christian ethical *reflection* takes cognizance of the specific ingredients in a given situation only in view of the priority of the decision and action of God which exercises sovereignty both *over* and *within* every particular context [2]. It follows, then, that Christian ethical *action* will consist in preparing for participation in the action of God, a preparation which receives concrete expression in the celebration of the Lord's Supper [3].

The responsibility placed upon man to respond to the command of God as it encounters him in specific contexts carries with it a demand for his actual involvement. The issue here, as always, has to do with man's obedience or disobedience to God's action and the determination this sets for him. It will thus be impossible to approach the matter in a spirit of detachment and objectivity. To assume this attitude would mean, as Barth expresses it in a studied play on words, that we remained "detached, not realizing that our *interesse* is an accomplished fact, but instead becoming idly 'interested' in this and that—a procedure which has nothing at all to do with our real *inter-esse*" [4].

The involvement required of man is, further, not isolated, but one which is defined specifically in the question, "What ought *we* to do?". Barth borrows from Kant at this point by way of illustration, with the familiar dictum that all human action is to be "the principle for a universal law". In the light of what we have already developed about the command of God, this can scarely be taken in a straightforward Kantian sense [5]. Here, it serves as no more than a reiteration of Barth's earlier point about the centrality of the community of God as the place at which God's action is recognized and accepted, and so witnessed to and proclaimed. Ethics in this context can never be a question merely of

---

[1] *Ibid.*, p. 711.
[2] *Ibid.*, p. 711f.
[3] *Ibid.*, p. 712f. The significance of the Lord's Supper, and of worship generally for Christian ethics, will be discussed in Chapter VI of this study.
[4] *Ibid.*, p. 728.
[5] *Ibid.*, p. 730. If Barth allowed substantive force to Kant's formulation, he would emerge with an ethics on the model of a rule-, rather than an act-deontology. Cf. Frankena, *Ethics*, p. 23f.

"my" actions, but always of the "I" which is at once placed beside and within the "we" of the congregation [1]. The command of God always encounters individuals in their particular circumstances and with their given capabilities. However, the possibility of a relativizing of the command through an unlimited appeal to the uniqueness of the individual and his situation is undercut by emphasizing his given identity as a participant in the covenant community, in the "body" (*Leib*) of which Christ is the head [2].

Within the context of the Christian community and the identity it imparts to individuals, ethical reflection will (and must) entail a doing, the carrying out of a specific action. Ethical reflection is in no sense a theoretical inquiry constituting a necessary pause between willing and doing, between ethical formulation or insight and the embodiment of that insight in a definite act. To pose the question of human response to the command already presupposes that one is on the way to action, since the concreteness of responsibility and the demand for obedience allow neither for separation nor detachment [3].

Barth's reading of the sovereignty of the divine command as God's decision on the human necessitates an analysis both subtle and complex of the notion of the "situation" or "context" within which ethical reflection and action take place, which will bring out the multi-dimensionality indicated by the former terms. The context within which man is called upon to render obedience to the command is not simply equatable with the historically and sociologically conditioned place he occupies within time and space. Two additional contextual levels must be added to the historical and the sociological before a complete description of the ethical situation is achieved: (1) the context provided by God's eternal decision and action in electing man to covenant, which was accomplished in Jesus Christ, which binds all temporal possibilities together into unity, and which provides the ontological, epistemological, linguistic, and behavioral ground of the human [4]; (2) the context of response provided by the emergence and continuity of the covenant community, Israel and the Church. An adequate understanding of the

---

[1] II/2, p. 731f.

[2] *Ibid.*

[3] *Ibid.*, pp. 732-737. Cf. I/2, p. 298f.: "That is how the children of God hear the Word of God. Their hearing is really the hearing of an order, and therefore obedience a *hearing* which as such and necessarily is a *doing* of the Word". Italics added.

[4] Cf. Ch. II above, Section A, "Theological Method".

importance of "context" for Christian ethical reflection and action, theory and practice, can occur only when these three levels are seen in their dynamic interrelationship.

Something of this interrelationship emerges in Barth's discussion of the definiteness of the command. What this underlines is the way in which the ethical situation in which man is called upon to act is shaped and determined primarily by the continual activity and presence of God in the command, and by man's participation in the covenant community, a participation which provides the basis for an obedient response to the command. Now, since it is the ethical situation in which man stands *in its totality* that is given shape and focus under the impact of the command, it follows that the anthropological, i.e., historical and sociological, factors in it cannot be isolated and given independent attention [1]. This is not to suggest that Barth reduces or eliminates the importance of these factors. However, it does indicate that they receive contextual significance only as they are placed within and under the shaping and transforming immediacy of God's command, not as independent variables whose relation to the command is discovered at the point of man's deliberation. The logical and operational tightness of the command excludes this sort of dichotomizing approach.

That Barth devotes a section to discussing the "definiteness" or "precision" (*Bestimmtheit*) [2] of the divine command reminds us, once again, that man's ethical decisions and actions do not rest on a consideration of universal norms or principles, but on something whose presentational immediacy is such that no distinction between form and content, prescription and application, is possible [3]. God's command is presented

---

[1] The same will be true, of course, of the inner, psychological structure and dynamic of the self as moral agent. See below, Ch. V. Both from the side of the command and from the side of human action, then, the ethical context is "formed" in such a way that there are *no* independent factors (Cf. III/4, pp. 18ff). The "horizontal" and "vertical" dimensions of ethics, in both its general and "special" significance, proceed exclusively out of the Word of God.

[2] II/2, pp. 737ff.

[3] "The command of God is an integral whole, so that form and content, universal prescription and specific application, are not two things, but one. The divine decision, which constitutes the execution of a sovereign judgment over our decisions, is a wholly definite decision. That means that in the demand and judgment of his command, God always confronts us with a fully precise meaning and intention, with a will which has considered everything and each thing in particular, and which has left nothing to chance or our caprice". *Ibid.*, p. 739. On Barth's view, the lesser possibility of "fixing" or

anew each moment as "always one and only one possibility in every conceivable determination of its inner and outer modality" [1]. An adequate understanding of human responsibility rests on our seeing that the command is given only in this sort of completeness. As the quite specific structure and content resulting from God's continuous activity within the full particularity of time and place within which man finds himself, it is not in any sense an open possibility requiring or receiving validation at the point of human interpretation. Rather, the command is self-interpreting down to the smallost detail [2].

It is clear that Barth's interpretation of the definiteness of the command effectively sets aside every possibility of human cooperation or "synergism" (*Synergismus*) [3]. The radicalness of this move can be appreciated only when we realize that it amounts to nothing less than a total exclusion of the necessity of *deliberation* in ethics. There can be deliberation only where there are formal rules or principles to be brought into conjunction with particular cases, so that a consideration of alternative possibilities for action is made a constant factor in the ethical situation. On this analysis, it would seem obvious that man as deliberator would contribute something toward the determination of morally appropriate actions. As Barth sets things up, however, it is impossible that man could contribute *anything* to the ethical situation. Even a term as traditionally freighted with moral significance as "conscience" is neutralized with respect to the definiteness of the command. The command is not given *by* but *to* conscience, so that the latter, along with "spirit", is given an eschatological, rather than an anthropological, grounding and function [4].

The only point at which man is faced with the necessity for decision lies in the question of his behavioral conformity or non-conformity, i.e., obedience or disobedience, to the command:

---

expressing the command in a "small" text of ethical law (*kleinen ethischen Gesetzestext*) is also decisively rejected (Cf. III/4, p. 9).

[1] II/2, p. 739.

[2] *Ibid.*, p. 741; Cf. III/4, p. 11.

[3] II/2, p. 745.

[4] *Ibid.*, p. 744. Barth's placing of conscience at an eschatological level is not a new development in the *Dogmatics*; it was given identical treatment in the lecture-outline given at Münster in 1928. Cf. above, p. 49 f. The consequences arising from Barth's apparent rejection of "spirit" as an immanent anthropological category for his views on man in the role of ethical agent will be examined in Chapter V, below.

It is in just this definiteness that the command is unconditional, so that it leaves us no other choice except that between obedience and disobedience. Its unconditional character consists in the fact that, independently of our opinions and in each moment and relationship in which I find myself situated, it has the form that God in all seriuosness always demands something specific from me ... The human decision that is mine in face of the divine command does not consist in a decision of the question whether this or that possibility is good, or whether the command demands this or that of me, or of whether I should do this or that—this question would be about as significant and fitting as the question whether there is indeed a God, who or what he is, and how and what we are allowed to think of him, where he has already decided all these things in his Word and revelation, and where our task can consist only in reflecting quite explicitly on what has been said to us in his Word. My decision, the human ethical decision, is whether, in my action, I conform to the command which encounters and confronts me in the most specific and pointed form, whether I shall be obedient or disobedient to it, whether for my part I shall meet it according to my election (the election of Jesus Christ!) as a believer or an unbeliever [1].

The accent in the notion of command thus falls consistently on the way in which God in Jesus Christ is present to man as the *living* and *acting* God whose impingement on the human is immediate, continuous, and explicit [2]. The command brings us face to face with the person of God himself. It is thus impossible to interpose the command *between* man and God as though it were an independent third entity, a kind of formal receptacle whose elaboration and application is left to the discretion of human self-determination [3]. The presupposition of action is never controlled by man. Human actions will therefore be purely casual, *ad hoc* actions indicative of an immediate response in particular situations under the impact of the (prior) formative actuality of God [4]. Ethically significant actions occur only as man is *told* what is required of him, and then decides in obedience to do it [5].

The fact that the command always encounters man contingently, i.e., in its specific definiteness within given contexts, does not, Barth insists, lead to a loss of structure or continuity. The reason for this is

---

[1] II/2, p. 745f.; Cf. III/4, p. 2: "Man's action is good to the extent that he is the obedient hearer of the Word and command of God".

[2] II/2, pp. 748; 753ff.

[3] *Ibid.*, p. 741f.

[4] " ... lauter höchst zufällige oder in ihrer Notwendigkeit doch nur historisch Kontingent begreifliche Handlungen und Verhaltungsweisen ...". *Ibid.*, p. 751.

[5] *Ibid.*, p. 786.

that the command occurs within, and is therefore an expression of, the embracing context of grace signalled in man's election [1]. The ethical task given man, accordingly, is that of participating in the continuing history of the covenant of grace. It is only within this framework (exemplified historically in the emergence of Israel and the Church) that God's command can be apprehended and acted upon in its full particularity:

> The history of this one and twofold people as the society of the man Jesus of Nazareth, the history of its preparation and arrangement to be the witness of this One, and thus to be the witness to the divine compassion for the whole world, the Bearer of this arising from the midst of this people, to be the source from which this people arises—this history is the history of the covenant of grace, to which the interest of the entire Bible in its two sections is inseparably directed ... Since that history is undoubtedly its theme and content, it can, in relation to the decision of God concerning human action and inaction, have only this for its testimony: God wills that human action and inaction should conform to that history, that it should subordinate itself to its purpose and follow its course. God wills that man should be called and gathered to this people of his choice, that he might participate in its office of witness. God wills that he should be and will and do and not do the particular thing required of him as a result of the particular thing God himself is and wills and does and does not do in Jesus Christ [2].

Within the context of the covenant of grace, and the covenant people resulting from it, it is clear that human ethical actions can in no sense be seen as falling under general prescriptions or norms. The activity of God in shaping man's situation (which is precisely the factor that lends ethical significance and substance to that situation) proceeds *immediately*, rather than mediately. Even such apparently obvious examples of ethical laws or rules as are found in the Ten Commandments or the Sermon on the Mount are to be understood dynamically, so that, relative to the divine command, they are given, respectively, the tasks of negative delimitation and positive indication. The function of the Old Testament decalogue is to mark off (negatively) those outer boundaries within which the commanding activity of God will take place [3]. In themselves, they say nothing about what man specifically is to do. In a pinch, one might say that they occupy the status of "range rules", provided this was understood strictly as an indication of established *limits* which in themselves are lacking entirely in substantive force. In a similar,

---

[1] *Ibid.*, p. 754f.
[2] *Ibid.*, p. 756.
[3] *Ibid.*, pp. 762ff.

though positive, fashion, the Sermon on the Mount stands as an indication of the "new man" (*neuen Menschen*) called into existence and
activity by Jesus Christ [1]. As such, it is significant first of all as the self-
disclosure of Jesus Christ [2], and then additionally as a description of
the conditions and direction of the life of the people of God (*die Lebens-
bedingungen der Gemeinde Gottes*) [3]. The Sermon on the Mount is thus
ethically significant as an indication of the lines along and within which
obedience will take place. Both the Ten Commandments and the Sermon
on the Mount, then, are ethically important not as independent "principles" or prescriptive rules, but rather as the negative and positive
lines marking out the context within which the commanding activity of
God, and the human response of obedience, will occur. On this analysis,
Barth is able to argue a continuity of both form and content between
the ethical thrust of the Old and New Testament [4]. What this entails for
theological ethics is the establishment of a unified differentiation between
Gospel and Law, indicative and imperative, as the *content* and *form*,
respectively, of the command of God.

The continuity holding between Old and New Testaments at the
point of their common (ethical) grounding in the covenant is exhibited
again when consideration is given to the behavioral question concerning
acceptable human action. What links human behavior together within
the Bible generally is that it occurs always as the obedient or disobedient
response to the immediate and particular formative presence of God in
the command. This continuity, however, extends beyond the Bible.
It applies to all men as they are placed under a similar option (i.e.,
obedience or disobedience) by the intrusion of God into their situation:

> Under the no doubt totally different external conditions of our situation,
> we are to act not only like Abraham, Peter, the centurion of Capernaum,
> the Israelites or the community of Corinth, but again are to behave
> as those who then and there were addressed by God, allowing the com-
> mand given to them to be the command given to us here and now in our
> totally different time and situation, thereby certainly ranking ourselves
> with them, and in their immediate situation before God including our-
> selves in the history and sequel of the divine covenant of grace, accepting
> and fulfilling our mission or partial mission not as something new and
> special, but as the repetition and confirmation of the commission given
> them [5].

---

[1] *Ibid.*, p. 774.
[2] *Ibid.*, p. 770.
[3] *Ibid.*, p. 778.
[4] *Ibid.*
[5] *Ibid.*, p. 788f.

This behavioral inclusiveness is enclosed within the formal and material continuity of the command. Barth explores this in his consideration of the final aspect of the command as God's decision, its pervasive and unifying *goodness*. This is treated under three points. First, the divine decision is good because of its own inner unity and continuity. This is evidenced by the fact that it always speaks to men of the goodness of God's gracious action, and the divine determination over the human resulting from it. In Jesus Christ, God has shown (and continues to show) himself to be unreservedly *for* man. It is this goodness that gains expression in the divine command, and that is "the particular and the universal thing that he has to say to each man and to all men together with his specific command, and which all men have to hear, and again is the one thing which is for each individual the constant factor in everything that God has to command and forbid him in the different stages of his way" [1].

This precludes the possibility of an atomized will or command of God which would speak differently to different men in varying epochs of history or in differing specific contexts. The goodness of the command does not adjust to the changing situations and spheres which characterize the human; goodness is its constant property wherever and whenever it makes itself known. A correct apprehension of the command will always involve our hearing it as a command of goodness [2].

The second aspect of the goodness of the command is that it unites

---

[1] *Ibid.*, p. 794; Cf. III/4, p. 16f.

[2] "Either we hear it as the command of his goodness (even when it is an order to shoot), or we do not hear it at all (even though it is a commission to preach)". II/2, p. 796. The full implications of Barth's position on this point may be seen in his treatment of ethics within the context of creation (III/4). In that, he takes issue with both Brunner and Bonhoeffer over their reading of the natural (under the rubric of "orders of creation" and "mandates", respectively), in that it is given at least an apparent partial autonomy in relation to the grace of God. Cf. Emil Brunner, *Das Gebot und die Ordnungen* (Zürich: Zwingli Verlag, 1939), Drittes Buch: "Die Ordnungen". The English translation is by Olive Wyon. *The Divine Imperative* (Philadelphia: The Westminster Press, 1947). Dietrich Bonhoeffer, *Ethik*, Eberhard Bethge, ed. (München: Chr. Kaiser Verlag, 1958). The English translation is by Neville Horton Smith. *Ethics* (New York: The Macmillan Co., 1955). Barth's movement beyond the employment of an ethic grounded in either "orders" or "mandates" is achieved through an inclusive description of the natural in terms of the sanctification of all life accomplished in Jesus Christ, which results in man's being provided with certain penultimate "spheres" within wh ch he can live in freedom. See below, Chapter VI.

men in fellowship. True, there are and will be conflicts between them, but these can never be absolutixed so as to secure a final breaking of relationships. Rather, the unity within the human evolving from the command is itself understood as a "reflection" (*Entsprechung*) of God's own proper unity [1]. The unifying thrust of the command gains expression at two levels. It is, first of all, an operational and behavioral predicate that applies to the Christian congregation. The fact that men are unified as believers existing under the command undercuts the possibility of a purely individualized treatment of the Christian life. Within the unity achieved by the command, the interplay between individual responsibility and corporate participation can occur without danger of collapsing into either simple conformity or anarchy [2].

Second, the unity exemplified within the Christian community adumbrates the unity of all men in love under the command. In making this claim, Barth is not advocating an easy or straightforward transition from *de iure* to *de facto* statements about the reconciliation of humanity as a whole. The point has to do, instead, with the attitude and activity of Christians within the world and toward men generally. Because the world stands already under a total and irrevocable determination, and because evil has been overcome decisively in Jesus Christ, Christians are free to remain open to a sustained activity and participation in the world. Or, to put the matter negatively, they are not free *not* to remain open in this way. The Christian congregation is thus incapable (in principle) of an isolationist withdrawal into itself, on the one hand, or of a polemical, agressive move into the world as a kind of ideological party, on the other [3].

Finally, the goodness of God's decision is shown in that it unifies each individual in himself. In God's grace given in Jesus Christ, every attempt of man to live out of his own resources and unto himself is overcome, and he is set free for a life lived under that grace, i.e., life in the Holy Spirit. As such, the command of God is the good word of God to man that he is to live in the peace and harmony of the grace offered

---

[1] II/2, p. 801.

[2] *Ibid.*, pp. 800ff.

[3] *Ibid.*, p. 804f. Barth speaks pointedly here of the *political* activity of the Christian congregation, and offers at least a partial view of the status and function of the State. I shall reserve consideration of this aspect of Barth's ethics until Chapter VI, where the various dimensions of "life under grace" will be examined.

him ¹. What this means, finally, is that the unity of the individual is
grounded in the unity holding between Christ and the community
established by the Holy Spirit. The individual can be seen and understood
in his unity, therefore, only in his relation to the community, never as
an isolated self ².

The third and final dimension of the command that Barth explores
has to do with the judgment it imposes on man. In God's judgment of
man, his real nature as the one against whom God maintains his command is made clear, for in his judgment on man God receives him as
his own. Judgment is thus to be seen and interpreted as a demonstration
of God's love for man:

> If his existence had no connection whatever with the will of God main-
> tained in his command, how could he be appealed to in this connection?
> How could he be sentenced, rejected, and condemned through the will
> of God? Authentic wrath is obviously possible only on the basis of,
> and in connection with, a primary and essential love. It is the judgment
> that is passed on man in God's command—whatever else it means—that
> is in all instances the proof of his love for man, even if it is only an angry,
> burning, consuming love ³.

But if the judgment under which man is placed by the command
confirms the fact that he is loved and called by God, this is not because
of anything he brings with him, but only on the basis of the judgment
already achieved in Jesus Christ. It is only because of God's judgment on
himself in this man that the threat of final and total judgment, i.e., of
annihilating alienation and rejection, which man might otherwise fear
from God, has been set aside ⁴. On this basis, man approaches God's
judgment in the light of his knowledge of his election by grace to the
community of God. In one sense, then, as something already completed,
the judgment embodied in the command stands as the reverse side of
the eternal decree of God's election of man ⁵.

The confrontation of man with God's judgment is for Barth the first
result of man's encounter with the command. What is revealed there is

---

¹ *Ibid.*, p. 812f.

² *Ibid.*, p. 814f. Barth's insistence on seeing the individual only in relation
to the community gains exemplification throughout the *Dogmatics*, in that
the discussion always proceeds *from* the community *to* the individual, never
the reverse. Cf. II/2, Pars. 34 and 35; IV/1, Pars. 62 and 63; IV/2, Pars. 67 and
68.

³ II/2, p. 821.

⁴ *Ibid.*, p. 824f.

⁵ *Ibid.*, p. 819.

man's persistent situation and condition as transgressor of the command. At this point, the earlier dimensions of the command as claim and decision are subsumed under the overarching reality of the judgment that falls on man in the command:

> We are not those who comply with and fulfill sufficiently the claim of the divine command. And we are not those whom we ought to be on the basis of the decision executed over us in God's command. We neither follow nor fulfill the command, and so the judgment in which we stand can consist in the first instance only in our condemnation [1].

Under the divine command man is judged and condemned, in that, knowing the reality of the claim and decision of grace, he continues to hold to the freedom of judging between good and evil, and to live out his life autonomously in terms of derived principles and norms which he feels competent to apply. In the end, he is neither responsible nor obedient (and therefore not free) before God's grace [2]. We neither know of, nor can we find at any point in our lives, the conformity with the unity of the divine command which is demanded of us.

The reality of the divine judgment, however, can never emerge as the result of our own introspective efforts and deliberations. It is in no sense a judgment which we can pass on ourselves. The reality of the judgment in the command is visible only in Jesus Christ, and it is communicated only through God's self-impartation in the Holy Spirit. Man's realization of God's judgment on him depends on an act of pure grace [3].

The fact that God judges us is not, however, the final statement concerning our situation before him. For Barth, judgment is the *penultimate* reality of our existence, which corresponds to the crucifixion of Christ [4]. The *ultimate* fact of our existence is that we are elected and loved by God, and this is the corollary to the resurrection. Together, these two events (crucifixion and resurrection) constitute the forgiveness of sin, and impose on man a radical summons to faith and obedience. To live in faith means simply that we live out of the grace continually offered to us anew each day. And this requires, in turn, that we recognize

---

[1] *Ibid.*, p. 829f.

[2] These points are treated in detail in Barth's later development, within the context of his Christology, of the phenomenon of man's sin. Cf. IV/1, Par. 60; IV/2, Par. 65; IV/3.1, Par. 70.

[3] II/2, pp. 836ff.

[4] *Ibid.*, p. 838.

the paradoxical quality of our position—that before God we are *semper peccatores* and *semper iusti* [1].

The meaning and purpose of the judgment embodied in the command, then, is that we are directed to live exclusively by grace. It is thus intended to shape man's life in accordance with the formative activity of God. The proper response to this judgment from man's side, accordingly, will be repentance, which occurs as a recognition of the final purpose of the divine judgment in the sanctification of man, and the behavioral consequences to which this leads, i.e., "his readiness, preparation, and exercise for the eternal life appointed and promised to him" [2]. The ethical life of the Christian will thus evidence a continual recognition of God's judgment on all his actions, and continued prayer for the direction of the Holy Spirit, that he might learn anew in each situation the one particular action that will correspond to the obedience demanded by the prior good accomplished by God in Jesus Christ.

At this point, we must draw together the various strands and nuances of our discussion sufficiently to enable criticism and questioning to take place. Perhaps the single most important aspect of Barth's discussion of the command is the way in which it is related consistently to the category of event. This has to be understood both inclusively and specifically, as indicating the way in which the command provides a *total* shaping and determination of man's *particular* situation. In its immediate impingement as claim, decision and judgment, the command sensitizes us to the continuing activity of God, and evokes our immediate response, which is exhausted by the possibilities of obedience or disobedience. This underlines the strictness of the connection, if not the identity, that Barth establishes between theory and practice, which excludes both the necessity and the possibility of ethical deliberation. The reason for this is that on Barth's analysis there can be no independent factors in the ethical situation about which to deliberate. The Law embodied within grace (as command), like the Gospel whose form it is, leaves nothing to human decision or cooperation.

What are we to make of this? The first step toward understanding what is implied in Barth's analysis is to notice that there are at least two ways of construing the word "event" as employed within theological ethics, neither of which is separable from the other. The "ethical event" in question can refer, first of all (and primarily) to the divine history in

---

[1] *Ibid.*, p. 846.
[2] *Ibid.*, p. 865.

its total movement from creation to redemption, which provides throughout a christological exemplification of the inclusion of the divine and
the human, and which serves as both the locus and the persistent point
of orientation for the directional thrust of the command of God. Beyond
this, the "ethical event" is signalled by God's continual revelation of
the command through the Holy Spirit, and the human response this
evokes of belief or unbelief, obedience or disobedience. At this second
level, there is both a "vertical" and a "horizontal" dimension to be
taken into account, which indicate the *continuity* of both God's
command and man's response under the total order and *telos* of the
divine history, while yet allowing for the given *differentiation* of individual
cases [1]. This differentiation is ordered along trinitarian lines, as man
encounters the command of God as Creator, Reconciler, and Redeemer,
and responds respectively as God's creature, as the sinner who is always
forgiven and justified (*simul iustus et peccator*), and, ultimately (i.e.,
eschatologically) as the child of God [2]. Here it must be emphasized that
Barth's understanding of the command within this trinitarian framework
is linear rather than punctiliar. This point has an importance beyond
that merely of removing the possibility of an atomization of the command. For Barth, it establishes the existence of "definite spheres and
relationships" (*bestimmte Bereiche und Verhältnisse*) [3] which manifest
the constancy of the "event" of divine command and human response,
and which make possible a "formed reference" (*geformten Hinweis*) [4]
to that event.

The accent on event in Barth's reading of the command eliminates every possibility of translating or reducing it into either universal or particular ethical principles or rules, which would seem
to entail that the command does not permit of fixed propositional
expression [5]. Even such ostensibly obvious examples of propositional
formation as the Ten Commandments and the Sermon on the Mount

---

[1] Cf. III/4, p. 17.

[2] *Ibid.*, p. 26f. Naturally, the notion of the *perichoresis* of these "moments"
of the command has to be kept clearly in view, as a corollary to the principle,
opera Trinitatis ad extra sunt indivisa. Once this point has been made, however,
there will then be a provisional differentiation and ordering within ethics in
its significance for creation, reconciliation, and redemption that unfolds in
precise continuity with the trinitarian being of God. *Ibid.*, pp. 34ff.

[3] *Ibid.*, p. 31.

[4] *Ibid.*, p. 18.

[5] *Ibid.*, p. 9.

indicate no more than negative and positive directional limits set by the command, within which human response will occur. They do not in any sense indicate fixed principles or rules to be "introduced" into specific contexts.

The impossibility of giving expression to the command in binding propositional form as either general or specific principles or rules underlines the oddity of Barth's use of the term. When the notion of command is joined to the category of event, it is removed from its ordinary, literal meaning, and invested with a special sense that borders on metaphor. For Barth, God's activity in commanding man consists of his continual shaping and structuring presence in the midst of the human, which makes us sensitive in a radically new (and unexpected) way to the realities of our situation under the aegis of God's total and particular action, and which nudges us toward a corresponding response, which will inevitably turn out to be either obedient or disobient [1].

There are difficulties in the dynamic meaning and content that Barth attaches to the notion of command as event. To get these clearly before us, it is necessary to recall the exceedingly tight relationship that Barth sets up between dogmatics and ethics. What this means, as we have seen, is that it is impossible to develop ethics independently of dogmatics, and that this lends a certain fluidity to the terms "dogmatics" and "ethics", in that they are to some extent interchangeable. This interchangeability carries both a *substantive* and a *linguistic* consequence. Substantively, it means that dogmatic formulation and ethical description fall into precise continuity under the single and unifying action of God, which always includes the human and its appropriate

---

[1] The limitation of human response to these possibilities is closely related to Barth's notion that in Christian ethics we are no longer concerned with attempts to distinguish between good and evil. This issue is now resolved at the point of God's judgment on our action. There are two questions that arise from this ordering: (1) Is it the case that there is no use whatever for the terms "good" and "evil" in Christian ethics? What is not clear at this point is that a *theological* dictum about our not knowing good or evil (or even *claiming* to) is sufficient to dispel their use, or that their continued use (in a limited, proximate fashion) would necessarily spell disaster. (2) What are the possibilities, empirically and existentially, for a realization of obedience? If obedience remains always an *unactualized* potential (except in Christ), then *this* would seem to spell disaster for the possibility of significant human action (i.e., action that makes a discernible *difference* relative to given contexts) as quickly as an easy assumption of either the ability or necessity to distinguish between good and evil.

response. On this analysis, the action of God ("divine ethics") and the action of man (as response) will exhibit analogical similarity, so that the distinction between them is relative rather than absolute [1]. Linguistically, the interchangeability between dogmatics and ethics means that "the propositions of Christian ethics are propositions of Christian dogmatics" [2].

The conclusion suggested by this continuity between dogmatics and ethics is that the *problems* encountered in each will be similar, and that they will be traceable, finally, to the inclusive methodological assumptions on which both dogmatics and ethics rest. In our earlier consideration of Barth's theological method, I argued that the basic difficulty in the *Dogmatics* arises from the persistent realist stance taken by Barth, and that this exhibits an ontological, an epistemological, and a logical dimension [3]. I shall focus here on the latter two of these, taking them in reverse order, and will reserve discussion of the (possible) ontological difficulty in Barth's ethics until the next chapter, where the status of man's being and existence as ethical subject and agent will be examined.

To get at the logical (i.e., linguistic) difficulty in Barth's ethics, it is necessary to recall that the command of God cannot be given fixed prescriptive form in either general or particular principles or rules [4]. The significance of ethical propositions, accordingly, will be entirely *descriptive* (i.e., indicative). It is only in this way that there emerges in Barth the (ostensible) possibility of talking about a "cognitive" ethics. At this point, however, it must be recalled that the *meaning* of dogmatic (and so of ethical) propositions, even at a descriptive level, is established only in the event of grace, and not at all on independent grounds either of meaning or usage. The statements and propositions of ethics, then, will inevitably share in the linguistic "crisis" surrounding the language of the Bible, preaching, and dogmatics:

---

[1] Cf. above, Ch. II, Section B.

[2] II/2, p. 670.

[3] Cf. above, Ch. II, Section A.

[4] Barth's position on this point is even more strict than that taken by Professor Lehmann, who will allow at least a limited *use* to the term "pirnciple" within the ethical vocabulary, provided the "distinction between 'principles and the situation', even as a difference of emphasis", is not allowed to appear. *Ethics in a Christian Context*, p. 154. Whether this amounts to a subtle recognition or a subtle rejection of principles, there at least appears to remain the possibility, after a fashion, of using the term.

The propositions of Christian ethics are propositions of Christian dogmatics. However, that means that their truth content, like that of all other propositions of dogmatics, rests and is contained in the Word of God, that it can be known only in the Word of God, and that it must be sought and taken again in the Word of God and so in faith [1].

The establishment of this sort of logical continuity between ethical and dogmatic propositions raises serious problems for an objectifying, cognitive approach to our attempts to give linguistic expression to the command of God. What was seen to be true of the propositions of dogmatics, that "the means of definition at our disposal are not sufficient, in relation to God, to reassure us when we have applied them to him, that we have thought what must be thought and said here" [2], will necessarily hold true for the propositions of ethics as well. But this can only mean that every attempt to give logical form and precision to the command will prove inadequate. Or, to put the matter in slightly altered form, our attempts will gain adequacy *only* under the impact of grace. But again, this leads straight to the difficulty encountered earlier in relation to the question of meaning in dogmatic propositions, which can now be translated into the context of theological ethics: If the propositions of theological ethics which attempt to give expression to the command of God have, in themselves, *no* meaning (and are, therefore, neither true nor false), then it is not at all clear what it means to claim that they are given a *true* meaning in the event of grace. And if this is the case, then the possibility of either an adequate or (cognitively) meaningful description of ethics as the command of God is excluded.

The logical difficulties occasioned for ethical language by Barth's realism may be seen as the consistent and necessary outcome of his adoption of an epistemology which lodges the condition for knowing exclusively in the event of revelation. So, if the question is asked, What is it to *know* the command of God?, the answer follows that knowledge of the command results from our being "readied" and "placed" to know it by the event of grace and the resulting establishment of faith as the requisite epistemic organ. The difficulty in this program is that faith, as the epistemic organ enabling us to respond to grace, evidences no direct continuity with ordinary epistemic and cognitive modes, or with

---

[1] II/2, p. 670.
[2] II/1, p. 210.

the usual subject-object relations encountered under those. It is, rather, a *unique* (i.e., miraculous) occurrence, which has as its counterparts an equally unique subject-object relationship (between God and man) and body of knowledge [1].

Now, it is precisely the uniqueness of these various factors that renders the possibility of a cognitively meaningful descriptive ethics at best dubious. Just as faith depends on the event of grace that creates the condition for, and brings us into contact with, the reality of God and his command, so too the capacity of language adequately to express either of these depends on the same miraculous event of grace. I have intentionally pushed this point to its limits, because I wish to argue that Barth's articulation of a theological ethics is at this juncture placed squarely between two options, only one of which will produce anything remotely approaching a cognitively meaningful ethics. The first option to recognize the logical difficulties involved in attempting to provide an apparently neutralized ordinary language with true meaning through the ingression of grace, and to opt for a non-objectifying, and so non-cognitive, view of ethical propositions along the lines of a metaphorical, poetic, or (perhaps) existential view of these. It was seen earlier that Barth's notion of command tends somewhat in the direction of metaphor as a result of its being interpreted strictly as event. This option, then, would consist in taking that point seriously by relinquishing any claim to provide objectively significant descriptive propositions to which cognitive status can be attached. If I have read Barth correctly, however, there is no indication whatever that he would have been willing to consider that sort of move, Heinrich Ott to the contrary notwithstanding.

The other option is to claim that the propositions of theological ethics indeed receive meaning only in the event of grace, but to follow this with the additional claim that grace is active *whenever* the theologian undertakes to give linguistic expression to the command. Of course, since the command flows directly out of the prior context

---

[1] The validity of the notion that faith is brought into proximity with, and (with certain appropriate limitations) given access to, a "body of knowledge", follows from Barth's insistence on the *objective* status of the events comprising salvation history. Since the command of God is enclosed within these events, it necessarily attains a similar status, which, I have argued, provides at least the ostensible possibility of the articulation of a cognitively meaningful ethics.

of salvation history, an identical claim would have to be advanced about linguistic efforts in that area. This option, however, would no doubt be as distasteful to Barth as the former, since it is hard to see how this position could be taken without incurring a trivialization of grace. The event of grace, on this view, would be moved from the miraculous to the ordinary. In the end, it would have to be read, perhaps, as some kind of indigenous aspect of the created order [1].

Since neither of the suggested options (presumably) would be acceptable to Barth, and since it seems clear that he does wish to provide descriptive cognitive status to the propositions of theological ethics, it would appear we are left with a dilemma. This does not necessarily render Barth's program for ethics impossible, but it surely makes it problematic.

The problems occasioned by Barth's delineation of theological ethics in exclusive reference to the command of God are not exhausted by the linguistic and epistemological difficulties to which it leads. These difficulties, I have suggested, expose the ambiguity of Barth's concern for the objectifying status and function of theological and ethical language, and, from the perspective of that concern, force us onto the boundary between a trivialized ethics that keeps intact the descriptive cognitive force of its propositions, and (from Barth's perspec-

---

[1] I have used the word "event" throughout this discussion in an essentially uncritical fashion. It is important to notice, however, that within the realism of Barth's ontology there are some ambiguities surrounding its use, so that its meaning in that context becomes less than perspicuous. Here we must recall the meaning normally attached to the concept of an "event", which also determines its use. For anything to be an "event" in the ordinary sense of the term means that it is spatially and temporally exhibited. As was pointed out, however, there is a certain ambiguity at this point surrounding Barth's treatment of the events comprising salvation history. The difficulty here arises out of Barth's notion that the events in question there are not susceptible to discovery and elucidation through the modes of "ordinary" historical investigation. They are appropriately known only as the condition for their being known is given. But then this suggests that Barth's notion of "event" falls somewhat outside the range of normal usage. It may be that the theologian needs to be able to claim this sort of discontinuity. When he does so, however, he ought to be aware of the linguistic shift involved in his use of the term "event", as well as the possible danger that he will have removed it so far from its ordinary meaning as to render his claims unintelligible. It is at least open to question whether this has not occured in Barth's notion that linguistic meaning is conferred only in the "event" of grace.

tive) no ethics at all. Apart from these considerations, there are problems that arise even when it is assumed that Barth's approach to ethics, and the content resulting from this, are essentially consistent and meaningful. These result from Barth's inclusion of the command under the category of event, and his description of the "definiteness" of the command, which seems to exclude any consideration of alternatives or options within a situation, for the simple reason that there are none to be considered. This entails an immediate and decisive exclusion of the role of practical, deliberative reason, which is underlined in Barth's insistence that the only options remaining are those of obedience or disobedience.

The upshot of this approach is that everything known and knowable about the ethical "situation" is provided by the command (i.e., by the Word of God). Particular ethical contexts, and the "linear continuity" of the command informing these (which provides the basis for "special" ethics), become simply extensions of the overarching and inclusive event of grace that moves the world inclusively from creation to redemption. Barth thus allows an exclusive and consuming priority to *theological* categories. It is impossible to extricate the notion of "event" at any point from that context. Within this ordering, the lack (and impossibility) of rational ethical deliberation is expressed clearly in the dictum that *sub gratia*, and within the ethical situation, man no longer knows, or claims to know, good or evil.

The restrictions against any knowledge of or sensitivity to good and evil within Christian ethics appears to be almost an incantational formula in Continental theology. However, it is certainly less than clear what is meant by saying this, or why it is necessary to say it as the most persistent and meaningful judgment on the human condition viewed from within theological ethics. If it means merely that *ultimate* Good is given and done by God in Jesus Christ, so that theological ethics cannot legitimately take part in the "search for the Good" exemplified within philosophical ethics, then it is doubtless true. But if the suggestion is extended to mean that our ordinary, proximate judgments have no *use* for this distinction (in a *relative*, not absolute or ontological sense), then it is clearly false. It is not at all evident why the categories of good and evil should not occupy a relative status indicative both of the given, empirical conditions and expressions within which man finds himself, and of the options and directions available to human action. A program which calls for the total elimination of the distinction between good and evil, so that these terms can no longer be given even limited significant use within theological ethics, must face the question whether the result is not a relativization of the human so radical as to make impossible the ordinary distinctions necessary to the maintenance of any sort of viable *human* context within which ethically significant decision and action can occur [1].

The difficulty in Barth's position at this point is that, while wishing to give adequate recognition to the decisiveness of God's action in Christ, he stands in danger of undercutting *human* sensitivity and responsiveness by providing an unreal delineation (in general terms) of man's ethical situation. The difficulty, I suggest, is that Barth has allowed his view of the *empirical* context within which the event of God's command and man's response occurs to be delimited entirely by the *ontological* context and event of the total movement of God outward from himself in creation, reconciliation, and redemption. And, since everything in the latter event is fixed and determined by God (grace), it follows that the same is true of human action, and the context(s) within which it unfolds. It is one thing, however, to make the latter point as an indication that God is decisively acting in all situations, and to draw from this the imperative, "So respond to all actions upon you as to respond to his actions" [2]. It is another matter altogether to mean by this that the situation in which we are called upon to respond is, as regards our precise decision and action, entirely uncluttered and free of ambiguities, so that it is immediately self-evident, without serious moral reflection on our part, what we are to do. When do we ever find ourselves in situations that meet these specifications? This is not a way of underlining the seriousness of the ethical context—it rather leads straight in the direction of its reduction to the trivial.

Further, is it really the case that there is *never* ambiguity about "the will of God" for a given situation? This is a locution that needs to be

---

[1] Barth's exclusion of good and evil from the range and possibility of human knowledge and concern reflect, as Charles West suggests, his overwhelming concern for the victory of grace in Jesus Christ, and the ontological transformation of man and the world resulting from it (Cf. *Communism and the Theologians*, pp. 244ff.). The Good is thus established exclusively by God's action, and sin and evil are viewed as ontologically impossible. The problem here, however, is that it is both philosophically and theologically unsatisfactory to allow ontological categories to absorb historical and existential realities. Where this occurs, the actualities surrounding man's immediate existence are both diminished and relativized, and he is bereft of the possibility of drawing important and necessary distinctions.

[1] Niebuhr, *The Responsible Self*, p. 25.

wielded with extreme care, lest it provide a basis for begging important questions. It is no doubt true that the most succinct answer that can be given within a Christian context to the question, "What am I to do?" is "The will of God!". As Paul Lehmann points out, however, a recital of this locution is "not a simple answer to a simple question but a complex answer to a complex question" [1]. It follows, then, that when men ask about the will of God, they do so not

> merely evasively, pretending that they do not know they are to do the will of God, when they really do know, but because they are genuinely perplexed by the diversity and complexity of human motivation and of behavioral options which make up the stuff of the ethical situation [2].

It is the apparent lack of attention to "the diversity and complexity of human motivation", and to the "behavioral options" which confront man that underlines the persistent difficulty in Barth's approach to ethics, and his delineation of the command. For if the assertion that the command is definite and self-interpreting down to the last detail is taken literally (as Barth clearly intends), then any possibility of giving attention to factors in a situation which are relatively "non-theological" (i.e., political, economic, sociological, psychological), and any discussion of "options", is excluded from the outset.

If this happens, however, it will indicate nothing more than a *reduction* of both the ethical context and the ethical agent under the aegis of an exclusive concentration on God's direct action in the situation, which somehow is presented with such force and clarity that the notion of *human* action (and responsibility) is channeled exclusively along the lines of either obedience or disobedience. It is only in reference to these possibilities that human actions will be "good" or "evil".

Barth's failure to take seriously the actual complexity of man's situation, and the variety of options presented for action, suggests an inadequate transition from the inclusive ontological indicative and imperative presented in the command (and fulfilled initially in Christ) to their behavioral manifestation amid the multiplicity of roles and contexts within which we are unavoidably entangled. What will it mean for us to "see" or "hear" the direction that freedom and obedience are to assume in a given situation? How are we to account for different "perceptions" and "hearings" of the command? Where do we ever

---

[1] *Ethics in a Christian Context*, p. 76.
[2] *Ibid.*

(even within the Christian community) achieve and exhibit unanimity, however subtle, immediate, or profound our assurances about "the will of God"?

The notion of command as employed by Barth is significant in that it marks again his concern to undercut every possibility of ideological construction and commitment, this time along the lines of a self-substantiating ethics grounded in principles and rules subject to rational manipulation from man's side. The underlying difficulty, however, is that the command functions to relieve man of every dependence on or reference to principles or rules, the distinction between good and evil, and, apparently, empirical analysis of the situation, and sets him instead within a total directing and shaping action that receives specific exemplification in the individual and corporate givenness of man's existence. The freedom which this provides is "openness for obedience", i.e., for immediate response along the lines of God's formative action. How this "freedom in obedience" is restrained from collapsing into either an oversimplification of actual situations, or into an unending series of individual responses or "hearings", which then provide the basis for summoning others to follow [1], is not clear.

Perhaps this dilemma is inadvertently recognized in Barth's emphasis on the command as judgment, which exposes the behavioral corollary of *repentance*. The question raised thereby is precisely the one faced at the end of our analysis of the *Römerbrief*: To what extent is man capable of obedience? Is there an exemplification of sanctification within the occurrence of justification in man's existence? Or does the former remain only an eschatological reality? Barth's initial delineation of the command does not appear to provide a resolution of this and other difficulties.

---

[1] Cf. III/4, p. 8f.

CHAPTER FIVE

MAN UNDER GRACE: THE CHRISTIAN
AS ETHICAL AGENT

The underlying concern of this chapter is to expose, as completely as possible, both the possibility and the actuality of obedience as the concrete manifestation of a sensitivity and response to the action of God in Jesus Christ. For Barth, the structure (form and content) of theological ethics reduces to the category of obedience, which receives initial fulfillment at a christological level. It is the obedience of Jesus Christ as the humiliated and suffering Son of God that provides the paradigm of appropriate human action. Now, neither the possibility nor the actuality of obedient human action can be discussed apart from the assumption that ethical agency is properly attributable to man. And this assumption rests on an implicit distinction between divine and human subjectivity. As was noted earlier, Barth's handling of this distinction suggests a certain ambiguity [1]. The issue about human obedience, accordingly, can be put in the form of a question: To what extent is it possible, on Barth's reading of the matter, to draw a real distinction between divine and human subjectivity and agency, and so between "the humanity of God" and "the humanity of man", so that man is established as a unique subject and agent capable of significant ethical action, i.e., obedience? The cruciality of this point becomes peculiarly transparent when it is recalled that on Barth's analysis, and in keeping with his view of God, man's identity is construed dynamically, as person-in-act [2].

A. THE STRUCTURE OF THE HUMAN

The approach to general anthropology lies in Christology, for it is in Christ that the authentic human is posited and determined. The

---

[1] Cf. above, p. 146.
[2] "Denn der Mensch existiert als Person, indem er handelt". II/2, p. 572; Cf. III/2, pp. 209ff.

movement from Christ to the general human does not signal a purely deductive transition trading on the assumption of a "direct equation" (*direkte Gleichsetzung*) between our humanity and that of Jesus [1]. It is simply an additional illustration of the pervasiveness of the "principle" of presupposition, and of analogy, in Barth's method. A discussion of the "structure" of the human, accordingly, will unfold as follows: Jesus Christ is the exclusive basis for developing a view of (1) "real man" (*wirkliche Mensch*) [2], and for understanding (2) the ontological distortion of the human in sin. In addition, Christ provides the ground for (3) a positive ontological description of the human along analogical lines.

1. *Real Man: Christological Anthropology*

The most trenchant indication of the importance of Christology for anthropology is given in the statement that Christ's "person, the person of the Son of God, and so of God himself", is "*the* human person" (*die menschliche Person*) [3]. So, just as the clue to the ontological determin- ation and goal of the human, ethically considered, is found in Christ, man's identity and subjectivity as person and agent are also given initially and exclusively in him. It is this point that invokes once again what we have seen repeatedly to be a necessary and irreversible order of priority governing the development of each phase of our discussion. It is impossible, within the *Dogmatics*, ever to begin with general con- siderations, whether these focus on God, the created order, the identi- fication of the Good, the destructive capacities and resources of evil, sin, and death, or the destiny and identity of man as elected recipient of, and ethical agent under, grace, and to provide these with some sort of independent elucidation and content.

When this point is brought into conjunction with the question as to the possibility of providing the notion of "real man" with descriptive adequacy and content, it will exclude the possibility of an approach to this issue along the lines of what Barth describes as "phenomena of the human" (*Phänomene des Menschlichen*) [4]. This exclusion takes the form

---

[1] III/2, pp. 54; 83; 264f.

[2] *Ibid.*, Par. 44, Part 3.

[3] II/2, p. 872; Cf. III/2, p. 49 : "This man is man. As surely as God's attitude toward sinful man is initially and properly entirely his attitude toward him, and only in and through him also his attitude to other men, so initially and properly he alone is man".

[4] III/2, Par. 44, Part 2.

of an initial, general "demarcation" (*Abgrenzung*) that establishes
a clear and fixed boundary between adequate and inadequate approaches
to the anthropological question:

> No definition of human nature can in any case be adequate to the issue
> with which we are concerned here, if it is finally only an assertion and
> description of the characteristics of his nature that are accessible and
> knowable to perception and thought, and that man takes as indicative
> of the nature of his fellow-men, and so of humanity in general. On this
> basis, human self-knowledge must, in view of all our criteria, denote
> only a circle, in which we can never approach real man [1].

Barth's ostensible point here is critical, not simply negative, and
centers on what he sees as the irremediable ambiguity surrounding both
the data emerging from a general approach to the human, and the
conclusions to which they lead. This holds true whether the approach
proceeds along the lines of the biological sciences [2], the givenness of
human ethical awareness and response [3], or, more recently, the emphasis
in existentialist thought on supposed "frontier situations" (*Grenz-
situationen*) [4] that expose man to "self-transcendence" amid the tensions
of suffering, guilt, and death. Barth is willing to recognize the possibility
that any or all of these can be *symptomatic* of real man, but insists that
their significance will be apparent only on the basis of a prior knowledge
of who and what man actually is [5]. The danger and limitation involved
in launching the inquiry from the side of the general human, aside from
the fact that it involves an obvious ignoring of the christological point,
is that it gives at best a partial, and therefore distorted, notion of man,
and (more importantly) that it can lead to the emergence of rigid,
inflexible interpretations that end by asserting and imposing conclusive
ideologies within the context of human self-understanding.

---

[1] *Ibid.*, p. 86f.

[2] *Ibid.*, pp. 92ff.

[3] *Ibid.*, pp. 106ff.

[4] *Ibid.*, pp. 132ff. It seems clear that Barth's delimitation of "real man"
from mere "phenomena of the human" would also rule out the possibility of
building a viable anthropology on the insights emanating from the social
sciences, i.e., sociology, history (political or economic), anthropology, psychology, and, more recently, psychiatry. Aside from the possible difficulties occas-
sioned for Barth's anthropology by this delimitation, it can be noted that
the question it poses for his ethics is crucial: To what extent (if any) can these
"phenomenological" factors be taken seriously into account at the point of
ethical assessment and action?

[5] *Ibid.*, p. 87; Cf. III/4, p. 47.

The way out of this development, Barth insists, is to recognize that man's authentic being and identity are disclosed not within the framework of generalized inquiries, but exclusively within the specific *history* that takes place between God and man as exemplified in Jesus Christ [1]. Only within that context can man's real difference and autonomy within the created order be described [2].

What is it, then, to talk about and describe "real man" from this center? What are the differentiating and identifying characteristics that emerge in Christ, and that extend, analogously, to all men? In our initial exploration of the determination given the human in the event of reconciliation, it was noted that the most important unifying and distinguishing property marking Christ's humanity was the utter *freedom* surrounding his action as Son of God and Son of Man. What makes Jesus real or "whole" man is indicated comprehensively by the freedom in which he is open and responsive to and for both God and man [3]. The identity and action of Jesus as the Son of Man cannot be separated from his identity and action as the Son of God. He *is* man only as the actualized eternal potential of the Son of God to become and be this particular man existing within the context, and under the conditions, of space and time. So, as Christ is both electing God and elected man, he exhibits conclusively both the freedom of God for man, and man's corresponding freedom for God and his fellows [4].

The dynamic import of the category of freedom as applied to the humanity of Jesus underlines again Barth's refusal to utilize fixed, static concepts and orderings. Human nature appears only within the *history* of Jesus, for it is only there that Jesus's own identity emerges. It is not, then, a matter of elucidating what is essentially a "neutral" (*neutrale*) humanity in Jesus, which permits the entertainment of a variety of options concerning its fulfillment or realization [5]. Jesus is man exclusively in his action as the "bearer of an office" [6], in his work as the Savior:

---

[1] III/2, pp. 90ff.; 143ff.; Cf. III/4, p. 44f.

[2] III/2, p. 90f.

[3] Cf. III/4, Par. 44, Part 1, "Jesus, Man for God"; Par. 45, Part 1, "Jesus, Man for Other Men"; Par. 46, Part 1, "Jesus, Whole Man". Barth's discussion of the anthropological point within the event of reconciliation is also relevant to our concern here. Cf. IV/2, Par. 64, Parts 3, "The Royal Man", and 4, "The Direction of the Son".

[4] II/1, pp. 356ff.; IV/1, p. 269f.; III/2, pp. 158ff.; 242ff.

[5] III/2, p. 66.

[6] *Ibid.*

Who and what man is is real and évident in its fulness in the fact that the
Son of God has become man in Jesus, and that man is placed so completely at the disposal of God in him. It is just here that man is real,
and is perceivable in his reality [1].

It is within the context of this specific history that man's openness
and availability for God is shown. So Jesus is to be seen as the creature
who is uniquely for God, whose existence takes place and continues
only in relation to the divine work of reconciliation and deliverance [2].
Jesus is the creature who exists only in the lordship of God. What this
means is that it is impossible to separate man's being (in him) from the
being of God [3]. And within this relation of dependence, the existence of
the man Jesus shows that the creature itself has significance for God,
that the relation in which it is placed is one involving reciprocity:

> Man is the being who is for God. In that respect, he surpasses all other
> creatures. At any rate, we do not know this to be true of any other
> creature. That makes man—this man—a unique form in the cosmos.
> For how does the creature come to be "for God"? In terms of its general
> reality, knowable in other forms, it indeed belongs to its essence that
> God is for the creature, that it owes him gratitude for everything. But it
> does not belong to the essence of the creature that (on its side) it is for
> God, that it should have significance for him, that he should expect
> something from it, that it should contribute something to his activity
> and being. This reciprocity is man's privilege. The privilege of *this* man,
> as we must indeed say here. Nor does it only *belong* to his essence that
> man is for God. Rather, his essence is constituted by, and consists exclu-
> sively in, the fact that he is for God [4].

Just as Jesus's identity as "real man" is marked, on the one side,
by the fact that he exists exclusively as the man for God, so too it is
marked, on the other, by the fact that he exists solely as "the man for
other men" [5]. The humanity of Jesus, on this side, is delineated totally
in his existence (in act) *"propter nos"*, i.e., *"propter salutem nostram"* [6].

> What interests him totally and exclusively is man, indeed other men
> as such, who need him and are directed to his help and deliverance.
> Other men are the object of his saving work, in the execution of which

---

[1] *Ibid.*, p. 74.
[2] *Ibid.*, p. 81f.
[3] *Ibid.*, p. 79f.
[4] *Ibid.*, p. 82.
[5] *Ibid.*, pp. 242ff.
[6] *Ibid.*, p. 251.

he himself exists. It is on their behalf that he takes God's place in the cosmos ... From the first, since he is himself man, Jesus is not without his fellow-men, but to them, with them, and for them. He is sent and ordained by God to be their deliverer. Nothing else? No, really nothing else. For whatever else may be said of the humanity of Jesus is reducible to this denominator, and finds here its key and explanation. The form of his humanity is in strict correspondence with his divinity—his being as it is directed to his fellow-men [1].

The being of Jesus as man is thus describable as both "from" and "to" his fellows, in the sense that his action (as Son of God) arises wholly *from* God's graciousness in dealing with man's need, and is directed exclusively *to* the fulfillment of reconciliation and a restoration of man to authentic humanity within himself, toward others, and before God [2]. The significance of Jesus' co-humanity (*Mitmenschlichkeit*), and the relationship this bears to his action as the Son of God, are brought together in Barth's description of Jesus as "the royal man" (*der königliche Mensch*) [3].

This description, as applied to Jesus, is designed to bring out the way in which his humanity "forms a parallel in the creaturely world to the plan and intention and work and attitude of God" [4]. Put succinctly, Jesus "exists as a man in analogy to the mode of existence of God" [5]. As the royal man, Jesus undergoes the "strange destiny" (*wunderliche Los*) falling to God and his people in the world [6]. His humanity, as being-in-act, represents a true reflection of the humiliation of the Son of God, thereby drawing attention to the "marginal" status of God's power and victory in the world (i.e., as weakness and defeat) which underlines the "pronouncedly revolutionary character" of its impact on man and society [7]. The revolution in question focuses on the encroachment of God on the world and man, an encroachment so radical and total that it calls into question all existing programs, and sets a limit to every established order. The questioning and limiting of the social that occurs in the action of Jesus signals "the freedom of the kingdom of God" (*die Freiheit*

---

[1] *Ibid.*, p. 249; Cf. pp. 257ff.
[2] *Ibid.*, pp. 257f.
[3] IV/2, pp. 173ff.
[4] *Ibid.*, p. 186.
[5] "Will sagen: er existiert als Mensch analog zur Existenzweise Gottes". *Ibid.*, p. 185.
[6] *Ibid.*, p. 186.
[7] *Ibid.*, pp. 186-191.

des Reiches Gottes) [1]. This freedom, exhibited in the humanity of Jesus, consists (1) in his identification with the poor and the outcast of the world, and in his ignoring or "overlooking" (*vorübersehen*) of the rich and the powerful [2]; (2) in his ability to move within and under established orders and structures [3]; and (3) in his total freedom from any final dependence on them [4]. The attitude and activity of Jesus within the established order neutralize the claims and sanctions it imposes on man, and so opens the way for a radical "reordering" or "transvaluation" of existing values [5]. And in all this, Jesus, as the creaturely reflection of God's own being-in-act, is never against, but always *for*, man. This is the first and last word to be said about his humanity as it is given form in his action [6].

Finally, the humanity-in-action (i.e., as history) [7] of Jesus provides the concrete instance of "whole man" (*ganzer Mensch*). What it means to be whole man, a unified being, emerges only on the far side of a

---

[1] *Ibid.*, p. 192.

[2] *Ibid.*, p. 188.

[3] *Ibid.*, p. 192.

[4] *Ibid.*

[5] "In Gemeinschaft und Konformität mit diesem in der Welt armen Gott ist der königliche Mensch Jesus selbst ein Armer und vollzieht er jene Umwertung aller Werte, bekennt er sich zu denen, die in dieser Welt, ohne darum bessere Menschen zu sein, in irgend einem Sinn arme Menschen sind". *Ibid.*, p. 188.

[6] "The word which is really first and last is undoubtedly that the man Jesus, like God himself, is not against, but for, men—and for men exactly in the full impossibility of their perversion, in their form as the men of the old world of Adam ... The man Jesus is decisively 'created after God' in that he is as man the work and revelation of the mercy of God, of his Gospel, his kingdom of peace, his reconciliation, and that he is thus the creaturely, earthly, human correspondence of God". *Ibid.*, p. 200f. Barth's analysis of the impact of Jesus on contemporary orders and structures, and the valuational results of this, is reminiscent of certain passages in his early essays and the *Römerbrief* (Cf. *WG*, pp. 299ff.; 316. *RÖM*, p. 275f.). What is suggested in this continuity, as Charles West has pointed out, is Barth's continuing acceptance of the socialist critique of "bourgeois" standards, and the inevitable tendency they exhibit in the direction of ideological ultimacy. Cf. *Communism and the Theologians*, pp. 200; 215; 317. Indeed, if one were to attempt a negative epitomization of the persistent thrust of all of Barth's theological and ethical thinking, it would consist in the immediate relativization and exclusion of all ideological pretensions and securities under the impact of God's grace in Jesus Christ.

[7] III/2, p. 64f.

consideration and elucidation of man's being as a being in covenant with God and in relation to his fellow-men [1]. Within this framework, the human constitution of Jesus emerges consistently as a *unity* so firmly established that it permits of only a provisional, relative differentiation between the "soulish" and "bodily" dimensions [2]. Barth borrows a term from Classical philosophy to describe the interconnection holding in Jesus between soul and body, and argues that it is "no chaos, but a cosmos (*Kosmos*), an ordered and formed whole" [3]. Thus, though there is an order to be observed and maintained between soul and body, or "inner" and "outer", which makes it necessary to speak of "a higher and a lower, a first and a second, a ruling and a ruled", these never fall into tension or discontinuity [4]. The humanity of Jesus exhibits continuous sovereignty, so that his life as soul and body is really his own. He is the origin of his own unity, so that he is at no point subject to alien, external control or determination. It is the sovereignty of Jesus as self and agent that accounts for the continuity of his being-in-act, and allows him to live for and in other men without ceasing to be uniquely himself:

> Jesus wills and completes himself. He is his own ground, his own in-tention. He lives in such a way that command and obedience, super- and sub-ordination, plan and execution, goal and purpose, proceed in the same way from himself, so that they are grounded alike in an inner necessity ... He lives in sovereignty. His life in the order of soul and body is really his own. He has complete power over it, and so he can make it the life of many others without its ceasing to belong to him, to be his life, and without its being diminished or lost to him [5].

---

[1] *Ibid.*, p. 391.

[2] *Ibid.*, p. 394. Barth employs the traditional Cartesian terminology, though apparently he does not wish to understand the distinction between body and soul along the lines of a dualist metaphysic of substance (Cf. *Ibid.*: " von zwei 'Substanzen' gar existierte, sondern als einiger und ganzer Mensch "). As Barth employs these terms, they designate the "rational and sensuous", or "inner and outer", or "invisible and visible", or "intelligible and empirical" aspects of man's being as man. Where the specific humanity of Jesus is under consideration, however, these distinctions do not have binding, absolute meaning, since in Jesus there is no "inner" or "rational" dimension that is finally distinguishable from an "outer" or "sensuous" counterpart (*Ibid.*). This would follow logically from the fact that Jesus *is* man (and so "a man") only as the Son of God.

[3] *Ibid.*, p. 399.

[4] *Ibid.*

[5] *Ibid.*, p. 400.

The unity that gains expression in the humanity of Jesus does not, however, rest merely on a consistently harmonious ordering of soul and body. The condition for this ordering, and the unity to which it leads, lies in the unique relation in which Jesus stands, as the Son of God, to the Holy Spirit. It is this relationship that forms "the special determination of the human constitution of Jesus" [1], and that guarantees that his life will be "personal", and so "permeated and determined by his I, by Himself" [2]. As *the* human person, whose humanity is simultaneously whole and real, Jesus, in that he not only has but is "spirit" (i.e., the Holy Spirit of God himself), is provided with a determination and an identity which cannot be attributed to men generally [3]. This point underlines, once again, Barth's refusal to treat the humanity of Jesus as an independent, isolable factor. He is man, and so spirit, only as the Son and Word of God:

> But the power and necessity in which Jesus is whole man are not grounded in themselves, but in the fact that he is first and simultaneously true God and true man. We have seen that they are the power and necessity of the Holy Spirit resting upon him. It is because he is the Son and Word of God that the Holy Spirit rests on him, that he exists in the fulness of the Holy Spirit, that he is whole man in a meaningfully ordered unity of soul and body [4].

In concluding this discussion of Jesus as real and whole man, I wish to draw attention to a difficulty that emerges in Barth's treatment of the distinction between the divine and the human in Jesus. In getting at this difficulty, it is necessary to bear in mind that, on Barth's view, the man Jesus represents no independent human person, but is understood to be man only as the actualized eternal potential of the Son of God to become and be this particular man. The humanity of Jesus, accordingly, is properly describable as God's own humanity. Given this orientation, it would appear to follow that the humanity of Jesus would exhibit identity with God, even though this would not amount to *logical* iden-

---

[1] *Ibid.*

[2] *Ibid.*, p. 403.

[3] *Ibid.*, pp. 402; 414ff. The question that arises here for Barth's anthropology, whether, and to what extent, man is to be understood as person and subject, since he is not, apparently, definable as spirit, is explored in Section C, below, "The Analogical Validation of Man".

[4] *Ibid.*, p. 410f.

tity [1]. And this would entail, further, (1) that no legitimate distinction can be drawn between the economic and immanent modes of God's being as Father, Son, and Spirit, or (2) between a "Logos asarkos" and a "Logos ensarkos" [2].

This interpretation of the relation between the humanity of Jesus and God is borne out in Barth's statement concerning the obedience of Christ:

> The One who in such obedience is the perfect image of the ruling God is himself—in distinction to every human, creaturely kind—*God by nature, God in his relation to himself*, i.e., God in his mode of being as the Son in relation to God in his mode of being as the Father, with this One, with this same essence" [3].

In view of the consistency and strenuousness with which Barth develops this point, it is surprising to find him making, within his discussion of "Jesus, Man for Other Men", what appear to be very ambiguous statements. The passage in question runs as follows:

> The humanity of Jesus is not only the repetition and imitation of his divinity, or of the governing will of God, but it is the repetition and imitation of God himself—no more and no less. It is the image of God, the *imago Dei*. The "image"—we must take account of the restriction implicit in this conception. Because the humanity of Jesus is the image of God, it follows that it is only indirectly (and so not directly) identical with God. It belongs intrinsically to the creaturely world, to the cosmos. Therefore, it does not belong to the inner sphere of the essence of God, but to the outer sphere of his work. It does not, then, present God as he is in himself and in relation to himself, but it presents him in his relation to the reality distinct from himself. In the former, we have to do with God and God. In the latter, with God and man. These are two different things. We cannot expect more than correspondence and similarity between them. We cannot maintain identity. Between God and God, between the Father and the Son, and the Son and the Father, there is a unity of essence, the complete satisfaction of self-grounded reality, a blessedness which is eternally generated and renewed out of itself. There can be no question of this between God and man, however, and so it cannot gain expression in the humanity of Jesus, in his co-humanity as the image of God [4].

---

[1] I/2, p. 177f.; IV/2, p. 78.
[2] I/1, pp. 351ff.; 426ff.; I/2, p. 170; III/1, pp. 53f.; 57ff.; IV/1, pp. 54, 70; IV/3.1, pp. 457ff.
[3] IV/1, p. 228. Italics added.
[4] III/2, p. 261f.

The baffling points that emerge in this passage are (1) an apparent
distinction and separation between an economic and an immanent view
of God's being; and (2) an apparent view of the relation between the
Father and the Son, as eternal modes of God's being, which proceeds
independently of the specific humanity of Jesus. On both points, Barth
is at odds with what has thus far been taken to be his orientation and
meaning. And the ambiguity and discontinuity present here are underlined in a statement immediately preceding the passage quoted above:

> God for man—if that is the eternal covenant which is revealed and
> powerful in time in the humanity of Jesus, then in this decision of the
> Creator for his creature there occurs a relation which is not alien to him
> as Creator, to God himself as God, but which is, we might say, appro-
> priate and natural to him. In this relation God repeats *ad extra a relation
> which is proper to himself in his inner divine essence* [1].

What Barth has in mind in stressing the humanity of Jesus as the
"image" of God, it appears, is a maintenance of the firm distinction he
has drawn between man and God, and so a preservation of the distinction
between creature and Creator. Where the development of a viable
anthropology along christological lines is in question, this distinction
becomes crucial, since it is exclusively from Christ that we are to draw
our clues as to the identity and structure of the authentically human.
That the preservation of this distinction is what concerns Barth here is
seen in his assertion that the "correspondence and similarity" (*Entsprechung und Ähnlichkeit*) holding within the being of God between the
Father and the Son, on the one hand, and between God and man in
Jesus, on the other, is an instance of the *analogia relationis* [2].

Now, where it is a matter of the relation between God and the creature *generally*, this is indeed, given Barth's ordering of the factors, the
only possible way in which the relationship can be construed. As such,
the *analogia relationis* constitutes a continuing emphasis on the priority
of grace, and the utterly dependent status of the creature corresponding
to it. Where it is a matter of the specific humanity of Jesus, however,
it is dubious that this move is open to Barth. The major consideration

---

[1] *Ibid.*, p. 260. Italics added. Cf. also Barth's statement in his lecture,
"The Humanity of God"; "God requires no exclusion of humanity, no non-
humanity, not to speak of inhumanity, in order to be truly God. But we may
and must, however, look further and recognize the fact that actually His deity
encloses humanity in itself". *The Humanity of God*, p. 50.

[2] III/2, p. 262; Cf. Bouillard, *Karl Barth*, Vol. II, p. 251.

against it, aside from the points already mentioned (i.e., the fact that Jesus is man *only* as the Son of God, the emphasis on the pre-existence of Christ, which precludes the possibility of a "Logos asarkos", and the continuity established between the economic and the immanent modes of God's being), is that Barth specifically asserts that the unity established between God and man, Creator and creature, in Christ, is absolutely *sui generis*, and so cannot be thrown into precise parallel with humanity or the created order, generally considered [1]. But this entails that the relation between God and man in Christ is only improperly described as an example (or even the prime example) of the *analogia relationis*. Besides, it may be recalled that the role Barth assigns to analogy is that of a vehicle permitting significant ontological description of the *creature* to take place.

It is true that Christ is *the* example of true creaturely being. It is also true, however, that he is this only as the actualization of the eternal potential of the Son of God to become and be "flesh" as this particular man. To put the matter in technical terms, it is improper, we feel, to apply the *analogia relationis* to Christ because, as the Son of God, and so God himself, he would necessarily function as the *analogue* rather than the *analogate* in any analogous relation. It is human nature generally, not the specific humanity of Christ, that would be accounted for on the basis of analogy. This holds true despite the fact that the humanity of Christ provides an ontological determination and goal for created human nature generally, so that the latter is viewed only from the perspective of the former. It should be noted, however, that if Barth *could* establish the relation between God and man in Christ as an instance of the *analogia relationis*, the difficulty mentioned at the end of the last chapter regarding an apparent (or possible) absorption of humanity might be forestalled. For the reasons indicated, however, it is necessary to reject the propriety of this move, and to underline the continuity and identity holding between the humanity of Jesus and God. If it is possible, within Barth's framework, to mark off a significant ontological distinction between the identity of Christ as Son of God, and man generally, it will have to proceed along different lines.

---

[1] I/2, p. 177; III/2, p. 264f.

2. *The Distortion of the Human in Sin*

It must be underlined at the outset that there can be no question here of a total and irrecoverable *loss* of humanity. This might occur, if Barth's analysis of human sin, and the consequences to which it leads, proceeded along independent anthropological lines. Since the discussion here, as at all points in the *Dogmatics*, moves along consistently christological lines [1], sin will constitute no more than an "episode", an unwarranted intrusion into the created order and human nature and action as originally posited by God. And since the totality of God's purpose and action toward man and the world is subsumed under his eternal election of man as his responsible covenant partner, it follows that man's breaking of the covenant, and the subsequent loss of genuine identity and selfhood resulting from this, will be related at all points to the fulfillment of the covenant, and the exemplification of authentic humanity, that occurred in Jesus Christ [2]. This approach precludes the possibility of granting ontological status to sin, and the consequences resulting from it for man. In referring to the "*distortion* of the human in sin*", then, recognition is given to Barth's insistence that sin influences or "determines" (*bestimmt*) man's being at all points, but does not result in a structural alteration of it [3]. There is thus a common "creaturely essence" (*geschöpfliches Wesen*) which is grounded in creation, and which persists "throughout the antitheses of sin, reconciliation and redemption" [4].

---

[1] IV/1, pp. 152-161; 395ff.; IV/2, pp. 423ff.; IV/3.1, pp. 425ff.

[2] IV/1, p. 154f.

[3] III/2, p. 46.

[4] *Ibid.*, p. 46f. With this point, Barth establishes a clear continuity between the orders of creation, reconciliation, and redemption, and so, anthropologically considered, between "nature" and "grace", or the "natural man" and the man of faith. Taken in one way, this could be interpreted as a modification of an earlier and stronger position in the *Dogmatics*, in which the fact of sin resulted in a *total* blurring and, finally, elimination of the *imago Dei* in man. This interpretation is taken by Professor Come in his book, *An Introduction to Barth's "Dogmatics" for Preachers*, p. 152f. As regards the question of a development or modification at this point in Barth's anthropology, I should like to suggest the following observations : (1) Barth's ostensibly stronger, earlier position on the question of the status of the *imago Dei* after the fall is explained, in part at least, by his concern to mark a decisive separation and distinction between his own position and those represented in contemporary protestant (i.e., Emil Brunner) and Roman Catholic theology, both of which trade, either implicitly or explicitly, on the (for Barth) forbidden assumption

Barth's analysis of sin proceeds within the context of the obedience of Jesus Christ, an obedience that gained expression precisely in his freedom for both God and man. Viewed from this perspective, man's sin will consist in his continued response of disobedience to the action of God, and the paradigm of appropriate human action posited therein, which carries with it a corresponding loss of freedom and authentic selfhood [1]. The precise dimensions of sin, accordingly, will provide the negative counterparts to (1) God's action of condescension and humiliation in Christ, in taking his place beside man within the context of world history and under the burden this imposed; (2) the exaltation of man to fellowship with God that occurred in Christ; and (3) the fidelity of God to man manifested in the action of Christ (through the Holy Spirit) as the witness to, and guarantor of, reconciliation. Descriptively, this amounts, respectively, to a delineation of the pride (*Hochmut*), sloth (*Trägheit*), and falsehood (*Lüge*) of man [2]. Pride and sloth form the "works" of man in sin, falsehood his "word" [3]. Barth takes it that in describing the tri-dimensionality of sin, he is describing man's *past*, his being in Adam which now (in Christ) lies wholly behind him [4].

---

of the *analogia entis*. Cf. I/1, p. 251; II/2, pp. 588ff. (2) Though Barth does speak of a certain "created constant" that is not obliterated by sin, it is clear that this cannot be given independent description or status outside the event of reconciliation. What remains of the *imago Dei* after the fall, furthermore, does not pertain to man considered exclusively as individual, but rather to certain modes of relationality, which are real and continuous enough, but only on the basis of the *analogia relationis*, or, more generally, an "analogy of grace". It is exclusively on the basis of grace that reconciliation represents and effects a "fulfillment" of created human nature. Seen in this light, it is possible that the earlier passages in question could be brought under this interpretation. (3) Even though continuity is maintained between "natural man" and the man of faith, it is clear that this cannot be used as a basis for independent constructions concerning the former, because (a) created human nature is seen in its constancy only from the perspective of its fulfillment in Christ, so that the movement, anthropologically, is always from Christ to Adam, and never the reverse; and (b) for Barth, the continuity between created and reconciled human nature is exemplified initially *only* in Christ, though it gains secondary exemplification in other men under the impact of the Holy Spirit. The conclusion to be drawn from these points is that it is possible to view the ostensible shift or development in Barth's anthropology as primarily a matter of emphasis, rather than substance.

[1] IV/1, pp. 459; 498ff.; IV/2, p. 459f.

[2] IV/1, pp. 156ff.

[3] IV/3.1., p. 430.

[4] IV/1, p. 559f.

Here the ontological significance of the Christ event comes again into view. It must be kept in mind, however, that this point functions primarily to indicate man's "real" destiny and determination, and so, to a measurable extent, eschatologically. It will therefore be the case that the history of man will be describable at all points as "Adamic history" (*Adams Geschichte*) [1].

Pride, as the first aspect of man's total reaction to grace, results in man's loss of openness for God. In dramatic contrast to God's action in becoming man (an action that can only be successful), man seeks to become and be "like God", (an action that is, from the outset, doomed to failure) [2]. There can be no explanation for this move on man's part, for it has no real basis, justification, or possibility. In wishing to be like God, man rebels against his given status and identity as the good creature of God [3]. In exchange for his place as God's elected covenant partner, and the openness and fellowship for God which this includes, man now attempts to function as his own standard, and so is led into serving the false god of his own self-contained existence [4].

The distortion involved here is immediately compounded by the fact that in his position of isolated self-sufficiency, man covertly becomes (in distinction to Christ, the Lord who became a servant) "the servant who wants to be lord", i.e., over the world and his fellow-man [5]. This is borne out in man's attempt to be his own judge, and the judge of others, concerning good and evil, right and wrong. The upshot of this can only be self-alienation and destruction, and a dissolving of any possibility of a realization of the co-humanity and freedom, which he has received in the judgment fulfilled in the obedience of Christ, to be *for* as well as with his fellow-man [6]. Man's only authentic possibility lies in the direction of following the action of God, which has already determined and drawn the proper distinction between what is good and what is evil, or what is right and what is wrong [7].

---

[1] *Ibid.*, p. 567.

[2] "It is not paradoxical or absurd that God becomes and is man. It does not contradict the idea of God; on the contrary, it fulfills it. It reveals the glory of God. But it is only paradoxical and absurd that man wishes to be God. It contradicts the idea of man. It destroys it. In wishing that, man ceases to be man". *Ibid.*, p. 465.

[3] *Ibid.*

[4] *Ibid.*, pp. 467ff.

[5] *Ibid.*, pp. 479ff.

[6] *Ibid.*, pp. 483f.; 494ff.

[7] *Ibid.*, p. 498f.

Stated comprehensively, the distortion involved in the response of pride is that it encourages man to imagine that he can establish and maintain himself as a free being and agent, and so provide himself with authentic life. The error becomes complete when, in adopting this posture, he seeks at the same time to enlist God's aid in its accomplishment and continuation [1]. The inevitable result of this orientation is that man becomes "fallen man—fallen to the place where God, who does not and cannot fall, has humbled himself for him in Jesus Christ" [2]. An understanding of man's situation here does not emerge from an analysis of the "natural man" as such, but only within the context of the Gospel [3]. Nor can man's fall signal an absolute separation from God—he cannot fall into total or "ontological" godlessness. The covenant between God and man continues in force. The difference is that God's "Yes" is now experienced as a "No", i.e., as the "wrath" (*Zorne*) of God [4]. Man continues to live before God, but in disobedience. Faith and obedience, and so freedom, are channeled into the wasteland of "religion", which functions precisely as an indication of man's "bad faith", of his continuing efforts to secure self-justification [5]. Man thus exists under a contradiction which he is powerless to resolve: He is at once (in terms of his response) totally sinner and totally bound by the covenant [6].

If man's response of pride signals a rejection of both the judgment brought to bear on man in the humiliation and obedience of Christ, and the way in which he is thereby freed for an authentic relationship with God, his response of "sloth" signals his rejection of the demand imposed on him in that action [7]. Whereas man ought to respond with alacrity to the divine claim, he falls instead into sluggishness or inertia, and so refuses to live in and under the freedom presented in Christ [8]. In rejecting this, he rejects his own proper nature and destiny, and so loses the possibility of experiencing or demonstrating real freedom at

---

[1] *Ibid.*, pp. 508ff.

[2] *Ibid.*, p. 531.

[3] *Ibid.*, p. 533.

[4] *Ibid.*, p. 545.

[5] *Ibid.*, p. 537f. The negative significance of Law, as the "outer" side of grace, of levelling a judgment against man's false attempts to secure his existence with God and man, may be recalled in connection with Barth's statement here on "religion". Cf. I/2, Par. 17, Parts 2, "Religion as Unbelief"; and 3, "True Religion".

[6] IV/1, p. 548f.

[7] IV/2, p. 455f.

[8] *Ibid.*, p. 457f.

any point in his life, whether in relation to God, his fellow-man, the created order, or his given limitation in time and history [1]. Taken together, these four points indicate the *"gestalt"* of man's inactivity and unresponsiveness when confronted with authentic freedom.

Furthermore, there is an interrelatedness and unity holding between these manifestations of man's failure properly to respond to grace. The consequences proceeding from this inaction, descriptively summarized as "stupidity" (*Dummheit*) [2], are, strictly speaking, entailed consequences indicative of both the totality and the inexorability of man's loss of freedom. Thus, a refusal to actualize the freedom given in Christ leads immediately to a loss of knowledge of God, which in turn leads to a loss of authentic co-humanity (since this relationship is grounded in God), a sundering of the unity of the created order (expressed within man) into a dualism of the psychical and the physical, and a temporality devoid of meaning or promise [3]. Or again, beginning with the second point, a loss of authentic humanity entails a loss of knowledge of God, which leads irrevocably to the collapse of order and unity between body and soul, and so to a loss of man's temporal place and significance in history [4]. Or, finally, a distortion of the unity of soul and body given man in Christ falls immediately over into "dissipation" (*Verlotterung*), a kind of total self-abandonment covered over with self-justifying appeals to "freedom" or "naturalness" [5]. Human existence at this level is locked within the circularity of disorder and unpredictability, which produces a loss of authentic knowledge of God (since God stands for order and peace), a loss through irresponsibility of man's given and destined co-humanity, and a dissolution of meaningful temporality through a process of unending striving toward infinity [6].

As with pride, so also with sloth, there is a way of indicating comprehensively what is involved in the loss of freedom, openness and responsiveness to which it leads: Man's life is marked and controlled at all points by an obsessive *care* (*Sorge*) [7]. To live one's life in care is

---

[1] *Ibid.*, p. 459. These four points are, as Barth points out (*Ibid.*), paralleled in his initial development of anthropology, and the development of a "special" ethics of creation. Cf. III/2, Pars. 44-47; III/4, Pars. 53-56.

[2] IV/2, p. 462.

[3] *Ibid.*, pp. 471-477.

[4] *Ibid.*, pp. 497-502.

[5] *Ibid.*, pp. 509f.; 517.

[6] *Ibid.*, pp. 519-524.

[7] *Ibid.*, p. 532f.

to exist in the domination of fear and desire [1], which can take the form either of an activist concern with the achievement of success in some activity or context, or a lapse into passivity through resignation and contemplation [2]. In the end, the loss of authentic freedom given in Christ is exemplified, amid the onset of a continuous disrelationship to God, himself, and his fellow-man, by the fact that man moves through his time, and approaches his end, without hope. Instead of a present and future filled with *hopeful* possibilities for existence and action, time presents itself as a burden and threat to be overcome and submerged [3].

The ontic counterpart to the response of sloth is misery (*Elend*), a total and consuming "sickness unto death" that embraces man's existence at every point [4]. The misery of man reflects the loss of the best that is his as the good creature of God. Having failed to act on the freedom maintained for him in Jesus Christ, human decision and action, as functions of will, manifest man's negative bondage to sin. An analytical pattern is thus set in motion, in which the initial response of inactivity (*peccatum originale*) falls over into particular actions exemplifying that response (*peccata actualia*), and so into "peccata in actione" [5]. The negative side of man's bondage is total, but not final. Beyond it, and prior to it, there lies man's liberation and sanctification, and so the possibility of freely willed and achieved acts, secured in Christ [6].

Both the pride and sloth of man are descriptively subsumed under the third dimension of sin, his falsehood. As a "movement of evasion" (*Ausweichbewegung*) [7], it constitutes the "word" of human response to God's action, which aims at its domestication and elimination, and so at its control [8]. The paradigms of human attempts to relativize the truth

---

[1] *Ibid.*, p. 532.
[2] *Ibid.*, pp. 534ff.
[3] *Ibid.*, pp. 527ff.
[4] *Ibid.*, p. 549f.
[5] *Ibid.*, pp. 558; 554f.
[6] *Ibid.*, pp. 558-564.
[7] IV/3.1, p. 500.
[8] "The discovery and effort of evasion in face of the firmness of the truth is the real artistic achievement and masterpiece of falsehood. The man of sin who to a certain extent reflects objectively asks himself why he should not make the attempt to use the truth, and the knowledge of the truth, for an evasive movement before its attack and gradual seizure of control. If one cannot overcome it, if it cannot be effectively denied, if its knowledge cannot be contained, and if one cannot escape from it into another place where one will have nothing more to do with it, then the solution might well be to canalize

presented in the person and action of Christ are found in Judas and Dostoevsky's Grand Inquisitor. The occasion for this response is provided by the total freedom in which God confronts man in Christ's obedience, a freedom that meets man as both grace and command [1]. Since the issue of man's own liberation is totally enclosed within the action of God, he can encounter God only from the position already established by God himself, and so only in the response of gratitude and obedience. Human truth will therefore consist exclusively in the acceptance of the freedom given man by God, in which man is "born again to freedom and self-determination, to that, namely, which belongs to him as the responsible covenant partner of the free and self-determining God, as his creature, as the one who is loved by him" [2]. Instead of accepting the action of God as the presupposition for authentic human freedom and action, man seeks to limit or obscure the total independence of God by importing human presuppositions into the picture, and so can end only in the "foolish freedom" (*Narrenfreiheit*) of attempting to ground his being and action in the necessity and ability that he possesses for independent self-determination in choosing from among the various alternatives which confront him [3].

The result of man's falsehood is his condemnation. In resisting and distorting the grace of God, man rejects his true being and destiny, and so falls under God's judgment:

> It is his condemnation really to be hopelessly bound by his pride and hopelessly enslaved by his sloth. That is the threat under which he comes to stand, and indeed places himself, as he lies, that he is subject to his lie, that he is taken seriously as a liar, that he will be granted and finally alloted a life by and in untruth as the portion which he himself has chosen, a life that can only be a lost life, and that can only be described as such [4].

In choosing to exist in falsehood, man opts for an impossible possibility which has already been met and overcome in Christ. Though

---

and transform to a certain extent its power. He will in no sense close his ears to it. He cannot do that, after all, for he already has it in his ears! But he will hear it only as he wishes to hear it. He will not deny it, indeed he will emphatically affirm it, but he will affirm it only in the sense in which it is held to be bearable and useful". *Ibid.*, p. 502.

[1] *Ibid.*, p. 511f.
[2] *Ibid.*, p. 515.
[3] *Ibid.*, pp. 515; 517f.
[4] *Ibid.*, p. 531f.

human existence is marked at all points by man's distortion and rejection of the truth, so that authentic human community is marred by continual hostility, this can never be the final word. The reality of the freedom of God, and the man freed for him and his fellows, cannot be displaced by man's falsehood [1]. The continuing witness of Jesus Christ to the truth which unfolds in the history of the activity of the Holy Spirit, insures that man will continue to be surprised by occasions of truth which occur both within and outside the Christian community:

> Manifestations of the truth are followed—for "the truth shall make you free"—by manifestations of the freedom of God and man. If the human situation is serious enough, it cannot be denied that it nevertheless might be more serious, and that it is not more serious because it is actually determined not only by its great painfulness, but also (openly or in secret) by the many occasions of goodness and beauty that fall in from above rather than ascend from below. For not only *intra* but also *extra muros ecclesiae* there are lights in the darkness, clarities in confusion, steadiness in the shifting dialectic of our existence, order in disorder, certainties in the great sea of doubt, genuine speaking and hearing in the labyrinth of human speech. They are all very wonderful, truly unforseeable and incalculable. When they occur, they are completely new. But they are never wholly lacking, even to men and Christians in our time. For this reason we should always hope and pray for them. For the reality of God and man in Jesus Christ is superior to the pseudo-reality into which we are delivered by our falsehood [2].

The negative dimensions of man's existence in sin are always superseded and overcome by the givenness of God and man in Christ, and the ineluctable destiny and direction provided therein for the human. Viewed from this perspective, there is not only room, but a positive necessity for optimism and openness regarding man's potentiality [3].

---

[1] *Ibid.*, p. 548f.

[2] *Ibid.*, p. 549.

[3] At this point, Barth knowingly exposes himself to the charge of "universalism", i.e., of a final, eschatological removal of the threat of condemnation under which man is placed, and a *de facto*, rather than merely *de iure*, inclusion of all men in grace. That Barth is unable to avoid this conclusion forms the substance of much of Thielicke's criticism of Barth. Cf. *Theologische Ethik*, Band I, Pars. 569, p. 19; 613, p. 209. Barth's own answer to this charge consists in emphasizing both the total "reach" of grace, and the freedom of God in his action. Cf. IV/3,1, pp. 549ff.; *The Humanity of God*, p. 61f. The upshot of this is that a "principle" of either inclusion or exclusion is replaced by confidence and hope in God's grace manifested in the continuing activity of the Holy Spirit.

With this, it is now possible to undertake a positive delineation of the status and identity accorded man under grace as this pertains to his ethical decisions and actions.

3. *The Analogical Validation of Man*

The reality of the human lies in the fact that man is summoned to obedience by God's Word. It is only on this basis that a positive description of man's identity as ethical subject and agent can be undertaken [1]. And it is only because of the givenness of the destiny of created human nature, decisively embodied in Christ, that the emergence of sin does not entail a total loss of being for man. An indication of the ontological status of the human under grace, accordingly, will proceed along two lines. First, it will be necessary to describe the constancy of human nature, i.e., of the "natural man", apart from the event of faith. What this amounts to is a delineation of the status and identity of man as he is involved in the event of reconciliation *de iure*. Second, the transition that occurs as man is moved, through the activity of Christ in the Holy Spirit, to a *de facto* participation in reconciliation as a member of the Christian community, and the ensuing categories of self-identity and presentation to which this leads (i.e., authentic freedom embodied in the response of faith, love, and hope).

Barth's insistence on grounding even the ontological identity of man outside the event of faith in grace underlines again his total rejection of the *analogia entis*. That both the general creaturely continuity of man, and his "special" status in faith, depend exclusively on grace, was clearly indicated in Barth's essay that appeared in 1930, *Zur Lehre vom Heiligen Geist*. And it was indirectly expressed in the outline of a lecture on ethics given by Barth at Münster in 1928. Thus, the specific contours of Barth's anthropology, as this applies to the generally human, are not unique to the *Church Dogmatics*.

The clearest indication of man's essential, general status and identity is given in Barth's discussion of the "basic form" (*Grundform*) of humanity [2]. The clue as to what makes man human is provided in the humanity of Jesus, which is inexplicable apart from his being with and for other

---

[1] III/2, pp. 180ff.; 195.
[2] III/2, Par. 45, Part 2, "Die Grundform der Menschlichkeit". Cf. Bouillard, *Karl Barth*, Vol. II, pp. 249-263.

men [1]. When this is laid down as the necessary and sufficient point of departure for a viable understanding of the human, the possibility of viewing man as an independent, isolated, self-sufficient being and agent is immediately excluded. The humanity of man is located only in the inescapable givenness of his "coexistence" (*Mitexistenz*) with other men [2]. It is only on the basis of this initial (and prior) point that attention can be given to man's individual identity, expressed in the unity of soul and body. There is an important distinction to be made here between the humanity of Jesus and other men. The co-humanity of Jesus is exemplified primarily by the fact that he is totally the man *for* other men. The most that can be said of humanity generally, however, is that man finds himself at all points *with* his fellow-man, placed beside him in ineluctable community and togetherness, though this does not exclude altogether the fact that there is also "a being for one another in the relation of man to man" [3].

The designation of man's essential givenness as co-humanity (*Mit-menschlichkeit*) does not signify a static quality or determination. It rather underlines the reality of continuous and unavoidable *encounter* (*Begegnung*) [4] between man and man, and is thus to be understood as a history, as an "existere", not an "esse" [5]. The "basic formula" (*Grundformel*) employed by Barth expresses the point succinctly: "I am, because you are" [6]. The use of the term "because" (*indem*) must not be construed as indicating either the cause or substance of the identity of the individual. Barth's utilization of Buber's terminology [7] is intended to underline the impossibility and impropriety of attempting an exhaustive description of man as independent self. It is thus not his intention to suggest that man's existential identity as "subject" is swallowed up

---

[1] III/2, pp. 269ff.
[2] *Ibid.*, p. 271.
[3] *Ibid.*, p. 291.
[4] *Ibid.*, p. 296.
[5] *Ibid.*, p. 297.
[6] *Ibid.*, p. 296.
[7] Bouillard suggests an additional indebtedness on Barth's part to the thought of Ferdinand Ebner and Gabriel Marcel, both of whom have explored the concept of the "Thou" in relation to the issue of authentic communication. In this respect Bouillard suggests that Barth has incorporated the results of philosophical reflection into the context of theological anthropology. *Karl Barth*, Vol. II, p. 259.

in the "object" of encounter [1], nor that the "I" and "Thou" merge into a higher unity as acting subject [2].

The givenness of man's being as co-humanity involving history and encounter serves as the formal condition establishing continuity and unity between human nature and human destiny under God's election of man to be his covenant partner [3]. Man's humanity, as co-humanity, does not itself provide *materially* significant insights for Christian ethics. What it does lead to, however, is an indication of the "categories of the distinctively human" [4] which provide for a limited and initial (but nevertheless real) "freedom in the being *with* one another of man and man" (*Freiheit im Miteinander von Mensch und Mensch*) [5]. In this connection, Barth cites the mutual openness that holds between persons, which permits them to see one another directly and honestly [6]; the dialogic engagement that takes place in the event of a mutual speaking and hearing, which proceeds on the implicit assumption of genuineness, and which results in a reduction of distance between persons [7]; the giving and receiving of assistance, which signals the beginning of a transition from "being with" to "being for" [8]; and the fact that these mutual transactions all "take place gladly" (*gerne geschieht*) [9]. These are all seen as "natural" determination of man. They do not, therefore, depend on revelation or the activity of the Holy Spirit [10]. The freedom to be *with* his fellow-man is precisely the co-humanity of man. This freedom does not depend on, nor is it to be confused with, Christian love (*agape*),

---

[1] III/2, p. 296; Cf. *Ibid.*, p. 293f.

[2] Though Barth does assert at one point that man and woman, as the unique embodiment of the I-Thou relationship, constitute "the acting and responsible subject man" (*das handelnde und in seinem Handeln verantwortliche Subjekt Mensch*). III/1, p. 352. Interpreted strictly, this would lead to disastrous and absurd consequences for both anthropology and ethics. It is clear from the context in which this occurs, however, thqt Barth is simply stating, in somewhat dramatic terms, the basic point in his position: That in both his being and his action (or his being-in-action), man cannot be seen apart from his fellow-man.

[3] III/2, p. 384f.

[4] *Ibid.*, p. 297.

[5] *Ibid.*, p. 332. Italics added.

[6] *Ibid.*, pp. 299ff.

[7] *Ibid.*, pp. 302ff.

[8] *Ibid.*, pp. 312ff.

[9] *Ibid.*, p. 318f.

[10] *Ibid.*, p. 332.

which represents a "new ... co-humanity" involving formal structure as well as positive content (i.e., both freedom *with* and *for*) [1]. The reality of man's freedom to be with his fellow-man constitutes the given and ineradicable dignity of man, a dignity which is not lost even in sin, and which, further, cannot be dissolved in the contrast between *eros* and *agape* [2]. The ethical significance of the formal givenness and continuity of created human nature is thus that it locates the human as a *tertium datur* between *eros* and *agape*, thereby providing a positive point of continuity between the Christian community and the world which must be taken into account in the proclamation and action of the former [3].

The paradigm of all creaturely co-humanity is found in man's differentiated identity as male and female [4]. This is a structural differentiation which cannot be eliminated or transcended. No one escapes the definiteness of his existence as both male *or* female, and male *and* female [5]. The importance of human sexuality as a model for man's extensive co-humanity becomes totally transparent in the marriage relationship, a specific connection between a particular man and woman which "is clear and strong enough for both parties to make their marriage possible and necessary as a particular and unique relationship to one another" [6]. Barth's insistence on the centrality of marriage at this point is almost suggestive of an ontological principle, so that the authentic identity of man and woman necessarily entails marriage. He asserts, for instance, that man's creation was completed "as he became and is ,man with his wife' ", and that "the only real humanity for woman is that which consists in being the wife of a male, and therefore the wife of a man" [7]. That Barth does not finally allow marriage to occupy this position seems clear from a later statement in which it is described as the *telos* under which all male-female encounters stand, although the sphere of male and female is itself wider than the marriage relationship [8].

I have already indicated the importance of man's co-humanity as the basic instance of the *analogia relationis* [9]. It remains now to specify

---

[1] *Ibid.*, pp. 332ff.; 338ff.
[2] *Ibid.*, pp. 335-338.
[3] *Ibid.*, pp. 337; 343f.
[4] *Ibid.*, pp. 344f.; 349; Cf. III/1, pp. 206ff.; 329f.
[5] III/2, pp. 344-349.
[6] *Ibid.*, p. 348.
[7] III/1, p. 353.
[8] III/4, pp. 154ff.
[9] Cf. above, p. 72f.

the way in which this is grounded and justified. The initial ground and justification for viewing created human nature in this way lies in the relation that holds between creation and covenant. Since it is the eternal election of man to covenant that lies at the basis of creation, it follows that man's existence in encounter as male and female will exhibit continuity with his destiny and goal as the elected covenant partner of God [1]. Within the created order, then, the givenness of man's humanity as cohumanity, the "mystery" of human togetherness, functions as a reflection, *analogia relationis*, of the covenant between Christ and the Christian community, which is itself a fulfillment and clarification of the relation between God and Israel [2]. It is the covenant relation between Christ and his community, toward which the "basic form" of humanity has been oriented from the beginning, that provides an ontological focus and goal that cannot fail of exemplification and completion, and which is therefore distorted, but not finally submerged and lost, by the emergence of sin [3].

The relation between Christ and the Christian community is not, however, the only analogans to which the co-humanity of man corresponds as the analogate. Behind this, and so prior to it, stands the eternal being of God, which itself encloses, in the relationship between the Father and the Son, the relationality, differentiation and confrontation of the I and the Thou [4]. It is the being-in-encounter of God that forms the decisive ground of the *tertium comparationis* holding between God and man, the existence of the I and the Thou in confrontation. Man is thus understood as the "repetition" (*Wiederholung*) of the inner life-form of God:

> Man is the repetition of this divine life form, its copy and reflection. He is this first of all in the fact that he is God's counterpart, and that the self-encounter and discovery that take place in God himself is copied and reflected in God's relation to man. And he is also this in the fact that he is himself the counterpart of his fellows, and that in his fellows he has his own counterpart, so that the fellowship and cooperation that occur in God himself are repeated in the relation between man and man.

---

[1] Barth's initial discussion of the unity holding between creation and covenant is found in III/1, Par. 41, Part 2, "Creation as the External Basis of the Covenant", and Part 3, "The Covenant as the Internal Basis of Creation". Cf. Bouillard, *Karl Barth*, Vol. II, p. 257f.

[2] III/2, p. 381f.

[3] *Ibid.*, p. 384f.

[4] *Ibid.*, p. 390f.; III/1, pp. 206ff.; 222ff.

Very simply, then, the *tertium comparationis*, the analogy between God and man, is the existence in confrontation of the I and the Thou. This is first constitutive for God, and then also for man as created by God ... God wills and creates him as he wills and creates the being between which and himself there stands this *tertium comparationis*, this analogy : the analogy of free differentiation and relation [1].

So, just as there is a necessary correlation and correspondence between creation and reconciliation that throws them into continuity within the totality of the being and activity of God, there is a parallel correlation and correspondence, and so continuity, between the I-Thou relationality of created human nature and that holding between Christ and the community, which finds its ultimate counterpart in the eternal being of God. Just as creation is the external basis of the covenant, created human nature is also the external basis of the existence of Jesus Christ [2]. And Jesus Christ in his humanity and with his community is the internal basis and meaning of created human nature. The natural being and activity of man is thus given a positive significance and function, which makes it unnecessary, as Henri Bouillard points out, to disparage man in order to exalt the graciousness of God [3].

The priority that Barth places on the I-Thou relationality of the human as the primary instance of the *analogia relationis*, obviously is not intended to subsume the human without remainder. It is thus both possible and necessary, within the context of the "basic form" of humanity, to give descriptive contour to the ontic structure of man's individuality [4]. This dimension of Barth's anthropology must be delineated here, since it provides the requisite basis for a discussion of individual ethical agency, and so of human subjectivity, within the framework of faith.

That Barth includes a discussion of the ontic dimensions of man's individuality in his initial, extended treatment of anthropology marks again the way in which the line running from reconciliation to creation signals a fully unified history between God and man that gains final exemplification in the eschatological event of redemption, and that permits of only a provisional (i.e., *de iure* and *de facto*) rather than an

---

[1] III/1, p. 207.
[2] *Ibid.*, p. 214.
[3] *Karl Barth*, Vol. II, p. 258; Cf. III/1, p. 214; IV/1, p. 94f.
[4] Cf. III/2, Par. 46, Pts. 2-5.

absolute distinction within the human. The continuity thereby established between Christians and non-Christians (which provides the basis for a continuous ethical framework) is schematically indicated at this point by the fact that Barth prefaces his discussion of the ontic aspects of the generally human with an indication of their christological grounding [1]. What this means is that, just as the model for the *analogia relationis* is seen initially in the relation between the divine and the human in Christ, and ultimately in the inter-trinitarian relation holding between the Father and the Son, so too human subjectivity, individually considered, is grounded initially in the subjectivity of Christ, which lodges ultimately in the eternal subjectivity of God. Strictly speaking, then, man "exists" as subject only because Jesus Christ exists, or, in Barth's somewhat dramatic statement, man "exists as a predicate of this Subject" [2]. Within the framework of the total teleological movement of grace, this holds true for both the "natural" man and the man of faith, since Christ stands as the center of that movement, and so as the point at which human nature as originally posited by God receives confirmation and examplification as existence in faith.

The existence of Jesus Christ thus provides, ostensibly, for continuity between the subjectivity of both created and reconciled human nature, a continuity which persists despite (and so beyond) the distortion and tension occasioned by the onset of sin. The impact of grace entails both a rejection and a restoration. It entails a rejection of man's distorted existence in sin, and a restoration of his originally intended status as the elected partner of God in the covenant [3]. This indicates an immediate and irrevocable continuity between creation and covenant, as this touches on the issue of man's ontic status in each. The anthropological counterparts to the terms "creation" and "covenant" are designated by Barth in terms of the distinction between man's "natural condition" (*natürlicher Beschaffenheit*) [4] as one who "lives and dies in the event of the livingness of God" [5], a condition which enables us to speak of man's "human form, and of his existence in this form" [6], and his "histor-

---

[1] Cf. III/2, Par. 46, Pt. 1, "Jesus, Whole Man"; Par. 47, Pt. 1, "Jesus, Lord of Time".
[2] II/2, p. 599, IV/2, p. 300f.
[3] II/2, p. 621f.
[4] III/2, p. 419.
[5] *Ibid.*
[6] *Ibid.*

ical standing" (*geschichtlichen Stand*)[1] devolving from the fact and event of the covenant. The continuity between these is occasioned by their common enclosure within the embracing framework of grace. On this basis, it is possible (and necessary) to assert that man is "determined by the one grace, that of his creation, for the other, the grace of the covenant, and he is referred by the one to the other"[2]. At this point, it is in order to indicate Barth's reading of the "natural condition" of man, as this relates to the issues of subjectivity and ethical agency.

The fact that created human nature is delineable only from the perspective of the covenant and its christological fulfillment in the event of reconciliation underlines an initial and fundamental thrust that persists throughout Barth's development of anthropology, and, finally, throughout the *Dogmatics*: the absolute and irreducible priority of the being-in-act of God. Where the discussion focused on the development of the doctrine of reconciliation, the priority of God was emphasized in Barth's decisive rejection of the *analogia entis*, a rejection that persistently informs the methodological stance taken in the *Dogmatics*. The ontic and behavioral significance of Barth's emphasis on the priority of God, and the rejection of the *analogia entis* this entails, appear in Barth's discussion of created human nature in the form of an unrelieved emphasis on the *dependent* status of man in his creaturely being. The dependent status accorded man may be seen both in his relationship to God (a relationship that proceeds always from God's side) and in his own existence as an ordered unity of "soul" and "body"[3].

---

[1] *Ibid.*

[2] *Ibid.*, p. 420. The order of priority, however, always runs from man's historical standing as the elected covenant partner of God to his natural condition—never the reverse. The reason for this lies in the fact that the historical standing of man is the "original and model to which the natural condition of man must succeed and correspond". *Ibid.*, p. 429.

[3] III/2, pp. 414, 420f., 502ff. The notion of dependence as utilized by Barth should not be taken as equivalent with Schleiermacher's concept of the "feeling of absolute dependence" (*Gefühls schlechthiniger Abhängigkeit*). As Barth sess it, Schleiermacher's reading of the relation between God and man inevitably "opens the door to the establishment of every kind of caprice and tyranny, and so to the profoundest disobedience to God". II/2, p. 614. Against this, Barth argues that man's dependence on God is not grounded in sheer power, and that a recognition and acceptance of his status as God's creature confronted with a definite claim leads to authentic freedom and obedience.

The former point may be indicated directly: "Man exists as he is grounded, constituted, and maintained by God" [1]. Man's existence and being are thus not to be seen as indigenous properties. They are rather the immediate results of the fact that ontically and noetically man is never without God, that he comes into being on the basis of a "transcendental determination" (*transzendente Bestimmung*) [2] that (as grace) is continually renewed. Now, it certainly comes as no surprise to find Barth arguing the continual dependence of man for his existence and being on the decision and action of God. Within the context of theological anthropology, this reading of the status of the human is both expected and defensible. We are thus well prepared, as it were, for Barth's assertion that the *creaturely* being of man is as much dependent on God's Spirit (as both its possibility and actuality) as his existence in faith as the elected and called recipient of that "special" grace [3]. This treatment of the function of God's Spirit in relation to both the creaturely and covenantal being of man follows logically from the relationship already posited between creation and covenant. It is the one God who by his Spirit links these together as the "external" and "internal" aspects of the total movement of grace. Thus, since creation serves as the "external" ground of the covenant, and the covenant illumines the "inner" meaning of creation, it is only to be expected that the anthropological counterparts to these would exhibit continuity through the creating and re-

----

Ibid., p. 612f. I shall be concerned to examine Barth's claim with respect to the possibilities of freedom and obedience as these receive form and substance within his anthropology. Meanwhile, it is perhaps well to recall Richard R. Niebuhr's warning against "a Barthian captivity of the history of modern Christian thought", if only because it draws attention to the possibility that Schleiermacher has not been given either a full or a fair hearing within the *Dogmatics*. Cf. *Schleiermacher on Christ and Religion* (New York: Charles Scribner's Sons, 1964), p. 11.

[1] III/2, p. 416.

[2] *Ibid.*, p. 418.

[3] "As the elected and called and to that extent 'new' man lives in the covenant by the fact that God gives him his Spirit, so too the natural man also and already lives in just the same way. It is the same Spirit who is there the principle of his renewal who is here the principle of his creaturely reality ... As he receives the Spirit from God he lives, he becomes and is soul, his material body becomes and is a physical body, and he is the soul of this body". *Ibid.*, p. 431.

conciling activity of the one Holy Spirit of God. It is in this respect that man's being and existence are always given a dependent status.

However, a decisive point emerges when the analysis is extended to cover man's ontic status as an ordered unity of soul and body. Here it must be recalled that the anthropological model for the discussion is given in Jesus Christ, who exhibits in a unique way this quality of order. The self-identity of Jesus rests not merely on the order maintained between soul and body, but rather on his unique relationship to the Spirit of God. It is this relationship that guarantees the "personal" quality of Jesus' existence, for it indicates that he not only *has* but *is* "spirit" [1]. It is at precisely this point that an ambiguity appears in Barth's anthropology, for it is not clear that spirit appears as an ontic category in any man except Jesus. In order to determine whether this ambiguity indicates a real or merely apparent difficulty in Barth's anthropology, it will be necessary to sketch in the way in which the category of "spirit" relates to those of "soul" and "body" in Barth's general anthropology.

The simplest way of describing man generally is to say that he is an ordered unity of soul and body whose basis or "ground" (*Grund*) is "Spirit" (*Geist*). The reference to "Spirit" does not refer to an indigenous property of the human, but rather underlines again the way in which man is "grounded, constituted and maintained by God" [2]. It follows, then, that "man exists, because he has Spirit" [3]. The theologically proper statement descriptive of man's ontic status would consequently appear to be that he *has*, rather than *is*, spirit. Man has spirit as an aspect of his natural condition only to the extent that it represents the original movement of God toward his creation [4], not as "a moment of his constitution as such" [5]. Spirit "belongs" (*gehört*) to man as the necessary and sufficient condition for his existing as the soul of his body (and therefore as *man*), a condition which, since supplied by God's own Spirit, serves as the "superior, determining and limiting ground" of his constitution [6]. Thus, although man needs spirit to be *man*, since without spirit he be-

---

[1] *Ibid.*

[2] III/2, p. 414.

[3] "Der Mensch ist, indem er Geist hat". *Ibid.* Cf. Bouillard, *Karl Barth*, Vol. II, p. 266f.

[4] III/2, p. 428f.

[5] *Ibid.*, p. 426.

[6] *Ibid.*

comes "a bodiless soul and a soulless body", it is also clear that spirit
"can be identical neither with man nor with a part of the being of man" [1].

It will be helpful here to describe, briefly, the interconnection and
order that emerge between soul and body when these are grounded in
spirit. The interconnection between soul and body is an immanent
distinction and antithesis lying wholly within the created order [2]. This
means that it is not an extension or embodiment of the distinction between Creator and creation, or Spirit and man. The being of man is
in its totality *creaturely* being. Relative to this, the "soulish" dimension
of man establishes him as a "*living* being" (*lebendes Wesen*) [3], while
the "bodily" dimension marks him as a "living *being*" (*lebendes Wesen*) [4].
The relationship holding between soul and body in man emerges as an
asymmetrical unity. Thus, though man is seen always as an irreducible
unity of soul and body, there is a sense in which soul, since it is equivalent
to "the independent life of a corporeal being" [5], enjoys a certain priority.
It is the quality of independence attaching to soul that invests man's
life with self-awareness and subjectivity. The dimension of soul marks
man as a "definite subject" (*bestimmtes Subjekt*) [6]. This is not allowed
to fall over into dualism, however, since, on Barth's analysis, soul and
body do not form two parts or "substances" that have somehow to be
conjoined. They function rather as "the two moments of the inseparably
one human nature" [7].

Soul and body together constitute an order (*Kosmos*) [8]. The order in
question is maintained through the functions assigned soul and body
within it: the function of soul is that of control or rule; the function of
body is service [9]. When this order is retained, man is then describable
as a "rational being" (*Vernunftwesen*), a description that cannot be
limited simply to man's ability to think. As Barth uses the term, it stands
for the fact that "it is proper to his nature to be in conscious order of

---

[1] *Ibid.*

[2] *Ibid.*, p. 441.

[3] *Ibid.*, p. 440.

[4] *Ibid.* I have followed the translators here in adding italics for emphasis.
Cf. *Ibid.* (Eng. trans.), p. 367.

[5] *Ibid.*, p. 449.

[6] *Ibid.*

[7] *Ibid.*, pp. 471, 519f.

[8] *Ibid.*, p. 502. The parallel here with Barth's elucidation of the humanity
of Jesus is immediately apparent, and is indicated by Barth himself.

[9] *Ibid.*

the two moments of soul and body, and thus to be a percipient and active being" [1]. The order in which man exists is grounded in God's addressing him as one who "rules" himself, so that "before God, he is not an improper, but a proper, i.e., a free subject" [2]. The condition for realizing this order and continuing in it, and so for activity as a free subject, is that God gives and continues to give his Spirit to man:

> As he acts in this freedom, as in thinking and willing he is his own lord and ruler, he is a spiritual soul. In order that he might be active in this way, he is given Spirit by God, and through the Spirit he is awakened to be a living being [3].

It is clear from the foregoing just how crucial it is for Barth's anthropology that man has Spirit. This cruciality becomes even more apparent when consideration is given to the significance of Spirit as regards the possibility of man's participation and activity as subject. Initially, the fact that man has Spirit means that he is given permission to live [4]. And this, in turn, signifies to man "that God is there for him" [5]. Man's freedom to live is not in any sense immanent to him, and this fact makes transparent his total dependence, as creature, on the event of God's giving him his Spirit. It is only because man has and receives Spirit from God that he is able to exist in his "fundamental determination" (*Grundbestimmung*), i.e., "the decisive possibility of his being as soul of his body" [6]. Spirit is to man what the center is to the circle, a "mathematical mid-point" that determines everything. What this means is that even though man is totally "of the Spirit", because "the Spirit is the principle of life and power of the whole man", the Spirit is nevertheless not "a third thing beside soul and body" [7]. Instead, Barth views Spirit as a kind of "augmentation" (*Vermehrung*) of man's creaturely constancy [8]. In this respect, it is allowable and correct to say that Spirit is "in" man, as "the nearest, most intimate and most indispensable factor to be considered for understanding his essence and existence", without being thereby identical with man [9]. Spirit is, finally,

---

[1] *Ibid.*, p. 503.

[2] *Ibid.*, p. 509. Cf. von Balthasar, *Karl Barth*, p. 139.

[3] III/2, p. 510f. The issue of human freedom will be examined in a later section of this chapter.

[4] "Geist haben heißt leben dürfen". *Ibid.*, p. 435.

[5] *Ibid.*

[6] *Ibid.*, p. 436.

[7] *Ibid.*

[8] *Ibid.*

[9] *Ibid.*, p. 437.

the "principle" (*Prinzip*) that establishes man as subject, as it stands in
direct relationship to man's soul, and in indirect relationship to his
body [1].

What does man's receiving Spirit from God entail for the possibility
of his activity and participation as subject? In order to get at this point,
we must keep in mind the priority that Barth gives to soul, over body,
within the order constituted by man's reception of Spirit. It is thus "not
without his body, but not as body", and so as soul, that man is a self-
conscious agent, the subject of his decisions, and, finally, a "person"
(*Person*) [2]. Soul and body are therefore distinguished as subject and
object, operation and work, center and periphery, in the being and
existence of man. From this variously expressed distinction, Barth
draws two significant points.

The first of these focuses on the perceptual capacity of man as subject
and agent. Barth does not mean here a general capacity for perceptual
awareness of the world. Man's capacity to perceive (*vernehmen*) instead
refers, initially at least, to his ability to perceive and be aware of God as
he reveals himself to man, encounters him, and provides him with his
Spirit [3]. It is this capacity in man that saves him from "a purely self-
contained self-consciousness", and that indicates his ability to posit
himself in relation to another, and to receive the other into his consciousness [4]. The occurrence of perception can be broken down into an

---

[1] *Ibid.*, p. 437f.

[2] *Ibid.*, p. 477.

[3] *Ibid.*, p. 471.

[4] *Ibid.*, p. 479. This would appear to constitute Barth's preferred solution
to the philosophical problems of epistemological solipsism and "other minds".
Both are set aside as problems by appealing to man's capacity for "perceiving"
God as he receives Spirit from him, and is made capable of an engagement
with the "other", i.e., objects and persons in the world generally. It is on this
basis that Barth criticizes and rejects the possibility of a general, philosophical
approach to the issues of perceptual awareness and thought (rationality).
Cf. *Ibid.*, p. 483. Aside from the ambiguities present in Barth's relating of the
category of Spirit to man's ontic structure, there is both an epistemological
and a logical difficulty in his treatment of "perception". The condition for
"perceiving" God (and so the "other"), for man in both his "natural condition"
and his "historical standing" in the covenant, is the occurrence of revelation,
i.e., the imparation of the Spirit. As was noted earlier, however, revelation
(the "event" of grace) brings about a totally new level of subjectivity, and
so (in this instance) of perception. How this evidences continuity with "ordinary" perceptual modes is not made clear. The logical difficulty noted in Barth's

"outer" and an "inner" aspect, which correspond, roughly, to the body's capacity for "noticing" or awareness (*Wahrnehmen*), and to the soul's capacity for "reflection" or thought (*Denken*) [1]. In the end, however, man's ability to perceive God and the other represents a function of the whole man (i.e., as soul of his body) under the ordering impact of Spirit.

The second point Barth makes focuses on man's activity as ordered subject. The fact that man is subjectively equipped to perceive God entails that he is also able to respond actively within the context of the knowledge he is given [2]. So, man is empowered by the Spirit not only to "perceive" God and the other, but is further enabled to become actively engaged with each at the point of decision, which will represent the ordered relationality of "desiring" (*Begehren*) and "willing" (*Wollen*) [3]. Man's ability to act in the world generally hangs on the primal action of acknowledging God, an acknowledgement fulfilled in man's obedience, belief, and love [4]. Although the analysis of human action displays the "outer" side of desiring, which has a "special relation" to the body, and the "inner" side of willing, which has a similar relation to the soul, these "moments" nevertheless constitute a unity, since the distinctions here are not indicative of a final dualism [5].

The fact that man has Spirit from God thus means that he is equipped to perceive and act in a certain way, with reference both to God and the world generally, and that he functions as an ordered subject and agent in these capacities [6]. Before proceeding to an analysis of the importance of Spirit for a "reconstitution" of man beyond the distorting impact of sin, and the consequences this carries for the possibilities of freedom and existence in faith indicated in actions embodying responsibility and obedience, it will be instructive to suggest some of the difficulties surrounding Barth's treatment of created human nature as viewed from the unifying center of christology.

---

reference to the "event" of grace would thus appear to be transposed here into his use of the word "perception", which now takes on a similar ambiguity. Cf. Bouillard's comments on this point. *Karl Barth*, Vol. II, p. 266f.

[1] III/2, p. 481.
[2] *Ibid.*, p. 487.
[3] *Ibid.*
[4] *Ibid.*, p. 491.
[5] *Ibid.*, p. 489.
[6] *Ibid.*, p. 499f.

It needs to be made clear at the outset that Barth certainly does not set out either to disparage the human, or to render ambiguous man's ontic status as subject and agent. That the latter occurs, implying thereby in some sense the occurrence of the former, rests on the following considerations. There is a terminological difficulty, to begin with, in Barth's use of the traditional distinctions of "soul" and "body" as descriptive vehicles capable of portraying adequately man's ontic structure and status. The problem here is that it appears virtually impossible to employ this terminology without importing a note of dualism (Classical, Cartesian, or other) into the discussion, however severely one warns against this possibility [1]. Admittedly, this difficulty is not easily overcome, since there appear to be at present no terms that might function as suitable substitutes [2].

However, the possible difficulties attendant upon the adoption of the traditional terminology are heightened when consideration is given to the role of "spirit" in Barth's anthropology. Where the specific humanity of Jesus is concerned, the category of spirit (i.e., the Holy Spirit of God himself) serves as the basis for a positive unity between the "soulish" and bodily dimensions, and thus forms the ground of his personal existence as subject. It is because Jesus not only *has* but *is* Spirit that his life is "permeated and determined by his I, by himself" [3].

Man generally, however, is whole man only as he *has*, and so receives, Spirit from God. It appears never to be the case that man is describable as one who *is* spirit. Moreover, the Spirit that man is capable of receiving and having is the Holy Spirit of God himself as he acts to quicken and substantiate both the "natural" man and the man of faith. Now, it is understandable why, in this particular context, Barth does not and cannot say that man is spirit. The reason for this is that the only spirit Barth speaks of here is the Holy Spirit. Hence, to assert that man *is* spirit would entail that man is either a direct extension of God, or that he is capable of some sort of divinization. It has been clear throughout our discussion that Barth will not allow even an ostensible

---

[1] As Barth repeatedly does, of course. Cf. III/2, pp. 455f., 479f., *et passim*. Cf. the comments by Professor Come on the difficulties attendant upon an adoption of the traditional terminology within the framework of theological anthropology. *Human Spirit and Holy Spirit* (Philadelphia: The Westminster Press, 1959), p. 34.

[2] Cf. Come, *Human Spirit and Holy Spirit*, p. 34f.

[3] III/2, p. 403.

"point of contact" between God and man, much less this sort of identity procedure.

It may be questioned, however, whether a similar difficulty does not appear within the present ordering. If man attains unity of self, and so subjective identity and continuity, only under the impact of God's Spirit, so that it becomes essential that man *has* that Spirit, then it is hard to see how this avoids making man's ontic structure as subject in some sense an exemplification of God's own subjectivity. At the very least, it exposes the difficulties occasioned for the possibility of man's achieving unity of self (i.e., between the "soulish" and bodily dimensions), and the accompanying threat of a collapse of unity [1]. This holds true, it seems, despite Barth's assertion that man, as "besouled body" or "embodied soul" is subject and person [2]. If this is the case, then it can only mean that man generally achieves subjectivity and selfhood in a fundamentally different way than Jesus. In a way, the reasonableness of this suggestion is obvious, since the humanity of Jesus is that of the eternal Son of God. At the same time, it renders obscure the precise way in which Jesus is to be taken as the paradigm of creaturely humanity in general. Even beyond this point, however, it is still clear that on Barth's analysis man does not achieve either authentic subjectivity or personality apart from the Spirit of God, which can only mean that the basis for his self-unity lies in a source outside himself. Where this is allowed to stand, however, it raises serious questions for both man's subjective unity as self, and his capacities as ethical agent.

These difficulties are encountered again when consideration is given to Barth's delineation of the "basic form" of humanity exemplified in the I - Thou relationality holding between men. Barth wants to see the I - Thou relationship holding between men as an analogy of the relationship between God and Israel and Christ and the Christian community. Now, it seems at least possible to get a reasonably clear notion of what Barth has in mind by the notion of analogy or similarity

---

[1] In the later volumes of the *Dogmatics*, however, Barth apparently modifies his position, for he makes reference to man's own spirit, and distinguishes this from the Holy Spirit: "The Holy Spirit, for whose work the community and the believing Christian in the community are thankful, is not the spirit of the world, nor the spirit of the community, nor the spirit of the individual Christian, but He is the Spirit of God himself ... He never is nor becomes man's own spirit". IV/1, p. 722. Cf. *Ibid.*, p. 836: IV/3.2, p. 1082.

[2] III/2, p. 477.

as it applies to these relationships. The difficulty that might emerge would fall at the point of determining what an application of Barth's "formula" for analogy, "complete similarity along with complete dissimilarity" [1], would mean here, and where the emphasis, respectively, would fall. I have already noted the difficulties in Barth's approach to theological language, and have argued that these appear to be nicely embodied within the definition of analogy given above. Where it is a matter of positing meaningful analogical assertions about man's ontic status (here established relationally), it is at least open to question whether we can form any clear notion of what is, in fact, being asserted.

The perplexities become more entrenched, however, when consideration is to given the third level of analogy posited by Barth, which serves as the basis for the other two. The ground for asserting an analogical relation between human co-humanity and the relation holding between God and man is given, Barth asserts, in the eternal relation that exists between the Father and the Son in the Trinity. Barth specifies the latter relationship as one embodying "free differentiation and relation". In short, the relation between the Father and the Son in the Trinity is posited as an I - Thou relationship [2]. It is quite correct to refer to this point as the most baffling and difficult in Barth's anthropology [3]. Now, there is clearly a way in which meaning can be given to the claim that man exists and receives his basic form in the I-Thou relationship. And though there is possibly a difficulty in Barth's assertion that that relationship is analogous to the one holding between God and man, it at least does not come into conflict with the central points in his position as those have been developed them thus far. With respect to the relation between the Father and the Son in the Trinity, however, it is hard to see how it can possibly be asserted that it is an instance, much less the basic instance, of I - Thou relationality, without running directly counter to Barth statement of the doctrine of the Trinity. In that Barth argues that the distinctions permissible within the Trinity do not designate "persons", but instead are indicative of eternal "modes of being" within the *one* Person of God.

It is clear, at this juncture, that Barth is in serious danger of compromising either his doctrine of the Trinity or his doctrine of man. If the

---

[1] IV/3.2, p. 612.

[2] III/1, p. 207.

[3] Come, *An Introduction to Barth's "Dogmatics"*, p. 156f.

relations between man and man and man and God are I-Thou relations, and if these are seen as analogues to the relation between Father and Son in the Trinity, then it is hard to see what sense can be attached to the latter notion unless Father and Son are treated as distinct persons, in which case Barth's doctrine of the Trinity is compromised. This move of course, is vigorously rejected by Barth, who remains firm in his insistence that the intra-Trinitarian distinctions designate no more than the *modes* in which God is present to himself and man. It thus becomes necessary, in carrying out the analogy to its basis, to be willing to credit the notion of an intra-Trinitarian relation between the modes of Father and Son with meaning as the supreme instance of I-Thou relationality. This, however, is an exceedingly queer formulation, and it is quite unclear what meaning *can* be attached to it. Nor will Barth's stipulated definition of analogy as "complete similarity along with complete dissimilarity" clarify things. An application of the logical principle of excluded middle would seem to be in order here: *either* the notion of I-Thou relationality between Father and Son partakes of the ordinary sense of "relationship", which automatically presupposes two subjective centers, in which case Barth's doctrine of the Trinity goes by the board; *or* the notion of I-Thou relationality is improperly applied to the intra-Trinitarian being of God, in which case some other ground will have to be set forth as the basis for human interrelatedness [1].

The difficulties occasioned by Barth's use of this pattern of analogy for his anthropology come clear when the notion of an intra-personal relation between Father and Son as eternal modes of God's being is taken (momentarily) at face value, and then read back into the context of the human. Here it must be recalled that the basis for the relationship between Father and Son in the Trinity is the Holy Spirit [2]. And, as we have seen, this same Holy Spirit is asserted to be the necessary and sufficient basis for man's individual identity as subject and agent. If, then, the basic relational form of the human is understood as analogous to the intra-Trinitarian relation holding between Father and Son and sustained by the Holy Spirit, it is hard to see how this can avoid compromising once again man's status as independent (i.e., ontically), and therefore responsible, subject and agent.

---

[1] Cf. Come, *An Introduction to Barth's "Dogmatics"*, p. 156f.
[2] I/1, p. 493f.; IV/1, p. 722.

It seems, then, that there is here at least a partial fulfillment of the warning sounded at the end of chapter three of this study. There does indeed appear to be operative in Barth's anthropology, if not a final or irremediable "absorption" of the human, at least a serious ambiguity about its status. Where the question of man's status as *ethical* subject and agent is at stake, however, any ambiguity may prove fatal. Thus far, the ambiguity has been confined to an analysis of the "natural condition" of man. The possible consequences this carries for Barth's treatment of the "historical standing" of man within the covenant must now be explored. The question raised thereby will focus on the degree to which man is capable of a realization and embodiment, as active subject, of faith, love, and hope, and so of freedom and obedience.

B. The Possibility and Actuality of Right Human Action

It is the activity of God as Holy Spirit that provides continuity, anthropologically, between creation and covenant. In this section I wish to explore the way in which man's encounter with the Holy Spirit moves him beyond the distortion of his being in sin, and into the positive context of a reconstituted relationship to God, himself, and other men that carries with it the possibility and actuality of actions that are both free and obedient.

1. *The Holy Spirit and Human Freedom*

At one point in the *Dogmatics*, Barth asserts that "the true *tertium comparationis*, and so the sign of the community already established between God and man at his creation", is the freedom to obey assigned to man [1]. The restoration of this freedom, beyond the occurrence of sin, rests on the event of revelation, i.e., the self-impartation of Jesus Christ through the Holy Spirit. Now, since the activity of the Holy Spirit provides the condition for a knowledge of Jesus Christ, and so for authentic self-knowledge, it follows that both the possibility and actuality of right human action (i.e., obedience in freedom) are enclosed within that activity, and man's acknowledgement and reception of the event of revelation. This means that man's participation through the Holy

---

[1] III/1, p. 302.

Spirit in the being of Jesus Christ eliminates any gap that might exist between the possibility and the actuality of his obedient response in freedom [1].

At the same time, it seems clear that apart from the activity of the Holy Spirit, man is capable neither of freedom nor obedience. It is only through the Holy Spirit that man is made participant in revelation, so that the Holy Spirit becomes, for Barth, both the "subjective reality" and the "subjective possibility" of revelation, and so of the particular freedom given man to be open to God [2]. This is not to say that man has *no* freedom apart from the special activity of the Holy Spirit. His freedom to be with his fellow-man as the irreducible dimension of the "basic form" of humanity, was described earlier [3]. And, in terms of the general activity of God's Spirit within the creaturely sphere, this provides the basis not only for a significant range of human activities and accomplishments, but also for the proper ethical action and word occasionally to occur [4]. It is also clear, however, that an analysis of created human nature does not, in itself, provide materially significant insights for theological ethics. At best, it uncovers certain formal conditions inhering in the human which derive from creation, and which are caught up and brought to completion, christologically, in the event of reconciliation. The event of the Holy Spirit, then, is both the reality

---

[1] Cf. IV/2, p. 297: "The freedom presented to us immediately and unconditionally and irrevocably in the existence of the kingly man Jesus wills as such to be known and used and lived out. The problem of the transitional reflection that must occupy us in this section is whether, and under what circumstances, this reality can and should and must take place, and whether it is possible to avoid a violation of this reality in which we stand—where the existence of Jesus, the kingly Son of Man, does not remain an open question ... We have to reckon seriously first of all with the fact that the anthropological sphere is dominated by the Son of Man as its Lord, and therefore that our self-knowledge is enclosed and included in the knowledge of Jesus ... He is the answer to the question of the distinctive knowledge and use and living of the freedom which he presents to us. He in whom the decision concerning us has already been made is, as the living and creative source of the change it signifies for our existence, also its measure and criterion. He determines its meaning, extent and depth. As the one who is with us and for us, he also decides what we can and should and must become and be in him".

[2] Cf. I/2, Par. 16, Pts. 1 and 2; IV/3.1, Par. 69, Pt. 4, "The Promise of the Spirit".

[3] See above, p. 223f.

[4] Cf. II/2, p. 632; IV/3.1, p. 549.

and the possibility of man's participation in authentic humanity, and so
of his having ethically significant freedom, i.e., freedom for obedience [1].

The possibility of ethically meaningful human action thus rests
on the action (and freedom) of the Holy Spirit, which invests the human
with a totally new kind of freedom which is in no sense intrinsically
present in man: freedom for God [2]. The freedom that is given man
through the Holy Spirit is not understood, in the first instance, on strictly
individual terms. It is rather the decisive ground for the being and existence of the Christian community, and it is only within that context that
the freedom of the individual receives meaning and content [3]. The
importance of the Christian community for the individual lies in its
serving as the locus of certain definite "signs" (Zeichen) that establish
the objective side of the subjective reality of revelation, i.e., preaching,
baptism, and the Lord's Supper [4]. These signs provide the answer to the
question "How does revelation come from Christ to man?" [5]. But since
they are all directly attached to the Church, it follows that the activity
of the Holy Spirit that awakens man to participation in revelation is
such that the individuals involved are always bound to the Church as
the visible community of Christ. It is within this visible "definite place"
(bestimmten Raum) that man is made a "recipient of revelation" [6].

---

[1] Created human nature would thus exhibit, as von Balthasar suggests, a
formal rather than a material freedom. Cf. Karl Barth, p. 140f. In this respect,
Ulrich Hedinger is correct in arguing that Barth distinguishes between creaturely freedom as such, and Christian liberty, though this distinction tends to
become blurred at points, due to Barth's insistence on viewing both created
and reconciled man from an exclusively christological center. Cf. Der Freiheitsbegriff in der Kirchlichen Dogmatik Karl Barths (Zürich: Zwingli Verlag, 1962),
pp. 93f., 98. As pointed out in the preceding section of this chapter, however,
it is open to question whether Barth succeeds in establishing man's ontic
status as independent subject sufficiently to insure the emergence of the sort of
freedom he wants to attribute to man at that level.

[2] I/2, pp. 223f., 265f.; IV/2, p. 344f.

[3] I/2, p. 229f.

[4] Ibid., pp. 248, 253ff. The ethical significance and function of these
signs will be explored in the following chapter of this study.

[5] Ibid., p. 242.

[6] Ibid., pp. 230f., 269. Cf. Ibid., p. 240: "The children of God are visible
men. A visible event brings them together. A visible unity holds them to one
another. The fact that they have received God's revelation is invisible, but
they themselves are visible as those who must remember that fact, and wish
to do so".

Within the context of the activity of the Holy Spirit, then, to be a man means to be "in Christ, as a hearer and doer of the Word of God, in the Church" [1]. To exist as a man in this way requires the addition of a "new thing" beyond the capacities of man's creaturely being. This underlines the fact that neither the possibility nor the actuality of man's participation in the event of revelation (on which his freedom rests) can be seen as simple extensions of his creaturely ontic structure. Participation in the event of revelation, and the freedom and liberation to which it leads, is something that is excluded from our being as such, and which therefore transcends it [2]. The power to become a Christian is in no sense our own. It is dependent exclusively on the power of the resurrection of Christ as this is given shape and substance in the second stage of his *parousia*, the self-manifestation of Jesus Christ to the Christian community in the Holy Spirit [3]. The reality of the Holy Spirit within the Christian community is thus the presence and action of Jesus Christ himself; it is the "self-expression" (*Lebensäußerung*) of the man Jesus [4]. The unity that emerges between Christ and the community, as this is provided in the being and action of God as Holy Spirit, thus becomes a reminder and reflection of the eternal triune being of God, i.e., of the "fellowship" (*Gemeinschaft*) between the Father and the Son that is maintained eternally by the Holy Spirit [5]. Or, to put the matter

---

[1] *Ibid.*, p. 281.

[2] *Ibid.*, pp. 281, 257. As I have argued, however, Barth does maintain ontological continuity between created and reconciled human essence, in terms of the "outer" and "inner" dimensions of the total sweep of the covenant initiated and sustained by God. This continuity is given primary exemplification in Christ, and (ostensibly) secondary exemplification in other men through the activity of the Holy Spirit.

[3] IV/2, p. 345f.

[4] IV/2, p. 370.

[5] "Why is the miracle and the mystery of the Holy Spirit so great, so oppressive, and yet at the same time—as we may at least allow the witness of the New Testament to speak—so liberating? ... The answer we now make is that it is because in the mystery of his being and work in our earthly history there is a repetition, representation and operation of what God is in himself. Precisely in his being and work as the mediator between Jesus and other men, in his creating, establishing and maintaining community between himself and us, God himself is active and revealed among us men, i.e., the fellowship, unity, joy and love which are in God, in which God was and is and will be God from and to all eternity. We speak of the fellowship of the Father and the Son". *Ibid.*, p. 380f.

in slightly different terms, the Holy Spirit, as the Spirit of the resurrected Jesus, is at the same time the Spirit of God the Son, "and as such he is not different from the Spirit of the Father, but on the contrary is the Spirit in whom the Father and the Son, eternally distinct, are also eternally united" [1].

Man's encounter with Christ through the Holy Spirit, his being placed within the context of the Christian community, is at the same time the condition for, and the fulfillment of, his own freedom as authentic subject and agent [2]. The condition for man's existence and activity as ethical agent, i.e., the realization, empirically, of obedience, rests squarely on this encounter, since it provides the exclusively specific matrix out of which human freedom emerges. In short, man's liberation, as Barth indicated in an address delivered to the *Gesellschaft für Evangelische Theologie* in 1953, is a "gift" that forms the "foundation of evangelical ethics" [3].

On Barth's view of human freedom, it is impossible for man *not* to be free [4]. A rejection of freedom is by definition, in continuity with Barth's reading of sin, an ontological impossibility. The logic of this assertion becomes clear when it is recalled, first, that man's freedom is inextricably bound up with the reconciliation accomplished in Jesus Christ, and, second, that the terms "freedom" and "obedience" are for Barth virtually equivalent [5]. Only the man who is free is capable of obedience. And the converse of this is equally true: Only the man who is capable of obedience is free. Now, both freedom and obedience received initial expression in the being and existence of Jesus Christ, who represents both the freedom of God for man, and man's corresponding freedom for God. It follows, then, that for man to reject freedom (and obedience) at an ontological level, he would have to be capable of an ontological rejection of his relationship to God

---

[1] *Ibid.*, p. 388.

[2] I/2, p. 296; III/2, p. 230f.; IV/2, p. 405f. Barth prefers to speak of the "liberation" (*Befreiung*) rather than the "freedom" (*Freiheit*) of man, since he considers the former to preserve more adequately the dynamic overtone of the encounter between God and man on which man's status as subject and agent depends. Cf. IV/3.2, p. 759f.

[3] Included in "The Gift of Freedom: Foundation of Evangelical Ethics", *The Humanity of God*, pp. 69-96.

[4] *Ibid.*, p. 76f.; II/2, p. 660f.; IV/1, p. 266f.

[5] Cf. II/2, pp. 669, 671.

secured in Jesus Christ. This, however, is precisely what he cannot do, for the line of continuity between creation and covenant, we have seen, is such that all men are included within the dynamic framework of grace. Within that framework, a rejection of freedom, and the obedience that it entails, is thrown into continuity with sin, which on Barth's analysis is no more than an "episode" in the total history between God and man, and so an ontological impossibility.

The positive point that emerges from this negative line of argument is that the distinction between Christians and non-Christians is epistemic, not ontological. Ontologically, all men share the same status [1]. This follows from the fact that in the life-act of Jesus Christ there occurred "the life of all men" [2]. This point is important for a complete delineation of Barth's reading of the human, for it establishes the needed point of continuity between the identity and status of created human essence in its *de iure* participation in the event of reconciliation, and the additional ontic significance for human subjectivity and agency that issues from the transition to a *de facto* recognition of and participation in that same event [3].

Since man is given liberation only through his inclusion in the being and action of God's own freedom, it is to be expected that human freedom will display both a positive and a negative dimension, i.e., both a freedom *for* and a freedom *from* which find their originals in God's own freedom to say both "Yes" and "No":

---

[1] IV/1, p. 98f.

[2] IV/3.1, p. 43.

[3] See above, p. 221. Barth draws this distinction nicely in the following: "But we must remember that what is to be said first of all of the Christian man as such has a general validity for all men to the extent that it could be said of them also if they came to know Jesus Christ and what they are in him ... The being of the man reconciled with God in Jesus Christ is reflected in the existence of the Christian. That is something that cannot be said of other men. They do not lack Jesus Christ and the being of man reconciled to God in him. But they lack a life in obedience to his Holy Spirit, eyes, ears and heart open for him, a knowledge and recognition of the conversion of man to God that took place in him, the new direction which those who have been given newness of being in him must conform to, the gratitude of life in and with his community, participation in its ministry, the confession of him and witness to him as its Lord and as the Head of all men. For these reasons the being of man reconciled in Jesus Christ is not—yet—reflected in them. To understand and describe it, therefore, we must confine ourselves to Christians and the Christian community". IV/1, p. 98f.

Human freedom is not to be understood as freedom to assert, to preserve, to justify and save oneself. God is primarily free *for*; the Father is free for the Son, the Son for the Father in the unity of the Spirit. The one God is free for man as his Creator, as the Lord of the covenant, as the beginner and perfecter of his history, his *Heilsgeschichte*. God says "Yes". Only once this "Yes" is said, He also says "No". Thereby he reveals Himself to be free from all that is alien and hostile to His nature. Only once this "Yes" is said, is He free for Himself and for His own glory. Human freedom is freedom only within the limitations of God's own freedom [1].

In correspondence to God's own freedom [2], then, the liberation that comes to man through the Holy Spirit does not mean that he is suddenly equipped with a neutral ontic capacity heretofore lacking. The freedom (as permission) that comes to man from God carries with it a precise obligation, so that human behavior is given a new focus and direction. The crucial problem in theological ethics, accordingly, focuses on the "use or *non-use*" (*Gebrauch oder Nichtgebrauch*) that man makes of the fact of his liberation, not on its possible misuse [3]. The freedom granted man cannot be misused. If it is used at all, it is used rightly [4]. And this will mean discerning the one particular action in a given situation that conforms to the command of God and human freedom under the direction of the Holy Spirit [5]. God's freeing of man thus entails at the same time a very strict and definite binding. Man is in no sense autonomously "free" [6]. His liberation for authentic subjectivity and ethical agency lies exclusively in his being irrevocably bound *to* God and his fellow-man, so that he can only exist *for* both.

---

[1] *The Humanity of God*, p. 78.

[2] The term "correspondence" indicates that we are involved again in an analogous relationship. It is still helpful, I feel, to indicate this in terms of both the *analogia fidei* and the *analogia relationis*, despite the fact that Barth seems to drop this distinction in the latest volume of the *Dogmatics*. Cf. IV/3.2, pp. 612f., 909f. Within the context of discipleship (the inclusive descriptive category applicable to the Christian community) freedom is exhibited first of all, in the act of faith, which provides the analogue to God's free self-knowledge in his eternal trinitarian being; and secondly, in the ability to be *for* as well as with his fellow-man, which forms the analogue to God's action in Jesus Christ.

[3] IV/2, p. 410. Italics added.

[4] *Ibid.*

[5] IV/2, pp. 410ff.

[6] IV/1, p. 108f.

The positive and negative dimensions of man's freedom (i.e., freedom *for* and *from*) may be indicated along the following lines. The most immediate consequence of God's self-impartation to man through the Holy Spirit is that man is free to rejoice. As man is liberated by the Gospel, he is set free for a joyous participation in its given reality, and for a celebration of his own (future) humanity as it impinges now on his being and existence in the present:

> And thus we can see that freedom is *being joyful*. Freedom is the great gift, totally unmerited and wondrous beyond understanding. It awakens the receiver to true selfhood and new life. It is a gift from *God*, from the source of all goodness, an ever-new token of His faithfulness and mercy. The gift is unambiguous and cannot fail. Through this gift man who was irretrievably separated and alienated from God is called into discipleship. This is why freedom is joy! [1]

Man's freedom for the Gospel expressed in his response of joy means also that he is now free for an existence dominated by the action of Jesus Christ. It is this action that forms the positive background and pattern for man's own free action as one who is justified and sanctified by God, and therefore capable of being both with and for his neighbor:

> From this perspective the liberation of the Christian consists simply in the fact that what has taken place in Jesus Christ becomes the concrete determination of his own existence and the dominating factor in his own life-history, that he may exist as a man who is justified before God and sanctified for him, that he may believe and love in spite of all his sin and guilt and need [2].

Under the impact of grace, man is thus drawn out of the possibility of an isolated existence, and is set in authentic community with his fellows, in precise imitation of God's own freedom, which is realized initially *pro nobis*, and only after that *pro me* [3]. In man's freedom for God, i.e., for the Gospel of Jesus Christ, which carries with it a corresponding freedom for the neighbor, we find exhibited a *précis* of the positive thrust of man's encounter by Jesus Christ in the Holy Spirit.

The negative side of human freedom under grace may be indicated, first of all, by the fact that man is liberated from the false security and imagined freedom of his own attempts at self-justification. He is no longer free to live at the level of that sort of activity, and the anxiety

---

[1] *The Humanity of God*, p. 78; Cf. IV/3.1, p. 284f.; IV/3.2, p. 757f.
[2] IV/3.2, p. 759; Cf. IV/2, p. 339f.
[3] *The Humanity of God*, p. 77; IV/3.2, p. 761f.

to which it leads [1]. In addition, man is set free from the possibility or
the necessity of considering himself a kind of indifferent spectator of the
world, achieving a degree of self-identity by placing himself in the
comfortable niche of detached neutrality. The Word of God removes
entirely this sort of imagined freedom as it liberates man for sustained
and genuine participation in the world on behalf of his neighbor [2].
As this occurs, the Christian is liberated from a dependence on and
concern for a variety of possibilities, and is directed instead toward the
one remaining necessity: obedience. This automatically insures, however,
that the Christian is additionally freed from a concern for "things"
(*Sachen*), and the desiring and demanding that accompany that concern [3].
In the end, man is set free for the human, and for it alone, which means
that he is liberated from indecision, the dialectic of the moral and the
immoral, and the anxiety that accompanies them, and is set free for
positive action within the context of grace, i.e., forgiveness and prayer [4].

It needs to be pointed out, finally, that the freedom that comes to
man through the Holy Spirit represents the impingement of his future,
irrevocably cast in Christ, on his present existence. But since his present
existence remains charged with the distorting overtones of sin (as pride,
sloth, and falsehood), it will be seen only within the continuing history
of Jesus Christ, a history which still moves toward final closure in
victory. What this means for human freedom is that it is always (and
at best) imperfectly realized:

> Certainly, man does not live up to this freedom. Even worse, he fails
> in every respect. It is true enough that he does not know any longer the
> natural freedom which was bestowed upon him in creation; he does not
> know as yet the ultimate freedom in store for him at the completion of
> his journey, in the ultimate fulfillment of his existence. It is true enough
> that man may presently know and enjoy this freedom through the abiding
> Spirit of the Father and the Son only in spite of sin, flesh, and death;
> in spite of the world, his earthly anxiety and his worldly nature; and in
> spite of himself in his persistent temptation [5].

Given the persistence of these negative aspects of man's existence,
it is less than clear what positive significance the event of freedom carries
as regards his identity as subject and agent.

---

[1] IV/3.1, p. 278f.
[2] *Ibid.*, p. 280f.; IV/3.2, p. 761f.
[3] IV/3.2, pp. 763ff.
[4] *Ibid.*, pp. 767-772.
[5] *The Humanity of God*, p. 78.

2. *The Marks of Freedom: Faith, Love and Hope*

This section seeks to describe the significance that Barth attaches to faith, love and hope as ontic modes of the Christian, and to determine from this something of the form and status of human action within theological ethics. In getting at these issues, it will be necessary also to indicate the importance of the categories of justification, sanctification and vocation, as these devolve from the action of God in Jesus Christ, and provide the positive conditions for the emergence of faith, love and hope. What is at stake here is an understanding of the degree to which man is capable of obedient actions that take him beyond the basic ethical action of repentance. This concern was expressed in the questions raised at the end of the fourth chapter of his study: Is there an exemplification of sanctification within the occurrence of justification in man's existence? Or does the former remain only an eschatological reality? A clear grasp of Barth's handling of these issues, and the questions to which they lead, will throw important light on his development of a "special" ethic, which will be examined in the following chapter.

It must be kept in mind that the possibility (and actuality) of man's subjective appropriation of faith, love and hope will, like his appropriation of freedom, be strictly dependent on the activity of the Holy Spirit. The reason for this is that we are again faced with the question of a transition from Christ to other men, and so of a transposition of man's *ontological* determination in Christ to its exemplification, ontically, within humanity which is signalled, initially, in the being and activity of the Christian community, and so in the lives of the individuals who belong to it [1].

The event of reconciliation occurs exclusively and completely in Jesus Christ. Although it is a totally unified event, it can nevertheless be analyzed into the three "moments" of Christ's humiliation as the suffering and crucified Son of God, his exaltation as the resurrected Son of Man, and his impartation of the communicational (i.e., revelatory) dimension of that event through the Holy Spirit. These "moments" of the completed event of revelation can also be described, more traditionally, as the priestly, kingly, and prophetic modes of God's action in Jesus Christ. It is to these distinctions within the unified event of reconciliation that the categories of justification, sanctification and vocation

---

[1] IV/1, pp. 95ff.

correspond, and their *general* ontic corollaries lie in the responses of
faith, love and hope evoked by the Holy Spirit.

Ontologically, the justification, sanctification and vocation of man
as these occur in Jesus Christ take form against the divine "verdict"
(*Urteil*) [1], "direction" (*Weisung*) [2], and "promise" (*Verheißung*) [3] under
which man is set. The realization of these in the history of Jesus Christ
signals a decisive and final "determination" for the human [4]. Temporally,
the divine verdict leading to the justification of man relates primarily
to his past as sinner which is overcome and rejected in Christ, and the
forgiveness which is his as a result; the divine direction entailed in
reconciliation corresponds to man's present existence under the command of God; and the divine promise is indicative of man's future
status as the redeemed child of God [5]. Man's temporality is thus securely
anchored in the eternal co-temporality of God, which receives exemplification and fulfillment in Jesus Christ, the Lord of time [6]. But since the
divine verdict, direction and promise receive *simultaneous* fulfillment in
Christ, it follows that the being and action of man will display a corresponding simultaneity and interpenetration of these factors. The justification, sanctification and vocation of man do not, then, indicate temporally
isolated (or isolable) "moments" of his being, which can be related in
serial fashion. They are rather the descriptive contours of man's being,
beyond sin, as the elected covenant-partner of God, which are realized
in Jesus Christ [7]. What we have here, then, is an account of reconciliation
as a completed forensic event providing ontological determination for
man, together with its movement toward eschatological closure in
redemption.

It is in relation to this completed event that the question of man's
subjective, existential identity and participation as ethical agent comes
into view. Ostensibly the issue of man's involvement in the event
of reconciliation at a subjective level is resolved through a delinea-

---

[1] IV/1, p. 99.

[2] *Ibid.*, p. 106.

[3] *Ibid.*, p. 117.

[4] Cf. above, Ch. Three, Section C, "The Determination of Man".

[5] IV/1, p. 99f.; IV/2, pp. 565ff.; IV/3.2, pp. 553ff.

[6] Cf. III/2, Par. 47, Pt. 1.

[7] IV/2, pp. 569ff.; IV/3.2, pp. 554, 581. The possibility of describing
the total event of reconciliation, as it is analyzable into man's justification,
sanctification, and vocation, along the lines of an *ordo salutis*, is thus decisively
set aside.

tion of the categories of faith, love and hope as these are produced in man by the presence and activity of Christ in the Holy Spirit. Now, it is precisely the introduction of the phrase, "in man", that provokes careful analysis, for unless it becomes unambiguously clear that these categories are descriptive of the way in which the event of reconciliation becomes (in some sense) directly predicable of human subjectivity, and not merely in a christological and eschatological way, then the possibility of giving descriptive cogency to man's status as subject and agent will be quite problematic, and the meaning of the phrase, "Christian ethics", will remain obscure [1].

Justification, as the initial dimension of the total event of reconciliation, displays the dual aspect of judgment and pardon, the "No" and "Yes" of God which together constitute the divine verdict on the human condition [2]. Anthropologically, this means that justification, like sanctification and vocation, is "the dialectic of a history" (*die Dialektik einer Geschichte*) in which man's wrong is completely behind, and his right, in Jesus Christ, always before him [3]. The pardon of God that secures man's justification thus entails a total rejection of his past, and the assigning of a definite promise to man as regards his future. In receiving this promise, man is "already the one, whom he will be" [4]. Stated comprehensively, the event of man's justification, viewed as the promise of his future already secured and maintained in Jesus Christ, consists in (1) the forgiveness of sins; the restoration of (2) his right as a child of

---

[1] Barth is himself quite aware of the danger involved here, and of the necessity to invest human subjectivity and agency with positive content. Speaking of the importance of freedom in relation to the being and activity of Christians, he remarks: "The positive element which is hidden in the limitation of their unholy being, the freedom which has become a factor in their lives, must also be understood as real. Otherwise there would be no such thing as the apostolic admonition issued to Christians in the New Testament. It is not issued as a law or ideal proclaimed in the void. It is not issued as if the question whether or not man is capable of obedience remained an open question, still to be answered. It is issued and proclaimed on the assumption that these men are free, and that they can make use of the freedom in which Christ has set them free ... Without this assumption, there would be no such thing as Christian ethics even for us". IV/2, p. 602f.

[2] IV/1, Par. 61, Pts. 2 and 3.

[3] *Ibid.*, p. 660.

[4] *Ibid.*, p. 664.

God, which goes beyond man's reconciliation as the elected covenant-partner of God, and falls over into its fulfillment in redemption; and (3) his being placed in a state of hope [1]. When viewed properly as history, justification provides the initial way in which the total event of reconciliation can be described. It is scarely surprising, therefore, that it exhibits the verdict (forgiveness of sins), direction (transition from past to future under the promise of God), and promise (the seizing of both verdict and direction in hope) of that event.

In describing the relationship that holds between man's identity and status experienced presently in himself, and his future promised and secured in Jesus Christ, Barth is at pains to avoid throwing the latter onto a purely eschatological plane. So, even though man knows and receives the forgiveness of sins, on which his justification rests, and the transition from reconciliation to his status as the redeemed child of God, *only* as promise, it is nevertheless true that the promise under which man stands is always immediately present to him. In this respect, it is even allowable to speak of a "realized eschatology" [2]. This does not mean, of course, that man is capable of a direct realization of the forgiveness of sins, his divine right as a child of God, or the fulfillment of hope, in his temporal existence and action. Within his own history, man is always caught in the dialectical position of being *simul peccator et iustus* [3]. An analysis of his past, accordingly, displays only a lack of forgiveness, a total obscuring of his status as a child of God, and a submersion of hope in despair [4]. It is only in relation to his future in Jesus Christ that man is justified and given newness of being.

It is at precisely this point that the event of faith becomes crucial, for it provides the needed transition between man's past and future, offering thereby at least the possibility of a viable participation, through his own being and action, in the event of reconciliation. It is clear, to begin with, that it is *only* through faith that man is made participant in his justification. As the action of God, the occurrence of justification is not open to direct inspection and elucidation by human self-understanding. It remains an "enigma" (*Rätsel*) [5] which can in no sense be demon-

---

[1] *Ibid.*, pp. 665ff.
[2] *Ibid.*, p. 668.
[3] *Ibid.*, p. 672.
[4] *Ibid.*, pp. 665, 670f.
[5] *Ibid.*, p. 610.

strated and controlled from our side [1]. Man knows of and participates in justification only as he is brought to this knowledge and participation in the action of the Holy Spirit. It is through this action that man is moved beyond pride to a new humility, in which he is equipped to be open, at the point of witness, to both God and his fellow-man [2].

This does not mean, of course, that the humility that comes with faith entails a total transition from man's former response of pride. It is man in his pride who, in faith, is made humble. As humility, faith is "a genuine, but a comforted despair" [3]. This indicates that faith does not in any sense constitute a completion of justification as one aspect of the event of reconciliation. Indeed, the recognition of justification that comes with faith is, strictly speaking, a *denial* of "the competence, sufficiency, power and value of all human action" [4]. It remains true, nevertheless, that faith, as the "obedience of humility" [5], is the basis for a positive freedom in man, a freedom grounded in his awareness both of his present existence in sin, and of his future being in Jesus Christ [6]. Faith is thus indicative of the way in which man's future, already completed event in God's action in Jesus Christ, falls over into his present through the action of the Holy Spirit, and invests it with new meaning and possibility. It is at this point that man is made participant in the ongoing history of salvation, becoming thereby the analogue to the continuing history of Jesus Christ, which provides the paradigm for the transition from reconciliation to redemption [7].

As the sign of man's participation in reconciliation, it is clear that faith does not, in itself, create anything. It is, rather, a recognition, acknowledgement and following of something that is already there, in Jesus Christ [8]. Through the Holy Spirit, man is brought to a necessary, though free, action, in which his own "yes" follows as a repetition of the divine affirmation of man, and so to the "subjectivization of an objective *res.*" [9]. As the free action of man, faith is "*the* act of the Christian life" [10],

---

[1] *Ibid.*, p. 682f.

[2] *Ibid.*, pp. 685, 690f.

[3] "Die Demut des Glaubens ist nämlich wohl eine ernstliche, sie ist aber eine getroste Verzweiflung". *Ibid.*, p. 692.

[4] *Ibid.*, p. 700.

[5] *Ibid.*

[6] *Ibid.*, pp. 707f., 866f.

[7] IV/3.1, p. 274f.

[8] IV/1, pp. 828ff.

[9] *Ibid.*, pp. 828, 835f.

[10] "Faith—like love and hope, viewed from other aspects—is *the* act of

in the sense that it, and it alone, qualifies every additional action. As an act of acknowledgement and recognition, faith displays both a theoretical and a practical side. As the act that signals man's epistemological participation in revelation, it provides the basis for correct thoughts and formulations concerning the event of reconciliation accomplished in Jesus Christ [1]. This knowledge does not remain abstract, however, but falls over immediately into the self-knowledge of the individual, and so gains practical import in relation to the decisions and actions that he undertakes [2]. The occurrence of faith is thus exemplary, at an individual, subjective level, of the unity that exists between dogmatics and ethics.

The ethical significance of faith lies in the fact that it establishes the action of the believer as an analogue to the action of God in Jesus Christ. In this respect, faith will display an inward *mortificatio* and *vivificatio* corresponding to the humiliation and exaltation of Jesus [3]. It is in filling out these concepts that Barth provides substance and clarity to the ethical significance of faith. The basic point here is that we are dealing, in both instances, with no more than an *analogy*. What is provided in the *mortificatio* and *vivificatio* of the Christian, then, is an emphasized and extended recognition of the reconciliation, and so justification, that has taken place *for* him in Jesus Christ, and that has come *to* him in the Holy Spirit, but which has in no sense occurred directly *in* him [4]. The difference, finally, is that man now exists as a disturbed sinner, as one alarmed and sorrowful at his condition (and that of the world), and as a hopeful sinner, i.e., as one who looks forward in confidence to his own future already secured in Jesus Christ [5]. The upshot of this is that man is positively equipped for the actions of repentance and confession [6], and so for the actions of trust, prayer and hope to which they lead [7].

---

the Christian life to the extent that in all the activity and individual actions of a man it is the most inward and central and decisive act of his heart, which —assuming it takes place—characterizes them all, as manifestations and confirmations of his Christian freedom, his Christian responsibility, his Christian obedience". *Ibid.*, p. 847. Cf. II/1, p. 433f.

[1] IV/1, p. 854f.
[2] *Ibid.*, pp. 855ff.
[3] *Ibid.*, pp. 863ff.
[4] *Ibid.*, pp. 861ff., 864ff.
[5] *Ibid.*, p. 867.
[6] *Ibid.*, pp. 867ff.
[7] *Ibid.*, pp. 865, 671.

In turning, now, to an analysis of man's subjective participation in the sanctification realized in Jesus Christ, we are again faced with the unfolding of a history, this time in the form of a dialectic between the slothful inactivity of the "old" man in face of God's action, and the obedience (in love) of the "new" man awakened to conversion [1]. As regards the possibility of a realization of sanctification in his actions, man continues to be "simul (totus) peccator" and "simul (totus) iustus" [2]. That these factors describe a total history in which man is ineluctably involved is underscored by the fact that his sanctification consists specifically in his being placed under the divine *direction*, i.e., the command of God [3]. As regards the motif of dialectic present in Barth's delineation of man's involvement as subject and agent in the total event of reconciliation (i.e., justification, sanctification and vocation), the discussion of justification and faith just concluded provides an instructive paradigm.

Man's sanctification consists essentially in God's turning man to himself as he turns to him, in spite of and beyond his sin, in Jesus Christ [4]. As an aspect of the completed event of reconciliation, sanctification cannot be separated from justification, though there is a sense in which sanctification "teleologically is placed over justification" [5]. Put more subtly, the relationship between sanctification and justification, viewed as a *Prius* and a *Posterius* within the one event of reconciliation, can be expressed as follows:

> In the *simul* of the one divine will and action justification is first as basis and second as presupposition, sanctification is first as goal and second as consequence—in this respect both are superior and subordinate [6].

The history of man's subjective engagement with the fact of sanctification begins with his "conversion" (*Umkehr*), in which he is awakened to "fellowship with Jesus the Son of Man, in the power of his summons, and in the freedom which he is given in the power of his Holy Spirit to look to him, and so to lift himself up in spite of the downward drag of his slothful nature" [7]. It is a part of the reality of God

---

[1] IV/2, p. 645f.
[2] *Ibid.*, p. 646.
[3] IV/1, p. 106f.
[4] IV/2, p. 565.
[5] *Ibid.*, p. 575.
[6] *Ibid.*
[7] *Ibid.*, p. 626.

himself that man is encountered by the "shock" (*Anstoß*) of conversion, and is thus awakened and placed in a new direction. The actuality of conversion is thus a function of the prior actuality of God [1]. As man is placed on the way toward a realization of his sanctification in Christ, he is simultaneously called to discipleship, readied for actions that reflect that call, and placed under the cross, which stands as the reality marking the outer boundary of the Christian's participation in Christ [2]. Within this total movement, conversion denotes a radical and continuous "altercation" or "falling out" (*Auseinandersetzung*) with oneself [3]. The unavoidability of this lies in the fact that man's movement toward sanctification unfolds in terms of a "twofold determination", i.e., he is at once the man who is turning toward God in repentance, and the man who stands in need of continual forgiveness [4]. This duality does not involve merely a continuous circularity, however, since man's true future and being are already established in Jesus Christ. As God turns to man and addresses him from this perspective, the "old" and the "new", past and future, serve to define, respectively, the *terminus a quo* and the *terminus ad quem* marking the beginning and end (teleologically) of the history in which he is made participant [5].

In conversion, then, man is provided with the very definite freedom of acknowledgement. He is given permission to recognize the good action of God in Jesus Christ, to accept what he already is (in him), and so to exist and act under the direction that is given him. It is clear, on this analysis, that neither sanctification nor the conversion attendant upon it are directly predicable of man in his given temporality. Strictly speaking, both sanctification and conversion take place only in Jesus Christ [6]. The question thereby raised focuses on the actuality of the liberation granted man under the direction given him as he is brought to a direct involvement in the event of his sanctification. Now, both the liberation and the direction of the Christian may at this point be drawn together in the question whether, and to what extent, man is capable of genuine acts of love, since the category of love is ontically related to the event of sanctification in the same way that faith relates

---

[1] *Ibid.*, pp. 630ff.

[2] *Ibid.*, Par. 66, Pts. 3, 5 and 6. A more extended discussion of these dimensions of the Christian life will be given in the following chapter.

[3] *Ibid.*, p. 644.

[4] *Ibid.*, p. 645f.

[5] *Ibid.*, p. 647f.

[6] *Ibid.*, pp. 597ff., 659.

to justification [1]. The correct response to the divine direction is Christian love, i.e., the act of self-giving which corresponds to faith as the act of initial reception [2].

Man's capacity to engage in acts of love is, like his conversion on which this capacity depends, grounded exclusively in the activity of the Holy Spirit. As God gives himself, as Spirit, into the context of human life, man is enabled to participate in the eternal love of God [3]. The activity of the Holy Spirit represents an overflowing of the love between Father, Son and Spirit within the being of God, a love whose reality as act was made explicit in Jesus Christ [4]. God's love is thus seen exclusively as act. It is not a "divine state" (*göttlicher Zustand*), but "the divine life-act, the act of his self-giving" [5]. As the totally free act in which God gives himself to man, the divine love signals man's status as the elected covenant-partner of God, the rejection of his misunderstanding and distortion of his being in sin (here seen as sloth), and the creation of the condition that makes possible a response on man's part, i.e., analogous actions that constitute a reflection of and correspondence to the love of God [6].

The Holy Spirit thus sets man free for his own limited but significant acts of love, which are not directly identifiable with God's love:

> The work of the Holy Spirit consists in the liberation of man for his own act, and so for spontaneous human love, whose littleness and fragility are not the responsibility of the Holy Spirit, but his own. As a human act, Christian love displays, after a fashion, a genuine correspondence to the act of God's love, thought it is indeed to be distinguished from it. It is an act in which man is active, not as God's puppet, but in his heart and soul and strength as an independent subject who encounters and replies to God, and who is responsible to him as his partner [7].

---

[1] *Ibid.*, p. 825f.

[2] *Ibid.*, p. 828f. Barth identifies the love of the Christian with *agape*, and draws a firm distinction between it and *eros*, its secular counterpart. *Ibid.*, pp. 831ff. The ethical consequences to which this distinction leads will be examined in the following chapter. Our only interest here is to determine whether, and to what extent, love is directly predicable of the Christian, and so determinative of his identity as subject and agent.

[3] *Ibid.*, p. 855f.

[4] *Ibid.*, p. 862f.

[5] *Ibid.*, p. 875.

[6] *Ibid.*, pp. 869-888.

[7] *Ibid.*, p. 891.

√   Put succinctly, the anthropological consequence of the activity of
the Holy Spirit at this point is that man is set free for a realization of
obedience, which here takes the form of love. The obedience of the man
sanctified by God centers in his total orientation on the will and command
of God [1]. Obedience is thus at once the action which is *required* of man,
yet wholly free. As act, the free obedience of the Christian represents a
movement beyond thought and will, and the beginning of a life lived
wholly in response to the continuing action of God in the ongoing
history of Jesus [2]. The possibility of the Christian's exercise of the freedom granted him for obedience in acts of love being channeled along
rigidly prescribed and systematized lines is thus excluded, and he is
made capable of definite actions exhibiting love toward both God and
man [3]. So, within the sphere of human action, there will be a representation and reflection of the one true action of God in Jesus Christ which
secures ontologically the love of man to both God and the neighbor [4].

     Here we must recall the importance of the event of faith, as a means
of providing contact and continuity between man's rejected past and his
promised (eschatological) future in Jesus Christ. Faith provides both
the possibility and the actuality of man's present participation in the
event of reconciliation viewed as justification. There is a corresponding
tension between man's rejected past and promised future where
reconciliation is viewed as sanctification, which is resolved (ostensibly)
as man is awakened to conversion, placed under the divine direction,
and equipped to perform acts of love demonstrating both his freedom
and his obedience. Love thus emerges as the second crucial ontic category
descriptive of man's status as subject and agent.

     The difficulty in Barth's treatment of man's participation in the
√ sanctification achieved and promised in Jesus Christ is that it never
quite becomes clear in what sense it is descriptive of something that
takes place *in* man. Both conversion and love, the central dimensions
of sanctification, are in the strict sense predicable only of Jesus in his
action as the Son of God. They are actualized as event *in* him alone [5].
It is in this event that man's past and future are decisively cast, and it is
through the immediate self-manifestation of Christ to the Christian

---

[1] *Ibid.*, p. 906f.
[2] *Ibid.*, p. 909.
[3] *Ibid.*, p. 909f.
[4] *Ibid.*, pp. 891f., 925f.
[5] *Ibid.*, pp. 658ff., 933ff.

community in the Holy Spirit that man is made participant, derivatively, in his sanctification in Christ, so that both conversion and love receive analogous confirmation in his actions. There will be, accordingly, a similarity and correspondence between the action of Jesus and that of the Christian. The introduction of analogy at this point, however, seems both to clarify and to confuse the issue. It provides a clarification to the extent that it indicates what Barth might mean when he asserts that there is, on the one hand, a sense in which love becomes, in our actions, a "real event" (real Ereignis), while remaining, on the other hand, "figurative" or "improper" (uneigentlich) [1]. It confuses the issue, however, when Barth's operational definition of analogy, "complete similarity along with complete dissimilarity" [2], is introduced, for this suggests that the event in which man's free obedience in love is actualized is dependent on the repeated occurrence of the event of grace, which is always coincidental with the activity of Christ in the Holy Spirit. What this entails for human agency, however, is that ostensible acts of love (as embodiments of freedom and obedience) are, in themselves, "improper", in that they stand under the negative side of analogy, and so exhibit "complete dissimilarity" to the action of God in Christ. It is only under the impact of grace that their corresponding "complete similarity" to that action emerges. But this can only mean that love, as the basic mode of man's participation in the event of reconciliation (viewed as sanctification), does not become ontically predicable of man in any direct sense. It is at best an indirect predicate of the human devolving from the activity of the Holy Spirit and the event of grace. The difficulty that surrounds Barth's concept of the "event" of grace has already been noted. This becomes even more entrenched when the attempt is made to forge a link between man's (eschatological) future

---

[1] Ibid., p. 935. Strictly speaking, it would seem the translators erred in rendering "uneigentlich" as "improper". Cf. Ibid. (Eng. trans.), p. 824. Although "eigentlich" does mean, among other things, "proper", "uneigentlich" is uniformly translated as "not literal" or "figurative" by both The New Cassell's German Dictionary (New York: Funk and Wagnalls, 1958) and The Pocket Oxford German Dictionary (London: Oxford University Press, 1955). For "improper", Cassell's lists the following: "ungeeignet", "untauglich", "unschicklich", "ungehörig", and "unanständig". However, there is perhaps justification for the translator's otherwise odd preference for "improper", when consideration is given to Barth's use and definition of analogy as it relates to human acts of love.

[2] IV/3.2, p. 612.

in Christ, and his present status as subject and agent. In the end, it appears that love, like faith, is not indicative of the sanctification that takes place *in* man. Love rather underlines the fact that the sanctification realized in Christ (for all men) has, in the Holy Spirit, come *to* him. To be sure, this does represent for Barth the incursion of man's future into his present. What remains unclear is that it establishes the subjective status of man sufficiently to enable the obedience demanded by Barth's reading of theological ethics to take shape.

We are brought, at this point, to a consideration of the possibility open to man for participation in the event of reconciliation, viewed here under the rubric of "vocation" (*Berufung*) [1], in terms of the corresponding ontic category of "hope" (*Hoffnung*) [2]. Here man is viewed as one equipped and posited by God as "the bearer of the divine promise" [3]. What is provided in this is the goal or purpose to which justification and sanctification lead. Thus, although man's calling or vocation under God, and the hope in which this is embodied, is simply a third dimension of the one event of reconciliation, it is nevertheless both possible and necessary to provide it with separate treatment, for it constitutes the point at which man's present reconciliation connects with his future redemption [4].

The event of vocation signals man's (ontological) removal from the context of falsehood, through the prophetic witness of Christ, and his being placed "in actual fellowship with Jesus Christ, namely, in the service of his prophecy, in the *ministerium Verbi divini*, of the word of reconciliation, and so in the service of God and his fellow-men" [5]. As an event actualized within both the eternal trinitarian being of God and the history of Jesus, it becomes actual once again in the concrete event in time in which man is called directly to service and participation in the history of salvation. It is the event that marks the incursion of the specific time and history of Jesus into the general human, and so the fulfillment of man's time and history [6]. This does not mean, however, that the event of man's calling and vocation occurs generally.

[1] IV/3.2, Par. 71, "Des Menschen Berufung".
[2] *Ibid.*, Par. 73, "Der Heilige Geist und die christliche Hoffnung".
[3] IV/2, p. 117.
[4] *Ibid.*, p. 122f.
[5] IV/3.2, p. 554.
[6] *Ibid.*, p. 575f.

Although the future of every man lies only in the call of Christ [1], so that there is, in effect, a *de iure* participation of man in his vocation under God, its actualization as concrete event moving him to a *de facto* grasp of that future in the present is dependent on the movement of God as Holy Spirit toward particular individuals [2]. The most immediate result of man's being encountered by Christ in the Holy Spirit, as regards the question of a subjective realization of vocation, is his "illumination" (*Erleuchtung*) or awakening, and so his advancement to knowledge of revelation [3]. Formally considered, the awakening of man to this knowledge constitutes "the totality of what makes a man a Christian" [4].

The event of vocation thus indicates the beginning of a process, as man is brought directly, i.e., subjectively, into the history of salvation, and so into the ongoing history of Jesus Christ. The goal of this process, the *telos* toward which man is moved, is "that he become a Christian, a *homo christianus*" [5]. Within this history the existence of the Christian is determined exclusively by Jesus Christ and his faith in him. It is because and as Christ remains the active Subject in the event of vocation, and the hope embodied in this, that man is given a new freedom, the liberation of the child of God [6]. Again, there is present here a dialectical movement, and so a continuation of man's past history of falsehood into his present existence under the future promised him in Jesus Christ. The freedom given man in his calling will not, then, indicate a static quality. As the sign of his new creation in Christ, it will need to be received anew each day [7]. When this freedom is grasped, however, man is enabled to exist in expectation and hope under his future in Christ as a child of God. Christians are thus equipped for actions in the present that will mark them as those who exist "in repetition, confirmation and revelation not only of the manner but also of the will and act of God as the One from whom they derive" [8].

The event of vocation, and the hope which accompanies it, provide the needed point of closure for man's justification and sanctification,

---

[1] *Ibid.*, pp. 559f., 578.
[2] *Ibid.*, pp. 573f., 576f.
[3] *Ibid.*, pp. 584ff.
[4] *Ibid.*, p. 588f.
[5] *Ibid.*, p. 599.
[6] *Ibid.*, pp. 604ff.
[7] *Ibid.*, pp. 610ff.
[8] *Ibid.*, p. 613.

as these are reflected in faith and love. Although Barth's development of justification, sanctification and vocation is designed to provide a complete description of the event of reconciliation, his treatment of vocation and hope underlines the way in which reconciliation moves toward redemption within the continuing history of the *parousia* of Jesus Christ. It is through the action of Christ in the Holy Spirit that the Christian (and the Christian community) is enabled to locate himself within this history, and so to become a participant in the future of Jesus Christ, which has now become his future as well. The mode of participation is the hope with which the Christian is invested, which enables him to exist in the present as a "child of light" (*Kind des Lichtes*) [1]. Temporally, the existence of the Christian in hope is qualified at every point by the "not yet" of the completed self-manifestation and declaration of Jesus Christ. It is hope, then, that provides substance and stability to faith and love. The time of the Christian is thus grounded at all points in God's own time manifested in Christ. He will exist, accordingly, as one who believes in Jesus Christ as the One who came, loves him as the One who now comes, and hopes in him as the One who will come [2].

In the hope of the Christian, as in his faith and love, Jesus Christ remains the primary subject. Hope will therefore always occur as the act and event in which man grasps anew the future (as promise) under which he stands. Along with faith and love, hope will not designate an existential capacity *in* man, but rather the continually renewed possibility of immediate existence in hope under the impact of the Holy Spirit [3]. The category of hope is indicative, finally, of both the possibility and the limitation (from man's side) set over his existence, the possibility of an actualization, both subjectively and objectively, of his future in Christ as it impinges on his present, and the limitation occasioned by the persistent overtones of his former existence in sin. The significance for theological ethics of Barth's emphasis on hope as a strict eschatological category is that it brings home once again the inability of man to achieve a consistent and direct embodiment of his ontological future in Christ (even though this operates as a future in the present), and his need always to be open and receptive to the judgment and forgiveness of God [4].

---

[1] IV/3.2, p. 1035.
[2] *Ibid.*, p. 1046f.
[3] *Ibid.*, p. 1048f.
[4] *Ibid.*, p. 1037f.

The upshot of this, of course, is that the existence of the Christian in hope derives entirely from God. No one is capable of living in hope out of his own resources. Through the activity of the Holy Spirit, the Christian is set free for hope, i.e., he is given *permission* to hope [1]. This permission provides the basis for action, for service in hope, which will always be grounded, finally, in the spontaneous action of the Christian in continually seeking, in prayer, the freedom which is given him by the Holy Spirit [2].

It is time now to draw together the various strands in Barth's anthropology that have been developed, and to indicate the points at which critical reservation becomes necessary. The question with which this chapter began concerned the possibility open to man for an actualization of obedience, and, as the requisite basis for meaningful talk about human obedience, the degree to which man's identity and status as subject and agent can be established apart from the humanity of God in Jesus Christ.

I have argued that there are ambiguities present in Barth's treatment of created human essence. These result from an attempted use of the *analogia relationis* as a means of grounding the basic I-Thou relationality in the eternal trinitarian being of God, and in the apparent restriction of the category of "spirit", as an ontic specification of man, to the humanity of Jesus. At each of these points, the issue of man's independent status was seen to be in certain respects unclear. In concluding this chapter, I shall focus on the status of the *Christian* as subject and agent. The cruciality of clarification on this point is apparent, for it is only on the assumption that God, through the continuing activity of Christ in the Holy Spirit, establishes men as independent subjects capable of genuine obedience, that Christian ethics is even conceivable, much less actual. In assessing the results of Barth's treatment of these points, I shall argue that the ontic structure and status of the Christian, and so his capacity for an obedience beyond the basic action of repentance, are surrounded with ambiguity, despite Barth's obvious intent to do justice to human subjectivity and agency. The reasons for this ambiguity may be located (1) in Barth's consistent utilization, in his description of both God and man, of an act-ontology; (2) in a continuation of the sort of realism that was discussed before, with its attendant ontol-

---

[1] *Ibid.*, p. 1079f.
[2] *Ibid.*, pp. 1081ff.

ogical, epistemological, and, at this point, *ethical* consequences; (3) in Barth's insistence on making Jesus the only instance of complete or "real" (ontically) man, and so the only real Christian [1], which entails that other men are real or complete only as "predicates" of Jesus; (4) in the sustained eschatological tension in which he sets man's present experience, which makes problematic the possibility of a realized transition, in specific acts, from man's past in sin to his future in Jesus Christ, even though, paradoxically, it is only *in act* that man *is*.

It comes as no surprise that Barth's description of the ontic status of the Christian is cast in the form of an act-ontology. This follows directly from his doctrine of God, and from the continuity that he establishes between christology and anthropology. Earlier, it was noted that Barth's approach to theology in the *Dogmatics* trades heavily on what may be described as the "principle" of presupposition, which serves to anchor every point of the discussion securely in Jesus Christ. From this, it follows that the clue to the being of both God and man will be given only "in act", i.e., in the specific history between God and man exemplified in the birth, life, death and *parousia* of Christ. God is God only in his action in moving outward from himself through the various "moments" of creation, reconciliation and redemption, a movement and history exemplary of God's eternal being-in-act as Father. Son and Spirit. And man is man only in the history of his response to the action of God, as he is engaged in the active fulfillment and realization of his status as the elected covenant partner of God, and so brought to freedom and responsibility in the acts of faith, love, and hope.

As regards the ontic structure of the Christian, the adoption of an act-ontology of this sort suggests a removal of the traditional distinction between potentiality and actuality, or potency and act. The reason for this is not hard to see, since Barth clearly rejects a substance ontology to which the categories of potency and act could be applied. There is, accordingly, no way to describe the Christian apart from his action, or his being-in-act, as this emerges in his responsibility, freedom, faith,

---

[1] IV/2, p. 933f. Barth's insistence on identifying Christ as the only real Christian may be seen as a rather striking echo of the position he took as early as 1919, in "The Christian's Place in Society": "*The Christian:* we must be agreed that we do *not* mean *the Christians*, not the multitude of the baptized, nor the chosen few who are concerned with Religion and Social Relations, nor even the cream of the noblest and most devoted Christians we might think of: the Christian is *the Christ*". *WGWM*, p. 273.

love and hope, which may be drawn together under the embracing category of obedience. This reading of the human is simply a reflection of the being of God, which is never separable from the divine action in which it is embodied. So, just as the love of God does not describe a "divine state", but "the divine life-act, the act of his self-giving" [1], in a similar way man's ontic status in faith, love and hope, and the freedom in obedience (and obedience in freedom) to which they lead, does not denote a static positioning of these factors, but rather those concrete acts in which man's being is established, demonstrated, and maintained [2]. The Christian *is*, then, only as he acts on the permission (freedom) given him in the Gospel, which places him in direct responsibility to God's command, thereby sensitizing him to the continuous shaping and directing activity of God in the world, a sensitivity exemplified in specific acts of love that always bear the additional modes of faith and hope [3].

The actualism of Barth's anthropology, as it touches on the specific issue of the ontic structure of the Christian, while clearly reflecting his view of the being-in-act of God (which is summarily describable as *Heilsgeschichte*), is also designed to safeguard the two central points of Barth's whole theology: (1) the irreducible sovereignty and freedom in which God is God in his act, and (2) the total dependence of the creature on God's initiative, in the Holy Spirit, in bringing him into direct participation in the event of reconciliation and the ongoing *parousia* of Christ. The being of the Christian, accordingly, will take shape in precise parallelism to the essence of the Church, and the possibility of theological knowledge that emerges there: It will be *actus purus*, and will appear only in the "present instant in which Jesus Christ himself speaks and is heard, and the divine light is created in our hearts" [4]. The being of the Christian, as act, is dependent at all points on the contingency of God's action through the Holy Spirit, an action which never allows God to become man's possession, but which underlines man's continual need to wait openly for the event of grace.

Where this is extended to cover the ontic predicates of the Christian, however, it raises doubt as to Barth's handling of the issues of human

---

[1] IV/2, p. 875.

[2] The following passages provide a good indication of the pervasive actualism of Barth's description of the Christian: II/2, p. 572f.; III/2, pp. 209ff.; IV/1, pp. 846ff.; IV/2, pp. 831f., 845f.; IV/3.2, pp. 1066ff.

[3] IV/2, p. 831f.

[4] I/1, p. 41.

continuity and existence [1]. This doubt can be expressed in the form of a question: What are the possibilities, on Barth's analysis, of speaking of a "state" of man, which, while not undercutting his total dependence on grace, nor assigning the freedom given in faith, love and hope as a direct and unqualified "possession" of man, would yet provide the needed indication that reconciliation not only comes *to* man as a gift in the Holy Spirit, but also takes place *in* him?

The difficulty in giving an unambiguously affirmative answer to this question centers in the total freedom of God's action as Holy Spirit, which indicates that man at best can "possess" the freedom given in that action (and so faith, love and hope) only contingently, never in a directly predicable fashion. As man acts in the moment in which he is addressed by the Holy Spirit, he *is* free. This clearly suggests, however, that man's being collapses into act, so that it is not altogether appropriate or possible to speak of a "state" of man. In a recent study of Barth, Herbert Hartwell argues against this interpretation, and asserts that "the idea of a 'state' is excluded only in so far as there can be no state apart from God's constant giving" [2]. As Hartwell clearly indicates, however, this merely underlines again the contingency of the being of the Christian, and aligns it strictly with the act of grace. It is only in

---

[1] A problem noted earlier by Bonhoeffer. Cf. *Akt und Sein* (München: Chr. Kaiser Verlag, 1956), pp. 76ff. Cf. also Eberhard Bethge's comment on the question raised against Barth by Bonhoeffer: "Bonhoeffer holds that Barth cannot secure the continuity and the concern for existence by his emphasis on contingency. Barth describes his revelation all the time with negations, and the revelation is atomized in pure acts ... Bonhoeffer cannot see how Barth can solve the problem of present faith and obedience which Barth only hints at". "The Challenge of Dietrich Bonhoeffer", The Alden-Tuthill Lectures, in: The Chicago Theological Seminary *Register*, Vol. LI, Number 2 (February, 1961), p. 9. It is important to note that Bonhoeffer's criticisms were directed primarily to the "early" Barth of the *Römerbrief*. What I am suggesting here is that Barth has not fully resolved the difficulties encountered during his dialectical period, despite a methodological shift into analogy and a positive development of the time of reconciliation between creation and redemption. There is still, I feel, a strong overtone of contingency present in the *Dogmatics* which threatens to vitiate, through the adoption of an unrelieved act-ontology, the continuing identity of man as subject and agent under the command of God.

[2] *The Theology of Karl Barth* (Philadelphia: The Westminster Press, 1964), p. 37.

reference to the action of God in which his being (in Christ) is event for man that he can be said to "have" and "possess" the ontic modes predicable of the Christian:

> Act and being are linked up in Barth's theology in such a way that there is no 'being' apart from God's continual action, and this action takes place in the freedom of the divine grace. Man can and does act freely and responsibly and he can and does 'have' and 'possess' provided that his acting, having and possessing is brought about *and* sustained by God's free and gracious action [1].

It is surely not incorrect to see in Barth's actualistic anthropology, in its exclusive dependence on the activity of the Holy Spirit, a transposition of his analysis of the (ostensible) cognitive status of theological language and the command of God into the context of ontology. On Barth's view it proved impossible to substantiate the cognitive (i.e., factual) status of either theological language or the command of God, except by appealing to the action of God in the "event" of grace, an appeal that elicited profound epistemological and logical obstacles. Now, when the ontic status of the Christian is made dependent on this same action of God in the event of grace, man's subjective identity and agency are vitiated in a reappearance of Barth's stringent realism.

As regards the ontic status of the Christian, the realism involved is indicated nicely in Barth's assertion that man exists as a "predicate" of the one Subject Jesus Christ. This, of course, is merely a continuation of his earlier assertion that "ordinary" history is seen properly only as a "predicate" of salvation history (*Heilsgeschichte*). It follows, then, that man in his concrete historicity and empirical givenness is viewed appropriately only in terms of his "transcendental determination" in Christ, a determination that is also operative for the non-Christian [2]. The totality of man's being, as history and act, is thus developed from within the embracing configuration of a divine history that links creation and reconciliation securely together, and moves toward eschatological completion in redemption. This provides for obvious continuity between created and reconciled human nature, as we have seen. And, what is additionally significant, it enables Barth to elaborate a common ethical context for both Christians and non-Christians.

The adoption of a realist reading of the human, however, appealing

---

[1] *Ibid.*
[2] III/2, p. 418.

though it may be from the standpoint of an adequate christology (and even here it is questionable whether a realist stance, as Barth develops it, is entirely necessary or defensible), raises serious difficulties when the attempt is made to elaborate an anthropology that does justice to man's independent being and action. I have already noted the problems connected with Barth's discussion of created human nature. Neither in his elaboration of the "created constant" of I-Thou relationality, nor in the view of man's subjective individuality that emerged from it, did Barth manage clearly to establish man as independent subject and agent. Given his approach to the doctrine of the Trinity, it is a clear mistake to attempt to locate an intra-trinitarian ground for the I-Thou relationship within the human. As regards Barth's handling of the issue of "spirit" in man, that appears, in his initial discussion of this (in III/2), to be present to man only through the activity of God as Spirit toward his creation, although Barth seems willing to credit man with this capacity in the later volumes of the *Dogmatics*. In view of the realist context within which these comments are placed, however, it is not an easy matter to make out the precise significance this carries.

The difficulties imposed by the adoption of a realist ontology for an adequate development of man's ontic status as Christian may be seen at two points. First, in the fact that the humanity of Jesus is that of the eternal Son of God. When this is made the ontological model for speaking of man's authentic humanity, which he "has" only as a future in the present in the action of God as Holy Spirit, it is less than clear that an effective transition has been, or can be, made from Christ to other men [1].

---

[1] Hartwell suggests a possible way out of this dilemma by arguing that a legitimate distinction can be drawn in Barth's thought between "the Son of God as the *designate* Godman Jesus Christ and Jesus Christ as very God *and* very man". *The Theology of Karl Barth*, p. 185. He then goes on to spell this out in more detail: "In speaking throughout of 'Jesus Christ', Barth obviously wants to stress the continuity between the Son of God and Jesus Christ and, in a sense, their identity; but the language used by him to that end is, theologically, open to question since according to his own teaching Jesus Christ, in contrast to the Son of God, existed before the Incarnation only in the form of God's thought and will". *Ibid.* The major consideration against this position is Barth's consistent refusal to allow a distinction between a "Logos asarkos" and a "Logos ensarkos". I have already argued against what appears to be an ambiguity in Barth's formulation of this point, in relation (as I see it) to an illegitimate attempt to establish the unity of God and man in Jesus Christ as an instance of the *analogia relationis*. In fairness to Hartwell,

And second, in the fact that Barth's delineation of the knowledge granted man in faith through the *analogia fidei,* and so (by implication) man's ontic status in the event of faith, trades implicitly on Kant's notion of the transcendental ego [1].

When this concept is extended to cover man's ontic status as participant in the event of reconciliation, it will follow necessarily that both the possibility and the actuality of man's free obedience, as embodied in faith, love and hope, will take form as a sheer miracle which can in no sense be his direct possession, but which can only be received as they are given to him in the action of the Holy Spirit. The upshot of this approach is that it becomes quite difficult to establish any clear line of continuity between man's empirical givenness and his new identity established in the miracle of grace. Barth's employment of a realist ontology, with the attendant notion of a transcendental determination and ego, explains, perhaps, why he finds it necessary to eschew completely an empirical approach to the human. Unlike Bonhoeffer, who made a conscious effort to employ sociological categories in his delineation of ecclesiology and anthropology [2], Barth categorizes the biological and social sciences, and existential philosophy, as "phenomena of the human". The reason for this, obviously, is that they all fail to provide insight into "real" man, which for Barth is developed along exclusively christological lines. What is not clear, however, is that even Barth's strict utilization of Christology at this point necessitates a complete ignoring of possible insights, hints or suggestions about the human that might come from these disciplines. Indeed, given the sort of continuity he establishes between creation and reconciliation, and so between created and reconciled human nature, it seems almost a deficiency on Barth's own terms that his treatment of these possibilities remains merely cursory. Where this is allowed to happen, however, it results in an empirically deficient anthropology, and renders ambiguous the sense in which statements about the reality of man in the event of grace are to be taken.

---

however, it is quite possible that this is simply one more point where Barth has failed to establish consistency.

[1] Given Barth's reading of the human in terms exclusively of a "transcendental determination", it is scarcely unexpected that man's "real" and "true" humanity touches his individuality only through an ego that is similarly transcendental, i.e., non-empirical.

[2] Cf. Bethge, "The Challenge of Dietrich Bonhoeffer", p. 9.

The lack of clarity surrounding Barth's analysis of the ontic status of the Christian may be seen, finally, in the persistent eschatological tension in which it is set. In a way, this point exhibits a continuation of Barth's actualism, since it indicates the intrusion of man's (promised) future into his present existence, and provides the needed ground and focus for the act of the Christian [1]. It is further important, however, as the establishment of a definite limit within which human action is placed. As was noted in developing the categories of faith, love and hope, these unfold within the (historical) dialectic occasioned by man's being decisively turned from his distorted past in sin and set on the way to a realization of his true being in Christ. What remained unclear, at the end of that discussion, is the degree to which man is capable of an actualization of obedience that takes him beyond the initial action of repentance. The difficulty here is that Barth sometimes speaks as though man's past in sin were really past, in the sense that reconciliation, and so faith, love and hope, not only come to man, but take form *in* him in specific actions constituting obedience to the command of God [2]. At other points, however, he appears to trade heavily on the negative side of the dialectical movement in which man is placed, with the result that the actualization of man's eschatological status becomes an impossibility [3].

There is, it would seem, both a positive and a negative point to be made concerning Barth's employment of eschatology. Positively, it establishes definite continuity between creation and reconciliation, and so between Christians and non-Christians. Eschatologically, all men are set under the same future. It is thus impossible for the Christian community ever to break away from the wider context in which it finds itself, and forfeit community with the neighbor [4]. Negatively, it results

---

[1] The fact that Barth's actualism unfolds within an eschatological framework sets it off clearly from the sort of actualism encountered in, say, Sartre. The eschatological point makes clear the fact that man is in no sense engaged in the independent creation of an "essence" out of existence through the employment of a radical freedom. As Barth states, man's status under grace is indicative of an "existere", not an "esse". III/2, p. 297. The crucial difference, however, is that man's act, as *existere*, is referred at every point to his promised future and being in Jesus Christ in its impingement on his present in the Holy Spirit.

[2] Cf. IV/1, pp. 111f., 131, 835f.; IV/2, pp. 626ff., 890f.; IV/3.2, pp. 612f., 1074ff.

[3] Cf. IV/1, pp. 861ff., 864ff.; IV/2, pp. 657ff., 933f.

[4] Cf. IV/1, pp. 870ff.; IV/2, pp. 618, 637f., 691f.; IV/3.1, p. 393.

in a lack of clarity as to the precise ethical significance of the epistemological difference marking Christians from their non-Christian neighbors. Ostensibly, of course, the difference would occur at the point of
the Christian's obedience to the command, which would make for a
positive bodying forth of the facticity of sanctification. In actuality,
however, the outcome of the difference of the Christian man, as Barth
develops it, appears to come down to the fact that Christians exist as
"disturbed" sinners who are uneasy about their past, and who recognize
and acknowledge their future in Christ [1].

The difference between Christians and non-Christians, finally, lies
in the fact that Christians confess and witness to the action of God in
Christ, and the ineluctable future of all men in that event. When confession and witness are translated into the context of ethics, the result
is that obedience takes the form of worship. Now, worship obviously
must occupy a central place in theological ethics, for the simple reason
that the action of God, as the paradigm of appropriate human action,
has an obvious priority. It is another matter, however, if theological
ethics is equated with worship without remainder, for it would then be
quite unclear that obedience could ever be embodied in actions that go
beyond the specific act of worship. Of course, Barth would agree with
this. The difficulty is that he never allows for a definite or persistent
enough embodiment of obedience (i.e., freedom exhibited in faith,
love and hope) in the action of the Christian to move him beyond the
basic act of worship, i.e., a reception of the judgment and forgiveness
of God, prayer for the continuing activity and presence of the Holy
Spirit, and a renewed recognition and celebration of God's action.
In this respect, the possibilities open to the Christian for an exemplification of sanctification within the occurrence of justification bear a
striking similarity to Barth's development of this point in his earlier
writing, *Zur Lehre vom Heiligen Geist*.

The upshot of the ambiguity surrounding the action of Christians,
in terms of a movement beyond worship, is that it makes problematic
the question of their obedience to the command. The difficulties involved
in Barth's formulation of the command, as the action in which God
provides substance and direction to the specific context in which ethical
action is demanded, were explored in an earlier chapter. Now, it appears,
there is a question whether, even allowing for a possible clarification

---

[1] Cf. IV/1, pp. 692, 867.

of these difficulties, the requisite obedience imposed on man as an actualization of his freedom could ever be forthcoming in such a way as to gain direct embodiment in his action.

CHAPTER SIX

LIFE UNDER GRACE: THE ETHICAL MODES OF
THE CHRISTIAN COMMUNITY

The concern here is to explore the interplay that emerges between
the Christian community and its secular environment at the point of
ethical decision and action. The background for this exploration was
established in the two preceding chapters, which provided an elucidation
of the command of God, and of the ontic structure of the human both
in the form of its "natural condition", and in its "historical standing"
within the covenant. Now, it is clear that both the reality of the command
and man's ability properly to respond to it are strictly dependent on
God's action as Holy Spirit, as this occurs within the Christian community. The remaining task, accordingly, is to determine the relation
holding between (1) Barth's general delineation of the command and
the ontic status of the Christian as subject and agent under it, and (2) his
elaboration of a "special" ethic focusing on specific contexts, and the
issues arising within them [1]. In this discussion, I shall consider, first,
the internal structure and order of the Christian community; and second,
the various modes and dimensions of its encounter with the secular
order.

A. THE STRUCTURE OF THE COMMUNITY

The importance of a clear apprehension of the internal order and
functions of the Christian community for understanding Barth's development of theological ethics should, at this point, be relatively clear.
The definition of dogmatics as a particular science attaching exclusively
to the Church, the firm connection established between dogmatics and

---

[1] Although it is true that in the published volumes of the *Dogmatics*
Barth's development of ethics beyond the general discussion of the command
centers in the "special" ethics of creation, I have chosen to expand the meaning
of the term as used here to indicate any aspect of theological ethics as exemplified in the life of the Christian community that provides insight into specific
contexts, responses and lines of action.

ethics, and the importance of the Christian community as the locus of man's response to the event of revelation have been described previously. It follows, then, that the various modes through which the Church engages its larger cultural setting will emerge directly out of the prior givenness it has as a free community grounded in the ethical action of worship.

1. *The Freedom and Authority of the Community*

Just as it is impossible to discuss the freedom of the individual Christian apart from the obedience it entails, so too it is impossible to describe the freedom of the Christian community apart from the authority in which this is grounded, and the obedience it requires: The Word of God given in Scripture as the primary witness to revelation [1]. Freedom in the community is expressed only in the obedience given to the authority of Scripture. Scripture is thus the source of both authority and freedom in the Church [2]. In this respect, obedience within the Christian community displays an outer and an inner dimension. Externally, obedience lies in the recognition of the authority of Scripture. Internally, it emerges in the freedom given man by the Holy Spirit for this recognition. The authority of Scripture is thus the external determination of man *from* God; freedom the internal determination of man *for* God [3].

Under the authority of Scripture, and the freedom which this brings, the Christian community is established in its own derivative, mediate, formal and relative authority, which takes form in its obedience in humility, in its willingly subordinating itself under the prior reality of Jesus Christ and the Holy Spirit as they are present to and for the Church in Scripture [4]. This means that the authority of the Church will receive expression only in the act of decision, i.e., in a recognition and confession of the Word of God. It is through such "common decisions" (*gemeinsamen Entscheidungen*) that past and present are linked together, and the life of the Church unfolds in history [5]. The continuity of confession and recognition within the Church is seen in (1) a common acceptance of the canon of Scripture; (2) a common acknowledgement

---

[1] I/2, p. 604f.
[2] Ibid., pp. 749ff.
[3] *Ibid.*, p. 599f.
[4] *Ibid.*, p. 653f.
[5] *Ibid.*, p. 664f.

of the authority of certain teachers within the Church (the Church "fathers", so-called); and (3) a common reception of the specific confessions that have emerged from time to time within the confessing community, and a willingness to work out new ones as these become necessary [1]. As regards the interrelationship of these signs of the unity of the Church's confession, Scripture enjoys an obvious priority as the primary witness to the action of God in Jesus Christ. The Word of God given to the Christian community in the action of the Holy Spirit is thus the sole criterion and norm of Church authority given in the teaching of individuals and confessions. The authority of the Church in its various forms rests entirely on the question of its service to that Word [2].

Because the freedom of the Christian community lodges exclusively in the authority it attains through the action of obedience to Jesus Christ as the living Word of God, it follows that neither the freedom nor the authority of the Church can be turned into a principle. The being of the Church, like that of the individual Christian, occurs only "in act". Freedom and authority do not, then, denote static possessions given to the community. The authority of the Church, and the freedom that goes with it, will be entirely "spiritual" (*geistlich*), and so contingent, in keeping with the ontological status of the Church as *actus purus* [3].

There is a distinction to be drawn here between the continuity and existence of the Church, and that of the world generally. Despite the fact that both "are" only by virtue of the *creatio continua* of God, this carries a different meaning for each [4]. The continuation of the world generally evidences the faithfulness of God in his "patience" (*Geduld*) toward it; the continuation of the Church depends on "the grace of the

---

[1] *Ibid.*, pp. 666ff.; III/4, pp. 79ff.

[2] II/2, pp. 685, 743f. Barth's expanded treatment of this point is given in his Gifford lectures, *The Knowledge of God and the Service of God* (London: Hodder and Stoughton, 1938). Cf. IV/2, pp. 781ff.

[3] I/2, p. 665f.; Cf. IV/1, p. 726f.

[4] I/2, p. 771f. Mr. Hartwell argues that in III/3 Barth drops the notion of a "creatio continua" in favor of an emphasis on the divine providence. *The Theology of Karl Barth*, p. 36. The difficulty in this argument is that it is unclear that Barth means anything more by the *creatio continua* in I/2, than he does by the divine providence in III/3. Both seem to relate to the issue of the continuance of the creature which results from God's grace and patience, and so bear no relation to a series of successive acts of creation. Cf. III/3, p. 77: "God is not obliged to preserve the creature, to give it *continuance* and to give time to its *continuance*". Italics added.

Word of rebirth and new creation spoken in the midst of the created world" [1]. Though the difference is that of a *de iure* as over against a *de facto* participation in revelation, so that the distinction is finally epistemological rather than ontological, it is nevertheless a crucial difference as regards the ontic status in freedom of the Christian community. The freedom of the community is dependently grounded in the freedom of the Word of God issuing from the resurrection of Jesus, and continuing through the second stage of his *parousia* in his prophetic witness. The Church is free only to the extent that it allows complete freedom, at the point of recognition and confession, to this Word through the sustaining and quickening presence of Scripture in its life [2]. It is only through an acceptance of the responsibility and action imposed by the authority of Scripture that the Christian community is free. The freedom of the Church is thus in no sense autonomous, but is achieved wholly and exclusively in obedience. It provides, therefore, the natural paradigm for the freedom of the individual Christian, just as Christ provides the paradigm for the freedom of the community and, ultimately, creaturely freedom generally [3]. The ramifications of the contingent freedom and authority of the Church may be seen in the various modes of its internal order and structure, which will constitute a kind of "first order" ethical action.

2. *Church Order and Worship*

In moving into this section of the discussion, there are two important points to keep clearly in mind. The first is that when Barth sets out to describe the internal order and structure of the Church, he does so with the individual congregation particularly in mind [4]. This does

---

[1] I/2, p. 772. This point is, of course, a further indication and restatement of the different ways in which both the non-Christian and the Christian are dependent on the activity of God's Spirit. It therefore exemplifies the continuity previously noted between creation and covenant, and the divine preservation and election of man, which issues in a single, comprehensive ethical context and demand for all men.

[2] I/2, p. 773f.; III/4, p. 91.

[3] I/2, p. 776f.

[4] This point retains validity, I feel, despite the fact that Barth also refers to the community of believers indifferently as "the Christian community, Christendom, the Church". IV/1, p. 726. The ethical importance of an underlying concern for the individual congregation within the general discussion

not indicate the adoption of a congregationalist form of Church polity, but serves rather to emphasize the being-in-act of the Christian community in its immediate context [1]. The second point to be remembered

of the Church in the *Dogmatics* is that it reminds us again of the persistent contextuality of Barth's approach to theological ethics viewed strictly as obedience to the command of God.

[1] The clearest indication of Barth's concern for the individual congregation occurs in a paper he wrote for the Amsterdam assembly of the World Council of Churches: "The Church—the Living Congregation of the Living Lord Jesus Christ", in: *Man's Disorder and God's Design*, The Amsterdam Assembly Series (New York: Harper & Brothers, 1948), pp. 67-76. Barth begins with a definition: "The title of this paper constitutes a *definition* of the idea, 'Church'. It is a positive description of what the Church *is* ... The definition describes the Church as a *congregation*, a subject, which is confronted by, and controlled by another primary subject: *Jesus Christ* as absolute Lord (Creator, Preserver, Owner, Governor); the Church (as 'congregation') is only a *living* Church in so far as it is filled with the life of this primary subject, and only if its life is based on this foundation is it a *real* Church". Although the definition given here does not amount to an adoption of a congregationalist form of polity, it does convey, as Barth clearly states in the paper, a certain regard for it over other possible forms (i.e., papal, episcopal, consistorial, and presbyterian-synodal): "Not even the *Congregationalist* church order is above criticism. Its representatives have not yet been able to offer a satisfactory answer to the problem of the unity of the Church and of the churches. This paper is not a plea for the uncritical adoption of this particular system. But the principle of Congregationalism—the free congregation of the free Word of God—is sound enough. At any rate, certain elements of Congregationalism are absolutely indispensable for other proposals for church order if these are not to lead to disorder, but to create real order. From this standpoint too the ecumenical unity of the Church can be seen more freely than anywhere else. It is obvious that the last remnants of sovereign authority in the idea of a *corpus christianum* are disappearing; this suggests that we should now look in this other (Congregationalist) direction. Indirectly, this argument receives further confirmation in the reflection that a Church formed on the basis of these principles would be an event of exemplary importance in the political world of the present day". *Ibid.*, p. 75f. These statements appear to constitute an important modification of Barth's remarks delivered to a group of pastors at Travers and Neuchatel, Switzerland in a series of lectures running from 1940 to 1943: "The government of the Church needs to conform with the foundation of the Church. The Church was not founded by men, by a few persons who, being on the right side of the fence, were gathered together to cultivate their spiritual needs. The Church was founded by the Christ, who called his disciples ... Nor is the government of the Church, consequently, the business of a human initiative. It is an act of obedience unto the Lord of the Church. The Lord of the Church is Jesus Christ alone,

here is that the action of the Church in its order and worship is, like the freedom and authority which it exhibits, continually dependent on the immediate presence and action of Christ in the Holy Spirit. This accounts for the fact that Barth's discussion of the various contours and dimensions of the being and existence of the Christian community, both internally and in encounter with the world, unfolds entirely within and under the prior actuality of God as Holy Spirit [1]. The being of the community, as *communio sanctorum*, the "living community of the living Lord Jesus Christ" [2], will therefore display a persistent eschatological overtone in keeping with its position "between the times" of the resurrection and the final coming of Jesus Christ [3]. In its position between the "no longer" of Easter and the "not yet" of Christ's final *parousia*, the existence of the community is marked by the simultaneity of weakness and strength. Its strength lies in the fact that it comes from the event of the resurrection, and moves, under the guidance of the Holy Spirit, into its future in Christ [4]. The Church is strong because it knows, in faith, the significance

---

such as he exists in time, that is, in the Scripture. Thus no government, either monarchical or aristocratic or democratic, of the Church shall be able, as such, to pretend to authority. Rather, it shall possess authority only to the extent to which it serves Jesus Christ, that is to say, concretely, in which it submits all its decisions to the criterion of the Scripture. We shall not then have any fundamental reason to prefer the aristocratic to the democratic system, or conversely. For in the Church we are not dealing with either 'someone' or 'some one' or 'everyone', but with the One: the Lord. The essential of Church government is not its outward form, but its submission to the Scripture". Stenographic notes of these lectures are printed in: *The Faith of the Church*. A Commentary on the Apostle's Creed according to Calvin's Catechism, Jean-Louis Leuba, ed., translated by Gabriel Vahanian (New York: Living Age Books, 1958). The quotation above is found on p. 145f. of this volume. It would appear obvious that the "fundamental reason" for Barth's move toward a more direct appreciation of Congregationalist polity in the Amsterdam paper was provided by the emergence of National Socialism in Germany, and the subsequent tension and split this engendered between the German Christians and the Confessing Church, which came decisively into focus in the Barmen Declaration. What I are arguing, then, is that Barth's concern that the Church exist exclusively as "the free congregation of the free Word of God" provides the background for his discussion of its structure and order in the *Dogmatics*. Cf. also IV/1, p. 751.

   [1] Cf. IV/1, Par. 62; IV/2, Par. 67; IV/3.2, Par. 72.
   [2] IV/1, p. 733; Cf. III/4, p. 559.
   [3] IV/1, pp. 356, 810.
   [4] *Ibid.*, p. 812f.

of the time in which it exists as it is bracketed by (and so enclosed within) the eternal co-temporality of God's time in Jesus Christ.

The weakness of the community arises from the strength of its knowledge of the time within which it is placed. The knowledge in question is given only in faith, which depends on the continual action of Christ in the Holy Spirit [1]. This means that although the Church will take form empirically as a definite socio-historical grouping of men, its true reality will in no sense be available to direct, visible analysis. The true character of the Christian community, "the truth of its existence in time and space, is not the subject of a general but of a very special visibility" [2]. What the Church is in itself will always remain hidden, despite the fact that it occurs as a visible event and action within the world. This indicates that the reality of the Church, as the body of Christ, the "earthly-historical form of the existence of Jesus Christ himself" [3], is in no sense an immediate possession. In itself, the Christian community can only witness to its future, and therefore invisible, being in Christ, and to the reconciliation that has taken place for all men in him [4].

In drawing a distinction between the "visible" and the "invisible" dimensions of the existence and action of the Christian community, Barth does not wish to articulate a simple dualism between historical and non-historical, or present and future. What is at stake here is a clear understanding of the material identity of the Church that infuses its empirical, formal givenness with meaning [5]. The material identity of the Church is provided by the action of Jesus Christ in the Holy Spirit in calling it into being and equipping it as the effective witness to revelation, and so to the true and irrevocable future of all men. Now, it is in the action of the Holy Spirit that the material dimension of the Church, though eschatological, falls over into the present at the point of man's epistemological participation in, and recognition of, God's action in Christ. This means that the Christian community lives wholly by and through the divine action, the event of grace in which it is called into existence and sustained in its temporal and spatial concreteness [6]. An analysis of the implications of the epistemological involvement of

---

[1] *Ibid.*, p. 813f.
[2] *Ibid.*, p. 731.
[3] *Ibid.*, p. 738.
[4] *Ibid.*, p. 734.
[5] *Ibid.*, p. 729f.
[6] IV/2, pp. 699, 737f.

the Church in the event of reconciliation will throw important light on the possibilities open to it for a concrete embodiment of the knowledge given in the action of the Holy Spirit, and will additionally bring into focus the ethical centrality of the order and worship of the community.

The fact that it is only as Jesus Christ acts in the Holy Spirit that the Christian community is brought into existence and made epistemological participant in the event of reconciliation indicates at once its dependent, secondary status as the body of Christ. Strictly speaking, this means that "the being of Jesus Christ is the being of the Church" [1]. Or again: "Jesus Christ is the community" [2]. Neither of these propositions is reversible, and both serve to emphasize in the strongest possible terms the derivative reality of the Church as constituted by the event of grace.

There are several important points that follow from these observations as regards the possibility of an embodiment, in the empirical, visible life of the Christian community, of the knowledge it receives through faith. To begin with, it is clear that the divine action on which the Church depends, and by which it is established as the true Church, can never become a quality of the Church [3]. This means that the true Church is never directly and objectively present or visible. It *becomes* visible as the true Church only through the action of the Holy Spirit [4]. In itself, the community can only witness to its invisible (and future) being as this is made visible through that action [5]. From this it follows that the "holiness" (*Heiligkeit*) of the community will also be a matter strictly of revelation and faith, and will constitute a reflection of the prior holiness of Christ. The action of the Church will always be only "a seeking and asking after holiness, a prayer for it" [6]. Stated emphatically, this means that the Church can never claim the predicate "Christian" for its actions. That there are human actions that may appropriately be described as "Christian", and so as "a holy activity of the community within the world", depends exclusively on the prior holiness of Jesus Christ as Lord of the Church, and his continual sustaining action within it [7].

---

[1] *Ibid.*, p. 741.
[2] *Ibid.*
[3] *Ibid.*, p. 699.
[4] *Ibid.*, p. 700f.
[5] IV/1, p. 733f.
[6] *Ibid.*, p. 775.
[7] *Ibid.*, p. 774f.

It is apparent that the knowledge given to the Christian community
in faith, on Barth's analysis, can take empirical form only as it is embodied in definite actions marking its derivative status, and the continuing history in which it is encountered and established anew, by the
immediate action of Christ in the Holy Spirit, as the people of God.
Within and under this history, the existence of the Church functions as
a "provisional representation of the sanctification of all humanity that
has taken place in him" [1]. The question of the holiness of the community
will therefore carry practical as well as theoretical significance. Within
the history of its encounter with the Holy Spirit and the world, it will
be called to continual reflection on the correspondence evidenced in its
actions between its external, visible side and its invisible identity as
the body of Christ [2]. The holiness of the community is presented as a
continual problem and responsibility because it throws into stark relief
the issue of its obedience or disobedience to the prior holiness of Christ,
which serves as the decisive "imperative and standard" (*Imperativ und
Maß*) of all its actions [3]. In the conduct of its affairs, both internal and
external, the Church must look directly to its invisible being and holiness
grounded and promised in Jesus Christ [4]. Of course, the community
itself cannot simply "have" obedience and holiness as its direct possessions, any more than it can possess freedom and authority, and the faith
in which they are grounded, in an immediate, unambiguous fashion.
The decision as to the reality of the obedience and faith of the Church
will take shape in precise parallelism to the decision about its freedom
and authority. It will be exlusively a function of the action of Jesus
Christ, the Lord of the Church, in the Holy Spirit [5]. This will mean,
however, that the invisible reality of the Church, its obedience and faith,
freedom and authority, will never become directly perceptible in its
visible history. Visibly, the Christian community in its action will
inevitably fall into continuity with, and constitute an aspect of, "sinful
history" (*sündige Geschichte*) [6]. The possibility of a direct manifestation
of its future identity received through the Holy Spirit, even though,

---

[1] IV/2, p. 701.
[2] IV/1, p. 782. Barth also focuses on this issue in his lecture, "The Real
Church", in: *Against the Stream* (London: SCM Press, Ltd., 1954), pp. 62-77.
This lecture was delivered at various places from March to June, 1948.
[3] *Ibid.*, p. 783.
[4] *Ibid.*
[5] *Ibid.*, p. 774f.
[6] *Ibid.*, p. 734.

ostensibly, it is a future impinging on the present, would appear, on
Barth's analysis, to be seriously compromised, if not excluded. To be
sure, there are, as Barth states, "manifestations and analogies" of the
invisible, spiritual character of the community in its visible forms and
actions. The correlation between visible and invisible depends solely
on "the will and the power of the act of God" [1], i.e., the event of grace
in which the Church is created anew as the body of Christ in the world.
So, the distinction that Barth draws between the visible, historical
dimension of the Christian community, and its hidden, invisible identity
given to faith in the action of the Holy Spirit, is not designed intentionally to leave us with a merely "eschatological" reading of its actuality,
in the pejorative sense of that term. What we have here is simply an
indication of the background and context within which the analysis
of the status of the Christian as ethical subject and agent given in the
preceding chapter can be placed. The fact that the Christian, as acting
subject, can never claim to have faith, love and hope as direct predicates,
but can only receive these through the continuing self-manifestation
of Christ in the Holy Spirit, may be seen as a reflection, on the individual
level, of the prior status of the community as a whole. So, just as there
are analogous actions performed by individual Christians that provide
an indication and reflection of their ontological status in Christ, there
are also analogous manifestations, in the visible forms and actions of
the Christian community, and particularly in its order and worship,
that provide partial embodiments of its invisible status as the elect
people of God. What is to be avoided at all costs is the attempt at a
direct identification, whether in the actions of the individual Christian
or the community as a whole, of the (mundane) historical with the
eschatological, the visible with the invisible. Barth's analysis of the
possibilities open to the Christian community for an exemplification,
in its empirical life and activity, of the knowledge given in faith, provides
a nice continuation of the central concerns of his theology: The absolute
priority of God, the total dependence of man on God's action, seen
here in terms of the quickening power and presence of the Holy Spirit
within the Christian community; and the strenuous withdrawal of every
possibility that would lead in the direction of an autonomous ideology [2].

---

[1] *Ibid.*

[2] All three of these concerns are captured in this statement: "No confession, theology or cultus; no party, tendency, group or direction in the
generally perceptible being of the community; nothing which can be confirmed

The question that remains, once these concerns have been noted, is whether the analogous status attaching to the internal and external visibility of the Church allows sufficiently for an actualization of obedience, or whether it leads again to an ambiguous and problematic treatment of the human under the command of God.

The fact that the primary difference marking the Christian community from the secular context in which it exists and acts is epistemological rather than ontological in nature leads, Barth insists, neither to quietism nor to withdrawal. In both its internal ordering and its external commerce with the world, the community is equipped for positive actions reflecting its status as the body of Christ. Descriptively, all the actions of the community fall under the category of "service" (*Dienst*) [1], and so are freighted with immediate ethical significance. It is thus necessary to assert that "the community realizes its true order as his body when and as its action is service" [2]. Within the Christian community, then, preaching, dogmatics, Church law, and worship will all be indicative of the fulfillment in service of the demand for obedience [3]. Since none of the actions undertaken by the community can be understood as extending or completing the event of reconciliation, it follows that the obedience manifested in the service of the community, whether internal or external, will constitute no more than the witness and proclamation of the Church to the fulfillment of reconciliation in Christ, and the future set for all men in that event [4]. In all its actions, the Church can do no more than provide a provisional representation and reflection of the history of

---

or delimited or counted or formulated in purely human terms, and, naturally, none of the persons assembled and active within it, can be directly identical with what the community is ... The preservation and fulfillment of the community, as the mystery of what its visible history is on that level, is in the hand of God as his own work, a spiritual reality constituting its third invisible dimension, and so cannot be perceived but only believed in ... According to the will and power of the action of God it can and should, even in its visibility, attest its invisible glory, i.e., the glory of the Lord justifying man and the man justified by him". *Ibid.*

[1] IV/2, p. 781; Cf. III/4, pp. 544ff.

[2] IV/2, p. 782.

[3] Cf. I/2, Par. 22, Pts. 1, "The Word of God and the Word of Man in Christian Preaching" and 2, "Pure Doctrine as the Problem of Dogmatics"; III/4, Par. 53, Pts. 1, "The Holy Day"; 2. "Confession" and 3. "Prayer"; IV/2, Par. 67, Pt. 4, "The Order of the Community"; IV/3.2, Par. 72, Pts. 3, "The Task of the Community" and 4. "The Ministry of the Community".

[4] IV/1, p. 349f.; Cf. IV/3.2, pp. 637ff., 956f.;

Jesus Christ. As the community is set in action by the Holy Spirit, and moved toward a fulfillment of its task of ministry and service, the modes of its internal order and worship become crucial, for they provide the visible means by which the Church is distinguished from its secular environment and reminded of its origin. thereby necessitating a re-affirmation of its given identity and self-understanding [1].

Viewed comprehensively, the order and worship of the community constitute the event in which it is built up and readied for a positive engagement with the world. The description of order and worship as a unitive event underlines the liturgical center around which all the internal modes of activity and self-expression of the community are gathered. And the mention of a "liturgical center" emphasizes again the fact that the Church devolves directly from Jesus Christ. This precludes the possibility of any particular aspect of the internal life of the Christian community receiving autonomous status or function, since they will all be directed toward the effective dramatization of the being of the community through the act of worship. In this respect, the act of worship emerges as the comprehensive event in which the various activities of ministry carried on within the community for its effective upbuilding (i.e., preaching, the various forms of theology, biblical studies, and Church law) are fulfilled and continued [2]. The act of worship thus constitutes the epitome of the ministry of the community in both its internal and external significance.

The act of worship embodies a recognition of the Lordship of Jesus Christ within the community and the world, a confession of human limitation and need, and a celebration of the promise and sufficiency of grace. It is, in short, demonstrative of man's "readiness for the Gospel" (*Bereitschaft für das Evangelium*) [3]. The definiteness of the event of worship is provided by the dimensions of confession, baptism, the Lord's Supper and prayer [4]; and by the fact that it occurs on a specific day of the week, the day of rest and celebration (*Feiertag*) that marks the completion of one week and the beginning of another [5]. The latter point is of particular importance in understanding the ethical thrust of

---

[1] IV/2, p. 790f.
[2] Cf. IV/2, pp. 772f., 800; IV/3.2, pp. 1007f., 1033f.
[3] III/4, p. 55.
[4] IV/2, pp. 790ff., 801f.
[5] III/4, p. 55; IV/2, p. 790.

the act of worship, for it makes clear that worship as a total act takes place in direct response to the divine command.

The legitimacy of the act of worship is grounded in the fact that God commands and directs man to the observance of a holy day [1]. The "command of the holy day" (*Gebot des Feiertages*) [2] indicates an interruption and limitation of man's activity. On that day, man is summoned "to celebrate, rejoice and be free, to the glory of God" [3]. The observance of the holy day demanded of man finds its counterpart in the biblical account of God's resting on the seventh day after creation, and in the resurrection of Christ as the fulfillment of the covenant between God and man inaugurated at creation [4]. In being summoned to an observance of the holy day as a day of rest, man is reminded again of the fact that his history under the command of God is grounded in the priority of Gospel over Law. As the definite sign of his freedom (in obedience) under the command, the observance of the holy day directs man from his own activities and achievements toward God's gracious affirmation of man in Jesus Christ. He is thus reminded that he comes from and returns continually to *grace* [5]. By being temporarily removed from the sphere of his own concerns and activities, man is freed for himself in a new way, as he is freed for God in the particular sense of "divine service", which is given positive embodiment and meaning in the assembling of the Christian community in worship [6]. The act of worship does not, in this respect, constitute a self-justifying or fulfilling "religious" observance guaranteeing a proper observance of the holy day and what it signifies. It is only as worship embodies a "renouncing faith" attesting man's responsibility and freedom under the command that it becomes a defensible and meaningful activity [7].

The event of worship in which the Christian community expresses and recalls its grounding in grace, and the reconciliation of man realized in Christ, takes place as divine service in response to the command of God. As an ethical action, worship will not in any sense be an exaltation and celebration of the community itself, but will be a recalling, re-

---

[1] III/4, p. 53.
[2] *Ibid.*, p. 54.
[3] *Ibid.*
[4] *Ibid.*, p. 56f.
[5] *Ibid.*, p. 59f.
[6] *Ibid.*, pp. 65ff.
[7] *Ibid.*, pp. 68ff.

affirmation, dramatization and rediscovery of the grace by which the community (and all men) is called into being and maintained, and in which it moves from the resurrection of Christ to his future (redemptive) coming. The event of worship will thus always be (1) an act of confession of the One who has brought men together in the community, which constitutes a public recognition and reaffirmation of the divine "Yes" addressed to all men against every human "No" [1]; (2) a common acceptance and trust between persons in the community grounded in their common baptism [2]; (3) a celebration and dramatization of the Gospel in the Lord's Supper, by which the community is reminded of its standing within the history of the *parousia* of Christ [3]; and (4) the action of prayer, in which individual and community, mankind and the world, are turned to God in petition and intercession [4].

It is apparent that Barth's development of a "special" ethic moving beyond his initial, general discussion of the command will rest squarely on the action of the Christian community in worship [5]. The action of worship represents a primary actualization of human freedom and obedience under the command of God, and serves to remind us again of the basically indicative character of Barth's reading of theological ethics (i.e., the priority of Gospel over Law), since it represents that event in which man is brought to recognition and action on the basis of his true being in Jesus Christ.

3. *Divine Service: Praise and Love*

Barth describes the action of worship as "divine service". The importance of this phrase is that it marks a distinction (though not a separation) between the service and ministry of the community as focused upon and directed toward its internal upbuilding, and as expressed in the movement of the community into engagement with its larger cultural setting. Of course, this distinction is not intended to

---

[1] IV/2, p. 792f.; III/4, p. 84f.

[2] IV/2, p. 794f.

[3] *Ibid.*, pp. 795ff.

[4] *Ibid.*, pp. 797ff.; III/4, pp. 121ff.; IV/3.2, pp. 1011ff.

[5] Barth's completed ethics of creation, for instance, begins with a section devoted to the holy day, confession, and prayer. Cf. III/4, Par. 53. And his treatment of the ethics of reconciliation, according to Professor Come, was built totally around prayer (with the Lord's Prayer as the model), baptism, and the Lord's Supper. Cf. *An Introduction to Barth's "Dogmatics"*, pp. 127ff.

suggest that the internal upbuilding of the community occurs as a private or hidden exercise. Since the establishment and growth of the Church, in the action of the Holy Spirit, is exemplified in the visible gathering of the community for confession, prayer, and a celebration of the sacraments, divine service carries an obvious public significance as a reminder to the world of its future in Christ. It is also true, however, that the divine service embodied in the act of worship serves to remind the community of its distinct identity and role within secular culture. The ethical importance of divine service for establishing and maintaining the identity and role of the Church becomes clear when it is viewed in relation to the task of the community to praise and love God.

As the body of Christ, the community is given the task of providing a paradigm, within the creaturely sphere, of the reality and decisiveness of God's reconciling action in Christ. To be sure, it will do this only imperfectly and ambiguously, and it will need the continual action of the Holy Spirit to achieve even a moderately appropriate reflection, in its own being and action, of the true paradigm of human response given in the exalted Son of Man, Jesus Christ. The discussion of the order and worship of the community in the preceding section underlined the continuing dialectic between its weakness (in itself) and its strength (in faith) as it is continually summoned and reconstituted by its Lord. When this dialectic (or oscillation) between weakness and strength is brought to bear on the praise and love of the community, it points up the terminological and existential equivalent to man's obedience: gratitude. And it also exposes once again the priority and sufficiency of God's action as the exhaustive condition for man's gratitude.

It is because God encroaches positively on man and the world in Jesus Christ, becoming thereby a "world reality" (*Weltwirklichkeit*) [1], that man is summoned to the corresponding action of praise and thanksgiving. And it is as he offers thanks, and so praises God, that man participates authentically in revelation [2]. As an act of "wondering awe" the praise of the community will manifest an acknowledgement of the goodness of God's action which does not seek in any way to equal or displace it [3].

The being of man expressed in the act of praise is thus a being in gratitude. Gratitude (*Dankbarkeit*) forms the precise and appropriate

---

[1] II/1, p. 232.
[2] *Ibid.*, pp. 243ff.
[3] *Ibid.*, pp. 247ff.

creaturely counterpart to the grace of God [1]. To offer thanks and praise
to God is the concrete actualization of the permission and freedom
given man. The divine service of praise carried on by the community
will therefore constitute a fulfillment of true human being, for it is only
as he is thankful that man becomes the man he really is under grace [2].
There is, then, a dual action to be noted in the upbuilding and preservation of the Christian community: On the one hand, the grace
of God given to the community by the action of Christ in the Holy
Spirit; on the other hand, the gratitude and praise of Christians as a
sign of their reception and acknowledgement of God's action, and their
total dependence on it [3].

The action of praise and gratitude exhibits direct continuity with
the love of the community directed toward God. The modal distinctions
of praise and love are understood properly only when viewed as analytic
derivatives proceeding directly out of the event and act of worship as
the center and focus of the witness and proclamation of the community.
So, to speak of the praise and gratitude of Christians entails an automatic reference to their love, both of which lodge in the worship of the
community, which leads, again, into the event of ministry and service.
It is in this sort of sustained, analytic continuity established between the
modal distinctions that emerge within the total response of the community that Barth guards effectively against the erection of purely
"religious" responses as ends in themselves, thereby insuring that the
Church, under the prevenient direction of the Holy Spirit, will provide
the persistent locus of "true religion" [4].

The continuity established between the community's praise and love
of God underlines the fact that the love here in question occurs only as
a function and result of grace, and so only in light of man's eternal
election and predetermination to be the responsible covenant-partner
of God [5]. The love of the community for God is not reducible merely
to sentiment or feeling, but is indicative of man's being and action
within the relationship grounded in the guidance, help and salvation that
encounters man as a sheer gift from God [6]. Nor is the love given to God

---

[1] III/2, p. 198f.; III/4, p. 764f.
[2] III/2, pp. 200ff.
[3] IV/2, p. 747.
[4] Cf. I/2, Par. 17, Pts. 2, "Religion as Unbelief" and 3. "True Religion".
[5] I/2, p. 409f.; IV/2, pp. 869ff.
[6] I/2, p. 415f.; IV/2, p. 891f.

representative of an autonomous human capacity. It is rather the sign
of man's repentance, and so of his recognition and acceptance of God's
action on his behalf [1].

In the action of love, man responds to the divine decision concerning
his present and future existence, and the claim this imposes. Love is
thus to be seen as the fulfillment of the command, which, although it
forms the one "categorical imperative" under which man stands, is
nevertheless in the first instance indicative rather than imperative [2].
Since the demand to love manifests precise continuity with man's true
future and being, it follows that the obedient fulfillment of that demand
will not be "hard" or "heavy" [3]. What *will* be difficult is the disobedience
of an existence lived in apparent ignorance of man's true future enclosed
within God's action and the demand this imposes. In loving God,
then, man is set on the way to an actualization and realization
of what, in Christ, he already is. It is the action in which he
chooses God as his Lord, and so becomes obedient to the command [4].
The action of love that occurs within the Christian community, as an
action directed first of all to God, is, like the action of praise, indicative
of man's answer to God's grace. As a witness to the work of God in
reconciling all men in Christ, it is itself man's proper work, and is
productive of additional actions embodying love between members of
the community. There is thus a mutual upbuilding and preservation that
occurs as an action of the community in its love to God, which takes
form under the prior decision and judgment embodied in God's eternal
love to man [5]. More specifically, the reality of love shown in God's
election of man and the responding love of the community for God, is

> in its concrete form identical with the action in which Jesus Christ builds
> his community, in which he calls men to himself, gathering them in it,
> permitting them a part in its faith and mission, thereby sanctifying them,
> and so treating them as his own, as members of his body [6].

It is through the action of praise and love that the common (horizontal)
vocation of Christians within the community is indicated, and that they

---

[1] I/2, p. 429f.
[2] *Ibid.*, p. 425.
[3] *Ibid.*
[4] *Ibid.*, p. 429f.; IV/2, p. 870f.
[5] I/2, p. 441f.; IV/2, pp. 859f., 876f.
[6] IV/2, p. 883.

are drawn into participation in the inner history and upbuilding of the community, expressed in a perpetual concern for the purity of the proclamation and doctrine of the Church [1].

4. *The Transition to Special Ethics*

The point that was established in the preceding section is that there is an aspect of the ministry of the community which, because it is directed specifically toward God, enjoys a kind of priority over those dimensions of its ministry that take it into the mainstream of its secular environment. I have argued that this special form of ministry can be described as "divine service", and that it is embodied centrally in the act and event of worship as an exemplification of man's response of praise and love to God. The priority of praise and love serves to draw attention to the fact that the ontologically decisive action, ethically considered, is performed only by God, who moves unerringly in Jesus Christ to sustain man's being in grace beyond the occurrence of sin by drawing him into the orbit of divine history (*Heilsgeschichte*). Human actions within this history will always be derivative, "answering" actions in which the judgment and forgiveness of God are received, and in which man's authentic future in Christ is grasped at the point of obedience to the command. By stressing the priority of praise and love as actions addressed initially to God, we are reminded once again that human action within the community (and elsewhere) will be essentially captured in the act of worship, and so in man's recognition of the absolute goodness of God's action, and his (continual) repentance before it. There is thus a priority, within theological ethics, to the action of love expressed in the community's praise of God that can neither be equated with, nor substituted by, the love it is enjoined to demonstrate to the neighbor [2]. This will mean that there is a certain priority attaching to the ministry and service of the community as this is directed in the first instance toward God.

It is clear, however, that the distinction I have been suggesting cannot result in a separation. Though the permission given man under God's command is realized initially in the praise and love of God reflected in the act of worship, it is also actualized in the service and ministry of the community in the world, which can be described com-

---

[1] III/4, pp. 565ff.

[2] I/2, p. 443f.; IV/2, p. 896f.

prehensively as a manifestation of love to the neighbor. In this respect, the praise of God and the love of the neighbor are inseparable [1]. Their inseparability, however, will always take form, within the unified ministry of the Christian community, in terms of a definite ordering that places the internal dimension of that ministry, the praise and love of God, and the upbuilding and preservation of the community as a distinct society within history, in a position of priority. It is only from this center that the larger socio-political context in which the community finds itself can be feasibly engaged at the point of service [2]. In its response of obedience to the command of God within the contours of special ethics, the Church will evidence concern for both the internal and the external dimensions of its service.

At this point, it will be helpful to indicate somethings of Barth's view of the "problem" of special ethics [3], as a means of indicating at least a formal continuity between the earlier discussion of the command of God [4] and the succeeding portions of this chapter.

Earlier, it was noted that Barth's reading of the command of God as event displays both a vertical and a horizontal dimension, which direct us to a linear rather than a punctiliar understanding of that event. In addition, we saw that it was because of the constancy of the command in its linear embodiment that a "formed" reference to the total event of God's command and man's response within the context of certain "definite spheres and relationships" is possible. It is in relationship to this formed reference that the task of special ethics comes into focus.

The task of special ethics is to provide an analysis of the particularity of the divine command within the spheres and relationships marking its horizontal thrust. Of course, since the structural continuities in question arise solely through God's activity as Commander, it follows that information about the horizontal will not be provided by *ad hoc* analyses, but will issue directly out of the Word of God [5]. It is only the Word of

---

[1] I/2, p. 442f.

[2] The most instructive discussion of this distinction, and its implications for the internal and external service of the community, is found in Barth's discussion of "the active life". Cf. III/4, Par. 55, Pt. 3.

[3] Cf. III/4, Par. 52, Pt. 1.

[4] Cf. Ch. Four of this study.

[5] III/4, p. 19f.

God that provides "instruction concerning the constancy of the divine command and human action as concerning the reality of the command in the ethical event" [1]. It is for this reason that Barth rejects the notion of "orders of creation" (*Schöpfungsordnungen*) employed by Brunner, and Bonhoeffer's handling of this issue in terms of the concept of "mandates" (*Mandaten*), both of which, Barth feels, are in certain respects inadequate to the task at hand [2].

In analyzing the particularity of the command, special ethics will always contain a reference to the two factors that make up the formative dimensions of the ethical event: The revelational activity of the Holy Spirit, in which God's claim, decision and judgment are presented; and man's response of belief or unbelief, obedience or disobedience [3]. The latter point is designed to bring out "the leap of choice, decision and action, which he must execute himself and on his own responsibility" [4]. Man's response to the immediacy of the command is therefore crucial, for it is in it that he actualizes his being as the one "who at all times and places is absolutely secondary and subordinate and yet is treated seriously by God as a being who is autonomous in relation to him" [5]. Of course, the question of human response is answered *comprehensively* in the options of obedience or disobedience. In this respect, the development of special ethics will display the same strictness observed in Barth's general discussion of the command. In order to grasp this point clearly, we must recall that the concept of command, as employed by Barth, is so far removed from association with rules, precepts or principles as to embody the overtones of metaphor. The "command" of God, on Barth's analysis, refers to the immediate presence of God as Holy Spirit in the action of shaping and structuring totally the context in which ethical decision is required. The upshot of this from man's side is that the command of God

---

[1] *Ibid.*

[2] Barth feels that Brunner's position leads inevitably to the establishment of *lex naturae*, while Bonhoeffer's approach, though more convincing because of its christological grounding (the mandates always appear *sub specie Christi*), is still too suggestive of "a slight touch of North German patriarchalism". *Ibid.*, pp. 20ff.

[3] *Ibid.*, pp. 15f., 24f.

[4] *Ibid.*, p. 16.

[5] *Ibid.*, p. 24.

leaves nothing to human choice or discretion. It thus requires no interpretation to come into force. To the last and smallest detail it is self-
interpreted, and in this form it confronts man as a command already
in force [1].

The consequence this carries for man's response is that it leaves
only the possibility of "instant obedience" [2], which appears to lead to
the startling conclusion that the possibility of rational deliberation
within the ethical situation is set aside, since there appear to be no viable
or real options about which one might deliberate [3]. In moving into a
consideration of Barth's treatment of special ethics, one obvious concerns
to determine whether any modification of this point occurs, and, if so,
on what grounds.

A final point to be noted about the possibility of a special ethics is
that it occurs only within the total history between God and man exhibited in Jesus Christ. So, despite the diversity and particularity of the
command, it is finally single and unitary, since it flows directly from the
one total action of God. And, since the being and action of man are
completely given in that action, it follows that man as acting subject
will be continuous throughout the multiplicity of actions he performs [4].
Special ethics, accordingly, will consist of an elaboration of the various
emphases and "movements" within the one action of God as Creator,
Reconciler and Redeemer, each of which will call forth an appropriate
corresponding mode of human response [5].

The task of theological ethics, then, is to provide an analysis of the
various spheres and relationships that emerge under the definiteness
of the command, and so to lead in the direction of an answer to the
ethical question. As a human enterprise which is itself continually
dependent on the event of grace, it cannot hope to supply the final
answer to the ethical question, nor a precise determination and definition
of the ethical event. The freedom of God in his action prohibits this
sort of finality. The articulation of a special ethics can, however, lead
toward a clarification of the ethical event by providing

> a reference to it by which it is generally described in a way which is gener-
> ally intelligible and so attested in a generally valid form [6].

---

[1] III/4, p. 11.
[2] IV/2, p. 613.
[3] Cf. above, pp. 182ff.
[4] III/4, p. 16f.
[5] *Ibid.*, pp. 31ff.;
[6] III/4, p. 33.

Theological ethics, accordingly, can supply an ethical lead and directive, and to this extent can provide significant "training in Christianity", i.e., practice in "keeping the command" [1].

B. The Community in the World

In concluding the discussion of the possibilities open to the Christian as ethical subject and agent, I argued that Barth's handling of that question displays a certain ambiguity, so that it never quite becomes clear in what respect human action is equipped to move in a positive way beyond the initial action of repentence embodied in the event of worship. The analysis of the internal ethical modes of the Christian community has thus far been confined to indicating the centrality of the act of worship for the upbuilding of the community and the divine service to which it is called. In moving, now, to a description of the resources and avenues open to the Church for a positive and creative encounter with the total cultural framework in which it is placed, careful attention must be given to the possibilities present for an actualization of obedience under the command.

1. World-History and the Christian Community

It is instructive to begin on the periphery of things, so to speak, by noting the position of the community in relation to history and events as these unfold in the world generally. An analysis of the witness and confession of the Church in this larger context will provide the proper setting within which the more specific issues and concerns of special ethics can be explored. The immediate theological background for this analysis was given in the discussion of the general co-temporality of God in his action of preserving the creature and its world, which occurs under the total movement of the divine history [2]. It is the preserving and sustaining action of God that throws light on the status and function of the community in world-history, and invests general history and occurrences with positive significance.

In an initial description of the *analogia relationis*, it was pointed out that one example of this is found in the continuity holding between

---

[1] *Ibid.*, p. 34.
[2] Cf. above, Ch. Three, Section B, "The Temporality of God".

creaturely history and occurrence and the movement of covenant-history. As it is coordinated with divine history, creaturely history "acquires the character of a mirror" [1]. The basis for this coordination and continuity is ontologically grounded in the relationship posited by God between creation and covenant. Creation provides the external basis of the covenant; and the covenant is the internal basis of creation [2]. The importance of the interrelationship between creation and covenant is that it establishes the place of the former, and so the history and action of the creature, as "not only the means, but also the object of the divine action" [3]. Creaturely history achieves this status, however, only through grace. This means that the function of creation and the creature in providing "time, space and opportunity for the divine will and action in the covenant of grace" [4] attains a relative rather than an absolute independence. This is seen in Barth's description of creaturely history as a "predicate" of salvation history, and in his further assertion that the history of the Christian community is "the true world-history" (*die eigentliche Weltgeschichte*) [5]. World-history can proceed only under the history of the community as its "somewhat remarkable accompani-

[1] III/3, p. 57.
[2] III/1, Par. 41, Pts. 2 and 3.
[3] III/3, p. 54.
[4] *Ibid.*
[5] IV/2, p. 373. Professor West has argued an implied but unexplicated distinction in Barth's thinking between *Weltgeschichte* and *Weltgeschehen*. *Weltgeschehen* is "the objective reality of the events which make up the history of man on earth, his life cycle, his attempts to set up order, his sinful destruction of order, his relations to his neighbor, and the rest". *Weltgeschehen*, he asserts, is positively coordinated with covenant-history. *Weltgeschichte*, on the contrary, "refers not to these events as such, which lie in the hand of God, but to these events in so far as man himself is their subject, sees himself as their creator, and endows them with meaning of their own". The implication here is that *Weltgeschichte* is "at odds with grace and *Heilsgeschichte*". *Communism and the Theologians*, p. 263f. I have not followed Professor West in this distinction, nor in the pejorative status he attaches to *Weltgeschichte*, for it seems clear that it is treated negatively by Barth only to the extent that it indicates the construction of an independent *philosophy* of history. When both the history and events of the world are viewed from the perspective of the embracing contours of covenant-history, they are provided with a positive content and meaning, even though these emerge only in faith. If Professor West is correct, it is hard to see what justification Barth finds in referring to the history of the community as "the true world-history".

ment" [1]. The relationship thus set up between world-history and the
history of the community establishes an immediate tone for the engagement of the community with the former. On the one hand, the Church
will celebrate in its attitude and action the goodness of creation as
posited by God, and so the full range of human history and events
that take place within it. In all the developments occurring within
creaturely reality, the Christian community will see (through faith)
that it is confronted with the activity of God [2]. On the other hand, it
will be obvious that in all the developments within world-history and
occurrence the community is faced with "the reality and activity of the
absurd, of nothingness, neither chosen nor willed by the Creator, but
existing only *per nefas*" [3]. In short, the community is confronted with a
continuous and profound *confusio hominum* alongside its faith in the
Dei providentia [4]. This does not mean, however, that the existence and
action of the community in world-history is placed under a perpetual
oscillation between positive and negative, so that it moves in circular
fashion from the positive affirmation of the providential activity of God
throughout the created order to a negative recognition of the "heart of
darkness" embedded and evident in human history and action. Because
both the positive and negative dimensions of creation are viewed exclusively in terms of "the reality and truth of the grace of God given to
the world in Jesus Christ" [5], the Christian community is enabled to
engage the created order positively in the actions of faith, obedience
and prayer [6]. In this way, the Church, by its recognition of the lordship
of God within history, provides an authentic witness to the true grounding and status of both the created order and the creature [7].

It is important to stress that the actions of faith, obedience and
prayer marking the engagement of the Church with world-history and
occurrence constitute a *witness*. The fact that the community knows and
accepts the lordship of God over creation does not provide it with a key
unlocking the secrets and meaning of the occurrences that make up the

---

[1] IV/2, p. 373.
[2] IV/3.2, p. 787f.; III/3, p. 50f.
[3] IV/3.2, p. 796.
[4] *Ibid.*, p. 793f.
[5] *Ibid.*, p. 808.
[6] III/3, pp. 278ff.
[7] *Ibid.*, pp. 271ff.

historical process. The community is not provided with an automatic "Weltanschauung" with which to categorize events in their appropriate order. On the contrary, the Christian will, like other men, be confronted daily by "the riddles of the world-process, with the precipices and plains, the blinding lights and obscurities, of the general creaturely occurrence to which his own life's history belongs" [1]. It is only by faith that the community knows of the final goal and meaning of all history. The faith of the community signals its deliverance from binding and limiting world-views and ideologies, and its liberation for authentic participation in the occurrences of world-history. The involvement of the community in the world-process will therefore be marked by a total openness, freshness and surprise. Far from engendering pessimistic withdrawal, the faith that distinguishes the Christian's approach to the world enables him to view it as the matrix of drama and adventure within which he is called upon to participate to the full extent of his capacities [2].

As it is called into being by the action of God in the Holy Spirit, the community is ordered to service and set in action within the world. The "sending" of the community provides a reflection of the initial sending of Jesus Christ, who, as the Lord of the Church, still precedes its action at every point [3]. This means that the community, in all its undertakings, will exist only for man and the world. It is called out of the world only that it might be set genuinely free for it [4]. The task of the community in witnessing to Jesus Christ is carried out in complete solidarity with the world. The event of God's reconciling action in Jesus Christ establishes the community and the world as a "firmly united whole" [5]. In this respect, it can be said that "man as fellow-man" is "the content of the task given the community" [6]. Apart from the world, the community lacks entirely a basis for existence. Like the discipline of theology within the Church, it is invested with penultimate rather than eschatological significance, and is viewed correctly as a "stopgap in an unordered cosmos" [7]. From a strictly eschatological perspective,

---

[1] *Ibid.*, p. 275.
[2] *Ibid.*
[3] IV/3.2, p. 878f.
[4] *Ibid.*, p. 874; Cf. III/4, p. 575f.
[5] IV/3.2, p. 946.
[6] *Ibid.*, p. 915.
[7] I/1, p. 8; IV/3.2, p. 947.

of course, the world *is* ordered, for it stands under the resurrection of Jesus Christ and the total inversion (and conversion) that it brings. This is the event marking the ontological reality under which all men stand. The "unordered" character of the world, and so of contemporary world-history and occurrence, is therefore epistemological rather than ontological in nature. It is this deficiency which is effectively met and overcome within the history of Christ's movement from his resurrection to his final *parousia*, a movement which does not issue in a new event, but in a total confirmation of what has been achieved and secured already in him [1]. And it is both within and under this history, and the hope issuing from it, that the Christian community is called into being and activity within the world through the continuing miraculous presence of Christ in the Holy Spirit. As the community is called into being and sustained in its action by the Holy Spirit, it is provided with certain condition and criteria that define the character of its participation in the world, and of its differentiated solidarity with it.

(1) The fact that the Church understands itself only in relation to the totally inclusive movement of divine history means that it is capable of knowing the world as it really is in the eternal covenant between God and man. The Christian community is thus provided with a proper perspective on human identity, temporality and historicity. To see and know man from the vantage point of the Gospel is to see and know him as one who is in no sense separated from or alien to God, but who is totally loved by God [2]. In Jesus Christ, man is simultaneously justified and sanctified, and set under the promise of his future being as the child of God. Through this event, his "improper" time is taken from him, and he is set within the givenness of created time, the time that God has and takes for man [3]. Man is thus rescued from the remoteness and unavailability of the past, the uncertainty of the future, and the speciousness of the present, all of which indicate the distortion of his true temporality and historicity under sin [4]. So, even though he has only "allotted" (*befristete*) time, a certain definite temporal span within an equally definite beginning and end [5], it is nevertheless a time that is "willed and

---

[1] III/2, p. 588.
[2] IV/3.2, p. 881f.
[3] III/2, p. 624; III/4, p. 652f.
[4] III/2, pp. 616ff.
[5] *Ibid.*, pp. 671ff., 695ff., 714ff.; III/4, p. 656f.

created by God, given by God to man, and so real" [1]. Man's true time
as the creature of God is totally enclosed within the "eternal time"
of the One in whom the destiny and goal of created human nature is
(for the first time) fully realized: Jesus Christ, the Lord of time [2].
And because man is the object of God's eternal love and election,
his own being in time is bracketed by the promise of authentic being and
time actualized in Jesus [3]. Viewed from this perspective, it is both true
and factual to assert that "humanity is temporality" and "temporality is
... humanity" [4]. As the community is placed "between the times" of
the resurrection and final *parousia* of Christ, and so made epistemological participant in the event of reconciliation, it is empowered to provide
an authentic service, through its witness, to man's true being in time.
Of course, since the temporality of man proclaimed by the Church is
discernible only within the total sweep of the divine history, it follows
that the insight given the community into the temporality of the world
will carry with it an understanding of the real nature of human history.
As we shall see, this carries important consequences for the engagement
of Christians with the particular issues, movements and crises of the day.

(2) The ontological unity of all men in Christ places the community
under an immediate demand to *practice* its solidarity with the world.
In carrying out its task of assisting man in a transition from his situation
of epistemic abnormality to the "normal" knowledge of himself as one
addressed by God and enclosed within the divine promise [5], the Church
will never justifiably indulge in sectarianism, nor in a concern only for
its own well-being within the world. On the contrary, it will be ready
to compromise itself with the world, if need be. As the people of God in
world-history and occurrence, the Christian community will be no
stranger either to the heights or the depths of the human, but will gladly
accept its solidarity with all its manifestations, good and bad [6]. It will
address all men as "virtual or potential" Christians (*christianus designa-
tus*) [7], and will remain at all points truly worldly. It is called into being

---

[1] III/2, p. 628.
[2] *Ibid.*, p. 555.
[3] *Ibid.*, p. 626.
[4] *Ibid.*, p. 629.
[5] IV/3.2, p. 923f.
[6] *Ibid.*, p. 886f.
[7] *Ibid.*, p. 927.

only for service to the world, and it must accept unreservedly the fact
that it belongs wholly to it [1].

Solidarity is not conformity, however. The unreserved commitment
of the community to the world will therefore contain an appropriate
tension. While the thrust of the community into the world is always
positive, so that it is not called upon to say both yes and no in any final,
eschatological sense (but only to proclaim the overarching "Yes" of
God), it will nevertheless on occasion find itself resisting particular
tendencies and movements that capture man's attention and commitment. Conversely, it may find it necessary, from time to time, to champion
an unpopular or minority position, or to articulate a completely new,
perhaps revolutionary, course of action. In all its actions, however, the
community will move exclusively on the basis of love. Since it can only
be *for* men, it can never be against them—not even individuals [2]. In
light of the confidence it is given concerning the future of the world
in Christ, and the signs it discerns within history that point toward the
coming kingdom of God, it is restrained from becoming either purely
pessimistic and reactionary, or purely optimistic and revolutionary.
Because the community does not act "on principle", but always within
specific situations demanding obedience to the leading action of Christ,
the developments and problems in world history will receive the attention
and seriousness they deserve as penultimate rather than ultimate concerns [3].

The Church displays its solidarity with the world neither in identification nor withdrawal, but in a subtle balance between freedom and
obligation, strength and weakness, reminiscent of its own status under
grace. The quality of relationship sustained between the community
and the world is seen, first, in the fact that with respect to its environment

---

[1] "It necessarily closes it eyes to the light which it may see in distinction
to the world, and so conforms again to the world, if it attempts to ignore or
deny in practice its total relationship to it, and thus does not wish to exist
in solidarity with it. It must necessarily flee from God's love if it flees from the
world, and does not wish to remain itself worldly within it ... Solidarity with
the world means full association with it, an unreserved participation in it,
in the promise given it in its creation, in its responsibility for the presump-
tuousness and sloth and falsehood that reign in it, in its suffering under the
resulting distress, but primarily and initially in the free grace of God demonstrated and addressed to it in Jesus Christ, and so in its hope". *Ibid.*, p. 884f.

[2] *Ibid.*, p. 820f.

[3] *Ibid.*, p. 821f.

the community is both totally dependent and wholly free [1]; and second, in the fact that within the context of world-occurrence the community is both totally strong and totally weak [2]. The former point is exemplified in the linguistic forms adopted by the Church, and in its sociological structure. So, although the Church has its own definite message to proclaim through its witness, and is therefore free from other "messages" that claim the interest and attention of men, it must express its messages in the linguistic forms provided by its secular context, and so is bound to it [3]. There are, accordingly, no particular speech forms constituting a definite "religious" as over against an equally definite, and so separate, "non-religious" language. Were this sort of strict demarcation possible, it would mean that the Christian community was empowered with a specific language of its own whose meaning and effectiveness would be guaranteed simply by the use to which it was put. Actually, of course, as we have seen, the meaning of the language used by the Church is dependent on the action of God as Holy Spirit. Meaning is therefore *given* to religious language; it is not an indigenous possession. Or, to put it differently, *all* language is potentially religious in that it carries the possibility, under the impact of grace, of becoming a sign of the reconciling action of God. Thus, even though a relative distinction can be drawn between the language of the Church and that of the secular community, this cannot be allowed to harden into rigidly specific linguistic "games". The language of the Church is always, at bottom, secular [4]. The community will thus be faced continually with the risks of misunderstanding and self-deception, as it makes free use of whatever forms of speech are available to it. Its witness in speech will take the form of obedience, and so of a waiting on the confirming action of God in the Holy Spirit through which meaning is conferred and the ministry of the community to the Word nf God is made event [5].

The community is also totally free and totally bound with respect to its sociological structure. There is no distinctive social form corresponding to its existence in world-occurrence [6]. The sociological form of

---

[1] *Ibid.*, p. 840.
[2] *Ibid.*, p. 849.
[3] *Ibid.*, p. 841f.
[4] *Ibid.*, p. 842.
[5] *Ibid.*, p. 843f.
[6] *Ibid.*, p. 845f.

the community does not spring spontaneously into being, but emerges in specific and varied contexts in which it is empowered by the Word of God to exist as his community [1]. The Church is thus not dependent on any particular form, even though it will inevitably fall under some sociologically specifiable pattern. The particular sociological form of the community will always express, however, its free obedience to its Lord [2]. The possibility of an "intrinsically sacred sociology" (*als solche heilige Soziologie*) is completely set aside [3].

The weakness and strength of the community arise, on the one hand, because of its uncertain position in the world; on the other hand, because it is constituted solely by the Word of God. The weakness of the Church in the world is representative of the fact that its place as a visible entity and event is not self-evident. Unlike the state, work, or cultural forms, the community exists as an "absolutely contingent phenomenon" [4]. It enjoys a merely "marginal" existence (*Randexistenz*), which in itself is indicative of the true status of all men, and so constitutes a further testimony to the solidarity of the Church with the world [5]. The only effective weapon the community carries with it in its encounter with the world is its witness.

It is the very weakness of the community in its witness that mirrors its strength, however, for it makes clear the fact that its concern is not with the obvious and directly discernible factors in human experience and action, but with the presupposition underlying all human action—the decision God has taken toward the world in Jesus Christ [6]. The weakness of the community demonstrates the strength of God, and so its own strength as it is upheld and directed by the Word of God. The strength of the Christian community sustaining its engagement with the world, and exposing the ground of its solidarity with it, is "the strength of the dawning truth of the general human situation under the judgment and

---

[1] *Ibid.*, p. 847f.

[2] *Ibid.*, p. 848f.

[3] *Ibid.*, p. 846. As we have seen, however, Barth gives at least a relative weight to a polity in which the free obedience of the congregation to its Lord is safeguarded. This brings him, at points, to a certain nervousness with governing structures in the Church that go beyond the individual congregation, and suggests a partial affinity for a congregationalist polity and form.

[4] IV/3.2, p. 850.

[5] *Ibid.*, p. 852.

[6] *Ibid.*, p. 857f.

grace of God" [1]. The concern of the community for the general (i.e., ontological) ground of human action does not remove it from an engagement with the specific issues of the day. Nor does it lead to a levelling process in which no significant distinctions can be drawn because the Church finds itself, historically, in "a night, in which all cats are grey" [2]. The emphasis on the ontological presupposition of all human being and action serves rather to qualify and define the possibility of an actualization of obedience in the actions of the community designed to articulate its solidarity with the world, and to provide an adumbration of the final and total unity of all men under God.

(3) The active involvement of the Church in the practice of its solidarity with the world draws it out of passivity and detachment and into immediacy and familiarity with the world in its various spheres and movements. It is set in motion by the direct action of Christ in the Holy Spirit, and is marked off from the world only to be made directly responsible for it in light of the responsibility assumed for it by God in Jesus Christ [3]. To be sure, the Christian community is allowed only a relative, proximate responsibility for the world, which will be continually ambiguous and fragmented in terms of its specific actions. Within its limited capacity, however, it is enabled to cooperate with and have a part in God's work. In the action of the Holy Spirit, divine and human action form a parallel history [4]. The decisive indication of this parallelism, and so of the coordination between the continuing history of Jesus Christ and the world (exemplified initially in the community) lies in the *obedience* of the Church.

Obedience is bodied forth in human actions that constitute a concrete doing of God's Word [5]. It forms the unrelieved *obligatorium* under which the Christian, and so the community, is placed [6]. As a consistent obligation, the obedience of the community can never be its own achievement, as might be the case were it under the rule of a merely external law or principle. Essentially, Christian obedience consists in "submission" (*Fügsamkeit*) to the directing activity of the Holy Spirit, and so in a justification of what has been decided already in Jesus Christ

---

[1] *Ibid.*, p. 853.
[2] *Ibid.*, p. 1027.
[3] *Ibid.*, p. 888f.
[4] *Ibid.*, p. 870f.
[5] III/3, p. 288.
[6] *Ibid.*

about man and the world [1]. Under the total determination set for man in that event, the Christian community is called to obedience in every area of world-occurrence.

It is clear that the basic factor in the obedience of the community is found in the encounter that occurs between it and the Holy Spirit. It is through the Holy Spirit that the command of God for a particular situation or sphere is made evident in the first place, and that the correct response of obedience takes place [2]. Obedience is thus actually achieved, if only in an ambiguous, fragmented way. The obedience of the community and the individual Christian is, strictly speaking, a necessity. But since neither the community as a whole nor the individuals within it are ever removed from the context of creaturely reality, and the distorting overtones of sin accompanying it, obedience can never be acquired as an immediate datum or possession. It can only be rendered again and again, as the Holy Spirit continues to speak and direct the actions of the community [3]. Obedience is therefore exclusively indicative of the centrality of grace. It follows from this that the movement of the community into the larger context of world-history and occurrence can take place only against the background of the gathering of the Church in baptism and its continual nourishment in the Lord's Supper, and of the petition and intercession manifested in prayer [4].

The persistent grounding of the community in grace provides a nice point of continuity between its ontological grounding and its specific need to act in given contexts. The knowledge given in faith does not lead to the erection of a world-view, nor to a theoretically balanced and correct interpretation of the total course of world-history and occurrence. If this were the outcome of the event of grace establishing the community, it would amount to no more than another addition to the already overcrowded ranks of ideologies, world-views and philosophies of history. The crucial difference here is that the knowledge of God's action in Jesus Christ given in faith leads neither to

---

[1] *Ibid.*, p. 289f.

[2] *Ibid.*, p. 291f.

[3] *Ibid.*, pp. 293ff.

[4] *Ibid.*, pp. 297ff. Cf. Barth's address, "The Christian as Witness", delivered at the International Summer Conference for students at La Chataigneraie, Canton Vaud, Switzerland, in August, 1934. Included in: *God in Action*, which contains five of Barth's early addresses, translated by E.G. Homrighausen and Karl J. Ernst (New York: Round Table Press, 1963), pp. 94-118.

speculation nor contemplation, but to *action* within the world. So, although the community cannot judge the results of its actions, it can never fail to act, i.e., to render obedience [1]. As it moves under the continuing history of Christ, it is rescued from an unrelieved emphasis on the eschatological, and freed for significant engagement with the penultimate spheres of secular culture. The community is at every point under direct obligation to hear and respond to "the living Word of its living Lord" [2]. The subtlety here, of course, is that this places the community under obligation to the *eternal* Word of God committed to it precisely in its impingement on a given point within the human where the command of God is to be heard and obeyed [3]. It is just this subtlety, and the ethical tension it evokes, that leads the community beyond the relative safety of a "timeless" Gospel, and into the risk of hearing and responding in obedience to the directing action of God. The involvement of the Church in world-history and occurrence will display, then, the two-pronged schematism of command and obedience; and it will eschew completely the utilization of principles or presuppositions imported from general culture [4]. It remains now to specify, in the succeeding sections of this chapter, the way in which this approach enables the ontological and eschatological dimensions of the reconciling action of God to fall over into various specific contexts and lines of action, investing these with penultimate structure and importance.

2. *Discipleship, Witness, Vocation and Work*

Human activity within the Christian community is designed to mirror (by grace) the action of God. It does so under the impact of the claim and will of God embodied in the command as it encounters man in his specific temporal and spatial determination and limitation. It is the determination and limitation of man in time and space that provide the "unique opportunity" (*einmalige Gelegenheit*) [5] for the occurrence of his discipleship and witness leading to a fulfillment of his vocation within a precise form of work.

---

[1] IV/3.2, p. 857f.; Cf. III/4, p. 586f.
[2] IV/3.2, p. 933.
[3] *Ibid.*, p. 935f.
[4] *Ibid.*, p. 940f.
[5] III/4, p. 648.

The community is thus designed to provide the model of genuine creaturely action. As man is encountered by the command, he is called to discipleship, and so bound directly to Jesus [1]. Human vocation and work must be seen initially as aspects of discipleship, and the freedom in obedience it brings to man. Man's response of belief and obedience to the call of Jesus forms "the one, total work that he is called to do" [2]. The locus and meaning of vocation, accordingly, is found within the Church, the actively obedient people of God [3]. A more detailed consideration of these points will make clear how the "freedom in limitation" (*Freiheit in der Beschränkung*) [4] that emerges in the discipleship and witness of Christians provides a positive content for the concepts of vocation and work, and their place in theological ethics. In addition, it will take us a significant distance toward understanding how the somewhat vexing question posed by the assertion and defense of individual integrity and honor is to be answered.

Although the ethical actions of the community occur in direct response to the command of God in its immediate impingement on a situation, and so are freed from a dependence on general principles or rules, it is still possible to provide an over-all indication of the direction these will take. The call to discipleship that comes to a man signals the movement of God against the "given factors" (*Gegebenheiten*) that direct and bind human existence and action unconditionally [5]. These represent the entrenchment of certain natural and historical orders and powers which, in their claim to absolute value and worth, block authentic community between God and man and man and his neighbor. Embodied concretely in an unmitigated concern for and allegiance to such things as property, possessions, family, and religion; and buttressed and defended by "lawful honor" (*gesetzte Ehre*), they identify the world as the context in which "slothful" man moves and acts with a total lack of freedom [6].

The call to discipleship that marks the beginning of the lordship of Jesus over the life of the community and the individual indicates a submersion of the independent rule of these factors, and a freeing of man for positive action within the spheres and relationships established

---

[1] IV/2, p. 606f.
[2] *Ibid.*, p. 607.
[3] IV/3.2, p. 780.
[4] III/4, Par. 56.
[5] IV/2, p. 615.
[6] *Ibid.*

under the formative impact of the command of God. Human activity, viewed as immediate obedience to the formative and decisive particularity of the command [1], will exhibit "certain prominent lines" along which it will move [2]. These are seen in a renunciation of any final attachment to possessions; in a refusal to rely on force as a kind of obvious necessity and good; in a rejection of the unlimited validity of "self-evident relationships" between men, and so a limitation of the autonomy of the family; in freedom from legalism in moral and religious matters; and in a loss of anxiety for the status usually attaching to these which leads to a compulsive defense of honor and fame [3]. While these do not indicate general principles to be taken from the New Testament and applied directly and without remainder to our situation, they nevertheless constitute an "evangelical commission" (*mandatum evangelium*) that demands an appropriate decision and action [4].

The placing of the community and the individual under this commission evokes the tension in which they stand within world-history and its structures, and indicates one facet of the limited freedom that characterizes the activity of Christians. And both the tension and the freedom that surround the action of the Church arise from their common origin in the obedience required to the command of God as it works to deflect world-occurrence from its present, distorted lines and toward the positive future set for it in Christ. The event of the command signals the intrusion of man's past and future realized in the resurrection and final *parousia* of Christ into the present moment in which he must decide and act. The external ministry and witness of the community embodied in service to the world will therefore take on a persistently prophetic cast [5]. In carrying out its commission to preach the Gospel and to proclaim the present reign of Christ over the world, it cannot expect to find continuity between its view of things and that of the world. The community, in its response to the command, is set free from dominating perspectives and attitudes. Its action in witnessing will thus "not be drawn *from* the depths of the momentary present", but will occur "*in* the present from the depths of that qualified past and qualified future" [6]. In this respect, the activity of the community will always be

---

[1] III/4, p. 683; IV/2, p. 613.
[2] IV/2, p. 619.
[3] *Ibid.*, pp. 620ff.
[4] *Ibid.*, p. 626.
[5] III/4, p. 583f.
[6] *Ibid.*, p. 585. Italics added.

timely, since it occurs "at the time shown to be the right time for a particular insight or judgment in the light of its orientation on eternity" [1].
From another perspective, however, its action will be "untimely" (Un-
zeitgemäßheit), since it will be discontinuous with the prevailing attitude
or spirit of the time [2]. The witness brought to bear on the given factors
present in a situation will inevitably occasion mistrust and hostility.
Although the community does not, in its activity, constitute a "Christian
party", it can never remain neutral toward its surroundings, and the
structures, programs and values that gain expression there [3]. In its
prophetic thrust into the affairs of the day, which itself gives at least a
moderately polemical cast to its actions,

> it can only direct attention, by a deeply involved and positive opposition
> to every human policy, to the politics of God, which is not a system but
> his sovereign, hidden action which the community must humbly but
> vigorously follow as it listens to his Word, and whose way it now attests
> both in strength and weakness [4].

The action of the Church will thus manifest a persistent "Auseinandersetzung" with its surrounding cultural milieu, which is designed
to draw attention to the unifying direction set for the world in the command. The total ministry of the community, as this is reflected in the
activity of the individuals within it, will at this point fall under the determination and limitation for death marking the existence of Jesus. Initially,
this is an ontological rather than an ethical point. It gains immediately
in ethical significance, however, for it underlines the fact that the participatio entis of the Christian in the passion of Christ involves the imperative of suffering and rejection. There is, accordingly, a secondary theo-
logia crucis that applies to the disciple individually, and to the Christian
community as a whole [5].

It follows, then, that Christian existence and action will be denoted
by "affliction" (Bedrängnis) [6]. The affliction of the Christian follows
unavoidably upon his witness, as this is grounded in his relationship
to Christ. There is thus both an inner and a outer ground of the suffering
and rejection brought about by the exercise of discipleship. Internally,

---

[1] Ibid., p. 586.
[2] Ibid.
[3] Ibid., p. 586f.
[4] Ibid., p. 587.
[5] IV/2, p. 291f.
[6] IV/3.2, pp. 704ff.

the affliction of the Christian arises from his epistemological participation in the (ontological) event of reconciliation, and the necessity this carries for the action of witness [1]. Externally, it is occasioned by the vulnerability of the Christian in his witness, which is also a sign of the limitation under which he stands. He is called to witness to the Gospel, and so to both the positive and negative sides of God's action. It is thus impossible for him to engage in temporizing movements or stratgems that might make his witness more palatable, and this insures the response of hostility and rejection from the world [2]. In its active ministry of witness and service, the Christian community stands at all points under the "dignity" (*Würde*) of the cross marking the outer boundary and limit of its movements. The suffering that comes to it will be indicative of both its continuity and its discontinuity with men. It will thus share in the general affliction of creaturely life in all its nuances, and it will accept its involvement in the more particular burden of suffering imposed by its specific witness to Jesus Christ, an activity which insures that the community "will never swim with the stream", but will always move against it [3].

It is against the background of discipleship and witness that the issues of the vocation, work and honor of the community (and, by implication, of the world) can be approached. The continuity becomes clear when we recall that on Barth's analysis the essence of the vocation to which Christians are called in discipleship consists in their being made witnesses to Christ [4]. It is in this way that the activity of the community is positively coordinated with the prevenient action of Christ in the Holy Spirit [5]. Within this setting, the human is invested with a genuine vocation, a legitimate "praise of works" [6], and an honor corresponding to these.

The event of man's vocation is grounded in the call to discipleship and witness issued by Jesus Christ. Since Christ is the future of every man, this means that man's vocation is eternally real in his election to covenant with God [7]. Ontologically, there is no man who is not confronted by the fact of his vocation. Vocation is therefore

---

[1] *Ibid.*, pp. 717, 726f.

[2] *Ibid.*, p. 710f.

[3] IV/2, pp. 676f., 690.

[4] "Sie sind nämlich—und daß ist das Wesen ihrer Berufung—von Gott zu seinen Zeugen gemacht". IV/3.2, p. 660.

[5] *Ibid.*, p. 685f.

[6] IV/2, pp. 660ff.

[7] IV/3.2, p. 558f.

real *de iure* for all men, even though its actualization in time depends specifically on the grace and calling of the Holy Spirit [1]. When the ontological and the existential dimensions of the event of vocation are kept clearly in view, the possibility of an abstract reading of it along the lines of an exclusive emphasis on either its objective, supra-historical givenness or its actualization as a concrete event in time is excluded [2].

At this point, it will be helpful to insert a parenthetical note about the occurrence of authentic witness beyond the Christian community in the world generally. Not only will this make clear the continuity between a *de iure* and a *de facto* participation in vocation; it serves also to underline again the unity between the Church and its secular environment, and enables Barth to distinguish between a "pure and absolute" and a "mixed and relative" form of secularism [3]. The line of continuity between Christians and non-Christians becomes particularly transparent at just this point, for Barth argues that these varieties of secularism are not confined to the "outer" world, but penetrate into the Church as well [4].

Earlier, we saw that the intrusion of falsehood as a mode of sin into the human does not lead to the annihilation of truth. That there are manifestations of truth even within the darkness of human falsehood depends strictly on the validity of the continuing self-manifestation of Jesus Christ, in which he shows himself to be actively for man outside as within the Christian community. The inadvertent witness appearing in the secular community that permits the Church to "eavesdrop in the world at large" [5] incurs no lapse into natural theology, but is evidence of the way in which the world as a whole is caught up in the divine history and grace, and marked indelibly by its future in Christ. In addition, it signifies the total freedom of the Word of God in its movement within the world. The Christian community, it is true, is marked off

---

[1] *Ibid.*, p. 564f.

[2] The latter tendency, Barth feels, gained prominence through the Pietism and Rationalism of the 18th century, and reached a kind of culmination in the theology of Schleiermacher. The former possibility, he seems to suggest, was present in his own early theology. The difficulty with both approaches is the same: An isolated God set over against an equally isolated man. Barth's adoption of an uncompromising insistence on the christological unity of God and man is designed to prevent an outbreak of either possibility. *Ibid.*, p. 572f.

[3] IV/3.1, pp. 132ff.

[4] *Ibid.*, p. 133f.

[5] IV/3.1, p. 131.

epistemologically from secular culture by the activity of the Holy Spirit, and so is enabled to move toward a more direct embodiment of vocation and witness. It does not follow from this, however, that the Holy Spirit is locked within the confines of the community. The power and freedom of the Word of God given in the ongoing history of the self-witness of Jesus Christ in the Holy Spirit are made dramatically apparent in the appearance of "extraordinary witnesses" (*außerordentliche Zeugen*) to the truth of that Word from within the secular sphere [1].

The criterion to be applied in testing and weighing the ostensible truth of the witnesses provided by the secular world is their material agreement with the witness of Scripture. When this criterion is kept clearly in mind, the community must continue to be open to the significance such words may carry for its own life and activity. It must be ready to hear and receive them as true words from its Lord which simultaneously comfort and unsettle, encourage and correct the community; and which also enable it to draw important qualitative distinctions within the developments, programs and actions taking place in world-occurrence [2]. Taken in this way, the words issuing from the secular community can lead the Church into a deeper confrontation with Scripture, and so to a more relevant enactment of its own calling and vocation [3].

The elusiveness of the line of demarcation between the Christian community and its secular surroundings, and the possibility of an authentic word of truth taking form in the latter on the basis of a *de iure*

---

[1] *Ibid.*, p. 132.

[2] *Ibid.*, pp. 141ff.

[3] *Ibid.*, p. 151f. It is worth noting that Barth makes no attempt to specify aspects of contemporary culture that might qualify as genuine words bearing positive significance for the Christian community. The reason for this, he tells us, is that his concern here is to raise and answer the general question as to the possibility of such words occurring. *Ibid.*, p. 152f. It is tantalizing to speculate on the particular aspects of culture that might be cited by Barth. It seems clear that he regards the socialist critique of bourgeois standards with favor. And he is at least partially indebted to certain existential and phenomenological thinkers, notably Martin Buber, for his description of I-Thou relationality as the "basic" form of humanity. Beyond these, however, the possibilities are unclear. Neither the more recent developments in Anglo-American philosophy, nor the contributions from the newer social sciences appear to have captured Barth's attention, and we are provided with no clues as to how he regards current art, literature or music.

participation in reconciliation, exposes again the ontological unity holding between created and reconciled human nature. The vocation and witness of man, and the honor that comes from these, represent a fulfillment and confirmation of his original status as the creature of God, despite the fact that they depend on the special event of grace provided by the Holy Spirit, and result in a wholly new level of existence, in service to God [1]. The action of the Holy Spirit simply enables man to recognize that, in both his given creaturely existence and in his special calling to discipleship and witness, he is equally dependent on the grace of God. The lines between created and called human nature, which intersect in Christ, are therefore both "unmixed and inseparable" [2]. So, although it is necessary to distinguish between what may be called the "normal" honor man has as the creature of God, and the special honor that comes to him as he is called directly to service under the command [3]; and between vocation as this describes man's full particularity in time and space constituted by God, and the special vocation given him in the divine summons of the command [4], these distinctions fall into unity within the total reach of covenant-history. Because man has a limited but definite share in creation, cosmos and history,

> he is pointed directly to the grace of divine calling, orientated on the covenant which God has completed with man, and disposed for participation in the salvation-history which proceeds from this covenant, and which constitutes the fulfillment of the particular decree and work and Word which forms the inner ground of creation and the center and meaning of the whole cosmos and history [5].

The event of man's special calling to vocation and witness represents the actualization of his limited freedom within the unique opportunity provided by the temporal transition from birth to death within which he is placed. The time given man within these limits constitutes his "limited portion in the existence of God's creation" [6]. Man's temporal limitation provides the appropriate context within which he is encountered by the command of God and summoned to obedience. The command thus meets man where is he, in the full circumstances of his

---

[1] III/4, pp. 684, 751.
[2] *Ibid.*, p. 751.
[3] *Ibid.*
[4] *Ibid.*, p. 686f.
[5] *Ibid.*, p. 660.
[6] *Ibid.*, p. 653.

particularity, and so "demands of him only what he himself must desire from the standpoint of his own creaturely existence and nature" [1].

Since man's unique opportunity occurs in his present time, he must "seize and use" it, and so claim the promise given in the command [2]. There is a pervasive eschatological urgency surrounding human action, for it stands before the "frontier" (*Grenze*) of God manifested in Christ. Man's time is given definiteness and importance as a "moment" in the time of Jesus Christ, and this fact provides the criterion by which human action is measured and tested [3]. Man is obedient to the command to the extent that he seizes and makes use of his opportunity, and so remains open and resolute in his appointed place, knowing that he has no time to lose; realizing that he will one day die, yet having no fear of death [4].

The particular, individual limitation of man in time, with all the additional restrictive nuances this implies, define man's vocation as it relates to his being as created and determined for a specific and limited responsibility and action under the command of God. The definiteness of the command finds its correspondent, at this point, in the definiteness of man's situation. Vocation is thus man's "place of responsibility", and so "the *terminus a quo* of all recognition and fulfillment of the command" [5]. Since it relates to the totality of man's situation, it cannot be equated with the particular profession or work he has chosen. Nor is it possible to grasp in its totality the vocation of any man, for the place of responsibility is for each person the special confluence of a variety of factors which, in their uniqueness, elude exhaustive description [6]. It is possible, however, to set out general, formal criteria that provide guidance in considering the question of obedience to the command of God within the special responsibility given to each man. These will not, Barth points out, provide the answer to the question of obedience, for "no ethics can answer this question" [7]. Theological ethics can, however, focus the general considerations that will inform an inquiry into the question of individual responsibility and obedience to the command.

The first general criterion bearing on the total context of vocation

---

[1] *Ibid.*, p. 664.
[2] *Ibid.*, p. 665.
[3] *Ibid.*, p. 670.
[4] *Ibid.*, pp. 671ff.
[5] *Ibid.*, p. 687.
[6] *Ibid.*, p. 688f.
[7] *Ibid.*, p. 697.

within which man is encountered by the call of God is the element of age [1]. In relation to the command of God, the factor of age does not result in the establishment of independent temporal periods or cycles. It rather serves as an indication and reminder to man of his continual movement from past to present, and so toward his future, under the sovereignty of God's directing activity. Theologically understood, a man's age signifies the freedom in obedience to which he is called in the present moment, as he relinguishes his past time to God and moves forward to successively new encounters with him [2]. What man brings with him out of his past is a "recollection" (*Erinnerung*) of his past encounter and acceptance of the command, which amounts to no more than an "opinion, not the truth as it is in the sight of God regarding his own obedience or disobedience" [3].

The various temporal periods or ages through which the individual moves are thus meaningful and important "only as the divine determination of his Now, as the constantly changing Henceforth, from which he has to set out for new shores according to the command as though it were the first and last time" [4]. This lends an immediate and unending eschatological cast to human action. Since man moves from birth to death without knowing the precise extent of his alloted time, every moment is charged with urgency and possibility. And, since it is the decision and verdict that God takes toward man in the command that lend substance to human existence and activity [5], it follows that the criterion that runs like a thread throughout the life-span of the individual and links his actions together in unity and coherence

> consists ... in the secret but real coinherence of the differing stages of life, in their unity which is given by the fact that it is the same commanding God who speaks with man concretely and yet differently at all the various stages, in order that he will and may be heard concretely by the same man, and therefore in the particular form of his one being [6].

Obedience to the command will, in this respect, take the form of a movement into freedom from the past. Although it is relatively less complex for a young man than an old to make this movement, since the

---

[1] *Ibid.*
[2] *Ibid.*, p. 698f.
[3] *Ibid.*
[4] *Ibid.*, p. 701f.
[5] *Ibid.*, p. 704.
[6] *Ibid.*, p. 702.

young man brings a shorter past with him into the situation of encounter, the free movement and response of man to the command remains at all stages the sole condition for judging youthfulness and maturity [1]. There is, however, a valid relative distinction to be drawn between the stages of youth, middle- and old-age. The young man, in his "youthful objectivity" can provide an example of the kind of openess and spontaneity that is to be retained toward the command [2]. The man of middle-age, who is "no longer young and not yet old" is in a position of "relative limitlessness of development", and so is made peculiarly capable of recognizing the urgency of the opportunity presented for obedience to the command [3]. The old man, because of his proximity to the end of his time, and so to the future promised him in Christ, is in a position to remind all men of the necessity of recognizing the mercy and grace of God, and so of calling his own autonomy and sovereignty into question [4].

The second criterion for vocation is provided by the special historical situation in which each man stands. This represents the "outer limit of his vocation" [5]. As such, it is also an indigenous part of man's vocation, which must be encountered and accepted. This does not mean that it is given autonomous metaphysical status, however, since the various aspects that make up the *milieu* within which man lives and acts from moment to moment are lodged securely within the total movement of covenant-history [6]. The fact that every individual is externally limited, and to that extent defined, by the factors of climate, family, class, his educational and cultural level, the various forms of relationship that impinge on him, and the prevailing behavioral mores of his environment, does not mean that he is determined by them. As Barth insists, the total givenness of man's specific situation does not make him a person, and so cannot be equated with the man himself [7].

Within covenant-history, and under the imperative of the command, however, the historical situation in which man is placed requires his attention and commitment, for it forms the *terminus a quo* of his respons-

---

[1] *Ibid.*, p. 702f.
[2] *Ibid.*, p. 704.
[3] *Ibid.*, p. 705f.
[4] *Ibid.*, p. 707f.
[5] *Ibid.*, p. 710.
[6] *Ibid.*, p. 714.
[7] "Das Alles ist aber nicht er selbst, ist auch nicht seine Bestimmung, macht ihn nicht zum Menschen". *Ibid.*, p. 713.

ibility, and marks out the contours within which his response of obedience
is to be given [1]. On the one hand, then, man is warned against attempting
to invest the peculiarities of his situation with absolute or mythological
status. The command of God that comes to him bears "a summons to
break down all historico-sociological systems, myths and dogmas" [2].
On the other hand, he must not seek arbitrarily to break out of his
situation. Since it is given to him by God, he is required "to hold and
occupy his position" [3]. It is only in the action of accepting his given
placement, and the good and promise it holds for him, that he can be
open to the contextuality and individuality of the command. He is at
all points ordered by, and so accountable to, God's command, not his
special environment. The proper ethical stance is therefore captured in
his "place of readiness" (*Bereitstellung*), as he is summoned "in freedom
to reflection and resolution, to a new decision and action which transcends the previous form of his position" [4]. Obedience to the command
within his historical situation will thus involve the possibility that man
is called upon for actions both positive and negative, and so for movements of either affirmation or rejection. It is in this way that man bears
witness to the centrality of the command under which he stands, and
to the concern required of him for the shape and direction that his
given historical context will take [5].

The third criterion of vocation follows from the second. To the
external limitation provided by his "place" within history, there is a
corresponding internal limit which is occasioned by the "personal
ability" or aptitude of the individual [6]. There is, Barth argues, a point
at which the external and internal dimensions of man's vocation "intersect" which, although it does not establish either of these as a simple
continuation of the other, does enable significant questioning about
the reality of "man himself" within the outer and inner modalities of
vocation to take place [7].

As every man finds himself placed within a certain specific historical
matrix, so too he is equipped with his own unique "virtue" or
strength [8]. He has this as he is posited and preserved by the creative

[1] *Ibid.*, p. 712.
[2] *Ibid.*, p. 711.
[3] *Ibid.*, p. 712.
[4] *Ibid.*, p. 714f.
[5] *Ibid.*, p. 715f.
[6] *Ibid.*, p. 716.
[7] *Ibid.*, p. 717.
[8] *Ibid.*

action of God. This ontological grounding of human capacity lends a degree of fixity to its structure, so that although man himself can effect partial modification or realignment of it, it will nevertheless manifest "indestructible and certain characteristics which persist in their form throughout all change" [1]. Since each man bears his structure as uniquely his own, there can be no justification for attempts to grade individuals on the basis of their particular abilities or gifts. The significance of individual abilities and gifts does not lie in the fact that they are possessed by certain men, but in the precise use to which they are put in the obedient service to which all men are called. Further, although the individual traits present in a man expose his mystery and uniqueness, they cannot legitimately form the basis of a mythology of types, capacities or structures [2]. The specific characteristics of an individual never reveal the man as he is, since the true being of every man is open only to God. At best, they provide, in continuity with the historical situation in which he is called to action, the internal *terminus a quo* from which the individual moves into freedom and obedience [3].

The one unavoidable question confronting every person is "whether my action corresponds to the fact that the command of God claims and seizes myself and therefore all of the ability with which I am endowed?" [4]. Obedience within the sphere of one's individual capacities must therefore be total. Continuous self-examination becomes a necessity at this point, as a means of achieving a critical awareness of the frontiers and limits of our present obedience. This awareness is needed not only because of man's tendency to suppress or ignore aspects of his ability, but also because he has, ultimately, neither knowledge of nor mastery over himself [5]. Man has to *receive* his identity, and so his true capacity, continually anew from God. In relation to his own estimate of his given aptitude and ability, then, he must always respond obediently in the form of

an action which is always and on all sides open, eager to learn, versatile; in continual readiness, in obedience to the exclusively sovereign command of God, to allow itself to be orientated anew, in a totally different manner than appeared possible or necessary on the basis of his previous conception of his knowledge and ability [6].

[1] *Ibid.*
[2] *Ibid.*, p. 718.
[3] *Ibid.*
[4] *Ibid.*, p. 719.
[5] *Ibid.*, p. 723.
[6] *Ibid.*

The fourth and final criterion of vocation that Barth discusses focuses on the "more or less clearly circumscribed sphere of activity" that each man has [1]. It is his involvement in such a sphere of activity that constitutes the technical side of man's vocation, though this is not always identical with his inclusion within the "process of labor" (*Arbeitsprozeß*) [2]. Whether or not this dimension of vocation finds expression in a definite job or work, however, it will remain generally true that each person has

> his circle of operation, the field of his tasks, questions, endeavors and cares, purposes, undertakings and accomplishments, which cannot be the sphere of anyone else, which can only be his own, and yet which stands as such in the most varied relationships to the spheres of others [3].

Although there is more of the element of choice operative in the technical side of vocation, it is still the case that this, too, comes from God. Man's choice of a sphere of operation is bounded by the sovereign, creative activity of God, and so "thickly surrounded by pure pre-suppositions and conditions which he has neither established nor chosen, but in whose sphere he has simply found himself" [4]. Human freedom and choice thus take shape within the prior freedom of God's decision for man. Man's choice and designation of a specific operational context will always of necessity follow the will and plan of God. In this respect, man's vocation forms an answer to his specific calling and service under God [5].

The interrelation between vocation and calling that emerges in the choice of a precise sphere of activity poses three questions of a practical nature which bring into focus the issues of (1) a "correct" or obedient choice of a given context of activity; (2) correct or obedient existence within the chosen sphere; and (3) the possibility of obedient change from one sphere to another [6]. The issue posed by the first arises from the fact that man finds himself confronted externally by a variety of possibilities, and internally moved by various dispositional factors within his total aptitude. A correct decision falls at the point of inter-section between external possibility and internal disposition, and is

---

[1] *Ibid.*, p. 724.
[2] *Ibid.*
[3] *Ibid.*, p. 725.
[4] *Ibid.*, p. 726.
[5] *Ibid.*, p. 729.
[6] *Ibid.*

identified and so taken correctly when a man moves into a certain sphere not on the basis of its attractiveness or enticement, but because he finds himself summoned to move in a given direction [1]. This entails, however, that the possibility of setting up a hierarchy from either direction between the external and internal factors surrounding such a decision is excluded. Instead, there will be a correlation of external opportunity and internal possibility under the command of God [2].

The second question points up the importance of an attentive answer to the first. Once a decision has been made, and a definite sphere of operation chosen, man finds himself confronted with all the specific demands and requirements it imposes, with which he must somehow come to terms [3]. What will keep him from falling into disillusion or despair at the possible hastiness and error of his choice is the fact and the recollection that, despite possible appearances or indications to the contrary, he has been placed in this situation by the directing presence of God. Although man must assume responsibility for his action, this does not mean that he now becomes a kind of master over his fate. At all points in his activity, he stands under the ordering lordship of God [4]. Within the sphere of his choosing, then, whatever promise or limitation it seems to indicate objectively, he "may and should expect the divine calling, and hear the Word and command of God" [5]. He is therefore called upon to recognize both the center and the periphery of his context, and keep to them. A necessary degree of restraint is the condition for an appropriate response of obedience at this point. What this means is that he is given a certain specific, limited function to perform. He cannot legitimately take over the functions of others for which he is unequipped; he can be *with* them, but not *for* them, in their operations [6]. The ethical task given the individual within his special calling and function is to remain attentive and open to the full range of possibilities and nuances it presents. As he does this, and so enters into a total relationship to the tasks presented, and the persons with whom he is brought into contact in their fulfillment, he is moved beyond the dialectic of subject and object through a persistent orientation on "the

---

[1] *Ibid.*, p. 730.
[2] *Ibid.*, p. 731f.
[3] *Ibid.*, p. 733.
[4] *Ibid.*, p. 733f.
[5] *Ibid.*, p. 735.
[6] *Ibid.*, p. 736f.

divine calling, the command of God, which comes to man in his sphere of activity and vocation" [1]. As he is encountered by the command, man is brought to a positive and urgent engagement with the problems, relations and persons his situation presents, and is nudged toward a fulfillment of the command in obedience [2].

The third question is answered by recalling the priority of the command of God, as it calls man to authentic service, over every special context and activity. It may well be the case, that a man will be called to a different sphere of endeavor, or at least that his present situation will take on an unexpected focus and significance which carry a corresponding alteration in his activity within it. At any rate, the ethical point involved centers on man's readiness to be directed to new possibilities, which, since he is called to service under the living God, always remain open and real for him [3].

A discussion of what Barth refers to as the "technical" side of vocation opens the way for an elucidation and analysis of his comments on the place of man's "work" (*Arbeit*) in theological ethics. Barth's treatment of the phenomenon of human work occurs within his larger discussion of "the active life" [4]. The development of the contours and content of vocation thus far has centered on the importance of human activity. The external, historical context in which man finds himself; his internal aptitude and ability; and his choice of a special sphere of operation all focus on the central issue of his obedient response within the totality of his vocation or place of responsibility marked off by these factors. It is within his vocation as provided by the providential activity of God that man is prepared and equipped to respond to the call issued to him in the command, and set on the way to a realization of his ultimate, ontological vocation as a witness to Jesus Christ. What follows, then will provide a further sharpening of the ethical nuances of the context of special activity within which he is placed.

It is important, at this point, not to lose sight of the larger framework within which man's special activity, his work, is placed, for it provides the needed perspective from which a theological assessment of its ethical importance can be undertaken. The previous discussion of vocation displayed a movement from the total periphery of man's

---

[1] *Ibid.*, p. 740.
[2] *Ibid.*, p. 740f.
[3] *Ibid.*, pp. 742ff.
[4] *Ibid.*, pp. 538-648.

historical situation to the more specific context within which he engages and carries out the tasks and responsibilities of the day. Obviously, the special context of man's activity does not form an end in itself. It is, rather, one of the more precise dimensions of the totality of factors constituting the "unique opportunity" facing each person. And it is as he seizes this opportunity, and lives out his life within and under the limitations it imposes, that man takes his place within the total sweep of creaturely history and occurrence. Nor is this the end of the matter. A full appreciation of the opportunity given the individual, his specific limitation in time, and his occupancy of a definite situation of activity and work, is possible only when the whole of creaturely history, and the "cosmic determination and interconnection of each individual person" [1] displayed therein, is projected against the inclusive background of covenant-history.

When this total perspective is kept in mind, it follows that obedience to the command entails much more than the daily occupation or work in which a man engages. Indeed, strictly speaking, "work is not, in itself and as such, that which is demanded of man" [2]. What is required is the "active" life, which means initially that man is to "align himself with something and then accomplish it" [3]. The criterion standing over all human activity, of course, is obedience, i.e., conformity to the action of God. This corresponds to the notion of "service", in which man, under the command, is brought to a recognition of both God and the neighbor [4]. The primary context within which human activity gains expression is provided by the Christian community. In relation to the active life, the initial goal of the command of God lies in man's "action as the covenant-partner of God—which for us means as a responsibly active member of the Christian community" [5]. The community provides the requisite framework of response in which the individual, activated by the Holy Spirit, begins to move into the actualization of his eternal vocation as the elected partner of God. It is his action within the community that constitutes his true work.

The larger contexts and patterns of work that serve to fill out and substantiate the individual's specific area of activity would, under the

---

[1] *Ibid.*, p. 660.
[2] *Ibid.*, p. 540.
[3] *Ibid.*, p. 542.
[4] *Ibid.*, p. 549f.
[5] *Ibid.*, p. 554.

impact of God's providential ordering of all world-history and occurrence, fall into continuity with his existence as a member of the Christian
community. In this respect, a man's work lies at the "circumference"
(*Umkreis*), rather than the center, of his activity [1]. Under his twofold
determination as a man and a Christian, work is simply "man's active
affirmation of his existence as a human creature" [2]. It is the actualization
of his ordered unity as an embodied soul, or a besouled body, and forms
the necessary prerequisite to his service in the Church [3]. All work is
therefore an act of synthesis in which man emerges from both a purely
somatic externality and an abstractive inwardness. When man, in obedience to the command of God, engages in work, "he simply retains
fidelity to God and to himself as God's human creature, actively affirming
his own existence as such in the form of the fulfillment of that synthesis
for which he is determined by his nature" [4].

As an act of self-affirmation, work is also an act of self-moderation,
in that it marks a line of demarcation between creature and Creator [5].
It does not attain meaning as an end in itself, but only through the
"teleological connection" given it by God to man's eternal vocation.
Work is viewed properly only as an incidental activity performed "in
the context of the service to which man is properly and essentially
called" [6]. By securely linking the phenomenon of work, in its various
manifestations and subtleties, to the divine decree and purpose binding
the whole of creaturely occurrence together, Barth forestalls the possibility of mythologizing or divinizing approaches to culture, thereby insuring
that it remains creaturely throughout. It follows, accordingly, that
theological ethics, while capable of relating work to the command of
God within the context of the service demanded of him as a Christian,
can offer no independent justification for it [7]. Strictly speaking, then,
it is "only as he is claimed for cooperation in the service of the Christian
community, and thus knows the meaning of work, that man finds
himself actually and seriously summoned to it" [8]. Outside the context
of faith and obedience, work always remains "in the shadow of the

[1] *Ibid.*, p. 593.
[2] *Ibid.*
[3] *Ibid.*, p. 594.
[4] *Ibid.*, p. 597.
[5] *Ibid.*, p. 597f.
[6] *Ibid.*, p. 599.
[7] *Ibid.*, p. 599f.
[8] *Ibid.*, p. 600.

deepest uncertainty" [1]. Naturally, this is, in the first instance at least, an epistemological rather than an ontological point. The connection laid down between work and service in the community is established and maintained through the providence of God, and so holds even where it is not recognized or known. This relationship is simply another instance of the internal bond between creation and covenant. On this basis, Barth can assert a "factual orientation" of all human work on the divine service of faith and obedience [2].

In general terms, the ethical significance of work is that it serves the quite legitimate end of self-preservation. It is thus to be taken seriously as the activity in which man "sets himself to do what he can to guarantee his existence" [3]. The limitation set over this, which serves to recall the functional and teleological grounding of work, is that it must always be "an activity which is specifically human in character" [4]. The aim of work within the sphere of creaturely activity is the humanization of man. There are, accordingly, important criteria that can be applied to existing forms of work as a means of assessing their proximity to a fulfillment of obedience under the command of God.

The first criterion focuses on the need for all work to evidence a certain "objectivity" (Sachlichkeit), as man involves himself in the effort to attain the specific ends emergent within the work at hand [5]. Man's engagement with these ends, and his participation in the rules and procedures governing their realization, constitutes a measure of the seriousness of his approach to work. Where this seriousness is lacking, the ends for which a particular form of work is undertaken are achieved only haphazardly and deficiently, if at all. This criterion, and those that follow, it should be noted, are applied as stringently to the work of the community in its worship, praise and proclamation as to purely "secular" work [6].

The second criterion raises a question as to the validity and justification of the ends promoted by specific forms of work. The issue here is whether the ends in question lead in fact to an enhancement, enrichment or advancement of the human, or rather to the maintenance of artificial, manufactured desires and needs? The specific ends sought in a particular

---

[1] Ibid.
[2] Ibid., p. 601.
[3] Ibid., p. 603.
[4] Ibid., p. 604.
[5] Ibid., p. 605f.
[6] Cf. Ibid., p. 606f.

form of work are brought critically into focus in the question of their "worth" (*Würde*) [1]. Within the framework of contemporary patterns in labor-management relationships, Barth feels that the responsibility for the worth of work, and so for the possibility of "honest" work, must fall more heavily on employers than employees. In the larger perspective, however, the question of an effective relationship between work and meaningful ends is political in nature, for it leads inevitably to an analysis of the total ordering of a society [2]. The movement toward a solution that Barth proposes, at a societal level, falls back onto the *collective* responsibility of employees to consider seriously the question of the worth and honor of their work, and (perhaps) to refuse to participate in an ordering of labor that excludes these [3]. The thrust of Christian ethics at this point is not, however, in the direction of setting out general categories. Rather, its task is to make clear that there are boundaries and choices presented to the individual in the context of his work, and that he must exercise his discretion in choosing in a responsible way [4]. Nor is the individual left to his own resources in this venture. The place where issues are joined and concrete decisions taken is "the living ethos in the Christian community" [5].

The question posed by the third criterion of genuine human work is whether it promotes coexistence and cooperation among men. Where these are eliminated or submerged, man's work becomes subjected to motives of profit and competition, which results in the illusion that work can be pursued atomistically, without taking one's fellow-man into account [6]. The upshot of this sort of orientation is that work as a free act is impossible. The occurrence of work is thus shot through with the onerous fact of exploitation. The command of God stands as a summons to direct "counter-movements" against such dehumanizing drives and tendencies, which means concretely to stand with the weak against the strong, with those who are exploited against those who exploit [7]. In this issue, Barth argues, the Christian community must keep to the "left", yet without identifying exclusively with any of the proposed

---

[1] *Ibid.*, p. 608.
[2] *Ibid.*, p. 610f.
[3] *Ibid.*, p. 611f.
[4] *Ibid.*, p. 612f.
[5] *Ibid.*, p. 613.
[6] *Ibid.*, pp. 613ff.
[7] *Ibid.*, p. 624f.

solutions to it [1]. In this, it will be constantly alert to the relativity of every attempted resolution, and will look for no more than proximate success. The obedience of the community to the command of God, as it is led into engagement with the total context of work confronting it, will at best provide a measure of restraint to the dehumanizing pull of sin in that context [2].

The two final criteria of work that is authentically human are, respectively, those of "contemplation" or reflection and of "limitation" [3]. The importance of contemplation in man's work is that it draws attention to the fact that all work manifests an inner as well as an outer aspect. As Barth sees it, the relationship between the outer and inner, the obviously productive and the reflective, dimensions of work displays a persistent subtlety that must be taken into account. In some forms of work, the reflective demands upon external production and results are such as to subsume virtually the whole of a man, leaving little or no time for activity beyond the immediate and total demands of work [4]. Other contexts of work, on the contrary, that demand for the most part a merely "mechanical" response from the worker, call forth little or no reflection. This is not necessarily indicative of a problem, for it might give the individual "space and freedom" for creative inward activity [5]. Finally, there is the work of the artist, the poet, the scholar and the philosopher, which is primarily reflective, and which produces results in only a limited, perhaps sporadic, fashion [6]. The importance of this criterion lies in its insistence that contemplation or reflection forms an inevitable and necessary component of authentic work. The important distinction here is that although all forms of productive work require a corresponding dimension of inwardness, there are legitimate and important spheres of human activity that are carried out at the level of reflection alone. It is therefore not a necessity that internal work always be accompanied by a corresponding external manifestation [7].

---

[1] *Ibid.*

[2] *Ibid.*, p. 625f.

[3] *Ibid.*, pp. 627, 633.

[4] Barth provides no examples of people whose work levels this sort of demand. In contemporary society, perhaps the clearest examples of this are found in the work of a corporation executive or head of state.

[5] *Ibid.*, p. 628.

[6] *Ibid.*

[7] *Ibid.*, p. 630.

The limitation set over man's work is designed to draw attention to the fact that he does not secure his existence independently through his activity. The "active affirmation of his existence demanded of man as his outward and inward work" takes place correctly only "in concrete respect for the affirmation of his existence which is not his own affair but wholly the affair of God" [1]. An acknowledgement of this requires that man not allow his time to be subsumed totally by his work; he is therefore ordered to specific periods of "relaxation" [2]. It is in the rhythm established between work and rest that man is drawn out of himself in contemplation, and readied for an encounter with God's Word. The genuine rest that comes to man when he turns from the immediacy of his work to other forms of activity (for rest is not equatable with sheer inactivity) is ultimately a gift from God, and so dependent on his mercy [3]. The action of the Christian community cannot, therefore, guarantee a proper observance or use of the time man spends away from his work. There are obviously a variety of options for the filling of leisure time which, from the perspective of the command, and its total thrust toward the humanization of man, can only be viewed as negative possibilities. What the community can do, again, is to stand with those whose present working conditions exclude altogether the possibility of rest and recreation. It can join in the struggle for "a free Sunday, a free week-end, a shorter working week, and effective holidays" [4].

It is only in relation to man's vocation and work under the command of God that his honor can be discussed. In himself, man has no honor. He *receives* honor in a twofold sense, as he is first posited as the creature of God, and then called to service under the command [5]. "Honorable" human actions will therefore be actions that correspond to and confirm the honor God has shown man in creating him and granting him individual recognition in the claim for obedience. Although the question of obedience at this point cannot be determined through man's insight and analysis, there are, again, certain relatively constant criteria that can help to indicate the general direction of obedience.

Since man's honor devolves wholly from the fact that God, in positing man and calling him to service, wills to need and use him,

---

[1] *Ibid.*, p. 633.

[2] *Ibid.*

[3] *Ibid.*, pp. 636f., 647f.

[4] *Ibid.*, p. 642.

[5] *Ibid.*, p. 751f.

honorable human action will, in the first instance, always bear the character of service [1]. Second, honorable human action will always raise the question of man's "modesty" (*Bescheidung*) [2]. Man's honor depends completely on the event and action in which he is addressed by God, constituted a man, and called to service. The only response left man, then, is that of "pure thankfulness", given in the modest recognition that his honor "is before God and comes from him" [3].

The fact that honor is determined wholly by God will also entail, third, that man is directed away from attempts to establish independent "concepts of honor" [4]; and, finally, that the possibility of undertaking a defense of one's honor will be severely limited [5]. The former point is not meant to exclude all possibility of a degree of congeniality between the honor given man by God, and what is normally understood as honor. Ethically, its importance is to indicate the necessity of man's continual readiness to receive honor from God—perhaps in ways that are totally unexpected, whether this involves his exaltation or abasement [6]. Whether man's honor occurs in a dramatic or a quite ordinary form, the important point, ethically, is that he has it only as a gift.

It is the status of honor as a gift that sets, finally, a sharp limit to either the necessity or the justification for a defense of honor. The only real threat to man's honor would have to come from God. But since God acts only to secure the honor of man, we are called to act in cognizance of this, and so to refrain from a hasty concern to defend our honor [7]. Although steps may legitimately be taken to see that one's actions in response to the command are not distorted or misinterpreted, this does not extend to situations in which personal anger or irritation is the only thing at stake [8]. And any defensive maneuver must proceed in light of the solidarity set up between men by God. The question of the other person's honor (which is also given by God) will thus occupy as important a place as our own. In the end, the best defense of honor is provided by "the phenomenon of the truth of Christian existence" [9].

---

[1] *Ibid.*, p. 755f.
[2] *Ibid.*, p. 766.
[3] *Ibid.*, pp. 764, 767.
[4] *Ibid.*, p. 770f.
[5] *Ibid.*, pp. 780ff.
[6] *Ibid.*, p. 776f.
[7] *Ibid.*, p. 781f.
[8] *Ibid.*, p. 782f.
[9] *Ibid.*, p. 785.

It would be premature, at this juncture, to attempt an assessment of the effectiveness or ineffectiveness of Barth's transition from a general delineation of ethics as the command of God to its manifestation in those specific contexts of history and society within which man is called upon to respond and act in obedience. On the basis of the analysis, in this section, of his treatment of vocation and work (in particular), it is perhaps not too early to suggest a reservation and a modification that are beginning to take shape.

It is apparent, to begin with, that Barth's development of the particular or "special" dimensions of theological ethics is consistently related to a general concern for the humanization of man within culture achieved under the command [1]. The reservation in question has to do with Barth's description of the more precise contexts of culture within which man is called upon to enter into decision and action. It is clear that these have been stringently separated from mythologizing tendencies that lead in the direction of ideological commitment and finality. The Christian community, and, by implication, all men with it, is, as Charles West points out, freed to be "the guardian of the objectivity and validity of phenomenological truth about humanity and nature, against all ideologies", precisely because, in Jesus Christ, it "knows more than others of its reliability, and its friendliness to man" [2]. It may be questioned, however, whether Barth adequately safeguards the "objectivity and validity" required in an ethically perspicuous phenomenological analysis of cultural spheres. The difficulties in Barth's discussion appear to be twofold. The first obstacle to a genuine phenomenological approach to culture lies, oddly enough, in the very aspect of Barth's method designed ostensibly to insure that this will take place: his insistence on viewing culture in its totality only from a christological perspective. The problem here is that Barth never quite manages to turn sufficiently from his christological commitment to undertake a genuine phenomenological analysis. The

---

[1] The notion that man's central task, within the inclusive contours of culture, is the achievement of authentic *human* existence, is by no means new in Barth's thinking. It formed one of the central points in his early essay, "Church and Culture": "The command revives the promise which from the creation lies dormant in the law of nature; the law of nature is given, just because of the promise, necessity ... Sanctification, election for God, doing the will of God, is always in content being human. Men are to become men, not more than men; but also not less". This essay, written in 1928, is included in the volume: *Theology and Church.*

[2] *Communism and the Theologians*, p. 232.

ethically significant insights about cultural spheres come, not from empirical data and interpretation, but from Christology [1]. This is, of course, merely a continuation of the approach noted earlier in Barth's anthropology. There too, Barth was willing to give a qualified recognition to "phenomena of the human". It was clear, however, that the theologically and ethically important aspects of his anthropology emerged from a christological, rather than a phenomenological and empirical, background. Thus, although the sort of empirical data provided by the behavioral and social sciences is invested, from the perspective of faith, with at least a relative, limited significance, it never becomes clear that Barth utilizes it to even this limited extent [1]. A similar reluctance to involve himself in straightforward empirical analysis may be seen in his development of the categories of vocation, work and honor. The problem is not that all reference to the empirical data that fills out these categories in their historical manifestation is omitted. It is rather that Barth seems finally unable to decide whether they are viewed most appropriately from the ontological reordering of all things, including human culture, secured and promised in Jesus Christ; or from the "per nefas" continuation of the ambiguity and distortion occasioned by sin, which has lost all final power, but which still manages occasional eruptions within the human. Herein lies the second obstacle to an adequate phenomenological approach to culture.

The upshot of this indecisiveness is that when Barth does attempt to move at the level of empirical analysis, the results tend to be lacking in subtlety and completeness, and so remain unconvincing. One of the best examples of this occurs in his discussion of work, and of the necessity for the Christian community to stand against all forms of "exploitation" as an essential step in the direction of a humanization of labor. Barth's analysis of this problem proceeds essentially in terms of the distance and tension between employer and employee that emerge within capitalist economic structures. Professor West has argued (correctly, we believe) that Barth's early socialist background shows through in the moral condemnation he makes of capitalism, and in his positing of socialism as a necessary counter-force to it [2]. When the

---

[1] The persistence of this approach becomes even more obvious in the sections of special ethics that take up the issues of marriage and the family, the protection of life, and politics. Cf. below, sections 3 and 4.

[2] *Communism and the Theologians*, p. 185f.

alternatives are posed in this way, it is understandable that the "cure" proposed for the injustices of the economic order trades heavily on the collective power that resides in "the awakening of the working classes to a consciousness of their existing power when properly organized" [1]. This does not mean, of course, that Barth equates socialism with a "Christian" answer without remainder. Here too, the Christian community is cautioned against unlimited commitment. The difficulty, however, is that Barth's critique of the implications that a particular economic ordering carries for the humanization of labor relies on an almost stereotyped reading of capitalist and socialist alternatives. This results, however, in a failure to deal with the more obvious empirical distinctions and developments that characterize these alternatives in their contemporary forms. Barth makes only passing mention of the modifications of capitalism resulting from governmental control and regulation of monopolies, the give and take of collective bargaining, and the deployment of the "means of production" over a larger base through various profit-sharing plans and corporate ownership vested in stockholders, many of whom, of course, are employees of the firms whose stock they hold. Nor does he analyze the obvious distinctions holding between socialism as it has evolved, say, in the Scandinavian countries, Great Britain, or even, incipiently, in the United States; and as it has taken form in specifically Communist countries [2]. Finally, no mention is made of the "hardening" process that has overtaken some groups within organized labor, which at times results in a defense of the injustices of the *status quo*, and in the elimination of the revolutionary fervor that marked their beginning [3].

It is this lack of attention to important empirical distinctions, and the resulting tendency to view the ethical issue of genuine human work primarily in terms of class conflicts, that leads Professor West to charge that Barth "makes little contact with the ethical problems of Christians

---

[1] III/4, p. 624; Cf. *Ibid.*, p. 611f.

[2] Professor West's catalogue of Barth's *lacunae*, as regards the question of the empirical cogency of his analysis, is even more extensive than our own. Cf. *Communism and the Theologians*, p. 186, note 1.

[3] The tendency of some labor unions to justify existing conditions is a peculiarly acute problem in American society at present, in view of the concerted effort on the part of many to secure equal employment opportunities for minority groups. The irony of this situation, as Reinhold Niebuhr would delight in pointing out, is that the federal government is proving capable, at certain points, of a more decisive ethical commitment and action than labor.

as they actually present themselves in the economic order today" [1].
The problem here is not that Barth's theology excludes the possibility
of effective social action. As we have seen, the guidance and knowledge
given in faith can only issue in action, never in abstraction or contemplation. The difficulty is rather that the line of continuity between
theological formulation and empirical analysis is not always clear,
so that the latter, instead of displaying the sort of total openness that
would seem to follow from Barth's ordering of the categories of creation
and reconciliation, appears to be deficient in presentation, and to bear a
merely external relation to the former. It is obviously crucial to Barth's
development of a special ethics that the relation between these remain
clear and intact, for it is only on this basis that the definiteness and
continuity of the command can be given the degree of descriptive completeness required to undergird ethical decision and action.

This exposes the modification in question. In initially exploring
the command, we saw that it could in no sense be interpreted
as having only general significance. Rather, the definiteness in which
it impinged on a situation was such as to provide an exhaustive indication
of the shape and direction of human action, and so an unambiguous
grasp of the will of God for a specific situation. The strictness of this
view of the command excluded both the possibility and the necessity
for rational deliberation, leaving only the options of immediate obedience
or disobedience. The definiteness of the command served at this point
to underline its unconditional status as an explicit demand that eliminated completely the notion of behavioral options and alternatives:

> It is in just this definiteness that the command is unconditional, so that
> it leaves us no other choice except that between obedience and disobe-
> dience. Its unconditional character consists in the fact that, independently
> of our opinions and in each moment and relationship in which I find
> myself situated, it has the form that God in all seriousness always demands
> something specific from me ... The human decision that is mine in face
> of the divine command does not consist in a decision of the question
> whether this or that possibility is good, or whether the command demands
> this or that of me, or of whether I should do this or that—this question
> would be about as significant and fitting as the question whether there
> is indeed a God, who or what he is, and how and what we are allowed
> to think of him where he has already decided all these things in his Word
> and revelation, and where our task can consist only in reflecting quite ex-
> plicitly on what has been said to us in his Word. My decision, the human

---

[1] *Communism and the Theologians*, p. 186, note 1.

ethical decision, is whether, in my action, I conform to the command
which encounters and confronts me in the most specific and pointed
form; whether I shall be obedient or disobedient to it, whether for my
part I shall meet it according to my election (the election of Jesus Christ!)
as a believer or an unbeliever [1].

I have intentionally quoted this passage again, because it leaves
no doubt as to the focus Barth wished to give the notion of command in
his original formulation of it. As man is encountered by the command in
its total particularity within a given context, he is also brought under the
unity and continuity it exhibits within the overarching movement of
covenant-history. It is precisely the diversity of the command within
this continuous unity which insures that the required specificity in which
it shapes the total operational matrix of the individual will not dissolve
into sheer atomism.

In the sections of special ethics that we have examined, there appears
to be a discernible modification of the stringency of Barth's initial
handling of the command. It is perhaps true that this occurs in spite
of, rather than because of, Barth's intentions, since, as noted earlier,
he begins the volume of the *Dogmatics* devoted to the special ethics of
creation by asserting that the command

> leaves nothing to human choice or discretion. It thus requires no inter-
> pretation to come into force. To the last and smallest detail it is self-
> interpreted, and in this form it confronts man as a command already
> in force [2].

If taken at face value, this would indeed exclude every possibility of
rational deliberation, leaving only the option of "instant obedience" [3].
Any modification of Barth's position on this point cannot result in a
lessening of the emphasis placed on the centrality of the notions of
command and obedience. Appropriate human action will still be identified exclusively with the submission and obedience of the Christian
community to the directing activity of the Holy Spirit [4]. Beyond this,
what I are suggesting is that Barth's exposition of the divine command
and human obedience in relation to the more limited spheres and relationships marked off by the action of God provides, perhaps unconsciously,
for a broadening of man's participation in the command at the point

---

[1] II/2, p. 745f.
[2] III/4, p. 11.
[3] IV/2, p. 613.
[4] III/3, p. 298f.

of rational deliberation, assessment and choice. Naturally, this is not to suggest that human reason is given an autonomous role in theological ethics. It functions only as a limited vehicle of recognition and assessment, which is always susceptible of distortion through an attempted elevation of itself beyond its valid capacities. That it has a valid place in special ethics is indicated by the way in which Barth seems willing to recognize the fact that man is confronted, within the sphere of creaturely occurrence and action, with a range of *empirical* possibilities that call forth a deliberation and weighing of alternatives, and so necessitate a choice. Actually, it is perhaps not altogether surprising that rational deliberation should find a place in special ethics, since confession and prayer, the basic ethical actions of the Christian community, are both described by Barth, in their relationship to man's knowledge of God, as "the basic act of human reason" [1].

The broadening of the ethical context to include (implicitly) rational assessment and choice can be seen, I feel, at the following points. To begin with, it is clear that the development of special ethics does not provide a final answer to the ethical question. This means, however, that *no* formulated ethics as such can exhaustively describe either the command, or human obedience under the command. The freedom of God, and the corresponding freedom in which man is placed, preclude that sort of finality. What special ethics can do is to indicate the more prominent lines that mark off the spheres and relationships within which creaturely action occurs. Barth does this by describing the various "contours" of vocation, work and honor. Within these, it is possible to detect a degree of flexibility, and a multiplicity of structural and behavioral options, that presuppose continuous rational moral deliberation if human action is to achieve any degree of conformity to the command. So, within his given temporality, man is counseled to "seize the day" and actualize the unique opportunity confronting him. He is reminded of the urgency surrounding the necessity of his moving freely from the past into the future, exhorted to remain sensitive and open to the precise configurations of his external, historical situation, and faced with the importance of continuous self-examination in order to discern, as fully as possible, his peculiar limitations of aptitude and ability. Although his precise sphere of activity is ultimately grounded in the providential ordering of all creaturely activity and occurrence by God, man remains responsible for a correct (i.e., obedient) choice of a particular vocation

---

[1] III/4, pp. 79, 95.

or work; for an existence within that context that is open and sensitive to the tasks and requirements it brings, as well as to the interrelationship between his own sphere of activity and those of his neighbors; and for a continual readiness to be drawn from one sphere of activity into another. Finally, he is called upon to work actively for the humanization of all spheres of creaturely life, and so for the securing and protection of man's genuine vocation and honor before God within the general contours of human culture. And all of this activity takes place in response to the simplicity of the command under which man is placed: service in love to God and the neighbor. Within the Christian community, then, and occasionally outside it as well, man is enabled to perform actions that provide him with a positive opinion as to his obedience or disobedience to that command [1].

It seems obvious that Barth's development of these points presupposes, implicitly, both the importance and the unavoidability of rational deliberation. The definiteness of the command to the contrary notwithstanding, the notions of awareness, sensitivity, openness and choice marking human decision and action all point in the direction of an awareness of the behavioral and empirical options that confront man. This entails, however, that the options open to Christians within human culture cannot be placed neatly within the simple either—or alternative of obedience or disobedience. This might do as an ontological description of man's condition under the command. When extended into the empirical matrix within which human behavior takes shape, however, it results in confusion, for unless man is faced with real alternatives, no sense can be attached to the notion of responsible choice. Empirically, of course, we are faced with alternatives at all of the critical junctures where action is required. Nor is the choice between these in any sense clear-cut. There are subtleties and shadings present that may place several alternatives in a favorable light. It is precisely this fact that calls forth the best use of our capacities. I would argue that rational deliberation can be given an appropriate place in theological ethics without falling into a dependence on rules or principles. Within the formative action of the command, a recognition of the legitimate place of reason in theological ethics can serve to indicate the complexity of the context in which we are called upon to act, thereby avoiding a reduction of the empirical factors and variables that surround human behavior. It is only when rational deliberation is included within theolog-

---

[1] III/4, p. 704.

ical ethics that Christians become, in Professor West's words, "simply
and truly human in a relative and practical way, objective, relative,
realistic in [their] thinking, and perceptively helpful in [their] actions
toward other men" [1]. I have argued that Barth provides, implicitly
at least, a legitimate place for moral assessment and choice within his
special ethics. That this remains for the most part implicit is indicative,
perhaps, of the fact that Barth is not wholly successful in bringing about
a transition from a general statement of human response under the
command to a description of the form this takes within the specific
empirical contexts of human culture. At any rate, it seems clear that an
emphasis on he command and obedience does not and cannot exclude
rational deliberation. As we shall see, this judgment will be borne out
in the succeeding sections of this chapter.

3. *Freedom in Fellowship and Life*

Human action under the command is directed at all points toward
the neighbor. Within this general determination, there are certain
relational structures that are central to the maintenance of human
fellowship: the "encounter" between man and woman, and the "relationship" between parents and children, and between near and distant
neighbors [2]. The fact that Barth discusses the ethical dimensions of
these levels of human encounter and fellowship before turning to a
description of the importance of the command for the givenness of
man's life and existence as such, reminds us again that the fundamental
pattern and determination of man's being is not his existence as an
individual, but his position within the created constant of I - Thou
relationality [3]. There is also an order of priority holding between the
three relational structures mentioned above. The encounter between
man and woman, and the relationship between parents and children,
are both informed by "a specific command and a specific obedience" [4].
This provides these relationship with an obvious and irreducible strictness, the importance of which is made clear in Barth's assertion that
"as concerns fellow-humanity, the necessary determination of human
nature by creation has its limit in the relationship between man and

---

[1] *Communism and the Theologians*, p. 233.
[2] III/4, p. 127.
[3] *Ibid.*, p. 367f.
[4] III/4, p. 345.

woman and parents and children" [1]. In the relationship between near
and distant neighbors, however, there is no specific command, and so no
specific obedience. It does not indicate a "constant determination" of
man, but serves only as one manifestation of God's providential ruling of
creaturely history and occurrence, and so as "the concrete presupposition
under which he must hear the command and will and do the right" [2].
Barth's refusal to invest national identities and interrelationships with
final or constant validity will carry important consequences for his views
concerning an adequate theological approach to the State, and the ethical
participation of Christians in the political order. Of course, the relatively
superior position and function of the relationships between man and
woman and parents and children does not mean that they can be legitimately apotheosized as divine orders. They remain throughout fully
human, and so natural and historical relationships within which man is
called to an appropriation and exercise of genuinely creaturely freedom,
and to responsibility and service to his fellow-man [3].

The first point that must be made, as regards the question of man's
obedience to the command within his differentiated identity as male and
female, is that this is an issue involving the whole man in the totality
of this encounter. By insisting on this point, Barth seeks to avoid a
reduction of the larger issue posed by this encounter for theological
ethics to the more limited questions of sex and marriage [4]. What is at
stake here is a recognition that the command of God within the sphere
of male-female relationships is correctly understood only as a summons
to freedom and responsibility. It is the concrete indication that man is
not left to his own devices and constructions, and the mythic restrictions
and absoluteness he tends to read into that sphere. Under the command
of God, the encounter between man and woman, and the being of man
in that relationship, is thoroughly relativized [5]. It is the relativizing
thrust of the command that enables man to exist with complete natural-

---

[1] *Ibid.*, p. 344.

[2] *Ibid.*, p. 343f.

[3] *Ibid.*, pp. 127f., 138.

[4] A tendency that Barth feels gained expression in Brunner's work,
Das Gebot und die Ordnungen, Vierte, Photomechanisch Gedruckte Auflage
(Zürich: Zwingli-Verlag, 1939). Brunner apparently manages to avoid the
sort of apotheosizing approach Barth finds in Schleiermacher, Walter Schubart
and Theodor Bovet. *Ibid.*, pp. 130f., 134ff.

[5] *Ibid.*, p. 133f.

ness, openness and spontaneity within the total reach of this encounter. The lines of obedient action within this sphere will fall under an embracing pattern of relationality that touches man's existence as male and female at every point, and that results in an initial "decentralization" of the rule of marriage [1].

Because the differentiated identity of man provided in the encounter between male and female constitutes a dimension of his vocation, a description of the order it displays under the command will fall within the same limitations Barth sets over anthropology and vocation as a whole. This means, first, that it will not be possible to describe and define exhaustively the differentiation of male and female, any more than man's vocation can be fully detailed; and second, that the point of departure lies in the knowledge provided by revelation and Christology, and not in a phenomenology or typology of the sexes [2]. Theological ethics at this point stands under the limitation and determination given man and woman as they are summoned to their true natures under the divine command. Authentic human existence within this relationship can only be discovered; it can never result from independent theoretical or empirical constructions [3].

The "disjunction and conjunction" of man and woman is set within the controlling framework of a definite order [4]. An elucidation of this order forms the first step in determining the precise contours of the command that insure a correct exercise of creaturely freedom within this sphere. The order in which man and woman are placed is one involving "succession", and so a definite "preceding and following, super- and subordination" [5]. This is not an order of "inner inequality", but one in which the equality of man and woman falls along the lines of a functional inequality. The equality-within-inequality of

---

[1] *Ibid.*, p. 155.

[2] *Ibid.*, pp. 166f., 168ff.

[3] "To what male or female nature must they remain true? Precisely to that to which they are summoned and obligated here and now by the command of God—to that which it imposes on them as it encounters them with its immediate requirement. As it encounters them, their particular sexual nature will not be hidden from them. In this way, the command of God allows man and woman continually and particularly to discover their special sexual natures, and to be faithful to it in this form which is true before God, without being bound to preconceived opinions". *Ibid.*, p. 170.

[4] *Ibid.*, p. 187f.

[5] *Ibid.*, p. 189.

this order is secured by the fact that its observance is imposed as an obligation on all [1]. The inequality of the order lies in the fact that within it man occupies a superior, and woman a subordinate, position. This does not mean that man is given privilege or advantage over woman, any more than it entails the belittling or degradation of woman. Rather, it indicates that man and woman approach a realization of their true co-humanity only as they recognize that this occurs within the definite place and function they are assigned [2].

The model for the order in which man and woman are placed in their co-humanity is found in the superiority of Christ over man, and his subordination before God [3]. The superiority of Christ is given continuation in the relationship that exists between him and the Christian community; and his subordination is ontologically grounded in the eternal relation between Father and Son in the Trinity. Analogically, the order in which man is male and female is established as a direct extension of the basic form of humanity. Man is thus the *kephale* of woman, just as Christ is the "head" of the community. This does not imply the construction of a metaphysical ladder, however; woman's relationship to God is mediated through Christ, not through man. Man and woman are both adapted, within their relationship, to an order in which Christ is the true head [4]. It is, accordingly, an order grounded in Gospel, not Law, within which both man and woman are called to responsible freedom.

The submission required of woman within this order stands as an analogue of the submission to Christ enjoined upon all Christians. In her submission to man, woman functions as the prototype of the community in its relation to Christ. Man, similarly, in his function as head of the woman, acts as a "copy and reflection" of the action of Christ [5]. Within this definite order and sequence, the functions of man and woman take shape. Their tasks can therefore not be exchanged or confused through either separation or equation. Nor can they be legitimately avoided by attempting to transcend one's identity as male or female [6]. It is only within the order of male *and* female that human

---

[1] *Ibid.*
[2] *Ibid.*, pp. 170f., 189f.
[3] *Ibid.*, p. 193.
[4] III/4, p. 193f.
[5] *Ibid.*, p. 195.
[6] *Ibid.*, pp. 173ff.

sexuality as male *or* female is realized, and the questions posed by the encounter between man and woman can be heard and answered [1].

The first thing required by the command, accordingly, is that man maintain this order [2]. The question of what this will mean, in terms of obedient action, cannot be decided on in advance. The order in question is always determined by the freedom of God in his action, not by attempts to elaborate final ethical systems. The emphasis thus falls primarily on the reality of the relationship in which man and woman find themselves. It is only against the background of this relationship that its order can be noted and discussed [3]. Against this background, man is enabled to move toward obedience by assuming responsibility for preserving and maintaining the order. And woman achieves a similar movement toward obedience through a continuous exercise of self-restraint [4]. In this fashion, both man and woman are brought into a creative and fulfilling dynamic, and so placed on the way to achieving a mature and responsible co-humanity.

The ordered relationship of man and woman provides the general contours within which a discussion of marriage and sex *per se* can take place. The order of the relationship between male and female, since it touches all persons, entailed a preliminary decentralization of marriage, since Barth views the latter as a special vocation to which only certain persons are called [5]. This does not mean that the ethical dimensions of the command within marriage are neutralized and isolated so as to carry no consequences for the larger context of male-female relationships. Marriage, on the contrary, is for Barth the "center and *telos*" of the whole sphere of male and female [6]. This will mean not only that the ethical lines laid down within the ordered relationship of man and woman apply to marriage, but also that marriage itself sets certain directions and requirements under the command that reach back into that larger sphere. In this respect, then, it follows that within the total sphere of male and female "everything is good which in the full and strict sense is compatible with marriage, and everything is bad which is not so compatible" [7]. As the "exemplary form of the encounter of

---

[1] *Ibid.*, pp. 185ff.
[2] *Ibid.*, p. 196.
[3] *Ibid.*, p. 182.
[4] *Ibid.*, pp. 197f., 201f.
[5] *Ibid.*, p. 205f.
[6] *Ibid.*, p. 202.
[7] *Ibid.*, p. 155.

the sexes", marriage provides a universal criterion for what can be said generally about that encounter [1]. In making this point, Barth is arguing the cruciality of marriage as an ethical paradigm, rather than some kind of social or psychological necessity within the human that makes it unavoidable. So, although marriage is the "natural home" of every man and woman, there may be good reasons for remaining outside it [2].

When marriage is set under the command of God, it emerges as "a supremely particular divine vocation" [3]. Initially, it is not a matter simply of human choice, but of the divine calling and decision that frees man for the obedience required by the command within the special context of marriage. Descriptively, marriage is "the special life-partnership established and maintained between a particular man and a particular woman" [4]. The fulfillment of this life-partnership forms the first task of marriage, and provides the criterion and center for the various desires, needs and goals that emerge within that relationship. The special relationship between two persons in marriage is not a means to achieving certain ends. Rather, it is viewed correctly as an end in itself, a *sui generis* relationship within which "husband and wife form a sphere of fellowship separate from children and family" [5].

Marriage as a life-partnership is marked by the qualities of fulness, exclusiveness and permanence. These qualities distinguish the marriage relationship sharply from other forms of encounter between man and woman, and indicate the special ethical requirements under which it is placed. The first requirement is that the persons involved exist in total mutuality as "one body" [6]. This means neither a loss of individuality nor a total knowledge of the other person. What is at issue here is the living out of a mutually total orientation of two persons on each other [7]. It is this "being and persistence in the orientation of a specific man on a specific woman, and vice versa", that provides "the determination and limit of that freedom" that follows the recognition and acceptance of the responsibility imposed by marriage [8].

---

[1] *Ibid.*, p. 203.
[2] *Ibid.*, pp. 203ff.
[3] *Ibid.*, p. 205.
[4] *Ibid.*, p. 209.
[5] *Ibid.*, p. 211.
[6] *Ibid.*, p. 212.
[7] *Ibid.*, p. 214.
[8] *Ibid.*

The fulness enjoined by the total orientation of two persons on each other in marriage provides the only proper context for considering the act of sexual intercourse. The specific problems this raises for theological ethics cannot be given independent treatment. The reason for this limitation lies in the "rule" governing all encounters between man and woman, which specifies that the sexual dimension of these encounters must always be seen in relation to the total context of the lives of the persons involved [1]. Sexual intercourse, accordingly, is not intelligible in itself. Even within the marriage relationship, Barth argues, sexual intercourse "for itself and as such" is "an inhuman business excluded under the command of God" [2]. The position Barth takes in this matter should not be taken as a sign of puritanical nervousness about the body. The command of God that calls man to freedom in his given co-humanity "requires no liberation from sex", much less a denial or repression of it [3]. What it does call for, however, is a rejection of the notion of "sovereign physical sexuality" [4]. In addition to demythologizing sex, Barth also undertakes to rid it of its demonic overtones of priority and control. The command of God "claims the whole man", and so brings about "the sanctification of physical sexuality and the sex relationship" [5]. Under the command, man is given the freedom to live in the ordered unity of soul and body as a person, and to encounter others on this basis. Man's being and activity in their specifically sexual manifestations fall under the command "only in its relationship with the whole historical being of man before God and in fellowship" [6]. The question of obedience to the formative action of God must always be assessed in relation to man's place in the total interplay and coordination between creaturely and divine history. When this is taken into account, it follows necessarily that "coitus without co-existence is demonic" [7]. The proper approach to the free obedience required of man lies in the direction neither of promiscuity nor legalism, but in a recognition of and participation in the humanizing action of God in the world. As man is drawn into the context of faith, and made a member of the Christian community, he is set loose from the destructive pull of both quasi-moral libidinal

---

[1] *Ibid.*, p. 144f.
[2] *Ibid.*, p. 302.
[3] *Ibid.*, p. 145.
[4] *Ibid.*, p. 146.
[5] *Ibid.*
[6] *Ibid.*
[7] *Ibid.*, p. 148.

repression and unfettered libidinal indulgence, and is readied for an acceptance and expression of sexuality that is informed by a persistent awareness of his own humanity and that of others [1].

The ethical issues that are raised when the exclusiveness and permanence of marriage are viewed as requirements of the divine command are, respectively, those of monogamy and divorce. Since marriage is a total orientation of two persons on each other, it clearly admits no third person to

> the mystery of that element of life and joy that forms the center of the whole, in relation to the task and work which is to be done by the couple, in the dialectic of freedom, community and order which it is the human destiny of these two and these two alone to live and suffer through, and for better or worse to master [2].

Marriage denotes the choice of a particular man or woman with whom one enters into a total relationship. Humanly speaking, it is an act of full commitment that is grounded in love. In itself, however, love provides an insufficient basis for monogamy, for although every marriage so grounded aims at the "right choice", as a human action it is always subject to error and disappointment. Monogamy, accordingly, becomes an unconditional requirement for love and marriage only when these are related directly to the command of God [3]. Viewed in this way, monogamy is "the content of the divine command ... to the extent that this is the command of the gracious God who is free, but who freely elects in his grace" [4]. Monogamy emerges as a binding norm for marriage only when it is seen, within man's co-humanity, as a reflection of the particularity of the covenant shown in God's election of Israel, Christ and the Christian community. Monogamy is thus secured on an ontological and transcendent, rather than an immanent, basis [5]. For the Christian community, this means that monogamy, love and marriage have no independent validity or authority. They become authoritative only through the command of God given in the action of Christ [6]. And, since the encounter between man and woman rests on the relation be-

---

[1] *Ibid.*, p. 148f. Professor Lehmann's treatment of sexuality shows a marked similarity to Barth's. Cf. *Ethics in a Christian Context*, pp. 133ff.

[2] III/4, p. 218.

[3] *Ibid.*, p. 221.

[4] *Ibid.*

[5] *Ibid.*, p. 222f.

[6] *Ibid.*, p. 225.

tween Christ and the community, monogamy, as an aspect of the command, will fall under Gospel rather than Law. Or, to put the matter more subtly, it will appear as the imperative dimension (Law) of the indicative (Gospel) pronounced in Christ on the totality of the encounter between man and woman. Monogamy, then, is

> an invitation, permission and freedom to represent and symbolize in this human form of fellowship the fellowship of God with man, in the choice of love his free, gracious election, in the covenant of marriage the faithfulness of his covenant ... [1].

There are two important restrictions placed over the rule of monogamy. The first of these underlines the fact that monogamy, like marriage and love, is in all respects a natural, creaturely structure and transaction. Its function, accordingly, is strictly penultimate; it neither has, nor can it legitimately be given, eschatological import. Ethically, this means that the possibility of a second marriage, following the death of one of the partners, is, if not automatic, at least defensible [2].

The second restriction has to do with the activity of the Church in cultures where polygamy is a social and legal institution. The task of the community at this juncture is limited to the proclamation of the command concerning monogamy. It is not called upon to defend monogamy as an institution against polygamy. The issue of correct action in this matter thus becomes a matter of the specific cultural context in which the Church operates, an awareness of the importance of existing social structures for the maintenance of human community and life within it, and a sensitivity to realistic options in the area of concrete actions [3].

Under the divine command, marriage becomes a "lasting life-partnership" [4]. The permanence required of marriage is grounded in the "fidelity" of God to man in establishing and maintaining the covenant. It is this fidelity that guarantees permanence to man and the world [5]. So "permanence", like monogamy, forms the content of the divine command. The ethical direction set by the command is thus decisively against the possibility of divorce. The act of marriage cannot legitimately be related to the notions of "erotic experimentation",

[1] *Ibid.*, p. 221f.
[2] *Ibid.*, p. 226f.
[3] *Ibid.*, p. 227f.
[4] *Ibid.*, p. 228.
[5] *Ibid.*, p. 228f.

"trial marriage", or "provisional association" [1]. It is important to stress that the command sets an ethical *direction* away from divorce. The New Testament restrictions on this matter cannot be turned into an inflexible law, for they are placed exclusively with the context of Gospel, and the responsible exercise of freedom to which it calls man [2].

However, the obedience required by the command cannot be guaranteed by man, for he cannot himself establish marriage as an indissoluble union. Every marriage stands under the question whether it has been sanctioned and joined together by God. The question of permanence must always be approached and answered in the act of faith that seizes the divine promise concerning marriage. When this attitude of seriousness takes hold, it is possible that the basis of a particular marriage will lie in human capriciousness rather than the action of God, so that "in spite of all appearance to the contrary it has never been genuinely concluded and established" [3]. It is this possibility that makes divorce, in certain exceptional cases, a defensible and appropriate action. This does not in any way authorize the sort of misguided calculation that surrounds the ease with which the decision for divorce is reached in contemporary culture. For the Christian, divorce will always be a "highly extraordinary decision" that can be undertaken only as an *ultima ratio* [4]. As an *ultima ratio*, however, even the Christian may find himself and his marriage placed before God's judgment, and so forced to recognize that his marriage was a mistake from the beginning. Such a recognition may even entail the final step of legally dissolving the marriage. Special care must be exercised at this point, for two reasons. First, because the entry into legal proceedings signals a point of no return for the marriage in question. The Christian is therefore cautioned to consider with extreme care every possibility short of legally ending his marriage, to see whether he might recognize the failure of his marriage without resorting to this final step, or whether he might, finally, decide to remain in patience and hope within it [5]. The second reason why special care must be shown in moving to the point of legal proceedings is that these are

---

[1] *Ibid.*, p. 231.

[2] *Ibid.*, p. 230.

[3] *Ibid.*, p. 236.

[4] *Ibid.*, p. 237.

[5] *Ibid.*, p. 237f. One is led to wonder, at this point, what Barth might have in mind when he asserts that there are ways other than that of legal dissolution to give effect to the fact that a marriage stands under the divine judgment.

not a part of the divine command concerning marriage. The action of legal dissolution, Barth argues, belongs to marriage only as an institution [1]. And, as an institution, marriage operates within a completely pre-eschatological context that trades on "the old hardness of heart" [2]. Within the context of faith, however, the prohibition against recourse to civil law cannot form a general principle. The believer will therefore move into that situation as a sign of his willingness to accept God's complete judgment on his marriage. Because of this, the attitude of the Christian community can only be one of extreme reservation, not an inclusive prohibition, against the legal dissolution of marriage [3].

The exclusiveness and permanence of marriage that issue in the ethical directives concerning monogamy and divorce, although grounded in the command of God, point obviously toward the external, visible dimensions of the relationship. When marriage is placed under the divine command, it necessarily assumes "the character of a responsible act outwards in relation to those around" [4]. We have already seen that the decision legally to dissolve a marriage can, *ultima ratio*, bear this character. The issue now centers on the more regular forms that govern the exercise and fulfillment of one's responsibility toward society in the event of marriage.

The transition from love to marriage brings about the establishment of "a new sociological unit", and so requires participation "in the nearer, the more distant and the most distant events in the surrounding, contemporary world" [5]. This participation is effected through a public recognition of "the domestic, legal and ecclesiastical institution of marriage" [6]. The recognition of these institutional structures centers

---

[1] *Ibid.*, p. 238.

[2] *Ibid.*

[3] *Ibid.*, p. 238f. Barth's distinction between marriage as an institution, and as a total, exclusive and permanent life-partnership under the command, is not entirely clear. Specifically, it is difficult to see why the "ultima ratio" of legal proceedings leading to divorce could not be brought under the command at the point of judgment. As we have seen, the command carries a persistent overtone of judgment, as well as a claim and a decision, against all human action. And the Christian, presumably, in taking the step of legal dissolution, would at that point, as everywhere, be acting in free obedience to the command—even though the dimension of judgment becomes piercingly central in his decision and action there.

[4] III/4, p. 251.

[5] *Ibid.*, p. 252.

[6] *Ibid.*, p. 254.

in the wedding ceremony, which forms a public declaration of marriage, but does not, in itself, constitute it. The declaration given in a wedding calls forth a reciprocal recognition and understanding from the surrounding structures it touches. For the parents, who as the domestic side of the institution of marriage are the "nearest neighbors" of the couple, this will take the form of an "intensive counseling" that steers clear of "command, prohibition or obligatory obedience" [1]. The legal recognition given by the State consists simply in the acknowledgement that the required ordinances and formalities of civil society have been fulfilled, and that the marriage in question is, in that respect, concluded [2]. The recognition given by the Christian community signifies that a particular marriage occurs as an event in its life. It is not necessary that this event occur as a church wedding. What is necessary and so central to the recognition given by the community is that it provide a "pastoral exhortation" declaring the marriage to be concluded before God and under his command, and so reminding the participants of the seriousness of the responsibility that is now theirs [3]. Finally, it must be noted that the observance of these institutional structures, and the recognition they provide for marriage, is a matter more of direction and desire than of binding ethical requirement. There may be legitimate cases where such observance is not possible, in which the marriage will have to occur without recognition by one or more of the institutional structures. These cases, however, will be the exception rather than the rule. The general direction set over marriage is toward a recognition of the validity of institutional forms, and so toward a seeking of their acceptance and affirmation of a marriage [4].

The discussion of the ethical contours of marriage thus far has centered primarily on what may be described as its eternal, ontological basis in covenant-history, and its objective, empirical basis in the recognition afforded by the domestic, legal and ecclesiastical communities. There is also an inner side to marriage that reveals the human basis of the life-partnership between two persons. The importance of this aspect of Barth's discussion is that it provides the appropriate context within which to explore the relationship that occurs in marriage between *eros* and *agape*, and to indicate the legitimate place of the former. As we shall

---

[1] *Ibid.*

[2] *Ibid.*, p. 255.

[3] *Ibid.*, p. 255f.

[4] *Ibid.*, p. 257.

see, it appears necessary to distinguish between Barth's comments on the acceptability of *eros* within marriage, and his discussion of the relationship, or, more accurately perhaps, the lack of relationship, between *eros* and the *agape* love the Christian community is required to embody in its service [1].

The fact that every legitimate marriage has its ontological origin and basis in the covenant between God and man exhibited in Jesus Christ, and the command issuing from this, must not obscure the "specific and mutual recognition, choice and love of two human beings of opposite sexes" [2]. It is the inner basis of marriage formed by the choice and love of two persons for each other that provides the proper counterpart to the free decision and election of God surrounding all creaturely occurrence, and, in particular, his calling of these persons to the special work of marriage [3]. The emphasis Barth places on the love that occurs between man and woman emphasizes again his refusal to invest marriage with quasi-metaphysical or apotheosizing overtones. The fact that the marriage ultimately rests on the decision and command of God leads neither to a determinism of "inspiration" nor to an undercutting of human decision and choice [4]. As a special vocation and calling, marriage remains a thoroughly human, creaturely relationship. The divine calling and union, then, can never be presumed beforehand; they can only be sought, in faith, at the point of free decision [5]. The love between two persons provides both the necessary and the sufficient condition for an actualization of this freedom. In this respect, Barth can argue that marriage "becomes and is and remains true marriage primarily and directly in virtue of its inner origin" in human love and decision [6].

The love in question consists in a "reciprocal understanding, self-giving and desire" [7]. In true love, desire has its correct place and function, for it is preceded and ordered by the self-giving of two persons to each other. True love will therefore be "reasonable love" (*vernünftige Liebe*), for it embodies a total orientation and concern that goes beyond mere physical attraction [8]. Within this sort of love-relationship, the idea of

---

[1] Cf. IV/2, Par. 68, Pts. 1 and 3.
[2] III/4, p. 240.
[3] *Ibid.*, p. 241f.
[4] *Ibid.*, p. 241.
[5] *Ibid.*, p. 244f.
[6] *Ibid.*, p. 242.
[7] *Ibid.*, p. 246.
[8] *Ibid.*, p. 247.

eros can be legitimately employed. True *eros* presupposes the mutual
agreement between two persons that moves toward its natural culmination in marriage. Marriage thus forms the criterion of true love, just
as true love forms the inner basis of marriage [1]. The final test of a love
which is obedient to the command, and which has the potentiality of
becoming "sanctified *eros*", lies in the relationship it has to *agape* [2].
Genuine love is grounded, finally, only in faith, and participation in the
community of faith. It thus presupposes that the persons involved move
toward the culmination of their love in marriage with a sense of responsibility toward God, so that they are united not only in *eros*, but in *agape*
as well [3]. When the necessary relationship between *eros* and *agape* is
made the criterion of the human in the area of true love, the genuineness
of mixed marriages, and marriages between unbelievers, is called into
question [4].

The interesting thing about Barth's discussion of the love that forms
the inner basis of marriage is that it allows for a positive treatment of
eros. When it is filled out and informed by the richness of a total commitment and orientation between two persons, so that their relationship
includes, but is not controlled by, physical desire, it is admissable,
within the context of faith, to speak of a "sanctified" *eros* that forms
the proper creaturely counterpart to *agape*. Both *eros* and *agape*, at this
point, relate positively to the freedom given man, in faith, to be open
and obedient to God, and to establish meaningful relationships with his
fellow-man. The line between created and reconciled human nature,
between man's freedom to be *with*, and his freedom to be *for*, his fellow-
man, is caught up and given expression in the possibility of a new and
complete co-humanity emergent in faith. Human nature is thus not
directly identified with either *eros* or *agape*, but, as Barth suggests in his
opening discussion of anthropology, is a *tertium datur* between these [5].
The important thing to notice here is that *eros* is, within the occurrence
of natural, creaturely love, given a positive significance and function.

---

[1] *Ibid.*, p. 248f.
[2] *Ibid.*, p. 249f.
[3] *Ibid.*, p. 250.
[4] The *particula veri* of the Pietist doctrine of marriage, Barth asserts,
is that "humanly speaking, it is difficult to see how two human beings can find
themselves in the true love which is the basis of marriage except in the common
consciousness of performing thus an act of communal responsibility towards
God". *Ibid.*, p. 251.
[5] III/2, pp. 337, 343f.

To be sure, it is here a matter of what Barth refers to as "sanctified *eros*", in which the element of desire has been placed within the ordering matrix of a total life-orientation and partnership. When this is kept in mind, *eros* has its legitimate place, and does not fall into conflict with *agape*. Indeed, at this point in the discussion, *eros* is filled out with the dimension of self-giving usually associated with *agape* love.

It is surprising to find, after the positive treatment given *eros* as an indispensable dimension of the inner genesis of marriage, that Barth appears to shift his position decisively when he moves into a discussion of Christian love. The movement in Barth's position occurs it seems, between his elaboration of the special ethics of creation (III/4) and his discussion of Christian love in the second volume of the doctrine of reconciliation (IV/2). In order to state clearly the difference between these, it is necessary to recall briefly the previous discussion of love as an aspect of the freedom given man in the action of the Holy Spirit [1]. There we saw that as man is encountered by the Holy Spirit and brought directly into the context of the event of his sanctification, he is provided with the directing impetus of the command, and enabled to engage in acts of self-giving. These are acts of Christian love, which form the immediate external counterpart to the act of faith in which man receives God's Word [2].

The act of love is, of course, directed toward both God and man. Although there is need to exercise caution lest the former result in religious eroticism, it is still true that there is a proper love that man is called upon to direct toward God that cannot be identified with love for the neighbor [3]. The exercise of love to the neighbor requires a certain "proximity" between the one who loves and the one (or many) who are loved [4]. The proximity required for the action of love is not a function simply of geographical or temporal factors, though these obviously come into consideration. What is required essentially for the act of love is a historical connection within the context of an event that places men together in love. The event that provides the required historical connection is, of course, the total sweep of covenant-history centering in the reconciliation accomplished in Christ. This means that the com-

---

[1] Cf. above, Ch. Four, Section B, Part 2: "The Marks of Freedom: Faith, Love and Hope".

[2] IV/2, p. 829.

[3] *Ibid.*, pp. 901ff.

[4] *Ibid.*, p. 910f.

mand to love falls within a "closed circle" [1]. In the Old Testament, the exercise of love is restricted to those within the community of Israel; in the New Testament, to members of the Christian community. There is, then, an initial ethical restriction placed on the enactment of love. Since the exercise of love, as Barth sees it, depends on the prior reality of a shared faith, it follows that

> the fellow-man can actually be loved only in the form of the other Christian who is directly associated with the Christian through the love of God and of Jesus Christ. In this form he can be loved with all the necessity of the love for God and for Jesus, but it is in this form alone that he can be loved [2].

As an act, "what the New Testament calls love takes place between Christians" [3]. This provides a certain internal, esoteric character to love. For although the love practised by Christians is performed on behalf of all man, it cannot be addressed to all. This is a practical rather than a theoretical restriction. Despite the fact that love as an act takes place only between Christians, the Christian community is required to maintain a continual and total openness to all men [4]. The exercise of this requirement precludes the possibility of drawing a rigid line of demarcation between the Christian and non-Christian communities. Towards those outside the context of faith and love, Christians are

> to be engaged in the exercice of humanity, in the confirmation of the specific fellow-humanity which is inalienably distinctive of the essence of man as such, not being caught unawares by omissions nor surpassed by others, but knowing how to practice humanity better than others. And humanity is indeed a good attitude always very definitely demanded and practiced by the Christian who knows what love is. Humanity as demanded by the New Testament is, as it were, latent love; the readiness of the Christian to love everyone [5].

The surprising thing about this discussion is not so much that Barth restricts the practice of love (which, in acts of self-giving, takes the form of *agape*) to the Christian community, although a question can be raised about the ethical necessity of that move. The problem here is the exceedingly tight distinction Barth draws between *eros* and *agape*, which

---

[1] *Ibid.*, p. 912.
[2] *Ibid.*
[3] *Ibid.*, p. 913.
[4] *Ibid.*, p. 917f.
[5] *Ibid.*, p. 913.

leads not only to their being placed, as regards the existence and action of the Christian, in a position of mutual exclusion, but which also eliminates completely the notion of a legitimate, sanctified *eros* that would gain exemplification in the exercise of humanity to which the Christian community is called within the world at large.

It is important to notice that Barth does not attempt to establish this distinction on purely conceptual grounds. Both *agape* and *eros* are instead treated by Barth, within his discussion of the doctrine of reconciliation, as "historical determinations of human nature" [1]. The "human nature" in question is in no sense a neutral factor; it refers precisely to "the nature of man chosen and willed and posited and ordered by God" [2]. In both *eros* and *agape*, then, we have to do with historical determinations of the whole man as posited by God. By setting both forms of love within the controlling framework of the authentic human nature posited and ordered by God, and exemplified in Christ, Barth is able both to satisfy the logical point raised by Heinrich Scholz, that "two forms can be compared only when they have at least one property in common"; and to avoid the sort of ontological antithesis implicit in Anders Nygren's treatment of the problem [3]. The antithesis remains, but it is now historically ordered and teleologically (i.e., eschatologically) removed in the irrevocable destiny given all men in Christ. This insures an independence and superiority to *agape* as against *eros*. Barth insists, that makes it unnecessary for Christian faith to insist on the antithesis [4].

As historical determinations of human nature, *eros* and *agape* constitute "two movements that proceed in different directions", between which "no harmony, but only opposition and conflict, can take place" [5]. *Eros* is grounded in self-love and desire; *agape* love in self-giving. Erotic love forms the basis of all that occurs in the world; the most abysmal and the most exalted manifestations of the human alike rest upon it. In this respect, the Christian community too is to a large extent determined by *eros* in its actions, although it is permitted and commanded to live by *agape* [6]. What *agape* love makes clear at the outset is the

---

[1] *Ibid.*, p. 841.

[2] *Ibid.*, p. 843.

[3] *Ibid.*, p. 840. Cf. Anders Nygren, *Agape and Eros* (Philadelphia: The Westminster Press, 1953).

[4] IV/2, p. 848.

[5] *Ibid.*, p. 835.

[6] *Ibid.*, p. 833f.

discontinuity between Christianity and the world. The Christian life can only be an "existence in the history of the distinction between these two types of love" [1]. This places the Christian in a position of continual tension between the freedom granted him by the Holy Spirit to practice *agape* love, and the continuing reality of *eros* in his life, which closes off that freedom. *Eros* is thus indicative of man's loss of authentic humanity and a perversion of human nature. It is grounded only in man's continuing "No" to the "Yes" of God's grace given in the possibility of a genuine humanity, as co-humanity, based on actions of self-giving embodying *agape* love [2]. The upshot of this is that man is at all points faced with an irreducible choice: either *agape* or *eros*.

The obvious difference in tone between Barth's handling of *eros* and *agape* in his discussion of Christian love as an operational dimension of the event of reconciliation, and in his treatment of the creaturely love that forms the inner basis of marriage within the special ethics of creation, makes for a certain lack of clarity as regards the precise ethical significance of *eros* love. In the love relationship that underlies marriage, *eros* is given a positive reading that places it in a kind of continuity with *agape*. At least, it is not set forth there as the contradictory of *agape*; indeed, within the context of faith, *eros* is sanctified and fulfilled in *agape*. It is difficult to see why, on this basis, *eros* should be given a merely negative treatment when the discussion turns to the question of Christian love. If there is a legitimate place within a natural, creaturely sphere like marriage for the notion of a self-giving *eros* that goes beyond the ethically inadmissable overtones of desire and control, then surely it would be possible to argue the validity of a similarly purified and extended *eros* as an aspect of the humanity the Christian community is enjoined to demonstrate to everyone. Barth allows the merest hint of this possibility in his discussion of Christian love when he asserts that both "humanity" and *agape* may be discerned, negatively, in *eros* [3]. This discernment is never allowed positive significance at the point of a transformed *eros*, however Indeed, it is clear that the removal of the suggestion of an ontological antithesis between *eros* and *agape* (as *per* Nygren) is simply replaced here by a historical antithesis which in its own way is presented just as uncompromisingly. Perhaps Barth's intention was simply to underscore the real difference between the two

---

[1] *Ibid.*, p. 835.
[2] *Ibid.*, p. 847f.
[3] *Ibid.*, p. 846.

forms of love. If so, then we have to contend with only an ostensible incongruity between the treatment of these in relation to the sphere of marriage, and in the act of Christian love. Otherwise, the discrepancy may be indicative of a more serious problem, namely, a failure to arrive at a satisfactory coordination between the created and reconciled dimensions of human nature within the context of action.

The concluding point to be made in this discussion of marriage focuses on the question of obedience to the command within that sphere. The first action that man is called to in face of the totality and precision of the command is repentance. He must accept the accusation and judgment the command brings against him as one who does not keep it [1]. The initial step of accepting God's judgment enables man to move, by grace, to a doing of those actions of which he is capable. The command of God both judges man, and calls forth his response, because it distinguishes between man as sinner under the judgment of God, and man as the creature preserved and maintained in his goodness by God. The action of God thus insures that man will be led beyond his position as a transgressor of the command to an observance of the order insured in the sphere of male and female by the command, which, although partial, is nevertheless real [2].

We turn now to an examination of the relationship that takes form under the divine command between parents and children. The first step in Barth's approach to this relationship consists in excluding the concept of "family" from serious ethical consideration [3]. The reason for this is that the ethically important lines in this sphere under the command run in terms of specific relationships between persons, i.e., father and son, child and parent, brother and sister, etc. That these relationships will inevitably fall within the larger framework of a group or clan is, from the standpoint of theological ethics, an expendable point [4]. Since every man is first a child and then, perhaps, a parent, Barth begins with a consideration of the relationship between children and parents.

The primary concern of the command is not with the physical relationship between parents and children, but with "a certain priority and commission with regard to their children which this relationship implies for the parents" [5]. As the immediate and primary "elders"

---

[1] III/4, pp. 260ff.
[2] *Ibid.*, p. 265f.
[3] *Ibid.*, p. 270f.
[4] *Ibid.*, p. 271.
[5] *Ibid.*, p. 272.

of their children, parents are equipped with a wisdom and experience that the child does not yet have. In general terms, then, what the command requires of children is that they "subordinate" themselves to their parents as their "apprentices" realizing that they are less experienced and wise than they, and willing to learn from them [1].

The priority and commission exercised by parents over their children corresponds to the being and action of God. This means that the instruction and guidance that parents give their children has no independent validity. It is grounded throughout in the prior validity of God's own Word. The place and responsibility of parents within the historical order of parent and child is a representation of "the free grace of the Creator turned toward them as parents" [2]. Ultimately, only God is "properly, truly and primarily Father" [3]. In fulfilling their responsibility toward their children, parents are called upon to imitate the action of God [4].

There is an important limitation placed over the exercise of parental responsibility and authority, which carries a corresponding limitation for the obedience required of children. The limitation in question is closely related, Barth suggests, to the fact that no separation was possible in the Old Testament between the first and fifth commandments of the Decalogue, so that the authority of the parent, and the child's recognition of it, were directly related to the child's recognition of God [5]. It was thus impossible for a separation or distinction to occur between the fifth and the first commandments. Honor to one's parents and fidelity to God are indistinguishable in the Old Testament.

In the New Testament, however, and so in the relationship between parents and children within the life of the Christian community, this order no longer holds. For the Christian community, this relationship is viewed *post Christum natum*, and so in light of the paradigm for "the fatherhood of God and the sonship of man" given in Jesus Christ [6]. As this is given expression in the relationship between Christ and the community, the natural modes of fatherhood and sonship are confronted

---

[1] *Ibid.*, p. 272f.
[2] *Ibid.*, p. 275.
[3] *Ibid.*
[4] *Ibid.*, p. 277.
[5] *Ibid.*, p. 277f.
[6] *Ibid.*, p. 278.

by an independent relationship that makes possible a separation between the honor required for one's natural parents and obedience to God [1].

This places the obedience required of the child to its parents on a different footing. First of all, it makes room for the possibility of a direct challenge to parental authority. Second, since obedience and honor to one's parents is no longer tied directly to the obedience given to God, the former becomes a "free and discriminating decision" [2]. This implies no weakening of the command, for the priority of the claim of God does not result in a simple cancellation of the honor required to one's parents. What happens is that the command to honor one's parents is now limited; man's first obedience is to God, not to his parents. Within this limitation, however, the obligation to honor one's parents and obey them is to be observed even more seriously [3].

Although the honor shown to one's parents depends generally on their taking seriously the priority of God over the relationship between parents and child, there is no one form that the required honor will take. The specific form of honor required must be grasped directly as the will of God for a particular relationship is sought and obedience given to it. It is only in response to the will of God in this definiteness that the decision to honor one's parents remains obedient to the command, and is a free and discriminating decision [4].

Within the ordered relationship between parents and children that occurs under the command, it is possible to describe, in somewhat general terms, the line of development along which honor is shown to one's parents, and the modifications it undergoes. There is a difference in the honor required of a child, an adolescent and an adult. The child stands in a relationship of almost total dependence to his parents. Lacking almost totally in experience and knowledge, he must look for guidance and instruction to his parents. The honor required at this stage of development begins with an unequivocal hearing and obeying, although even here the responsible parent takes care to prepare his child for an exercise of the awareness and responsibility that are beginning to appear [5]. Even in the child, then, it is possible to inculcate an attitude of free response that goes beyond mere conformity and submission to parental wishes, which prepares the child for a genuine encounter with

---

[1] *Ibid.*
[2] *Ibid.*
[3] *Ibid.*, p. 280f.
[4] *Ibid.*, p. 282f.
[5] *Ibid.*, p. 283.

the command of God, and which sets him on the way to an exercise of a freedom and responsibility that are really his own. The child honors its parents to the extent that he is provided with, and accepts, a mode of conduct that is "relatively free of immediate parental directives" [1].

The adolescent stands mid-way between the (relative) heteronomy under which the child necessarily stands, and the (relative) autonomy of the adult [2]. Honor to one's parents for the adolescent takes the form of accepting the parental authority under which he stands, while at the same time beginning a movement in the direction of independent reflection and action. It is within a balanced relationship between imposed and free obedience, between heteronomy and autonomy, that the adolescent moves toward a recognition and acceptance of the authority of the command of God that underlies the legitimate authority exercised by his parents. As a transitional stage between childhood and maturity, adolescence marks the point at which God emerges as "a distinct authority *sui generis*" beyond the parents [3]. It is here that the issue of autonomy emerges with full clarity and force, even though it still remains within the framework of direct parental guidance and instruction.

For the mature adult, the balanced relationship between autonomy and heteronomy ends. Heteronomy, in the form of parental permission and limitation, is replaced by the independence of maturity. This does not signal an end to the requirements of the command in relation to the child-parent relationship, however. The command to honor one's parents continues in force. The form this takes for the adult, however, is precisely that of becoming mature, and moving away from the sort of parental supervision and guidance required for the child and the adolescent. Parents now become "senior friends" who still provide, within a mature relationship, that sort of counsel that seeks to be genuinely attentive and helpful without in any way attempting to undercut the independence of their child [4].

The obligation to honor parents under which children stand cannot be arbitrarily set aside, even though, within a specific relationship, the parents appear to the child to be inadequate and deficient in fulfilling their responsibility. The command acts in this sphere as a sign of the patience and providence of God that replaces the potentially chaotic

---

[1] *Ibid.*
[2] *Ibid.*, p. 283f.
[3] *Ibid.*, p. 284.
[4] *Ibid.*, p. 284f.

results of man's rejection of his authentic humanity within a dependable order. Since children as much as parents participate in both the potential disorder and the "normal" order established by the command within the human, they are incompetent to decide, on their own, that their parents are only failures. Even the most glaring and serious inadequacies in parents do not absolve children from showing them the honor required by the command [1]. So long as the relationship between children and parents remains within the "ordinary" contours of the provisional order maintained by the command, it cannot justifiably be set aside [2].

It is a different matter, however, if this relationship and order are superseded by the direct action of Christ in which one is called to immediate discipleship [3]. When this occurs, the individual may find himself called to a life and an obedience that results in a "teleological suspension" of the normal relationship between parents and children. This possibility emphasizes in a peculiarly dramatic way the eschatological thrust of Christian ethics. The advent of God's Kingdom signalled in the reconciliation between God and man accomplished in Jesus Christ "has foreshadowed the end of all human occurrence, and so also of what (normally) takes place between children and parents" [4]. The eschatological edge of the obedience required by the command may be seen in both the ordinary and the extraordinary circumstances in which a man is placed, and to which he is called. So, within the ordinary sphere of the child-parent relationship, the eschatological dimension gains expression in the fact that this sphere, together with the whole of creaturely history and occurrence, is placed "between the times" of the resurrection and final *parousia* of Jesus Christ. It therefore moves within the grace of the time alloted man within the total sweep of covenant-history, and so is invested with a seriousness and urgency that prohibits its being taken for granted [5].

The eschatological thrust of the command may take a more dramatic form, however, which results in a special calling and vocation in which a man is made directly responsible to Christ in such a way that he is removed from the ordinary sphere of the child-parent relationship [6].

---

[1] *Ibid.*, pp. 285f., 287f.
[2] *Ibid.*, p. 288f.
[3] *Ibid.*, p. 290f.
[4] *Ibid.*, p. 291.
[5] *Ibid.*, pp. 291, 294f.
[6] *Ibid.*, p. 291f.

The special calling and freedom given to certain individuals does not mean that they now stand in opposition to the order of parent and child; it means only that they now confront it independently [1]. When such exceptional callings do become manifest, they serve as reminders that "the Lordship of Jesus Christ in his community, and through it in the world, and the direction of the Holy Spirit, cannot be canalized and limited to a single form and shape" [2]. The freedom of Christ and the Holy Spirit that leads to the removal of a man from the normal order between parent and child can in no sense be made into a general rule governing human action. The individual will always need to exercise care at this point, to avoid the unwarranted assumption of a special calling. As Barth remarks, "truly prophetic men, or even men with only passing prophetic vocations, are unusual phenomena" [3].

When the relationship between parents and children is viewed, now, from the side of parents, the first point to be made is that, *post Christum natum*, it is no longer a misfortune, in itself, to be without children [4]. This is true on a simple human level because, from a Christian perspective, "the true meaning and the first aim of marriage is not to be an institution for the rearing of children" [5]. This merely confirms the point made earlier by Barth, that the marriage relationship is an end in itself independent of children and family. The second consideration concerning childlessness is christological, and so eschatological. Stated bluntly, the lack of children in a marriage can no longer be treated as the serious issue it once was (i.e., in the Old Testament), for in Jesus Christ "the Child who alone matters has been born" [6]. From a christological perspective, childlessness can even be a good thing, for it makes possible a carrying out of the responsibility to the surrounding world that falls to the married couple. And even where a marriage does not result in direct, physical parenthood, there is ample opportunity, Barth suggests, for the exercise of a kind of spiritual parenthood in the role of elders to those children whose real parents are either deceased or incapable of carrying out their legitimate functions as parents [7].

Although childlessness is not, in itself, an ethical problem, the

---

[1] *Ibid.*, p. 292.
[2] *Ibid.*, p. 295.
[3] *Ibid.*, p. 297.
[4] *Ibid.*, p. 298.
[5] *Ibid.*, p. 300.
[6] *Ibid.*, p. 299.
[7] *Ibid.*, p. 300.

practice of voluntary childlessness through birth control requires special comment. *Post Christum natum*, and in view of the problem of over-population, Barth asserts, "there clearly can be no serious objection to the freedom of birth control" [1]. Within the more specific contours of marital fellowship, however, there is an important point to be considered, that might necessitate a restriction of this freedom. This has to do with the implicit possibility of a widening of the marriage relationship through children that occurs whenever sexual intercourse is undertaken as an unobstructed expression of the "physical completion of life-partnership in marriage" [2]. Where the possibility of children is removed through the deliberate practice of birth control, the question must be faced whether this does not entail a rejection of the "offer of divine goodness made by the One who even in this last time does not will that it should be all up with us" [3]. The point at issue here, as Barth sees it, is that since the marriage relationship normally includes sexual intercourse, the *possibility* of parenthood, at least, necessarily follows. The adoption of birth control techniques that eliminate this possibility is acceptable only to the extent that they are used with a sense of responsibility to God under the command [4]. Where efforts at birth control are under-taken simply on the basis of pleasure, expediency, or selfishness, it becomes automatically an evil practice. This does not mean, of course, that birth control is excluded as a legitimate action under the command. Indeed, the failure to take proper and necessary precaution against conception can, if grounded in the wrong motives, be just as evil as a prolonged refusal to have children [5]. The correct approach to this issue lies in the direction neither of legalism nor permissiveness, but only in a free and responsible decision based on "rational reflection". A deci-sion in either direction that seeks to be obedient to the concrete will of God for a particular marriage will inevitably incur the risk of error [6].

As regards the precise method of birth control to be used, Barth

---

[1] *Ibid.*, p. 302.

[2] *Ibid.*

[3] *Ibid.*

[4] *Ibid.*, p. 303. Bonhoeffer makes the same point by arguing that a marriage in which the possibility of children is consistently excluded results in a violation of "the right of nascent life", and an exclusion of the blessing God gives to marriage in the birth of children. Cf. *Ethics*, Eberhard Bethge, ed. (New York: The Macmillan Company, 1955), p. 131.

[5] III/4, p. 304f.

[6] *Ibid.*, p. 304.

finds that no absolute preference or rejection can be given to any of the options. However, although in the end it is a matter of individual choice and discretion, there are "a few certain, universal principles" that control the choice made [1]. First, the choice must always be made with a clear conscience. Second, the decision must be one in which both husband and wife partake to the full measure of their corporate freedom and responsibility. And third, the husband must be willing to assume responsibility for whatever painfulness, discomfort or danger a particular method of birth control may bring [2]. When these rules are observed, the decision may be made freely and the risk of error run, for, as a responsible decision made before God and under the imperative of the command, it is already surrounded and buttressed by the divine forgiveness [3].

The correct fulfillment of parenthood involves an awareness of both the honor and the obligation it brings. This applies to unmarried parents as well as married. The fact that a couple is not married in no way relieves them of the responsibility and duty the child brings to them; any more than it diminishes their honor as parents [4]. Although there is an interdependence between the honor and the obligation of parenthood, it is nevertheless a "good mutual arrangement" if the mother experiences more directly the joy and honor of the child, while the father remains more immediately aware of the seriousness and obligation it brings. This arrangement constitutes for Barth the "formal point of departure" of the discussion [5].

Basically, both parents "are summoned to view their children from the angle of the divine will, and to deal with them, to live with them and for them, accordingly" [6]. In this respect, parents are to function as the first representatives of God to their children, though this need not be done in any deliberate or studied way. What is important is that they carry out their responsibility on the assumption, and in the knowledge, that "God sees and knows and loves and maintains and guides themselves and all men" [7]. Against the background provided by this knowledge, the traditional notions of parental authority, the "upbringing"

---

[1] *Ibid.*, p. 309.
[2] *Ibid.*, p. 309f.
[3] *Ibid.*, p. 309.
[4] *Ibid.*, p. 311.
[5] *Ibid.*, p. 312.
[6] *Ibid.*
[7] *Ibid.*

of children, the place and significance of punishment, and the scope of parenthood undergo important modifications. Under the command, the authority of parents can be given no autonomous status. Nor does its exercise consist in keeping children "in their place" within a rightly established and maintained hierarchy. Parental authority is genuine and effective only when it points the child beyond itself to the authority of God on which the whole parent-child relationship rests [1]. Similarly, parents will "be there" (*da sein*) for their children in an authentic way not by easing them through every difficulty, nor by imposing their own preferences on them, but by directing them to a responsible adaptation to, and realization of, their own unique possibilities, and so witnessing to the fact that it is primarily God alone who is there for both children and parents. The proper exercise of parental responsibility in directing the child toward God will thus mark the beginning of a "divine *paideia*" [2]. Within this context, punishment can serve only a secondary function; the priority of Gospel over Law penetrates directly into the parent-child relationship. The eschatological overtone given to a pedagogy that is now placed under the *parousia* of Christ excludes the possibility of making punishment and discipline ends in themselves. They perform a valid function only to the extent that they attest the imperative given in and with the Gospel [3]. Finally, the proper exercise of parenthood requires a willingness to accept the limitation under which it stands. Humanly speaking, the office of parents is restricted to offering possibilities and opportunities to the child; parents cannot themselves "make something" out of their children. Beyond this human limit, parents must remain open to the restriction that may be imposed on their function by the "exceptional case" in which Christ himself intervenes and calls the child to a wholly new task that sets him completely outside the normal order of parent and child [4].

The final relational structure exhibited within the general givenness of humanity as co-humanity is the relation that exists between near and distant neighbors. The "near" neighbors to which man is related consist in the particular race and people to which he belongs. The "distant" neighbors are those groups of persons having a different

---

[1] *Ibid.*, p. 314.
[2] *Ibid.*, pp. 313f., 315.
[3] *Ibid.*, p. 316f.
[4] *Ibid.*, p. 319f.

natural and historical basis, to which one has no immediate attachment [1]. These latter groups form the "outermost circle" by which one's own immediate group is bounded. As such, they form the "wider humanity to which he and his people also belong, and to which he can now be in some way bound and committed as a fellow human being" [2]. As the command of God calls and sanctifies man in all his relationships, it issues a claim, judgment and decision concerning his action in these spheres as well.

The fact that man is addressed by the command as a member of a particular people is indicative of the ethical significance of the definite "natural-historical place" he occupies [3]. As a member of this or that particular national group, he is provided with an "allotted framework" within which his obedience will take shape [4]. The question of obedience to the command within the spheres of near and distant neighbors is much more problematic than it is within the relationships of male and female and parents and children. The reason for this increased difficulty is that the relationships between differing ethnic and national groups are not governed by a specific form of the command [5]. As we shall see, this lends a certain fluidity to the lines of demarcation between these groups, and so extends considerably the range of possibilities open to man at the point of obedience.

The relationship in which a man stands to his immediate ethnic and national context is built up on the basis of a shared language and speech, and a common history that unfolds within a more or less specified geographical location [6]. None of these factors can legitimately serve as the basis for a mystique or ideology of "home, fatherland and people", nor for the positing of a blood unity that unites persons in a certain group [7]. Although the command of God sanctifies the particular dimensions of the national context in which man finds himself, and so provides him with the appropriate conditions for service and obedience, these can in no sense be invested with final meaning and reality. This does not mean that man is relieved of all responsibility toward his own context.

---

[1] *Ibid.*, p. 321f.
[2] *Ibid.*, p. 322.
[3] *Ibid.*, p. 323f.
[4] *Ibid.*, p. 324.
[5] Cf. *Ibid.*, p. 343.
[6] *Ibid.*, pp. 325ff.
[7] *Ibid.*, pp. 330, 332.

He approaches the possibility of obedience only within the matrix of specific economic, social, cultural, political and religious commitments and forms, and he is not released by the command from a legitimate and proper concern for these [1]. The command calls for a positive and consistent engagement with the whole range of one's given context.

The relationship in which man stands to the "near" neighbors of his own people leads out immediately to the larger sphere of "distant" peoples. The history and development of a particular people, and the assumptions, values and goals to which this leads, inevitably points beyond itself to an involvement with the history of other peoples. So, although the command encounters and prepares man for obedience within a specific ethnic and national structure, it sets a definite limitation over his commitment to it. The obedience required by the command results in man's being nudged beyond the restrictive confines of his own people, and placed on the way to encounter and action within the total sphere of humanity [2].

Even the transition, ethically, from near to distant neighbors does not constitute an irreducible framework within which obedience occurs. The notions of "near" and "distant" neighbors are "correlated concepts" (*Korrelationsbegriffe*) which ultimately form "one and the same reality" [3]. The distinction between different national groups, and the encounters that take place between them, does not constitute a *natural* form of fellow-humanity. They are not "permanent orders" within the sphere of crea-turely occurrence and history [4]. Their independent status is wholly provisional, and the relations between them entirely fluid and reversible. So, although man is "actually led into the sphere" of near and distant neighbors, he belongs to it "only provisionally and temporarily" [5]. The issue of obedience to the command within this sphere, although it will occur only within a recognition and limited acceptance of differing national identities, and the relationships holding between these, cannot be finally bound to them. This insures that man's obedience within this sphere will be genuinely free, since he stands "originally and finally" in a position of independence over against it [6].

---

[1] *Ibid.*, p. 331f.
[2] *Ibid.*, p. 334f.
[3] *Ibid.*, p. 337.
[4] *Ibid.*, pp. 337, 341.
[5] *Ibid.*, p. 341.
[6] *Ibid.*

We turn now from the definite relational spheres marking man's existence in co-humanity to a consideration of the contours laid down by the command, and the direction set for free obedience, in relation to the simple givenness of life. Barth's discussion of this aspect of theological ethics focuses first on the "reverence" toward life that is required under the command; and second, on the "protection" or "care" of life [1].

Human life comes into being as God addresses man and establishes his full particularity as a specific being placed within an alloted temporal span, and called to the responsible exercise of a real, though limited, freedom, in community with his fellow-man. In addition to the freedom for God and man that he is given, there is also a freedom for existence, grounded in the fact that God commands man to live [2]. Within the total sphere of existence or life, the freedom to which man is summoned is "the freedom to treat both the life of all men with his own, and his own with that of all men, as a loan from God" [3]. That man has his life and existence only as a loan from God reminds us again that the ethical issues raised by the givenness and vitality of life, in both its human and non-human forms, emerge only against the background of the total history between God and man. The ethical decisiveness of life, and the seriousness with which it is invested under the command, become fully transparent in the Incarnation, which provides the decisive indication of the cruciality of life when placed within the embracing contours of creation and covenant [4].

To recognize and treat life as a loan from God is, first of all, to show reverence toward it. Generally speaking, the attitude of reverence is "man's astonishment, humility and awe before a fact in which he meets something superior—grandeur, dignity, holiness, a mystery which

---

[1] *Ibid.*, Par. 55, Pts. 1 and 2. I have chosen to translate "Ehrfurcht" as "reverence" instead of the weaker "respect" used by the translators of this volume. Not only does the word "reverence" convey more precisely the seriousness of intent and concern that Barth gives to this section of ethics; it also provides a way of suggesting the proximity-*cum*-remoteness in which he stands to the position of Albert Schweitzer, with whom he continues, in this volume, the "Auseinandersetzung" started in the 1929 "Outline" of ethics.

[2] III/4, p. 367.

[3] *Ibid.*, p. 380.

[4] *Ibid.*, p. 382ff.

compels him to withdraw and keep his distance, to deal with it modestly, circumspectly and carefully" [1]. In itself, life does not bring about the required attitude and action of reverence; the command of God creates this. Under the command, reverence for life becomes a decisively practical matter having to do with man's "determination and readiness for action in the direction of its confirmation" [2]. It is the *whole* of life that is to be affirmed and reverenced. This includes the full range of man's vital and psychic life, and the life of plants and animals as well [3]. The reverence called forth by the command also includes an awareness of the limitations set over life by the Creator. As a loan, life has certain definite limits within which it takes shape. Specifically, this means that reverence for life cannot replace reverence for God [4]. In certain situations, this can mean that the reverence required both toward one's own life and the life of others will be restricted. When this occurs, however, it will always take the form of an *ultima ratio* indicating the presence of a truly exceptional case. At any rate, man is in no sense free to turn these possible limitations of life into general principles that result in a weakening of the command. For this reason, the explicit form of the command given in the Decalogue is to be taken with strict seriousness: "Thou shalt not kill" [5]. Within these general contours, there are various specific points at which reverence to life will receive concrete expression.

The psycho-physical structure of human life insures that it will be first of all a "life of impulses" [6]. This vital, dynamic side of life is also to be taken seriously, and so given its due reverence. The important thing is to live within the vital, impulsive side of life "humanly", so that it takes the form of "a physical process guided and ruled by the soul as awakened by the divine pneuma" that proceeds in terms of "freely chosen and executed decisions" [7]. The impulsive life is given its proper recognition and place when set within, and limited by, the totality of man's being as an order of soul and body. When this order is maintained, and the required priority given to the "soulish"

---

[1] *Ibid.*, p. 384.
[2] *Ibid.*, p. 387.
[3] *Ibid.*, pp. 385f., 399f.
[4] *Ibid.*, p. 388f.
[5] *Ibid.*, p. 389f.
[6] *Ibid.*, p. 391.
[7] *Ibid.*, p. 392.

dimension of man's life, his instinctual needs and drives receive fulfillment within a valid freedom for life that eludes the abuses of both
excess and deficiency [1].

The vital, instinctual side of man's life provides a feasible point in
the discussion for raising the question of his relationship to non-human
forms of life that also exhibit the processses of reproduction,nourishment
and rest. What does the command require of man in his relationship
to animals and plants? Is there a proper form of reverence demanded
toward these levels of life as well? This question must be answered
affirmatively. The command of God recognizes no areas of life that
stand outside the demand for reverence. To this extent, Schweitzer's
assertion that "Ethics is infinitely extended responsibility to everything
that lives" [2] has an obvious *prima facie* validity and weight. The crucial
limitation set over this dictum is that neither life, nor the command to
reverence life, can properly form independent, self-substantiating requirements or principles within theological ethics. What is at issue here
is obedience to the command of God within the givenness of life, not to
life in itself as a kind of undifferentiated continuum [3]. The command of
God meets man within the context of different life forms, which must be
taken seriously into account at the point of decision and action. So,
although the command says something quite definite about a proper
attitude toward animal and plant life, it is clear that these forms do not
convey as stringent an ethical imperative as human life. As regards the
showing of reverence to the life of animals and plants, man is faced with
"a serious secondary responsibility" [4].

Man's responsibility toward plant life is relatively less complicated
than his obligation to animals. The reason for this is that animals encounter man as a series of distinct beings complete in themselves. This
provides for relational nuances between animals and man that cannot
occur between man and the plant world [5]. Because of this, man can use
plants for food as a legitimate exercise of his relative, creaturely sovereignty over them. The only obligation here is that the use made of plants
be held in check by a sense of responsibility; man is not free to engage

---

[1] *Ibid.*, p. 394f.
[2] *Ibid.*, p. 397. The quotation is from the second part of Schweitzer's
philosophy of civilization, *Kultur und Ethik* (Bern: P. Haupt, 1923).
[3] *Ibid.*, p. 366f.
[4] *Ibid.*, p. 399.
[5] *Ibid.*, p. 400.

in the wanton destruction of plant life [1]. The relationship between man and animals is more subtle. Consequently, his responsibility toward animals becomes more serious. Generally speaking, man owes animals, as his fellow-creatures, "careful, considerate, friendly and above all understanding" treatment [2]. As regards the question of a legitimate killing of animals, this may be undertaken only as "an appeal to God's reconciling grace, as its representation and proclamation" [3]. The killing of animals takes place only within the "interim period" of human history between creation and consummation, when the inherent peace between man and the animals is disrupted by sin. Man is therefore faced with the necessity and the responsibility to kill animals in order to live [4]. This can be carried out with a clear conscience only when it is done in consciousness of the reconciliation of creation achieved in Jesus Christ, and the fulfillment and consummation of all things that it promises [5].

Barth now returns to the question of reverence for life within the human sphere, and takes up the question of health. Although a persistent concern for physical well-being may indicate either a deficiency in health or an unwarranted attempt to secure it as an end in itself, there is nevertheless a legitimate will to be healthy, which is "demanded by God and is to be seriously achieved in obedience to this demand" [6]. Since the health in question is simply "the strength to be as a man" [7], there is no absolute antithesis between sickness and health. Neither health nor sickness, in themselves, are final determining factors. The healthy person is marked by a readiness to exist fully as an ordered unity of soul and body, and to "continue this history in its unity and totality" within the limits of the power given him by God [8]. The person who is not obviously sick may lack this sort of openness and responsiveness to his total being as a unified subject, and so be on the way to deterioration despite his apparent "health". Conversely, the person who has suffered an impairment or loss of his physical capacities may continue to be essentially healthy in his attitude toward whatever strength remains to him [9].

---

[1] *Ibid.*, p. 399.
[2] *Ibid.*, p. 400.
[3] *Ibid.*, p. 403.
[4] *Ibid.*, p. 401f.
[5] *Ibid.*, p. 404.
[6] *Ibid.*, p. 406.
[7] *Ibid.*
[8] *Ibid.*, p. 407f.
[9] *Ibid.*, p. 406f.

This does not mean that the reality and seriousness of sickness are minimized or ignored. Within the good creation of God, sickness is an "unnatural and disorderly", though real, manifestation of the chaos of sin against which God's "No" has already been pronounced [1]. Although it continues only *per nefas* as an aspect of the "Nichtige" rejected and overcome in Jesus Christ, the proper attitude to it does not lie, as in Christian Science, in a rejection of its reality. This reaction is rejected by Barth as firmly as the response of lethargy and despair [2]. The command of God requires that man at all points continue to will to live, and to seek the physical and psychical strength necessary to do this as a man. Faith and prayer form the essential, though not the exclusive, means of a legitimate will to health [3]. Beyond these, the knowledge and techniques of the medical profession have an important part to play, provided it is kept clearly in mind that the doctor can at best remove or modify whatever obstacles stand in the way of the will and strength to exist as a man; he cannot himself impart these [4]. Finally, the social dimensions and ramifications of sickness and health must not be overlooked. The will to exist fully as a man can be threatened as much by inadequate social and living conditions as by individual deficiencies. Attention must be given to securing and maintaining the general conditions that will enable the individual to experience the health and strength to exist as a man as real possibilities [5].

The reverence for life given expression in man's affirmation of himself and others calls forth a corresponding joy and happiness, a sensitivity to the importance of "character", and an appropriate "will to power" (*Willen zur Macht*) [6]. The anticipation that surrounds man's life as a movement through his allotted time arises in relation to the various programs he undertakes, the ends to which these are related, and the "ideas, wishes, obligations, responsibilities and hopes" by which these are guided [7]. As a sign either of anticipated or fulfilled expectations, joy embodies an eschatological overtone. The reverence for life demanded of man requires that he "continually hold himself in readiness

---

[1] *Ibid.*, p. 416f.
[2] *Ibid.*, pp. 414ff., 417f.
[3] *Ibid.*, p. 419.
[4] *Ibid.*, pp. 401ff.
[5] *Ibid.*, p. 413.
[6] *Ibid.*, pp. 426ff., 439ff., 445ff.
[7] *Ibid.*, p. 428.

for joy" [1]. Real joy will take the form of gratitude, for it will be present to man at those points where he is enabled to recognize his life as a manifestation and gift of God's grace. The occurrence of joy is signalled by man's grateful acceptance of those events, situations and times in his life that bear the character of fulfillment. Since the experience of fulfillment, and so of authentic joy, depends on the action of the Holy Spirit, it will always have the overtones of surprise and spontaneity [2]. Although there can be a legitimate preparation for joy, it cannot simply be guaranteed and produced through regulated holidays and observances. Nor can it be experienced in isolation. Like health, joy has a social dimension. Real joy will always be marked by a movement toward one's fellows [3]. As joy cannot be removed from the solidarity in which man exists, so too it cannot be isolated from the remaining determinations of life. We cannot experience joy at the expense of our work, or in detriment to health, or in a temporary loss of conscience and sense of agreement with God [4]. Finally, since real joy is a matter of God's gracious action towards man, we must be prepared to experience joy even in times of sorrow and misfortune. The capacity to enjoy life must also include a willingness to bear the burden of suffering it imposes [5]. The experience of joy in life, and the acceptance and celebration of it demanded by God, can never be more than provisional. Joy is properly accepted and experienced only within the expectation of eternal life. Against this background, the will for joy required of man will be

> the faith, sustained by hope, which holds to what has been accomplished as the future in every present, and so to God himself, who is the source of every good thing, who from and to all eternity, and therefore also here and now in time, intends good for us, and has dealt, deals and will deal kindly with us, so that we may be thankful to him [6].

The sensitivity to character required by the command as an aspect of a proper reverence toward life consists simply of man's "resolute will to be himself" [7]. Reverence for life includes a proper measure of self-affirmation, and a respect for one's individuality. This does not mean the simple justification of whatever general or anonymous levels of self-

---

[1] *Ibid.*, p. 430.
[2] *Ibid.*, p. 431f.
[3] *Ibid.*, p. 432f.
[4] *Ibid.*, p. 435f.
[5] *Ibid.*, p. 436f.
[6] *Ibid.*, p. 439.
[7] *Ibid.*

understanding man achieves, or assumes he has achieved. The only acceptable self-affirmation is one which moves, in somewhat reversed fashion, from the "Thou" posited and addressed by God to the "I" that takes form from this in the full particularity of its individual history and character [1]. The act of self-affirmation is thus a matter of obedience, rather than the assertion of a claim or a right. It is an acknowledgement of the "I" that "can exist only in its assumption into the Thou-I, which is the man himself before God, and the soul only in its connection and surrender to the Spirit of God who makes it a living soul" [2]. The attainment of "character" through the exercise of self-affirmation, when seen in this way is obviously a question of the effect of God's grace on man. Man's character occurs as the obedient action in which he wills and moves toward an embodiment of what he already is in reality before God, an action that necessitates a continual "struggle of the Spirit (of God) against the flesh on behalf of the soul which must be saved at all costs" [3]. It is the action of God as Holy Spirit that keeps man in sight of his center as a unique person addressed from eternity by God, and that provides him with the necessary ability to discriminate between what is genuinely, and what is merely apparently, a fitting actualization of his uniqueness. Because man is posited and determined in his identity by the living God, his character is not given him as a timeless quantity; it is rather found in the historical process of discovery and examination that leads to a deepened self-knowledge. The character of a man, in the end, will be directly related to, and embodied in, the special form of service to which he is called [4].

The final thing that the "will to life" demanded of man requires is a proper measure and exercise of power. The power in question is in no sense an abstract end in itself. It is simply the "necessary capacity for experience, knowledge and action" that underlies and informs his encounter with the various forces and powers that surround him in the world [5]. It is man's power as a definite subject that keeps him from falling prey to alien powers of control, and that enables him to respond obediently to the command. The criteria by which this sort of genuine power is identified are, first, that it is a power "given to him with the

---

[1] *Ibid.*, p. 441f.
[2] *Ibid.*, p. 442.
[3] *Ibid.*
[4] *Ibid.*, p. 443f.
[5] *Ibid.*, p. 445.

loan of his life in general and as such" by God [1]. Man's recognition of his power will thus begin as an act of gratitude and reception of the ability given him to do what is necessary for life, an ability which he never possesses directly or finally, but which he can only receive again and again from God. This power is "a genuinely elevating and liberating power", and so "can be affirmed and used only in humility" [2]. Second, the power given to man by God is in continuity with his special capabilities and limitations. This means that man must not try arbitrarily to extend his power in illegitimate ways, and also that he must not attempt to define his abilities exhaustively, nor allow them to be so defined by others. The full extent of power and ability given to man is decided only by God [3]. Third, the power that comes to man is to be accepted and used as a necessity, not a luxury. This fact enhances, rather than weakens, the cruciality of a decision about the immediate necessity of power that is to be used in a given program or direction. The concept of service provides the guiding criterion for assessing the correct use of power, and for distinguishing between what is and what is not necessary [4]. Finally, it must be remembered that the presence of power will at times take the negative form of weakness and silence. When this occurs, it can serve as a useful and necessary reminder that power in all its forms is a gift of God, so that man is relieved of any necessity to insist stubbornly on a certain kind of power. In keeping with the paradigm of a fitting exercise of power given in Christ. which involved his humiliation and death as well as his resurrection and exaltation, man's will for power must always remain flexible [5].

The reverence for life demanded of man, and the legitimate will for life to which this leads, provide the requisite background against which to explore the question of the protection or care of life. As noted earlier, the protection of life is comprehended inclusively in the biblical prohibition against killing. As Barth interprets it, this is not an unqualified exclusion of the "extinction" of human life, but refers more directly to acts of murder [6]. This distinction serves to in-

---

[1] *Ibid.*, p. 447.
[2] *Ibid.*, p. 448.
[3] *Ibid.*, p. 448f.
[4] *Ibid.*, p. 450f.
[5] *Ibid.*, p. 452f.
[6] *Ibid.*, p. 454.

tensify rather than relieve the ethical tension and ambiguity surrounding those situations in which the taking of human life seems to have some basis of justification. The theological ethics is therefore summoned to a special vigilance at this point, for it must, on the one hand, remain faithful to the decisive movement of the *kerygma* away from the possibility of a legitimate taking of human life; and, on the other hand, it must do justice to those situations in which obedience to the command requires, *ultima ratio*, the taking of human life [1]. The task of theological ethics, then, is to explore those ostensibly "exceptional cases" where killing becomes permissible, and to stress repeatedly their status as *exceptional* cases that stand on the outermost boundary of action permitted under the command.

Barth's discussion focuses generally on the two possibilities of suicide and homicide. Under the latter, consideration is given to abortion, euthanasia, killing in self-defense, capital punishment, and war.

The possibility of suicide exposes the final, irrevocable action of destruction that a man may take against himself. The act of suicide is given incipient expression in the fact that man can and does place himself in situations that endanger his life. He may do this unwittingly or in full realization of the possible consequences. The problem of suicide or self-murder is already present in these situations [2]. The command of God places a sharp restriction on man's ability to place his life in jeopardy, whether this occurs through an insensitivity to or ignoring of the dangers in one's surroundings, or in the deliberate act of suicide. Man may take his own life only where it is unambiguously commanded that he do so [3].

Humanly considered, suicide represents the most radical attempt possible to secure recognition, justice and freedom. It provides the final means whereby the individual may surmount the indifference of environment and a sense of personal failure. The fact that a man can find himself at the point of making this sort of estimate about his life underlines the ethical inadmissability of suicide. It is an illegitimate action because man has his life only as a loan from God. He cannot, then, decide on his own that it is without meaning and worthless, and that he is justified in ending it. Since God gives life to man, and commands him to live in freedom, only God has the right to require that man give up his life.

---

[1] *Ibid.*, p. 454f.
[2] *Ibid.*, p. 457.
[3] *Ibid.*, p. 458.

The basic judgment that must be levelled against suicide, then, is that "self-destruction as the exercise of an assumed and usurped sovereignty of man over himself is a frivolous, arbitrary and criminal violation of the command, and therefore self-murder" [1].

The rejection of suicide is grounded in Gospel, not Law. The God who brings man into being and gives him the freedom to live is the gracious God who continues to bear responsibility for man's life, surrounding it with his providential care and leading it to a fulfillment and realization of its appointed destiny. Man is never alone with his life, for God continues to be with him and for him throughout its duration [2]. Suicide is wrong because it constitutes a rejection of God's mercy and love. It is excluded as an acceptable action by the "Yes" of God proclaimed to all men in the death and resurrection of Christ [3]. The action of God provides the only possible effective counter to the possibility of a decision to take one's own life.

When human life is related consistently to the Gospel, the possibility arises of an obedience to the command that requires the act of suicide. Where this occurs, self-destruction is not equivalent to self-murder. The God who gives man life may, on occasion, require the extreme action of relinquishing it. This can only be undertaken in free obedience, in response to the direct command of God [4]. There is thus no way of deciding beforehand what situation will be commensurate with this decision. The legitimate act of self-destruction can occur only as immediate and irrevocable obedience to God. This means, however, that "the possibility of a limiting case is here as elsewhere the particular possibility of God himself" [5]. This insures that the possibility of self-destruction, while not absolutely excluded, remains *extreme*, and so remote.

The prohibitions surrounding the exceptional situation in which homicide is a permissible action under the command must be even more stringently set forth, for every murderer tries at least implicitly to justify his action in the belief that "the exceptional case has been reached when he may let the wolf howl and then break loose" [6]. Further, the overt

---

[1] *Ibid.*, p. 460f.
[2] *Ibid.*, p. 463f.
[3] *Ibid.*, p. 466.
[4] *Ibid.*, p. 467f.
[5] *Ibid.*, p. 470.
[6] *Ibid.*, p. 472.

murderer is simply an exemplification of the tendency to murder present in all men, which stands as a mark of the distortion and corruption of human nature, since men also have an awareness that they are to respect human life. The possibility of marking out contexts in which the taking of life may be a required action grounded in free obedience to God's command is fraught with peril, for it inevitably moves in extreme proximity to murder [1]. Because of this, it is to be expected that the guidance provided in those contexts by the divine command will be essentially a decisive prohibition against every form of killing. It is this initial rejection placed against every situation in which the taking of human life is thought to be a legitimate and necessary action that calls for extreme caution in marking off the boundaries of the exceptional case, and that necessitates careful distinction between the various forms it might take.

The first form of homicide that Barth discusses is the practice of abortion. Despite the widespread growth of this act, particularly among the more technologically advanced nations, it remains a fact that everyone involved in this practice is "engaged in the killing of human life" [2]. The developing embryo that is removed by abortion has from the beginning a life that is independent of its mother. In the act of abortion, man "kills a man, and so ventures the monstrous thing of decreeing concerning the life and death of an unknown fellow-man whose life is given by God, and which, like his own, belongs not to himself but to God" [3]. A recognition of the seriousness of the act of abortion forms the only suitable basis on which to discuss its possible legitimacy in certain situations.

What is needed at the outset is a sense of the profound mystery surrounding all life as a gift from God. This awareness provides the only feasible basis for the "definite No" against abortion that is the basis for further consideration of the issue [4]. The negation and rejection of abortion arises from the permission to live that God gives to man. The problem of abortion cannot be settled on legalistic grounds, despite the almost frightening respectability with which the Roman Church has stood its ground on this point. The movement beyond legalism is achieved through a renewed recognition and proclamation of the permission to live that comes to man from God. It is only in relation to the positive

---

[1] *Ibid.*, p. 473.
[2] *Ibid.*, p. 474.
[3] *Ibid.*
[4] *Ibid.*, p. 476.

thrust of the Gospel that the full seriousness of abortion as an ethical problem comes into view [1]. When the ethical situation is informed by Gospel rather than Law, it is cut loose from the debilitating restrictiveness of an unrelieved legalism, and set under the liberating direction of the command. Within this renewed context, the risk of free obedience can be taken in good conscience, even when obedience to the command entails, *ultima ratio*, the act of abortion [2].

How does one decide, in a given situation, for or against abortion? Ultimately, there is simply no way to provide an unambiguous answer to this question. The risk of free obedience becomes particularly transparent at this point, for the possibility of a legitimate taking of human life, here as everywhere, is finally not a prerogative of man. It lies exclusively in the immediate decision of God given in the command [3]. There are, however, certain criteria that can be set forth as guiding considerations. First, in any situation where abortion is contemplated, there must be a genuine issue of life against life [4]. This does not mean that the life of the mother is always to be given preference over that of the unborn child, which would be simply a reversal of the Catholic position [5]. The intended significance of this criterion is that of removing the decision about abortion from the realm of purely subjective motivation, thereby opening the way for a calm, objective appraisal of the given factors in a situation. The decision as to whether the life and health of the mother is to be maintained at the expense of the child is not for the mother (or father?) alone to make, but is finally "a matter for the experienced and trained physician" [6]. The remaining criteria can be summarized quickly. In addition to the existence of an actual tension of life against life, the ethical context in which abortion appears as a responsible action is further characterized by (2) an exceedingly careful analysis of the factors involved, and a resolute decision that proceeds

---

[1] *Ibid.*, pp. 475ff.

[2] *Ibid.*, p. 479f.

[3] *Ibid.*, p. 480.

[4] *Ibid.*, p. 482.

[5] *Ibid.*, p. 480f.

[6] *Ibid.*, p. 481. Barth's position here is surprising, to say the least. It is clear that the physician would be the logical person to clarify the situation and the alternatives it presented from a strictly medical point of view. Barth seems to suggest, however, that the actual decision to save the life of the mother (or child) would fall to the physician. It is hard to see how this could fail to place the doctor in a quasi-priestly role as the one who dispenses life to some and withholds it from others.

from a conscience that is wholly bound and wholly free; (3) an awareness that the decision in question takes place "before God and in responsibility towards him"; (4) a readiness to receive God's forgiveness for the elements of sin that inevitably surround such a decision [1].

Related to the possibility of legitimate abortion is the issue of euthanasia or "mercy killing". There are, Barth asserts, no exceptions whatever here. Euthanasia is unequivocally prohibited by the command of God [2]. The reason for this inclusive prohibition is that the arguments advanced in favor of euthanasia all display an unconscionable degree of arbitrariness and sophistry. Further, there appears to be no way to set limits to the practice, once it is admitted. Whether as a subtle form of suicide, or more generally as a justification for legalized murder, euthanasia inevitably involves a loss of reverence for life [3]. The only possible exception to the restriction against euthanasia might be the legitimate refusal by the physician to prolong life artificially through drugs that stimulate the action of the heart. Actions of this sort would not be guilty of an arbitrary employment of euthanasia. They would rather constitute passive failure to apply drugs, and so would amount to a recognition of "the respect, which may be claimed by even the dying life as such" [4].

Although the killing of another person in self-defense is a justifiable action under civil law, the command of God in the first instance leads away from an exercise of that freedom. The legitimacy of self-defense must not be assumed as a matter of course. It can occur only at the point of obedience in those situations where one is specifically commanded to kill the attacker [5]. When and if the command takes this form, it will not amount to a recognition of the validity of the "primitive reaction" of every man to protect possession and life. As in the case of honor, the protection of one's possessions and life cannot be the first word in Christian ethics, for these are not viewed as ultimate goods to be preserved at all costs. Under the command, the normal, natural response will be the renunciation of the "right" of self-defense [6]. The "radical defenselessness" of man before God's grace implies a corresponding

---

[1] *Ibid.*, p. 482.
[2] *Ibid.*, p. 483.
[3] *Ibid.*, pp. 485ff.
[4] *Ibid.*, p. 488.
[5] *Ibid.*, pp. 489f., 496f.
[6] *Ibid.*, p. 493f.

defenselessness before the neighbor—even the neighbor who apparently seeks to take our possessions and life [1].

The limitation here that gives rise to the possibility of a legitimate exception to the prohibition against killing in self-defense lies in the necessity to maintain order within society. The injunction of the Gospel against an unrelieved exercise of self-defense must not result in the removal of all restraints on those who move aggressively against their neighbors. At this point, the "No" pronounced by God upon disorder may legitimately gain expression in the form of resistance to these who threaten the order and stability between men on which human life depends [2]. Even here, however, there are important distinctions to be made. There is a difference between moving against someone who threatens the property and life of the neighbor, and taking steps to secure oneself against attack at these points. And there is a difference between the decision of the State to execute certain individuals, and a decision to kill another person individually reached and carried out. These considerations serve merely to underline again the extreme seriousness of killing in self-defense, and insure that due consideration will be given to every alternative short of this that is offered under the command [3].

The problem of capital punishment arises naturally at this point. Does the State have the right to put persons to death? If so, under what conditions? The issue is complicated by the fact that capital punishment, or legal execution, proceeds in terms of a "twofold delegation" [4]. The individual who has been wronged by his neighbor now transfers his "right of defense or counter-attack" to society, which in turn transfers the decision as to the punishment required to appointed judges. At the end of this process, the executioner, in carrying out the sentence, acts on behalf of the individual and society [5].

Although this arrangement has the positive result of deterring to some extent the arbitrariness of individual action, it has the more serious consequence of heightening individual responsibility. Each man must now hold himself directly responsible for the way in which society deals with the offender.

From the perspective of the Gospel, capital punishment is ruled out

---

[1] *Ibid.*, p. 496.
[2] *Ibid.*, p. 496f.
[3] *Ibid.*, p. 498f.
[4] *Ibid.*, p. 499.
[5] *Ibid.*, p. 499f.

as a generally necessary and acceptable way of dealing with offenders against society. It cannot, then, be defended as part of the "regular and normal" order of the State that operates to some extent in recognition of the command to protect life [1]. Nor can it be supported by resorting to the more traditional arguments advanced in its favor. The death sentence serves neither a legitimate pedagogic nor retributive function. And as an ostensible means of protecting society, it falls into ethical inconsistency. The pedagogic approach to capital punishment fails because, while pretending to a concern for the hopefully positive impact that the encounter with "justice" will have on the offender, any such impact is cancelled immediately by the absolute finality of the sentence [2]. In Christian ethics, a retributive view of capital punishment is excluded on christological grounds. In the death of Christ, the full measure of "retributive justice" required to overcome and remove man's sin was given. All men are now placed under the divine mercy and forgiveness [3]. Finally, the notion that capital punishment provides a feasible way of protecting society is ethically inconsistent because it fails to take seriously the status of the offender as a member of that society, and so as its "inner enemy" [4]. Society cannot validly renounce its solidarity with the criminal, but must remember, in its efforts to mete out justice, that he is a product of both its benefits and its limitations. It must be willing to accept at least part of the responsibility for what he has become [5]. When these reservations are brought together, the only course of action left open to the Christian community is that of working for the legal abolition of the death penalty [6].

There is, however, the situation that arises on the far boundary of ethical possibilities where, *ultima ratio*, the only action that can express conformity to the command of God will be the imposition of the death penalty. Situations of this sort will be highly irregular, and will occur only when it is a matter of protecting the stability and continuity of the State [7]. The invoking of capital punishment will in no sense represent an appeal to a normal part of the penal machinery. It will be called into play only when the State is threatened by external forces, so that those

[1] *Ibid.*, p. 509.
[2] *Ibid.*, p. 503f.
[3] *Ibid.*, p. 505f.
[4] *Ibid.*, p. 507.
[5] *Ibid.*, p. 508f.
[6] *Ibid.*, p. 509.
[7] *Ibid.*, p. 510f.

responsible for the preservation of the order represented by the State are faced with a clear necessity to act *in extremis* [1]. Such an action can be undertaken only in the "extraordinary threefold recognition" that (1) it is better to sacrifice one life than that of the nation; (2) christologically, the person put to death becomes a companion of the thieves put to death with Jesus; (3) the only mercy that can be shown this person is death [2]. There are apparently only two situations where the exceptional case arises, and capital punishment becomes mandatory in obedience to the command: cases involving high treason in war; and situations in which tyrannicide is ethically defensible and necessary as a means of preserving the well-being of the State from within [3].

The final point that must be considered under the protection of life is the problem of war. As regards the possibility of a "just" war that takes place as an act of obedience to the command, the restrictions are, if possible, even more stringent than those surrounding suicide, abortion and capital punishment. Modern warfare has lost every vestige of the notions of limited killing, and the defense of honor and justice, with which it was once given a kind of relative sanctity and dignity [4]. In the contemporary world, war is a total event in which all the members of one society are pitted against those of another, and in which the dominant value and goal, stated bluntly, is the killing of as many of "the enemy" as possible. In face of this, the first task of Christian ethics is "to experience and make evident itself a distinctive horror of war and a definite aloofness from it" [5].

Viewed in this way, war can in no sense form a part of the legitimate operations of the State, nor of the political order required under the command. The State has, it is true, a power vested in it which can be used when the occasion demands. Theological ethics must emphasize, however, that the exercise of this power is not the primary function of the State. It is an *opus alienum* which cannot, under any circumstances, provide a *carte blanche* for organized mass slaughter [6]. The central task of the State is the formation and maintenance of peace. The Christian community must therefore stand against every tendency within the political community that moves contrary to this basic task and goal.

---

[1] *Ibid.*, p. 511.
[2] *Ibid.*, p. 512.
[3] *Ibid.*, p. 512f.
[4] *Ibid.*, pp. 516ff.
[5] *Ibid.*, p. 522.
[6] *Ibid.*

Its first responsibility, in this respect, is the firm rejection of every suggestion of "a relapse into a post-Constantinian theology of war" [1]. The Church will, so far as possible, guard against the creation of "standing armies in which the officers form *per se* a permanent danger to peace" [2]. Above all, it will never stand among those who agitate for war, but will calmly insist that "relatively if not absolutely, in practice if not in principle, war can be avoided to a very large extent" [3]. In the first instance, then, the Christian community is called upon to take seriously the strength of the pacifist position, and to align itself with it.

There are two points, however, at which this position must be qualified, which provide for the occurrence of a just war undertaken as an act of faith and obedience. The pacifist position must be qualified when it is a question of defending the independence of the State against external encroachment. And it must be qualified if the State finds itself summoned to the aid of a weaker nation similarly threatened to which it is obligated by treaty or some other agreement [4]. To be sure, neither of these possibilities can be automatically sanctioned. They will always be exceptional cases marking the outer boundary of the action of a State. The actualization of either of these possibilities can occur only after the most stringent appraisal of the situation, and only after all other alternatives have been explored. Despite the seriousness with which the entry of the State into war is surrounded, it may still be the case that it is forbidden directly by the command of God to renounce either its internal sovereignty or its commitment to other nations, and so finds itself summoned to provide open resistance and aid [5]. A decisive mark of the just war that takes place under either of these possibilities is that it is entered into "unconditionally", with no attempt to answer beforehand the question of success or failure [6].

When war takes place in fulfillment of the State's obligation to defend itself or other nations, and when the decision is made unconditionally, then the Church can do its part to support and encourage the effort required to carry the decision through to completion. While not forgetting its first responsibility to preach the Gospel of peace, it can

---

[1] *Ibid.*, p. 527.
[2] *Ibid.*, p. 526.
[3] *Ibid.*
[4] *Ibid.*, p. 529f.
[5] *Ibid.*, p. 528f.
[6] *Ibid.*, p. 530.

also issue "a call to martial resolution which can be righteous only as an act of obedience but which as such can be truly righteous, and which can be powerful only as an act of faith but which as such can be truly powerful" [1].

The possibility of a just war also raises the problem of individual responsibility and decision, which is epitomized in the conscientious objector. Ultimately, the decision to engage in the destruction of human life, even where it is a question of a just war, can be made only by the individual. The Church must stand firm at this point in its insistence on the sanctity of persons. There can be no legitimate loss of individuality in a general hypostasis of the State [2]. The individual must consider carefully what the State asks of him at that point, and make his decision either for or against participation, as a citizen of the State, in this particular venture. In this respect, there is no basis for distinguishing between individual and social ethics [3]. There is a distinction that must be made, however, between the command of God that may lead the State to a legitimate preparation for and entry into war, and the requirement of military service placed on the individual. Barth argues that military service cannot be given "the dignity of an inviolable divine command" [4]. Military service can only be placed before each citizen as a specific question which he must answer. The State is not God; it can require only proximate, never absolute, obedience to its requirements. The individual citizen must therefore remain free to make his decision before God, keeping clearly in mind his obligation as a citizen. If he finds himself led in the direction of conscientious objection to the military action of the State, then he must be prepared to take that position resolutely. The two criteria set over his action are (1) that he take this position in loyalty to the State and his status as a citizen, and not in an effort to

---

[1] *Ibid.*, p. 531. Two of the clearest examples of Barth's application of his position on war are found in *This Christian Cause* (New York: Macmillan Company, 1941), and *The Church and the War* (New York: The Macmillan Company, 1944). Both of these, of course, are from the period of Barth's decisive encounter with National Socialism. I shall attempt, in the following section of this chapter, to analyze the differences, and their basis, between his attitude toward the menace posed by Hitler and his position on Communism.

[2] III/4, p. 532f.

[3] *Ibid.*, p. 532. Barth is perhaps suggesting a corrective to the position adopted by Reinhold Niebuhr in: *Moral Man and Immoral Society* (New York: Charles Scribner's Sons, 1955).

[4] III/4, p. 534.

evade his responsibility; and (2) that he be ready to accept the consequences that will inevitably follow from his action [1]. And he must carry
through in his decision with a certain measure of humility that manifests
itself in a willingness to be instructed and brought to a different appraisal
of the situation and the form his own action within it will take. Conscientious objection, in short, must not be turned into an absolute
principle [2].

Throughout the situation engendered by war, the Church stands
ready to assist and encourage both the State and the individual citizen.
It is crucial to keep in mind here that the service rendered the State by
the Church will not display the tidy consistency that might be found in
other groups within society. It may or may not stand with the State in
its preparations for war, depending on its own appraisal of the situation
at hand, and the direction given by the command. Again, the State must
not expect the Church to champion its cause against the conscience of
the individual, although the Church has fallen into this questionable
practice often enough in the past. The Christian community has its own
task and responsibility, its specific identity and calling, and a distinctive
perspective from which it views things and makes decisions. From which
it follows that the State must not count on the unqualified support and
allegiance of the Church; nor must the Church under any condition
give this to the State [3].

The preceding sections provide an initial description of the freedom
that comes to man under the command within the spheres of fellowship
and life, and the general contours of the direction in which human
behavior is set as a result of that freedom. Although an overall estimate
of the adequacy or inadequacy of Barth's development of special ethics
must await the completion of the final section of this chapter which deals
with the relationship between the Christian community and the State
(some intimation of which has already been given), there are some
provisional observations that can be made here.

The first observation concerns the relationship between the christological and phenomenological dimensions of Barth's analysis. At the
end of the discussion of Barth's treatment of vocation and work, I
indicated a reservation about his handling of the phenomenological

---

[1] *Ibid.*, p. 535f.
[2] *Ibid.*, p. 536.
[3] *Ibid.*, p. 537f.

realities that flesh out the context of work in which christological insights are brought to bear. To make the Husserlian point, Barth's analysis of the context of work, and the ethical options available to Christians within it, was phenomenologically (and so empirically) deficient, because it failed to pay close enough attention "to the things themselves" [1]. Instead of actually engaging the various forces and counter-forces, shifts and modifications that characterize the whole matrix of labor-management relationships in their contemporary setting, both his description and his recommendations appeared to trade heavily on almost stereotyped notions borrowed for the most part from his earlier involvement with the socialist movement. The result, I argued, was an inadequate sensitivity to the complexity and subtlety of the empirical factors that shape the context within which man's work is carried on.

A similar judgment can be made about Barth's handling of the contexts we have just examined, within which man's freedom in fellowship and life under the command takes shape. The basis for this judgment, however, is slightly different, for it does not rest, in the first instance at least, on Barth's providing a deficient phenomenological analysis of these contexts. It lies rather in his insistence on deriving the insights and directions that provide them with ethical shape and substance from exclusively christological considerations. When this insistence is placed alongside Barth's two-dimensional view of human nature [2], the result is that the subtlety and complexity of these contexts tend to be

---

[1] "Zu den Sachen selbst". This phrase formed a kind of *leitmotif* in Husserl's early concern to develop a phenomenology free of prior philosophical assumptions. William Barrett has provided a good summation of Husserl's point "For Husserl, phenomenology was a discipline that attempts to describe what is given to us in experience without obscuring preconceptions or hypothetical speculations; his motto was 'to the things themselves'—rather than to the prefabricated conceptions we put in their place". *Irrational Man* (New York: Doubleday Anchor Books, 1962), p. 213. Barth's problem, of course, is not identical with Husserl's. The question Barth must face is whether an exclusively christological approach to things allows, at the same time, for an empirico-phenomenological analysis of the contexts in which man is called upon to exist and act that does justice to their irreducible givenness and complexity.

[2] Cf., III/4, p. 407, where man is described as "the soul of his body, the rational soul of his vegetative and animal body, the ruling soul of his serving body". Although Barth insists on the *unity* of soul and body, it is still hard to see how this two-dimensional approach does justice to the inner complexity of the human.

reduced. This leads, in turn, to an unevenness in the degree of persuasiveness in the ethical judgments Barth makes. I shall now attempt
to support these contentions.

If there was ever any doubt as to the pervasiveness of Barth's
employment of the christological principle, a reading of his discussion
of the formative thrust of the command within the spheres of fellowship
and life would be sufficient to dispel it permanently. Barth argues a
christological basis for everything from the relationship between man
and woman (with marriage as the "apex" instance of this) to the killing
of animals. Again, a christological view of marriage establishes its
exclusiveness (*pro* monogamy) and permanence (*contra* divorce); and
excludes childlessness as a serious problem. Aside from the question
whether any part of dogmatics can legitimately be made to bear this
sort of weighty extension, there is the further question whether a strict
utilization of the christological principle does not have the net effect
of letting the theologian off too easily. Professor West's judgment on
Barth's efforts to construct a theology free of ideological commitment
is applicable here: "Barth has made his case, as a theology free of
ideology. And yet one has the feeling that he has made it only because
Christ has made it for him ..." [1].

The surprising thing, perhaps, is not so much that Barth fails to do
complete justice to the actual contexts and situations in which men are
called upon to act, as that he is able, on a strictly theological basis,
to provide as such substantial guidance as he does. There are perceptive
comments scattered throughout his discussion of the direction
set by the command within the spheres of fellowship and life.
The sections dealing with marriage, near and distant neighbors, and
capital punishment, are particularly forceful and illuminating. Thus,
in suggesting that there is an *unevenness* of persuasiveness in Barth's
discussion, I am not asserting that it has *no* persuasiveness. Nor do
I wish to imply that Barth reveals no sensitivity to the reality of the
situations in which men are called upon to act. His own broad background in the mainstream of Western culture, and his concern to sketch
in the outlines of a human community within which man can be open to
himself and his neighbor, and move toward a proper reverence for and
protection of life in its communal and individual manifestations, are
enough to insure that Barth does not indulge in merely abstract theolo-
gizing about ethics. Even with these allowances, one still feels that

---

[1] *Communism and the Theologians*, p. 243.

Barth has missed opportunities provided by his own theology for a more sustained engagement with the empirical dimensions of the ethical context, and that these omissions lead him into ethical formulations that are lacking in sensitivity and subtlety.

There is an important distinction that must not be forgotten in raising questions about Barth's description of the "ethical context". For some thinkers, the primacy of context (over principles or norms, for instance) is argued on the basis of the importance, for decision, of the precise empirical factors that make the situation what it is. The necessary prerequisite to moral judgment, then, is a careful description and weighing of those factors. It is obvious that this sort of emphasis on the empirical is not what makes Barth's ethics contextual. For Barth, a contextual or situational ethics is necessitated on theological rather than empirical grounds. It is because the ethical question takes form only in God's immediate action of giving instruction, in the command, and man's equally immediate response of obedience or disobedience, that he is led to emphasize the priority of context [1]. Under the impact of the command, however, the *total* situation within which man must act is provided and shaped. When this point is recalled, it is not out of order to question the empirical cogency of Barth's formulations, since the empirical forms part of the total context given by the command.

The general criticism that must be brought against Barth, I feel, is that he makes virtually no attempt to use the suggestions and insights that might be provided by the various "secular" disciplines whose task it is to deal with "phenomena of the human". To be sure, Barth *mentions* these disciplines (some of them, at least). There is a difference, however, between mention and use. One looks in vain for the sort of positive use the theologian might make of the insights provided by the social sciences —anthropology, sociology, psychology and political science, in particular—and by some of the more recent experiments and developments taking place in the biological sciences. One can appreciate Barth's concern that the concreteness of man in his individuality and social relationships not be lost in sociological or psychological abstractions [2]. It is hard to see, however, why the theologian should not be open to

---

[1] James H. Gustafson has also drawn attention to the difference between Barth's contextualism and other varieties in a perceptive article: "Context Versus Principles: A Misplaced Debate in Christian Ethics", in: *New Theology No. 3* (New York: The Macmillan Company, 1966), p. 75f.

[2] III/2, p. 301.

whatever positive suggestions those disciplines (including anthropology), might shed on man's givenness, in both its individual and corporate forms; just as it is hard to see why the treatment given to the question of national identities and interrelationships, and the specific problem of war that inevitably emerges in that context, would not profit from a more serious engagement with the disciplines of the political scientist and the historian.

Further, if the theologian is going to ground his approach to the givenness of life in the notions of reverence, mystery, and protection, shouldn't he at least wonder whether the possibility of synthesizing life in the laboratory (viewed by some biochemists, at least, as a possibility that might well be realized in the near future), not to mention the more recent (and somewhat frightening) research into acquired characteristics, the planned introduction or elimination of genes, and the creation of new individuals from a laboratory union of sperm and ova stored indefinite lengths of time in appropriate "banks", might not result in a whole new concept of life and the human that he would need to take into account in his formulations? Barth confines his consideration of the latter possibilities to a short footnote in which he mentions Huxley's *Brave New World*, and expresses disapproval of the humanity and world it portends [1]. At this juncture, however, Huxley's vision is closer to reality than to dream, and a simple dismissal of it will not do.

Perhaps the most significant and, in its way, far-reaching, of Barth's omissions lies in his failure to utilize the insights into the human provided by psychology, particularly as it has developed, beginning with Freud, in a somewhat non-behavioral direction. Again, the problem is not that Barth ignores this development altogether. It is that his treatment of it is confined to making the pejorative point that Freud's theories allowed for a separation between sex and the whole man, a deficiency that has since been corrected from within the ranks of medical psychology [2]. Barth apparently sees no importance in that whole unconscious, sub-rational level of the psyche suggested by Freud's work, nor the implications it might carry for the theologian's approach to the problems of the relationship between man and woman, parents and children, and the reverence and protection of life. A sensitivity to Freud's contribution would certainly not entail accepting all of his notions. What it would do is restore a sense of the complexity and ambiguity

---

[1] III/4, p. 449.
[2] *Ibid.*, p. 150f.

that surrounds human relationships and decisions, that seems, for the most part, to be missing in Barth.

Professor Rieff has suggested recently a way of understanding the importance of Freud that goes beyond the issue about sexuality to a heightened awareness and appreciation of the ambivalence in human motivation and action that any ethic must come to grips with if it is really to make contact with the full situation in which man moves. He writes:

> Freud's most important ideas finally may have less to do with the repression of sexual impulses (which explains neither the past discontents of our civilization nor the present ones), than with ambivalence. It is their capacity to reverse feelings that is the human problem and hope. What hope there is derives from Freud's assumption that human nature is not so much a hierarchy of high-low, and good-bad, as his predecessors believed, but rather a jostling democracy of contending dispositions, deposited in every nature in roughly equal intensities. Where there is love, there is the lurking eventuality of hatred. Where there is ambition, there is the ironic desire for failure. Although he wishes not to know it, a sore loser may be sore mainly because he almost won and is reacting against his wish to lose. Psychoanalysis is full of such mad logic; it is convincing only if the student of his own life accepts Freud's egalitarian revision of the traditional idea of an hierarchical human nature [1].

Of course, it might be argued that Barth's early attraction to existentialism, and his appreciation for the novels of Dostoevsky, provide the needed balance to his omission of any serious grappling with Freud [2]. This argument might be acceptable, if it could be shown that Dostoevsky's character analyses, and the complexity and ambiguity of man they reveal, led to a more perspicuous treatment of the ethical contexts and problems in which man finds himself immersed. Unfortunately, they do not; Barth refers to Dostoevsky, as to Freud, only by way of mentioning a point. He apparently sees no need to use the insights they might provide about man to open up the full complexity of the ethical. The result is that the phenomenological side of ethics is diminished, and so fails to receive its due. Barth achieves a certain measure of unity and simplicity, on christological grounds, at the expense of empirical completeness.

The explanation for Barth's failure to deal fully with the empirical,

---

[1] Philip Rieff, *The Triumph of the Therapeutic* (London: Chatto and Windus, 1966), p. 55f.

[2] Barth cites Dostoevsky on the ambivalence of the human in his opening remarks on the problem of homicide. III/4, p. 471.

phenomenological side of the ethical context, at least where Freud is concerned, lies in the fact that he works exclusively with an hierarchical view of human nature [1]. When man is defined as "the rational soul of a vegetative and animal body", and when the motifs of super- and sub-ordination resulting from this ordering are grounded and sustained in the immediate action of the Holy Spirit, there is no room left for a serious consideration of factors that come into conflict with an excessive rationalism in ethics. The result is that Barth's approach to the issues that arise within the spheres of fellowship and life does not deal convincingly with the ambivalence and opaqueness, and so the complexity, present in human structures and decisions. The "downward drag" of sin resolves essentially into a failure to will the appropriate action at the point of moral decision. The unconscious, irrational factors that impinge on human motivation and the exercise of responsible choice, are obscured within a hierarchic ordering in which the superiority of the rational is assured by simple definition [2]. It is this aspect of Barth's thought, which informs throughout his approach to the various contexts in which man is called upon to render moral decisions, that is scored by Stanley R. Hopper in a trenchant comment:

> Barth's use of language is rationalist, his logic is rationalist, his psychology is rationalist. He does not distinguish, as Kierkegaard does, between a "first self" and a "deeper self", or between the conscious ego and the unconscious, as the depth psychologist does. Therefore he cannot recognize that the disrelationship with God is in the first instance made "dialectically" manifest as alienation, or disrelationship with ourselves. He does not recognize with Kierkegaard, in that passage so decisive for Kierkegaard's understanding of the Self, and thereby for his entire "theology", that the Self becomes a Self by relating itself to its own self, and by willing to be itself the self is grounded transparently upon the Power which posited it [3].

---

[1] This may account also for Barth's reluctance to look seriously at the insights afforded by the social and biological sciences—though here there is the additional factor of a persistent concern to avoid falling into ideological assumptions. Perhaps a firmer distinction between the descriptive legitimacy and the occasional prescriptive assertiveness of those desciplines would guard sufficiently against that danger.

[2] I am not suggesting that rational deliberation might be replaced by pure feeling or spontaneity, nor that it is impossible to achieve, given the unconscious, irrational factors in man's make-up. I am arguing that a proper assessment of the place of reason in ethical decision can occur only when the latter aspects are recognized and accounted for in one's anthropological assumptions.

[3] "The Modern Diogenes: A Kierkegaardian Crochet", in: *Religion and Culture*, Walter Leibrecht, ed. (New York: Harper & Brothers, 1959), p. 106.

Professor Hopper's comment goes somewhat beyond our concern here, for he is ultimately concerned to call into question the overall authoritarian cast of Barth's theology. I shall have something to say on this point, in assessing the total impact of an ethics of command and obedience, as that is related to Barth's anthropology. For the moment, I are concerned only to argue the inadequacy of an approach to the ethical that elevates the rational at the expense of ignoring the unconscious, irrational, and surd dimensions of the human.

A good example of this inadequacy is suggested in Barth's short comment on the phenomenon of homosexuality. Although he begins by describing homosexuality as a "physical, psychical and social sickness" requiring the attention of "the doctor, the pastor trained in psychotherapy, the legislator and the judge", Barth ends by asserting that what is needed (presumably from theological ethics) is a clear statement of the command that will warn men away from attempting to exist independently of women, and vice-versa [1]. The upshot of this is that homosexuality is made to appear as though it were grounded in some sort of *decision* that moves one away from an authentic humanity, and that this might have been made initially on aesthetic grounds. Now, perhaps homosexuality arises in this way, for some people. It surely does not, however, for most who find themselves in this situation.

If theological ethics wants to do justice to this problem (and the others that arise within the spheres of fellowship and life), it will have to take more seriously than Barth the full complexity of factors from which it emerges. Barth says much that is helpful and instructive, in terms of setting a direction for ethical action, about the relationships between man and woman and parents and children; and about the problems raised by abortion, suicide, killing in self-defense, and war. By treating the soul in exclusively rational terms, however, and failing to develop fully the impact that the unconscious, irrational dimension of the self has on the exercise of reason, he obscures the complexity of those issues. A little more of Kierkegaard's sensitivity on this point, and less of an emphasis on the Classical model (Plato and Aristotle), would illuminate the internal ambiguities of the human that must be accounted for if justice is to be done to the full reality of the ethical context.

I turn now to a specific issue that Barth deals with in this section

---

[1] III/4, p 184f.

of special ethics: the possibility of an "exceptional case" in which war could be justified. Barth argues two situations in which a nation might justifiably enter into war: when its internal security and sovereignty is immediately threatened, and when it is under obligation to assist another nation similarly threatened. It must be remembered that Barth does not imply that these guidelines provide automatic justification for war. The precise situation in which either of these conditions is present must be stringently examined to determine whether war is really the one remaining course of action open to a people. In spite of this cautionary note, there are difficulties in Barth's position.

The first difficulty with these conditions is that they are altogether too self-evident. They are precisely those that every nation state appeals to when it seeks to provide a modicum of respectability to its involve-ment in war. Both the United States and North Vietnam, for instance, appeal to the second criterion to justify their presence in South Vietnam. And every nation state would claim that its particular history, life and independence constituted a sacred trust which it could under no circum-stances surrender. Barth's sentiments about Switzerland would find their echo in every national context [1]. It may be that the Christian community would be capable, in a "crisis" situation, of discerning between a legitimate and an illegitimate use of these conditions, but surely this cannot be assumed without an equally strong emphasis on the ambiguous position in which it is placed as a result of its involvement in a particular national ethos.

Actually, it is not clear that the first condition, that of defending the territorial integrity and independence of a nation, has much appli-cation outside the context of relatively small political units. The major confrontations taking place in the world today that could lead to war are not situations in which one country threatens the immediate borders of another (i.e., the United States and Russia; or China and the United States). They arise, instead, because of conflict over common areas of interest, power and commitment, i.e., Berlin and Southeast Asia. What application Barth's criteria would have in these situations is unclear. Perhaps different conditions could have been suggested if Barth had been assisted in his analysis by the insights of political scientists concerning the very real displacement of power beyond the immediate geographical boundaries of a nation, which results in an extension and diffusion of

---

[1] *Ibid.*, p. 529.

that power. At least the first of Barth's criteria sounds as if it were written with Switzerland particularly in mind.

Even if the criteria suggested by Barth could be reformulated or replaced, there would still remain the question whether any attempt should be made to spell out the identifying marks of the just war. There are two considerations that weight against this undertaking. First, any attempt to set forth criteria, conditions or guidelines that permit a distinction between the just and the unjust war tends in the direction of a reduction of the ambiguity and tension of the ethical context in which war becomes a possibility. Second, no matter how strenuously these criteria are articulated merely as guidelines that in no way minimize the importance and necessity of immediate obedience to the command, it is difficult to avoid the overtones of an ethic of rules or principles [1].

4. The Church and the Political Community

The problem of the relation between the Christian community and the State has been indirectly suggested in Barth's discussion of the relationship between near and distant neighbors; and it was encountered more directly in considering the problem of war, and the attitude and function of the Christian community in a time of national emergency. In this section, I wish to examine this problem in more detail. There are two difficulties that limit the possibility of a complete treatment of it. The first is that Barth had not yet gotten to the point of providing a full discussion of the State when the Dogmatics was terminated with his retirement from Basel. The second difficulty, as Professor West remarks, is that Barth's views on church and state were, for the most part, "forged in the heat of political controversy" from 1933 to the present [2].

With these limitations in mind, I shall try to do two things in this section. First, I shall describe the legitimate role assigned the State vis-à-vis the Christian community, as set forth primarily in Barth's shorter works beyond the Dogmatics. Second, I shall examine the positions Barth has taken toward National Socialism and Communism, respectively. This will provide some notion of what obedience to the command looks within the political sphere.

While there is no specific command and obedience governing the relations between near and distant neighbors, and so no final structures

---

[1] Cf. Paul Lehmann's comments on this point. *Ethics in a Christian Context*, p. 143f.

[2] *Communism and the Theologians*, p. 212.

and loyalties in the area of international relations, there is a "political form" of the command that is addressed to the State [1]. The command of God to the State does not fall within the special ethics of creation, because the State is not an order of creation (*Schöpfungsordnung*), but "a genuine and specific order of the covenant" (*Bundesordnung*) [2]. This means that the State, and the command of God to it, form a part of the doctrine of reconciliation. They are ordered exclusively along the lines of the reconciling grace by which man is justified in Jesus Christ. The State is given continuance and meaning only as an aspect of the "kingly rule" of Christ over the world [3].

When the State is viewed from the perspective of redemption rather than creation, it is placed in a definite parallelism with the Christian community. Both the Christian community and the State are provisional orders established by grace. They are indicative of the patience of God in allowing man time to respond to the event of reconciliation, and so form the counterparts, in the anthropological sphere, to the continuing prophetic witness and self-manifestation of Christ in the Holy Spirit [4]. Within the present action of Christ, the Christian community and the political community are each provided with their special responsibility and task. The Christian community is that place within the human at which God's action is recognized, accepted and proclaimed. The witness and service of the community provide one side of the patience of God, the side that participates directly in grace, and is sustained and guided exclusively by it [5]. The State forms the other side of God's patience, and provides the ordered context within which the collective life of man can be maintained, and the Gospel preached. Although the State is established only by the grace of God's patience, it is itself a "graceless order" that lives by compulsion and fear, and that is directed by the rule of law [6].

The fact that the State and the Christian community are both placed under the present rule of Christ over the world means that they will

---

[1] III/4, p. 342.

[2] *Ibid.*, p. 343.

[3] II/2, p. 806.

[4] *Ibid.* Cf. *Christengemeinde und Bürgergemeinde*, Theologische Studien, Heft 20 (Zürich: Evangelischer Verlag A.G. Zollikon, 1946), p. 97. Hereafter referred to as *CGBG*. A translation of this by Stanley Godman appears in: *Against the Stream* (London: SCM Press, 1954), pp. 15-50.

[5] II/2, p. 806.

[6] *Ibid.*, p. 806f.

not be free or able to carry out their activities independently of each other. There is a mutual orientation of the Christian community on the State, and of the State on the Christian community. Each in its own way, and in continuous interaction with the other, is put to the direct service of God. Naturally, this will mean rather different things for each, for the State participates in reconciliation, and so in the kingly rule of Christ, only *de iure*, while the existence and action of the Christian community marks the occurrence of a transition from a participation "in principle" in reconciliation to an involvement in it "in fact". It follows from this that the State will have a real, though unrecognized and unacknowledged task to perform vis-à-vis reconciliation, which places a corresponding task upon the Christian community as regards the State's fulfillment of its task. It is at precisely this point that the *political* responsibility of the community becomes clear, and that its distinctive service to the State, which is correlated with the service of the State to the Church, can be indicated.

The Christian community is called to the political service of the State by virtue of its knowledge that the latter "belongs originally and ultimately to Jesus Christ" [1]. In its "relatively independent substance, dignity, function and purpose" it is "to serve the person and work of Jesus Christ and the justification of the sinner that occurred in him" [2]. The power of the State is legitimate because it comes wholly from God. The State manifests "the operation of a divine ordinance ... an *exousia* which is and acts in accordance with the will of God" [3]. Even the power of a corrupt State, such as that represented by Pilate, is still ordained and preserved by God. Just as there are no perfect political systems, so too there are no "wholly diabolical" States that have fallen completely away from their grounding in God [4].

The service of the Christian community to the State is directed toward the establishment and maintenance of a just political order. Christians can "will and affirm only a State which is based on justice" [5].

---

[1] *Rechtfertigung und Recht*, Theologische Studien, Heft 1 (Zürich: Evangelischer Verlag A.G. Zollikon, 1948), p. 18. Hereafter referred to as *RR*. A translation of this by G. Ronald Howe, entitled "Church and State", appears in: *Community, State and Church* (New York: Doubleday Anchor Books, 1960).

[2] *Ibid.*

[3] *CGBG*, p. 9.

[4] "The Christian Community in the Midst of Political Change", in: *Against the Stream*, p. 81. Cf. *RR*, pp. 9ff.

[5] II/1, p. 435.

It is in light of this criterion that the community recognizes and accepts the authority of the State, and intercedes for it in prayer. This does not mean that the Church retreats into quietism in the political sphere, nor that it is prepared to sanction any form of political order. The fact that the service of the community to the State is marked initially by subordination and prayer indicates that the Church brings no ideological program of its own into the political sphere. It does not need—indeed, is forbidden—to play off opposing ideologies against each other [1]. Although the State has a service to perform to the Church, and so to all men, the subordination and prayer which the Christian community gives the State is not dependent on the State's prior fulfillment or recognition of the service required of it. Indeed, "the most brutally unjust State cannot lessen, but can only increase, the responsibility of the Church for the State" [2]. The Church will always hope for and expect the best from the State, but it will continue to render obedience to it, and pray for it, regardless. The prayer and obedience of the community function as signs of its recognition of the divine grounding of the State, and of its willingness to be actively *for* its well-being.

The freedom of the community from ideological commitment in the political sphere does not mean that it has no criteria by which to measure the validity or invalidity of a given political form. The recognition and obedience given by the Church to the political community do not always mean active support and encouragement for its practices. Indeed, the "intercession" of the Christian community on behalf of the State can, on occasion, take the form of criticism, opposition, and, in extreme cases, revolt [3]. In order to appreciate the point Barth is making, it will be helpful to inject here a word about the legitimate service of the State, as it relates to the task of the Church.

The relation between the Christian community and the civil community may be likened to two concentric circles whose center lies in the event of reconciliation accomplished in Christ [4]. Their respective responsibilities and tasks will thus be directly related to the redemption of man secured in that event, which establishes the fulfillment of the

---

[1] *CGBG*, pp. 12ff. Cf. *RR*, p. 34f.

[2] *RR*, p. 35.

[3] *Ibid.*, p. 36f. Cf. *The Knowledge of God and the Service of God*, pp. 229ff. Hereafter referred to as *KGSG*.

[4] *CGBG*, p. 23. Thielicke also calls attention to Barth's use of this simile in his discussion of his political thought. Cf. *Theologische Ethik*, Band II/2, Pars. 4122-4125, p. 720f.

created order. Within the creaturely sphere, both Church and State are placed in the service of God as "agents of reconciliation" [1], for both are called into existence at the point of man's justification. The task of the Christian community is the continuous proclamation of that event in its witness and service to the world in its varied activities: preaching and teaching, the celebration of the sacraments, prayer, and its common participation with all men in the spheres and relationships that make up the context of creaturely occurrence. The task of the State is that of providing and maintaining a framework within which the common life of man may be carried on in an atmosphere that is marked by an active concern for, and defense of, justice. The correct order of the State will thus be "outward justice, outward peace and outward freedom" [2]. As it is claimed by the Christian community for this service, the State must "remain within the bounds of justice and within the bounds of its tasks" [3]. Put succinctly, the service to which the civil community is called is

> the safeguarding of both the external, relative and provisional freedom of the individuals and the external, relative and provisional freedom of their community, and to that extent the safeguarding of the external, relative and provisional humanity of their life both as individuals and as a community [4].

When the State remains faithful to the service required of it, and provides a political order in which man's individual and corporate life is grounded in a concern for justice, it also insures the one thing needed by the Church for its particular activity of proclamation: freedom [5]. When this condition is fulfilled, the Christian community can cooperate actively in the life of the State—praying for it, encouraging it, affirming its general policy and direction. It can do this only when

> the significance of the State as service of God is made clear and credible to (it) by the State itself, by its attitude and acts, its intervening on behalf of justice, peace and freedom and its conduct towards the Church [6].

---

[1] I have borrowed this pregnant phrase from the title of a book by Arnold B. Come, *Agents of Reconciliation* (Philadelphia: The Westminster Press, 1960).

[2] *KGSG*, p. 221.

[3] *Ibid.*, p. 224.

[4] *CGBG*, p. 4.

[5] *KGSG*, p. 226.

[6] *Ibid.*, p. 227.

The State cannot claim more than the cooperation of the Church. It cannot legitimately make an *inward* claim upon men either through the imposition of a particular world-view, or by exacting the response of love from its people [1]. Nor can there be any confusion or exchange of the respective tasks given the State and the Christian community. The State cannot undertake to instruct the Church in the performance of its task of preaching the Gospel, nor seek to effect a reform in its order and life. By the same token, the Church cannot attempt to become a political power in its own right, lobbying for special attention and privilege. Nor can it wish to turn the State into an extension of itself by fostering the development of a "Church-State" (*Kirchenstaat*) [2]. Its sole task lies in the proclamation of the Gospel; in a continuous testimony to what God has done and continues to do for man in Jesus Christ. Within the political order, the Church will always be a "παροικία", an "establishment among strangers" [3].

In keeping with Barth's disdain for merely theoretical constructions in ethics, and his emphasis on the need for continuous action in obedience to the command of God, the concept of the "just" State is not allowed to harden into an abstraction that is wielded independently by the Christian community, or that applies exclusively to a given political order. No State, as such, is wholly just or wholly unjust. There are, however, in the political sphere as elsewhere, guidelines that enable the community to distinguish between the relative merits of possible arrangements, and to participate "in the human search for the best form, for the most appropriate system of political organization" [4]. It is by participating in an ordinary, human way in the search for a political order in which justice is given at least a relative, provisional embodiment that the Church "subordinates" itself to the political community, and "calls the political community from neutrality, ignorance and paganism into co-responsibility before God" [5].

The most complete statement of the guidelines marking the direction in which justice is to be sought in the political order is given in Barth's 1946 essay, "Christengemeinde und Bürgergemeinde". The particular interest of this essay lies in the way in which Barth establishes these

---

[1] *RR*, p. 42.
[2] *CGBG*, p. 19f.
[3] *RR*, p. 26; Cf. *CGBG*, p. 14f.
[4] *CGBG*, p. 15.
[5] *Ibid.*, pp. 16, 25.

guidelines. They are derived by analogy. The justification for this procedure lies in the fact that the Christian and civil communities are neither
completely homogeneous nor completely heterogeneous, as regards their
relationship. They are unified ontologically in Jesus Christ, and the
reconciliation of all men that has taken place in him. The only option
remaining, then, is to view the State "as an image, as a correspondence
and an analogue to the Kingdom of God which the Church proclaims
and believes in" [1]. The hope of the Church in the future promised to
man in Christ, in the "new age" already beginning to dawn in the world,
provides the point at which the Christian community is united with the
State, and enables it to discern the activity of God in the provisional
efforts of men to secure justice in the political order [2]. In choosing from
among the alternatives open to it in the political sphere, the Church will
favor those that most clearly express continuity with the content of the
Gospel entrusted to it. The concern of the Christian community is that
the political decisions taken by the State correspond, however remotely,
to the politics of God, and that they point toward the Kingdom of God,
not away from it [3]. In general terms, the Church proceeds to the task
of political decision by making "its knowledge of the Lord who is Lord
over all its criterion", and by distinguishing

> between the just and the unjust State, that is, between the better or worse
> political form and reality exhibited at a given time; between order and
> caprice; between government and tyranny; between freedom and anarchy;
> between community and collectivism; between personal rights and
> individualism; between the State as described in Romans 13 and the
> State as described in Rev. 13 [4].

These general considerations can be brought closer to specific cases
by drawing more heavily on the principle of analogy. Because the Church
is grounded in the Incarnation, and the compassion God shows to man
in Christ, the Christian community will be primarily concerned, in the
political sphere, with the human, with man in the full range of his
individual and collective life, rather than with principles, programs or
causes. It will have no interest in policies that overlook the human in
favor of abstractions—not even when the abstraction in question is
labelled "progress" [5]. The human counterpart to divine justification

---

[1] *Ibid.*, p. 23.
[2] *RR*, p. 23.
[3] *CGBG*, p. 24f.
[4] *Ibid.*, p. 16.
[5] *Ibid.*, p. 25f.

is the relative, provisional justice that can be secured in the context of
politics. The Church, as the "witness of the divine justification", will
favor the State that is grounded in constitutional law providing equal
protection to all men [1]. The action of God in Christ was directed toward
man in his weakness. The Church will therefore concern itself particularly
with those who are poor and weak, economically, socially and politically,
in society, and will speak out for the "socialistic" possibility that insures
the greatest measure of social justice [2]. The Christian community is
grounded in the freedom of God's Word of grace, which calls man to
a corresponding freedom and maturity. In the political sphere, it will
be concerned with the safeguarding of individual liberty of expression
and decision. It will not necessarily oppose a partial, temporary restriction
of these freedoms, but it will stand resolutely against the "dictatorship
in principle of the totalitarian State" [3]. The individual and corporate
dimensions of the Christian community are creatively united through
the common loyalty of its members to Christ. The analogue to this in
the civil community is that neither individualism nor collectivism can
be given ultimacy. Both the claims of individuals and the prerogatives
of the State as a total unit are subordinated to their common responsibility to find and establish that form of civil law that will best limit and
preserve man's life in both its individual and corporate manifestations [4].
The Christian community is a visible sign of the unity of all men in
Christ. Within the political sphere, then, there can be no legitimate
restriction of the equality of all persons under the law, whether this is
based on considerations of religion, ethnic background or sex [5]. The
Church manifests in its life a diversity of callings, abilities and functions.
The analogue to this in the State is that the proper separation be maintained between its various functions and "powers"—legislative, executive
and judicial. Justice in the body politic is more readily approximated
when these are decentralized [6]. Since the Church lives by the truth
revealed to all men in Jesus Christ, it will oppose "all secret policies
and secret diplomacy", and will work for the creation and preservation
of a political order in which officials are willing (and able) to answer

---

[1] *Ibid.*, p. 26f.
[2] *Ibid.*
[3] *Ibid.*, p. 27f.
[4] *Ibid.*, p. 28.
[5] *Ibid.*, p. 29.
[6] *Ibid.*, p. 29f.

openly for their actions [1]. The Christian community is grounded in the completely free Word of God. It will therefore stand for freedom of expression in the civil community, and will oppose attempts to regulate or censor this freedom [2]. The Church, as the provisional representation in the world of the action of God, is called into existence only to serve God and its fellow-men. Legitimate ruling in the State will always be in the interests of service to the people. The Church will therefore oppose political orders grounded only in the exercise of "naked power" (*Macht an sich*) [3]. As the people of God called to service in the world, the Christian community is by nature ecumenical, and so open to all men without limitation. The corollary to this in the political order is a sensitivity to the wider contexts and dimensions of political responsibility that lead beyond a merely "parochial politics" (*Kirchturm politik*) [4]. Finally, although it may be necessary from time to time to sanction "violent solutions" to conflicts that arise within the political community—whether in the form of the more regular operation of the police and the courts, or the less frequent possibility of an armed uprising against an unjust State—these will always need to be undertaken only as final, extreme measures. A definite restriction of force to those situations in which, *ultima ratio*, no other course of action is possible, forms the analogue, in the political order, to the fleetingness of God's anger as contrasted with his mercy, which is "for eternity" [5]. The Christian community performs its necessary service to the State when it assists in the formation and maintenance of a political order in which these guidelines have at least a partial embodiment. In this way, the State is assisted to a fulfillment of the command of God set over the political community: that it strive to achieve *justice*.

It is obvious that the directions set by Barth in "Christengemeinde und Bürgergemeinde" lead toward a democratic state. In "Rechtfertigung und Recht", Barth makes this point explicit, and argues that the "democratic conception of the State" represents a legitimate extension of the thought of the New Testament [6]. Although the distinctions between

---

[1] *Ibid.*, p. 30.

[2] *Ibid.*, p. 31.

[3] *Ibid.*, p. 31f.

[4] *Ibid.*, p. 32.

[5] *Ibid.*, p. 32f. The last two points have, of course, been given more extended treatment in III/4, in Barth's discussion of the relation between near and distant neighbors, and the limitations set over capital punishment and war.

[6] *RR*, p. 44.

various political orders are relative, they are nevertheless real and
important. Barth marks both the reality and the importance of these
distinctions, and the crucial importance of the direction in which one
chosses to move, in a trenchant footnote:

> The statement that all forms of the State are equally compatible or in-
> compatible with the Gospel is not only outmoded but false. It is true
> that one may go to hell in a democracy, and achieve salvation in a mobo-
> cracy or dictatorship. But it is not true that the Christian can affirm,
> desire and strive after a mobocracy or dictatorship as earnestly as he
> can a democracy [1].

Barth has been criticized both for his general approach to the State,
and for attempting to provide ethical guidelines, by means of analogy,
that will assist the Christian community in the "discernment of spirits" [2]
necessary to moving among the available political options in the direction of justice. Thielicke is critical of Barth's insistence on viewing the
political order christologically, as an order of the covenant. The main
difficulty in this approach, Thielicke argues, is that it overlooks the fact
that the modern secular State stands not only for "constitutional justice"
(*Naturrecht*), but for "the power of the fallen angels and the Antichrist"
as well [3]. When this criticism is coupled with the additional charge that
Barth's view of the State betrays supra-lapsarian overtones [4], and with
Thielicke's rejection, noted earlier, of Barth's ordering of Gospel and
Law, it is not surprising to find Barth charged with having ordered
the relationship between Church and State in such a way that their
basic over-againstness is lost [5].

Barth's rejoinder to these criticisms would probably be something
like the following: The fact that both the Christian and the civil communities are viewed properly only as dimensions of the kingly rule of
Christ over the world leads neither to facile assumptions about the
justice or injustice of a particular State, nor to an ignoring of the "principalities and powers" that continue to distort the aim of justice. The
State, like every other aspect of the world, is set under the total affirmation and reconstitution of things accomplished in Christ [6]. It is given

---

[1] *Ibid.*, p. 43, note 30b.
[2] *Ibid.*, p. 19.
[3] *Theologische Ethik*, Band I, Par. 2139, p. 690f.
[4] *Ibid.*, Band II/2, Par. 4090, p. 714f.
[5] *Theologische Ethik*, Band II/2, Par. 4093, p. 715.
[6] Here Barth would take direct issue with the "two Kingdoms" view of
Church and State implied in Thielicke's criticisms.

a special function, however, as the context and structure in which the ordinary justice that forms the counterpart to man's justification in Christ proclaimed by the Church can be sought and, to a degree, achieved. To be sure, this is a limited undertaking, subject to misunderstandings and errors, and capable finally only of a relative, provisional realization of its goal. There are indications, however, of the direction in which justice will lie. The fact that these indications are derived *analogically* is evidence for the continuing activity of Christ in the political sphere. It is the presence of Christ in the Holy Spirit working to lend shape and substance to the political order that insures that the negative forces that continue there will have only a limited, not an ontological, significance. Thus, there can be only relative, proximate, not ultimate, eschatological crises in the political sphere. Under the guiding activity of the Holy Spirit, the Christian community is called to authentic participation in the search for justice. It is precisely Barth's emphasis on the process of weighing alternatives and making decisions in definite contexts, against the background of the analogical guidelines already indicated, that insures that the necessary tension between Church and State remains intact. The way is always open, in the decisions taken by the Christian community, for critical reservation, opposition and (in rare instances) revolt against the established or evolving State to occur. Of course, this will never result in a separation between the Church and the political order *per se*. It will simply be an enactment of the prophetic responsibility facing the Christian community *at that point* to oppose the State, and so to recall it to its legitimate place and ordering, in correspondence to the command of God in the political sphere. The action of the Church, whether in support or in criticism and revolt, is never *against* the State but always *for* it [1].

Thielicke is also critical of Barth's use of analogy to derive guidelines in the political order, on the ground that *any* political form or practice can be defended by this means. The "Messianic secret" can be used to justify the practice of "secret diplomacy", and from the relation between Christ (as Head) and the Christian community (as the "body" of Christ), the political concepts of "people, kingdom and leader" used by the German Christians can be derived [2]. It is hard to take Thielicke's criticism

---

[1] *RR*, p. 38.
[2] *Theologische Ethik*, Band I, Par. 1241, p. 411f. Emil Brunner has raised the same criticism against Barth's use of analogy to derive political norms. Cf. *The Christian Doctrine of Creation and Redemption*, p. 319.

altogether seriously. Of course, analogy can be put to improper as well as proper uses. And there is surely no difficulty in finding examples of the former. What Thielicke overlooks is the total context within which Barth places and justifies the use of analogy. It is only in relation to the total being-in-act of God, and the ethical consequences resulting from it, that the question of valid analogical relations and forms in the creaturely sphere can be raised. One is not free, then, to derive any or every possibility by analogy. Here as everywhere, a limit is set by the overall direction in which man is placed by the action of God in Christ. In the event of reconciliation, man is restored to his original and proper place as the covenant partner of God, and is set on the way to authentic cohumanity and fellowship with all men. The only legitimate use of analogy, therefore, will be in providing suggestions as to the consequences this might carry for an ordering of man's common life within the political order.

The difficulty in Barth's use of analogy at this point arises because of his failure to allow the guidelines drawn from it to inform consistently his sensitivity and response to the specific political contexts within which man finds himself. On at least one occasion, this leads Barth perilously close to suggesting an analogical justification for totalitarianism:

> God above all things! Sovereign even over the legalistic totalitarianism of your state! You fear it? Fear it not! The limits of that system where its representatives must halt or else be destroyed is set not by its totalitarianism, but by its legalism which makes the state totalitarian in an ungodly and inhuman way. "Totalitarian" also, in a way, is the grace of the gospel which we all are to proclaim, free grace, truly divine and truly human, claiming every man wholly for itself. To a degree the Communist state might be interpreted and understood as an image of grace —to be sure, a grossly distorted and darkened image. Indeed, grace is all-embracing, *totalitarian* [1].

The disconcerting thing here, in view of the guidelines Barth derived for the just State in "Christengemeinde und Bürgergemeinde", which led clearly in the direction of constitutional democracy, is that Barth implies that there might be such a thing as a *godly* and *human* totalitarianism. We shall need to keep this apparent discrepancy in mind, for it simultaneously throws light on the nature of Barth's encounter with specific political issues, and raises a question as to the adequacy of his handling of the precise empirical factors involved in them.

---

[1] With Johannes Hamel, *How to Serve God in a Marxist Land*, Thomas Wieser, trans. (New York: Association Press, 1959), p. 58.

The guidelines set forth by Barth provide, as it were, a sense of the direction in which Christian political decisions will move. They also suggest, roughly, the contours of a political order in which the importance of justice is both recognized and given provisional exemplification. The qualification set over all the indications and suggestions derivable by analogy is the necessity for continuous obedience to the directing presence of God in the command. None of the guidelines that Barth sets forth can legitimately be taken as more than that—they are not unyielding principles or rules to be applied automatically to the political situation. If they indicate a direction, they do not supply the Church with an ideology of the "just" State. As we shall see, this limitation has important consequences for understanding Barth's own quite different reactions to Nazism and Communism, respectively. Before turning to this, it will be helpful to sketch out the way in which, as Barth sees it, Christians go about the business of making political decisions.

Barth spells this out in some detail in a monograph he wrote in 1952, "Political Decisions in the Unity of Faith" [1]. The discussion unfolds against the specific question of political responsibility posed by the imminent remilitarization of Germany, and its inclusion within NATO [2]. This provides the model for saying something generally about the nature of Christian political decisions. The first thing to be said here is that political responsibility is made real at the proper times and places primarily in the action of individuals, not in official Church pronouncements insuring a degree of unanimity. Barth writes:

> If the political mission of the Church is to be turned to practical account at all and in good time, it can only take the form of comments and declarations by individual members of the Church, made in the freedom and commitment of their personal responsibility as Christian [3].

The individual Christian does not act in isolation from the Church, however. His action will always constitute "a call and a summons *in* the Church *to* the Church" [4]. It will inevitably provoke controversy and opposition, however, and may even lead to a definite crisis within the Church, for it will be an action grounded in the immediate response of faith and obedience that the individual finds unavoidably required of

---

[1] In: *Against the Stream*, Stanley Godman, trans., pp. 149-164. Originally published as No. 34 in the series: *Theologische Existenz Heute*.

[2] *Against the Stream*, p. 150.

[3] *Ibid.*, p. 151.

[4] *Ibid.*, p. 157.

him at a given point. The action of the Christian must therefore proceed
without regard to the issue of unanimity, for it will represent his particular judgment about a situation in which he is called upon "to choose
between life and death, God and idols" [1]. This does not mean that he
has no concern for the Church—indeed, it is precisely because of his
concern that he must proceed in his decision and action:

> The unity of the faith can maintain its spiritual truth and reality only by
> constant renewal. It can and will be renewed only if Christians do not
> try to avoid crises in their fellowship with one another, but are determined,
> whatever the outcome, to see them through [2].

As they are addressed to the Church, the political decisions of
individual Christians will manifest the openness and joy, but also the
resoluteness, indicative of the freedom in which they (and all men) stand.
Of course, no one has the right to speak out on issues affecting the life
of the Church unless he has, so to speak, done his homework. Effective
decisions and actions—those that manifest the clear overtones of authority and truth, will always be marked by "a good deal of common sense
and a spark of prophecy" [3]. In one respect, the political decisions of
Christians will resemble those of their non-Christian neighbors. They
will always be grounded in a careful assessment of alternatives, and in
a consideration of the arguments for and against the particular issue at
hand. Thus, they will demand the full employment of the powers of
rational deliberation at one's command [4]. The point of difference between
Christian and non-Christian political decisions is that the former take
place

> not in a space apart from his Christian faith, but before God—and not
> before any god, but before the God who speaks to the world, to the

---

[1] *Ibid.*, p. 154. The note of crisis Barth injects into political decisions,
and the necessity to move ahead regardless of the threat they might pose
to the unity of the Church—momentarily, at least—are the result of his own
experience in opposing Hitler and National Socialism. There too, it was a
question of immediate obedience and action that simply could not wait for
the affirmation of the Church as a whole—which, indeed, never came. Cf.
Ibid., p. 156, note 1: "If in 1934 we had had to wait for the unanimity of all
the groups and circles in the Church which were not even adherents of the
'German Christian' school—or even merely for the understanding and agreement of the wise men of Erlangen and Tübingen, etc., either nothing at all
would have been said in Barmen or only a lot of vague mumbling".

[2] *Ibid.*, p. 159.

[3] *Ibid.*

[4] *Ibid.*, p. 152.

Christian community and therefore to the individual Christian, in the gospel of Jesus Christ [1].

In his political decisions, then, the Christian "will look for a decision which is not arbitrary or just clever in a human sense, but which is made in the freedom of obedience to God's command" [2]. There is thus an unavoidable tension and risk present in the political decisions of Christians, for they are placed on "the extremely narrow frontier that divides the world from the Kingdom of God", and must aim at hitting the precise point "where common sense speaks the language of the Holy Spirit and the Holy Spirit the language of common sense" [3]. It is clear, however, that even when the latter coincidence occurs, there can be no guarantee of a favorable reception by the Christian community at large of what the promptings of common sense and the Holy Spirit suggest to the individual to be the best (indeed, the *required*) course of action. In the end, political decisions always entail the willingness to take a confessional stance, "and to summon other Christians (and non-Christians!) at all costs to take the same decision (since God, known or unknown, is the God of them all)" [4].

At this point, we are in a position to consider Barth's own engagement with the political order, and the decisions to which this has led. Obviously, this will mean focusing on his stand toward National Socialism and Communism, respectively. Now, both of these, formally considered, can be classified as totalitarian political systems. And, since the guidelines set forth by Barth in "Christengemeinde und Bürgergemeinde" lead clearly in the direction of a constitutional, democratic State, it would appear to follow logically that he ought to take an identical stand toward both these systems. It is just here that the request for logical consistency is exposed as a bad criterion when applied to theological ethics—at least where Barth's ethics are under scrutiny—for it has been his firm insistence on drawing a distinction between National Socialism and Communism that has confounded and provoked the critics [5]. Let us

---

[1] *Ibid.*

[2] *Ibid.*

[3] *Ibid.*, p. 160.

[4] *Ibid.*, p. 154. The ethical framework linking Christians to non-Christians is clearly indicated here. The necessity for taking a position, ethically, and summoning others to that position, is also expressed in Barth's special ethics of creation. Cf. III/4, p. 8f.

[5] For a sampling of the critical response to Barth's refusal to respond to Communism in the same way that he did to National Socialism, cf. Brunner's

look more closely at these distinctions, and the grounds on which they are drawn.

One of the clearest statements from Barth on the difference between National Socialism and Communism is found in a short letter written in 1948 in reply to Brunner [1]. The first thing to remember in assessing political movements, Barth asserts, is that the Church "never thinks, speaks or acts 'on principle' " [2]. It makes its evaluations and judgments "spiritually and by individual cases" [3]. The importance of this point, of course, is that it underlines the freedom of the Christian community from every sort of ideological preoccupation and commitment. The ethical and political importance of this point is that the Christian community is always justified, initially, in adopting a "wait and see" attitude toward political changes—even where this means the institution of a radically new order. Barth's refusal to issue a blanket condemnation of Communism as a political form was, in this respect, n precise continuity with the position he adopted during the early years of the National Socialist experiment. The patience that the Christian community can allow to political experimentation is lodged in a firm distinction between the dogmatic task of the Church and the provisional loyalty required by the existing or changing form of the State. The Church was justified in remaining at first relatively neutral and open toward Hitler and National Socialism, because "the Church did not consist of seers and further she could not, as the Church, consider and treat as dogma either the political system displaced by the revolution or that taken up by it as such" [4]. Gradually, however, the situation changed. The overall direction of the State under Hitler became unmistakably clear. The time for neutrality and waiting was past:

> Everything has its own time. It was first of all fair and just to give even the political experiment of National Socialism as such its time and

---

"An Open Letter to Karl Barth", in: *Against the Stream*, pp. 106-113; and Reinhold Niebuhr's article, "Why is Barth Silent on Hungary?" in: *The Christian Century*, Vol. LXXIV, No. 19 (January 23, 1957), pp. 108-110.

[1] In: *Against the Stream*, pp. 113-118. This is Barth's reply to Brunner's "open letter". Translated by Mrs. E.M. Delacour.

[2] *Ibid.*, p. 114.

[3] *Ibid.*

[4] *The Church and the Political Problem of Our Day* (New York: Charles Scribner's Sons, 1939), p. 34. This appeared originally as "Die Kirche und die Politische Fragen von Heute", and is included in: *Eine Schweizer Stimme* (Zürich: Evangelischer Verlag A.G. Zollikon, 1945). Translator's name not given.

chance. What its aim was could certainly then be guessed, but could *not* be known in such a way that the Church, on the basis of *this* knowledge, must or even might take up her stand in relation to it with Yes or No ... Today it is senseless to continue to close one's eyes and deny that the import and character of National Socialism as a political experiment, is a dictatorship which is *totalitarian* and *radical*, which not only surrounds and determines mankind and men in utter totality, in body and soul, but abolishes their human nature, and does not merely limit human freedom, but annihilates it [1].

What this statement gives, of course, is a précis of the transition in the Church from an initial attitude of neutrality, pending a fuller indication of the direction the State would take under Hitler, to one of opposition and resistance, Barth himself being the central figure in calling the Church to this transition. This does not mean that the Church was *inactive* during the early years of the Hitler regime. The period of preliminary neutrality, of patiently waiting to see what the new order would bring, meant, for Barth, that the Church was called to the task of "testing the spirits", and of carrying on even more vigorously its *theological* task of witnessing to the triumph of God's Word in Jesus Christ. This was indeed the specific counsel Barth gave in 1933, when the Church was faced with the problem of the "German Christians" and the threatened election of a "Reichs-Bishop". The proper stance in face of these, Barth declared, was "to carry on theology, and only theology, now as previously, and as if nothing had happened" [2]. The concern for a properly sustained theological existence took precedence over all others. Friend and foe alike were marked by whether they assisted or hindered the Church in carrying on this task:

> No concern can be more pressing, no hope more moving than the concern and hope of our ministry. No friend can be dearer than one who helps us in this ministry, no foe more hateful than he that wants to hinder us in this ministry [3].

Far from being a call to passivity, Barth viewed the faithfulness of the Church to its theological responsibilities as the one thing needed to insure proper *ethical* engagement with the political situation. Only by keeping to its theological tasks (i.e., the elucidation, in dogmatics

---

[1] *The Church and the Political Problem of Our Day*, pp. 35ff.

[2] *Theological Existence Today!*, R. Birch Hoyle, trans. (Lexington: American Theological Library Association Committee on Reprinting, 1962), p. 9.

[3] *Ibid.*, p. 13.

and preaching, of the victory of God's Word of reconciliation) would the Church be adequately equipped to assess the ethical significance, for its own life and that of all men, of what was happening in the political sphere [1].

The culmination of this concern for the priority of theology in the life of the Church came in the formulation of the Declaration of the Synod of the German Confessional Church meeting at Barmen in 1934. In the six theses that form the body of the Declaration [2], the "No" that theology and the Church must present to National Socialism, and its basis, are clearly set forth. Even here, however, the theological niceties are kept intact. It is not National Socialism as *named* that is rejected, but National Socialism as *represented* in the "German Christians" and "the present Reich Church government which are devastating the Church and are also thereby breaking up the unity of the German Evangelical Church" [3]. The specific errors addressed by the Barmen Declaration are the false notions that there are other sources or figures of revelation besides Jesus Christ, that demand unconditional loyalty and obedience in certain areas of life (Theses 1 and 2); that the message of the Church can legitimately be turned to ideological purposes which require the appointment of leaders with special power and authority in the Church for their execution (Theses 3 and 4); that the State can become an all-embracing system controlling every facet of life and replacing the Church, and that the Church can subvert its message to the purposes of the State, becoming thereby its extension (Theses 5 and 6) [4].

---

[1] Barth's answer to his critics, who accused him of passive withdrawal into theology in 1933, is given in his reply to Brunner in: *Against the Stream*, p. 118: "Incidentally, it is a legend without historical foundation that in 1933 I recommended 'passive resistance' when I urged the Germans to fulfill their duties of Christian witness 'as though nothing had happened', i.e., ignoring Adolf Hitler's alleged divine revelation. If they had consequently done so, they would have built up against National Socialism a political factor of the first order".

[2] As Barth points out, this document was not referred to as a "confession" (*Bekenntnis*), but as a "theological declaration" (*Theologische Erklärung*). I/2, p. 701. However, its genuine status as a confession can scarcely be questioned. Cf. Arthur C. Cochrane's comments on this point. *The Church's Confession under Hitler* (Philadelphia: The Westminster Press, 1962), p. 188f.

[3] *The Church's Confession under Hitler*, Appendix VII, "The Declarations, Resolutions and Motions Adopted by the Synod of Barmen, May 29-31, 1934", p. 239.

[4] *Ibid.*, pp. 239ff.

These points are precisely the ones we would expect Barth to make against the totalitarian claims of National Socialism. From this point on, his opposition to the Hitler regime continued to develop, and by 1938 was total, unrelieved, and, in some respects, strident. The totalitarianism of the Nazis was seen as a *sui generis* manifestation of evil. The judgment that must be made against it "is not something to be said of every dictatorship as such" [1]. The National Socialist State no longer carries out a divine commission. It is not a "higher power" in the sense of Rom. 13 [2]. It is a "fundamental dissolution of the just state", and so, in short, it is "no state" [3]. The prayer of the Church directed toward the State in this context can only mean "to beseech God that he may let his free, unmerited grace become visible to us in the suppression and casting out of this need, and hence in the suppression and casting out of National Socialism" [4].

The severity of Barth's opposition was tempered somewhat by his awareness of the role played by the Treaty of Versailles in contributing to the general climate in Germany that made possible the emergence of Hitler. The framers of that treaty must share in the guilt incurred by the Germans [5]. And he called upon the Allies to realize that they were dealing with "a sick man", and that compassion would be required when the war ended [6]. However, these points refer more to the situation of Germany as a whole than to the National Socialist government. At any rate, the judgment that the latter had failed to provide any measure of justice led Barth unequivocally to proclaim the war in progress against Germany a just war [7]. The defense of the war against the Germany represented by Hitler is, Barth asserted, "the only way" to cure the Germans of their present sickness [8]. The war marks

---

[1] *The Church and the Political Problem of Our Day*, p. 38.

[2] *Ibid.*, p. 39.

[3] *Ibid.*, pp. 52, 55.

[4] *Ibid.*, p. 61.

[5] Cf. *This Christian Cause*, First letter to French protestants (New York: The Macmillan Company, 1941). This contains Barth's first and second letters to the French Protestants, written in December, 1939, and October, 1940; and his letter to Great Britain, written in 1941. There is no pagination in this volume. The same point is made in: *The Church and the War* (New York: The Macmillan Company, 1944), p. 25.

[6] *This Christian Cause*, First letter to French protestants.

[7] *The Church and the War*, pp. 14f., 26, 29.

[8] *The Only Way* (New York: The Philosophical Library, 1947), p. 53.

the solidarity of those who oppose the unjust State in the name of the just. The Church must not only support the war effort, but must participate actively in military duty. Every man who fights against Hitler fights in the cause of Jesus Christ—the Czech soldier as well as the Christian [1].

Such is the nature of Barth's encounter with National Socialism. In it, the lines of Christian responsibility in the political sphere were set forth in trenchantly straightforward terms. The only possible response, ethically, to the threat posed by Hitler was the *ultima ratio* of armed resistance. Indeed, Barth seems at times to invest with almost eschatological urgency the necessity of overcoming the National Socialist government. It represents a totally corrupted form of the State, lacking entirely in those features associated with the just State. The possibility of compromise is completely rejected, as is the possibility of different forms of resistance to Hitler [2]. To be sure, one still finds Barth, even with the note of definite crisis in his statements during this period, reminding us of the christological basis of his position, and indicating that the struggle against Hitler is a penultimate venture necessitated by the exigencies of the day. Thus, although the war is a definite task and necessity laid upon all men [3], it must not be presented as a crusade. It is no war of religion, and calls for no fanaticism; indeed, what is needed more than ever are "clear heads" [4]. Further, there are no ideological necessities projected onto the peace that will follow the war. The actions and decisions of the present are not shaped by future expectations [5]. What is needed, in addition to armed resistance, is a remembrance of the present kingly rule of Christ that "confronts and overrules with sover-

---

[1] *The Church and the Political Problem of Our Day*, p. 77.

[2] Charles West has drawn attention to these points in Barth's position: "One looks in vain for any recognition that there was still, even under the Nazis and through their administration, a solid core of uncorrupted state service. One fails to find any recognition that different positions in society required different kinds and degrees of resistance to the Nazi corruption". *Communism and the Theologians*, p. 290.

[3] In his letter to Great Britain, Barth stated that Christians who did not see the necessity of the war "have slept over their Bibles as well as over their newspapers". *This Christian Cause.*

[4] *Ibid.* In: *The Church and the Political Problem of Our Day*, however, National Socialism appears as the "new Islam", i.e., a "proper *Church*" against which decisive and final action must be taken (p. 43).

[5] *Ibid.*

eign dignity the principalities and powers and evil spirits of this world" [1].
Even the power of the National Socialists is "completely disarmed" [2].
Finally, in a comment that is hauntingly evocative of the position he
would later work out in detail in the *Dogmatics*, Barth firmly identified
that present crisis as a momentary, limited outbreak of the evil that has
already been completely vanquished in Jesus Christ:

> The enterprise of Adolph Hitler, with all its clatter and fireworks, and all
> its cunning and dynamic energy, is the enterprise of an evil spirit, which
> is apparently allowed its freedom for a time in order to test our faith
> in the resurrection of Jesus Christ, and above all to test our obedience
> to that faith [3].

Before turning to consider Barth's quite different estimate of Communism, it is important that we recognize clearly the poles between
which his political thought moves, both of which are indicated nicely
in the quotation above. On the one hand, there is the fact of the resurrection and lordship of Christ over the world, and so over every occurrence
and development within history. On the other hand, there are those
situations within history that call for immediate and total involvement
and action, as life and death issues confronting not only Christians
but all men. I have already drawn attention to this polarity, more
indirectly perhaps, in discussing the presence and involvement
of the Christian community in world occurrence and history [4]. It is the
way in which these poles are held firmly together in Barth's thought that
leads, as Charles West notes, to a certain quality of paradox, but not
to contradiction [5]. The paradox arises in the necessity facing Christians
to take seriously the crises and problems that occur within history,
because, not in spite of, the present, total victory of Christ's resurrection
over all historical movements and occurrences. When both poles of the
paradox are held together, we have, in West's suggestive phrase, "a
forceps with two prongs" enabling significant decision and action to
take shape within a proper sensitivity to both theological and historical
realities [6]. It is against the background of this paradox, as West correctly
argues, that an assessment of the validity of Barth's movement from

---

[1] *Ibid.*
[2] *Ibid.*
[3] *Ibid.*
[4] Cf. above, this chapter, Section B, Part 1.
[5] *Communism and the Theologians*, p. 279.
[6] *Ibid.*

theological construction to social realities must be made. I would also argue that it is at the decisively critical juncture where theological insight and empirical context meet in ethical decision and action that the relevance or irrelevance of the notion of the command of God for the ethical situation will be determined.

It is instructive, at this point, to return to Barth's short reply to Brunner's letter, for it is there that we are informed simultaneously of the main consideration behind both Barth's active condemnation of National Socialism, and his subsequent neutrality toward Communism —a neutrality, it should be noted, that appears to have gone considerably beyond the normal "wait and see" period required of Christians in the face of any political change. The major threat in National Socialism— what made it an unmitigated evil to be opposed at all costs—lay in the fact that both in Germany and elsewhere, men "had succumbed to Hitler's spell" [1]. It was the fact that the pseudo-religious ideology put forth by the National Socialists had captured the imaginations and minds of people, and threatened to become the ruling loyalty of their lives, that overshadowed, finally, even its obvious totalitarianism, its virulent anti-Semitism, and the militarism that brought about its extension throughout Europe:

> Whether the essence of National Socialism consisted in its 'totalitarianism' or, according to other views, in its 'nihilism', or again in its barbarism, or anti-semitism, or whether it was a final, concluding outburst of the militarism which had taken hold on Germany like a madness since 1870 —what made it interesting from the Christian point of view was that it was a spell which notoriously revealed its power to overwhelm our souls, to persuade us to believe in its lies and to join in its evildoings [2].

The danger posed by National Socialism, then, was not simply "a matter of declaiming against some mischief, distant and easily seen through" [3]. As we have seen, it was a matter of life and death, a historical crisis of the first order, and it called for resolute and unyielding resistance:

> For that very reason I spoke then and was not silent. For that very reason I could not forgive the collaborators, least of all those among them who were cultured, decent and well-meaning. In that way I consider that I acted as befits a churchman [4].

---

[1] *Against the Stream*, p. 114.
[2] *Ibid.*, p. 115.
[3] *Ibid.*
[4] *Ibid.*

The situation posed by Communism, however, is different. To be sure, it is still totalitarianism, and if anyone wishes from Barth "a political disclaimer of its system and its methods", he "may have it at once" [1]. This would not really amount to much, however, since there is no present danger of anyone being tempted by Communism. Since Communism is generally condemned and rejected, it would mean nothing for the Church openly to enter the lists against it; it would *cost* nothing, for there is no clear and immediate danger confronting the Church that demands unequivocal rejection and resistance:

> What is given cheaply can be had cheaply. Surely it would cost no one anything—not even a little thought—certainly nothing more, to add his bundle of faggots to the bonfire? [2]

Behind Barth's reluctance to be drawn into the general chorus of opposition to Communism lay, of course, his emphasis on the uniqueness of each situation as it is shaped by the command of God, together with the necessity for the Church always to move in its own direction, independently of prevailing opinion, "in fear and trembling, not with the stream but against it" [3]. The additional danger Barth sees in the Church's opposing Communism at this point is that it will be drawn into the ideological assumptions of the West, and so find itself moving "in principle" against it as simply one more instance of totalitarianism:

> Must the Church then move with the stream and thus side with America and the Vatican, merely because somewhere in the textbooks of its professors—ever since 1914—it has rightly been said that 'totalitarianism' is a dreadful thing? [4]

When the principles and ideology of the West are set aside, and the Church surveys the situation from its perspective of the total victory of

---

[1] *Ibid.*, p. 116.

[2] *Ibid.* In "The Church between East and West" (in: *Against the Stream*, pp. 127-146), Barth expands on this point: "Ten years ago it cost something to say the one-sided, unequivocal 'No' that it was necessary and imperative to say at that time. For anyone who said that 'No' was not able to whistle it with all the sparrows from the rooftops. At that time he saw himself surrounded by the careful silence of most of the fine people who are so excited today, saw himself criticized, by the same papers that shout so loudly today, as a prejudiced fanatic, saw himself accused of infringing the law of Christian love with his speeches, and of endangering Swiss neutrality" (p. 137). First published in: *Unterwegs*, June and July, 1949. Translation here by Stanley Godman.

[3] *Against the Stream*, p. 116.

[4] *Ibid.*, p. 117.

the Gospel over all human claims and pretensions, and the immediacy of the command, it is led of necessity, as regards the issue of Communism, to a position of continued patience and, for the moment, aloofness:

> I am of the opinion that the Church today—contrary to its action between 1933 and 1945—ought to stand quietly aloof from the present conflict and not let off all its guns before it is necessary but wait calmly to see whether and in what sense the situation will grow serious again and call for speech [1].

The Church, then, must stand "between East and West", and refuse to participate in what is essentially no more than a power struggle between Russia and the United States. That conflict, Barth tells us, is "not a genuine, not a necessary, not an interesting conflict" [2]. It is conducted in terms of purely standardized ideological points of view, which the Church must at all costs resist becoming involved in [3]. This will be an exceedingly difficult undertaking, for "geographical and natural circumstances inevitably lead us to take sides with America and the Western hemisphere" [4]. The primary task of the Church, for the moment, is to resist this easy alignment with the Western value structure and interpretation of history, and to insist, in spite of criticism, that "the Church is *not* identical with the West, that the Western conscience and judgment is not necessarily the Christian judgment" [5]. At the same time, it must not be seduced into identifying itself with the East. In its political decisions, the Church is called to a responsible discernment of the cause of God, which lies entirely beyond the conflict between East and West [6].

Barth was even willing to cite qualitative differences between the totalitarianism of the Nazis and that of the Communists. Communism, for all its inhumanity (and Barth did not deny this), has wrestled seriously with the social question—something the West has yet to do with any degree of consistency and conviction. The ideological and philosophical grounding of Communism in Marxist thought makes it and its leaders (i.e., Stalin) more appealing than Hitler and the propaganda the Nazis passed out as truth. And Communism, unlike National

---

[1] *Ibid.*

[2] "The Church Between East and West", in: *Against the Stream*, p. 131.

[3] Just how standardized Barth feels the respective viewpoints are is indicated in the summary he gives of them. Cf. *Against the Stream*, pp. 132ff.

[4] *Ibid.*, p. 134.

[5] *Ibid.*, p. 135. Barth makes this same point in his letter to a pastor in East Germany. Cf. *How to Serve God in a Marxist Land*, pp. 51ff.

[6] *Against the Stream*, p. 136.

Socialism (and for Barth this point was crucial) has made no move to replace Christ and the Church by claiming for itself the status of a new revelation [1]. These differences make it impossible for the Church to view its encounter with Communism as "a matter of a good Christian-political confession" [2].

Speaking in Hungary in 1948, Barth counseled sensitivity to the mixture of good and evil in all political systems, and argued an appreciation of the remnants of good to be found in even the worst political systems—a point that dropped out entirely in his analysis of National Socialism:

> There is no such thing as a perfect political system. There are only better and worse systems ... But something of God's wisdom and patience ... will be revealed by even the worst political system ... It may well be that even in the best State Christians will never be able to express their gratitude for God's gift and ordinance except in the form of serious opposition. But this implies that they will never be able to regard and treat even the worst State as wholly diabolical. If they have to remember on the one hand that it would be pure foolishness to expect any political system to be the Kingdom of God, they must not forget that 'the devil has already lost his ancient right to the whole human race', so that, much as he would like to, he does not in fact stand a chance of incarnating himself in any political system [3].

How is the obvious (and sometimes baffling) difference in Barth's position toward National Socialism and Communism to be interpreted? Perhaps a few preliminary observations of a general nature are in order. Political decisions are always open to question, for the simple reason that they embody a certain degree of ambiguity and elusiveness. The basis for their ambiguity and elusiveness lies in the complexity of the situation in which they are made. On the one hand, there are the objectively present factors in the situation that must be recognized, evaluated, and decided upon. From among the various alternatives present, a choice must be made, and the risk of error and misunderstanding taken. On the other hand, there are the less tangible (but nevertheless real) factors of internal motivation and interest, the necessity to achieve a degree of impartiality in making a decision, and the consequences implied by

---

[1] *Ibid.*, p. 139f.

[2] *Ibid.*, p. 143.

[3] "The Christian Community in the Midst of Political Change", in: *Against the Stream* (pp. 77-93), p. 81. Originally delivered in Sarospatak and Budapest in March, 1948. Translation by Stanley Godman.

specific courses of action or inaction. Christians, however, stand under an additional burden and responsibility in making a political decision —or any ethical decision. Beyond the normally present factors, obvious and subtle, that make up the context of decision, they must keep continually in mind the significance of the reconciling action of God in Jesus Christ for every specific decision. Where the ethics of Barth are concerned, this means nothing less than remaining open and sensitive to the way in which the resurrection of Christ, as the central ontological event under which all human activity and history is set, impinges on the totality of a given situation and invests it with ethical meaning and direction. The goal at which ethical decision aims, within the context of Barth's ethics, is immediate obedience to the will of God embodied in the command, i.e., the total formation of the situation that occurs in the present activity of God. And the possibility (and actuality) of achieving obedience, as we have seen, is dependent on the specific action of the Holy Spirit.

It is against this background that an appraisal of Barth's political thought can be undertaken. The crucial issue in this has to do with his success or failure in unifying theological insights with the empirical givenness of particular situations. The first thing to notice is that Barth's theological reading of the State remained remarkably consistent, despite the dramatic difference in his ethical response to National Socialism and Communism. By placing it under the category of redemption rather than creation, he avoided the possibilities both of inflexible ideological commitment to some particular form of political organization, and of the Lutheran "two kingdoms" distinction. As an order of the covenant, the State—that whole "outer circle" of communal order and structure insured by law—is brought within the stretch of time created for man by Christ's resurrection, and his ongoing *parousia* in the Holy Spirit and is thus related positively to the Christian community. Christians are set free to accept the civil community with its definite order and limit as an aspect of the gracious action of God in preserving space and time in which it can carry out its ministry of witness and reconciliation in light of the justification that has come to man in Christ.

At the same time, there are certain relative distinctions that inform the prophetic action of the Church in its service to the State, just as they indicate the general direction in which the State is to move in order to fulfill its service to the Church. The ordering category here is "justice". Not as an absolute, of course, nor as a principle that the Christian community brings to bear in approving or condemning particular forms of political order. As we discovered, justice for Barth works dynamically. It is sought after and formed in a relative, provisional way in the concrete process of giving substance and structure to the political community. There are analogical guidelines that provide assistance here, though again, they cannot be abstracted and handled as final principles. The just State is more readily discernible, perhaps, in a constitutional democracy, but the Church need not insist on this specific form in order to exist. Judging from the analogies to human justification that Barth argues ought to follow in the political community, the main consideration, after all, is what happens to persons within a particular order. Pending an answer to this question, the Church can always afford to be patiently open to political changes, regardless of the direction they assume initially. Within history, the Church will never encounter the perfect State, nor one that is completely diabolical. It will always be faced with a political order that falls between these extremes. Whatever crises must be lived through in the political sphere, the Church will view them in the light of the resurrection, and so refuse to invest them with final importance. They will be no more than relative, temporary complexities within a history whose future has already been irrevocably decided in Christ.

When Barth's theological perspective on the State is brought into conjunction with specific cases, several things can be noted. First, the major concern manifested in Barth's encounter with both National Socialism and Communism appears to lie more at the level of the ideological bearing these have on the self-understanding of the Church than in the question of their impact on persons. His rejection of Hitler and the Nazi program took shape initially as a theological criticism of the "German Christians", which later became an all-out attack against the perverted religious ideology of the Nazis. In retrospect, it is the temptation that National Socialism carried for the Church that Barth cited as the major factor in his opposition. His refusal to take a straightforwardly negative position toward Communism was grounded, in part, in a similar ideological concern, this time in the fear that a rejection of Communist ideology would lead the Church too easily to embrace that of the West. Thus, although both movements (National Socialism and Communism) were responded to only after an initial period of waiting, the results were radically different.

The second point of importance for understanding Barth's position on these different political developments was his persistent refusal to be trapped into utilizing totalitarianism as a principle. Situations are to be judged individually, under the impact of the command of God. Thus, although formally considered National Socialism and Communism are both totalitarian systems, the Church's response must not be grounded in this consideration. Totalitarianism exhibits important material differences in its historical manifestations which theological ethics must take into account in making assessments and reaching decisions. As we have seen, Barth was especially impressed by the concern of Communism with restructuring the social order, and its refusal (ostensibly) to proclaim itself a replacement or extension of Christ and the Church.

When Barth's rejection of principles is joined with the ideological thrust of his encounter with both National Socialism and Communism, the question arises whether these concerns dulled, to a degree, his perception of the actual situation under which people are placed in these regimes, and the precise form the State assumes. Charles West has raised this question most pointedly, and argues that Barth is not entirely successful in making the transition from theological insight to social and political realities [1]. The reason for this, as West sees it, is that Barth has refused to enlist the aid of social scientists and politicians in forming a complete picture of the internal dynamics and configuration of specific political and historical realities. The resulting *lacuna* is filled by Barth's general knowledge of culture, generalizations out of his "very limited personal experience in the politics of Germany and Switzerland, and information and judgments from friends whose theology he trusts" [2]. The upshot of this, West argues, is "confusion and ineptitude in Barth's theology of politics, where he faces the difficult decisions which Christians must make in crisis situations" [3].

I would agree with West's contention that Barth pays insufficient attention to the sort of empirical grounding that might be provided by the social sciences. Barth's tendency to rely on the insights, for specific problems, that can be derived from theological categories and analyses has been noted both in his general delineation of the command, and in the preceding sections of this chapter. Admittedly, the theologian would need to be alert to possible ideological or self-justifying overtones in these disciplines. It is also clear, however, that theological ethics cannot

---

[1] *Communism and the Theologians*, p. 287.
[2] *Ibid.*
[3] *Ibid.*

itself provide the detailed, accurate analyses of specific developments, structure and contexts required for a sensitivity to the direction in which obedience to what God is doing in the world at those points lies. As regards Barth's political thought in particular, the question can legitimately be asked whether he has been as sensitive to the particular situations in which men find themselves, and the ethical demands and tensions these impose, as his own exclusively contextual approach to ethics requires. Barth may have been quite right in refusing to make a decision either for or against either side of the ideological conflict between East and West. Indeed, perhaps the single most important contribution that he has made to the ethical sensitivity of the Church lies in his insistence that the reconciling action of God in Jesus Christ set men free once and for all from the need to make any ideology a life or death issue.

When this point has been granted, however, the question still must be faced, on the ground of Barth's own concern for maintaining and protecting the basic givenness of man's common life with his fellows, what a given political order means for those living under it. On occasion, Barth expressed real sensitivity to the plight of the individual under Communism [1], a sensitivity that moved considerably beyond the clash of ideologies. To be sure, individuals can and do suffer under Western governments as well, and they achieve at best only a fragmented, ambiguous approximation of social and economic justice. The fact that injustice to an extent flourishes in both the East and the West is not, however, a sufficient basis for deciding, as Barth did, that the conflict between them is merely ideological, and therefore not a conflict in which the Church has any stake. Obviously, the future of the Church is not tied inextricably to the fate of Western civilization. It has been demonstrated often enough, in the past as well as in the present, that the Christian community can exist under both totalitarian and democratic forms of government. On the basis of Barth's own analogical suggestions as to the direction in which political justice lies, however, a more precise awareness of the empirical realities occasioned by Communism would appear to be in order. Barth was impressed with the concern for social justice embodied in the Marxist critique of Western culture, which has received a certain actualization in the political order of Communism. The question here, however, is whether it is not important to draw a

---

[1] Cf., for example, his comments in: *How to Serve God in a Marxist Land*, pp. 70ff.

distinction between political order (and justice) and economic justice? In non-Communist socialist countries in the West, for instance, the social problem has been successfully tackled without the oppressive political results usually attached to Communist governments. Further, it is not clear that Barth was sufficiently sensitive to the way in which Communist ideology can be used to justify and prolong practices which have essentially no relationship whatever to the question of social and economic justice.

In short, Barth's application of theological insights to specific political contexts suggests a lack of appreciation of the complexity and subtlety surrounding those contexts, which lends an overtone of cavalierness to some of the proposals he has advanced. It is perhaps not altogether possible, in the end, to avoid the feeling that Barth's major preoccupation, in the area of political and social action, was to safeguard the Church against ideological confinement, and that he moved into action primarily at those points where the freedom and purity of the Church's witness and proclamation were threatened. What is not clear is that his action (or inaction) has always shown an awareness of the subtle as well as the obvious ways in which the existence and activity of the Christian community can be threatened, or of the complete dimensions and meaning of the empirical context in which individuals find themselves. Barth's insistence on deriving ethical directives from christological considerations, and his insufficient development of the empirical complexity and subtlety of specific contexts, are themselves, in some respects, suggestive of an ideological overtone in his thinking on political questions.

At the end of the discussion of Barth's treatment of vocation and work, I argued that it exhibited a modification of his earlier development of the ethical event (i.e., God's command and man's response), in that it opened the way, implicitly at least, for the employment of rational assessment and deliberation. In order to see clearly what is involved here, it will be helpful to step back a moment from the context of special ethics, and recall the perplexities that emerged at the end of our discussion of the command in its general meaning and form. There, we recall, the notion of command was developed exclusively in relation to the category of event. Barth's insistence on viewing the command as event led to certain difficulties. First, it made unclear the sense, if any, in which Barth could be said to have established a cognitive ethics. Given his emphasis on the objective status of the events of revelation, it seemed feasible to expect that he would develop an ethic whose cognitive, factual status would be evident. As it turned out, however, it was difficult to see, on inspection, how that could be maintained. The difficulty arose because of Barth's unification of dogmatics and ethics. The result of this was that the epistemological and logical problems that placed the cognitive status of dogmatic propositions in jeopardy now extended to the propositions of ethics as well. Whatever meaning attached to the notion of command, and the attempts made to give linguistic expression to it, occurred only in the event of God's immediate action in the Holy Spirit. The upshot of this, we saw, is that the "event" in which man is confronted by the command in a specific situation displays no continuity with ordinary epistemic modes. Like faith, it requires the presentation of a new level of subjectivity. The Holy Spirit thus supplies both the command, and the condition for its being apprehended. In the end, it was difficult to see in what way the command makes contact with empirical realities, and the possibility was raised that an elucidation of the command might end, like the doctrine of the Trinity, by saying nothing at all.

Another result of Barth's general statement of the command was that it appeared to exclude the function, normally assigned practical reason in ethics, of a deliberation and assessment of alternatives. This was clearly the case insofar as such deliberation might consist in relating formal principles or rules to specific contexts requiring moral action. As Barth developed the command as the specific event that shapes the total situation in which man is placed, it also appeared to exclude a more modest sort of appraisal of alternatives and options, in order to decide, in a given context, what the command of God was. The command issued directly out of the total context of the gospel, and, like it, left no undecided factors, no loose ends, so to speak, that might present a certain range of possibilities for human choice and discretion. The definiteness of the command made this sort of open-textured view of the ethical situation impossible. Down to the last detail, the command presented itself as a totally self-interpreting imperative—a complete and final shaping of the context—before which only the possibilities of obedience or disobedience remained. The upshot of this approach was that it tended to undercut the actual complexity of the ethical situation, and to exclude the quite obvious range of behavioral options that lie before us at the point of decision. In addition, it failed to account satisfactorily for the different ways in which the will of God given in the command is interpreted.

I have argued that a modification of this position is discernible in Barth's treatment of vocation and work. This modification continues and deepens in the sections of special ethics that deal with man's freedom in fellowship and life, and reaches a culmination, of sorts, in Barth's approach to the question of obedience within the context of politics. It might be assumed that the explanation for this modification lies in the fact that in special ethics attention focuses primarily on the horizontal thrust of the command that gives rise to those spheres and relationships within which man is called to responsible freedom. As an explanation, however, this will not do. None of the spheres and relationships that take form under the command are themselves equatable with the command. The command occurs *within* these, and it does so as a "formed reference" consisting of both the immediacy of the command and the equally immediate response of obedience or disobedience required of man. Barth was quite clear in his insistence that within the different contexts of special ethics, man is still faced with the necessity for "instant obedience", which again would seem to exclude the possibility of there being viable options between which a choice must be made.

Despite this apparently continuing emphasis on the immediacy and stringency of the command, and the requirement it places upon man for immediate obedience, Barth quite obviously allowed considerable latitude in special ethics to rational discrimination, assessment and choice. There is more of a sense of the actual complexity of the ethical situation, and of the options that lie to hand within it. Even here, Barth's insistence on deriving ethical guidelines along christological lines sometimes resulted in an oversimplification of the situation, and his two-level view of man as moral agent failed to take note of the complexity of the self at the point of motivation and decision. However, the implications that a heightened sensitivity to the place of rational deliberation in ethics carries for the notions of command and obedience can be examined in relative isolation from these points.

When Barth tells us that the political decisions of Christians aim at hitting the point "where common sense speaks the language of the Holy Spirit and the Holy Spirit the language of common sense" [1]; or that the apprehension of the command in relation to the issue of birth control requires "rational reflection" [2]; or that there are situations in

---

[1] "Political Decisions in the Unity of Faith", in: *Against the Stream*, p. 160.

[2] III/4, p. 304.

which war is justified, but each individual must analyse fully the prevailing conditions and make his own decision [1], it is difficult to avoid concluding that rational deliberation has a definite importance, from man's side at least, in determining what the command of God is for a given situation. However, if I have understood correctly Barth's initial development of the command, the latitude given reason (understood informally) in special ethics raises certain questions. To begin with, the relationship thus posited between the activity of reason (i.e., "common sense") and the command is not clear. In the context of politics, Barth comes close to suggesting the possibility of a direct coincidence between these—if we may assume that the activity of the Holy Spirit and the immediate actuality of the command are identical there. And in the remaining contexts of special ethics, there is clearly a certain proximity intimated between the process of rational deliberation and decision and the formative thrust of the command. Even when allowance has been made for the fact that the statement about the relationship between common sense and the Holy Spirit taken from Barth's political thought falls outside the context of the more studied tone of the *Dogmatics*, so that it would be perhaps ill-advised to base too much on it, there is still a general impression running throughout the sections of special ethics that to an extent at least the Holy Spirit speaks through the channel of ordinary rational discernment and choice.

The difficulty with this, however, is that Barth, so far as I can see, has not prepared us for this move in his earlier description of the command, nor in his doctrine of man, nor in his development of the "event" of grace. At none of these points was there a discernible basis for the sort of continuity between man's rational capabilities (as moral agent) and grace that Barth allows in his special ethics. Thus, there seems to be a difficulty in Barth's transition from his general delineation of the command to its ramifications for specific ethical contexts. This has to do, perhaps, with the fact that his initial statement of the command follows immediately out of the extensive discussion of the doctrine of election, and so remains relatively abstract or removed as regards specific ethical situations.

To put the matter somewhat differently, in his initial treatment of the command, Barth moves directly out of the context of what may be described as "divine ethics". At that point, the discussion of the command aimed more in the direction of the *total* ethical context resulting.

---

[1] *Ibid.*, p. 533f.

from the reconciling action of God, and the eternal election of man accomplished by it. Now, there obviously can be no alternatives vis-à-vis man's election. That event provides a total ontological determination for the human within all men are enclosed. It is scarcely surprising, then, that when the command is formulated initially against that event, and the determination it brings to the human, the "definiteness" of the command excludes the possibility of rational assessment and deliberation. At an ontologically inclusive level, there is simply no need for Barth to concern himself with either the complexity of structures or the range of alternatives and behavioral options that make up the concrete ethical context.

When he moves to develop the sections of special ethics, Barth still wants to claim the definiteness of the command, and the necessity for immediate obedience. It is apparent, however, that, from man's side at least, the definiteness of the command cannot be maintained in quite the same way. There are alternatives that must be recognized; possibilities to be agonized over; the thin line dividing the world from the Kingdom of God to be aimed at in decision and action. In special ethics, Barth necessarily moves out of a strictly *theological* development, and into the business of rational analysis and explication. Whether or not his elucidation of the guidelines within which the direction of the command falls—either the relatively "normal" range of possibilities, or the more infrequent action required "ultima ratio"—depends, as Bouillard claims, more on the ordinary judgments of reason than on the Word of God and the divine command [1], the point I have been arguing remains constant. In special ethics, the process of rational deliberation occupies a place of definite importance, in contrast to its virtual exclusion in Barth's general discussion of theological ethics as the command of God.

This modification raises a question, however, as to the final significance of the command for ethics. What does it mean, for instance, to refer to God's command beyond the process of deliberation leading to a choice? Is the command to be seen as something "in" the ethical situation over and above the factors discerned by reason? If it is taken as the total "gestalt" of the situation, in what sense is it "there" as a form or direction capable of embodiment either linguistically or behaviorally? We have already noted the difficulty in providing the command with linguistic precision in the framework of its general contours.

---

[1] *Karl Barth*, Vol. III, p. 256f.

Barth's development of special ethics moves us no closer to a direct expression of the command. Indeed, this possibility is ruled out from the beginning, because the command is always viewed as immediate event; the point at which God's Word is addressed directly to man, and the response of obedience or disobedience follows. As event, the command remains *actus purus*, in continuity with the action of the Holy Spirit in providing the possibility (and actuality) for the existence of the Christian community, and the individual Christian, and for the occurrence of theology.

The most that can be achieved, as regards a direct expression of the command and human obedience, is an indication of the lines along which these normally fall. Here we are helped to a degree by the fact that the command displays both a vertical and a horizontal dimension. The importance of the latter is that it provides for the emergence of definite spheres and relationships within which obedience occurs—although it is not strictly limited to these. Descriptively, then, it is possible, after a fashion, to given an account of Christian action as it takes form within the horizontal thrust of the command. Negatively, the usual direction in which obedience lies might be formulated this way: As a rule, or generally, or for the most part (these locutions being approximately the same, logically) Christians do not divorce, kill, go to war, commit suicide, condone capital punishment, or renounce (even temporarily) solidarity with their fellow-men. There are, for most of these usual directions, limiting or exceptional cases where the normal "rule" of human behavior undergoes a kind of teleological suspension under the impact of the immediate action of Christ in the Holy Spirit. This is not to suggest that the general direction discernible within the horizontal movement of the command provides a set of principles or rules that are "applied" ethically by being introduced into specific contexts. The spheres and relationships created by the command of God, and the general direction set for human behavior within them, must be distinguished. The definite orders and structures of co-humanity that emerge under the command are not static, inflexible contexts that determine in themselves what appropriate human action will be. They are, rather, concrete situations within which man is called to a responsible exercise of freedom. What is to be done, specifically, will depend on a proper openness and responsiveness, on man's part, to the precise configuration given a situation by the formative presence of God through the command. Thus, although it is possible to provide an indication of the direction in which the command of God and human obedience will normally lie, in the end neither can be directly specified.

The immediacy of the command insures that human action remains (relatively) free of ideological constraint and confusion, and provides for a total openness to each situation. The difficulty, however, is in getting clear what a reference to the command beyond the process of rational deliberation leading to ethical choice and action is to mean, for it is clear that although Barth allows for the importance, in special ethics, of the function of deliberative reason at the point of coming to some conclusion as to what the command of God is for a specific context, the two are not directly equatable. In what sense is the command present in the situation? To whom is it present? The Christian community? The individual Christian? All men? The answer, of course, is that it is present at all three points, but in perhaps different ways. The command is present for all men *de iure*, as an aspect of their ontological determination in Christ. It is there *de facto* for the Christian community as a whole, since it recognizes and accepts the total direction under which human life is set by the action of God. And it is there for the individual in the immediacy of the situation in which he must decide and act.

It is possible to get a relatively clear sense of the meaning of the command in its inclusive significance for man, whether at a *de iure* or a *de facto* level. For there it serves to indicate the *direction* in which human existence and action is set under the reconciling action of God, and provides a common ethical framework for the human. It is when we move to the level of individual judgment and action that the precise meaning of the command becomes opaque, for two reasons: First, because it is not clear how the unity of the command, and the initial action of the Holy Spirit toward the Christian community as a whole, are to be reconciled with the variety of specific "hearings" that are claimed, particularly where supportive appeal is made in each case to the Holy Spirit! Second, because it is not immediately evident what basis there is in men outside the community to hear and receive the summons to obedience issued by the individual members of the community. The problem here is that although Barth provides for a common total ethical framework for all men at an ontological level, it is not clear how this is capable of expression within *specific* ethical contexts. Barth's ambiguity about the precise relationship between the command of God and rational deliberation poses a difficulty at this point. Although practical reason is given more of a place in special ethics, its relationship to the command remains elusive. A more serious difficulty is posed, however, by Barth's ambiguity as to the ontic status of man—both the "natural" man and the Christian [1]. Until this is clarified, both the place of rational deliberation in ethics, and the line of continuity, within a particular ethical situation, between Christians and non-Christians, will remain dubious. Indeed, at this point in the discussion, it seems that the latitude Barth allows to rational deliberation in special ethics occurs in spite of, rather than because of, his anthropology.

---

[1] Cf. above, Ch. V. Cf. Bouillard, *Karl Barth*, Vol. III, p. 235f.

CHAPTER SEVEN

QUESTIONS, ISSUES AND PROJECTIONS:
CHRISTIAN ETHICS BEYOND BARTH

A. QUESTIONS AND ISSUES

The concern in the preceding sections of this study was to elucidate and analyze the structure and substance of Barth's ethics, and to draw critical reservations where these appeared necessary. Because of the exceedingly tight relationship that Barth establishes between dogmatics and ethics, an adequate treatment of the latter requires a full sensitivity to the theological framework in which it is placed. When Barth's ethics is displayed within the rich architechtonic of the *Church Dogmatics*, its credibility and effectiveness are vitiated by a series of recurring problems that render ambiguous the status of man as subject and agent, the meaning of the command, and the possibility of obedient action that goes geyond the basic act of worship. It will be helpful to indicate these here, for it is against their background that suggestions must be made about the direction in which theological ethics beyond Barth will need to move.

1. *The Adequacy of Barth's Method*

The most general reservation I have about Barth's ethics centers in the overtones of transcendentalism and actualism that run throughout it. Although Barth is obviously at pains to bring the ethical content of the *Dogmatics* into meaningful contact with the empirical world, his aim is frustrated by objectionable points in the method he adopts to do this. The two central aspects of theological method in the *Dogmatics* lie in the employment of the "principle" of presupposition, which derives from Barth's concern to ground the various "loci" of dogmatics in Christology; and in the use of analogy, which provides the means whereby epistemological and ontological basis and continuity are given to the human. In wielding these two aspects of his method, Barth is led into a strong realist position, which produces ontological epistemological and logical difficulties. These center, respectively, on the question of the independent status of creation (i.e., man and history); the relationship of faith (as the epistemic mode of the Christian), and the knowledge of revelation given in faith, to the knowledge of the human derivable through ordinary epistemic modes; the relationship between the logical form and the meaning of theological and ethical statements.

These problems reflect the strictness with which Barth insists on the analogical grounding of man and history against the background of the christological presupposition. Thus, man and history within the created order are ontologically grounded (*analogia relationis*) in the relationship between God and man in Christ, and between Father and Son (through the action of the Holy Spirit) in the eternal trinitarian being of God. The knowledge of God man has in faith is grounded (*analogia fidei*) in God's own self-knowledge. And the way in which meaning is given to theological and ethical statements reflects the "real similarity along with complete dissimilarity" that holds between God and the world. This means that meaning is conferred on these statements in the immediate, direct action of the Holy Spirit (*actus purus*).

Barth's use of analogy is designed to overcome every suggestion of an immanent line of continuity or point of contact between man and God that would permit a "natural" development of theological ontology and epistemology, thereby insuring that theological language has the capacity, in itself, to speak of God. The rejection of the *analogia entis* that runs throughout the *Church Dogmatics* marks the culminating statement of Barth's persistent concern, beginning about 1911, to break away from the assumptions governing nineteenth century theology. The initial impact of this concern, methodologically, appeared in the second edition of the *Römerbrief*. Barth's thinking at that time was marked by an emphasis on the total transcendence of God over the world, the employment of dialectic as the major vehicle in theological method, and the utilization of Kantian (or neo-Kantian) categories. In the *Church Dogmatics*, Barth moves out of dialectic into analogy, drops the emphasis on the "wholly other" character of God in revelation in favor of "the humanity of God" exhibited in Christ, and replaces Kant (for the most part) with Hegel. Although Barth wishes to maintain the line of distinction between God and the world as strictly in the *Dogmatics* as in the *Römerbrief*, the former, by its unrelieved emphasis on the humanity of God in Christ, allows for a genuine participation of man in the event of revelation. And, by developing fully the time of reconciliation between creation and redemption, provides (ostensibly) for an embodiment of man's knowledge of revelation in meaningful action. In short, the use of analogy in the *Dogmatics* is designed to make possible what was obviously impossible in the *Römer-brief*: a viable theological ethics that enables man to move beyond the "crisis" occasioned by the inbreak of God into history, freeing him for obedient involvement in the structures and events of his world.

I have argued, however, that Barth's use of analogy, when placed against the pervasive christological grounding of things in the *Dogmatics*, tends to obscure, rather than clarify, the status of the creature. Ontologically, the confusion results, initially, from Barth's description of the created order, and the structures, relationships and actions within it, as "likenesses" of the eternal relationship between the Father and the Son in the Trinity. When to this are added his statements about the "eternal" fulfillment of salvation history in the union between the Son of God and the humanity of Jesus in the Trinity; and about the inclusive temporality of God's being, which entails that all the events of the creaturely order are known beforehand to God, the independent status of ordinary history is obscured, and its dynamic configurations and unpredictability are reduced. This is not to suggest that Barth ends by identifying God and the world. The analogical relationship between creation and God, salvation history and ordinary history, involves both similarity and dissimilarity; and the former is established only from God's side, in grace. Even so, we have seen that Barth fails to develop adequately the sort of insights that might be expected to come from a created order that is really distinct from the being and action of God. In particular, Barth tends to minimize, and occasionally to over-look, the empirical givenness and complexity of the creaturely, historical sphere, in favor of the insights that come directly out of salva-tion history, i.e., christological description. Thus, while not excluding entirely the significance of the "phenomena" of man's historical, political and social life, and the disciplines concerned with their study, he never quite arrives at the point of indicating directly their bearing on the theo-logical venture.

In addition to making ambiguous the independence of the created order and human history, Barth's use of the *analogia relationis* leads, interestingly, to another sort of difficulty: When Christ is made the presupposition for understanding the relation between sacred (i.e., *Heilsgeschite*) and human history, there is confusion as to how salvation history makes contact with the ordinary space-time context of nature and history, since the former lodges at an essentially transcendent level. The ostensible exception to this, of course, is the specific history of Christ. We discovered, however, that Barth is ambiguous in his reading of the central event of Christ's history, the resurrection. That event is somehow both "historical" (*Historie*) and "unhistorical" (*Geschichte*). It is an event that occurred in space and time whose meaning lies on a transcendent plane, inaccessible to the working historian. The confusion is merely deepened when Barth tells us that the creation "event" is similarly "historical". The upshot of this is that Barth is forced to fall back on dogmatic assertion, and tends to ignore the pressing question of evidence and verification. Even the investigation of the evidence provided by the New Testament accounts of the resurrection, for instance, is curtailed somewhat by Barth's view of the relationship between hermeneutics and dogmatics [1].

The epistemological problem to which Barth's realism leads arises out of his stringent rejection of every suggestion of an immanent ground or "point of contact" in man which enables him, on his own, to know God. It follows from this that man is not himself notically active in the event of revelation. Just as Christ forms the presupposition of being, he is also the presupposition of knowing. Thus, revelation supplies its own epistemology. This occurs through the immediate and continuous activity of Christ in the Holy Spirit, and results in man's receiving an appropriate, though limited, knowledge of God (*analogia fidei*). In the action of the Holy Spirit, man is provided with the condition for a knowledge of revelation, and is made participant in it, noetically, in faith.

The problem with this, however, is that faith, as a cognitive mode given man in the "event" of grace, evidences no obvious relationship or continuity with ordinary epistemic modes, or the knowledge resulting from them. On the contrary, faith for Barth apparently constitutes a wholly new subjective level in man. The latter point is in some ways reminiscent of the Kantian notion of a transcendental ego. Thus, the unique transcendental reality of salvation history requires a correspondingly unique mode of apprehension. Aside from the difficulties this appraoch carries for Barth's anthropology it also has the consequence of drastically reducing the possibility of a concern for the apologetic question. By overruling every suggestion of an immanent point of

---

[1] I shall return to the ontological problems connected with Barth's methodological assumptions, and the transcendental and actualistic overtones they embody, when we examine the results of his anthropology in the next section.

continuity between God and man, and by lodging the epistemological basis for a knowledge of revelation in the event of revelation itself, Barth is led to a rejection of the questions generated by that event by absorbing epistemology into ontology.

The third major difficulty with Barth's realism lies in the effect it has on the statements of dogmatics and ethics. Here again there are strong intimations of transcendentalism and actualism. Barth takes it that these statements have no meaning in themselves. The impact of sin is such that the possibility of a direct appropriation of creaturely language for the purpose of talking about God is excluded. This means that meaning is not an indigenous property of language when put to the task of describing the reality of God in revelation, and the ethical implications that follow. Meaning, Barth seems to say, is conferred directly, in the action of the Holy Spirit (*actus purus*). Apart from the event of grace, theological and ethical statements have no meaning.

The difficulties in this approach to the question of meaning are as follows. First, it is self-defeating for Barth's whole theological program, for it renders ambiguous the objective status of the events of salvation history. If theological language in itself has *no* meaning, then it is neither true nor false, since meaning (of some sort) is a necessary criterion for deciding the truth or falsity of any statement or proposition. However, if this is the case, then theological language cannot be supplied with a *true* sense or meaning through an appeal to the miraculous event of grace. The result is that the cognitive force of such propositions is seriously compromised. And if the statements and propositions of theology (and ethics) are finally non-cognitive, it is unclear what would be meant by referring to the *objectivity* of the events of salvation history. In order for the latter point to hold, theological statements would have to function, logically, as *assertions*. Barth's approach rules out this possibility.

Second, Barth's analysis results in an intolerable separation between the logical form of language and its meaning, and suggests that theological language might actually be meaningless without the benefit of a special divine illumination. This is a totally inadequate approach to the statements of theology, for it makes the meaning of such statements dependent simply on the assertion of the theologian about the activity of grace. If Barth's actualistic derivation of meaning is adopted, both his dogmatics and his ethics cease to have descriptive force, and become poetic or metaphorical expressions. As regards Barth's ethics specifically, we saw that this was indeed the case. The notions both of the "event" of grace in which the command is made real to man, and of the command itself, bordered on metaphor, and so remained at least partially ambiguous.

Thus Barth's method tends in certain respects to defeat his purposes. The use of the principle of presupposition and the method of analogy invest his theology and ethics with the overtones of transcendentalism and actualism, and make ambiguous the precise status of the created order, history and the knowledge derived from ordinary cognitive modes, and the relationship these bear to the events of salvation history. Nor does the relationship Barth establishes between created and reconciled human nature succeed in alleviating these difficulties.

2. *Man as Subject and Agent*

The ontological difficulties attendant upon Barth's use of the *analogia relationis* are nowhere exposed more clearly than in his anthropology. We have found that man's status as subject and agent is threatened alternately in the *Dogmatics* by (1) an insufficient distinction between God and man, and the possibility of an "absorption" of humanity; (2) an inadequate reading of the structure of the human, and the suggestion that man is only deficiently person and agent; (3) an ambiguous treatment of faith, love and hope as ontic modes of the Christian, which, together with freedom, appear at times to be thrown onto an essentially eschatological level, as regards their temporal embodiment in human action.

The paradigm for the "basic form" of humanity—the I - thou relationality of male and female that signifies their being placed with one another in creation—is given in the relationship between God and man in Christ, and in the relationship between the Father and the Son in the Trinity. Even at a purely analogical, level, there are serious obstacles confronting this program. The major difficulty is that Barth wants to locate the point of similarity between these relations in the fact that they are all I - thou relations. This notion, however, is unacceptable on Barth's own terms, for it comes into sharp contradiction with his doctrine of the Trinity. In that Barth rejected the notion of Father, Son and Spirit as three divine "persons", and substituted instead the term "modes of being" to describe the intra-trinitarian distinctions. On this interpretation, man's independent status as the creature distinct from God is immediately jeopardized, for, if the relation between Father and Son is not that between two persons, but rather (by Barth's own formulation) that between two modes of the one Person of God, it is hard to see what sense can be attached to either the independence or the personal quality of the I - thou relation within the human. Barth is faced here with the compromise of either his anthropology or his doctrine of the Trinity.

When consideration is given to Barth's handling of the individual subjectivity and identity of man, equally serious difficulties are encountered. Here the model set over all men is the appearance of "real" man in Jesus Christ. There is the immediate suggestion of a loss of distinction between God and man at this juncture, for the specific humanity of Jesus is that of the *eternal* Son of God. Thus, Jesus is no independent person, but the second mode of God's own being. It is hard to see how this can be made the paradigm for all men, both Christians and non-Christians, without losing either the independent status of man over against God, or the uniqueness of Jesus as the Son of God.

Beyond this basic issue, we discovered ambiguity in Barth's description of both the "natural" man, and man under grace. At both points, the possibility of speaking meaningfully about human being and action is vitiated by an unsatisfactory analysis of man's ontic structure. The normal status of man as creature (i.e., apart from the specific grace of the Holy Spirit), taking Christ as the model, is analyzable into the categories of body, soul and spirit. The problem, however, is that Barth is equivocal about the category of spirit in man. Jesus, as an ordered unity of soul and body, *is* also spirit, and so a "person". Other men, it appears, are persons only as they *have* spirit (the Spirit of God himself), and so are grounded and maintained as a unity of soul and body. The upshot of this is that man's status and identity as person are lodged at a transcendent level, in the determination given him as he receives and has God's own Spirit. By apparently making man's status as subject and person dependent on the immediate action of God, Barth obscures again the distinction between God and man, and man's status as independent agent. Although Barth seems willing, in the later volumes of the *Dogmatics*, to speak of man's spirit, and to distinguish it from the Holy Spirit of God, he never explores the difference in an informative way. The result is that the relationship between his earlier and later statements on this point remains unclear.

As regards the ontic status of man under grace (i.e., the Christian), we discovered that it was made problematic by a continuation of Barth's realism, an unrelieved act-ontology, the eschatological tension in which Christians are placed, and the restriction of the predicate "Christian" to Jesus. The result of this approach is that it never becomes clear in what sense reconciliation (as completed event) not only comes *to* man, in the Holy Spirit, but also takes place *in* him, i.e., in his actions. Thus, we saw that the freedom for obedience given the Christian, and the faith, love and hope to which they lead, seemed continually to lie before him as a possibility to be actualized.

Now, it must be admitted that Barth's insistence that it is only "in act" that man's being is established would seem, *prima facie*, to lead in the direction of a strong empiricist reading of the self, which would be somewhat at odds with the motif of transcendentalism. Taken by itself, the employment of an act-ontology to describe the being of both God and man would place Barth in proximity to the left-wing Hegelians. The difficulty with this move is that the act in question that (at any point) establishes man's being depends on the "event" of grace supplied in the action of the Holy Spirit. Here the transcendental motif intrudes again, just as it does in the notion of the command of God as "event".

One way of reducing the tension in Barth's anthropology between the actual and the transcendental would be to interpret the latter meta-phorically, so that the "event" of grace that presents the command of God to man and provides the condition for his being-in-act would be a kind of synonym for the total configuration of any situation in which decision and action are required. This is tempting, but scarely appro-priate to the underlying concern for the objectivity of God in his revela-tion that runs throughout the *Dogmatics*. To suppose that the notions of grace and command as event can be aligned with the total *gestalt* of a context, so that there is nothing to talk about beyond that, is to miss Barth's whole point. The contextual character of Christian ethics, and the being-in-act of man depend, for Barth, on the revelational immediacy with which God-in-act impinges on any and every situation calling forth human action. The result would seem to be, then, that Barth's actualism, as regards the being of man, cannot be separated from his transcendentalism, as regards the event of grace and command. The ambiguity surrounding the ontic status of the Christian arises precisely because the act that establishes his being appears to lie at a transcendental level, and to evidence neither a simple nor an immediate continuity with the empirical givenness of the self.

The uncertainty found in Barth's treatment of the ontic status of the Christian applies as well to the existence and action of the Christian community. Like the propositions of theology and ethics, its status occurs as *actus purus*, and depends on the continuing, immediate action and presence of the Holy Spirit. The difficulty of a transition to a realization of obedience in freedom to the command of God, and so of an embodiment of faith, love and hope in concrete actions, is as problematic for the Christian community as a whole as it is for the individual Christian.

This raises the question, however, not only of the place of the Christian community in the world, in relation to the reconciling action of God, but of the possibility of Christian ethics as well. The problem here, I suggest, lies in the relationship that Barth establishes between the Christian community and the world. Barth is emphatic in insisting that the reconciliation that took place in the birth, life, death and resurrection of Jesus Christ resulted in an immediate and final ontological transformation of the human. Man *is* reconciled now, whether he realizes this fact or not. Both Christians and non-Christians stand under the same ontological determination which establishes a common ethical framework for all men. The distinction between the Christian community and the world is epistemological, not ontological, in nature. Or, in Barth's terminology, the distinction is between a *de iure* and a *de facto* participation in revelation. Christians are different from non-Christians because they have been brought to a recognition and acceptance of the rightness and goodness of God's action and its meaning for all men.

It remains ambiguous, however, whether the epistemological distinction given the Christian community can be given embodiment, ontically, in concrete actions that go beyond the basic action of worship. In addition to the ontological determination that encloses the human, there is also a persistent ontic motif that Barth applies to describe the relation between man's accomplished future in Christ and the distorting impact of sin, which now lies in his past. Man is always *simil iustus et peccator*. This means that although sin and evil are no longer part of man's future ontological being, they continue to thwart and subvert human efforts and achievements within history. What remains unclear in Barth's ethics is the degree to which man's future, in its impingement on his present through the action of the Holy Spirit, allows for an embodiment of the freedom it brings in actions that manifest faith, love and hope.

Barth refuses to draw rigid lines of separation or distinction between the Christian community and its secular environment. The freedom of Christ in the Holy Spirit insures that there will be actions and words in the latter that correspond to man's future being in Christ. And the continuing impact of sin, historically, insures that the actions of the community will remain at best partial, fragmented, and ambiguous. Their status as "right" actions conforming to man's ontological determination is not in any sense secured through human resources, but is determined in the immediate action of the Holy Spirit. Human action receives analogous validation at that point.

The problem with this move, however, is that it does not manage, finally, to "save the appearances". We recall that the "formula" Barth arrives at for analogy is "real similarity along with complete (or all) dissimilarity". The "real similarity" reflects the analogous transformation of human action by the Holy Spirit from its otherwise "complete dissimilarity" to the action of God, and man's true future given in that action. The possibility and actuality of correct human action is thus described, again, along *both* transcendental and actualistic lines.

The upshot of this is that although Barth insists that the transition from unbelief to faith requires a new creation of man as subject and agent, it remains unclear that this can be realized historically. This throws the notion of Christian ethics into obscurity, however, and leaves us wondering once again whether Barth has made a sufficient or a successful transition from divine ethics, and the ontological transformation of the human this brings about, to the context of human action. The degree to which eschatology connects meaningfully with history is obscure, and the relation between salvation history and the context of human action is described too much in transcendental and actualistic terms.

3. *The Relation between Creation and Reconciliation*

The questions that have been raised about the relation between the Christian community and the world, and the possibility and necessity of Christian ethics, unfold against the larger background of the relation Barth establishes between creation and reconciliation. Creation is set within the embracing contours of the covenant. Creation for Barth is the "external basis" or ground of the covenant; the covenant, the "internal basis" or ground of creation. And, since the covenant is fulfilled in the event of reconciliation, it follows that creation is viewed entirely from the perspective of that event, i.e., christologically. I have suggested that Barth's grounding of the history between God and man in the eternal trinitarian being of God obscures somewhat the independent status of the created order. Also, that the utilization of the christological principle results in a certain lack of sensitivity to the subtlety and complexity of the empirical situations in which decision and action must be taken; and to a failure to utilize the sort of descriptive information about those situations that might be provided by, say, the social sciences.

I wish to raise one additional question here. When creation is set exclusively under the event of reconciliation, and the "ontological impossibility" of sin and evil to which this leads, it may be wondered whether this does not have the result of so flattening the context of human history as to make difficult an appropriate ethical sensitivity to the relative evil that persists within it. Barth is insistent that the ontological transformation of the human secured in reconciliation not be taken as eliminating the importance of the historical, and the relative tensions and crises that occur within it. What it does insure is that these will be met as penultimate rather than ultimate developments and problems, and that they will not be invested, therefore, with ideological or metaphysical overtones. So far, so good. I have argued throughout this study that one of the most significant points in Barth's approach to ethics is his insistence that the inclusive action of God that moves the world irrevocably forward to its appointed future redemption results in man's being set free for open, sensitive, relative participation in the world. He is thus able to give events and situations their due without falling back on restrictive assumptions of an ideological nature. The action of God has to this extent, and positively, relativized all occurrences within history.

The problem here is that it is not clear that Barth's anthropology—in particular, his reading of man under grace, and the relation between reconciled and created human nature—allows sufficiently for the emergence of the freedom required for this openness and sensitivity. Given the persistence of sin even for the man under grace, might the result not be an insentivity to issues and crises, or a tendency, perhaps, to invest them with more significance than they can bear? Might not the result be that Christians would continually fail to achieve the proper balance and relation between their own relative affirmative or negative response to situations and issues, and the overarching "Yes" of God under which the world as a whole is placed? On Barth's reading of the human, there is no clear indication why this should not happen. It is at this point that a question can be raised about Barth's handling of the relation between Gospel and Law.

4. *Ethics as Command and Obedience*

Barth's ethics is stringently contextual in character, excluding any reliance on principles, rules or norms that are "applied" by reason to the ethical context. The basis for this contextualism does not lie in a concern for clarifying the situation *per se*. A contextual approach to ethics arises for Barth out of a consideration of the nature of revelation. God encounters man immediately in the Holy Spirit, and presents him with the command. It is the immediacy of the command, and the necessity it imposes on man for an equally immediate response of obedience, that provides the structure of contextuality in Barth's ethics.

We discovered difficulties in Barth's notion of the command, and the way in which it relates to the empirical facets of the ethical situation. Because of the relation Barth sets up between dogmatics and ethics, and the linguistic problem that surrounds the former, it is not possible to give cognitive status to the statements of theological ethics. In short, a description of the command is, at best, a limited possibility. Of course, this limitation is established by Barth himself. Theological ethics, he tells us, cannot give complete expression to either the command or obedience. The most it can do is indicate (primarily in special ethics) the general lines along which they will fall.

Beyond this limitation, there are additional difficulties in attempting to formulate the command, or even to get clear what it is supposed to mean. Since the command coincides with the immediate action of God in the Holy Spirit that provides a total shape and direction to the ethical context, it must be interpreted as event. This means, first, that it will be impossible to give propositional form to the command. Barth's use of the term at this point takes on the overtones of metaphor. But second, and more important, it means that the notion of event, when related to the command, will share in the ambiguity that was seen to surround Barth's notion of the "event" of grace. Knowledge of the command is provided by the Holy Spirit, and takes place, again, as *actus purus*. This not only throws the notion of command onto a transcendental level; it also results in a lack of clarity as to how the command relates to the empirical dimensions of the ethical context, and to the role of deliberative reason.

We saw that the question of the place of rational assessment and choice in Christian ethics underwent a modification as we moved from Barth's general delineation of the command (in II/2) to his elucidation of special ethics. In the former, the command was presented as something completely definite and self-interpreting. No room was left for questions about the will of God expressed in the command for a particular situation. The only option was either immediate obedience or disobedience.

In the sections devoted to special ethics, Barth appears to modify the stringency of his initial statement concerning the definiteness of the command. In part, this is because he is analyzing the spheres and relationships that appear under the horizontal thrust of the command. This is only part of the solution, however; Barth insists that even within special ethics, the command still requires "instant obedience". Nevertheless, there is an obvious latitude permitted, which allows for rational assessment, weighing and decision. This means that man now has a responsibility in deciding, *from his side*, what the command is, specifically, for a given context. In addition, Barth describes a series of guidelines, contours and norms along which obedience within the context of special ethics will ordinarily occur. These do not function as abstract principles. Nor can they be absolutized. They indicate nothing more than the *general* direction of human action under the command. The command for a specific context, however, may well require a temporary suspension of these. This occurs where the situation turns out to be, on inspection, what Barth describes as an "exceptional case".

There are two problems that attend Barth's transition from general to special ethics. First, the increased role given to rational deliberation in the latter. Second, the relation between the guidelines and the specificity of the command in special ethics. Both of these may be indicative of the fact that Barth has not been wholly successful in moving out of the general statement of the command developed against the background of election, to a description of the special contexts that emerge under the horizontal thrust of the command. It is possible, then, either that Barth has not been fully consistent in deriving ethical guidelines on exclusively theological grounds, or that he has been unsuccessful in relating theological categories to empirical realities. At some points, Barth suggests a rather clear affinity between rational assessment and the command. We noted this particularly in his political thought, where the goal in ethical analysis was described as the achievement of coincidence between the promptings of common sense, and the action of the Holy Spirit. At other times, the command seems either to preclude the possibility of rational deliberation, or to stand essentially disrelated to whatever it might turn up. At any rate, the precise relation between the empirical factors in the ethical context, and the stringency of the command, remains finally unclear.

There is a further aspect of Barth's contextualism that must be noted. This has to do with his rejection of principles or rules, and his insistence that obedience occurs immediately, in response to the directing action of God. The rejection of principles in ethics is epitomized in Barth's reformulation of the Law-Gospel question. For Barth, the Law forms the "outer" side of grace, and provides the behavioral counterpart to the indicative of the Gospel—the "inner" side of grace. This means that the imperative of the Law does not impose alien restrictions or demands on man, but directs him toward the action that will most appropriately embody his status under grace. The Law thus presents the possibility for a correct actualization of freedom, along the lines of faith, love and hope.

Again, the difficulty here is that Barth's anthropology makes ambiguous the possibility of a realization of the authentic demand of Law in concrete actions, i.e., a living out of man's indicative under the Gospel. Further, it raises the question whether man—even Christians—should be completely free of the ordinary restrictions and limits provided by principles and rules. Perhaps Barth has recognized this problem. It is possible to view the guidelines he sets forth in special ethics as *descriptive* norms. The question, however, in view of the relation that Barth sets up between Christians and non-Christians and the continuing impact of sin for each, is whether these would not, in fact, function more as prescriptive guidelines.

5. *The Relation between Theological and Philosophical Ethics*

The question as to how Barth relates theological and philosophical ethics leads to the question of his positioning of theology and philosophy *per se*. In the end, we are brought into the context of the apologetic question.

Barth's approach to philosophy and philosophical ethics is both conciliatory and polemical. It is conciliatory to the extent that theological ethics undertakes to speak inclusively. The basis for this attempt is established theologically rather than anthropologically, in the eternal election and reconciliation of all men in Jesus Christ. This provides a common ethical framework within which theological ethics moves toward its counterpart in philosophy on the basis of "annexation". The polemical side of the encounter is occasioned by the inability of theological ethics to take seriously the claims of the philosopher to be legitimately engaged in the search for the Good. As regards Barth's attitude toward philosophy *per se*, we saw that this was ambiguous. On the one hand, philosophy apparently has no continuing importance *post Christum natum*. The theologian (Barth, at least) can only express wonder and amazement that the philosopher persists in his outmoded approach to reality, knowledge and the issues of correct behavior and its ground. On the other hand, philosophy is allowed a relative significance as a kind of "Hilfswissenschaft" to theology. The philosopher, by emphasizing the importance of the human, can keep the theologian from becoming too narrowly focused on the reality of God, which could result in a failure to do justice to man and the world.

I argued that Barth's approach to philosophy is inadequate, because it tends to exclude any serious consideration of the apologetic question. The theologian needs to do more than simply claim the right of annexation over philosophical ethics. And he ought to be willing to go beyond a mere assertion of final insight into the true basis of reality and knowledge. Further, Barth's position suggests an improper sensitivity to the way in which the theologian is dependent on the conceptual tools and apparatus provided by philosophical construction and analysis. It is doubtful that Barth could have structured the *Römerbrief* or the *Church Dogmatics* without the assistance of Kantian and Hegelian categories. At least, the theologian ought to be open to discussing why he prefers one philosophical approach and statement to another. It is clear at any rate, that the theologian is not so independent of or indifferent to the activity of the philosopher as some of Barth's comments imply.

Beyond the question of a more open and fruitful exchange between philosophy and theology, Barth's general rejection of the possibility of apologetics—or rather, his identification of apologetics with dogmatics—leads to difficulties in other areas of human endeavor. Barth makes no attempt to utilize the insights that might come from the social sciences, with the result that his anthropology and his analysis of the specific contexts of special ethics manifest a certain lack of attention to empirical realities. In particular, Barth's analysis of man in terms of the traditional distinction between soul and body, despite his insistence that they are always present only in their unity, carries a rationalistic overtone that seriously minimizes the complexity of the self and the ambiguities that surround ethical decisions. In this respect, Barth's failure to allow Kierkegaard to accompany him into the *Dogmatics* in a more creative way must be judged a mistake.

6. *The Unity of Barth's Ethics*

We must begin by noting a paradox. Part of the difficulty with Barth's ethics is that it is altogether too unified. By insisting on virtually identifying dogmatics and ethics, Barth fails, at points, to make an effective transition out of the context of "divine ethics" and into the empirical framework where the stuff of *human* decision and action must be wrestled with. The motifs of transcendentalism and actualism that run through his presentation do not clearly make contact with the human, and such contact as they do manage is vitiated by the relation Barth sets up between created and reconciled human nature. The result of this is a certain ambiguity about the status and meaning of Christian ethics, and human action generally, beyond the one inclusive action of God in Christ. To this extent, at least, it would appear that the difficulties noted in the ethics of the *Römerbrief* and the shorter writings that follow it, have not been completely overcome in the *Dogmatics*.

Where the unity of Barth's ethics is open to question, I feel, occurs at the point of his transition out of the general development of the command against the background of election, and into the specific spheres and relationships of special ethics. The difficulty here lies in the extended role given deliberative reason in assessing options and making decisions. The suggestion is clearly given that man is noetically involved, from his side at least, in deciding what the command of God (and so God's will) is for a given situation. This appears, however, to conflict with the strictness with which the command was initially developed. Neither Barth's discussion of the total definiteness of the command, nor his completed anthropology, provide clear justification for the role assigned deliberative reason in special ethics.

B. PROJECTIONS: CHRISTIAN ETHICS BEYOND BARTH

The issues raised in the preceding section suggest the areas in Barth's approach to theology and ethics that call for additional reflection, if not reformulation. My intention here is not to suggest that Christian ethics must somehow proceed "in spite of" rather than "beyond" Barth. It is rather to call attention to those areas in Barth's formulations that press for continuing attention and an alternative development. Needless to say, it is quite possible that the resources for moving theological reflection about ethics beyond Barth are provided already, incipiently, by Barth himself.

The first area that requires additional attention is the method and extent of the theological enterprise. As regards Barth's method, we have seen the difficulties involved in his use of the principle of presupposition and of analogy. What I would suggest here is the need to explore the possibilities for both a reassessment and a redirection of the role assigned these in Barth's program. The principle of presupposition serves to underline the fact that Jesus Christ is the center from which the whole of experience and reality is to be viewed. But for Barth, this means nothing less than that the whole sweep of God's action from creation to redemption, and all that occurs within it, is understood and assessed correctly only from the center of that action: the reconciling action of God in Jesus Christ. What needs to be emphasized, however, is that the principle of presupposition does not function in Barth's thinking as the axion from which experience and reality are to be deduced. Its utilization, therefore, need not result in a loss of sensitivity to the givenness of things in their richness and variety. In short, it would appear to be possible to take Barth's principle of presupposition seriously and still provide a thorough and convincing treatment, at a phenomenological level, of the created order. That Barth does not entirely succeed in providing this is the result, I feel, both of his failure to take as seriously as he might his own insistance on the importance of the secular and its various disciplines, and of his concern lest theology fall prey to ideology. Thus, Barth fails to provide a convincing treatment of the empirical and pragmatic range of human experience because he fails to take seriously the insights that might come from those disciplines devoted to its analysis and explication. A move beyond Barth at this point would involve an expansion of the "sola Scriptura" emphasis of the Reformers as the source of the theologian's insight and wisdom.

Barth's approach to the problem of analogy is designed to make clear the centrality of grace as the necessary and sufficient condition for man's participation (noetically and ontically) in the event of reconciliation. This entailed a stringent rejection of the Catholic doctrine of the *analogia entis*, and an exploration of man's status as participant in revelation in terms of the *analogia fidei* and the *analogia relationis*. In the later volumes of the *Dogmatics*, Barth drops this distinction while retaining the intent embodied in his approach to the question of analogy, viz., to emphasize the fact that there is no "point of contact" in created human nature that provides a preparatory basis for the event of grace. What remains unclear, however, is how the created and the reconciled dimensions of human nature are to remain unified at an experiential or existential level. That they do so at a Christological level is clear. On this point, it is less clear that Barth's approach can be reformulated so as to overcome what seems to be a discontinuity between the empirical self and the self established by grace. It would rather appear that a rethinking of the whole question of analogy and analogous discourse is in order.

The question as to the scope or extensiveness of the theological venture also becomes important in reflecting on the possibilities for moving Christian ethics beyond Barth. The difficulty in Barth's program, as Bonhoeffer saw it [1], was that he found it necessary to say everything that could possibly be said in theology, and to build this into a balanced "system". I have deliberately put that last word in quotation marks, for it is clear that Barth did not move in this direction out of consideration purely for the demands of logic and reason, but rather on the basis of what he took to be the legitimate task of theology in carrying out its responsibility to the witness of Scripture and the Christian community.

The question that must be raised is whether theology in fact needs to be cast in so comprehensive and inclusive a form? Granted, there will always be a need for theology to spell out the stance from which the Christian community undertakes responsible and obedient action in the world. What is not clear is that the articulation of this stance needs to be as complete, in all respects, as the *Dogmatics*. Perhaps it is time to explore the possibilities and resources for theological construction that retains a sense of the casual, even *ad hoc*, status of the theological venture itself. If theology, like ethics, is in continual process of being formed and reformed under the impact of God's present activity in the world, then this insight might legitimately be reflected in the scope of the task theology sets for itself. Despite Barth's warnings against taking the *Dogmatics* as the final word in theology, there is inevitably an aura of completeness and finality associated with so inclusive a program.

The second area that requires attention is the relation between theology and ethics. Obviously, Christian ethics inevitably will be grounded in theology. What is needed is an exploration of theological grounding and ethical context that will show how theology touches ethics at every point, yet which will not endanger the subtlety and complexity of the empirical and behavioral dimensions of the ethical. As regards Barth's handling of this issue, it needs to be strengthened by a more

---

[1] *Prisoner for God*, p. 126.

perspicuous treatment of the full dimensionality of the horizontal thrust of the command exhibited in special ethics. Again, the need is for closer attention to the task of concrete, empirical analysis.

Third, there is a need to overcome the ambiguities present in Barth's anthropology. The central task here, of course, is to state the importance of Jesus Christ for all men without vitiating their subjective status and agency. In this respect, it is not clear that Barth is justified in his assumption that all relevant insights about the human can be developed out of Christology. True, this is not set forth as a deductive program. It is, nevertheless, an approach that makes it difficult to take seriously the kinds of data and insights that are provided by phenomenological description. Insofar as the "phenomena of the human" produced by the social and behavioral sciences can be freed of metaphysical overtones, there is no reason why the theologian should not allow himself to be instructed by them. The same point, incidentally, could be made about artistic creativity and insight in its impingement on the human. Barth's failure to take these as seriously as he might is not the result of his having rejected them in principle. It is, rather, due to his failure to remain consistent with the implications of his own assumptions.

The fourth area where additional reflection is required centers in Barth's development of a contextualist ethics. Despite the attention that this reading of ethics has received in recent theology [1], it still remains unclear that the issues between "context" and "principles" have been explored sufficiently. Part of the difficulty, as James Gustafson has pointed out, is that there has been a lack of attention to the range of possibilities that exist within both approaches [2]. A decision as to the validity or invalidity of principles in Christian ethics, and of the adequacy of an unrelieved emphasis on context, must await further exploration. In terms of Barth's own position, however, it is interesting to note that Paul Ramsey, who would not, certainly, be mistaken for a contextualist, finds his own emphasis on "in-principled love" to be congenial with

---

[1] Cf. Bonhoeffer, *Ethics*; Lehmann, *Ethics in a Christian Context*; Niebuhr, *The Responsible Self*; Joseph Sittler, *The Structure of Christian Ethics* (Baton Rough: Louisiana State University Press, 1961); Albert Rasmussen, *Christian Social Ethics* (Englewood Cliffs: Prentice-Hall, 1956); Gordon Kaufman, *The Context of Decision* (New York: Abingdon Press, 1961).

[2] "Context Versus Principles: A Misplaced Debate in Christian Ethics", in: *New Theology No. 3*, pp. 69-102.

Barth's development of the horizontal continuity of the command in special ethics [1].

Fifth, there is the question of history as dealt with by the theologian. In Barth's theology, this question has two dimensions. First, there is the problem surrounding his use of the category of salvation history. The difficulty here lies in getting clear what meaning is to be attached to that notion of history. As Barth employs it, it describes a series of events that have (paradoxically) a transcendental objectivity. Now, it is difficult initially to see how the concept of history can be applied legitimately to events that have no obvious relation to the ordinary space-time framework of nature and history. When we are further informed that the totality of salvation history occurs initially as a movement within the eternal trinitarian being of God, the difficulty deepens considerably.

The second dimension of the problem has to do with the status of ordinary history and occurrence. On Barth's view, this appeared to be in some ways compromised, in that its dramatic configuration and complexity were reduced under the impact of salvation history. What is needed is both a reformulation of the relation between salvation history and ordinary history, and a stringent analysis of the logic of these terms. Part of Barth's difficulty is the result of a lack of sensitivity to the logical and categoreal distinctions that exist between terms like "history", "salvation history", and "eschatology".

Finally, it is tantalizing to conjecture what a post-Barthian venture into the area of apologetics might look like, or whether such an undertaking is even possible. This is a subtle issue indeed for a theology that undertakes to move beyond Barth at this point, and to provide a new basis for apologetic encounter. The paradox in Barth's position (i.e., that the best apologetics is a sound dogmatics) is that while it quite deliberately rejects both the possibility and the necessity of apologetics, it has at the same time won the respect of non-theologians. Philosophers, for instance, as Ninian Smart points out, respect Barth because "he does not compromise, and he does not play around with dubitable metaphysics" [2]. Any venture into apologetics, then, will have to abide by these limitations if it is to be theologically respectable.

---

[1] Cf. *Deeds and Rules in Christian Ethics* (Edinburgh: Oliver and Boyd, 1965), pp. 61ff.

[2] "The Intellectual Crisis of British Christianity", in: *New Theology No. 3*, p. 21. Barth, it would seem, has gotten more of a hearing from the

There are possibilities, however, that involve, *prima facie*, neither compromise nor dubitable metaphysics. One approach, for instance, would consist in an exploration of suggestions from other disciplines that might have bearing on theological method and construction. We already have an example of this sort of engagement with non-theological disciplines in Paul van Buren's book, *The Secular Meaning of the Gospel*, where the attempt is made, without complete success perhaps [1], to apply the methods of contemporary linguistic analysis to theological doctrines. And there might be other possibilities, as yet unexplored, that would bring theology into a more direct and dynamic relation with the full spectrum of human endeavor.

In suggesting that these areas will require additional attention as theology moves beyond Barth, I make no claim to have arrived at even preliminary answers. There is one observation that can be made, however, that would apply to at least some of these points. Many of the concerns that have been indicated were also problems in nineteenth century theology. The movement of theology beyond Barth, then, might well take a turn back to that context. To be sure, it will not be a matter simply of looking at what was done in nineteenth century theology for answers to these issues. It could mean, however, that theology will find itself needing to go back and pick up some of the threads left hanging there, and pull them forward into a new theological fabric. There are indications that such a move has already begun. Some of the so-called "radical theologians" have expressed a renewed interest in the nineteenth century. And good critical studies have appeared recently on Schleiermacher and Troeltsch [2], in addition to a recent volume of readings in nineteenth century Christology [3]. It is fascinating indeed to contemplate

---

philosophers than Tillich. Cf. the discussion of Barth's theology in: *Faith and the Philosophers*, John Hick, ed. (New York: St. Martin's Press, Inc., 1964), Ch. IV. Unfortunately, what the discussion reveals is the lack of insight and understanding that a contemporary philosophe—Brand Blanshard—is capable of in the area of Protestant theology.

[1] Cf. the article by Jerry Gill, "A Case of Mistaken Identity: Paul van Buren as Linguistic Analyst", in: *The Christian Scholar*. Vol. XLIX (Summer, 1966), pp. 147-151.

[2] Cf. Richard R. Niebuhr, *Schleiermacher on Christ and Religion* (New York: Charles Scribner's Sons, 1964); and Benjamin A. Reist, *Toward a Theology of Involvement* (Philadelphia: The Westminster Press, 1966).

[3] *God and Incarnation in German Theology*, Claude Welch, trans. (New York: Oxford University Press, 1966). This contains selections from the works of Thomasius, Dorner, and Biedermann.

what new soundings might be found in the efforts of nineteenth century theology that would bear significantly on contemporary efforts in theology and ethics to move the discussion beyond Karl Barth.

BIBLIOGRAPHY

A. *Primary Sources*

Books

Barth, Karl, *Against the Stream: Shorter Post-War Writings, 1946-1952*. Translated by Mrs. E.M. Delacour and Stanley Godman. Edited by Ronald Gregor Smith. London: S.C.M. Press, 1954.

——, *Christ and Adam: Man and Humanity in Romans 5*. Scottish Journal of Theology Occasional Papers No. 5. Translated by T.A. Smail. Edinburgh: Oliver and Boyd, 1956.

——, *Christengemeinde und Bürgergemeinde*. Theologische Studien, Heft 20. Zürich: Evangelischer Verlag A.G. Zollikon, 1946.

——, *Christliche Ethik*. München: Verlag Chr. Kaiser, 1946.

——, *Der Römerbrief*. Zürich: Evangelischer Verlag A.G. Zollikon, 1940. English title: *The Epistle to the Romans*. Translated from the sixth German edition by Edwin C. Hoskyns. London: Oxford University Press, 1957.

——, *Die Kirchliche Dogmatik*. Vols. I/1-IV/4. Zürich: Evangelischer Verlag A.G. Zollikon, 1955-1959. English title: *Church Dogmatics*. Translated by various scholars under the general editorship (excluding vol. I/1) of G.W. Bromily and T.F. Torrance. Edinburgh: T & T Clark, 1955-1961.

——, *Evangelium und Gesetz*. Theologische Existenz Heute, Heft 50. München: Verlag Chr. Kaiser, 1956.

——, *Fides Quaerens Intellectum*. London: SCM Press, 1960.

——, *God in Action*. Addresses given in the early 1930's. Translated by E.G. Homrighausen. New York: Round Table Press, 1963.

——, and Johannes Hamel. *How to Serve God in a Marxist Land*. Translated by Thomas Wieser. New York: Association Press, 1959.

——, *Rechtfertigung und Recht*. Theologische Studien, Heft 1. Zürich: Evangelischer Verlag A.G. Zollikon, 1948. English title: "Church and State", in: *Community, State and Church*. Translated by G. Ronald Howe. Edited by Will Herberg. New York: Anchor Books, 1960.

——, *This Christian Cause*. Contains Barth's first and second letters to French protestants (1939 and 1940), and his letter to Great Britain (1941). Translator's name not given. New York: The Macmillan Company, 1941.

——, *The Church and the Political Problem of Our Day*. Translator's name not given. New York: Charles Schribner's Sons, 1939.

——, *The Church and the War*. Translated by Antonia A. Froendt. New York: The Macmillan Company, 1944.

——, *The Faith of the Church: A Commentary on the Apostle's Creed According to Calvin's Catechism*. Made up of stenographic notes taken during a series of lectures delivered at Travers and Neuchatel. Switzerland, from 1940 to 1943. Translated by Gabriel Vahanian. Edited by Jean-Louis Leuba. New York: Living Age Books, 1958.

——, *The Humanity of God*. Translated by Thomas Wieser and John Newton

Thomas. Richmond: John Knox Press, 1960. Originally published as
separate monographs in the series, *Theologische Studien*. Zürich: Evangelischer Verlag A.G. Zollikon.

Barth, Karl, *The Knowledge of God and the Service of God According to the
Teaching of the Reformation*. The Gifford Lectures delivered in the
University of Aberdeen in 1937 and 1938. Translated by J.L.M. Haire
and Ian Henderson. London: Hodder and Stoughton, 1955.
——, *Theological Existence Today*. Translated by R. Birch Hoyle. Lexington:
American Theological Library Association, 1962.
——, *Theologischen Fragen und Antworten*. Gesammelte Vorträge, 3. Band.
Zürich: Evangelischer Verlag A.G. Zollikon, 1957.
——, *Theology and Church: Shorter Writings, 1920-1928*. Translated by
Louise Pettibone Smith. New York: Harper and Row, 1962.
——, *The Only Way: How Can the Germans Be Cured?* Translated by Marta
K. Neufeld and Ronald Gregor Smith. New York: Philosophical Library,
1947.
——, *The Word of God and the Word of Man*. Translated by Douglas Horton.
New York: Harper and Brothers, 1957. German title: *Das Wort Gottes
und die Theologie*. München: Verlag Chr. Kaiser, 1924.
——, and Heinrich Barth, *Zur Lehre vom Heiligen Geist*. München: Verlag
Chr. Kaiser, 1930.

Articles

——, "How my Mind has changed in this Decade", *The Christian Century*,
Vol. LVI, Nos. 37 and 38 (September 13 and 20, 1939), pp. 1097-1099,
1132-1134.
——, "How my Mind has Changed, 1939-1948", *The Christian Century*,
Vol. LXVI, Nos. 10 and 11 (March 9 and 16, 1949), pp. 298-300, 333-334.
——, "The Church—The Living Congregation of the Living Lord Jesus
Christ", *Man's Disorder and God's Design*. The Amsterdam Assembly
Series. New York: Harper and Brothers. No date given.
——, "Philosophie und Theologie", *Philosophie und Christliche Existenz:
Festschrift für Heinrich Barth*. G. Huber, ed., Basel: Verlag Helbing und
Lichtenhahn, 1960.
——, "Recapitulation Number Three", *The Christian Century*, Vol. LXXVII,
No. 3 (January 20, 1960), pp. 72-76.

Secondary Sources

Books

Barrett, William, *Irrational Man*. New York: Doubleday Anchor Books,
1962.
Bartsch, Hans Werner (ed.). *Kerygma and Myth: A Theological Debate*.
Vol. I, Translated by Reginald H. Fuller. London: S.P.C.K., 1953.
Berkouwer, G.C. *The Triumph of Grace in the Theology of Karl Barth*. Trans-
lated by Harry R. Boer. London: The Paternoster Press, 1956.
Bonhoeffer, Dietrich. *Akt und Sein*. München: Verlag Chr. Kaiser, 1956.

English title: *Act and Being*. Translated by Bernard Noble. New York: Harper and Brothers, 1962.

Bonhoeffer, Dietrich, *Gesammelte Schriften. Band III: Theologie-Gemeinde*. München: Verlag Chr. Kaiser, 1960.

——, *Prisoner for God: Letters and Papers from Prison*. Translated by Reginald H. Fuller. Edited by Eberhard Bethge. New York: The Macmillan Company, 1957.

Bouillard, Henri. *Karl Barth*. Three volumes. Paris: Aubier, 1957.

Brown, James. *Subject and Object in Modern Theology*. New York: The Macmillan Company, 1955.

Brunner, Emil. *The Christian Doctrine of Creation and Redemption. Dogmatics, Vol. II*. Translated by Olive Wyon. Philadelphia: The Westminster Press, 1952.

——, *The Christian Doctrine of God. Dogmatics, Vol. I*. Translated by Olive Wyon. Philadelphia: The Westminster Press, 1950.

——, *The Christian Doctrine of the Church, Faith, and the Consummation. Dogmatics, Vol. III*. Translated by David Cairns in collaboration with T.H.L. Parker. London: Lutterworth Press, 1962.

Castañeda, Hector-Neri, and Nakhnikian, George (eds.). *Morality and the Language of Conduct*. Detroit: Wayne State University Press, 1963.

Cochrane, Arthur C. *The Church's Confession under Hitler*. Philadelphia: The Westminster Press, 1962.

Come, Arnold B. *An Introduction to Barth's "Dogmatics" for Preachers*. Philadelphia: The Westminster Press, 1963.

——, *Human Spirit and Holy Spirit*. Philadelphia: The Westminster Press, 1959.

Copleston, Frederick. *A History of Philosophy*. Vol. 2, Part II. New York: Image Books, 1962.

Cullberg, John. *Das Problem der Ethik in der Dialektischen Theologie*. Uppsala: Appelbergs, 1938.

Diem, Hermann. *Dogmatics*. Translated by Harold Knight. London: Oliver and Boyd, 1959.

Ferré, Frederick. *Language, Logic and God*. New York: Harper and Brothers, 1961.

Frakena, William K. *Ethics*. The Foundations of Philosophy series. Edited by Monroe and Elizabeth Beardsley. Englewood Cliffs: Prentice-Hall, Inc., 1963.

Gill, Theodore A. *Recent Protestant Political Theory*. Great Britain: Hunt, Barnard, and Co., Ltd., 1953.

Gustafson, James M., *Christ and the Moral Life*. New York: Harper & Row, 1968.

Hartwell, Herbert. *The Theology of Karl Barth*. Philadelphia: The Westminster Press, 1964.

Hedinger, Ulrich. *Der Freiheitsbegriff in der kirchlichen Dogmatik Karl Barths*. Zürich: Zwingli Verlag, 1962.

Hick, John. *Faith and the Philosophers*. New York: St. Martin's Press, 1964.

Kaufman, Gordon D., *Systematic Theology: A Historicist Perspective*. New York: Charles Scribner's Sons, 1968.

Lehmann, Paul. *Ethics in a Christian Context*. London: S.C.M. Press, 1963.

Leibrecht, W., Religion and Culture: Essays in Honor of Paul Tillich. New York: Harper and Brothers, 1959.

Long, Edward Leroy, Jr., *A Survey of Christian Ethics*. New York: Oxford University Press, 1967.

Marty, Martin E., and Peerman, Dean (eds.). *New Theology No. 3*. New York: The Macmillan Company, 1966.

Michalson, Carl. *The Rationality of Faith*. New York: Charles Scribner's Sons, 1963.

Niebuhr, H. Richard. *The Responsible Self*. New York: Harper and Row, 1963.

Niebuhr, Richard R. *Resurrection and Historical Reason*. New York: Charles Scribner's Sons, 1957.

——, *Schleiermacher on Christ and Religion*. New York: Charles Scribner's Sons, 1964.

Oden, Thomas C., *The Promise of Barth*. New York: J.B. Lippincott, 1970.

Ramsey, Paul. *Deeds and Rules in Christian Ethics*. Edinburgh: Oliver and Boyd, 1965.

——, (ed.). *Faith and Ethics: The Theology of H. Richard Niebuhr*. New York: Harper and Brothers, 1957.

——, *The Just War*. New York: Charles Scribner's Sons, 1968.

Rieff, Philip. *The Triumph of the Therapeutic*. London: Chatto & Windus, 1966.

Robinson, James, ed., *Dialectical Theology*. Richmond: John Knox Press, 1967.

Smart, James. *Revolutionary Theology in the Making*. Richmond: John Knox Press, 1964.

Thielicke, Helmut. *Theologische Ethik*. Three volumes. Tübingen: J.C.B. Mohr, 1951-1958.

Tillich, Paul. *Systematic Theology*. Vol. III. Chicago: University of Chicago Press, 1963.

Torrance, Thomas F. *Karl Barth: An Introduction to His Early Theology, 1910-1931*. London: S.C.M. Press, 1962.

Torrance, Thomas F., *Theological Science*. New York: Oxford University Press, 1969.

Toulmin, S., Hepburn, R., and Macintyre, A., *Metaphysical Beliefs*. London: SCM Press, 1957.

Von Balthasar, Hans Urs. *Karl Barth: Darstellung und Deutung seiner Theologie*. Köln: Verlag Jacob Hegner, 1951.

Van Buren, Paul. *The Secular Meaning of the Gospel*. New York: The Macmillan Company, 1963.

Van Oyen, Hendrik. *Theologische Erkenntnislehre*. Zürich: Zwingli-Verlag, 1955.

Weber, Otto. *Grundlegen der Dogmatik*. Zweiter Band. Moers: Neukirchener Verlag, 1962.

Welch, Claude. *In This Name*. New York: Charles Scribner's Sons, 1952.

West, Charles C. *Communism and the Theologians*. Philadelphia: The Westminster Press, 1958.

Wittgenstein, Ludwig. *Tractatus Logico-Philosophicus*. Translated by C.K. Ogden. London: Routledge and Kegan Paul, 1922.

Wolf, Ernst, Ch. von Kirschbaum, and Rudolph Frey (eds.). *Antwort*. Zürich: Evangelischer Verlag A.G. Zollikon, 1956.
Yoder, John H., *Karl Barth and the Problem of War* (New York: Abingdon, 1970).

Articles

Bethge, Eberhard. "The Challenge of Dietrich Bonhoeffer's Life and Theology", The Alden-Tuthill Lectures, The Chicago Theological Seminary *Register*, Vol. LI, No. 2 (February, 1961), pp. 1-38.
Gill, Jerry. "A Case of Mistaken Identity: Paul van Buren as Linguistic Analyst", *The Christian Scholar*, Vol. XLIX (Summer, 1966), pp. 147-151.
Hamilton, William. "Thursday's Child: The Theologian Today and Tomorrow", *Theology Today*, Vol. XX, No. 4 (January, 1964), pp. 487-495.
Harvey, Van A. "A Word in Defense of Schleiermacher's Theological Method", *The Journal of Religion*, Vol. XLII, No. 3 (July, 1962), pp. 151-170.
Jonas, Hans. "Heidegger and Theology", *The Review of Metaphysics*, Vol. XVIII, No. 2 (December, 1964), pp. 207-223.
Niebuhr, Reinhold. "The Quality of Our Lives", *The Christian Century*, Vol. LXXVII, No. 19 (May 11, 1960), pp. 568-572.

INDEX OF NAMES

Imprimerie Orientaliste, Louvain (Belgium)